KNOWLEDGE, TRADITION AND CIVILIZATION

Festschrift in honour of Professor Osman Bakar

KNOWLEDGE, TRADITION AND CIVILIZATION

Essays in honour of Professor Osman Bakar

Edited by Khairudin Aljunied

BEACON BOOKS

Published in the UK by Beacon Books and Media Ltd
Earl Business Centre, Dowry Street, Oldham, OL8 2PF, UK.

www.beaconbooks.net

ISBN: 978-1-915025-41-8 Paperback
ISBN: 978-1-915025-42-5 Hardback
ISBN: 978-1-915025-43-2 eBook

Cataloging-in-Publication record for this book is available from the British Library

Cover design by Raees Mahmood Khan

Cover image by Slaunger, under Creative Commons Licence.
BY-SA 3.0, https://commons.wikimedia.org/w/index.php?curid=35203662

Contents

Acknowledgements vii

Preface, *Seyyed Hossein Nasr* ix

Foreword: Parallel Paths with Osman Bakar, *Anwar Ibrahim* xi

Introduction: Why Osman Bakar Matters, *Khairudin Aljunied* 1

Part 1: The Production and Problem of Knowledge 17

Chapter 1: An Engaged Scholar: An Intellectual Biography and Bibliometric Study of Osman's Intellectual Contributions, *Muhammed Haron* 19

Chapter 2: Faith and Modern Science: A Journey of Rediscovery with Professor Osman Bakar, *Tengku Mohd Azzman Shariffadeen* 39

Chapter 3: Osman Bakar and the Renewal of Islamic Classification of Knowledge, *Jasser Auda* 57

Chapter 4: Narrating the West for the Malays: Syed Shaykh al-Hady and *al-Imam*, *Ahmad Murad Merican* 67

Chapter 5: Inventing Adversaries: Orientalism and the Arabs in Colonial Southeast Asia, *Farish Noor* 87

Chapter 6: Nasir al-Din Tusi's Ethics and Concept of Social Class, *Mohammad Faghfoory* 105

Chapter 7: Synergy of Knowledge in the Formation of Islamic Jurisprudence: The 5 Categories of Legal Rulings, *Yasushi Kosugi* 127

Chapter 8: Religion and Science: Selected Views of Iqbal and Bohm, *Suheyl Umar* 145

Chapter 9: Osman Bakar and the Dialogue with the Chinese Civilization and Philosophies, *Nevad Kahteran* 163

Chapter 10: The Making of a Korean-Islamic Tradition, *Hee Soo Lee* 175

Chapter 11: The Muslim Art of Management: Zheng He (1371–1433) and his Maritime Expeditions, *Lee Cheuk Yin* 189

Part 2: Civilizational Unity and Renewal **201**

Chapter 12: Knowledge of Unity and the Thrust of the Esoteric in Religion, *Patrick Laude* 203

Chapter 13: Renewal (*Tajdid*), Reform (*Islah*), and *Ijtihad* in Islamic Civilization, *Mohammad Hashim Kamali* 217

Chapter 14: Sufism In Indonesian Islam: A Brief History and a New Typology, *Azyumardi Azra* 237

Chapter 15: What Makes a Family and Its Values: A Critical Response to Professor Osman Bakar's Thoughts, *Zaleha Kamaruddin* 251

Chapter 16: Spiritual Knowledge and Humanities as Foundation for National Development and Peaceful Existence, *Md Salleh Yaapar* 263

Chapter 17: Bridging Religious Studies and Sustainable Development Goals via the Idea of Guardianship of the Environment, *Azizan Baharuddin* ... 275

Chapter 18: Reclaiming Philosophical Sciences in Muslim Education, *Rosnani Hashim* 293

Chapter 19: Ars Sine Scientia? Integral Aesthetics and Islamic Metaphysics, *Reza Shah-Kazemi* 309

Chapter 20: Scientific Realism and Islamic Science, *Mohd Hazim Shah* .. 335

Chapter 21: Bridging Civilizational Divides: Osman Bakar's Life-Long Quest for the Middle Ground, *Peter T. C. Chang* 361

Chapter 22: Islamic Science, Epistemology and the Space for Religion, *Oliver Leaman* 375

Afterword: Osman Bakar and Islamic Thought, *John L. Esposito* 387

The Works of Professor Osman Bakar **389**

Index **405**

Acknowledgements

This book would not have been published without the encouragement and support from the Center for Islam in the Contemporary World (CICW). I thank Yaqoub Mirza for his kindness and generosity. Ermin and Younos gave many useful insights and suggestions. I would like to express my deepest appreciation to Maryam Osman for the fine work she put in to make the manuscript sharper. The University of Brunei Darussalam, and Georgetown University provided the space and resources to see this book project through to its completion.

I am forever grateful to the contributors for sacrificing their time away from family to make this publication possible. I hope that this humble volume will add to the ocean of knowledge about Islam and Muslim societies, and about a great scholar of our time, Professor Osman Bakar.

Preface

Seyyed Hossein Nasr
University Professor of Islamic Studies at The George Washington University, USA

My first encounter with Dr. Osman Bakar occurred some forty years ago when he came in late 1981 to Temple University in the United States where I was teaching. I was then at the beginning of my exile after the Iranian Islamic Revolution. Dr. Osman came from London to Temple to do the PhD under my supervision. I found him to be a most gifted young scholar who soon became one of the best students I had ever trained. He wrote his doctoral thesis under my supervision on the classification of the sciences in Islam, a work that was later published and was immediately recognized as an important contribution to the notable subject. During the past four decades, I have met him nearly continuously in Malaysia and here in America where he taught for some time at Georgetown University. I have followed his academic and intellectual life closely and kept abreast of his numerous writings.

After returning home, Dr. Osman soon became a major intellectual figure in Malaysia. He was and is still highly respected as both teacher and writer as well as a "public intellectual." The influence of his work also spread to other parts of the Malay world especially Indonesia, Brunei, and Southern Thailand, in academic circles in the West, as well as in Islamic countries. His writings, moreover, went beyond his initial field of specialization, that is, Islamic science and its philosophy, into Islamic philosophy in general, civilizational studies, Malay culture and history, and many other domains.

Of special interest and important to note is his study of the relation between the Confucian tradition and Islam in which he was a pioneer in the Islamic world. Until a few decades ago, this subject was practically an unknown intellectual continent in the West as well as in the Islamic world itself. It is now a field of exploration into which many scholars are delving. Osman Bakar paved the way for this new field of study at the same time as Japanese scholars such as Toshihiko Izutsu and Sachiko Murata. Murata's early efforts were supported by the famous Chinese scholar, Tu Weiming, who was then a professor at Harvard University. While Osman Bakar was pursuing this matter in Kuala

Lumpur, Tu Weiming and I organized a conference on this subject at Harvard. Each of us invited several scholars that included Murata and William Chittick in my group. The two scholars have been collaborating on scholarly projects till today. The interactions and comparisons made between Confucianism and Islam owe much to the works of Osman Bakar, Sachiko Murata, and Toshihiko Izutsu who are the real founders of this very important subject. They have played a significant role in expanding the scholarly interest on the contemporary cultural and intellectual relations between China and the Islamic world.

Fortunately, Dr. Osman remains very active in the academic world through his teaching, lecturing, and writing. He was the Shaykh al-Kulliyyah of perhaps the most important center of research in Islamic studies in Kuala Lumpur, Malaysia – the Institute of Islamic Thought and Civilization (ISTAC). Founded by the notable Malay scholar, Dr. Naquib al-Attas, who personally supervised the beautiful architectural design and interior decoration of the ISTAC, this institution has played a major role in the intellectual life of Malaysia. Many young and prolific scholars have been trained there. May God make possible many years of service by Dr. Osman Bakar to the cause of scholarship in various institutions and provide him with the health and energy to continue his own scholarly and philosophical activities. He has left an indelible mark upon Malay-Islamic intellectual life and has served as a mentor to a whole generation of young aspirants. I pray that as an inspiring example for the new generation of Malaysian students and scholars, Dr. Osman is endowed with the strength and vitality to continue in this role for many years to come.

Wa'Llāhu a'lam

Seyyed Hossein Nasr

Foreword

Parallel Paths with Osman Bakar: The Polymath

Anwar Ibrahim

Former Deputy Prime Minister of Malaysia and Chairman Emeritus,
International Institute of Islamic Thought (IIIT)

There is a refrain that pops up at an alarming frequency, particularly in Muslim societies, that an antagonism must exist between politicians and scholars. This imagined clash of ignorance holds a peculiar irony where both hold as their ideal aspiration one who embodies the highest qualities of each, such as in Plato's notion of the philosopher-king, originally put forward in his work, *Republic*. This is an interesting dilemma that transcends the East–West divide as Al-Farabi adopted Plato's philosopher-king in his conceptualisation of *al-Madina al-fadila* (The Virtuous City), granted that this philosopher-king ought to also embody more theological qualities than Plato's first iteration. And this is not simply a sentiment of a bygone era. It lives on in our contemporary world when Ayatollah Khomeini sought to actualise this theoretical ideal in his role as the *Vilayat-e Faqih* of Iran, and his attempts at defending the democratic Shia doctrine of Ayatollah Shariat-Madari. Noting this curious contradiction, I have spent almost my entire career in public service raging against the idea that the scholar and the politician must be in perpetual conflict, although I do understand the roots of this clash.

From early on, I found myself entrenched in a rigorous debate about civilisational change. Prophet Muhammad demonstrated how this can be accomplished in the course of one generation within a relatively short period of twenty to twenty-three years. Yet the debate has become a chicken-or-egg argument. Is civilisational change accomplished through strong political will, good governance and effective leadership, or through an educational infrastructure that would enable the minds of the people to think critically in the pursuit of truth and justice?

I am also beholden to a philosophy that dictates the company I keep, a philosophy often attributed to a variety of business leaders and entrepreneurs that dates back to the sayings of Confucius (551–479 BC). Paraphrased, it states that if you are the smartest person in the room, then you are in the wrong room. And in surrounding myself with luminaries, I am often on the defensive as they insist that civilisational change begins with education, either through the empowerment of institutions or skilled teachers. My retort has been: how can an educational system go about instigating change without the will and direction provided by the state? The sting of poignance resonates particularly in a context like Malaysia's where historically the state and education have been intimately interlinked. Yet, my wise scholar friends are never quite satisfied, responding with an inquiry as to how political leaders are to know how to change or in which direction to steer a society without a robust educational system to enable such an intellectual facilitation? I have to admit that this is a good point. And round and round we go, the debate rarely reaching a gratifying conclusion for the parties involved.

While this debate may be unwinnable by either side, I remain committed to living out a clear example arguing for my side through my actions as someone dedicated to public service. Undoubtedly, so do my luminary friends in their scholarly work and educational endeavours. I have had the privilege of being challenged throughout my more formative years by Syed Muhammad Naquib al-Attas, who introduced me to Plato's *Republic* and instituted an unmatched scholarly rigor in my studies, as well as by his brother Syed Hussein Alatas and Ismail al-Faruqi, who brought me into IIIT (International Institute of Islamic Thought). IIIT continues to keep this debate alive and refuses to give in to my persuasions. That said, the three scholars afforded me countless hours of their time and an innumerable wealth of insight, their wisdom taking my education to a whole new level. They set me on my present intellectual trajectory. Indeed, so few have mirrored my life and career trajectories as a bona fide educationalist as Prof. Datuk Dr. Osman Bakar. And I can think of few individuals more worthy of being the subject of a Festschrift than Osman. This arises not just out of Osman being one of my oldest friends and colleagues or that our biographies are entangled since our rascal boyhood days at the Malay College Kuala Kangsar (MCKK), but that since our MCKK days—the final chapters of our own age of innocence—where our trajectories diverged. I walked from one political struggle to another, championing causes and serving their just rewards of a few prison sentences. Osman walked from one scholarly challenge to another, traveling the world both geographically and intellectually. Both of us hoped to make the change we desired. We aspired to the continuation of the projects we took on. Though our lives and journeys constantly intersected, from him being a member of the Central Committee and Secretary-General while I was President of ABIM (Malaysian Youth Movement) in the 1980s where together we promoted educational reform, to the stint we had in the United States, and finally to today, where both of us are impressively active with our respective projects here in Malaysia, which may take decades in the making. In this volume, the demonstration of Osman's influence is more than apparent. The variety and diversity of the contributions before you speaks not only to Osman's role as one of the great scholars of Islam, but also a scholar amongst all the other worlds Islam has come in contact with. Osman is more than a Muslim scholar, but a great scholar beyond modifiers.

In attaining such a global status, Osman sets an example for what all Muslim scholars ought to strive to be. In our tumultuous world of chaos and uncertainty, the forces of division, isolationism, xenophobia, and individualistic nationalism are rearing their ugly heads. While these trends shine brightest in society, they do not elude our educational systems which bear their own siloed and rigid disciplinarians, whose intellectual hubris has robbed them of the values of humility and curiosity required to produce original and revolutionary thought. And while many of us in the Islamic tradition dream for a return to the romanticised golden age of Islamic thought, unfortunately, too many of those who desire it the most often embody fullest that close-minded, unchanging conservatism that nailed shut the coffin on those glory days years ago. Yet, a noble few stand as a foil to this stereotype of the Islamic scholar, knowing and living an open, curious, and constructive framework for knowledge creation. These noble few know that the Islamic golden age was founded in openness and a desire for truth. Contradicting this, far too many take on a closed fundamentalist worldview built on proving their approach right or disproving others, regardless of the actual truth. They seek paradise while leaving the Earth to its own devices. Their concerns are solely based on a lasting intellectual legacy, unfazed by the people and communities they leave impoverished around them in their pursuits.

The course of history saw a decline of robust and new Islamic scholarship due to the machinations of those who justify mediocrity and stereotypes that persist up to today. Series of events and emerging hostility have grown into an artificial factionalisation of the world. They feed predominately global calls for clashing civilisations and this too often results in the sacrifice of essential Islamic tenets. Luckily, a noble few kept alive the Qur'an's call for critical thought and inculcated that call in almost all of our rituals down to the prayers we repeat five times each day. The Qur'an enjoins us to question, to keep open our minds and to build upon our prior knowledge. "Oh mankind! Verily we have created you all from a male and a female, and have made you into nations and tribes that you may come to know one another" (Chapter 49:13). The *Us* versus *Them* mentality that pervades the world order these days is a slap in the face for us when we reflect on this verse. Osman stands in direct opposition to the strict traditionalism that had ossified Islamic civilisation, removing its ability to have any impact on the world we presently live in. Osman raises critical questions instead of rallying troops for some fated apocalyptic battle. Whereas others desire conflicts and clashes, Osman looks to the world from all points of view and diverse traditions, seeing opportunities for advanced learning.

Osman embodies a child's sense of wonder. Not childish in terms of ignorance; far from it. Rather childlike in its innocence and incorruptibility in a world bent on poisoning the mind. This sentiment echoes the lost image of scholars during the Golden Age of Islam. It equips anyone with a potent tool to deal with the confounding state of the world, enabling him or her to operate in the throes of complexity, to work through seemingly unascendable contradictions. This approach to scholarship is incredibly powerful in tearing down engrained stereotypes both about and within Muslim scholarship, while offering solutions and contributions to the great questions of our day.

The foundations of such a scholastic philosophy rarely arise out of the typical pedagogical experience. And to say Osman's path has been atypical is but the tip of the iceberg. Predating Malaya's independence and the formation of Malaysia, great Malay scholars were not necessarily readily-made. While good schools were available, the success rate of Malay students was low, thanks to the double impediment of financial scarcity and the rigours of daily life which affected any Malay child's endeavour to get ahead in a system that demanded a strong command of English. This was a major hurdle for many young Malay students, particularly from rural areas. Academics and scholars tended to come from families with financial means or scholarly bloodlines. It was highly unlikely that a great Malay scholar could simply arise out of poverty and paucity. Yet, Osman did the unthinkable. Born to a poor and rural farming family from a small traditional village, Bukit Lada, Pahang, the prospects of becoming one of Islam's great scholars seemed an impossibility for Osman. I can still vividly remember chatting with Osman's father on a number of occasions. A simple farmer in the eyes of many, he instilled in Osman a strong sense of ethics in his upbringing. When matched with his preternatural curiosity and a high aptitude for learning, a path towards greatness was set before him. I remember from my own primary school days in Penang watching other kids from my community struggling to keep up with the demands of schooling life and how easily they were left behind. Luckily, Osman earned himself a spot at MCKK and the rest, as they say, was history. I cannot say it for many but Osman never forgot where he came from. He has tremendous pride in his parents and the rural community that raised him. His educational achievements were not a matter of chance but the product of the hard work, grit, and value his parents put into learning.

His divergence from the typical path would not falter even as he rocketed and found himself engrossed in the best education a young Malay could receive at the time. Even though a wide array of fields were open to us in the university, very few would pursue a degree in mathematics and eventually earning a Masters of Science. Osman did just that. More unusual was a shift in academic careers from mathematics to a PhD in the philosophy of science. Such a path was uncommon among Muslim scholars in the Malay world, but Osman took on the challenge in response to the revival of science education going on at the time throughout the Muslim world. Remarkably, Osman excelled in expanding the appeal of a highly specialized field, like the philosophy of science, to a wider audience and propounded it as a much needed area for Islamic scholarship. This is articulated well in one of Osman's best known works, *Classification of Knowledge in Islam: A Study in Islamic Philosophies of Science*. In reviewing the history of Islamic philosophy of science, he not only shines light on the field, but also investigates themes that would define his career, from the hierarchy and unity in science, to the distinction between revelation and reason, to the relationship between religion and philosophy.

It was here that Osman faced yet another age old artificial clash of ignorance, that which pits the people of science against those of faith. For Osman, ultimately, this manufactured dichotomy spoils the aims of each, which, at a fundamental level, are parallel pursuits or higher truths towards a greater understanding of our reality. And where both the Islamic and Western thinkers struggled to marry science and the divine, Osman saw it as an ideal arena for collaboration and discussion. While the two groups of thinkers may find it hard, nigh impossible, to reconcile certain worldviews, Osman found a commonality in the ethical underpinnings that unify their problem solving methodologies. A domination of one over the other has resulted in no victory thus far, and likely, never will. But from each other's strengths they can seek a better and more ethical understanding of the world. Instead of science as a distraction from faith, science can be a way to enhance one's faith. Deep devotion can enhance one's scientific quest. It is a balancing act that Osman takes on. He gives the perception that such a gargantuan task is simple and straightforward when the reality is somewhat different.

Anyone who listens to Osman's lectures can hear echoes of this integration reverberating. Within a few sentences, he will seamlessly jump from discussing Ibn Sina and al-Ghazali to the twentieth century theoretical physicist, Albert Einstein, and nineteen century naturalist, Charles Darwin, and not think twice about it. Interestingly, Darwin, along with Isaac Newton, remain in their final resting places of Westminster Abbey, a particularly holy place for two revolutionary heathen scientists who one would assume were of the greatest enemies to the faithful in the UK. Perhaps this assumed animosity between science and Christianity, like that between science and Islam, requires a bit more nuance.

Darwin, being a particularly conflicted man between his observations and faith, became an interesting subject for study to Osman in a series of papers on the theory of evolution. Where modern Western history has been rife with conflicts and strict dichotomy between the church and Darwin's theories, the Islamic perspective called for an understanding of the connectedness between the intelligent designer and evolutionary processes. Osman sought to prevent the rise of unproductive binaries in Islamic thought while also providing new solutions that Western thinkers would be wise to take a page from.

Osman even began to carry himself as an embodiment of the long overdue dialogue needed between Western and Islamic thought. To this day you still can see it in his outward appearance, developed during his days at the University of London, where he received his Bachelor's degree in mathematics. Upon receiving his degree, he would return to teach at the National University of Malaysia (UKM) in Kuala Lumpur and being the man of the world he was in our eyes, we gave him the nickname "Osman London." While I think he took the moniker with a good deal of pride, there was a bit of jest in the label as we would joke that he had become a Briton. The unforgiving cold that accompanies the winters of the UK is quite a shock to the Malay physique, its only recognized seasonal change being the monsoon. It is therefore perfectly understandable that a suit coat would become a regular fixture of Osman's wardrobe in London. But even when he was back in Malaysia, he insisted on wearing the suit coat, regardless of the more unforgiving heat encountered here! He insisted that he felt more comfortable wearing it and so, to this day, you rarely see him out in public without his coat. It has become his identity.

In his investigations into Darwinian theories and his adoption of a global, metropolitan aesthetic and intellectual lifestyle, we can trace the roots of Osman's greatest contributions to knowledge. Osman contributed to civilisational dialogue that I feel does not receive enough credit. It is masterfully displayed in *Islam and Confucianism: A Civilisational Dialogue* (1997). A much greater project, I hope, will continue well into the future with far larger aims. There are at least three major trans-civilisational projects at play here. The first project, which from Osman's perspective adds to a great dialogue that spans centuries is the one between the West and other dominant worldviews, especially between Islam and Chinese thought. This particular dialogue resides at the heart of numerous knowledge building pursuits. Al-Farabi and the thought of Plato and Aristotle may have been separated by centuries, but the interplay between their ideas represents the beauty and productivity of such a pursuit. In fact, the West, with their love of classical thought from Ancient Greece, owe early Islamic thinkers such as Al-Farabi a great debt. Thanks to Al-Farabi's hunger for all knowledge, many Greek works survived the numerous interregnums between the classical and renaissance ages in Europe. Today, Osman is always quick to cite the importance of Einstein's contributions to physics and why his theory of relativity needs further elaboration and development, particularly from the perspective of Islamic science. At the moment we see the need for academic collaboration in the fields of epidemiology and virology as the great minds of the whole world are coming together to rapidly develop a vaccine for the ongoing Covid-19 pandemic. These experts ought also to go further in preparing us all for the next pandemic that lurks just over the horizon.

The second aspect of the civilisational dialogue was spearheaded by Osman in the 1980s and 1990s. This is the civilisational dialogue that was particularly overdue, that is, the dialogue between the various civilisations who make their home here in Malaysia and have throughout history in the archipelago. While the first aspect of dialogue with the West was always present on the backburner of Osman's mind, this second aspect really came to form as he was conducting his doctoral studies in the US at Temple University. I recall one time when I stayed with him in Philadelphia in the early 1980s, when in spite of my jetlag, I was made to sit in a multi-hour long lecture on the eleventh century Persian scholar, al-Biruni's *Taḥqīq mā li-l-hind min maqūlah maqbūlah fī al-'aql aw mardhūlah (Verifying All That the Indians Recount, the Reasonable and the Unreasonable)*. Osman insisted I must hear his thoughts. Thankfully, his wife, Badariah Ahmad, saved me with her gracious hospitality. Badariah was savior to many of Osman's students and colleagues and her patience and support cannot be credited enough for its essential role in Osman's achievements.

Al-Biruni is largely considered one of the first Muslim scientists to open up a dialogue with Hindu thought and who struggled with Hinduism through the Islamic lens. It had always struck me how two civilisations that had grown up next door to each other throughout history, had so rarely attempted to understand one another. Osman explored this piece of Islamic intellectual history with so much passion, unpacking its deeper importance. Then as it is now, I take great interest in where he would take this, making it a great scholarly project.

The civilisational dialogue al-Biruni was tapping into, was also one of the earliest encounters in what we contemporaneously consider Malaysia. While the dialogue with the West worked to quell the conflict and clash, the dialogue here at home holds that same aim, but advances beyond the resolution of violence towards the peace found in unity. Through the Confucianism dialogue, which also sought to initiate dialogues with the other worldviews present here in Malaysia and throughout Asia like Hinduism and Buddhism, the similarities and common values unpacked in the project surfaced a deeper Asian identity. A most timely investigation for the dawn of what was at the time commonly considered to be the Asian Century. Economic and political factors could well have sunk the whole notion of the twenty-first century being the "Asian Century.' The civilisational dialogue project not only keeps this idea alive, but offers hope that great things lie ahead for the many years remaining in this century. The third dimension of Osman's civilisational dialogue project provides this avenue of opportunity through an additional layer of complexity.

While the dialogues needed amongst various present civilisations have a ready-to-hand pragmatism, a deeper and more connective exploration lies in the civilisational dialogues that exist across time. The present world is ensnared in narratives that obscure, if not completely erase our history, leaving the mind no other option but to accept what remains, which is the death of progress. This goes doubly here in Malaysia and throughout Southeast Asia. In Osman's latest publication, *Colonialism in the Malay Archipelago: Civilisational Encounters* (2021), the civilisational dialogue is extended beyond its contemporary station to explore the intersections that have occurred throughout history and rippled through into the present. The Malaysian sense of history has always been problematic. Alarmingly, recent narratives would have it that history began when the British arrived. Others would not care for the state of this beautiful land before the arrival of Islam. Yet all through time, the thought and culture that made its home here is important and requires unpacking as we seek to tear down divisions and respect difference in an attempt to know one another and advance our society together. While Osman is certainly not the first scholar to suggest a more elaborate approach to our history here in Malaysia, his additions are critical in clarifying elements of our knowledge that are often taken for granted.

In this refusal to accept taken for granted knowledge, we see the scholar and intellectual at the heart of Osman Bakar's being. Always curious, Osman leaves no question left unasked, no idea or theory left unscrutinised, but considered with openness and respect. Such an attitude has helped Osman to defend a figure of Islamic thought who has become a source of contention and division among Muslim thinkers. The Persian polymath Abu Hamid al-Ghazali, the namesake of the chair that Osman held at the International Institute of Islamic Thought and Civilization (ISTAC), was without a doubt, a towering thinker in the Islamic tradition, but no less a divisive figure. While his thought is held in high regard here in Malaysia, the insights of al-Ghazali are highly criticised, especially his critique of the philosophers. His cross-generational feud, if you can call it that, with Ibn Rushd concerning certain levels of incoherence illustrates well the debate. Osman is always quick to note that their rivalry was not a developed one as ibn Rushd was born just over a decade after al-Ghazali had died. Yet such a historical dialogue fits right into Osman's project. But instead of siding with the newer thinking, Osman digs deeper, considering the context of al-Ghazali's notion of *falsafa*. Osman rightly defends al-Ghazali, who saw a context where philosophical investigations were removed from their truth-seeking origins, which were in line with the Qur'ānic teachings, to be demented and used as a tool of contrarianism, ultimately undermining the *Sharī'a*, which philosophy in the classical sense was meant to support and further embellish. Al-Ghazali, like Osman, only sought to prevent sloppy thinking and populism from rotting our knowledge, something he saw as an existential threat; a threat that remains present in the unreflective world that stands on the other side of educational degradation and the handing over of our thought readily to technological convenience and selfish delights.

In his grand project of encouraging and engaging in civilisational dialogue, Osman also embodies the nomadic sentiment of the classic scholars of Islam's golden age. Ibn Khaldun travelled from the south of modern day Spain all across Mediterranean North Africa, onward to Mecca for *hajj*, to meet the infamous Tamerlane at the gates of Damascus, and spending his last days in Mamluk Egypt. Throughout his travels he not only encountered an immense wealth of peoples from innumerable backgrounds but also came to develop his theory of historiography which remains essential reading now. Journeying vast areas of land was almost requisite for the academics. Such travels produced the likes of Ibn Sina, Ibn Rushd, Al-Farabi and countless other golden age thinkers across Asia and North Africa. Mirroring their sojourns in the contemporary world Osman has studied all across the world, diving into the thoughts and theories the wider world has to offer. In his pursuits he puts forth another model which scholars ought to emulate. Unfortunately, Malay scholarship has been plagued by dastardly stereotypes which Osman has sought to put to rest. That is that a Malay scholar is only locally-oriented. On the contrary, a certain level of globe trotting is already inherent to Muslims of Southeast Asia. Peril and distance garners a greater respect for our brother and sister globetrotters out here than what is seen in the Middle East. To be sure, until recently, going on *hajj* from the Archipelago was quite the perilous journey. Hence here in Malaysia, we already find ourselves at the crossroads of a great many cultures and worldviews, thanks to the journeys which people from all over the globe made to this part of the world and the journeys of Malays here into the wider world. The revival of a golden age standard of scholarship must begin with such journeys which Osman has been among a noted exemplar.

Indeed, as the proceeding pages will testify, Osman not only presents us with a model by which the golden age of Islamic thought we long to see a return to may come about, but a new scholarship, which curious minds from the East to the West can embody. His objection to stagnation and arrogance in Muslim scholarship, is a beacon for all to build bridges with others in thought and society. His work ethic is admirable to all, remaining highly active well into his seventies. Even a global pandemic could not keep Osman from lecturing. He continues the scholarly conversations via Zoom and social media. He does not seem to be anywhere close to retirement. And what greater transformation could we hope to achieve?

Dr. Osman Bakar is a polymath who demonstrates the power of the Islamic tradition and the potential of scholarship and education in the Malay Archipelago. And what is most inspiring is not just what he has achieved, but the vigour with which he seeks to spread the transformative and uplifting power of education. Osman has not only pursued his own glory, but has been there every step of the way to assist us to build the educational ecosystem in Malaysia and to transform education into a tool for the Malays to succeed along with all the children of Malaysia. Osman's assistance and support was crucial in the formative years of ABIM. As Head of the Educational Bureau of ABIM, his efforts to reform education in the country were inspirational. He was instrumental in the establishment of Yayasan Anda Akademik, a project aimed at breaking the cycle of Malay youth being left behind by the old education system that denied many the opportunities they deserved. And he has left an indelible mark with each post he has taken through his teaching and going beyond to improve the system here in Malaysia from his lectureships at UKM, to his professorships and administrative posts at the University of Malaya (UM), as well as the positions he holds at the International Islamic University Malaysia (IIUM), and ISTAC. I only hope that I can inspire as much political discourse and reformist thinking as Osman.

But both Osman and I have many more miles to walk along our parallel paths of knowledge, wisdom, and progress. And while I and my like-minded principled colleagues will continue to work on bringing about transformation through political means and leadership, it is good to know that Osman and his fellow luminaries will keep our educational pursuits and institutions set on the path towards betterment as well. While the great debate I opened this piece with may never be satisfactorily resolved, I am hopeful that scholars and politicians will soon enough bridge their artificial differences to achieve civilisational transformation and renewal for a better future for all of humankind.

Introduction

Why Osman Bakar Matters

Khairudin Aljunied

Professor of Southeast Asian Islamic and Intellectual History at the University of Brunei Darussalam and Senior Fellow, Georgetown University, USA

This collection of essays is a tribute to the lifetime achievements of an erudite Muslim scholar-activist, Osman Bakar. Recognized as among the world's most influential Muslims, Osman is currently the second holder of the prestigious Al-Ghazali Chair at the International Institute of Islamic Thought and Civilization (ISTAC), Malaysia. He is the author and editor of close to three dozen books and hundreds of articles as well as commentaries, many of which have been translated into several languages. *The Classification of Knowledge in Islam* (1998) and *The History and Philosophy of Islamic Science* (1999) are now standard texts for anyone interested in the study of Islamic epistemology and civilization. Osman's prodigious scholarly career is also evidenced in a long list of keynote addresses and plenary speeches delivered in over forty countries. He has served as a chair professor in major Southeast Asian and North American universities and appointed as an expert advisor in many international organizations such as West-Islamic World Dialogue Initiative (known as the C 100), the UNESCO (The United Nations Educational, Scientific and Cultural Organization), the Qatar Foundation, and The European Science Foundation. An expert on contemporary developments in the Muslim world, his incisive and frank analyses have been sought after by major international media outlets such as *The New York Times, The International Herald Tribune, The Washington Post, Wall Street Journal, ABC News, BBC World Service, CNN* and *Al-Jazeera.*

Featuring established scholars based in North America, Europe, Africa, and Asia, the more than two dozen essays in this volume explore two key themes that pervade Osman Bakar's oeuvre: the production and problem of knowledge in Islam as well as the civilizational unity and renewal. In pursuit of these themes, this volume underlines Seyyed Hossein Nasr's view of his protege as the "most gifted young scholar who soon became one of the best students I had ever trained...His writings went beyond his initial field of specialization, that is, Islamic science and its philosophy, into Islamic philosophy in general, civilizational studies, Malay culture and history, and many other domains."[1] The former Deputy Prime Minister of Malaysia, Anwar Ibrahim, is barely exaggerating when he describes his childhood friend and fellow movement-leader as "a polymath," "a towering thinker," "a noted exemplar," and "a beacon for all to build bridges with others in thought and society."[2] Osman has set a high standard for budding scholars, intellectuals, writers, and activists. This volume is a humble attempt at honoring his multifarious achievements.

The Production and Problem of Knowledge in Islam

A dominant strand of Osman's scholarship pertains to how knowledge has been produced in Islam and the attendant problems that developed as Muslims encountered other systems of thought and ideologies. Muhammed Haron in his bibliometric study shows that one can only fully understand Osman's voluminous intellectual output by looking at his enquiries over the ways in which knowledge has been conceptualized and classified as well as the knowledge crisis which Muslims experienced in the face of colonialism, modernity and globalisation. It is almost commonplace nowadays to argue that the knowledge crisis confronting the Muslim world since the last two hundred years has no antecedent in the long career of Islamic thought.[3] Osman is among the modern Islamic thinkers who takes on this view. His response to that predicament has been, as Haron suggests, to take up the mantle of an engaged scholar "who is part of an academic structure such as the university and uses that opportunity to lower the academic walls by interacting with those in other disciplines."[4]

The essays in the first part of this volume engage fully with this facet of Osman's career. Together, the eleven contributors register the various circumstances and ideas which sensitized Osman with the issues relating to knowledge in Islam. They track and expand the intellectual pathways that Osman took. Clearly, Osman's ideas developed not only through the scholarly environments which he was situated in and an active participant of. Rather, his thoughts and scholarship are shaped by his experiences living with communities and querying the ideas of scholars he admired. As such, this section provides a brief sketch of Osman's intellectual biography and connects his life story to the theme of the production and problem of knowledge as discussed by the various contributors.

---

1 See: Preface by Seyyed Hossein Nasr in this volume.

2 See: Foreword by Anwar Ibrahim in this volume.

3 Abdul Ḥamid A. Abu Sulayman, *Crisis in the Muslim Mind* (Herndon: International Institute of Islamic Thought, 1993); Hishem Djait, *Islamic Culture in Crisis: A Reflection on Civilizations in History*, trans. Janet Fouli (New Brunswick: Transaction Publishers, 2011); Ali A. Allawi, *The Crisis of Islamic Civilization* (New Haven: Yale University Press, 2009).

4 See Chapter 1 of this volume.

Osman was born in 1946 from a poor peasant family in the edges of Pahang, Malaysia. He attributes his scholarly beginnings to his parents who imbibed in him the importance of hard work, the virtue of giving back to society, and the passion for knowledge and learning. A naturally gifted child, Osman was always fascinated with the wonders of nature. The Malaysian Nobel Laureate, Keris Mas, depicts life in rural Pahang in the pre-independence period in vivid terms as one that was challenging, yet at the same time, inspiring. The splendour of nature piqued the minds of anyone who cared to observe and reflect. Rural Pahang was a haven for thinkers, writers, and scholars.[5] Osman once related to me that, as a young child, he spent leisurely moments outside school admiring the sprawling flora and fauna. He memorized the names of all sorts of fruits found in abundance throughout the plantations and forests in close proximity to where he lived. That innate sense of curiosity and love for knowledge enabled him to excel in his studies. In 1963, he earned a place at the Malay College Kuala Kangsar (MCKK), a premier all-boys school established by British as the "Eton of the East." There, his interest for all things scientific deepened. "It would not be an exaggeration to say," according to Tengku Azzman who became his close friend since college days, "that we were totally dazzled and mesmerized by science. Its apparent objectivity, borne out of systematic methods of discovery, and the clarity of its findings inspired us like no other subject of study. The efficient way that science could reveal facts about natural phenomena was nothing short of magical."[6] Together, they were among the elite group of Malay-Muslims who entered British universities and, later on, became renowned academics in Malaysian universities. In the intervening period, Osman was actively involved in ABIM (Muslim Youth Movement of Malaysia) where he met and collaborated with other future Muslim scholar-activists such as Fadzil Noor, Anwar Ibrahim, Siddiq Fadhil, Mohd Nor Manuty, Razali Nawawi, among many others. The confluence of scholarly quest and activistic commitment became a trademark of Osman's writings in the ensuing years.

Trained as a mathematician specializing in algebra during his Bachelor's and Master's postgraduate studies in London, Osman switched to a life-long immersion in Islamic studies for his postdoctoral degrees at Temple University in the United States of America. This shift from the study of shapes, arrangements, and quantities to reflexive analyses of religious thought came about during his interactions with the renowned scholar of Islam, Seyyed Hossein Nasr. To Katherine Nielsen, Nasr exercised the greatest influence on Osman's thought. Nasr's call for the revival of sacred science in the modern world structures a core part of Osman's oeuvre.[7] My assessment of Osman's works points

5 Keris Mas, *Jungle of Hope* (Kuala Lumpur: Institut Penterjemahan Negara Malaysia Berhad, 2009).

6 See: Chapter 2 of this volume.

7 Katherine Nielsen, "The Philosophy of Osman Bin Bakar," *International Studies in the Philosophy of*

to a slightly different inference. Granted that Osman utilizes much of Nasr's ideas and is well-acquainted with all of his teacher's writings. But unlike Nasr, Osman is not concerned only with the fusion of science and religion. He envisions a total reconstruction of the architecture of knowledge in the modern world where science forms a constitutive but not a totalizing part of that reconstituted knowledge. As Jasser Auda rightly noted: "In our analysis, he [Osman] rather took a trans-disciplinary approach, in which the Qur'ānic knowledge lies at the center and as the basis. This was a significant step in the road towards a contemporary renewal in Islamic thought."[8] Osman seeks to expand the horizons of modern thought, particularly modern science.[9]

To be sure, there were a plethora of thinkers that fashioned Osman's ideas, among which was Syed Shaykh Al-Hady (1867–1934) whom Ahmad Murad sees as a precursor to Osman's project of providing Muslims with a renewed "sense of identity, unity, and new directions to overcome the problems of belief and domination by colonialists and Western civilization."[10] Osman also regarded the Malaysian intellectual, Naquib Al-Attas, as most prominent in shaping the direction of his early scholarship. During Osman's early years as a lecturer in the 1970s, he was Al-Attas' "student in philosophy and mysticism (*tasawwuf*), his colleague and friend, and at times also his sparring partner in the intellectual area, that is how I would describe myself in my then relations to him."[11] Al-Attas' sibling and intellectual antipode, Syed Hussein Alatas (1928–2007), too exerted some degree of influence on Osman. Alatas' critique of colonial ideology and the forms of knowledge that it had spawned made Osman attentive to the epistemic violence which western imperialism has effected on Muslim societies.[12] In an incisive essay that furthers Osman's concerns over the effects of colonial forms of knowledge on Muslims, Farish Noor puts into sharp relief selected Anglophone Orientalists' images of Arabs in Southeast Asia. Racism against the Arabs was justified through "the theory of racial polygenesis, which argued that the human race was not a single species but rather consisted of different races/species that resembled one another but which were nonetheless separate and distinct."[13]

Osman utilized widely the works of other classical and contemporary Muslim and non-Muslim thinkers in developing his own narratives of knowledge

---

Science 22, no. 1 (2008): 81–95.

8 See: Chapter 3 of this volume.

9 Pervez Hoodboy, *Islam and Science: Religious Orthodoxy and the Battle for Rationality* (London: Zed Books, 1991); Osman Bakar, "Nature as a Sacred Book: A Core Element of Seyyed Hossein Nasr's Philosophical Teachings," *Sacred Web* 40 (2017): 33–59.

10 See: Chapter 4 of this volume.

11 Osman Bakar, *Advancing Comparative Epistemology and Civilisational and Future Studies* (Kuala Lumpur: ISTAC-IIUM Publications, 2019).

12 Hussein Alatas, *The Myth of the Lazy Native* (London: Frank Cass, 1977).

13 See: Chapter 5 of this volume.

production and crisis in the Muslim civilization. The visions of Al-Farabi (872–950), Ibn Sina (980–1037), Al-Ghazali (1058–1111), Qutb al-Din al-Shirazi (1236–1311), Mulla Sadra (1572–1640), Muhammad Iqbal (1877–1938), Frithjof Schuon (1907–1998) and Ismail Al-Faruqi (1921–1986) are evident in Osman's works. Other than this list of thinkers, Osman admires Nasir al-Din Tusi (1201–1274) and his powers of observation and experimentation. Mohammad Faghfoory's chapter examines Tusi's ethical visions and theory of social classes which influenced generations of Muslims scholars and shaped the governing framework of Muslim empires. Like Osman, Faghfoory calls for a revival of Nasirian Ethics in the contemporary age since "modern politics and politicians have turned their back on ethics and ethical values in the realm of politics."[14] Beyond Tusi, the Muslim scholar that exerted a profound intellectual impact on Osman was Al-Ghazali.[15] In Chapter 7, Yasushi Kosugi pays homage to Al-Ghazali and other Muslim thinkers in synergizing primordial and adopted knowledges to define and refine the science of Islamic jurisprudence (*'ilm usul al-fiqh*). Kosugi agrees with Osman that Al-Ghazali was a master synthesizer who incorporated aspects of "Greek sciences, absorbed already in the form of speculative theology, and integrated them into the body of *usul al-fiqh*."[16]

At home with Western and Asian thoughts and philosophies, Osman benefited much from the insights of the eminent American historian of ideas, Arthur Lovejoy (1873–1932), particularly Lovejoy's notion of the cumulative traditions of knowledge within and between civilizations.[17] Harry Wolfson (1887–1974), in turn, provides Osman with insights into the expansive and intensive transmission of the works of Muslim theologians and rationalists into the Western civilization. Osman too was impressed with the ideas of the physicist, David Bohm (1917–1992), who propounded the theory of the wholeness of existence.[18] Suheyl Umar explores this strain of Bohm's thought and compares it with Muhammad Iqbal who preceded Bohm in arguing for "the ultimate ground of all experience."[19]

Indeed, Osman mined volumes of Iqbal's writings and many other thinkers from South Asia and East Asia. He was particularly moved by Confucianist thought and organised a landmark conference to encourage thinkers to compare Chinese thought with Islamic philosophy. For Osman, it is not excessive to suggest that Confucius was a prophet sent to the peoples of what later came to be known as China, Korea, Taiwan, and Japan.[20] Another East Asian scholar

14 See: Chapter 6 of this volume.
15 Interview with Osman Bakar, 20 March 2022.
16 See: Chapter 7 of this volume.
17 Osman Bakar, *Classification of Knowledge in Islam* (Cambridge: Islamic Texts Society, 1998).
18 Osman Bakar, *The History and Philosophy of Islamic Science* (Cambridge: Islamic Texts Society, 2012).
19 See: Chapter 8 of this volume.
20 Osman Bakar, "Confucius and Analects in the Light of Islam," in *Islam and Confucianism: A*

that exposed Osman to the shared features of the Buddhist, Taoist, and Muslim civilizations, the interactions and shared methodologies between them was Toshihiko Izutsu (1914–1993).[21] In Chapter 9, Nevad Kahteran explores Osman's long-standing interest in Chinese thought which has inspired "the establishment of an Islamic-Confucian-Daoist dialogue in the Balkans."[22] Similarly, inspired by Osman's call for the study of the interactions between East Asian thought and Islam, Hoo See Lee explores the making of the Korean-Islamic tradition that is firmly rooted in Confucian teachings and that are in line with Islamic basic principles.[23] Lee Cheuk Yin in his contribution directs our attention to the management genius of Admiral Zheng He, bringing to light how a deep analysis of this significant figure in Chinese history can reveal the close interactions between the Islamic and Chinese civilizations. Such interactions have survived for many centuries. Zheng He's "emphasis on harmonizing the ideals of Islam and that of other civilizations form the core of Osman Bakar's lifetime works which we are celebrating in this volume."[24]

All in all, the chapters in this section highlight the intellectual building blocks which Osman benefited from to explain the production of knowledge in Islam across space and time and the intractable problems that came with that process. Osman's trepidation was over four intertwining crises of knowledge in the modern Muslim world: secularism, materialism, universalism, and the problem of disequilibrium. On secularism, Osman agrees with Syed Naquib Al-Attas that the ideology has brought severe deformations in Muslim minds, one of which was the decoupling of spirituality from all intellectual pursuits.[25] In marking the dissonance between the sacred and the profane, Osman reprehends secularized Muslims for taking the step of reducing the meaning of human life to the earthly domain alone and of emptying it of its spiritual content. "All the ideals of human perfection and human happiness that religion in general and Islam in particular associates with the posthumous life became transferred at the hands of secularism to terrestrial life in the now-familiar form of a societal quest for progress and peace. A contest for influence between the two notions of societal salvation, one religious and the other secular thus became inevitable."[26]

Civilizational Dialogue, eds. Osman Bakar and Cheng Gek Nai (Kuala Lumpur: University of Malaya Press, 1997), 61–74.

21 Interview with Osman Bakar, 13 March 2020.

22 See: Chapter 9 of this volume.

23 See: Chapter 10 of this volume.

24 See: Chapter 11 of this volume.

25 Khairudin Aljunied, "Deformations of the Secular: A Rejectionist Conception and Critique of Secularism," *Journal of the History of Ideas* 79, no. 3 (2019): 643–63.

26 Osman Bakar, "Exclusive and Inclusive Islam in the Qur'an: Implications for Muslim-Jewish Relations," *Journal of the Interdisciplinary Study of Monotheistic Religions (JISMOR)* 5 (2010): 8.

Materialism forms the second component of the knowledge crisis faced by modern Muslims. Here, Osman foregrounds material wealth and prosperity as driving forces for the production of knowledge in the modern world. Osman sees this as a grave intellectual error on the part of many Western thinkers. This error permeates the works of Muslim scholars just as well to a point that they place technological and scientific progress above other equally important aspects of progress. Enamored by the achievements of the west, the modern Islamic thinker "ignores, belittles or denies altogether the metaphysical, spiritual, qualitative, and aesthetical aspects of nature."[27]

To be added to the issue of materialism is western universalism that dominates contemporary notions of knowledge. By this, Osman refers to the preponderant domination of European theories and truth claims as yardsticks to assess all civilizations. This claim to universality could be traced to the Enlightenment period and it became even more belligerent with the coming of colonization and, subsequently, with western military, political and economic hegemony in the era of nation-states. European forms of knowledge dictated the minds of the rest of the world. Rapid developments in science and communications in the west have made this universalism even more powerful than ever before. Western science positioned itself as "the most objective knowledge of the natural world ever attained in the history of human civilizations."[28]

Finally, Osman punctuates the problem of disequilibrium and, in this, he draws from Seyyed Hossein Nasr.[29] By prioritizing science and technology over other aspects of civilizational growth, Osman castigates modern Muslims for relegating religion, morality, ethics, culture, and values into becoming mere shibboleths. The Scientific Revolution that happened from the sixteenth century onward was, to Osman, imperialism of science and technology over all humankind. The world became subservient to the west. Muslims, in particular, became consumers rather than producers of western science and technology, imitators rather than inventors, and party to the very forces that hold them hostage. Osman laments:

> Contemporary civilisation whether in the West or the East is not well and is abnormal, because it has lost its equilibrium through various kinds of disorders and disproportions. Some of the diseases are unique to Western societies, some others to Eastern societies, and there are diseases that are common to both. The problem of restoring equilibrium in contemporary human societies is made worse by the fact that those individuals, institutions or functional groups on whom society traditionally relies to undertake the task are themselves in a state of crisis.[30]

---

27 Osman Bakar, *History and Philosophy of Islamic Science*, 64.

28 Osman Bakar, *History and Philosophy of Islamic Science*, 8.

29 Seyyed Hossein Nasr, *The Need for a Sacred Science* (Surrey: Curzon Press, 1993), 45–52.

30 Osman Bakar, *Islamic Civilisation and the Modern World: Thematic Essays* (Gadong: University Brunei Darussalam Press, 2014), 320.

Osman was however not a scholar who merely analyzes trends and challenges of knowledge within Islam. His other overriding aim was to bring together Muslims and non-Muslims to join hands in proposing reforms towards a renewal of their shared civilization. This theme is explored in the second part of this volume.

Civilizational Unity and Renewal

Unity (*Tawhid*) is, to Osman, a prerequisite for the renewal of civilization. He describes this as the "*Tawhidic* epistemology or vision of knowledge that affirms the view that all true human knowledge ought to be ultimately related to the unity of God, since all things are ontologically related to their Divine Origin."[31] Because unity forms the core of Muslim thought and the raison d'être of Muslim civilization, Muslim scholars pursued knowledge to deepen their quest to unveil God's wisdom. They studied forces, energies, music, arts, nature and wrote mathematical, scientific, historical, anthropological, and philosophical treatises to unlock the secrets of nature which they regarded as another form of divine revelation. The laws of nature were, to them, divine laws.

Osman believes that the effervescence of knowledge production among premodern Muslims had much to do with them embodying the spirit of Islam that encouraged *wasatiyyah* (balance) between technological progress and environmental preservation, between material prosperity and metaphysical fulfillment, between universal concern for humanity and particular wellbeing of Muslims, and between skepticism in worldly matters and certainty in faith. Guided by the *Tawhidic* epistemology, Muslim scholars and thinkers also outlined the functions of different fields through sophisticated classifications. They sought to live up to God's divine name, *al-'Alim* (The Omniscient), and became pathfinders of many scientific discoveries.[32] Or as Patrick Laude puts it in his exposition of Osman's *Tawhidic* epistemology: "Thus, a metaphysical understanding of Unity implies that multiplicity finds reality and meaning only through "unification" (*tawhīd*) or the "making one" of the (apparently) many. All the components of faith retrace aspects of this unification, the major ways in which multiplicity is "re-integrated" into Unity.... In other words, the soteriological and the eschatological are essentially included in the metaphysical, and they unfold from it, or rather they are various modes of its very unfolding."[33]

The remaining essays in this Festschrift advance Osman's views on the urgency of civilizational unity and renewal. In Chapter 13, Hashim Kamali

31 Osman Bakar, *Islamic Civilisation and the Modern World*.

32 Osman Bakar, *History and Philosophy of Islamic Science*.

33 See: Chapter 12 of this volume.

bridges Osman's thought with various efforts of *tajdid* (renewal), *islah* (reform) and *ijtihad* (independent reasoning) by modern thinkers in the likes of Muhammad 'Abduh, Yusuf al-Qaradawi, Muhammad al-Ghazali, Abu'l A'la Maududi, Isma'il Raji al-Faruqi, Hasan al-Turabi, Taha Jabir al-'Alwani, Abdullah bin Bayyah, and Fazlur Rahman. "The recourse to *tajdid*," according to Hashim, "is contingent on such existing norms and praxes and the renewers would usually prioritize which aspects require immediate attention and be restored to their original states." The inner dimensions of human life as emphasised by *tasawwuf* (Sufism) scholars, Osman suggests, must be spotlighted.[34]

To him, the Sufis provided Muslims with the rational and spiritual acumen that enabled Muslims to achieve great heights in all realms of life and to bind the hearts of communities. In the Malay world, Sufism inspired the creation of flourishing Islamic civilization for over five centuries.[35] Azyumardi Azra's chapter maps the contributions of Sufism in Southeast Asia in promoting unity among peoples in the region and in agitating for renewal and reform. There existed a variety of Sufi thought in Southeast Asia. Azra constructs an original typology to grasp the diversity of Sufi praxis: "collectivist Sufism," "individualist Sufism," "philosophist Sufism," "transnationalist Sufism," "televangelicalist Sufism," and "perennialist Sufism."[36] Such typology cements Osman's point that no unity can be achieved without recognizing and respecting the diversity of thought within civilizations. No unity can be achieved without reforming the family and educational system in ways that would underscore the spiritual dimension of Islam. In a searching review of Osman's thoughts, Zaleha Kamaruddin emphasizes the role of the family in creating "a harmonious balance for spiritual and moral development and focuses on the achievement of the twin goals of existence, i.e. servitude to God (*'ubudiyyah*) and the fulfilment of societal roles as *khalifah* on earth."[37]

In the same vein, Salleh Yaapar encourages the repositioning of the humanities in the educational system in an age when science and technology are given utmost attention. The neglect of the humanities, to Yaapar, has led to the creation of soulless societies. "Indeed, without the humanities—with their emphasis on values, ethics, the spiritual dimension of life and man-nature-divine relationship – STEM (Science, Technology, Engineering, and Mathematics) subjects can only produce humanoids, not humans!"[38] Azizan Baharuddin and Rosnani Hashim echo the same argument in urging for the return of religious and philosophical sciences as foundations for all educational pursuits. While

34 See: Chapter 13 of this volume.
35 Osman Bakar, "Sufism in the Malay-Indonesian World," in *Islamic Spirituality: Manifestations*, ed. Seyyed Hossein Nasr (New York: Crossroad, 1991), 259–89.
36 See: Chapter 14 of this volume.
37 See: Chapter 15 of this volume.
38 See: Chapter 16 of this volume.

Azizan makes the case for scholars of religious studies to "work together with scientific and philosophical studies and the humanities in general to help promote the ideals of sustainable development,"[39] Rosnani Hashim reiterates and magnifies Osman's stress on marrying the various sciences to avoid the pitfalls of later Muslims. The gulf between religious sciences and *Tawhidic* sciences which Muslim thinkers during the declining phase of Islamic history created led to intellectual stagnation. What intellectuals such as Osman tried to do, according to Rosnani, was remedy this problem by laying out a theoretical framework drawn "from the Islamic philosophical, religious and scientific traditions, the Qur'an and Prophetic Traditions, and also the current modern scientific thoughts and practices."[40]

The theoretical framework which Rosnani refers to could be termed as "dual consilience." Elsewhere, I have argued that Osman's idea of dual consilience refers to a judicious blend of overlapping methods, theories, themes, and questions posed within humanities, social sciences, and the natural sciences; three domains of knowledge that are often regarded as distinct from each other.[41] Such a vision parallels his contemporary, Edward O. Wilson. To quote Wilson here: "If the natural sciences can be successfully united with the social sciences and humanities, the liberal arts in higher education will be revitalized....The search for consilience might seem at first to imprison creativity. The opposite is true. A united system of knowledge is the surest means of identifying the still unexplored domains of reality. It provides a clear map of what is known, and it frames the most productive questions for future inquiry."[42]

The difference between Osman and Wilson lies in the latter's belief that all religions are a mere "ensemble of mythic narratives that explain the origin of a people, their destiny, and why they are obliged to subscribe to particular rituals and moral codes."[43] Islam is barely mythical to Osman. It is a rational faith that generated a flourishing civilization of knowledge. Moreover, Osman expands the notion of consilience to include religious sciences. The unification of various sciences was apparent in the Islamic civilization. In his chapter, Reza Shah-Kazemi explains how Muslim artists and thinkers in the medieval period struck a balance between different fields of knowledge in their endeavour to express the beauty of God's creation. "For traditional Muslim artists who lived, worked, and thought in a spiritual ambience governed, to some degree or another, by the worldview of *tawhid*, there was no compartmentalisation of thought and life. There was no artificial separation between the inner significance of things and their practical utility."[44]

39 See: Chapter 17 of this volume.
40 See: Chapter 18 of this volume.
41 Khairudin Aljunied, *Shapers of Islam in Southeast Asia* (New York: Oxford University Press, 2022).
42 Edward O. Wilson, *Consilience: The Unity of Knowledge* (New York: Vintage, 1999).
43 Wilson, *Consilience: The Unity of Knowledge.*
44 See: Chapter 19 of this volume.

To achieve consilience between different fields, Osman proposes a rethinking of the idea of "science." Modern science, in Osman's assessment, departs from science as it was understood and practiced by Chinese, Indian, Islamic, and other civilizations in the premodern period. These civilizations did not separate natural sciences from the humanities, social sciences, and the religious sciences. They drew and learnt from other civilizations to reach a middle ground. According to Peter Chang, this middle ground whereby all sciences were placed in equal importance to achieve a synthesis has been sidestepped since the advent of western secularism and colonialism. Hence, Chang posits that Osman's proposal for "the cross-fertilization of cultural ideas and scientific knowledge with the Greek, India, and Sinic civilizations" is much needed now. In that way, modern civilizations could once again recover the God-centric worldview that "was abandoned in favour of the man-centric worldview where the vision of the whole man has been lost."[45]

A renewal of interactions between civilizations is, to Osman, the key to realizing what he calls an "Islamic science" which embodied the ideal of dual consilience. Osman uses the term Islamic science "not just because it happened to be largely produced by Muslims but more importantly because it was based on the universal and particular principles of the Qur'an."[46] It follows then that Osman's definition of Islamic science stands in stark contrast to a noted historian of science in Muslim civilization, George Saliba, who refers to "Islamic science" to represent a body of knowledge that should be decoupled from *al-'ulum al-islamiya* (Islamic sciences). The term "Islamic" is used in a "more complex civilizational sense and not in the religious sense."[47]

Both Osman and Saliba are on the same page in maintaining that Islamic science—whatever the definition might be—reached its apogee by the seventeenth century. In Chapter 20, Hazim Shah explains that, since the outset, Islamic science has been instrumentalist in its philosophy, aims, and methods. For Muslim scholars during the heydays of the Muslim civilization, science "is largely utilitarian and served as a handmaiden to religion….The instrumentalist nature of Islamic science, and the non-integration of (Greek) natural philosophy with mathematics and experimentation, kept Islamic science immune from the kind of epistemological-cultural crisis that was later to beset the West."[48] Be that as it may, decline took root when Muslim empires gave less emphasis to philosophical and scientific pursuits than on religious dogma that promoted blind obeisance to authoritarian caliphates and, following that,

45 See: Chapter 21 of this volume.

46 Osman Bakar, "Islamic Science, Modern Science, and Post-Modernity: Towards a Synthesis through a *Tawhidic* Epistemology," *Revelation and Science* 1, no. 3 (2011): 13–20.

47 George Saliba, *Islamic Science and the Making of the European Renaissance* (Massachusetts: MIT Press, 2007).

48 See: Chapter 20 of this volume.

autocratic colonial, and postcolonial regimes. The resurrection of an eclipsed Islamic science is still possible, in Osman's estimation, "by virtue of their [Islamic science] universal and perennial worth." [49] However, such attempts at reviving Islamic science are never without challenges. Oliver Leaman makes apparent the philosophical and practical problems of any claims to bring back religion into science. He observes: "Scientists often do admire what they discover in their inquiries yet without assigning any particular spiritual meaning to it beyond the aesthetic. This may but need not have a religious basis, and what we are talking about here is not so much whether scientists claim a religious underpinning to the universe and to their work, but whether they really operate in accordance with such a principle." [50] Osman's rejoinder might be that the dialogues and debates over the relationship between science and faith must first be made mainstream before the idea and practice of Islamic science can be operationalised in earnest. He urges peoples from all traditions to be part of this process towards achieving consilience in knowledge and in realizing civilizational unity and renewal.

Conclusion

This collection of essays bears testimony to Osman Bakar's prolific career, his versatility of thought, and the impact that he has had on the minds of numerous fields of modern scholarship. His interventions into the question of what went wrong in the Muslim civilization and how it can be set aright cannot be glossed over. He is among the few Muslim intellectuals based in Southeast Asia who has consistently sought to address epistemological as well as ethical, cosmological, and ontological problems in contemporary knowledge that have shaped Muslim minds. Osman is, as John Esposito sums up so well in his Afterword, "one of the leading Muslim scholars of the late twentieth and early twenty-first century. He diagnosed and advocated the critical need for Islamic renewal (*tajdid*) and reform (*islah*), and promoted interfaith relations. Like Muhammad Iqbal, Sayyid Ahmad Khan, Seyyed Hossein Nasr, Ismail Al-Faruqi, Syed Muhammad Naquib al-Attas, and Hamka (Abdul Malik Karim Amrullah), to name a few prominent Muslim scholars and reformers in the modern Muslim world, Osman Bakar recognized the need for Islamic renewal."[51]

In highlighting the production and the problem of knowledge in the Muslim world and the possibilities of civilizational unity and renewal, Osman points to some interesting pathways that should be broached and given serious

49 Osman Bakar, "Towards a Postmodern Synthesis of Islamic Science and Modern Science: The Epistemological Groundwork," in *The Muslim 500: The World's 500 Most Influential Muslims, 2020* (Amman: The Royal Islamic Strategic Studies Centre), 197–201.

50 See: Chapter 22 of this volume.

51 See: Afterword of this volume.

thought. A courageous and yet unassuming man, he is a friend, a teacher, a comrade, and a role model to many in search of the higher truth in their bid to enhance human understanding. Osman Bakar matters, now and in the many years to come.

Bibliography

AbuSulayman, AbdulḤamid A. *Crisis in the Muslim Mind.* Herndon: International Institute of Islamic Thought, 1993.

Alatas, Hussein. *The Myth of the Lazy Native.* London: Frank Cass, 1977.

Aljunied, Khairudin. "Deformations of the Secular: A Rejectionist Conception and Critique of Secularism." *Journal of the History of Ideas* 79, no. 3 (2019): 643–63.

Aljunied, Khairudin. *Shapers of Islam in Southeast Asia.* New York: Oxford University Press, 2022.

Allawi, Ali A. *The Crisis of Islamic Civilization.* New Haven: Yale University Press, 2009.

Djait, Hishem. *Islamic Culture in Crisis: A Reflection on Civilizations in History.* Translated by Janet Fouli. New Brunswick: Transaction Publishers, 2011.

Hoodboy, Pervez. *Islam and Science: Religious Orthodoxy and the Battle for Rationality.* London: Zed Books, 1991.

Keris Mas. *Jungle of Hope.* Kuala Lumpur: Institut Penterjemahan Negara Malaysia Berhad, 2009.

Nasr, Seyyed Hossein. *The Need for a Sacred Science.* Surrey: Curzon Press, 1993.

Nielsen, Katherine. "The Philosophy of Osman Bin Bakar." *International Studies in the Philosophy of Science* 22, no. 1 (2008): 81–95.

Osman Bakar, "Exclusive and Inclusive Islam in the Qur'an: Implications for Muslim-Jewish Relations." *Journal of the Interdisciplinary Study of Monotheistic Religions (JISMOR)* 5 (2010): 8.

Osman Bakar. "Towards a Postmodern Synthesis of Islamic Science and Modern Science: The Epistemological Groundwork." In *The Muslim 500: The World's 500 Most Influential Muslims, 2020.* Amman: The Royal Islamic Strategic Studies Centre.

Osman Bakar. "Confucius and Analects in the Light of Islam." In *Islam and Confucianism: A Civilizational Dialogue*, edited by Osman Bakar and Cheng Gek Nai, 61–74. Kuala Lumpur: University of Malaya Press, 1997.

Osman Bakar. "Islamic Science, Modern Science, and Post-Modernity: Towards a Synthesis through a *Tawhidic* Epistemology." *Revelation and Science* 1, no. 3 (2011): 13–20.

Osman Bakar. "Nature as a Sacred Book: A Core Element of Seyyed Hossein Nasr's Philosophical Teachings." *Sacred Web* 40 (2017): 33–59.

Osman Bakar. "Sufism in the Malay-Indonesian World." In *Islamic Spirituality: Manifestations*, edited by Seyyed Hossein Nasr, 259–89. New York: Crossroad, 1991.

Osman Bakar. *Advancing Comparative Epistemology and Civilisational and Future Studies.* Kuala Lumpur: ISTAC-IIUM Publications, 2019.

Osman Bakar. *Islamic Civilisation and the Modern World: Thematic Essays.* Gadong: Universiti Brunei Darussalam Press, 2014.

Saliba, George. *Islamic Science and the Making of the European Renaissance.* Massachusetts: MIT Press, 2007.

Wilson, Edward O. *Consilience: The Unity of Knowledge.* New York: Vintage, 1999.

Part 1

The Production and Problem of Knowledge

Chapter 1

An Engaged Scholar: An Intellectual Biography and Bibliometric Study of Osman's Intellectual Contributions

Muhammed Haron

Former Professor of Theology and Religious Studies at the University of Botswana
Associate Researcher: Stellenbosch University, South Africa

Over a period of about four decades, Professor Osman gradually established himself as a remarkable scholar within and beyond the Muslim world. Apart from having placed Southeast Asian scholarship on the map as a respected scholar, he has also been recognised as one of the region's foremost Muslim philosophers. Osman's curriculum vitae reflects his passion for philosophy in general and Islamic philosophy in particular. He has a longstanding interest in the intersection between religion and science as well as in civilizational studies. As a tribute to Osman's critical scholarly interventions, this chapter undertakes a bibliometric analysis of his intellectual contributions. While the study intends to graphically highlight Osman's significant research outputs as an active and passionate academic, it also wishes to review and analyse selected texts that remain noteworthy.

Introduction

Islamic Studies has emerged as a distinct field of inquiry within western academia. Jacques Waardenburgs is correct to state that "there is no generally accepted definition of the discipline of Islamic Studies, that its boundaries are not clearly fixed, and that there are no uniform and generally accepted programmes … It constitutes a field of studies employing various disciplines."[52] It is perhaps appropriate to refer—albeit briefly—to Siddiqui[53] who defined

52 Bustami Khir, "Islamic Studies within Islam: Definition, Approaches and Challenges of Modernity," *Journal of Beliefs & Values* 28, no. 3 (2007): 260.

53 Ataullah Siddiqui, *Islam at Universities in England, Meeting the Needs and Investing in the Future*

Islamic Studies in two ways. The first is that Islamic Studies should be viewed as a discipline that is academically rigorous, that critically analyses Muslim communities in their respective regional settings and evaluates Islam as a complete civilization. The second is that Islamic Studies covers every aspect of Islam (i.e., it deals with, among other matters, the cultural and religious, the economic and political, the social and philosophical, the past and present, the regional and universal dimensions).[54]

Keeping these definitions in mind, it may be argued that it is a vast field of inquiry that is multi-disciplinary and, because of this, it has attracted the attention of a range of scholars from various areas of specializations within and outside the Muslim world. The contribution of scholars outside the Muslim world has recognizably added value to the expansive and growing field and this has been well-captured in the ongoing *Index Islamicus* project.[55] Anyone who browsed through its copious volumes, would give ample credit to the multitudes of scholars who ventured to pursue and open new areas of interests.

Undoubtedly, the field of Islamic Studies has been enriched because of the input of these creative scholars over many decades. It has since included many new areas of inquiry such as bioethics. More importantly, it may be submitted that Islamic Studies would not have blossomed if it had not been for a coterie of creative and inquisitive modern Muslim scholars who ventured into unknown territories. Individually and collectively, they continued to create new knowledge and enlarge the scope of Islamic studies.

This chapter's focus turns to one such scholar who is an eminent and respected professor, Osman Bakar. He has plied his trade with a scholarly zeal, with a desire for knowledge gathering, with a yearning to open pathways for younger scholars, and with a longing to leave a rich legacy. He is listed within the well-known and widely circulated publication *The Muslim 500: The World's 500 Most Influential Muslims*.[56] Since 2009, Prof. Osman Bakar (and from hereon: Osman) remained part of that exceptional register of scholars, many of whom come from inside the Muslim world, and some who come from outside that domain.

Hailing from Malaysia where he studied and worked for much of his life, Osman emerged as a noted reputable scholar, along with several other

(Leicester: Markfield Institute for Higher Education, 2007).

54 Muhammed Haron, "Southern African Islamic Studies Scholarship: A Survey of the State of the Art," in *African Traditions in the Study of Religion in Africa: Emerging Trends, Indigenous Spirituality and the Interface with other World Religions*, ed. A. Adogame, E. Chitando, and B. Bateye, 219–238 (London: Ashgate Publishing, 2012).

55 Geofrey J. Roper, "Index Islamicus," *History Compass* 36 (2003): 1–4; Sean Swanick, "Advisor Reviews – Standard Reviews: *Index Islamicus*," *Charleston Advisor* 14, no. 2 (2012): 29–31; Rosalina Othman and Ashraf A. Salahuddin, "Relevance Status of Value Model of *Index Islamicus* on Islamic History and Civilization," *International Journal of Web Information Systems* 11, no. 1 (2015): 54–86.

56 S. Abdallah Schleifer, ed., *The Muslim 500: The Most Influential Muslims 2022* (Amman: The Royal Islamic Strategic Studies Center, 2021), 123.

Malaysian social scientists and legal scholars such as Prof. Muhammad Naquib al-Attas (b.1931) and Prof. Kamal Hasan (b.1942). Presently, it may be argued that Osman remains one of Malaysia's foremost philosophers. He belongs to a select group of Muslim philosophers that have given a face-lift to a subject that has been neglected, if not ignored, as a critical area of study. Osman's enthusiastic and engaged scholarship has also inspired many young researchers and activists from the Southeast Asia region where a huge Muslim population resides.

This chapter aims to assess Osman's scholarly contributions using a bibliometric study approach, outline his luminous biography,[57] and comment on his scholarly acumen. Prior to embarking on that path, I take a slight detour by unpacking the notion of "an engaged scholar." I use this term as a theoretical concept to illustrate Osman's standing as a distinguished scholar within Asian academia and the contemporary Southeast Asian community that he served and continues to serve through his appealing scholarship.

Osman Bakar: An Engaged Scholar

It should be stressed that with all the evidence at hand there is little doubt that Osman may be described as an "engaged scholar" in and outside the Muslim world. The term "engaged scholar" or "scholarship of engagement" was first coined by the American scholar, Ernest Boyer.[58] Since then, the idea of "an engaged scholar" was popularized in and across academic circles. Boyer identified a few foundational principles of engagement, some of which many academics were already familiar with. This type of scholarship meant that a scholar who is part of an academic structure such as the university uses that opportunity to "lower the academic walls" by interacting with those in other disciplines. Through this, he/she opens spaces for intellectual and communal engagement. In the process of undertaking his/her academic tasks as an engaged scholar, he/she becomes accountable to the academic authorities and to various representative groups in civil society that are in pursuit of positive reforms and transformation.

The South Africa's University of the Free State defined "engaged scholarship" as a process in which "the application of academic scholarly work and professional expertise" are intentionally and purposefully directed at the public.[59] The scholar seeks and wants to reap mutual benefits from academia as well as the public. In other words, it cultivates a relationship between academic

57 Radu Iliescu, "Biography of Osman Bakar (b.1946–)," April 17, 2005, http://elkorg-projects.blogspot.com/2005/04/biography-of-osman-bakar-1946.html

58 Ernest Boyer, "The scholarship of engagement," *Journal of Higher Education Outreach and Engagement* 20, no. 1 (2016): 15–27; "The scholarship of engagement," *Journal of Public Service and Outreach* 1, no. 1 (1996): 11–20.

59 University of the Free State, "Engaged Scholarship Strategy," 2020, https://www.ufs.ac.za/supportservices/departments/community-engagement-home/community-engagement-at-the-ufs/engaged-scholarship

and non-academic stakeholders. Through these ties, the scholarship of engagement will generate new knowledge, enhance the application of knowledge, and disseminate knowledge to those that will gain positive benefits from it.[60] Hence, when Boyer pointed out that "the academy must become a more vigorous partner in the search for answers to our most pressing social, civic, economic, and moral problems, and must affirm its historic commitment to what I call the scholarship of engagement," he reminds us of Osman.[61]

Anyone who started out in academia from a relatively young age, would have encountered numerous challenges moving up the academic ladder while remaining committed to being an engaged scholar. Osman's path was, however, slightly different from the norm. Instead of following a career in the pure sciences with mathematics as the focus area, Osman opted out and turned to the social sciences as the alternative. Within this broad field, religion became his area of specialization. It is assumed that whilst he was busy with his doctoral studies thesis concentrating on Algebraic group theory, he read far beyond the subject. In that process, he realized the critical role that religion played in societies and the cosmos. Having read widely and extensively, he did not think twice of making the switch from the pure sciences to the social sciences. According to Kersten, he showed deep interest in examining the epistemological aspects of the relation between science and religion namely, Islam.[62] He never had regrets over this academic shift, but did not expect that he would be handsomely rewarded via various public recognitions over the years.

Osman's walk-over from one science to another, where philosophy and religion were key subjects for academics and society, caused him to devise informative exciting teaching courses (such as Science and Technology in Contemporary Muslim World, Religion and Quantum Physics, and Epistemology and Research Methodology) at the University of Malaya (UM).[63] He pursued teaching and research with great passion. It was his telling research outputs that had an enormous socio-scientific-cum-intellectual benefit for those within and outside the academia. Having always been a proud and honourable Malaysian, he had no qualms in dedicating his life serving Malaysian society via the local and international universities for fifty years.

On top of that, while in that position where he set himself up as a thought leader (*tokoh pemikiran*) he saw the glaring gaps within the academic system

---

60 Also see Dorothy Holland et al., "Models of Engaged Scholarship: An Interdisciplinary Discussion," *Collaborative Anthropologies* 3 (2010): 1–36; Matthew Flinders, "The Politics of Engaged Scholarship: Impact, Relevance, and Imagination," *Policy & Politics* 41, no. 4 (2013): 621–642; Lynette Shultz and Tania Kajner, eds., *Engaged Scholarship: The Politics of Engagement and Disengagement* (Rotterdam: Sense Publishers, 2013).

61 Boyer, "Scholarship of engagement."

62 Carool Kersten, "Reviving the 'Islamization of Knowledge' Project?" 2012, https://caroolkersten.blogspot.com/2012/01.

63 Iliescu, "Biography of Osman Bakar."

and worked towards bridging them. He noted the gaping holes that existed among religious traditions, on the one hand, and between science and religion, on the other. In response to the latter, he organized seminars and wrote essays for publications; these authored texts and co-edited works have since become significant reads and prescribed texts for students, interested researchers, and emerging scholars. One of these was *Tawhid and Science: Essays on the History and Philosophy of Islamic Science* in 1989 which was translated into Bahasa Indonesia under the title *Tauhid dan Sains* during 1994.

As for inter-religious dialogue, Osman, with Cheng Gek Nai co-edited *Islam and Confucianism: A Civilizational Dialogue* in 1997 (reprinted in 2019), the publication demonstrated Osman's interest in bringing religious communities towards a common ground. Related to this publication, it is appropriate to mention another title, *Islamic and Civilizational Dialogue: The Quest for A Truly Universal Civilization*. This book revealed Osman's passion for open and critical dialogue. Due to his recognized standing and interest in that theme in 2000, he was appointed as a member of the West-Islamic World Dialogue Initiative (known as the C 100), a structure that was set up by the Davos-based World Economic Forum while serving as UM's Research Fellow at its Center for Dialogue of Civilizations.[64]

Osman's appointment as C 100 member and other activities underlined his commitment to dialogue and overcoming the existing differences between faiths. In 2013, Osman became an Advisory Board member of the Centre for Buddhist-Muslim Dialogue that is housed in the College of Religious Studies at Thailand's Bangkok-based Mahidol University. And one of the most recent activities in which Osman was a participant was the "Online Islam-Buddhism Forum" with the theme "Compassion and Mercy as the Common Values between Islam and Buddhism" on 28 September 2020. Important to record is the fact that these were and still are some of the themes and topics that Osman engages with throughout his career as a scholar.

Besides having immersed himself in his academic surroundings to serve all stakeholders, Osman proved that he was loyal towards the communities that he dutifully served. This was through, among other activities, presenting various public lectures and pursuing academic activities. One of the critical themes/approaches that Osman broached in his books and articles was "Islamization of Knowledge," a theme that was advocated by Professor Naquib al-Attas as well as Professor Raji Al-Faruqi (d.1986). In an interview with Osman, Kersten rhetorically titled his blog: *Reviving the "Islamization of Knowledge" project?*[65] Azizan Had, another Malaysian scholar, was registered at King's

64 Muhamad Razak Idris, "Malaysian Scholars' Perspectives on the Role of Dialogue of Civilizations as an Approach in Promoting World Peace," *Malaysian Journal of Islamic Movements and Muslim Societies* 1, no. 1 (2021): 59–73.

65 Kersten, "Reviving the 'Islamization of Knowledge' Project?"

College London for a PhD to evaluate the project of Islamization of Knowledge since it was advocated by Osman and others as well.

He once responded to Kersten who held the view that the "Islamization of Knowledge" project had run out of steam. Osman retorted that this was due to "the over-politicization of the project at the expense of its academic rigour."[66] Osman intimated that, "the epistemological aspects surrounding the issue of how religion and science relate to each other have not been pushed far enough." As a result of this and in response to former Prime Minister Abdullah Badawi's request in 2008, Osman gave his support for the implementation of the *Islami Hadhari* project; it was a plan that Osman considered, during that period, "an opportunity to blow new life into the Islamization of Knowledge."

Osman's interest in the subject gained him a Fulbright Visiting Scholarship at Harvard University (circa July–December 1992) and position as Guest Research Fellow (circa 2006–2011) at the Kyoto-based Doshisha University in Japan. In addition to these academic appointments, Osman was offered invitations to deliver lectures at different tertiary institutions in and outside Malaysia. During these stints, he shared and exported his ideas to a variety of academic audiences globally. Since the start of the Covid-19 pandemic in March 2020, Osman has been consistently invited to participate in their online seminars and similar events that were open to a global audience; these underlined Osman's commitment as an academic activist and an engaged scholar. From what has been tabulated thus far, it can be argued that over the past two decades, Osman's academic profile skyrocketed; and this has secured his status as one of the most influential scholars in and beyond the Muslim world.

Osman created communal spaces and institutional partners to advance knowledge. One example that may be referred to is Osman's March 2021 presentation titled "Futuristic Vision of the Discipline of Islamic Studies." This virtual meeting targeted the staff at the Central University of Kashmir. Osman weeded out the misconceptions that were pervasive about Islamic Studies while stressing the difference between the "Discipline of Islamic Studies" and the "Study of Islam." He proposed that Departments of Religious Studies should consider introducing fresh courses such as "Spiritual Anthropology" and "Ummatic Studies."[67]

Besides engendering partnerships, Osman made ample use of online platforms to pursue this. In addition, during this challenging period Osman's continuous academic virtual participation is evidence of his engaging manner. He adopted a creative and responsive stance in face-to-face and virtual lectures. He dealt with complex topics by sharing them with diverse audiences in a

---

66 Kersten, "Reviving the 'Islamization of Knowledge' Project?"

67 Greater Kashmir, "Futuristic Vision for the Discipline of Islamic Studies," March 16, 2021, https://www.greaterkashmir.com/kashmir/futuristic-vision-for-the-discipline-of-islamic-studies-prof-osman-bakar-delivers-online-extension-lecture-in-cuk

comprehensible manner. Unlike other scholars that considered the university their ivory towers where knowledge is produced in isolation from social issues, Osman belonged to those that activated and shared knowledge beyond the university's walls.

Now that a definition and an explanation of engaged scholar has been proffered, it is time to take a closer look at Osman's scholarship in Islamic Studies; a scholarship that lends itself to interdisciplinary approaches and that cross-pollinates ideas from one discipline to the other. In unpacking this, there is a need to return to Osman's educational background to emphasize that he was exposed to different sciences and schools of thought; and because of that rich and energetic exposure, he made many efforts to bridge the knowledge gaps.

Osman's Islamic Studies Scholarship: Pursuing Goals, Advancing Academically

Via oblique reference, aspects of Osman's academic background were pointed out in the aforementioned section. This segment, however, intends to fill some of the glaring gaps. It refers to selective academic advances that he accomplished as he moved up the academic ladder in, and even far beyond, Malaysian academic institutions. While the first part re-narrates, albeit briefly, Osman's educational voyage, the second concentrates on his research records.

Osman's Academic Journey

Osman completed a BSc degree and an MSc from the University of London (UOL) in 1970 and 1971 respectively before completing his doctorate in Islamic philosophy from Temple University in 1987. He was lecturer at the National University of Malaysia (UKM) for several years (circa 1970–1977) and moved to the University of Malaya thereafter (circa 1977–2000). In 1977, Osman founded the Malaysian Academy of Islamic Sciences (MAAS). Between 1977 and 1981, he was its Secretary-General and a key member of the Angkatan Belia Islam Malaysia (ABIM: Malaysian Islamic Youth Movement est. 1971). Apart from demonstrating his leadership qualities, he was enthusiastically publishing several academic articles. From 1981 to 1986, he embarked on his PhD at Temple University (TU) and upon his return to Malaysia, he was elected MAAS' President in 1987; a position he held until 1992. And on two occasions, UM appointed Osman as the Faculty of Science's Deputy Dean. The first was from 1990 to 1992 and the second from 1994 to 1995.

In 1992, UM accorded him a full professorship post and this appointment was in view of a few books he had already published. Between 1992 and 2000, he took up the prestigious "Philosophy of Science" chair at UM. From 1995 till 2000, he was selected to be UM's Deputy Vice-Chancellor of Academics,

Research, and Human Resources. He was conferred the title of Datuk by the then King of Malaysia and too, formally retired. UM recognized him as its Emeritus Professor of Philosophy of Science because of his immeasurable academic leadership in both teaching and research.

He then journeyed to USA's Washington DC where he took up the Malaysia Chair of Southeast Asian Islam at the Prince Alwaleed Bin Talal Center For Muslim-Christian Understanding, Georgetown University (GU circa 2000–2005). This was a chair that he, interestingly, was commissioned to establish in 1994; the same year in which he was conferred the title Dato' by the Sultan of Pahang. While still at GU, he was invited in 2001 to be a member of University of Pennsylvania's Religious Working Group; it focused on Genetically Modified Food at its Center for Bioethics. Soon after Osman completed his contract at GU, he moved back to Malaysia when ISTAC-IIUM (Institute of Islamic Thought and Civilization-International Islamic University of Malaysia) conferred on him a professorial post. He stayed there until 2008.

He then moved on to become the Deputy Chief Executive Officer (circa July 2008–September 2012) of Malaysia's International Institute of Advanced Islamic Studies (IAIS). During this time, Osman was also a Senior Research Fellow at UM's Center for Civilizational Dialogue from 2007 until 2010, and he was thereafter appointed as its consultant from January 2010 to June 2012. In 2012, Osman received another offer to be the Distinguished Chair Professor and Director of Sultan Omar Ali Saifuddien Centre for Islamic Studies (SOASCIS) at the Universiti Brunei Darussalam. After he headed the Centre for five years (circa January 2013–July 2017), he was appointed as ISTAC's Shaykh al-Kulliyyah in September 2018; and he then took up the ISTAC-IIUM Al-Ghazali Chair of Epistemology and Civilizational Studies.

Osman's Intellectual Influences

Osman was exposed to important developments and influences that shaped his career as an engaged scholar. He entered Islamic Studies during the phase of resurgence across the Muslim world. During this period, many Muslim reformist movements such as Egypt's Muslim Brotherhood (est.1928) and Pakistan's Jama'at al-Islami (est.1941) were active in triggering the spirit of revival. These movements inspired the creation of several Muslim student organizations in countries such as Britain's Federation of Students Islamic Societies (FOSIS est. 1963) and Malaysia's ABIM.

While at the University of London, Osman was engrossed in reading on Muslim civilization and the philosophy that underpinned it. Since Osman embarked on reading extensively, he grasped the importance in combining science and religion. He then abandoned his UL Algebraic group theory doctorate for a religious studies doctorate (circa 1981–1986) at TU. At TU, Professor

Seyyed Hossein Nasr (b.1933) and Professor Raji al-Faruqi were the doyens of Islamic Studies since the 1970s. Under Nasr, Osman was profoundly influenced intellectually and morally. Iliescu[68] pointed out the deep impact that the following works of Nasr, namely *Introduction to Islamic Cosmological Doctrines* (1978), *The Encounter of Man and Nature: The Spiritual Crises of Modern Man* (1968), and *Science and Civilization in Islam* (1987) had on Osman's philosophical thought. Apart from these texts, Osman also benefitted from Al-Faruqi's writings.[69] The latter's book titled *Al Tawhid: Its Implications on Thought and Life* (1982) explicated the notions of God from diverse dimensions, which Osman built on.

The influence of Nasr was more palpable. Like Osman, Nasr was trained in the pure sciences at MIT and had a passion for religion. Because of Nasr's insights and understanding of God, human beings, and the Islamic cosmology, he adopted a traditionalist outlook. He proudly promoted traditional ideas and was part of a group that subscribed to a perennial philosophy. As Nasr's protégé, Osman understandably adopted the same approach. A proof of this was when Osman edited an informative collection of essays under the title *Critique of Evolutionary Theory.* The book bears testimony to Nasr's direct influence and of other perennial thinkers; among them were Martin Lings [d.2005] and Titus Burckhardt [d.1984].[70]

Armed with insights from these thinkers, Osman made creative contributions in the History and Philosophy of Science. These came to the fore whilst he was still attached to UM where he wrote and published a few books such as *Science, Technology, and Art in Human Civilizations* (1992), *Bibliography of Islamic Manuscripts at Islamic Museum* (1992), and *Islam and Civilizational Dialogue: Quest for a Truly Universal Civilization* (1995). He also devised new courses, such as Philosophy of Islamic Science (UKM), Qur'ānic Foundation of Islamic Science (ISTAC), Religion, Medicine and Health (Universiti Brunei Darussalam), and Contributions of Islamic Civilization to Science (Universiti Teknologi Mara) and taught many subjects such as Religion and Science (UM), Professional Ethics (Universiti Utara Malaysia), and Inter-Civilizational Dialogues in Southeast Asia (GU). In both teaching and research, Osman maintained a high standard. Despite moving from one academic post to another, Osman's active mind remained occupied with serious scholarly writings and establishing an impeccable research record.

---

68 Iliescu, "Biography of Osman Bakar."

69 M. Kamal Hassan, "Faruqi's Vision of a *Tawhidic* Worldview," keynote address, International Conference on The Legacy of Isma'il al Faruqi, October 22, 2013, http://irep.iium.edu.my/32621/1/FARUQI_KEYNOTE_Paper.pdf

70 Radu Iliescu, "Bibliographies and Biographies: Traditional Thinkers," August 30, 2006, http://elkorg-projects.blogspot.com/2005/05/bibliography-osman-bakar.html; Kersten, "Reviving."; Muhammed Yusuf, "Book Review: *Critique of Evolution Theory*," *Iqbal Review,* 1988, http://www.allamaiqbal.com/publications/journals/review/apr88/15.htm

Osman's Research Record

As already stated, Osman had made an important switch at the post-graduate studies level. At that stage, Osman did not actually turn his back on the pure sciences but approached it from a different angle; he used the TU doctorate project to mend a bridge between science and religion that appeared to have been broken. Phrased differently, he thus did not quit the pure sciences for the social sciences but simply employed his acquired research skills to demonstrate the synergy that existed between science and religion.

Midway during Osman's stint as UKM lecturer and while active in ABIM in 1974, Osman produced an education memorandum. It proposed, among others, the formation of a Muslim university. Osman also penned an academic paper that reflected on *The Problem of Malay-Muslim Progress in Science*. He addressed the twin topics of religion and science. He proposed the idea that in wanting to solve the Malays' backwardness in science education, there is a dire need for a Muslim intellectual cum cultural framework. The paper was presented at the "First Islamic World Conference in Science and Technology" in Riyadh in 1975, and it was published in the Proceedings of the Conference. Osman seems to have the former Prime Minister Mahathir bin Mohamad's book *The Malay Dilemma* (1970) in mind when he wrote this paper.

From that period onwards, Iliescu observed that Osman wrote primarily on "Islam and science." He published, among others, the *Meaning and Significance of Islamic Science* (1976), *Islamic Conceptions of Science* (1978), the *Fundamental Differences Between Traditional Islamic Science and Modern Science* (1978), and the *Relationship Between Science and Spiritual Values* (1979). Osman's papers have had a considerable impact on Malaysia's Muslim students because they concretely "proposed that science as conceived and cultivated in Islamic civilization exhibits characteristics that differ significantly from those of modern science." [71]

Osman's *Islamic Conceptions of Science* (1978) was later reprinted in ABIM's newsletter, *Risalah* and the *Majalah* of the Australian Federation of Malaysian Students' Association's (AFMSA). In 1979, Osman worked on a related symposium essay by reviewing *The Role of Science Education in the Spiritual Development of Man*. This featured in the 1979 *PKPIM Collection: Symposium on Islamic Education*, a Kuala Lumpur-based National Union of Muslim Students of Malaysia (PKPIM) publication. He turned these into publications that included book chapters and accredited journal articles.

It is interesting to observe that Osman penned four essays that covered different topics in different journals in his early academic years; these illustrate Osman's early attempts at engaging with diverse intellectual circuits in the Muslim world. Secondly, each of them appeared in journals that were established

71 Iliescu, "Biography of Osman Bakar."

by Muslim individuals/organizations. The Cambridge-based *Muslim Education Quarterly* (MEC est. 1983) was edited by Prof. Ali Ashraf (d. 1998) who was a renowned Muslim educationist. The Pakistan-based *Hamdard Islamicus* (HI est. 1978) established by the Hamdard Foundation (est.1954) and edited by Ḥakim Moḥammad Saʿid (d.1998). The Aligarh-based Muslim Association for the Advancement of Science (MAAS est. 1985) issued its first volume of *MAAS Journal of Science* (MAAS JIS) in the same year, and *The Islamic Quarterly* (IQ) was a periodical circulated by the London-based Islamic Cultural Centre since 1954. While the latter was edited by Gai Eaton (d.2010) who was a diplomat, the former was edited by one of MAAS' executive members.

These journals, in fact, welcomed contributions from emerging scholars such as Osman who dealt with themes and topics that the journal editors were eager to publicize and circulate because of their refreshing content. Though MEC, MAAS, and JIS were new journals then, HI was gaining traction and IQ was well-recognized; it was literally years ahead of them all. Via these, Osman's writings were exposed to a wide readership. Established Muslim scholars were introduced to Osman through these journals while they were sourcing material for their research projects. As significant platforms for young Muslim researchers during the period who were moved by the resurgence of Muslim identity across the globe, these journals enabled Osman to develop his research topic while he was doing his doctorate.

Indeed, each of these journal publications and several others in which Osman's essays featured placed Osman on the map of Islamic and scientific studies since he covered an area that few scholars were able to write on. Osman's steady but definite academic journey in the publishing industry was an important step towards increasing his impact and gaining readership. It may therefore be confidently argued that from the mid-1980s, many of Osman's essays illustrated his willingness to share his ideas as a thought leader. In fact, after having produced numerous essays, Osman collated and edited them into books that have been oft-cited and become important reference works. Altogether, he published seventy papers; most of which were in English. The three main subjects covered were religion, philosophy, and science. They contained topics such as evolution, bioethics, philosophy of medicine, and natural theology. Later in this essay, I will provide a bibliometric perspective that assesses some of these articles since it will not be possible to cover them all in a satisfactory manner.

Osman also authored and edited books. While some of the edited books consisted of essays that had previously appeared in journals, the authored books were fresh thoughts that impacted on those who latched onto Osman's insightful and perceptive ideas. There was a rapid output of books when he was at the UM in the 1990s. At one stage, he had a total of ten books, six in

English and four in Malay, which boosted Osman's standing as a scholar. In addition, Osman's books were also translated into other languages ranging from Persian and Turkish to Japanese and Spanish.

Turning to his authored and edited books, it is observed that Osman—being bi-lingual—used that linguistic skill to his advantage. Osman's first single authored publication appeared in both Bahasa Malaysia and English. If he did not publish Al-Farabi's text in both languages simultaneously, then his readership would have been limited to one set of readers only. He, however, wisely produced an English version and this meant that it became available to a much wider readership since the English-speaking world outnumbers Bahasa speakers.

Osman, being a specialist in Muslim philosophy and its advocates, inventively sought ways of giving life to these classical Muslim philosophers. He selected, among them, Ibn Sina (d.1037) and al-Ghazali (d.1111). While he might have been subtly influenced by each of these classical scholars, he chose to write a lengthy text on Al-Farabi (d.950) whom he admired and whose ideas he intuitively comprehended. This modest biographical text on Al-Farabi was significant in terms of the content's coverage; it, by and large, yielded positive results as has been observed from those who commented online about the book. According to one online reviewer, Osman offered "the non-specialist an accessible account of the philosopher's life and a breath-taking overview of the vast canvas of his thought."[72]

The second entry reflected is Osman's edited English text. Osman brought together a collection of essays that were essentially a *Critique of Evolutionary Theory*. He included prominent authors in this compilation, for example, Michael Negus and W.R. Thompson. He also inserted an essay penned by his former supervisor and mentor, Seyyed Hossein Nasr. While these were a mixed bag of scholars, they all critiqued the theory of evolution.

The third entry consists of a collection of previously published essays; the very first edition appeared under the title *The History and Philosophy of Islamic Science* (1999). A few years later, it was published under an altered title, namely *Tawhid and Science: Essays on the History and Philosophy of Islamic Science* (1991). That being the case, it should be remembered that Osman's authored book appears under two different titles. Reviewers gave very interesting comments. Walbridge commented that: "This book is not, as its title would indicate, an account of the history and philosophy of Islamic science … but rather a contribution to an internal Islamic debate about what the attitude of the modern Muslims should be towards modern science…"[73] He, however,

72 Iqbal Academy Pakistan, "Book Review: *Al Farabi: Life, Works, and Significance*," *Iqbal Review*, 1989, http://www.allamaiqbal.com/publications/journals/review/oct89/18.htm

73 John Walbridge, "Book Review: *The History and Philosophy of Islamic Science*," *Philosophy of Science* 68, no. 1 (2001): 273–274.

reminded the reader that it was a United Kingdom reprint of the 1991 *Tawhid and Science,* Malaysian edition. And he too hastily recalled that these were essays that were published during the 1980s.[74]

Leaving Walbridge's critique aside, the book comprised of, inter alia, major themes; the first focused on Islamic science's epistemological foundation; the second reflected on the position and relationship of "Man, Nature and God in Islamic science"; the third discoursed about "Islamic science and the West"; and the fourth conversed about "Islam and modern science." The work underscored Osman's desire to show and prove the strong interconnection between religion and science and through these discussions, he brought to the fore the Muslim intellectual and spiritual approach to science.

Worded differently, these edited chapters discoursed about the various principles of science. They contributed towards the cultivation of an understanding from the early period onwards and offered an insight into the place of science in relation to other branches of Muslim learning. Osman explained how these sciences were and are organically connected to Islam's fundamental teachings. The text included all the natural and mathematical sciences, and it illustrated what "Islamic science" shared with modern science. In this work, Osman highlighted the distinction between the Muslim approach vis-à-vis the modern approach to science.[75]

The last entry consists of a set of seminar papers; these were compiled by Osman under the Bahasa title *Islam dan Pemikiran Sains Masa Kini* (Eng.: *Islam and Contemporary Scientific Thought*). It was essentially a collection of essays that were delivered at a symposium at UKM during 1987. These reflected and interrogated the status of Islam, or rather Muslim, thought in relation to the current trends in scientific thought. The edited monograph underlined to what extent Muslim scholars felt the need to engage in these debates, and it demonstrated the underlying ties between religion (in this instance "Islam") and science.[76]

Osman's Classification of Knowledge in Islam: A Case Study

The *Classification of Knowledge in Islam* (1998), a text that was based on his doctorate and that went through several editions/prints, is Osman's crowning achievement.[77] The Kuala Lumpur-based Institute of Policy Studies first

74 See Hans Daiber, *Bibliography of Islamic Philosophy: Supplement* (Leiden: Brill, 2007); and Eric Winkel, "Review Essay: *Tawhid and Science*," *The Muslim World* 83, no. 3–4 (1993): 329–335.

75 Katherine Nielsen, "The Philosophy of Osman Bakar," *International Studies in the Philosophy of Science* 22, no. 1 (2008): 81–95; Mahdawi Abu Hassan et al., "The Perspective of Four Muslim Scholars on Islamization of Science," *Science International* 28, no. 2 (2016):1359–1362.

76 Osman Bakar, "Reformulating a Comprehensive Relationship between Religion and Science: An Islamic Perspective," *Islam & Science* 1, no. 1 (2003): 29–44.

77 Idris Samawi Hamid, "Book Review: *Classification of Knowledge in Islam: A Study in Islamic Philosophies of Science*," *Review of the Middle East Studies* 36, no. 2 (2003): 206–207.

printed it during 1992; six years later, it was reproduced with the same title during 1998 by the Cambridge-based Islamic Texts Society (ITS). Shortly thereafter (in 2000), it was—with permission—republished by Suhail Academy in South Asia's Lahore. I mention this point since there were/are publishing houses that ignore, transgress, and infringe copyright rules of books published outside Pakistan by reputable institutions such as ITS.[78]

More importantly, the work addressed "the classification of knowledge" or worded alternatively, knowledge's hierarchical structures. This was, and remains, a recurring theme within Muslim scholarship. For this book, Osman selected al-Farabi (870–950), al-Ghazali (1058–1111), and Qutb al-Din al-Shirazi (1236–1311) to demonstrate their respective inputs. These three thinkers were respected representatives of major think tanks of their time. They made an indelible intellectual impact, a noteworthy impression that no contemporary scholar can afford to ignore and sidestep. Osman gave life to their ideas and contributions via this work. As mentioned, this text was originally completed under Nasr's supervision; and since Nasr was his mentor, he was approached to write the Foreword.

The published text gained traction as noted by Google Scholar since several book reviews appeared; these featured in different well-established journals, and these reviews helped to give the book distinction in and outside academia. When it was republished in 2019, it was accompanied by a new preface. Osman had it reprinted under a modified sub-title: *Classification of Knowledge in Islam: Islamic Schools of Epistemology;* this version was also published by ITS.

The book, as indicated, went through reprints and was also translated into other languages such as Turkish. In this instance, it was translated by Purwanto in 1997 into Bahasa Indonesia with the following title: *Hierarki Ilmu: Membangun Rangka-Pikir Islamisasi Ilmu Menurut al-Farabi, al-Ghazali, Qutb al-Din al-Syirazi.* The Bandung-based Mizan Press in Indonesia republished it, and soon, it was sold out. It went through a second print run during 1998. It was strange to find on the Google Scholar website two separate entries; they were not lumped together although it is the same book published by the same printing press and in the same year.

The information shared here was extracted from Google Scholar and Good Reads. While the latter provided the ratings of readers, the former offered online figures of the number of those who visited/read the text online. The two complement one another; the one online figure revealed the number of readers that visited the online text per annum. The Good Reads site, however, gave one an indication how the reader rated the book. The thirty-three readers who responded gave it 4 or 5 stars; a minuscule number of 2 rated it 1 and the rest

78 Lee Wilson, *The Copyright Guide: A Friendly Handbook to Protecting and Profiting from Copyrights*, 3rd ed. (New York: Allworth Press, 2003); Stephen Fishman, *The Copyright Handbook: What Every Writer Needs to Know*, 13th ed. (Berkeley: NOLO Law for All, 2017).

rated it 3. The personal commentaries, which the readers shared online, underlined their reactions and appreciation of Osman's works.[79]

Before rounding off this brief case study, it should be restated that the information was extracted from Google Scholar. The data assisted in viewing Osman's profile on his broad research canvas. While Google Scholar has been the most popular site that placed researchers on the virtual map, others such as Research Gate and Plubons complemented it in other ways; and these were not factored in here. They captured aspects of the scholar's output at regular intervals, and the administrators of these sites usually remain in touch via email with the researcher. These sites generally track journals and other platforms by recording and verifying the necessary details.

When this researcher visited Google Scholar on 11th and 18th of Nov 2021, the site illustrated that the publication—that was accompanied by a specific edition and date—was cited 274 times; this meant that the data did not change. The latter, however, changes whenever it picks up information online about the book or journal that cited it. The problem that the data system encounters is when there are multiple authors; and another is that when the same book appears more than once on the system, Google Scholar fails to track this. This was the case with *Hierarki Ilmu* when the site was scanned.

Taking *Hierarki Ilmu* as an example, it will be noted that it was catalogued fourth on the online inventory, and that it was cited 121 times. Then as one scrolls down, one observed that another was inserted in the eleventh spot with forty-eight having cited it. Now, if one puts together all the figures, then the number of citations come to 169 and it thus pushes the book up the ranks. And if the text and the translated work are considered together, then the new tally would be 443. This then reveals that (a) the book has indeed attracted scores of readers, (b) it has become an important reference for researchers; and (c) it has moved up the non-fiction book ranks as a key source on classical Muslim philosophy.

Nevertheless, it may be argued that these online metric sites are not 100% accurate in recording the data; but despite their inherent shortcomings, they do provide reasonably good information that may be used by researchers. The data does assist in placing and ranking the researcher/scholar within the scholarly hierarchy. From what was shared, it can be underlined that *Classification/Hierarki* is indeed one of Osman's significant books. Essayists who reviewed it and readers who shared limited comments on public book sites were all positive. It is useful to turn the broad research canvas that inserts the aforementioned section in a wider research context.

79 "Hierarki Ilmu: Membangun Rangka-Pikir Islamisasi Ilmu," Goodreads, https://www.goodreads.com/book/show/7071218-hierarki-ilmu

Osman's Academic Outputs: From Supervisory Tasks to Professorial Publications

Osman was also a supervisor of many postgraduate students. A few words about the process of supervision is in order. Beckett opined that the supervisory system involves a fair degree of "accountability" from both the supervisor and the supervisee.[80] He further pointed out that along with that, the supervisor or the supervisory team should factor in the notions of "power and authority." Osman ensures a fair degree of accountability in his students. He acknowledges his position as an authority within the supervisory relationship. But he would permit the candidate to exercise his/her individuality or rather his/her individual personal power to demonstrate his/her abilities and achieve his/her goals as an emerging scholar/researcher.

In this context, one may describe Osman as someone who is determined and focused despite being a soft-natured individual. Being an accommodative, approachable, and gentle person, he cultivates a positive and an open relationship with the supervisee. He adopts an open-door policy that promotes a personal connection with him as the supervisor.[81] To be sure, Osman is an empathetic scholar who readily lends an ear, reflects deeply upon the candidate's thesis problem statement and other related matters. He shares his scholarly insights so that the candidate grasps and comprehends the shared ideas.[82]

Instead of feeling intimidated by the supervisor's inputs, the candidate is stimulated and energized to forge ahead with the research project. In the process of doing this, Osman—as the supervisor—generally adopts a healthy and engaging relationship with the supervisee. He normally encourages the candidate to "think-out-of-the-box." This approach is adopted so that the candidate is not solely dependent upon him as the supervisor but that he/she is one that uses his/her research skills to attain the set postgraduate goals.

During his long career Osman has had thirty-one postgraduate students under his supervision. Indeed eight completed their master's degrees and twenty-three finished their doctorate degrees; in all, the total number that completed was thirty-one. Osman currently supervises eleven postgraduate candidates. This is indeed an incredible feat. It may, however, be surmised that if all the current set of candidates should manage to complete within the next three to five years (say by 2025), then the overall number of postgraduates who would have completed under his supervision, would be forty-two. And that, one may contend, is a reasonable number for someone who has been in the academic arena since the 1980s barring the periods when Osman was busy completing his graduate studies in Malaysia, UK, and the USA. All in all, the data affirms that.

80 Chris Beckett, *Supervision: A Guide for the helping Professions* (London: Sage Publishing, 2020).

81 Sapna Kumar, Vijay Kumar, and Stan Taylor, "A Guide to Online Supervision," *UK Council for Graduate Education*, 2020, https://supervision.ukcge.ac.uk/resources/ukcge-guide-to-online-supervision/.

82 Alexander Bulat, *The Good Supervision Guide: A Guide for New and Experienced Supervisors* (London: University College London, 2018).

In regards to Osman's journal essay publications, it was noted that most of these featured in journals that were based in Southeast Asia in general and in Malaysia in particular. Some might argue that Osman did not reach out, as he should have, to other journals published in the UK and the USA where scholarship on themes that he usually writes on are in demand. For example, religion and science remain topical. UK/USA-based journals would welcome Osman's essays. Despite this minor point, Osman has done well and for that he has been recognized by national and international institutions. That said and in ending this assessment, one can describe Osman as one of Malaysia's active engaged scholars.

Towards a Conclusion

The purpose of this essay was to undertake an intellectual biography and bibliometric study of Professor Osman Bakar's scholarly contributions. I prefaced it with a brief theoretical backdrop that unpacked the notion of an engaged scholar. This was then followed by an exposition of Osman's academic voyage. Osman made a necessary intellectual detour, one that eventually rewarded him handsomely as he moved along the academic path. His move from the pure sciences to the social sciences gave him a great deal of satisfaction. This change meant that he could passionately and creatively contribute to both areas of specialization in a meaningful manner.

By bravely shifting into a related discipline, Osman managed to reach several goals. On a personal level, he developed into a prolific scholar and a productive researcher. On top of that and as a result of his participation in various conferences and seminars, Osman assertively reached out to national and international audiences, demonstrating tangibly that he was an extraordinary engaging scholar. In fact, the existing evidence pointed to the fact that Osman was literally and figuratively engaged on different levels: as supervisor, as an administrator, and as a scholar who was and remains intimately connected to his areas of specialization through regular scholarly outputs of books, book chapters, journal articles, conference proceeding essays, and seminar papers.

This chapter underpinned Osman's standing as a distinguished scholar within the Muslim world in general and contemporary Southeast Asian community in particular. Osman's scholarship helped shape the areas of Islamic Studies through the production of knowledge process over many decades. In fact, anyone who has browsed through the well-known Brill publication *Index Islamicus* would be able to notice Osman's presence. The *Index Islamicus* has helped to monitor and track the expanding and growing scholarship on Islam and Muslims for more than a century. Osman has not only filled knowledge gaps, but he has left us a rich scholarly legacy that others can improve and build on.

Bibliography

Ahmad, Ahmad Atif. *Pitfalls of Scholarship: Lessons from Islamic Studies*. New York: Palgrave MacMillan, 2016.

Beckett, Chris. *Supervision: A Guide for the helping Professions*. London: Sage Publishing, 2020.

Boyer, Ernest. "The scholarship of engagement." *Journal of Public Service and Outreach* 1, no. 1 (1996): 11–20.

Boyer, Ernest. "The scholarship of engagement." *Journal of Higher Education Outreach and Engagement* 20, no. 1 (2016): 15–27.

Bulat, Alexander. *The Good Supervision Guide: A Guide for New and Experienced Supervisors*. London: University College London, 2018.

Daiber, Hans. *Bibliography of Islamic Philosophy: Supplement*. Leiden: Brill, 2007.

Fishman, Stephen. *The Copyright Handbook: What Every Writer Needs to Know*. 13th ed. Berkeley: NOLO Law for All, 2017.

Flinders, Matthew. "The Politics of Engaged Scholarship: Impact, Relevance, and Imagination." *Policy & Politics* 41, no. 4 (2013): 621–642.

Greater Kashmir. "Futuristic Vision for the Discipline of Islamic Studies." March 16, 2021. https://www.greaterkashmir.com/kashmir/futuristic-vision-for-the-discipline-of-islamic-studies-prof-osman-bakar-delivers-online-extension-lecture-in-cuk

Haron, Muhammed. "Southern African Islamic Studies Scholarship: A Survey of the State of the Art." In *African Traditions in the Study of Religion in Africa: Emerging Trends, Indigenous Spirituality and the Interface with other World Religions,* edited by Afe Adogame, Ezra Chitando, and Bolaji Bateye, 219–238. London: Ashgate Publishing, 2012.

Holland, Dorothy, Dana Powell, Eugenia Eng, and Georginia Drew. "Models of Engaged Scholarship: An Interdisciplinary Discussion." *Collaborative Anthropologies* 3 (2010): 1–36.

Idris Samawi Hamid. "Book Review: *Classification of Knowledge in Islam: A Study in Islamic Philosophies of Science*, by Osman Bakar." *Review of the Middle East Studies* 36, no. 2 (2003): 206–207.

Iliescu, Radu. "Bibliographies and Biographies: Traditional Thinkers." August 30, 2006. http://elkorg-projects.blogspot.com/2005/05/bibliography-osman-bakar.html

Iliescu, Radu. "Biography of Osman Bakar (b.1946–)." April 17, 2005. http://elkorg-projects.blogspot.com/2005/04/biography-of-osman-bakar-1946.html

Institut Alam dan Tamadun Melayu (ATMA). "Osman Bakar." *One Stop Resource Centre for Malay World Research*. http://malaycivilization.com.my/exhibits/show/tokoh-pemikir-alam-melayu/osman-bakar

Iqbal Academy Pakistan. "Book Review: *Al Farabi: Life, Works, and Significance*." *Iqbal Review*. 1989. http://www.allamaiqbal.com/publications/journals/review/oct89/18.htm

Kersten, Carool. "Reviving the 'Islamization of Knowledge' Project?" 2012. https://caroolkersten.blogspot.com/2012/01/

Khir, Bustami. "Islamic Studies within Islam: Definition, Approaches and Challenges of Modernity." *Journal of Beliefs & Values* 28, no. 3 (2007): 257–66.

Kumar, Sapna, Vijay Kumar, and Stan Taylor. "A Guide to Online Supervision." *UK Council for Graduate Education*. 2020. https://supervision.ukcge.ac.uk/resources/ukcge-guide-to-online-supervision/

M. Kamal Hassan. "Faruqi's Vision of a *Tawhidic* Worldview." Keynote address, International Conference on The Legacy of Isma'il al Faruqi, October 22, 2013. http://irep.iium.edu.my/32621/1/FARUQI_KEYNOTE_Paper.pdf

Mahdawi Abu Hassan, Safiah Sadek, Shahrulanuar Mohamed, and Norliah Kudus. "The Perspective of Four Muslim Scholars on Islamization of Science." *Science International* 28, no. 2 (2016):1359–1362.

Muhamad Razak Idris. "Malaysian Scholars' Perspectives on the Role of Dialogue of Civilizations as an Approach in Promoting World Peace." *Malaysian Journal of Islamic Movements and Muslim Societies* 1, no. 1 (2021): 59–73.

Nasr, Seyyed Hossein. *Islamic Philosophy from its Origin to Its Present: Philosophy in the Land of Prophecy*. New York: SUNY, 2006.

Nielsen, Katherine. "The Philosophy of Osman Bakar." *International Studies in the Philosophy of Science* 22, no. 1 (2008): 81–95.

Osman Bakar. "Reformulating a Comprehensive Relationship between Religion and Science: An Islamic Perspective." *Islam & Science* 1, no. 1 (2003): 29–44.

Roper, Geofrey J. "Index Islamicus." *History Compass* 36 (2003): 1–4.

Rosalina Othman and Ashraf A. Salahuddin. "Relevance Status of Value Model of *Index Islamicus* on Islamic History and Civilization." *International Journal of Web Information Systems* 11, no. 1 (2015): 54–86.

Schleifer, S. Abdallah, ed. *The Muslim 500: The Most Influential Muslims 2022*. Amman: The Royal Islamic Strategic Studies Center, 2021.

Shultz, Lynette, and Tania Kajner, eds. *Engaged Scholarship: The Politics of Engagement and Disengagement*. Rotterdam: Sense Publishers, 2013.

Siddiqui, Ataullah. *Islam at Universities in England, Meeting the Needs and*

Investing in the Future. Leicester: Markfield Institute for Higher Education, 2007.

Swanick, Sean. "Advisor Reviews – Standard Reviews: *Index Islamicus.*" *Charleston Advisor* 14, no. 2 (2012): 29–31.

University of the Free State. "Engaged Scholarship Strategy." 2020. https://www.ufs.ac.za/supportservices/departments/community-engagement-home/community-engagement-at-the-ufs/engaged-scholarship

Walbridge, John. "Book Review: *The History and Philosophy of Islamic Science.*" *Philosophy of Science* 68, no. 1 (2001): 273–274.

Wilson, Lee. *The Copyright Guide: A Friendly Handbook to Protecting and Profiting from Copyrights.* 3rd ed. New York: Allworth Press, 2003.

Winkel, Eric. "Review Essay: *Tawhid and Science.*" *The Muslim World* 83, no. 3–4 (1993): 329–335.

Yusuf, Muhammed. "Book Review: *Critique of Evolution Theory.*" *Iqbal Review.* 1988. http://www.allamaiqbal.com/publications/journals/review/apr88/15.htm

Chapter 2

Faith and Modern Science: A Journey of Rediscovery with Professor Osman Bakar

Tengku Mohd Azzman Shariffadeen

Senior Fellow and Former Vice President,
Academy of Sciences, Malaysia

Aspiring for a future in science

My first encounter with Osman Bakar was in 1963 at the Malay College, Kuala Kangsar. I had entered the school in 1960 as a form one student, while he joined when we were in form four. We had both dreamed of becoming scientists, and were privileged to be assigned to the science stream. But one may ask why were students then so excited about becoming scientists? The answer lies in the changing circumstances of the country we called home. It had just become independent from British colonial rule six years earlier in 1957. As a young independent nation, there was much confidence in the power of science to develop the country. Schoolchildren were encouraged to study science. A system of streaming was practised, whereby selected students were channelled to the "science stream," while others were placed in the "arts stream." On the one hand, this ostensibly meritocratic system created a competitive spirit among students. However, it was openly elitist and produced several unintended consequences. Science students often held the "arts" courses as of lesser value. It also created a sense of inferiority among some who did not gain admission into the science stream. The effects of this are felt till this very day and Osman dedicated much of his writings on bridging the gaps between different disciplines and attitudes towards these bodies of knowledge.

The British had left as a legacy an education system that used English as the medium of learning and instruction. Science education, based on modern scientific discoveries of the western world, largely projected the western worldview. Teachers had been trained from this intellectual perspective, while teaching materials and textbooks without fail expressed ideas and concepts emanating from western civilization, in particular the Enlightenment, the Scientific Revolution and the Industrial Revolution. The fact that none of these cultural, social and economic upheavals had been experienced by the Malaysian people did not seem to matter. Indeed, colonial officers felt no need to understand or appreciate the cultures of the peoples that they were tasked to govern. They were generally unconcerned about the fact that we had our own civilizational perspectives based on a completely different belief system.

Islam was taught as independent religious classes in the curriculum. These classes focused on the fundamental principles of Islam, especially the ritualistic aspects of faith and practice. This fragmented educational approach facilitated specialization in the study of science in the western frame of thinking that reflects its worldview, while the religious subjects were taken in isolation. No thought was given to the intellectual link between them or to the integration of knowledge in general. The separation between the scientific and the religious aspects of learning and knowledge largely shaped the nation's thinking process of the day, and strongly influenced the minds of the youth such as ourselves.

Growing up in Malaysia then provided a good introduction to the world at large. In particular, when television became available, we were not only entertained with movies and serials, but also cultural, civilizational and political content that celebrated the overwhelming success and superiority of the west. I was among those who had watched on TV probably every single launch of America's Apollo space mission orchestrated by NASA. The triumphs of science as found in books and magazines, and in particular as shown on TV, convinced many of us that science was indeed the path to development and progress.

It was within such a context that Osman and I shared a common quest to become scientists, specifically in the physical sciences. It would not be an exaggeration to say that we were totally dazzled and mesmerized by science. Its apparent objectivity, borne out of systematic methods of discovery, and the clarity of its findings inspired us like no other subject of study. The efficient way that science could reveal facts about natural phenomena was nothing short of magical. Initial stirrings of apprehension did not constrain our desire to be scientists. Science appeared as an all-powerful field of study that could unravel the laws of nature without recourse to any other source of human knowledge beyond itself. It stood on its own, head and shoulders above other fields of study, to be almost independent and self-sufficient. It sounded too good to be true, but our belief in science was unshaken. Indeed, we were fascinated by it as we sought to understand the world purely from the point of view of scientific reason.

Our peers who chose the biological sciences perhaps dreamed of becoming doctors or teachers. For those who were in the arts stream, I had supposed that they would largely join public service. I had dreams of becoming an engineer from an early age. Osman and I shared thoughts and ideas, but at that juncture I had no inkling what Osman wanted to be. Still, not everything appeared so rosy. The Cold War between the West and the Soviet Bloc was understood to be an existential threat to all of humanity. America was waging war in neighbouring Vietnam, using weapons that were not nuclear but just as deadly. Science clearly was not only used for good, but was being abused for control and domination. Anti-Vietnam War protests raging in America and elsewhere did not go unnoticed. Hippies and the Flower Power movement, aided by the rising new pop culture, showed an unflattering face of the West. The younger generation of the west were questioning the claim that their societies were just, democratic, progressive and prosperous. They wanted their leaders to own up and be accountable. Leaders were expected to admit that there had been mistakes which had to be corrected. Change was in the air. The rising generation wanted more freedom and they demanded the right to make it happen. I saw myself as part of that generation.

Rediscovering Islam

We did well enough in school to gain admission to UK universities. Osman went to London to study mathematics, while I went to Manchester to pursue electrical engineering. We continued to be in touch and met on and off while there, but largely went on with our separate lives to fulfil one single-minded objective: to succeed in our respective studies. In an ironic twist of events the colonial system that had projected Western science also unwittingly unravelled its flaws. It was the colonial system that had brought us to study in England, one of the most important historical centres in the establishment of modern science, and subsequently modern industry. Yet by being exposed to its actual foundations, principles, and assumptions, and the kind of development that it produced, we began to see its weak points. Most importantly, being able to observe at close hand the social and cultural attributes of modern civilization demonstrated the stark reality of the actual impact of science on human society, both positive and negative.

In my first few days in Manchester towards the end of 1967, I sought to discover what opportunities lay ahead in life as a student. As I wandered through the corridors of the Students Union building, I was handed a copy of Mawdudi's *Towards Understanding Islam* (1960) by a member of the Muslim Students Association. I was surprised that there was such an association to begin with. More surprising was to find many Muslim students from all over the world, a large number of whom were already doing masters or doctoral degrees.

The pressures of attending lectures and completing assignments initially did not encourage me to read the book. I had also assumed that the book would not contain anything new. However, upon reading the book, things took a dramatic turn. A completely new vision of Islam began to reveal itself to me. Mawdudi peeled layer after layer of the key concepts to address issues that had lain dormant in my mind. Allah as the One and Only Supreme Creator became more coherent and concrete. Man, as an intelligent being created to fulfil the Will of Allah, is given the attributes of reason and knowledge for a specific purpose and role. Nature is His creation that unceasingly follows His laws, and which He sustains and controls with precision, balance and harmony without any break. In nature, humankind is provided with all the necessary instruments and enabling conditions to fulfil his mission. The Prophet's role as the last messenger of the final phase of revelation is woven into a unified and integrated knowledge framework, logically consistent and complete. Tawhid, the unity of the Creator and His creation, captured my complete attention in mind and spirit.

The principle of *tawhid* became coherent for the first time in a way that went beyond anything I had learned in the past. As a student of science, I was particularly moved to uncover the principle of humankind that has been created with an innate ability to think logically and rationally. Working from this foundation, man uses the freedom conferred to discover the "laws" of nature, rules which ultimately obey the *sunnatullah*, unceasingly manifesting the Will of its Creator.

Reading the book was nothing short of life-changing. In a quest to learn more, I began to increasingly engage with other Muslim students in Manchester and elsewhere. I had come to England at a fortuitous time. Just a few years earlier the Muslim students in the UK had organized themselves nationally by establishing an umbrella body called FOSIS (Federation of Student Islamic Societies). I regularly attended their programmes, especially their annual meetings, and read publications that they published and disseminated. Through these interactions I began to discover progressive authors and their works, at a time when science from the Islamic perspective was not yet in the mainstream.

My personal objectives also changed. My ambition to become a successful engineer was largely driven by the conventional wisdom of the day: to become wealthy. Now I treasured a new objective. By the second undergraduate year I had decided that the single-minded pursuit of material wealth was a flawed and false objective and had to be rejected. In its place, I resolved to become a person with knowledge, without fully appreciating its serious implications. Still, I had envisioned that knowledge would enable me to do many things, for my own good as well as for others with whom I would engage in life. In order to fulfil this new objective, it was only logical that I should position myself in an environment of learning. I was determined that I should gain higher degrees and pursue research. Then other opportunities would open themselves to me.

Opening the door to knowledge: unlearning and relearning

My new path proceeded with relative ease. After undergraduate studies, I completed a masters degree in one year and a doctoral degree in another two years. On my way home on Christmas day in 1973, I ran across a friend at Heathrow airport, an American Muslim then teaching in Malaysia. He was on his way home to California for vacation. I shared that I would be joining a newly-established technological university. He advised me not to accept that job, but instead join the University of Malaya as it would provide greater opportunities. I followed his advice, not fully appreciating that I had been guided beyond my understanding or anticipation.

I was pleasantly surprised to learn that Osman had returned before me after completing a masters degree and had joined the National University of Malaysia (UKM) to teach mathematics. We immediately started engaging on a topic of great mutual interest and concern: the concept of modern science as we had been exposed to and its contradictions with Islamic principles. We knew that we lacked sound knowledge or understanding of the subject. But where do we start?

At a dinner that I hosted in 1975, the few friends gathered collectively agreed to form the Islamic Academy of Science Malaysia (ASASI). I was persuaded to act as pro-tem President while Osman was Secretary. It became a forum for a small group of like-minded thinkers to share ideas. At about this time, Osman told me about a professor at UKM, Professor Syed Muhammad Naquib al-Attas, who was knowledgeable about Islamic philosophy, in particular the philosophy of science from the Islamic perspective. More interestingly, he was willing to engage with us at his home when we could be free to attend, which was at night. We both jumped at the opportunity.

Many nights were spent listening to Prof Naquib explaining the concept of knowledge in Islam, and how it subsumes and relates to scientific knowledge. Using a vocabulary that was completely new to our ears to expound on philosophical principles that were equally alien, he opened our minds to a way of thinking that we had not experienced before. In particular, these principles were presented in an accessible manner despite the fact that they were highly complex for most of us who had not taken any formal training in the relevant disciplines. We could sense our mental models shift radically, transforming our worldview about man, nature and science. At its centre stands the One and Only Creator of the cosmos.

A significant amount of the material from his talks were later published. In 1977, he presented an important paper *Preliminary Thoughts on the Nature of Knowledge and the Definition and Aims of Education in Islam* at the First World Conference on Muslim Education in Mecca. This was later expanded into a commentary entitled *The Concept of Education in Islam* (1999). Al-Attas' *Islam and Secularism* (1978) was soon published. His books were widely read by the younger generation and influenced much of the intellectual discourse in subsequent decades. Our confidence rose to such an extent that we decided to hold our first conference in 1977. Naturally, we invited Al-Attas to be our Keynote Speaker, to which he graciously agreed. It was a small conference yet very meaningful. Many of the early fellow travellers in ASASI have gone on to do great work in their respective fields, while at the same time maintaining close alignment with the true vision of Islam.

Hijrah

The decade of the 1980s proved to be the most seminal period in our mutual journey of rediscovery. Again this came about through serendipity rather than meticulous planning. I would even venture to say that we were guided by the All-Wise. For Osman, it began with a casual conversation that I had in the late 1970s with the late Royal Professor Ungku Aziz, Vice Chancellor of the University of Malaya. Ungku Aziz shared his plan to introduce a required undergraduate course in world civilizations. He believed in a broad educational foundation, whereby students could be exposed to the social, cultural, and philosophical ideas that underpin past and contemporary societies and civilizations. He knew that I was a strong supporter of the idea. He asked if I knew someone who could handle Islamic civilization, in particular Islamic science and its underlying philosophy. Osman immediately came to mind, and so I suggested that I could make the connection.

Osman needed no persuasion and readily moved from UKM to UM. This was his "hijrah," marking the beginning of his migration from the world of mathematics to the wider world of the Islamic faith and its philosophical and epistemological foundations based on tawhid. Our modest efforts up to this stage seemed to be coming together in a form that was completely unplanned and unanticipated. To me he was embarking on a new path to fulfil a destiny. Meanwhile in 1981 a national conference was held on *The Concept of Development in Islam,* organized by the Prime Minister's Department. I was asked to speak on science and technology, and settled on the topic of *Science and Technology for Development.* This was an opportunity that I had dreamed of, despite apprehensions that I was not fully ready to synthesize the traditional with the modern understanding of science and technology. Nevertheless, I proceeded to present a more balanced perspective of science and technology and its role in development that is in greater harmony with Islamic precepts. Expecting at most a lukewarm reception, I was surprised and moved by the enthusiastic response. The positive reaction of traditional scholars in Islamic studies was particularly heart-warming.

One key conference resolution caught the eye of the new Prime Minister, Dr Mahathir. It recommended the establishment of an International Islamic University by Malaysia to serve the developmental needs of the Ummah. This university would pursue knowledge comprehensively and integrate all branches of knowledge in a holistic framework, consistent with Islamic principles. A committee was set up to formulate a detailed proposal to which I was invited to be a member. As it turned out, this became the "birth certificate" of the International Islamic University Malaysia (IIUM). Subsequently I was also asked to formulate the curriculum of the Kulliyyah of Engineering. One of my contributions was for IIUM to offer a course in Mechatronics Engineering, combining mechanics and intelligent electronics. In hindsight, this was an agenda-setting move, given current developments in artificial intelligence, robotics and advanced automation that underpin Industry 4.0.

More significantly, in 1987 IIUM was to become the academic host of ISTAC (International Institute of Islamic Thought and Civilisation). Al-Attas, our illustrious teacher, became ISTAC Founder-Director, and Osman would subsequently also spend two stints as its leading staff member. ISTAC assumed a prominent role in the further advancement of knowledge in Islam.

In the early 1980s the Muslim Youth Movement of Malaysia (ABIM), founded and led by Anwar Ibrahim, our schoolmate, began to engage with prominent Muslim scholars from around the world. I was invited to meet the late Ismail al-Faruqi on his first visit to Malaysia sponsored by ABIM.

Just like al-Attas, al-Faruqi was not a natural scientist but was at ease and clearly very well-versed with philosophical ideas surrounding science. I suspected that their knowledge and understanding of the philosophy of science would put many practising scientists to shame. Al-Faruqi was particularly good at exposing the philosophical and epistemological principles of science in western thought, in stark contrast with Islamic principles. At our first meeting he explained the ideological underpinnings of Western science by expressing them as the "-isms": empiricism, materialism, determinism, reductionism, evolutionism, and so on, reserving a special place for scientism itself. The central idea of this ideology is that science has no need for God in nature, as all causal relationships are in and from the world.

In contrast, the central idea in Islam is that God is the final cause, who makes things happen. Al-Faruqi was fond of the word "usufruct" in clarifying the divine right given to mankind to use nature's resources. This right is however limited, in the sense that man is not entitled to waste or worse still, to cause nature's own destruction. This fundamental principle is particularly relevant in modern times, given the destruction of the natural world and the atmospheric pollution that is causing climate change, and other contemporary crises.

In 1982 ABIM reproduced for Malaysian readers *Tawhid: Its Implications for Thought and Life* which was deeply studied within the intellectual community. Al-Faruqi was a powerful source of inspiration and enlightenment, providing thought-provoking ideas that were revolutionary to those who were privileged to engage with him. His talks and writings provided some of my most memorable and transformative moments, revealing the diverse yet integrated dimensions of *tawhid* that light the way to the true teachings of Islam.

For Osman, the connection with al-Faruqi became even more meaningful and personal. In order to prepare him for the new agenda, UM sponsored his masters studies in comparative religion. I was elated to learn that he chose to work under the supervision of al-Faruqi at Temple University. He later continued with doctoral studies under the supervision of Seyyed Hossein Nasr, another intellectual giant. Although I had not met Nasr, he was one of the prominent writers I had been acquainted with as a student in UK. I had come across his book *Ideals and Realities of Islam* (1966) which explains and clarifies the distinction between the Real and Absolute and the relative. In preparing my conference presentation in 1981, I had consulted his other books, namely, *An Introduction to Islamic Cosmological Doctrines* (1964) and *Science and Civilisation in Islam* (1968).

Just like Osman, I too undertook a hijrah to chart a new path forward. At the end of 1984, after nearly 11 years as an academic, I left UM to become the founding head of a new national research institute, MIMOS, devoted to microelectronics and information technology. To put the initiative in proper context we should note the following factors. In the mid-1980s the personal computer was only in its infancy. The Internet had not been unleashed on the unsuspecting world, and the Worldwide Web had yet to be invented. The term information technology (IT) was not widely known even among specialists in computer science and engineering, let alone other disciplines. Despite this general lack of awareness about the rising importance of information and knowledge enabled by digital technology, some of us in UM were enthusiastic about the future potential of computer networks. We conducted initial research, sensing that networks could soon be globally interconnected, and if this were to happen, nothing short of revolutionary change would be unleashed upon human society.

Unknown to most, by 1987 MIMOS had begun R&D work on the Internet. Early experiments were initiated with close support from the actual inventors of the Internet protocol in the US. We had registered the country code top-level domain ".my" for Malaysia, the sixteenth country in the world to do so, just after Switzerland. This made us a world pioneer in developing and using the Internet. In 1988 I was invited to deliver a special lecture by a prominent member of the Institution of Engineers Malaysia. To suit the occasion, I chose the title *Microelectronics, Information Technology and Society.* I framed IT as the future enabler of societal advancement and progress, with microelectronics as its core technology. More so, I went on to propose that IT would be the new technological cornerstone of the emerging society which will be based on information and knowledge. All aspects of human life will be touched. Just like the Industrial Revolution three centuries ago, human societies will be restructured as economic activities are transformed and new kinds of work and employment become dominant.

My audacious idea of linking IT with social advancement and progress, and placing microelectronics as its foundational technology, was perhaps too much for my listeners to swallow. Judging from the reception of the audiences (three lectures were delivered in all), I could sense that many were mystified and intrigued but few could or were ready to accept the essence of the world that I was anticipating or its implications. Most were puzzled and skeptical, if not cynical. My claims had been too far ahead of contemporary thinking.

Putting knowledge to work

In the late 1980s Osman returned to commence teaching at UM after having completed his PhD. Even before his return he had published a collection of essays under the title *Critique of Evolutionary Theory* (1987). It was the first book published by the Islamic Academy of Science Malaysia. The modern theory of evolution, especially its derivative ideology of evolutionism, had been troubling many of us. Darwinian evolution claims to be scientific truth when in reality it is a hypothesis that still needs to be scientifically proven. Even more troubling was our observation that some of our learned scientists, especially academic friends, and colleagues, were strong proponents of evolutionary theory.

To be sure some may not have perceived or appreciated the contradiction with faith and belief. Just as the Newtonian model of dynamics reduces all natural phenomena to only material and physical form, the mechanistic model of evolution would likewise render God a *deus otiosis,* one who has withdrawn from governing the world after having created it, in the words of al-Faruqi. Osman assembled a wide collection of works by renowned scientists and metaphysicians, mainly from the West, who oppose evolutionary theory based on intellectual, philosophical, and scientific grounds. His own chapter summarises these objections in a clearly reasoned and rational exposition. Convincing arguments were presented in rejecting the notion that complex living forms arise from simpler forms. Osman asserts that the theory of evolution may even have borrowed ideas from metaphysics, a traditional discipline which provides a stronger integrative framework for life on earth. The metaphysical idea of the gradation of being links species in a chain, each with its own attributes which are immutable, finally leading to the Creator.

The decade of the 1990s proved to be the most productive period for both of us. What we had learned in the last two decades began to bear fruit as each of us in our own way became drawn into a world of change based on knowledge. We gained comfort from the fact that there exist influential counter currents among ranking contemporary scientists. Osman convincingly demonstrates that true knowledge influences the intellectual climate of society and often redirects the worldview of its members. Intellectual honesty and integrity, and openness to objective arguments, should be the primary guideposts in the search for truth.

In quick succession Osman published two more books in the early 1990s, *Tawhid and Science* (1991) and *Classification of Knowledge in Islam* (1992). I was privileged to receive copies as gifts from Osman. *Tawhid and Science* is a compilation of Osman's essays produced over a period of seven years spanning much of the time he spent pursuing his masters and doctoral degrees at Temple University. Several essays were written specifically for this compilation. This work addresses many of the concerns and questions that have arisen among our circle of thinkers in science and technology. Modern science is shown to share many of the attributes of Islamic science which predates it and to which it owes many key features of the scientific logical framework, methodology, and processes. However, Islamic science has several differences. Most importantly, it maintains an organic link to the fundamental teachings of Islam, the most important of which is the principle of unity or tawhid. To quote Osman: "Islamic science is at the same time of a religious nature in the sense that it is consciously based upon the metaphysical, cosmological, epistemological, and ethical and moral principles of Islam." [83]

The loss of these principles in modern science is reinforced in *Classification of Knowledge in Islam*. This book was his doctoral thesis which delved into classifications produced by three prominent philosopher-scientists in Islam: al-Farabi, al-Ghazali and al-Shirazi. Osman's thorough intellectual work brings out clearly the two main features of Islamic science. First is the unity of knowledge and its hierarchical nature. Second is the distinction between religion and philosophy, which is related to the distinction between revelation and reason. In contrast, this study reveals important facts about the nature of modern science. The loss of integration, excessive specialization, lack of a moral framework and loss of metaphysical principles, are key features leading modern science towards the pursuit of knowledge for the main purpose of human exploitation, manipulation, control and dominance of the natural world.

83 Osman Bakar, *Tawhid and Science* (Kuala Lumpur and Penang: Science University of Malaysia and Nurin Enterprise, 1991), ix.

Osman's teaching and research at UM elevated his standing within the intellectual community. He was duly promoted to full professor and appointed to leadership positions. One initiative that set him apart was his pursuit of civilisational studies and intercultural dialogue as a strategic academic and intellectual programme. I participated in some of these activities at his invitation and began to see a strong link between his work and my own.

In 1994 the National Information Technology Council (NITC) was established through a cabinet decision. It was chaired by the Prime Minister, and as the head of MIMOS, I became its Ex-Officio Secretary. The burgeoning impact of the Internet was acknowledged by national leaders. It did not take much convincing to propose that a robust national proactive response was urgently needed. Very quickly a study was commissioned, conducted by a globally-recognized consulting company. I became a member of the consulting team. This work resulted in a visionary national programme which came to be called the Multimedia Super Corridor (MSC). Launched in 1996, it sought to restructure the nation's economy and society through the application of "multimedia technologies" to develop new economic activities and industries, and thereby accelerate the nation's progress towards a more advanced state. Despite the technological focus implied in the programme's title, the actual strategic driving force is the content that underlies the new industries envisaged, which is knowledge.

Observing that the MSC's focus was economy and industry, I initiated work to add a complementing programme that focused on the development of the people. This resulted in the National Information Technology Agenda (NITA) whose objective was to initiate the creation of a values-based knowledge society resting on three key pillars: infostructure as the technological foundation, content and applications to provide solutions for work and life, and most importantly, people for whom comprehensive human development is the final objective. The MSC and NITA became the twin strategic programmes for the transformation of the nation towards becoming a knowledge-based economy and society. The impact of the Internet was wide-ranging, cutting across all kinds of human activity, as it democratizes access to knowledge and enables application of knowledge in creative ways to address humanity's challenges and problems. One of the key challenges was how to confront a world of plurality in all its varied forms.

What I had anticipated in my 1988 lecture was becoming the future reality. During the first decade of the Internet's introduction, the issues confronting human society rapidly surfaced. Although much good has come from ICT adoption, many cases of misuse, abuse and manipulation have been perpetrated by various parties, including sovereign governments. Much like the Industrial Revolution, sectarian forces have appropriated knowledge and used powerful knowledge-based technologies to gain advantage. Exploitation and marginalization of the less prepared or less capable is leading to a more inequitable world.

I attended a major global event, the World Summit on the Information Society, hosted by the UN and its agency the International Telecommunications Union. The first phase was held in Geneva in 2003, followed by the second phase in 2005 in Tunis. It was clear from the intense discussions that participants acknowledged and accepted the fact that information and knowledge, facilitated by the Internet, was fundamentally changing the world as we knew it. However, there was no consensus on how humanity could embark on a mutually beneficial journey of development. Indeed, I could not have expected a more positive outcome. The main reason is that knowledge does not have the same meaning and purpose among the diverse actors. Each was pursuing its own agenda and vested interests. Expecting to see unity, even for such a life-changing and transformative set of technologies as presented by ICT, was not feasible. Humankind has not been able to come together on a shared understanding of the philosophical and epistemological foundation of knowledge and its key role in human development. In short, humanity is facing a civilizational crisis.

A nomadic life

Osman began a nomadic life as an itinerant scholar. In 2000 he left UM to take up the Malaysia Chair of Islam in Southeast Asia at Georgetown University. He invited me to participate in one of the meetings held there, where I met many prominent scholars in the field of religion and philosophy. I was given an opportunity to share some of the programmes we had initiated in Malaysia to address the powerful forces unleashed by ICT and knowledge in development. Despite the novelty of our approach, I was not convinced that the participants could see much relevance to their work, as we are too far removed from the specific concerns of their world. Even so I observed that Osman had succeeded to build a circle of academic and intellectual sparring partners in a major centre of civilizational dialogue. This is a step forward in our quest for intercultural understanding based on rational and objective engagement.

On his return after the Georgetown stint, Osman joined ISTAC. When I discovered that he was giving lectures on the philosophy of science to graduate students, I asked to be allowed to attend. About a dozen doctoral students were taking his class, coming from various disciplines. Immediately I could sense that they were not only keenly interested in the subject, but more significantly, they had acquired the foundational knowledge to appreciate the meanings of words and expressions commonly used in philosophical discourse on science.

Only three decades ago Osman and I were struggling to comprehend these terminologies. Now Osman had become a recognised scholar in the field, and I had at least a passing acquaintance with the subject. Most gratifying was to engage with the rising generation of scholars who can be expected to go beyond conceptual analysis towards the new synthesis that we were seeking.

I too left MIMOS in November 2005 and began to do consulting work, starting with the Islamic Development Bank (IDB) in Jeddah. While on assignment at IDB, I sought to meet Dr Umer Chapra, a renowned pioneer of Islamic economics. I had read his book *Islam and the Economic Challenge* (1992) and came across the *Maqasid al-Shari'ah* for the first time. To quote from the book: The goals of Islam *(Maqasid al-Shari'ah)*, unlike those of the predominantly secularist systems of the present-day world, are not primarily materialist. They are rather based on its own concepts of human well-being *(falah)* and good life *(hayat tayyibah)* which give utmost importance to brotherhood and socio-economic justice and require a balanced satisfaction of both the material and the spiritual needs of *all* human beings.[84]

I was greatly impressed with his application of the *maqasid*, which beautifully and concisely encapsulates traditional knowledge, to the challenges of contemporary economic development. I had to know more by meeting the author himself. He proved to be most gracious and engaging. He was surprised when he discovered that I was an engineer by training. Perhaps this was the reason he decided to provide me with the draft copy of a new book he was working on, *The Islamic Vision of Development in the Light of the Maqasid al-Shari'ah* (2008), subsequently published by IIIT.

Through IDB, I was introduced to a Saudi think-tank run by influential leaders in Saudi society. They asked me to conduct a series of workshops to formulate a national strategic plan to transform Saudi Arabia into a knowledge society. Since I had done similar work in Malaysia, I felt fully prepared for the task. However, I confronted a unique challenge that I had not faced before. My work in Malaysia had always addressed the needs of a multi-cultural and multi-religious society. On the other hand, Saudi Arabia is exclusively Muslim, and more prominently, it is home to the two most holy places in Islam, Mecca and Madinah. I had no choice but to stage the workshops with a compelling formulation of knowledge-based development which is true to the Islamic spirit. It had to be *Tawhidic* and ummatic and, at the same time, modern in approach.

By the Grace of Allah, I found an answer in the work I had done previously with Osman, and lately with Chapra. Building from the latter's modern interpretation of the *maqasid* in development, I used my engineering background

84 M. Umer Chapra, *Islam and the Economic Challenge* (Herndon and Nairobi: International Institute of Islamic Thought and The Islamic Foundation, 1992), 6.

to conceptualise a systems diagram that integrates all the five elements, *din* (faith), *nafs* (self), *'aql* (intellect), *mal* (wealth) and *nasl* (progeny), into an interconnected system for human development based on knowledge which is at once balanced and sustainable. Three workshops were conducted in three different cities, drawing participation from about three hundred movers and shakers, covering top Saudi leaders in government, industry, academia and civil society. With the approval of the think tank, I tested the systems diagram during the first workshop in the presence of Dr Chapra who also presented his ideas on comprehensive development. I had requested the participation of renowned Saudi scholars of traditional knowledge. To my great relief and satisfaction, I was informed that participants, in particular the traditional scholars, had no objection to my unusual use of the *maqasid,* and actually welcomed it. I was humbled by Chapra's comments. He was pleased with what I had done, and commented that I had gone beyond what he himself had thought about. To be sure the same systems diagram was used in all three workshops to introduce basic principles of knowledge-based development to three different sets of participants. All expressed support, and this was amply demonstrated by the inspiring results achieved. The think-tank presented the strategic plan to the government, which I was later informed, approved at the highest level.

Osman moved again in 2008 to become the Deputy CEO of the International Institute of Advanced Islamic Studies (IAIS). I was a founder member of IAIS and regularly met him there at various events and functions. Consistent with the objective of IAIS our discussions began to turn towards the idea of civilizational renewal. Indeed, Osman can be considered a leading intellectual in the field with many scholarly writings on the subject. However, it was only after he moved to Universiti Brunei Darussalam (UBD) to establish the Sultan Omar Ali Saifuddien Centre of Islamic Studies in 2013 that we actively pursued the subject. In 2014 Osman invited me to deliver a lecture under the ISESCO Knowledge Economy Forum. Osman had given me a copy of his latest book *Islamic Civilisation and the Modern World* (2014). The book's theme is Islamic Civilisation and its relevance to the modern world. I was pleasantly surprised that he too had adopted the *Maqasid al-Shari'ah* as the basis for the new science of civilization, which is worth quoting: "The proposal made here is to utilize *maqasid* as the source of the fundamental assumptions of the new science of civilization …"[85]

For the lecture I chose the title *Islamic Education in the Network Society.* I wanted to highlight the importance of education and learning in the emerging world of knowledge, and the fact that this world is being constructed as an open global network that connects active participants communicating through

85 Osman Bakar, *Islamic Civilisation and the Modern World* (Brunei Darussalam: UBD Press, 2014), 326.

intensive application of digital technologies. I used the systems diagram that I had developed for the Saudi workshops to propose an integrated and comprehensive process of knowledge-based development. I also quoted Prof Naquib on the concept of education and its purpose in Islam, highlighting that the end of education is to produce a good man, as opposed to simply producing a good citizen.

I took the opportunity to quote from Osman's book[86] the four key elements of the *tajdid hadari* (civilizational renewal):

1. The preservation of principles, ideas, and institutions that are permanently needed by human beings both in individual and societal life;
2. The rediscovery and the restoration of principles, ideas, and institutions that have been lost through the vicissitudes of time, but that are still needed for the well-being of societies;
3. The acceptance of necessary changes in the light of permanence;
4. The synthesis of tradition and modernity or the integration of acceptable modernity into tradition.

Global networks that democratize access to thoughts, ideas and knowledge will have rising importance in creating a shared vision of the world under construction.

Response from participants was very positive and encouraging. One comment in particular from a non-Muslim participant was most comforting to me. He had assumed before the forum that the talk would be focused on traditional Islamic principles and practices. However, he had found that the ideas presented were universal in nature and could find wide application across all belief systems. This again serves as a demonstration that fundamental Islamic principles are indeed shared among varied cultures and civilisations. What could be more fundamental than the *maqasid*?

In 2018 Osman made one final move in his nomadic life to take up the Al-Ghazali Chair of Islamic Thought at ISTAC. He had asked for my opinion before accepting, and I strongly recommended that he should. This was a golden opportunity to pursue one of the most important intellectual challenges that he had identified in his lifetime of work in knowledge rediscovery: civilizational renewal. I was unable to attend his inaugural lecture but was duly impressed as I went through the text. He had set out the agenda of ISTAC as covering three broad areas: comparative epistemology, comparative civilizational studies and comparative futurology. I felt particularly well-positioned to "connect the dots," as it were, between the three focus areas. The ultimate agenda is civilizational renewal, which, given contemporary developments, must be based on knowledge in its true essence. Hence epistemology is the key

86 Osman Bakar, *Islamic Civilisation*, 312.

enabler to renewal. Futurology is something I had not fully expected, but welcomed most warmly. The structured process of understanding the alternative trajectories that may lead to the future is contained in futurology or futures studies. This then constitutes my understanding of ISTAC's integrated agenda.

There is a common thread between Osman and me in the story behind our affinity for futures studies. During the early-2010s I had become more active in the Academy of Sciences Malaysia (ASM), of which I was a founding Fellow at its establishment in 1995. For many years I was a dormant Fellow due to other demands. One of the major projects initiated in the mid-2010s was a foresighting exercise to produce alternative futures for Malaysia in 2050. I was invited to Co-Chair the Study Team and readily agreed. Scenario planning was one of my interest areas, having been introduced to the process by the IDRC of Canada which hosted an international event in the mid-1990s in the UK facilitated by the head of scenario planning at Shell, the oil company. It is common management lore that Shell is a pioneering company in correctly using scenario planning for business success and sustainability in a rapidly-changing global system.

Wanting to build a more balanced and nuanced framework for futures analysis and synthesis, we invited Osman to deliver a talk. We were delighted to learn that futures studies are a legitimate part of Islamic philosophy, and that Islamic principles exist to guide the process. This provided a powerful justification for the study and reinforced the legitimacy of its findings. The ASM foresight study ultimately engaged more than a thousand people from all walks of life, and was published in 2017 under the title *Envisioning Malaysia 2050 – A Foresight Narrative* (2017). Four alternative futures were conceived, out of which one was seen as the desired future, called "Synergised in Harmony" where good leadership and governance results in a growing economy with equitable distribution of wealth. The vision for Malaysia in 2050 is expressed as a "progressive Malaysia that is harmonious, prosperous and sustainable." Being the first ever foresighting exercise conducted, it received wide recognition and support among leaders and the community.

Upon accepting the Chair at ISTAC, he invited me to join the group looking into technological futures. This is a work in progress that may hopefully yield path-breaking ideas. Linking traditional knowledge to address contemporary challenges in knowledge-based development is not within the intellectual expertise or capacity of many institutions, even established ones. ISTAC can aspire to stand out from the crowd to become a successful pioneer in futures studies based on Islamic principles, given the right support.

The journey continues

Osman and I have enjoyed a close intellectual and spiritual journey for close to sixty years. Both of us started from the same initial conditions as far as education, science and religion are concerned, then pursued careers that seemed to diverge. Yet as we traversed the trajectory of learning and rediscovery we were drawn to the same path. He has become a renowned scholar in his chosen discipline, while I have been nudged into the technologies of information and knowledge.

The fact that humankind is reinventing itself by means of knowledge discovery and its application is clear to all. What is less certain is whether this new world of relentless innovation will possess the right attributes to bring about more happiness and well-being for humanity. Early signs seem to indicate the opposite. By wrongful use or plain abuse of knowledge to meet limited sectarian interests, the world is more likely to become less stable and less equitable, and indeed less just for most.

Twenty-first century crises for humanity will continue to mount if the basic principles of knowledge are left unchecked. The Covid pandemic is only the beginning. We have yet to see what other disasters await us as humanity continues to celebrate the triumphs of science without proper acknowledgment of its limitations.

Osman has much more to contribute, and indeed, all scholars and thinkers who are mindful of the great impact that knowledge could, and should have, in renewing human civilization for the better. For more than half a century he has resolutely stuck to his mission to understand, and then to propagate, the *Tawhidic* conception of man and his relationship with nature. His vision has now expanded into the realm of civilizational renewal, wherein science and technology will assume a primary role. In the process he has become a widely-acknowledged and respected scholar. Through our close friendship, I am truly privileged to have gained so much insight from his long and arduous intellectual journey. I speak for countless fellow travellers by thanking him for the gift of perennial knowledge and wisdom that would not have been so easily rediscovered without his pioneering spirit and inspiring leadership.

Bibliography

Academy of Sciences Malaysia. *Envisioning Malaysia 2050 – A Foresight Narrative*. Kuala Lumpur: ASM, 2017.

Al-Attas, Syed Muhammad Naquib. *Islam and Secularism*. Kuala Lumpur: Muslim Youth Movement of Malaysia (ABIM), 1978.

Al-Attas, Syed Muhammad Naquib. *The Concept of Education in Islam: A Framework for an Islamic Philosophy of Education*. Kuala Lumpur: International Institute of Islamic Thought and Civilisation, 1999.

Al-Faruqi, Ismail Raji. *Tawhid: Its Implications for Thought and Life*. Herndon: International Institute of Islamic Thought, 1982.

Chapra, M Umer. *Islam and the Economic Challenge*. Herndon and Nairobi: International Institute of Islamic Thought and The Islamic Foundation, 1992.

Chapra, M Umer. *The Islamic Vision of Development in the Light of the Maqasid al-Shari'ah*. Herndon: International Institute of Islamic Thought, 2008.

Mawdudi, Abul A'la. *Towards Understanding Islam*. Translated by Khurshid Ahmad. Birmingham: U.K.I.M. Dawah Centre, 1960.

Nasr, Seyyed Hossein. *An Introduction to Islamic Cosmological Doctrines*. Cambridge: Harvard University Press, 1964.

Nasr, Seyyed Hossein. *Ideals and Realities of Islam*. London: Allen and Unwin, 1966.

Nasr, Seyyed Hossein. *Science and Civilisation in Islam*. Cambridge: Harvard University Press, 1968.

Osman Bakar, ed. *Critique of Evolutionary Theory*. Kuala Lumpur: Islamic Academy of Science and Nurin Enterprise, 1987.

Osman Bakar. *Tawhid and Science*. Kuala Lumpur and Penang: Science University of Malaysia and Nurin Enterprise, 1991.

Osman Bakar. *Classification of Knowledge in Islam*. Kuala Lumpur and Penang: Science University of Malaysia and Nurin Enterprise. Kuala Lumpur: Institute for Policy Research, 1992.

Osman Bakar. *Islamic Civilisation and the Modern World*. Brunei Darussalam: UBD Press, 2014.

Chapter 3

Osman Bakar and the Renewal of Islamic Classification of Knowledge

Jasser Auda

Executive Chairman of the Maqasid Institute, London,
and a Visiting Professor of Islamic Law at
Carleton University in Canada

Introduction

Amongst Professor Osman Bakar's contributions to Islamic scholarship is in the realm of the Islamic classification of knowledge. The Aristotelian classification of knowledge has probably been the most prominent for many centuries, influencing generations of Muslim scholars, albeit in different forms. Two dominant streams could be identified, namely, classifications based on a modified Aristotelian approach by Al-Farabi (d. 339 H/950 CE) and Ibn Sina (d. 428 H/1037 CE), and classifications based on new non-Aristotelian approaches by Ibn Hazm (d. 456 H/1064 CE) and Ibn Khaldun (d. 808 H/1406 CE). Today, western academic disciplinization is most prominent and has impacted the definition of disciplines including Islamic studies. In his *Classification Of Knowledge,* which is originally his doctorate thesis from Temple University, the United States of America, Osman offers a unique and detailed discussion of classical Islamic classifications of knowledge, especially Al-Farabi, Al-Ghazali, and Al-Shirazi (1003–1083). This book and the many other studies that followed contributed to a Qur'ān-based approach that transcends current secular and Islamic classifications. Here, I analyze Osman's contribution towards the need to develop an alternative classification for Islamic Studies today.

The need for an Islamic classification of knowledge

In his introduction of Osman Bakar's book on the classification of knowledge, Seyyed Hossein Nasr writes:[87]

87 Seyyed Hossein Nasr, "Introduction," in *Classification of Knowledge in Islam: A Study in Islamic*

> Islamization of knowledge [is] being carried out throughout much of the Islamic world today. How can one Islamicize knowledge without being concerned with the traditional Islamic classification of the sciences? How can an Islamic education system accept a situation in which there is no hierarchy between the knowledge of the angels and of molluscs or between the method of knowledge based upon reason wed to the external senses and knowledge which derives from the certitude (*yaqin*) derived from heart-knowledge? The views of classical Islamic thinkers ably analyzed by Dr. Bakar here speak very directly to the current debate on the Islamization of knowledge and in fact provide an absolutely necessary dimension without which talk of this subject cannot proceed much beyond mere chatter.

These statements summarize the significance of Osman's contribution to the Islamization of knowledge project and—in my view—to the wider movement of renewal in Islamic thought in contemporary times. Currently, neither the dominant classifications of knowledge from a secular perspective nor the historical Islamic classifications of knowledge are adequate for the needs of current educational and research institutes of Islamic Studies. Osman's writings on the classification of knowledge, as well as his other contributions to Islamic thought, did not fall squarely under any of the current secular or Islamic classifications. In our analysis, he rather took a trans-disciplinary approach, in which the Qur'ānic knowledge lies at the center and as the basis.[88] This was a significant step in the road towards a contemporary renewal in Islamic thought.

The continued influence of Greek classifications

Aristotle's classification of knowledge has had a strong influence over many classical and contemporary classifications of disciplines/sciences, Islamic and non-Islamic, until today. His main categories were: theoretical, productive, and practical sciences.[89] Theoretical sciences are "knowledge for its own sake," in his words, which included metaphysics, mathematical sciences and natural sciences. This is the category that some Muslim philosophers, such as Al-Farabi, adopted while interpreting "metaphysics" to mean theological or Godly sciences (*'ilm ilahi*).[90] Productive sciences aim at the creation of products through craftsmanship. This is also a category that Muslim philosophers adopted. Al-Farabi included in productive sciences the Islamic philosophy of religion (*kalam*), and Al-Ghazali who included logic as a "tool" science (*'ilm aalah*).[91] Aristotle's practical sciences covered the knowledge of action, which

Philosophies of Science by Osman Bakar (Cambridge: Islamic Texts Society, 1998), xiv.

88 Refer for a clear example to the approach he took in his: *Qur'ānic Pictures of the Universe: The Scriptural Foundation of Islamic Cosmology*, as well as: *Tawhid and Science*.

89 Jonathan Barnes, "Introduction," in *The Nicomachean Ethics* by Aristotle (Harmondsworth: Penguin, 1976).

90 Osman Bakar, *Classification*, 128–132.

91 Al-Ghazali, *Al-Mustasfa fi 'Ilm Al-Usul*, 1st ed. (Beirut: Dar al-kutub al-'ilmiya, 1413 AH).

included ethics, judgement, politics, and arts. This category impacted classical Islamic classifications as well.

Al-Farabi categorized sciences into: (1) science of language (*'ilm al-lisan*), (2) logic (*'ilm al-mantiq*), which was divided similarly to Aristotle's books on logic, (3) mathematical or propaedeutic sciences (*'ulum al-ta'alim*), including arithmetic, theory of numbers, practical science of numbers, geometry, optics, stars, music, weights, ingenious devices, (4) natural science (*al-'ilm al-tabi'i*), (5) metaphysics or theology (*al-'ilm al-ilahi*), (6) practical sciences, including civil science (*al-'ilm al-madani*), jurisprudence (*'ilm al-fiqh*), and Islamic philosophy of religion (*'ilm al-kalam*).[92] Osman's analysis demonstrated the strong impact of Aristotle's classification on Al-Farabi,[93] despite the "Islamic" categories added such as *fiqh* and *kalam*. For one example, he analyses the categorization of logic given by Al-Farabi as follows:[94]

Logic (*'ilm al-mantiq*). This is divided into eight parts that deal with the following:

1. Rules governing simple intelligibles or ideas and simple expressions which signify these intelligibles, corresponding to Aristotle's Categories.
2. Rules governing simple statements or propositions composed of two or more simple intelligibles; and composite expressions signifying the composite intelligibles, corresponding to Aristotle's On Interpretation.
3. Rules of the syllogisms which are common to the five syllogistic arts – the demonstrative, the dialectical, the sophistical, the rhetorical, and the poetical, corresponding to Aristotle's Prior Analytics.
4. Rules of demonstrative proof and the special rules by which the philosophic art is constituted, corresponding to Aristotle's Posterior Analytics.
5. The means of discovering dialectical proofs, questions and answers, and the rules by which the art of dialectic is constituted, corresponding to Aristotle's Topics.
6. Rules governing matters which are such as to turn man away from truth to error and to lead him to deception, corresponding to Aristotle's On Sophistic Refutations.
7. The art of rhetoric. It deals with the rules by which rhetorical statements may be examined and evaluated, corresponding to Aristotle's Rhetoric.
8. The art of poetry, corresponding to Aristotle's Poetics.

92 Osman Bakar, *Classification*, chapters 5–6.
93 Osman Bakar, *Classification*, 10–19.
94 Osman Bakar, *Classification*, 120–121.

Ibn Sina's classification of sciences is even closer to Aristotle's. He did not include *fiqh* or *kalam* in his classification of knowledge.[95] He strictly followed the theoretical-practical classification, and included under them: nature, arithmetics, and theology; and ethics, governance of the household, and civil politics, respectively.

"Knowledge for its own sake," however, is not Islamic. There is a web of objectives that is tied to knowledge (*'ilm*) in the Islamic worldview, as Osman elaborates in his *Tawhid and Science*.[96] Therefore, it is obvious that the above two Islamic classifications, and many others similar to them,[97] are not relevant to a much-needed renewal of classification of disciplines for the sake of renewal of contemporary Islamic thought.

Ibn Hazm and Ibn Khaldun, amongst others, introduced classifications of disciplines that were significantly different from Aristotle's and the rest of the Peripatetics (*mashsha'iyyun*) and the Asharites and Mutazilites who were influenced by them.[98] However, Ibn Hazm and Ibn Khaldun were influenced by the dichotomous logic of the Greeks in general, including the theoretical-practical and physical-metaphysical categories. They also did not consider *fiqh* nor *Sharī'a* to be related to the sciences that they considered "common amongst nations," in the words of Ibn Hazm, or "not specific to any faith," in the words of Ibn Khaldun. However, Ibn Hazm included in this latter category philosophical sciences, whereas Ibn Khaldun included metaphysics. They both included in this "neutral" category: medicine and engineering (or mathematical shapes).

According to Osman, the Islamic worldview based on the revelation does not consider any science to be "neutral," valueless, or unrelated to faith. Philosophy, "metaphysics," medicine, and engineering are "all spheres of life" linked to beliefs. He writes that in Islam "the idea of hierarchy of human needs and of values of human acts in all spheres of life is based upon the ethico-legal teaching of the Shari'ah."[99]

Ibn Hazm also divided sciences into useful (*nafi'*), in which he included *Sharī'a*, language, *fiqh* and history, and detested/blameworthy (*madhmum*), in which he included alchemy, magic and astrology. Al-Ghazali has a similar category, which Osman referred to for its blameworthiness to causing harm. He writes:[100]

95 Osman Bakar, *Classification*, 9, 14, 25, 27, 29.

96 Osman Bakar, *Tawhid and Science: Islamic Perspectives on Religion and Science* (Shah Alam: Arah Publications, 2008), "Part 1: Epistemological Foundations of Islamic Sciences."

97 Such as those offered by: Al-Kindi, Al-'Amiri, Ibn Rushd, Tusi, A-Shirazi, Al-Ghazali, etc. Refer to: Osman Bakar, *Classification*.

98 Osman Bakar, *Classification*, 9, 11, 57, 174, 184, 215.

99 Osman Bakar, *Classification*, 47.

100 Osman Bakar, *Classification*, 216.

Al-Ghazali's three types of blameworthy knowledge may be described as corresponding to three different degrees of blame-worthiness. These degrees are understood not in a qualitative but quantitative sense. What I mean by "quantity" refers to the number of people who are subject to the harmful effects of each of the above three types. The first type, exemplified by the science of magic, produces the greatest degree of harm in the sense that no one, not even a prophet or a saint, is immune from the evil of magic. The second type, exemplified by astrology, corresponds to a lower degree of blameworthiness because there is a group of people, namely those "who are well grounded in knowledge" for whom the science is harmless although useless. As for the third type, exemplified on the one hand by trivial sciences and on the other by the science of divine mysteries, it is associated with the least degree of blameworthiness in the sense that it is harmful to the least number of people.

Ibn Khaldun divided knowledge into rational (*'aqli*), in which he included chemistry, magic, geometry, and music, and transmitted (*naqli*), in which he included exegesis, hadith, *fiqh, kalam,* sufism, and the Arabic language. It is interesting how "chemistry" and "magic" were considered one and the same at that time. Chemistry is now a standard science. But Muslim scholars such as to Ibn Hazm equated it with "magic" (*sihr*) (Qur'ān 2:102, 7:116, 10:81, 15:14–15, 20:66, 28:48) because both were seen as unexplained phenomenon or invention. Until a century ago, chemical reactions, and even telephones and bicycles were regarded as *sihr* by the jurists of Arabia.[101]

The impact of Ibn Hazm, Al-Ghazali, and Ibn Khaldun's categorizations, especially the categories of useful (*nafi'*) versus detested (*madhmum*), and rational (*'aqli*) versus transmitted (*naqli*), has been everlasting. However, it is also obvious that both classifications of disciplines, and similar classical classifications cannot meet the needs of the desired contemporary Islamic scholarship to deal with all disciplines of knowledge. Today, western academic disciplinization is most prominent, and it has impacted the definition of sub-disciplines within disciplines as well. However, none of the above categories of classifications is compatible with the disciplinization needs for a contemporary Islamic scholarship, hence the need to propose an alternative classification. Inspired by Osman's analysis of both, western academic as well as traditional Islamic classifications of knowledge, we propose the following critique of secular and Islamic classification.

Contemporary classifications of disciplines – secular and Islamic

Currently, the western academic classification of disciplines is prevalent worldwide. The dominant classification is: (1) Humanities, which typically

101 Hassan Al-Saffar, "'Aqliyat al-tahrim wal-tanfir min al-din" (The mentality of prohibition that made people reject religion), March 17, 2018, www.saffar.org/?act=artc&id=4072.

includes: arts, history, languages, literature, law, philosophy, and theology; (2) Social Sciences, which typically includes: anthropology, economics, geography, politics, psychology, and sociology; (3) Natural Sciences, which typically includes: biology, chemistry, earth science, astronomy, physics, and (4) Applied Sciences, which typically includes: business, engineering, health, computer science, and perhaps mathematics.

The above classification does not put "theology"—in this case Islamic Studies—in the right place as the fundamental basis of all sciences. Osman writes in his *Classification of Knowledge*: "The term "science" (*'ilm*) is used in this study in the comprehensive sense of an organized body of knowledge that constitutes a discipline with its distinctive goals, basic premises, and objects and methods of inquiry. I am therefore referring to a philosophy of science which embraces a far wider meaning and domain of study than does the modern discipline of the same name."[102] Therefore, the integrated nature of knowledge (*'ilm*) in Islam requires systematic ways of combining disciplines and not treating them as silos. This is especially so across the four categories, i.e. across humanities, social, natural and applied sciences, which is typically inadmissible and would discredit scholars and scholarship. Finally and most significantly, many of the basic premises of the above sciences require critique from the Islamic point of view and therefore have to be part of a bigger picture of the classification of disciplines.

Islamic Studies today, on the other hand, is divided into three broad classifications, which we can call: (1) historical Islamic Studies, (2) contemporary Islamic Thought and (3) Islamic Studies in secular academia.

Under historical disciplines, students specialize primarily in the history of one of the inherited Islamic branches of knowledge, such as exegesis (*tafsir*), narrations (*hadith*), jurisprudence (*fiqh*), philosophy (*falsafah/kalam*), history (*tareekh*), *Sharī'a*-based governance (*siyasah shar`iyah*), etc. Students study the fundamentals (*usul*) associated with each of these disciplines as the methodology or approach to it.

Under contemporary Islamic thought, students learn about an Islamic approach to a modern academic discipline, such as finance, psychology, art, law, education, or architecture. The approach is usually historical, while attempting to answer current questions in these disciplines based on the current literature in Islamic thought. There is a growing reference to *Maqasid Al-Sharī'a* in these programs, albeit generally manifesting the limitations mentioned earlier.

Islamic Studies in secular academia is a spectrum of programs that range from theology, religious studies and philosophy to political science, history and social studies. A few of these studies are still following the old orientalist approach, i.e. studying Islam's original texts with a pre-assumption of their

102 Osman Bakar, *Classification*, 5.

"biblical origins" and within the colonialist purposes of the old orientalist school.[103] Some of these studies moved from orientalism to what we can call a "neo-orientalism" approach, in which Islam is defined via its social, political or historical manifestations and studied through one of the typical secular social sciences approaches. The general purpose also moved from a colonialist agenda to a neo- or post-colonialist agenda.[104] However, over the past decade, we have observed a growing number of "confessional" approaches to Islamic Studies within secular academia in which professors and students are searching for an "Islamic approach" that is both genuine and commensurate with the complexity and demands of today's questions and challenges. Islamic "law" is offered as an alternative in this search for an Islamic approach, although there is a general awareness of the insufficiency of the Islamic classical schools of jurisprudence to answer today's questions in all disciplines.

Generally speaking, contemporary Islamic Studies experience a number of methodological drawbacks. The most significant are the following three:

First, there is a general lack in studying the original sources of Islam, i.e. the Qur'ān and Sunnah themselves, in all of these contemporary trends. Most of the attention is given to what scholars have said—past and present—while attention to the Qur'ān and Sunnah is virtually subordinated except for occasional references. A cursory look at what a student of jurisprudence studies today in a "Sharī'a College," for example, reveals the limited portion that revelation features in their studies. To study the revelation means to study the Qur'ān and Sunnah directly, not what scholars have said about it. Even when students are required to memorize parts of the Qur'ān and Sunnah, they are rarely taught to use what they memorize as criteria for evaluation of what they study. A similar problem manifests in all other branches and projects of Islamic Studies.

Contemporary Islamic thought is largely apologetic towards methodologies, outcomes, and organizations of modern academia. As such it lacks a critique of the boundaries of modern disciplines in western institutions. Yet, the ideological and philosophical foundations of these disciplines and the organizations that house them stem from a reality and worldview that contradicts with Islam in some aspects. For example, Islamic economics emerges from the same philosophies, theories, and organizations of western economics and does not seriously challenge neoliberal capitalism, which is the current trend, but rather on the whole attempts to accommodate it. Likewise, Islamic political theory is by and large a product of the philosophy, theory, and institutions

103 Compare for example: Joseph Schacht, "Foreign Elements in Ancient Islamic Law," *Comparative Legislation and International Law* 32 (1950); and Mohammad Al-Azami, *On Schacht's Origins of Mohammadan Jurisprudence* (Riyadh: King Saud University and John Wiley, 1985).

104 Refer to the discussion in: Jasser Auda, *Maqasid al-Sharī'a as Philosophy of Islamic Law: A Systems Approach* (London: IIIT, 2008), Section 5.5.

of modern western academia. The original contribution of Islamic political thought is still nascent and Islamic methodologies have been incapable of participating in critical discussions and offering real alternatives.

The pedagogic division of disciplines into Islamic and non-Islamic reinforces the secular ideology in the Muslim mind and society more broadly. It is a division that diminishes the domain and function of Islam—as a *din*—from its all-encompassing concept in the Revelation as applicable to more than theology, spirituality, and ethics. The average person will then live his entire life based on the philosophies, definitions and organizations that define the world by materialistic measures. Some Muslims even apologize for this serious methodological flaw by arguing that Islam is a rational religion that encourages "pure" and "factual" sciences and that the worldly sciences are value neutral, which is obviously a view that lacks sufficient analysis.

The future of Islamic classification of knowledge

Based on Osman's contributions to the development of an Islamic classification of knowledge, as well as our above critique of the current dominant "Islamic" and "secular" classifications, we find that the essence of Osman's approach in his seminal works promotes what we can call a trans-disciplinary approach. Rectifying the classification of contemporary disciplines and sciences in today's academic and educational systems does not mean rejecting them *in toto,* nor denying the major contributions that they have offered to humanity. However, trans-disciplinary studies involve studying phenomena from all dimensions based on an Islamic framework. Commenting on Al-Farabi's approach, Osman writes:

> In al-Farabi's account of natural science and political science, there is some overlapping between the two disciplines with respect to their subject-matters. This overlapping pertains mainly to psychology. Al-Farabi's natural sciences discusses the different faculties of the human soul and establishes the conclusion that man's final perfection is intellectual in nature, namely the perfection of the theoretical intellect. Political science incorporates this idea of man's final perfection into its body of knowledge and makes it the central theme of its inquiry. For natural science does not deal with the question of how man, in the context of his terrestrial existence, may attain that perfection. To conclude, it may be asserted that the subject-matter of al-Farabi's political science occupies a kind of intermediate ontological position between the subject-matters of natural science and metaphysics. Being an intermediate science, political science shares certain things in common with the highest science (metaphysics) and with the lowest science (natural science). However, the greater part of the subject-matter of political science clearly lies, ontologically speaking, between the subject-matters of natural science and metaphysics.[105]

105 Osman Bakar, *Classification*, 106.

This trans-disciplinary and integrating approach is where the future of Islamic classification of knowledge occurs. This is Osman Bakar's primary contribution to the wider project of a contemporary renewal in Islamic thought.

Bibliography

Al-Azami, Mohammad. *On Schacht's Origins of Mohammadan Jurisprudence.* Riyadh: King Saud University and John Wiley, 1985.

Al-Farabi. *Ihsa al-'Ulum*, edited by U. Amin. Cairo: Dar al-Fikr al-Arabi, 1949.

Al-Ghazali. *Al-Mustasfa fi `Ilm Al-Usul*, 1st ed. Beirut: Dar al-Kutub al-'Ilmiya, 1413 AH.

Al-Saffar, Hassan. "`Aqliyat al-tahrim wal-tanfir min al-din" (The mentality of prohibition that made people reject religion). March 17, 2018, www.saffar.org/?act=artc&id=4072.

Auda, Jasser. *Maqasid al-Sharī'a as Philosophy of Islamic Law: A Systems Approach.* London: IIIT, 2008.

Barnes, Jonathan. "Introduction." In *The Nicomachean Ethics* by Aristotle. Harmondsworth: Penguin, 1976.

Ibn Hazm. *Maratib al-ulum* (Manuscript), http://al-maktaba.org/book/1038/924.

Ibn Khaldun. *The Muqaddimah: An Introduction.* Translated by Franz Rosenthal. Princeton Classics, 2015.

Ibn Sina. *Risalah fi aqsam al-ulum al-`aqliyah* (Manuscript), http://ketabpedia.com.

Osman Bakar. *Classification of Knowledge in Islam: A Study in Islamic Philosophies of Science.* Cambridge: Islamic Texts Society, 1998.

Osman Bakar. *Qur'ānic Pictures of the Universe: The Scriptural Foundation of Islamic Cosmology.* Kuala Lumpur: Islamic Book Trust, 2018.

Osman Bakar. *Tawhid and Science: Islamic Perspectives on Religion and Science.* Shah Alam: Arah Publications, 2008.

Schacht, Joseph. "Foreign Elements in Ancient Islamic Law." *Comparative Legislation and International Law* 32, no. 3/4 (1950): 9–17.

Chapter 4

Narrating the West for the Malays: Syed Shaykh al-Hady and *al-Imam*

Ahmad Murad Merican

Professor of Social and Intellectual History at International Institute of Islamic Thought and Civilisation, Malaysia

Modern Muslim thought emerged as a reaction to the impact of the West upon Muslim society. Through colonialism, the west intervened in the epistemological space of Muslim nations, including that of Malay society. An altered sense of modernity developed. The thinking then (and also now) was that to be a modern Muslim was to be Western. The way to progress was assumed to be the Western way. The adjustment to modernity thus took the form of accepting or adopting Western solutions before formulating specifically "Muslim solutions" that brings to the fore Muslim culture and a Muslim system of values.

It was against such a condition of the West inducing the rest to mobilize itself through various forms of expression that the Muslim reform school emerged. Its main aim was to:

> provide solutions to allay Muslim conscience and permit Muslims to adopt and partake in scientific development. It was in a sense a resistance to European cultural penetration, and in another it was a yielding to what was considered science and technology... Those who opposed change called every departure from the old tradition westernization, that is imitation of the hated enemy, the infidel West. Those who supported change called every aspect of it modernization, however irrelevant the particular innovation might be to the needs of the man in the scientific and technological age. The problem arising from this controversy touched upon both theology and ethics.[106]

This is the position taken by the founders of the *al-Imam* periodical in colonial Malaya (1906–1908). From the outset, the founders of *al-Imam* declared its purpose to be the fulfilment of their duty as Muslims to: (1) impart

---

106 Mohamed Aboulkhir Zaki, "Modern Muslim Thought in Egypt and Its Impact on Islam in Malaya," PhD diss., University of London, 1965.

knowledge to their Muslim brethren in the East; (2) give advice and show the way to be a good Muslims and to remind those who are idle, awaken those who are asleep and lead those who have lost their way.[107]

Abu Bakar Hamzah, in his study of the role of *al-Imam* in Malay society, lists the objectives as follows:[108]

1. Establish a "Kingdom of God" on Earth.
2. Introduce and advocate Islamic political philosophy.
3. Help achieve independence for every Muslim umma from colonial powers and Satanic forces acting behind the curtain in every secular state.
4. Create political zeal and attitude amongst the Muslims individually and collectively.
5. Cooperate with other Islamic movements for the common good of all Muslims wherever they may be.

Undoubtedly, *al-Imam*, unlike other previous Malay periodicals, emphasized the political dimensions of life. It is the key to understanding the period both in Malay society, and in Europe and what we called the Middle East then.

This chapter seeks to address the intellectual and political influence upon al-Hady which informs his concept of journalism, specifically his belief and deployment of journalism as a tool for social reform, cultural and political expression. To be sure, the *al-Imam*'s visions mirrored that of the Egyptian reformist journal *al-Manar*. Both journals derived some inspiration from the European Reformist movement of Martin Luther. In many ways, the *al-Imam* disseminates religious values through the mode of journalism similarly to what had developed in early-modern Europe. The impetus was arguably due to the foundations of Arab Occidentalism in Egypt. Roff described the *Al-Imam* as a "radical" departure in the field of Malay publication, and journalism, distinguishing itself from its predecessors both in intellectual stature and intensity of purpose and in its attempts to formulate a coherent philosophy of action for a society faced with the need for rapid social and economic change.[109] The *al-Imam*, a notable reformist project of Al-Hady can be said to be the intellectual descendant of the *Al-Manar* designed to address the challenges faced by Muslims in the Malay World.[110]

Like Munshi Abdullah through his *Hikayat* and *Pelayaran Abdullah*, al-Hady, through *al-Imam* and other periodicals founded by him, made

107 *Al-Imam*, July 23, 1906.

108 Abu Bakar Hamzah, *Al-Imam: Its Role and Functions* (Kuala Lumpur: Pustaka Antara, 1991).

109 William R. Roff, *The Origins of Malay Nationalism* (Kuala Lumpur: Penerbit Universiti Malaya, 1974), 19.

110 Charles C. Adam, *Islam and Modernism in Egypt* by Muhammad 'Abduh (New York: Russell & Russell, 1968).

journalism an instrument of criticism focussing on Malay society. Apart from Abdullah and Pandita Za'ba, al-Hady can be described as the other significant figure in Malay society before the formation of Malaya, to have openly criticized the *umat*, the *bangsa* and the *kerajaan* of the day through his writings. This chapter seeks to address the following critical questions: What did al-Hady hope to achieve through his journalism? How was he influenced by the reformist and modernist thought in the Arab world at that time? How did that affect his views of the significance of journalism? How was al-Hady's journalism similar to that of the craft in Malaya and elsewhere in the world? Was he influenced by the journalism of Europe through the Arab world? What were his attitudes towards Europe and the colonizing powers, and how has that been expressed in its relation to Islam and the Malays?

The Al-Imam and Syed Shaykh Al-Hady's Milieu

The *Al-Imam* (The Leader) emerged in 1906. The periodical was conceptualized as a politico-religious newspaper, and identified itself with the reformist movement in the Arab world that engaged with Western modernity. One of its founders, and editor, Syed Shaikh bin Ahmad al-Hady, who set up the newspaper two years after returning from his studies in Egypt, was also a student of the West.[111] A dialogical reading of Al-Hady's writings in the *Al-Imam* would find one traversing through discourses of resistance against the Occident from the perspective of a reformist Muslim. Al-Hady's exposure to the West, through his education in Riau under Raja Haji Ali and tutelage under the Egyptian theologian Shaikh Mohamed Abduh made al-Hady an informed subject who was conscious of his milieu. According to his son, Syed Alwi al-Hady, his father founded *Al-Imam* to bring social and religious reforms into Malaya along the lines promulgated by Abduh. Al-Hady wanted to purify Islam from malpractices and non-Islamic influence and to eradicate despondency, inertia and feelings of inferiority that were predominant among the Muslims in Malaya. According to Nik Ahmad, although *Al-Imam* survived for only three and half years, it influenced Malay journalism in 1920s and 1930s Malaya.[112]

Al-Imam's editor, Haji Abbas Taha, was a staunch advocate of modernism in Islam. An editorial on 10 May 1913 argued that: "The neglect of our religion is the root cause of our present weakness. Does not our Holy Qur'ān enjoin upon us to help each other? Do we follow it and practice it as other advanced nations? We lack co-operation and *espirit de corps* which is regrettable for co-operation is the basis for and key to progress and development."[113]

111 Nik Ahmad Nik Hassan, "The Malay Press," *Journal Malayan Branch Asiatic Society* 36, part 1 (1963): 37–78.

112 Inclusive of Singapura. See Nik Ahmad, "Malay Press."

113 Nik Ahmad, "Malay Press."

Between 1906 and 1941, Muslims in the Malay world lived under conditions of colonialism and imperialism. The Malays then faced the problematics and consequences of what Makdisi (2000) describes as "Western dominated modernity." Major periodicals during the period, namely *Al-Imam* (1906–08), *Majallah Guru* (1924–1941), *Saudara* (1928–1941), *Warta Malaya* (1930–1941), and *Majlis* (1932–1941) highlighted the concerns and anxieties of Muslims during that time.

In studying these periodicals, it is important to reiterate Roff's argument about Malay's sharp criticisms and responses to the West that bespoke of some "ideological" currents that flowed in the Malay world then.[114] The editors and writers were informed subjects and were "producers" and not just "produced" by the West. The discourses were produced between two previously separate cultures. There was cultural crossing in the form of Occidental expeditions, missionary work, trade, leisure travel, etc.[115]

As "modern Muslim men" living under the conditions of imperialism, the writers of *Al-Imam* would have noticed the gulf in "progress" between the British and Malay subjects. Given the overwhelming dominance of the British which made them seemingly far more "superior," the founders of *Al-Imam* internalized and accepted some ideas and values from the colonizers as "true," even admirable.[116] The existence of ideological hegemony resulted in a congruency of ideas between contributors of the *Al-Imam* and the colonial government. The French philosopher Michel Foucault, who drew from the Gramscian notion of hegemony, describes such willing embrace of ideas and values by the subordinated group as "power effects at the level of desire."[117] Illustrative in *Al-Imam* is a letter from a reader ruminating about Malay backwardness. The letter remarked: "Everyone knows of the existence of the Malays but not everyone, it seems, has seen how a Malay man looks like. Why, just look in *Wonders* magazine—the stories of Sir Frank Swetenham; and the artistic depiction of the murder of Mr. Birch. The Malay figures are depicted by European artists as dressed in *cawat* (loincloths)."[118]

Was the birth of *al-Imam* induced by developments in Europe? Although *al-Imam*'s main concern was with religion and not directly with social, "even less with political, change" its editors and writers shared the traditional Islamic concept of the undifferentiated *umat* or community in which spiritual, social, and political well-being and ends are subsumed under divine law. Their

114 Roff, *The Origins of Malay Nationalism.*

115 M. Fairoz Ahmad, "Orientalism and Integrative History: A Study of An Early 20th Century Islamic Periodical in Singapore," Master's thesis, National University of Singapore, 2010.

116 M. Fairoz, "Orientalism and Integrative History."

117 D. Stephen Brookfield, *The Power of Critical Theory: Liberating Adult Learning and Teaching* (San Francisco: Jossey-Bass, 2005), 138.

118 Cited from *Surat Kiriman* (Letter from Reader) 3, no. 3 (August 1908), in "Orientalism and Integrative History" by M. Fairoz.

attention was tuned in to the state of Malay society. In all 31 issues, the periodical contains articles analysing the ills of the community—pointing out to the backwardness of the Malays, their domination by other races, their laziness, their complacency, their bickering among themselves, and their inability to cooperate for the common good.[119]

Works about Syed Shaykh al-Hady (1867–1934), *al-Imam* (1906–8) and that of early Malay periodicals are not new. Many have captured al-Hady as a reformist and a modernist, and also have written about the man in terms of his literary contributions, as well as in referring to him as an advocate of education through the many schools, and *madrasahs* he started.[120] In what follows, I explore a well-known but little explored facet of the Malay journalistic narratives in *al-Imam* associated with al-Hady's Occidental conceptualization of journalism in the context of Malay society during the colonial period. The various streams of ideas both from Europe and the wider Muslim world to which al-Hady was exposed was reflected in *al-Imam*, and also *Saudara*. These ideas inform us of his deployment of journalism as a tool for cultural and political expression.

Although not original in his diagnoses of the problems facing Muslim society, Al-Hady made a conscious effort to reflect on the question of backwardness, drawing very much upon the ideas of contemporary Muslim reformers in the Western part of the Muslim world. While al-Hady played a major role in the emergence of nationalism in colonial Malaya, al-Hady's ideas did not result in the formation of an intellectual class like that in Indonesia. Syed Farid Alatas argues that unlike his contemporary, H.O.S. Tjokroaminoto, whose ideas and organization inspired a mass movement in Indonesia, al-Hady did not have such an effect in Malaya.[121] Nationalist and other ideologies that developed never had the intellectual rigour of al-Hady's, whose death in 1934 was universally lamented. Indeed, in writing on Malay journalism in Malaya, Zainal-Abidin Ahmad, known as Za'ba, describes al-Hady as atypical, especially in regard to his uncompromising criticism of Malay life and advocacy of social and religious reformation for Muslims.[122] What were the contexts that motivated Al-Hady to vehemently push for these reforms?

In the early decades of the twentieth century, the Malay Peninsular witnessed the revival of Islam. The essence of the revival is *islah* (reform) with the

119 Roff, *Origins of Malay Nationalism*, 57.

120 Ibrahim Abu Bakar, *Islamic Modernism in Malaya: The Life and Thought of Sayid Syekh al-Hadi 1867–1934* (Kuala Lumpur: University of Malaya Press, 1994); Marina Merican, "Syed Shaikh Al-Hadi dan Pendapat-pendapat-nya Mengenai Kemajuan Kaum Perempuan" (Syed Shaykh al-Hady and His Views on the Advancement of Women), Unpublished B.A. Hons. diss., University of Malaya, 1961.

121 Syed Farid Alatas, "Ideology and Utopia in the Thought of Syed Shaykh Al-Hady," unpublished paper, 2003.

122 Zainal Abidin Ahmad, "Malay Journalism in Malaya," *Journal of the Malayan Branch Royal Asiatic Society* 19, no. 2 (1941): 244–50.

purpose of cleansing society from *tahayul, khurafat* and *bidaah.*[123] Being the first such Malay publication, it has to also be noted that *al-Imam*, although seen as integral to the transformation process of the Malays, was not entirely a response to the impact of British presence in the Peninsula, nor was it the colonial educational system which instilled in al-Hady an awareness of the rapidly changing demographic, economic and political environment.

Arguably, *Al-Imam* is more a manifestation of the general temperament of the Malays, in what Khoo Kay Kim refers to as "a mood for change" which was brought back by students studying in West Asia.[124] This mood for change, and much more than that, induced by the currents of new thinking in the Arab world emerging in the later part of the nineteenth century was certainly felt with some force by al-Hady. At that time, al-Hady was already engaged in the thinking of Sayyed Jamal al-Din al-Afghani, Muhammad 'Abduh and Rashid Rida. Al-Hady had visited Makkah and Cairo several times and was reported to have met Muhammad 'Abduh and certainly did meet Rashid Rida.[125] It seems that al-Hady was impressed by 'Abduh's progressive interpretation of Islam and came home with a sense of discovery and mission.[126]

Al-Hady used journalism as a *Perjuangan* (struggle) to propagating reform. It is instructive to trace further the historical context in the tension between religion and polity in the Malay world before colonial conditions in order to further understand al-Hady's ideas as manifested in *al-Imam* and subsequent periodicals. Clearly, he was subverting Islam as endorsed and patronized by the *rajas* and *sultans. Al-Imam's* denunciation of the *kerajaan* is to some extent the product of the tension between Islam and kingship.

Apart from the developments in Europe, the forces that gave character to the journalistic ethos of al-Hady and *al-Imam* and its successive periodicals were the external circumstances in the Muslim world, among which was the *Wahhabi* movement that probably reached the Malay Archipelago through the pilgrimage to Makkah and by means of Arab settlers and travellers. The *Wahhabi* impact was evidenced in the so-called *Paderi* campaigns in the Minangkabau heartland of West Sumatra, beginning in 1803. The Minangkabau *Paderi* leaders were in close contact with Islamic developments in the Arab lands.[127] It is noted that the *Al-Imam* editors, including al-Hady, to a large extent,

---

123 Fadhlullah Jamil, "Syed Syeikh al-Hadi: Pemikiran terhadap Islam dan Perubahan," *Dewan Sastera* 28, no. 6 (1998): 21–25.
124 Khoo Kay Kim, *Malay Society: Transformation and Democratisation* (Petaling Jaya: Pelanduk Publications, 1991), 176.
125 Syed Alwi Al-Hady, "The Life of My Father," in *The Real Cry of Syed Shaykh al-Hady*, ed. Alijah Gordon, 69–83 (Kuala Lumpur: Malaysian Sociological Research Institute, 1999).
126 Linda Tan, "Syed Shaykh: His Life and Times," in *The Real Cry of Syed Shaykh al-Hady*, 109–162.
127 William R. Roff, "South-East Asian Islam in the Nineteenth Century," in *The Cambridge History of Islam* (Cambridge: Cambridge University Press, 1978), 166.

encountered the stimulus second hand, by means of their relationship with the reformers.[128]

These were to serve as a model for later generations of reformers throughout the Muslim world, including in early Malaya, as seen in the activities of Syeikh Tahir Jalaludin, and the *modus operandi* of al-Hady. The influence of the three intellectuals of Islam on both leaders of *al-Imam* manifested a kind of renaissance, especially in the ideology of al-Hady. In accepting that change is inevitable and proceeding to justify them in religious terms, al-Hady's thought may be regarded as ideology that justified capitalism. Drawing upon al-Hady's *Ugama Islam dan Akal* to illustrate his ideological leanings, Shaharuddin Maaruf argues that al-Hady advocated a rational and individualistic approach to religion, which are also the defining features of a capitalistic ethic.[129] He suggests that al-Hady's emphasis on the Malays, on the rights of the individual, justice, equality and welfare, and on objectivity and independent reason "represents a justification of the new Western style of administration and the capitalistic social order with its ideas of social contract, individualism and the rule of law, as against feudalism, its social inequalities and the arbitrary powers of its leaders."[130]

As we shall see later, al-Hady and his group used journalism to forward religion as "guidance for man on earth and not salvation through the rejection of the world."[131] There is the trait of utilitarianism in al-Hady's thought in viewing Islam as an ideological force "propelling man along the path of worldly asceticism and progress on earth, besides ensuring salvation in the world hereafter." According to Shaharuddin, al-Hady's interpretation of Islam serves to develop the spirit of capitalism amongst the Malays.[132]

Al-Hady's main thrust was to change the mindset of the Malays.[133] That thrust was later to dominate the whole theme of *al-Imam*; also *al-Ikhwan* and *Saudara*. As al-Hady's son recounted, this was the basic theme. That was why he and others started *al-Imam*; that was why he started *al-Ikhwan*. Of course, in doing this with real missionary, extra-missionary zeal he offended the thousands of these *pondok* teachers and "ulama" who had the backing of the sultans and the religious councils.[134] Al-Hady called upon the Malays to face the realities of their situation; he broke down the wall of conservatism and opened up new ideas.

128 Anthony Milner, *The Invention of Politics in Colonial Malaya* (Cambridge: Cambridge University Press, 2002), 181.

129 Shaharuddin Maaruf, *Malay Ideas on Development: From Feudal Lord to Capitalist* (Singapore: Times Books International, 1988), 63.

130 Shaharuddin, *Malay Ideas on Development*, 66.

131 Shaharuddin, *Malay Ideas on Development*, 66–67.

132 Shaharuddin, *Malay Ideas on Development*, 67.

133 Syed Alwi, "Life of My Father."

134 Syed Alwi, "Life of My Father."

Conceptualizing a Malay Reading Public

Al-Hady's journalism in effect created a new Malay-Muslim public sphere. Roff describes *al-Imam* as the first radical (read: political) periodical different from previous Malay journalism which saw a marked absence of discussions of religious and related social and economic issues.[135] Nik Ahmad Nik Hassan sees *al-Imam* as marking a new stage of development in Malay journalism.[136] What is significant to note here is that al-Hady transformed Malay journalism from being event-centred to a medium of education, persuasion, opinion, discourse, and polemics. It was the commentary and the essay. News was secondary. *Al-Imam* assumed the role of an educator and an ideological organ, espousing the ideology of al-Hady and the journal's editors. The reach of *al-Imam* during the two years of its existence was very significant. It showed that the Malay-reading public was vibrant, with the periodical having an estimated circulation of 2000 copies per month in 1906 and 1,500 in 1907.[137] The periodical was read all over the Malay Archipelago including Pulau Pinang. If we account for the range of circulation of Malay periodicals and newspapers in the first two decades of 1900, the range was between 500 to 1200. The circulations figure implies an audience of more than 12,000 readers weekly or monthly.[138]

Al-Hady's journalism reflected the mood of writing and expression prevalent in Asia in the wake of modernization and resistance to colonialism. It can also be seen to be quite similar to the Lutheran Reformation. Did al-Hady, through the Muslim reformists in the Middle East, also have knowledge of pamphlet literature in early-modern Europe, particularly in the context of the Italian wars of the later fifteenth century, the German Reformation, and the French Revolution?

Al-Imam functioned similar to the European pamphlet journalism. It is a genre unto itself. Pamphlets are inseparable from polemic and contestation and are aimed at influencing opinion. Chisick argues that it is fair to characterize pamphlets as a literature of disjuncture and contestation.[139] They occur in large numbers when a significant segment of the population feels the need for change in some feature of public life, or wishes to prevent or limit a change that it perceives as threatening. Pamphlets were produced on any subject of broad interest, but they constitute a pre-eminently political genre. They were normally addressed to the public, with the purpose of winning public opinion

135 Roff, *Origins of Malay Nationalism*, 52, 59.

136 Nik Ahmad, "Malay Press."

137 William R. Roff, *Bibliography of Malay and Arabic Periodicals Published in the Straits Settlements and Peninsular Malay States 1876–1941* (London: Oxford University Press, 1972), 21.

138 This assumes a readership of 10 or more people per periodical, and discounting opinion leaders who would transmit what they have read to the larger society. The consciousness would be exponential.

139 Harvey Chisick, "The Pamphlet Literature of the French Revolution: An Overview," *History of European Ideas* 17, no. 2/3 (1993): 149–166.

in favour of their point of view. Pamphlets have predominantly been used as a means for persuasion.

Al-Hady was, as Passin speaks of Bengali philosopher Rabindranath Tagore, the embodiment of politics, literature and journalism.[140] But then, al-Hady would probably not have liked to think of himself as a journalist, "at least in the narrow sense of the scribbler, preoccupied with the immediate, the trivial, and the superficial." Like Tagore, al-Hady uses his writing as a form of criticism of society – its political conditions, social problems, its quality, its standards, its aspirations, its shortcomings, needs, hopes. Al-Hady has indeed informed us on some salient features of journalism. In the chapter "Writer and Journalist in the Transitional Society," Passin observes: "Each nation that enters the cycle of modernization must at some point break through in three fields: political and social reform, language and journalism. The breakthroughs may take place simultaneously or at separate times within a broad historical period."[141] Passin notes that under such historical circumstances, the nations (including those of the Arab states and that of South East Asia) bring with them a literary tradition and a mode of the writer as artist. In other words, the journalists are also legitimately seen and accepted as a writer. A tension is created. We have the creative artist with a vision and a vocation, and at the same time, we have the technician of words, the scribe preoccupied with the immediate, the surface. The reality is much like a continuum where the moment we leave the extreme, the distinction is blurred; and this is where the journalist becomes a commentator, essayist, propagandist: a "writer." On the other hand, the writer who leaves pure fiction becomes a commentator or essayist, thus meeting the journalist moving in the other direction.

The journalist becomes a writer, even if not a creative writer, and the writer, as a commentator with views on philosophy, aesthetics, politics and social reform, becomes a journalist.[142] Al-Hady never went to the extreme, as a scribe in the sense of being a technician of words. Nevertheless in him we see the merging of journalism, philosophy, ideology, social reform and utopia. It may even be argued that the utopia when used with journalism as an instrument points out to the future, transcending the reality of the present that it attempts to explain.[143]

140 Herbert Passin, "Writer and Journalist in the Transitional Society," in *Communications and Political Development*, ed. Lucian W. Pye, 82–123 (Princeton: Princeton University Press, 1963).

141 Passin, "Writer and Journalist in the Transitional Society."

142 Passin, "Writer and Journalist in the Transitional Society."

143 Syed Farid Alatas, "Ideology and Utopia in the Thought of Syed Shaykh Al-Hady." Alatas in explaining the utopian dimensions of al-Hady's thoughts in terms of Karl Mannheim's concept of utopia, refers to Shahruddin Maaruf's list of traits of utopian thinking as they apply to Muslims in Southeast Asia. These are (a) the rejection and denial of the existing order, (b) the posing of a radical alternative to the existing order, (c) the distortion of certain aspects of current realities which challenge their ideas; (d) the role of ideas in mobilization rather than for the purpose of diagnosis, and (e) its populist rather than intellectual nature. Quoted from Shaharuddin Maaruf, "Religion and Utopian Thinking Among the

Al-Hady writes history. In fact, through his writings, we see the beginnings of an ambivalent resistance—ambivalent because on the one hand, he advocates for emancipation of Malay-Muslim thought; and does not explicitly propagate an anti-colonial stance. He has, according to Alatas, merely perpetuated the mode of colonial capitalism. Through the periodicals, and including *Saudara*, which began to be published in 1928, al-Hady was plugging the same theme of changing religious interpretations and changing religious education. *Saudara*'s aim was to capture the secular reading market.[144] Al-Hady also ran the Jelutong Press. His grandson Syed Mohamed Alwi recalls that it was difficult to run a newspaper as a one-man show.

The periodicals at issue were al-Hady's most often used platform for advocating religious reform. The magazines of *al-Imam* and *al-Ikhwan* are most deserving of attention. *Al-Imam* surpassed all previous Malay publications from *Jawi Peranakan* (1876–96), and perhaps a total of 30 other Malay periodicals before the period. These periodicals called upon the Malays to bestir themselves and to take their due share in the activities of modern life. There was a surge of new interest and new ambition, with a new current of ideas penetrating literary life, expressed in the form of journalism. In this case, *al-Imam* was clearly the leader.[145]

The Projection of Watan by Syed Shaikh al-Hady

Al-Imam was instrumental in illustrating an epistemological transition from the colonial Malay world to the new nation state. This can be seen in an elaboration of the concept of *Watan*. *Watan* (Arabic *Watan* or homeland, Malay *Tanah air*), as advocated by Syed Shaikh Al-Hady, had a modern and secular connotation, posing a challenge to the prevalent worldview of the Malays and the *kerajaan* (kingdom). Ismail F. Alatas, in debating the thoughts of Al-Hady on *Watan*, brings attention to the novelty of the concept for most Malays.[146] Al-Hady, through *Al-Imam*, brought in his writings the incompatibility between *watan* and *kerajaan*. Whereas identity to the Malays was constructed predominantly in relation to the particular state in which a person resided, al-Hady's conceptualization of *watan* came to mean the pivotal basis for the construction of a modern nation-state. In this way, Alatas contends, al-Hady played an important role in facilitating the fusing of Malay receptivity with modern European political thought, in the form of a nationalist ideology. Loyalty, to al-Hady, was no longer exclusively to "the *kerajaan* but to a *spatial homeland* inhabited by the Malays." In this sense, *watan* necessitates the secularization of mind in the Malay psyche.

Muslims of Southeast Asia," unpublished manuscript, 1999, 2–3.

144 Syed Alwi, "Life of My Father."

145 Zainal Abidin, "Malay Journalism in Malaya."

146 Ismail F. Alatas, "Circumlocutory Imperialism: Watan in the Thoughts of Syed Shaikh bin Ahmad al-Hady," *Studia Islamika: Indonesia Journal for Islamic Studies* 12, no. 2 (2005): 247–297.

Alatas proposes the general theory of what he calls *circumlocutory imperialism*. Following Syed Hussein Alatas, he defines imperialism as "the subjugation of one people by another for the advantage of the dominating one." In the strict sense, imperialism is used in the context of the growth of capitalism and the emerging world system. We are more concerned here with intellectual imperialism as manifested in the form of epistemological domination of the subjugated. The subjugated, as mentioned earlier, experienced the "gap" between what is termed as "tradition" and "progress," and along with it general sentiments of deprivation relative to social, economic and political structures inherent. The Malays saw the incompatibility and the contradictory dynamics between the *kerajaan* and the colonial governments. Accordingly, the subjugated not only questioned their traditional epistemological framework, but also sought alternatives, including European thought. Alatas describes the situation of the political and economic structure of imperialism as generating "a parallel structure in the way of thinking of the subjugated people."[147] At the same time, the founders of *al-Imam*, being aware of the spiritual and metaphysical nature in the foundation of the *kerajaan*, awaited the secularization of the Malay worldview—in the form of a liberal and modern polity to substitute the *kerajaan*. Those men were aware that they were writing a new epistemology for the Malays.

It has to be noted that the adoption of Western epistemology for the Malays did not come directly from Europe. It came through Egypt. It was in Cairo that the alien values were veiled with an Islamic mantle, in what Michael Laffan calls "Cairene discourse," inducing a fundamental shift in the Islamic worldview.[148] The "Cairene discourse" refers to a reconciliation between modern Western values with Islam. The urge was brought about by the perceived political, economic and technological superiority of Western European power, first witnessed during the Napoleonic conquest of Egypt. Dissatisfaction with traditional Islamic thought and values was further solidified by the collapse of the Mamluk dynasty in Egypt at the hands of the French armies. Ironically, in the efforts to impede secularization, the Islam of Muhammad Abduh, Jamal al-Din al-Afghani and Rashid Rida was itself the product of colonial encounters.

It is significant here to note that in attempting to reconcile Western and Islamic thought, both 'Abduh and Afghani especially, pushed Islam into the colonial discourse. Alatas put it as Islam entering the colonial sphere and religion remoulded in the image of the progressive and enlightened Europe. Aspects of Islam that did not fit the model were discarded while those which were suitable were accepted. What was applied by the writer founders of *al-Imam* was a secularization of Islamic thought. The Islamic overtones, such as the sustained

147 Ismail Alatas, "Circumlocutory Imperialism."

148 Michael Laffan, *Islamic Nationhood and Colonial Indonesia* (London: Routledge, Curzon, 2003), 149.

usage of Islamic key-terminologies, possessed very different connotations after its semantic transformations to a more secular denotation. In this way, notes Alatas, the modification of religious doctrines was the direct result of the political and economic hegemony of Western European states. The Cairene discourse morphed the philosophies of nineteenth-century Europe into Muslim history and doctrines.

Al-Hady was beneficiary of the Cairo-educated Muslim reformists. The ideology from the West via Cairo arrived to the peninsula, introducing an alien worldview with its accompanying concepts to the Malay population. *Al-Imam*'s project was epistemological as much as journalistic. It required the restructuring of the epistemological framework. In addition, the language, saturated as it was with the traditional worldview, had to be reformed and was undertaken in a subtle and delicate way to guarantee its positive reception. The ideology had to give an Islamic "face" and to "sugarcoat" Qur'anic verses to win acceptance. Fazlur Rahman refers to the approach as the "janus-faced attitude."[149]

According to Alatas, the epistemological foundations of the new polity was very much derived from the West. The Cairene discourse had subversively conditioned the Malay mind into accepting an alien epistemology, contrary to the pre-existent worldview. In this respect, what is called the second front of imperialism occurred from within. As such, a power relationship between Europe and Malaya, facilitated by Egypt, was projected. In arguing that the theory of circumlocutory imperialism serves as a template for understanding the thoughts of al-Hady, Alatas traces the origin of *watan*, and its politicization in the light of colonial encounters in the Middle East. *Watan* is argued as the direct result of modernization and the diffusion of European thought into the Muslim world.

Al-Hady's idea of history and civilization through *al-Imam* was much borrowed from Europe. *Al-Imam* might well be described as a radical departure in the context of the quiet Malayan Islamic scene. Its appearance was the first consistent opposition to dogmatic and orthodox views. From that time, the group behind the periodical was given the pejorative stamp of *Kaum Muda* (New Group or Young Faction) with all its innovationist, deviationist, unorthodox, even heretical implications. Al-Hady was known to be the *Ketua* or *Khalifa Kaum Muda* (The Leader of the *Kaum Muda*).[150] Roff describes *Al-Imam's* first concern, and notes that it was religious, rather than social or political change.[151] Roff notes that the distinction (between religion and the non-religious) would have been in some measure foreign to the editors and

149 Ismail Alatas, "Circumlocutory Imperialism."

150 Tan, "Syed Shaykh: His Life and Times."

151 If "religion" is used in the social scientific post-Enlightenment sense, as Roff has understood it, then that description may not be entirely correct.

writers of the journal, who, following al-Afghani, 'Abduh and Rida, shared the Islamic concept of the undifferentiated *ummat* or community in which spiritual, social and political well-being and ends are subsumed under the one head—the good and profitable life lived according to Divine Law.[152] However, it was Japan, with her symbol of the Rising Sun, which gave impetus to the first issue of its editorial: Those who know the affairs of the world realise that the Europeans could not have extended their rule from West to East without the weapon of knowledge. And the Japanese, fewer than 50 million people, could never have defeated her enemies who were hundreds of millions strong if they were not in possession of the same knowledge.[153]

Al-Hady and the writers of *Al-Imam* noticed the gulf in "progress" between the British and Malay subjects. The perceived British and Western institutions as far more superior, and therefore have come to internalize and accept some of the ideas and values from the colonizers as "true," even admirable. It was suggested that a level of hegemony would have existed that would make some of the opinions and commentaries in *Al-Imam* congruent with the ideas of the ruling class—the colonial government, and Western civilization.[154] Their acceptance of "Other ideas" manifests the Foucaldian notion of the production of power contrary to the ideas of reform and liberation, what Brookfield describes as power producing the "effects at the level of desire."[155]

The concern of the threat of alien races and Malay backwardness, and the larger context of the plight of the *umat* brought *al-Imam* to the concept of *tamaddun* or "civilization." In acknowledging "civilization" as a criterion for progress, *al-Imam* agreed that Japan had a claim to be "civilized," especially considering its spectacular military victory of 1905 over a European country, Russia.[156]

True to the spirit of self-criticism, which Roff observes as "an orgy of self-vilification and self-condemnation," *al-Imam* points to the backwardness of the Malays, their domination by alien races, their laziness, their complacency, their bickering among themselves, and their inability to cooperate for the common good. Roff's approach was significantly different from Milner, in that although the former acknowledges *al-Imam's* religious orientation, he was at that time, assessing the journal primarily in the context of the origins of Malay nationalism. Milner, on the other hand, focuses on the text of Malays themselves, analyzing the discursive transition of the phases of Malay awareness of himself and society.

152 Roff, *Origins of Malay Nationalism*, 57.
153 *Al-Imam* 1, no. 1 (23 July 1906): 3–4.
154 M. Fairoz, "Orientalism and Integrative History."
155 Brookfield, *Power of Critical Theory*, 138.
156 Milner, *Invention of Politics in Colonial Malaya*, 168.

Milner sees the dynamic view of Malay society as manifested by the likes of Abdullah Munshi and the writers of *Utusan Melayu* and *al-Imam*. In associating the *bangsa* with *tamaddun*, *al-Imam* described it as the "movement" or "course" (*perjalanan*) of people in the past, not unlike Guizot's notion of movement in describing the Reformation. According to Milner, the word "movement" certainly gives a clear impression of the dynamic view of the past encountered in *al-Imam*. The dynamic historical perspective into which *al-Imam* draws its readers conveys above all the idea of dramatic and beneficial transition. It speaks of *moden* and *tamaddun*, of Japanese success and of parliaments. It draws attention to the invention of electricity and the telegraph and reminds its readers that in 1906 events taking place 7,000 or 8,000 miles away might be known within a day.[157]

It is evident that al-Hady and the editors of *al-Imam* were the earliest journalists in the Malay world advocating for change through journalism. To them, the process of journalizing is synonymous to chronicling the life and times of the day, of the modern. Journalism becomes the purveyor of change and innovation. Here again we see the influence of the reformers, in particular that of Muhammad 'Abduh. It is in the nineteenth century that "the evolutionary concept of historical development" was beginning to influence Muslim thinkers in West Asia. European contribution to this change was significant. For example, in the later nineteenth century, Muhammad 'Abduh not only read, but actually lectured on Guizot's *History of Civilization in Europe* which had been translated into Arabic in 1877. From Guizot, he appears to have gained a strong sense of historical movement, of people "pressing forward… to change… their condition."

Al-Hady's first appeal was made in an article in July of 1907 titled "Menuntut Ketinggian akan Anak2 Negeri."[158] Typical of al-Hady's genre, his writing was particularly notable for its forceful expression. He began by refuting the argument that people in the East were weaker or inferior to those in the West or that it was God's will that they should suffer. For such was the deception which the traditional leaders and the *ulama* of the community had tried to perpetuate in order to continue "squeezing the blood of the poor." He pointed to the Chinese in Malaya as an example of a people who had, by dint of hard labour and thrift, accumulated considerable wealth which they used to build schools to educate their children in order that they might compete with other peoples in modern life. He asked whether it was right that Muslims should be less hard-working, less intelligent, less learned, and less loving to each other, while their religion tells them to excel in all of these. Islam is not, says al-Hady,

157 Milner, *Invention of Politics in Colonial Malaya*, 173.

158 Milner translates it as "The Pursuit of Greatness of Our People," while Tan's translation is "Demand for the Improvement of the Sons of the Soil." See Milner, *Invention of Politics in Colonial Malaya*, 159; and Tan, "Syed Shaykh: His Life and Times."

as its detractors allege, hostile to knowledge and progress such as is exemplified by the West.[159]

Following upon its diagnosis, *al-Imam* goes to practice, so far as it can, what it preaches—though Roff argues that there is in its columns more exhortation than prescription. The Malays, and more especially the rulers and traditional leaders (*raja2 dan orang2 besar*) are urged to form associations to foster education, economic development, and self-awareness. Milner, in analyzing the journal's perceptions of the Malay sultanates, describes the attitudes of Shaikh Tahir and al-Hady towards the *kerajaan* of the royal courts appear to some extent surprising. He notes that historical scholarship on the period "has not prepared us for the severity of their critique."[160] Roff, for example, makes a subtle remark with regard to *al-Imam's* position, in the traditional practice of Islam in Malaya, adulterated by impurities of custom and belief derived from *adat* (referring to the royal courts) and from other religions, and inimical to progress, must be cleansed of these elements, and the *ulama* who transmit the imperfections brought to a sense of their errors and obligations.[161] In effect, *al-Imam* has stressed the central role of the sultans in Malay Islamic experience; apart from the known concentration of the journal's contribution to the development of Malay modernism and nationalism itself. With reference to earlier studies, especially by historians of Malay society, Milner notes that the journal's articles have been read in what was described as a retrospective rather than a prospective context.[162]

Al-Imam covered the *kerajaan* in places like Trengganu and Patani, describing the Malay rulers as "despotic," and "unorthodox." Faced with such negligence and injustice, *al-Imam* urges the rajas to follow the leaders of Japan who, as the journal explains, devote themselves to expanding education in their country.[163]

Concluding Remarks

In his role as a journalist, al-Hady's greatest success was in using his milieu, and his ideology through the periodicals he founded and led. He created a public sphere, and an audience during the formative years of Malay society under British rule. Through journalism, he challenged the *ancien régime* of the *kerajaan* and the *ulama*. His audience were the Malays.

He enabled new ideas and new values to be introduced against the orthodoxy of the *ulama* and Malay society. By doing so, he gave the Malay Muslim community a sense of identity, unity and new directions to overcome the

159 Tan, "Syed Shaykh: His Life and Times."
160 Milner, *Invention of Politics in Colonial Malaya*, 139.
161 Roff, *Origins of Malay Nationalism*, 58.
162 Milner, *Invention of Politics in Colonial Malaya*, 139.
163 Milner, *Invention of Politics in Colonial Malaya*, 139.

problems of belief and domination by the colonialists and Western civilization. However, he falls short of creating a mass intellectual movement through journalism, and his other ventures. Even if that were to happen, it could be argued that it would only perpetuate colonial capitalism in that the ideological bearing of al-Hady merely reinforces the structures of European civilization upon the Malay Muslims.

Bibliography

"Hal yang telah terjadi di negeri Iran." *Al-Imam,* January 16, 1907, 119–221.

"Huraian Melayu." *Al-Imam,* August 1908, 103–105.

"Islam dan Jepun." *Al-Imam,* July 23, 1906, 27–31.

"Islam dan Jepun (II)." *Al-Imam,* August 21, 1906, 56–63.

"Kembali cahaya ke pihak Timur." *Al-Imam,* December 18, 1906, 190–191.

"Penindasan Belanda di Hindia Timur." *Al-Imam,* September 1907, 92–95.

"Perkhabaran: Jepun dan Amerika." *Al-Imam,* February 1907, 253–259.

"Turki dan Jepun." *Al-Imam,* July 23, 1906, 30–31.

'Abduh, Muhammad. *The Theology of Unity.* Translated by Ishaq Musa'ad and Kenneth Cragg. Kuala Lumpur: Islamic Book Trust, 2004.

Abu Bakar Hamzah. *Al-Imam: Its Role and Functions.* Kuala Lumpur: Pustaka Antara, 1991.

Adam, Charles C. *Islam and Modernism in Egypt: A Study of the Modern Reform Movement Inaugurated* by Muhammad 'Abduh. New York: Russell & Russell, 1968.

Ahmad Murad Merican. "Pemikiran pergerakan Reformasi Eropah melalui kewartawanan Syed Shaykh al-Hady." *Melayu: Jurnal Antarabangsa Dunia Melayu* 4, no. 2 (2005): 96–108.

Al-Hady, Syed Alwi. "The Life of My Father." In *The Real Cry of Syed Shaykh al-Hady*, edited by Alijah Gordon, 69–83. Kuala Lumpur: Malaysian Sociological Research Institute, 1999.

Al-Hady, Syed Sheikh. *Ugama, Islam dan Akal.* Kota Bharu: Perchetakan Pustaka Dian, Not dated.

Alatas, Ismail F. "Circumlocutory Imperialism: Watan in the Thoughts of Syed Shaikh bin Ahmad al-Hady." *Studia Islamika: Indonesia Journal for Islamic Studies* 12, no. 2 (2005): 247–297.

Alatas, Syed Farid. "Ideology and Utopia in the Thought of Syed Shaykh Al-Hady." Unpublished paper, 2003.

Alatas, Syed Farid. *Alternative Discourses in Asian Social Science: Responses to Eurocentrism.* New Delhi: Sage, 2006.

Aljunied, Syed Muhd Khairudin. "British Discourses and Malay Identity in Colonial Singapore." *Indonesia and the Malay World* 37, no. 107 (2009): 1–21.

Azman Md Zain and Kamaruddin Ahmad. "Fenomena Dunia Islam Abad ke-19M: Satu Pandangan daripada Sayyid Jamal Al-Din Al-Afghani." *Jurnal Yadim* 2 (2001): 81–98.

Bayoumi, Alaa. "Occidentalism in late nineteenth century Egypt." M.A. diss., Duquesne University, 2005.
Brookfield, D. Stephen. *The Power of Critical Theory: Liberating Adult Learning and Teaching*. San Francisco: Jossey-Bass, 2005.
Chisick, H. "The Pamphlet Literature of the French Revolution: An Overview." *History of European Ideas* 17, no. 2/3 (1993): 149–166.
Fadhlullah Jamil. "Syed Syeikh al-Hadi: Pemikiran terhadap Islam dan Perubahan." *Dewan Sastera* 28, no. 6 (1998): 21–25.
Gordon, Alijah, ed. *The Real Cry of Syed Shaykh al-Hady*. Kuala Lumpur: Malaysian Sociological Research Institute, 1999.
Ibrahim Abu Bakar. *Islamic Modernism in Malaya: The Life and Thought of Sayid Syekh al-Hadi 1867–1934*. Kuala Lumpur: University of Malaya Press, 1994.
Khoo, Kay Kim. *Malay Society: Transformation and Democratisation*. Petaling Jaya: Pelanduk Publications, 1991.
Laffan, Michael. *Islamic Nationhood and Colonial Indonesia*. London: Routledge, Curzon, 2003.
M. Fairoz Ahmad. "Orientalism and Integrative History: A Study of An Early 20th Century Islamic Periodical in Singapore." Master's thesis, National University of Singapore, 2010. http://scholarbank.nus.edu.sg/handle/10635/18808.
Makdisi, Ussama. *The Culture of Sectarianism: Community, History, and Violence in Nineteenth-Century Ottoman Lebanon*. Berkeley and Los Angeles: University of California Press, 2000.
Marina Merican. "Syed Shaikh Al-Hadi dan Pendapat-pendapat-nya Mengenai Kemajuan Kaum Perempuan" (Syed Shaykh al-Hady and His Views on the Advancement of Women). Unpublished B.A. Hons. diss., University of Malaya, 1961.
Milner, Anthony. *The Invention of Politics in Colonial Malaya*. Cambridge: Cambridge University Press, 2002.
Nik Ahmad Nik Hassan. "The Malay Press." *Journal Malayan Branch Asiatic Society* 36, part 1 (1963): 37–78.
Passin, Herbert. "Writer and Journalist in the Transitional Society." In *Communications and Political Development,* edited by Lucian W. Pye, 82–123. Princeton: Princeton University Press, 1963.
Roff, William R. *Bibliography of Malay and Arabic Periodicals Published in the Straits Settlements and Peninsular Malay States 1876–1941*. London: Oxford University Press, 1972.
Roff, William R. *The Origins of Malay Nationalism*. Kuala Lumpur: Penerbit Universiti Malaya, 1974.

Roff, William R. "South-East Asian Islam in the Nineteenth Century," in *The Cambridge History of Islam.* Cambridge: Cambridge University Press, 1978.

Said, Edward W. *Orientalism.* New York: Vintage, 1979.

Shaharuddin Maaruf. *Malay Ideas on Development: From Feudal Lord to Capitalist.* Singapore: Times Books International, 1988.

Soedjatmoko et al., eds. *An Introduction to Indonesia Historiography.* New York: Cornell University Press, 1965.

Tan, Linda. "Syed Shaykh: His Life and Times." In *The Real Cry of Syed Shaykh al-Hady,* edited by Alijah Gordon, 109–162. Kuala Lumpur: Malaysian Sociological Research Institute, 1999.

Zainal Abidin Ahmad. "Malay Journalism in Malaya." *Journal of the Malayan Branch Royal Asiatic Society* 19, no. 2 (1941): 244–50.

Zaki, Mohamed Aboulkhir. "Modern Muslim Thought in Egypt and Its Impact on Islam in Malaya." PhD diss., University of London, 1965.

Chapter 5

Inventing Adversaries: Orientalism and the Arabs in Colonial Southeast Asia

Farish A. Noor

Professor at the Department of History, Faculty of the Arts and Social Sciences FASS, University Malaya

> The existence of the disabled native is required for the next lie and the next and the next.[164]
>
> Homi K. Bhabha,
> *Articulating the Archaic: Cultural Difference and Colonial Nonsense*

> The (Western) traveller begins his journey with the strength of an empire sustaining him—albeit from a distance—militarily, economically, intellectually; he feels compelled to note down his observations in the awareness of a particular audience: his fellow country-men.[165]
>
> Rana Kabbani,
> *Imperial Fictions*

The nineteenth century was a turning point in the history of the region now commonly known as "Southeast Asia." As rivalry in Europe intensified, the Western powers expanded their sphere of control across the region, colonising many parts of it and, in due course, discursively invented a place rendered known to fit with European sensibilities. Through modern techniques of cartography, the region's borders were demarcated and policed to serve the ends of racialised colonial capitalism (Farish 2016, 2018, 2020). Most major European powers scrambled for territories in the region and would soon be joined by the United States of America (Farish 2018).

164 Homi K. Bhabha, "Articulating the Archaic: Cultural Difference and Colonial Nonsense," in *The Location of Culture* (London: Routledge, 1994), 183.

165 Rana Kabbani, *Imperial Fictions: Europe's Myths of the Orient* (London: Pandora, 1986), xi.

Western expansion paralleled the growth of a new form of knowledge termed as "orientalism." British, American, French, Dutch, Spanish and Portuguese authors—many of whom were themselves directly involved in the process of empire-building and colonial data-gathering—would write about the region for their respective audiences back home.

This chapter brings into sharp relief the writings of British colonial authors, namely Stamford Raffles and John Crawfurd who were employees of the militarised British East India Company. Following the lead of Alatas (1977), I focus on the manner to which these colonial authors wrote about the native communities of Southeast Asia and other Asian communities in nineteenth century Southeast Asia. In so doing, these colonial writers invented and reproduced negative stereotypes that persist till this day. My attention will be focused on how Raffles, Crawfurd, and other Anglophone writers after them depicted and represented the Arab community in Southeast Asia. We can see a deliberate and systematic attempt to represent the Arabs of Southeast Asia as an *adversarial Other* against the aims and objectives of Western colonial capitalism. Algadri (1994) has expertly written about Dutch attitudes towards the Arabs in the Dutch East Indies. This essay builds upon his insights through an examination of British colonial authors and their host of prejudices and biases, some of which are stated openly, some cunningly understated. My argument will be that in the negative representation of Arabs by the likes of Raffles and Crawfurd, we can see the divisive logic of racialised colonial capitalism at work. The intention was to render alien a community that had closer relations with native Southeast Asians. But this demonisation could only be fully made more cogent through the discursive slight-of-hand that lumped all the various Arab communities together as a singular homogenous mass.

Perhaps it need not be mentioned here that "Arabs" appear repeatedly in the writings of Raffles and Crawfurd. But who were these Arabs and where did they come from? To be sure, the term "Arab" was used loosely in a somewhat generic and reductive manner. The Arab in the works of Raffles, Crawfurd, and subsequent authors who perpetuated this stereotypical image was distinguished mainly by his religious identity and language, and yet, none of these authors specified which part of the Arab world they came from. They were also seemingly oblivious to the fact that most of the Arabs who were present in maritime Southeast Asia then hailed from lands that were under either direct or indirect Ottoman rule. Most British colonial authors remained curiously silent about the existence and influence of the Ottoman Empire or the Turks as a different ethnic-religious community altogether. The same authors were also relatively silent about the presence of Persians in Southeast Asia during the period.

Indeed, British colonial authors failed to account for the origins of the different Arab communities in that part of the world. This gave the mistaken impression that Arabs were somehow homogenous, and that the Arab community was a distinctly singular one. Yet, it should be noted that Raffles and Crawfurd were writing at a time when many parts of the Arab lands were under Ottoman rule, in some instances as provinces, and in other moments, as vassals. By the end of the eighteenth century, the Ottoman Empire stretched all the way to the Balkans and into the Arabian Peninsula and North coast of Africa (Deringil 2011). Raffles' *History of Java* (1817) was published soon after the Serbian Revolution against the Ottomans (1804–1815), and the Arab uprising in the Arabian Peninsula that began in 1811 and ended with the defeat of the Emirate of Diriyah in 1818. By the time that Raffles and Crawfurd were writing their works the Arabs across the Ottoman Empire were already rising up against Ottoman rule and formed political communities of their own. None of these complex developments were touched upon by these authors. The readers of their works would not have been able to appreciate the extent to which Arab society then (as it is now) was both complex and internally differentiated along cultural, linguistic and historical lines. As such, it is difficult for us today to know if the Arabs that featured in their writings were from the Arabian Peninsula, Yemen, Egypt, or the North African coast.

Be that as it may, the two works that were, at their time of writing, considered among the most authoritative works on Southeast Asia by British colonial writers then were Stamford Raffles' *The History of Java* (1817) and John Crawfurd's *A History of the Indian Archipelago* (1820). Both of these works were written during Britain's brief occupation of Java (1811–1816), as a result of the Anglo-Dutch rivalry in the midst of the Napoleonic Wars in Europe (Carey 1992; Hannigan 2012; Farish and Carey 2021). In them is a storehouse of detailed information collected for the sake of colony-making. More than that, they reveal loaded prejudices and stereotypes of various non-Western communities that were active and present in Southeast Asia at the time.

Stamford Raffles and the Fear of the Arab as Competitor-Adversary

> Since the reduction of the Dutch influence in the East, several of the ports formerly dependent upon them have almost become Arab colonies.[166]
>
> Thomas Stamford Raffles,
> *The History of Java (1817)*

Thomas Stamford Bingley Raffles' (1781–1826) tenure as Lieutenant-Governor of Java (1811–1816) has come under much scrutiny by critical

166 Thomas Stamford Raffles, *The History of Java*, 2 vols., (London: Black, Parbury and Allen, publishers for the Honorable East India Company, Leadenhall Street; and John Murray, Albemarle Street, 1817), 228–229.

historians such as Wurtzburg (1949), Alatas (1977) and Carey (1992). My concern here is the massive two-volume work that he produced at the time, namely *The History of Java*, which was finally published in 1817. John Bastin (1965) in his introduction to *The History of Java* noted that "Raffles lacked William Marsden's linguistic mastery and contextual understanding of Javanese sources."[167] Though Raffles' *History of Java* was criticised by many others including John Crawfurd for numerous errors in dating and other facets of Javanese life, what is of interest to us here is how he attempted to provide a broad ethno-racial survey of the different communities in Java and its neighbouring islands. The portrait of the Arab community that he painted for the benefit of his fellow Englishmen back home is perhaps most problematic of all.

Voluminous and complex, *The History of Java* enumerates several objectives and agendas for its readers. Raffles did not hide his contempt for the Dutch, writing in the most candid way in his introduction: "I have often been obliged to condemn the principles and conduct of the Dutch colonists."[168] Notwithstanding his personal reservations about the Dutch and their East Indies Company, Raffles did state that Western (read: Dutch) intervention in Javanese affairs was a necessary evil, for the Dutch ruled Java with the assistance of local Javanese elites and kept their traditional local institutions intact. He noted that

> [...] arguments in favour of this system may perhaps be drawn from the respect due to the native usages and institutions, and from a supposed want of power, on the part of the (Dutch East Indies) Company, to assume any direct control over the native population. But whatever influence these ideas may have had on the conduct of the Company, it may be affirmed that an European government, aiming only to see right and justice administered to every class of the population, might and ought to have maintained all the native usages and institutions, not inconsistent with those principles; and that the power, for want of which it withheld its interference, would have been supplied and confirmed by the act of exercising the power which it possessed, and by the resources it might have been the means of drawing from the country.[169]

In his view, the Dutch system could only deliver mediocre results because it was overly committed to working with the local elites of Java. There is, according to Raffles, "the propensity inherent in every native authority to abuse its influence, and to render it oppressive to the population at large."[170] Read in the light of recent developments in global geopolitics, Raffles' justification for the British invasion of Java was like a propagandic tool for a "mission

167 John Bastin, in the 1965 edition of *The History of Java* by Raffles, iii.
168 Raffles, *History of Java*, vol. 1, xi.
169 Raffles, *History of Java*, vol. 1, xl–xli.
170 Raffles, *History of Java*, vol. 1, xli.

of liberation." He wrote that the invasion was an impetus of change and emancipation:

> The (Javanese) peasant was subject to gross oppression and undefined exaction: our object was to remove his oppressor, and to limit demand to a fixed and reasonable rate of contribution. He was liable to restraints on the freedom of inland trade, and to personal services and forced contingents: our object was to commute them all for a fixed and well-known contribution. The exertions of his industry were reluctant and languid, because he had little or no interest in its fruits: our object was to encourage that industry.[171]

The History of Java remains a somewhat complex work that foregrounds two distinct and identifiable narratives. On the one hand, it was a systematic critique of Dutch colonial management and praxis, where the "adversarial Other" was the Dutch, who were then the political enemies of Britain and the British East India Company's economic interests, thanks to the geopolitics of the Napoleonic Wars (Farish 2014). On the other hand, the work can also be read as a systematic and deliberate effort to build and sustain what Alatas (1977) has called the *Myth of the Lazy Native*. Raffles summarily clumps together the Javanese as a distinct racial type, and who are "an agricultural race, attached to the soil, of quiet habits and contented dispositions, almost entirely unacquainted with navigation and foreign trade, and little inclined to engage in either."[172]

Our concern here is the treatment meted out by Raffles to another non-Western community that was then present in Java and the rest of the archipelago in significant numbers: the Arabs. Raffles created not only a fixed and arrested stereotype of the "docile" and "degenerate" Javanese, but also the stereotype of the Arab as "outsiders." His stereotype of the Arab as adversary-competitor to Western colonial-capitalist interest would be reproduced in other writings by other Western colonial authors.

We need to look carefully at how Raffles saw and presented the Arabs in his work in order to understand and appreciate his aim of painting an imagined divisive landscape upon which British rule in Java would be rationalised and justified. Raffles projected himself as a sort of coloniser-curator who sought to "rescue" Javanese history (Farish 2014). For him Javanese history had begun its process of decline with the coming of the Arabs. Raffles makes this clear at the beginning of his work, when he wrote about how "the Mahometan institutions had considerably obliterated their (Javanese) ancient character, and had not only obstructed their improvement, but had accelerated their decline. Traditional (Javanese) history concurs with existing monuments, in proving them to have formerly made considerable advances in those arts, to which their

171 Raffles, *History of Java*, vol. 1, 154.

172 Raffles, *History of Java*, vol. 1, 57.

industry and ingenuity were particularly directed, and they still bear marks of that higher state of civilisation *which they once enjoyed.*"[173] (Emphasis mine.)

He begins his work by drawing a simplistic and divisive socio-cultural-religious map that divides the Javanese from the other non-Europeans in their midst, notably the Chinese and Arabs. The Chinese were presented by Raffles as a race of people who were "supple, venal and crafty," "without being very scrupulous" in their dealings with others.[174] Raffles stated that "the monopolising spirit of the Chinese was often very pernicious to the produce of the soil, as may be seen [...] at all the public markets farmed by them, and the degeneracy and poverty of the lower orders are proverbial."[175] In a similar vein, the Arabs were cast as a negative influence on the Javanese for they "inculcate the most intolerant bigotry."[176] Raffles insisted that through the propagation of their faith, language and culture, the Arabs had influenced the Javanese to the extent that the latter no longer appreciated their own past and former greatness.

While Raffles was undoubtedly suspicious of the Chinese in general, he noted that they were important actors in the local Javanese economy,[177] as were the Arabs.[178] There was, however, one very obvious and important difference between the Chinese and Arabs. The Arabs were all co-religionists with the Javanese who had, by then, also converted to Islam. It was this sense of religious brotherhood and fraternity that irked Raffles. Raffles' barbed accusations against the Arabs were often *ad hominem*, as he constantly undermined the character and credentials of the Arabs in Java. In his words: "Among the Arabs are many merchants, but the majority are priests. Their principle resort is *Gresik*, the spot where Mahometanism was first extensively planted on Java. They are seldom of genuine Arab birth, but mostly a mixed race, between the Arabs and the natives of the islands."[179]

Raffles' preoccupation with the racial "purity" of the Arabs in Southeast Asia was in keeping with the emergence and rise of pseudo-scientific theories

173 Raffles, *History of Java*, vol. 1, 57.

174 Raffles, *History of Java*, vol. 1, 224, 225.

175 Raffles, *History of Java*, vol. 1, 224–225. In his other writings Raffles clearly distinguished between the Chinese and the Japanese. In an account of the trade between Japan and Java, he noted that 'the Empire of Japan has, for a long period, adopted and carried with effect all the extensive maxims of Chinese policy, with a degree of rigour unknown in China itself. [...] the Japanese trade was reckoned by far the most advantageous which could be pursued in the East, and very much superior to either the Indian or Chinese trade.' Raffles noted that Dutch trade with Japan exceeded the value of 300,000 dollars, while 'their only profitable returns are Japan copper, and a small quantity of camphor.' Raffles, *History of Java*, vol. 1, xvii.

176 Raffles, *History of Java*, vol. 1, 228.

177 Raffles, *History of Java*, vol. 1, 74–75.

178 The extent of Chinese, Bugis and Arab commerce in and around Java at the time, according to Raffles, was extensive, and that the Arab merchants were most active in Surabaya, Semarang and Gresik. Arab merchant vessels were large and they navigated 'square-rigged vessels from fifty to five hundred tons burthen.' Raffles, *History of Java*, vol. 1, 202–204.

179 Raffles, *History of Java*, vol. 1, 75.

of racial difference and racial hierarchies from the eighteenth to the nineteenth century, and would also be reflected in the laws and regulations that he introduced in Java as its Lieutenant-Governor.[180] The notion that most of the Arabs in the archipelago then were not "pure" in the racial sense would later be taken up and repeated again and again by other Western writers such as John Crawfurd and Henry Keppel. It is interesting to note that the other Asian communities then present in the region—such as the Chinese and Indians—were not subjected to the same exacting standards.

The need to classify the Arabs into a neat typology may have stemmed from Raffles' awareness that they, as a merchant community, played a complex role in the political economy and overall success of colonial Java. Raffles was aware that the Arab merchants were among the pivotal trading communities that guaranteed the profits for the British East India Company that he served.[181] At the same time, he resented their cultural-religious proximity to the Javanese which gave them an advantage that he and his fellow Europeans did not possess.

Raffles penned his strongest criticism of the Arabs in general in the fifth chapter of the first volume of the *History of Java*. This came right after his lengthy critique of the Chinese:

> Some of these observations regarding the Chinese are, in high degree, applicable to the Arabs who frequent the Malayan countries, and under the specious mask of religion prey on the simple unsuspicious natives. The Chinese must, at all events, be admitted to be industrious; but by far the greater part of the Arabs are mere useless drones, and idle consumers of the produce of the ground: affecting to be descended from the Prophet and the most eminent of his followers, when in reality they are commonly nothing better than manumitted slaves, they worm themselves into the favour of the Malay chiefs, and often procure the highest offices under them. They hold like robbers the offices which they have obtained as sycophants, and cover all with the sanctimonious veil of hypocrisy.[182]

Wilfully oblivious to his own hypocrisy, which included his own record of theft of antiquities after the sacking of the royal city of Jogjakarta, Raffles' portrayal of the Arabs in Java was negative from start to end. Notwithstanding the negative labels he attached to the Arabs *in toto*—as drones, idlers, sycophants, manumitted slaves and robbers—there is evident tension in the stereotype he created. While presenting them as a race apart, crafty and drone-like to the core, he was also forced to admit that the Arabs occupied a position of leverage

---

180 Among the many regulations Raffles would introduce was the extensive and wordy 1814 *Regulations for the Better Governance of Java*. The *Regulations* of 1814 defined who was a foreigner to the land and people of Java: Article 149 stated the term 'foreigner' applied only to Europeans, Chinese, Arabs and the 'Mussulmen from the various parts of India,' and not to other ethnic groups from across the archipelago – such as Malays, Bugis, Madurese, etc.

181 Raffles, *History of Java*, vol. 1, 204.

182 Raffles, *History of Java*, vol. 1, 228.

above their European competitors: "It is seldom that the East is visited by Arabian merchants of large capital, but there are numerous adventurers who carry on a coasting trade from port to port, and by asserting the religious claim of Sheikh, generally obtain an exemption from all port duties in the Malayan states. They are also not infrequently concerned in piracies, and are the principal promoters of the slave trade."[183]

Within a couple of sentences, Raffles laid bare his true concern about the Arabs, namely that they enjoyed a privilege in local trade that the Europeans did not. Also, by virtue of being co-religionists with the Javanese and other Southeast Asian Muslim nations, they were seen and treated as members of the same faith (and trading) community. It was this cultural-religious and economic proximity that vexed Raffles to the point that he warned that "if the Arabs, under religious pretexts, are entirely exempted from (local) duties, *they may baffle all competition, and engross the trade of all the Malayan countries to the exclusion of European traders altogether*."[184] (Emphasis mine.)

Here, then, lay the cause and logic behind the stereotype of the Arab-as-adversary. Raffles may have heaped upon the Arabs every negative label that he could lay his hands upon but his primary concern was geostrategic as well as economic. For if Britain were to keep Java for posterity, the East India Company must reign supreme and its economic interests should not be jeopardised by any other competitors, be it the Dutch, French, Spanish, or the Arabs. The one thing that the Arabs had in common with the people of Java as well as Sumatra, Borneo, Sulawesi and the Malay Peninsula was their religion, and as it turned out, faith was thicker than blood. Raffles' inability to weaken this bond of faith between the Arabs and the Javanese, Bugis, and Malays was the thing that animated his pen. It led him to the conclusion that Arab trade in the region must be brought under Company control, lest the ports of Southeast Asia end up becoming "Arab colonies." In his words:

> Let the Chinese and Arabs still trade to the eastward. Without them, the trade would be reduced to less than one-third of even what is at present. [...] But let their trade be regulated; and above all, let them not be left in the enjoyment of immunities and advantages, which are neither possessed by Europeans nor the indigenous inhabitants of the country. *Since the reduction of the Dutch influence in the East, several of the ports formerly dependent upon them have almost become Arab colonies.*[185] (Emphasis mine)

Although largely a product of an imperial and racist imagination, the negative stereotype of the Arab was an *instrumental fiction*. But being a fictional stereotype did not render it entirely useless, and instrumental fictions often

183 Raffles, *History of Java*, vol. 1, 228.
184 Raffles, *History of Java*, vol. 1, 228.
185 Raffles, *History of Java*, vol. 1, 228–229.

had instrumental uses. Unlike the negative stereotypes of the other communities of Southeast Asia that were reduced to essentialised racial types by other orientalists such as John Crawfurd who we will encounter later—the Arab was *not seen as something inferior to the European.* Rather, they were an adversary, competitor, and ultimately, threat. The threat posed by the Arab came in the form of the cultural, theological and psychosocial bonds with the other Muslims in the region. The Arab threat straddled boundaries: between the inside and the outside, between being local and foreigner.

In the years to come, this notion of the Arab as insider/outsider and competitor/adversary would be further developed in the writings of other Western colonial authors. We now turn to a contemporary of Raffles, John Crawfurd, who was likewise an East India Company-man, and who promoted and defended the pseudo-scientific theories of polygenesis and racial hierarchies in Southeast Asia.

Racialised Colonial-Capitalism and the need for Adversaries: John Crawfurd's Fear of the "Mixed Arab"

> Of all the nations of Asia who meet on this common theatre, the Arabs are the most ambitious, intriguing, and bigoted. [186]
>
> John Crawfurd,
> *A History of the Indian Archipelago (1820)*

In the year 1820, John Crawfurd (1783–1868) published his account of the islands, peoples and history of maritime Southeast Asia entitled *A History of the Indian Archipelago.*[187] Having published a somewhat disparaging review of Raffles' *History of Java* (1817), Crawfurd had gone out of his way to be as thorough and systematic as possible. He produced a three-volume work furnished with tables, categories, and typologies that divided and subdivided the region of Southeast Asia. He presented a picture of a region that was complex and yet thoroughly classified and mapped out in his terms. Crawfurd projected his belief in the theory of polygenesis and racial difference. He divided Southeast Asia geographically, racially, politically, and socially. In the first volume, he distinguished four different island groups, each with its own society that existed at different levels of human civilisational development.[188] In the third

186 John Crawfurd, *A History of the Indian Archipelago, containing an Account of the Manners, Arts, Languages, Religions, Institutions and Commerce of its Inhabitants,* 3 vols., (Edinburgh: Archiband Constable and co., and London: Hurst, Robinson and co., 1820), vol. 1, 139.

187 Crawfurd, *History of the Indian Archipelago.*

188 In the introduction to the first volume Crawfurd mapped out the social-civilisational geography of the region he was writing about, and claimed that maritime Southeast Asia could be divided into four distinct groups of islands, ranked according to size: The first rank consisted of the larger islands of Borneo (Kalimantan), New Guinea and Sumatra; the second consisted of the islands of Java and (oddly enough) the Malayan Peninsula; the third rank consisted of the islands of Bali, Lombok, Sulawesi (Celebes), the

volume, he categorised five different types of native government—from the primitive to the absolute and tyrannical —as well as six different social classes.[189] This was a massive work that classified all of Southeast Asia and located everything in it within a system of rigid and totalising typologies.

While recognising the complexity and diversity of the region, Crawfurd maintained that *all* the communities in Southeast Asia were inferior when compared to the Europeans, for "no nation, indeed, inhabiting a warm climate has ever known how to reconcile freedom and civilisation."[190] Crawfurd's inclination to paint the communities of Southeast Asia in a decidedly negative light was clear from the beginning of his work. For him, maritime Southeast Asians were a "people in the lower stages of civilisation," "defective in personal cleanliness," "wanting in reason," and "to a wonderful degree credulous and superstitious."[191] In his view, most Southeast Asians then lived "in a state of turbulence and anarchy, where the empire of law is next to nothing, where death is familiar to the people," and "the great body are in such a state of degradation, that they neither value the lives of each other."[192]

Like Raffles, Crawfurd was well aware of the fact that the Southeast Asian archipelago was an integral part of the global trading network for centuries, long before the arrival of the British. To that end he sought to understand and analyse the role of Asian communities that had settled there, notably the Chinese, Indians, and Arabs. Of the Arabs, he noted that they were present in large numbers and that they shared a common bond of religious identity with most native communities of the region. Arabs had played a crucial role in international trade and "formed, in early times of Oriental commerce, the third link of commercial voyages by which the ordinary commodities of the Indian islands were transmitted to the farthest nations of the West."[193]

An interesting characterisation of the Asians in general and, more specifically the Arabs, can be seen in the writings of Raffles and Crawfurd. Raffles had entertained the notion that the Javanese were once a highly civilised nation

---

Moluccas and the islands of the Philippines; and the fourth rank consisted of all the other smaller islands of the region (pp. 3–7). Additionally Crawfurd divided the region into five distinct sea zones (p. 5), and introduced an explicit ethnic-cultural hierarchy that distinguished between the 'more civilised' and 'less civilised' natives of the archipelago. He maintained that the development of civilised communities across the region was not equal: The islands of Sumatra and Java, along with the Malayan Peninsula were, for him, the 'most civilised' parts of Southeast Asia (p. 8), while civilisation had only begun to develop in the second division of the archipelago, in places such as Celebes (Sulawesi) (pp. 8–9). The third division of the archipelago was seen as the least developed and civilised. Conversely the fourth division (which comprised of Sulu and other parts of Southern Philippines) was regarded as being 'more civilised than the third, but less civilised than the first and second' (p. 10).

189 Crawfurd, *History of the Indian Archipelago*, vol. 3, 2–28, 29–44.

190 Crawfurd, *History of the Indian Archipelago*, vol. 3, 2.

191 Crawfurd, *History of the Indian Archipelago*, vol. 1, 38–39, 47. Later Crawfurd would claim that generally maritime Southeast Asians were 'wholly ignorant of arithmetic as a science' (vol. 1, 253).

192 Crawfurd, *History of the Indian Archipelago*, vol. 1, 70.

193 Crawfurd, *History of the Indian Archipelago*, vol. 3, 199.

that declined, attributing this decline on the influence of the Arabs. This was linked to Raffles' own prejudices against Islam and Muslims in general. Crawfurd, on the other hand, was not inclined to reinvent his image as a colonial scholar-curator like Raffles, and was less concerned about the decline of Hinduism and Buddhism among the peoples of the archipelago. What mattered more to him was the commodities and products that could be traded, and how the East India Company that he served could dominate the local markets. He wanted the British to gain an advantage over their other European rivals, notably the Dutch, Portuguese and Spanish. The pragmatic and commercial-minded worldview of Crawfurd openly lamented the loss of the potential markets which the East India Company could have dominated.

To that end, the Chinese, Indians, and Arabs loomed large in Crawfurd's work, as he saw them as both potential allies as well as adversaries to the colonial-capitalist enterprise. Like Raffles, Crawfurd regarded the Chinese as industrious and useful, but a potential threat if allowed to grow in large numbers. But what worried Crawfurd even more was the role played by the Arabs who were both traders and co-religionists of the Muslim communities of Southeast Asia. Like Raffles, Crawfurd resented the fact that the Arabs were seen as members of the same faith community as the Javanese, Bugis and Malays.[194]

Crawfurd stated his concern about the Arabs early in his work. Though Crawfurd, like Raffles, clearly harboured contempt for Arabs in general, the *mixed* Arabs were those whom he was doubly suspicious of. In the first volume, he noted that "the Arab settlers are more considerable from their influence than their numbers," and that "Arab adventurers have settled in almost every country of the archipelago, and (by) intermarrying with the natives of the country, begot a mixed race, which is pretty numerous."[195] That many Arabs had married native Southeast Asians and "begot a mixed race" was something that irked Crawfurd, as he was himself a stickler for fixed identities that were not ambiguous or hybrid in any way. Crawfurd's belief in the importance of racial purity was oft-repeated, and at one point, he specifically identifies mixed Arabs as a subgroup of potential troublemakers in the region: "Of all the nations of Asia who meet on this common theatre, the Arabs are the most ambitious, intriguing, and bigoted. They have a strength of character, which places them far above the natives of the country. [...] They are, when not devoted to spiritual concerns, wholly occupied in mercantile affairs, and *the genuine Arabs are spirited, fair, and adventurous merchants. The mixed race is of a much less favourable character, and is considered a supple, intriguing, and dishonest class.*"[196] (Emphasis mine.)

194 Crawfurd did concede that in many ways the Arabs had brought about positive changes to Southeast Asian society, as when he noted that 'the Mahometan religion brought with it, as it did in India, a more manly and sober style of thinking' which he detected in the language and literature found in Muslim parts of the region. Re: Crawfurd, *History of the Indian Archipelago*, vol. 2, 27, 259–271, 288–289.

195 Crawfurd, *History of the Indian Archipelago*, vol. 1, 138–139.

196 Crawfurd, *History of the Indian Archipelago*, vol. 1, 139.

Crawfurd's tendency to dismiss those of mixed racial identity was the result of his own pseudo-scientific convictions and his belief in the theory of racial difference that was rooted in biology, and not culture or ethnicity. Yet even as he summarily relegated all mixed Arabs to an inferior rank in the chain of being, he admired the Arabs in general whose mode of interaction and commerce had endeared them to the local communities of Southeast Asia, and opened the way for the spread of Islam. Aside from adhering to theories of race, Crawfurd was an ardent believer of colonial-capitalism in view of his role as a functionary of the British East India Company. For him, commercial expansion was paramount and crucial for the company he worked with to out-manoeuvre European and Asian competitors. In the second volume of his work, he wrote at length about the success of the Arab merchants in the region, who had succeeded in obtaining two entwined objectives: To gain access to the local markets and polities of Southeast Asia, while also being able to integrate themselves into the fabric of native communities through their missionary work and intermarriage:

> The success of the Mahometan missionaries, contrasted with the failure of the Christians, it is not difficult to trace the true cause. The Arabs and the other Mahometan missionaries conciliated the other natives of the country, acquired their language, followed their manners, intermarried with them, and, melting into the mass of the people, did not, on the one hand, give rise to a privileged race, nor on the other, to a degraded cast (sic). Their superiority of intelligence and civilisation was employed only for the instruction and conversion of a people, the current of whose religious opinions was ready to be directed into any channel into which it was skilfully diverted. They were merchants as well as the Europeans, but never dreamt of having recourse to the iniquitous measure of plundering the people of the produce of their soil and industry. This was the cause which led to the success of the Mahometans, and it was naturally the very opposite course which led to the defeat of the Christians. The Europeans in the Indian archipelago have been just what the Turks have been in Europe, and the consequence of the policy pursued by both may fairly be quoted as parallel cases.[197]

The Arabs were, in the eyes of Crawfurd, successful precisely because they were willing and able to adapt themselves to the socio-political-economic realities of Southeast Asian society. They integrated with the local communities on a number of levels: religious, cultural, economic, political, and via intermarriage. Yet we see an apparent contradiction in Crawfurd's racialised logic of difference. While lauding the Arabs for being able to assimilate, he condemned them for begetting a mixed Arab-Asian race that confounded his neat typology of races and the racial hierarchy. The Arabs were thus vilified in the writings of Crawfurd because they were able to do what he and other Europeans could not.

197 Crawfurd, *History of the Indian Archipelago*, vol. 2, 275.

Because Crawfurd was convinced that European and Asian races stood apart as distinct biological groups, there was no way that he could have ever recommended the same course of action for his fellow Westerners. Yet this very inability to accept the idea of a singular human race—*unigenesis as opposed to polygenesis*—meant that all Europeans would remain in a disadvantageous state when compared with the Arabs who were their competitors. More crucially, Crawfurd's jaundiced image of the Arab as mixed racial hybrid and as economic-political adversary which was borne out of the heated logic of racialised colonial-capitalism was compelling. It would later be taken up and reproduced in the writings of successive British and American authors for the rest of the nineteenth century. At a time when racial hierarchies were deemed acceptable thanks to the rise of scientific racism in the West, the nineteenth century witnessed a significant development of pseudo-scientific theories of racial difference that divided humanity into categories of "higher" vs. "lower" races, "martial races" vs. "feminine races" (Farish and Carey 2021; Sinha 1997). The Arabs of Southeast Asia would find themselves slotted into such violent hierarchies in due course.

After Raffles and Crawfurd: The Recurring Image of the Arab as Adversarial Other

> The image of hatred and of the other, the foreigner is neither the romantic victim of our clannish indolence nor the intruder responsible for all the ills of the polis. [...] Strangely, the foreigner lives within us, he is the hidden face of our identity.[198]
>
> Julia Kristeva,
> *Strangers to Ourselves*

The legacy of Raffles and Crawfurd reverberated in the works of several European authors who came in their wake. The negative portrayal of Arabs can be found in scientific works, diaries, and recollections of military expeditions. In his reminiscence as the commander of the British Royal Navy warship HMS Dido, Henry Keppel wrote about the tribes in Borneo with whom the British waged a so-called "war on piracy" from the 1830s to 1846. In his opinion, these natives were under the influence and control of Arabs and half-Arabs who had settled in the kingdoms of Brunei, Sulu, and the coastal settlements of Mindanao and Sarawak. Citing the colonialist James Brooke, Keppel singled out the "half-Arabs" whom he considered to be the biggest threat for they were the leaders of these pirate bands: "The pirates on the coast of Borneo may be classed into those who make long voyages in large heavy-armed prahus, such as the Ilanuns, Balagnini, etc. and the lighter Dayak fleets, which make short but destructive excursions in swift prahus [...] A third, and probably the

198 Julia Kristeva, *Strangers to Ourselves* (New York: Colombia University Press, 1991), 1.

worst class, are usually half-bred Arab Seriffs, who, possessing themselves of the territory of some Malay state, form a nucleus for piracy, a rendezvous and market for all the roving fleets."[199]

Keppel and Brooke's obsession with "half-Arabs" echoes the views of Crawfurd, who had introduced the notion that half-breeds in general were an untrustworthy lot and that half-Arabs were more dangerous than their purer counterparts. A similar stance was taken by another British colonial author, Spenser St. John, in his writings on Sarawak where he argued that the people of Sulu were "lax and ignorant" in their religious beliefs and "half-bred Arabs" had "corrupted" the natives.[200]

Again and again, Arabs and mixed half-bred Arabs were seen and cast as the enemy within, who had settled in the region, married into local families and accumulated power for themselves with the intention of turning that power against Westerners. In the writings and opinions of men such as Keppel, Brooke and St. John, the Arab could only be seen as a lingering potential threat since they shared a common religious identity with the Malays, Suluks, Javanese, Bugis and other communities of the region. This negative image of the Arab did not simply materialise out of nowhere, but had its genesis in the colonial-capitalist enterprise that can be dated as early as the eighteenth century. Raffles and Crawfurd were among the first to present the Arabs of Southeast Asia *as a race apart*, and from there the othering of the Arab persisted till the end of the twentieth century. The effects of this is still felt today.

Conclusion

By way of concluding, I would like to highlight some of the salient points that can be made about the demonization of the image of the Arab in Southeast Asia found in colonial-era writings of the nineteenth century.

First, it should be noted that the blatantly racist overtones in the works we have looked at earlier were in keeping with the tone and tenor of nineteenth century scientific racism at the time. While Raffles and Crawfurd, as well as other writers such as Henry Keppel, Rodney Mundy, James Brooke, Albert S. Bickmore, and Spenser St. John, were explicit and unrestrained in their negative comments, slights and insults towards Arabs in general, this was not simply casual racism of a pedestrian variety. These men believed in the theory of racial polygenesis, which argued that the human race was not a single species but rather consisted of different races/species that resembled one another but which were nonetheless separate and distinct. This belief in the *separation* of different races also accounts for the disdain towards mixed/half-Arabs that

199 Brooke, in *The Expedition to Borneo of the HMS Dido for the Suppression of Piracy*, by Captain the Hon. Henry Keppel (London: Chapman and Hall, 1846), vol. 2, 144–145.

200 Sir Spenser Buckingham St. John, *Life in the Forests of the Far East* (London: Smith, Elder and Co. Cornhill. 1862), vol. 2, 183, 192.

we see in the writings of Crawfurd and some others. The very same pseudo-scientific theory of polygenesis was used as one of the justifications for slavery in the colonies and antebellum America then, for it was assumed that Africans were a separate species altogether, as were Asians and Arabs. The negative depiction of Arabs in the works of Raffles and Crawfurd should therefore be located in a broader historical-cultural context where these men validated the ideas of other like-minded Western colonial writers, who all shared the belief that racialized colonial-capitalism was the necessary and logical outcome of Western cultural-racial supremacy.

Second, it should be noted here that the negative image of the Arabs that we find in the works cited above was a complex one, that brought together and comingled considerations about economic necessity as well as strategic concerns about maintaining the primacy of Western colonial rule. Though the Arabs in Southeast Asia were often depicted in unflattering terms by the likes of Raffles and Crawfurd, neither of these men denied or underplayed the importance of Arab trade in the region, and the important role played by Arab merchants in maintaining trade links between maritime Southeast Asia and the Arab lands to the West. As functionaries of the militarised British East India Company, these orientalists presented the Arab as a double-edged sword so to speak. Arabs had played a visible and important role in the economic development of the region which in turn made Southeast Asia increasingly important and valuable to the Western colonial powers; but their success at commerce also made them a potential rival and threat to the expansion of Western colonial-capitalist power. In the writings of both Raffles and Crawfurd, this anxiety and tension were made visible. Both lauded the economic contribution of the Arab (and Chinese) merchants in the region which contributed to their company's earnings, but both were also keen to keep the very same Arab merchants under their control, for fear that Arab trade might eventually rival or supersede European trade in the region. The orientalist image of the Arab was littered with contradictions and paradoxes.

Third, accompanying the racist overtones was also a palatable sense of *envy* towards the Arabs. In the works of Raffles and Crawfurd, and others cited above, we come across passages that are laced with *jealousies*. Raffles and Crawfurd expressed their disdain over Arabs possessing an advantage which they, as Christian Europeans, would never get to enjoy. This was the fact that the Arabs belonged to the same faith community as the other Muslim communities of Southeast Asia and the common religious identity between them meant that the Arabs of Southeast Asia were not seen by the local communities as "foreign," as had the Europeans. That the Arabs could be accepted by the Javanese, Malays, and Bugis as fellow Muslim brothers was something that annoyed Raffles and Crawfurd. This may also account for why these Western authors were wont to dismiss and downplay the religious credentials of the Arabs at every given opportunity.

Citing "unfair practices" as the basis of their complaint, Raffles and Crawfurd would pour scorn upon all Arabs of Southeast Asia, and in due course, both men would be responsible for the demonization of the image of the Arab in the region. Notwithstanding the complaints of Raffles and Crawfurd against the "unfair advantage" enjoyed by the Arabs, the history of the East-West encounter in Southeast Asia was a case of unequal power differentials between the East and the West, with the latter having the most advantage due to military superiority. Raffles and Crawfurd may have bemoaned that the Arabs were seen as "brothers"and "fellow Muslims" and may have regarded this as being unfair to their Western interests. But Britain's own involvement in Southeast Asian affairs was hardly a peaceful or fair enterprise. From the invasion and occupation of Java (1811–1816) to the First, Second and Third Anglo-Burmese Wars (of 1824–1826, 1852–1853, 1885), to the numerous incursions and interventions across the Malay World, Britain's imperial venture was hardly fair or peaceful by any stretch of the imagination.

It is against the backdrop of racialized colonial-capitalism and the racial wars of the empire that we need to understand the development of the negative image of the Southeast Asian Arab as enemy-adversary-competitor. The negative image of the Arab was indeed an instrumental fiction that was put to serve the ends of divisive colonial politics and empire-building. This was not an instance of mundane, casual, and unreflective racism at work. The demonised image of the Arab as the adversarial Other was a discursive construct that was invented and instrumentalised in and by the workings of racialised colonial-capitalism. By reviewing its efficacy and utility today, we are reminded of how racism and colonialism were mutually supportive of one another during the era of European global dominance.

Bibliography

Syed Hussein Alatas. *The Myth of the Lazy Native: A Study of the Image of the Malays, Filipinos and Javanese from the 16th to the 20th Century and its Function in the Ideology of Colonial Capitalism.* London: Frank Cass, 1977.

Algadri, Hamid. *Dutch Policy against Islam and Indonesians of Arab Descent in Indonesia.* Jakarta: LP3ES, 1994.

Bhabha, Homi K. "Articulating the Archaic: Cultural Difference and Colonial Nonsense." In *The Location of Culture.* London: Routledge, 1994.

Carey, Peter B. R. *The British in Java, 1811–1816: A Javanese Account.* London: Oxford University Press, 1992.

Crawfurd, John. *A History of the Indian Archipelago, containing an Account of the Manners, Arts, Languages, Religions, Institutions and Commerce of its Inhabitants.* 3 vols. Edinburgh: Archiband Constable and co., and London: Hurst, Robinson and co., 1820.

Deringil, Selim. *The Well-Protected Domains: Ideology and the Legitimation of Power in the Ottoman Empire, 1876–1909.* London: I.B. Tauris, 2011.

Hannigan, Tim. *Raffles and the British Invasion of Java.* Singapore: Monsoon Books, 2012.

Kabbani, Rana. *Imperial Fictions: Europe's Myths of the Orient.* London: Pandora, 1986.

Keppel, Captain the Hon. Henry. *The Expedition to Borneo of the HMS Dido for the Suppression of Piracy.* London: Chapman and Hall, 1846.

Kristeva, Julia. *Strangers to Ourselves.* New York: Colombia University Press, 1991.

Farish A. Noor, and Peter Carey, eds. *Race and the Colonial Wars of 19th Century Southeast Asia.* Amsterdam: Amsterdam University Press, 2021.

Farish A. Noor. *Data-Collecting in 19th Century Colonial Southeast Asia: Framing the Other.* Amsterdam: Amsterdam University Press, 2020.

Farish A. Noor. *America's Encounters with Southeast Asia 1800–1900: Before the Pivot.* Amsterdam: Amsterdam University Press, 2018.

Farish A. Noor. *The Discursive Construction of Southeast Asia in the Discourse of 19th Century Colonial-Capitalism.* Amsterdam: Amsterdam University Press, 2016.

Raffles, Thomas Stamford. *The History of Java.* 2 vols. London: Black, Parbury and Allen, publishers for the Honorable East India Company, Leadenhall Street; and John Murray, Albemarle Street, 1817; Oxford and Kuala Lumpur: Oxford University Press, 1965.

Sinha, Mrinalini. “Colonial Masculinity: The ‘Manly Englishman’ and the ‘Effeminate Bengali.’” *Albion: A Quarterly Journal Concerned with British Studies* 29, no. 2 (Summer 1997): 367–379.

St. John, Sir Spenser Buckingham. *Life in the Forests of the Far East.* London: Smith, Elder and Co. Cornhill, 1862.

Wurtzburg, C. E. “Raffles and the Massacre at Palembang.” *The Journal of the Malayan Branch of the Royal Asiatic Society* 22, part 1 (1949).

Chapter 6

Nasir al-Din Tusi's Ethics and Concept of Social Class

Mohamad Faghfoory

Professor of Islamic Studies at the
George Washington University, USA

Traditional Islamic society was a hierarchical society where the population was divided into social groupings based on economic activities and occupational divisions. The Islamic social structure established in Iran was a continuation of the pre-Islamic model that prevailed in the Persian Empire prior to the advent of Islam with some changes and modifications. Islamic understanding of social groupings and the ways in which a new socio-hierarchical system was created evolved somewhat differently from the Sassanid model especially in terms of ethical standards, attitude towards economic functions, the relationship between social groupings, and the role of the state in establishing and maintaining the new pattern. What particularly changed after the advent of Islam was the nature and pattern of the relationship between social groupings in light of the injunctions of the Qur'an, the guidelines provided by the Prophet's tradition, and the writings of Muslim philosophers and political thinkers.

In this chapter, I shall examine the ways in which Islam and early Muslim thinkers understood social hierarchy and discuss briefly the views of the leading thinkers on this subject that influenced Khwajah Nasir al-Din Tusi's (1201–1274)perspective. I will focus on Tusi's comprehensive theory of social classes, which became a model that was adopted and implemented by several Islamic empires including the Ottoman and Safavid empires.

Before examining Tusi's views on social stratification and groupings, it is appropriate to discuss the opinions of leading Muslim scholars before him who wrote on the subject to demonstrate continuity and/or change, and show how the idea of social hierarchy was seen and debated in the Islamic world and how their discussion contributed to the development of Tusi's views and influenced his formulation of a systematic and complete theory of social classes.

The Concept of Class

There is a consensus among Muslim thinkers that class as perceived in pre-Islamic Persia or the Roman Empire did not exist in Islamic society.[201] The exploitation of one class by another as it became a standard practice under the European feudal system was not condoned in Islam.[202] The Qur'an sets piety and fear of God as the only criterion for superiority of a human being over another and clearly rejects any idea of superiority on the basis of wealth, power, or kinship.[203] By and large, this Qur'anic principle was acknowledged by the majority of Muslims and Islamic governments, and if not in practice at all times, was at least articulated in theory during most periods of Islamic history.

The social system pattern that appeared in the Islamic world as a result differed from the pre-Islamic Persian and Roman societies as well as from theories of class that developed after the Industrial Revolution and especially in nineteenth century Europe. Many European philosophers wrote extensively on the emerging social classes and changing patterns of relationship among them before the nineteenth century. But it was Karl Marx's theory of *class* that in fact dominated the latter part of nineteenth century discourse on this issue according to which "societies had been structured to promote the interests of the economically dominant class.... and that history of all hitherto existing societies is the history of class struggles."[204] As it is clear in this paradigm, different and often conflicting economic interests in modern societies would lead to an antagonistic relationship between economically dominant classes and those who are dependent on them. Therefore, according to this theory there is a constant tension and struggle between those who own the means of production and the working classes.[205] As will be demonstrated in the coming pages, the Islamic model of social "class" system and class relations were profoundly different. Since Islam placed much emphasis on the value of work and economic activity, it was a set of religious and ethical values and principles and not conflicting economic interests of different groups that defined the nature of "*class*" relationship. I must add here that in this article the term class (or *tabaqah* in Arabic) is used as identical with social and occupational groupings and very different from the meaning of the term in modern Western discourses.

201 On Tusi's classification of the types of societies see, *Aklaq-i Nasri*, 237–257.

202 Abdulhossein Zarrinkoob, *Karnameh-yi islam*, 5th ed. (Tehran: 1998), 135.

203 Qur'an, 49:13.

204 Lewis S. Feuer, "Marx and the Intellectuals," in *Encyclopedia Britannica*, accessed June 10, 2021.

205 "The political economy of social relations is important in understanding the causes of conflict. A basic assumption of Marxism is that a social and political structure is determined by the mode of production and those who control the means of production such as labor, land, and factory facilities. The economic structure determines forms of social consciousness as well as types of legal and political institutions." Ho-Won Jeong and Eleftherios Michael, "Theories of Conflict" in *Encyclopedia of Violence, Peace, & Conflict*, vol. 3, 2nd ed. (New York & Oxford: ELSEVIER, 2008).

Social Hierarchy

The oldest classification of population in Islamic societies is found in the *Nahj al-balaghah* where 'Ali ibn Abi Talib divided the population of the society into three categories based on the degree of their faith and knowledge of the truth. They included the divinely guided scholars (*'ulama' rabbani*), seekers of knowledge on the path of salvation *(muti'allim 'ala sabil al-najah),* and the common people (*hamaj al-ra'a*). The last group by definition is the unthinking majority.

Similarly, in their discussion on social hierarchy early Muslim philosophers used knowledge as the criterion to define the place of the individual in society. They often used two terms when they talked about social grouping, one being the selected few (*khawass*), i.e. the intellectual-religious-spiritual elite, and the other the ignorant majority (*'awam*). In this classification it was the mental and intellectual capacity of the individual along with his piety that determined his place in the society. Contempt for the majority is in fact hidden in the meaning of the term *'awam*. Gradually these terms acquired socio-economic and cultural connotations referring to the highly educated and the well to do and the uneducated and poorer segments of society respectively.[206] So wrote Muhammad ibn Jarir Tabari (224–310/839–923) in his commentary on the Qur'an (43:32) that "God had made people different in terms of appearance, character, and livelihood so that they would serve one another."[207] In view of another scholar who commented on the same verse, each person was born with certain qualities and talents suitable for a special function or craft. This, according to him, was the proof of monotheism because "...if every man wanted to be a builder or a tailor or scholar, the world would not survive."[208]

By the middle of the tenth century social stratification was accepted as an extension of the hierarchy that "pervaded the universe from the cosmos at large to human body and should therefore be exemplified at the level of human society as well." Hierarchy in fact guaranteed the order in society. "It was only in the tenth century that political thinkers began to describe hierarchy in their societies in terms of *tabaqat*," i.e. classes with reference to occupational divisions and economic standing and without reference to ethnic origin or affiliation. [209]

---

206 Patricia Crone, *God's Rule: Government and Islam* (New York: Columbia University Press, 2004), 335-336.

207 Muhamma ibn Jarir Tabari, *Tafsir*, xiii, 67, as quoted in Crone, *God's Rule*, 341.

208 Abu'l-Hasan Ali ibn Ibrahim al-Qummi, the Shi'a scholar argued in his *Tafsir*, vol. 2 (Beirut: 1991), 257, as quoted in Crone, *God's Rule*, 341. Another scholar observed that "God made everyone subservient (*sakhkhara*) to a particular craft by giving people different natures, so that everyone liked his own occupation, as was true even of weavers and cuppers (whose work was regarded as demeaning); if God had not done this, we all *would* have chosen the same occupation." Raghib Isfahani, as quoted in Crone, *God's Rule*, 342.

209 Crone, *God's Rule*, 334–336.

Abu Nasr al-Farabi (d. 339/950) addressed issues related to social structure and the necessity of hierarchy in every society. According to him human societies came to exist because man is a social being by nature (*al-insan madaniyun bi'l tab'*) and he cannot attain perfection by himself. When societies are formed each man is given a function in consideration with his natural disposition.[210] This necessitates the division of labor and leads to division of society in consideration with the economic function each person performs. Al-Farabi's classification was one based also on theoretical knowledge and ethical conduct. The most virtuous in his view were those who possessed speculative knowledge which were philosophers and scholars of religion. The second group composed of those who transmitted such knowledge and wisdom like secretaries, teachers, and poets. The third category constituted of people who applied the knowledge they learned from teachers, such as accountants, physicians, soldiers, property owners, merchants, and farmers. Here Plato's influence is visible who in fact divided society into three main groups each containing sub-groups. [211]

Ibn Sina's (369–428/980–1037) ideas on the necessity of formation of society were similar to al-Farabi's views. In Book Ten of *Shifa (namat–ten)-Kitab al-Siyasah* he discusses his views on politics. For Ibn Sina, division of labor is an instrument of establishing order and economic justice in society whereby redistribution of wealth from the wealthier to the poorer segments is facilitated under the supervision of the government and in accordance with the injunction of the Shari'ah.[212] His classification is similar to the Platonic division of labor and includes three professional groups composed of administrators, craftsmen, guardians, and soldiers.[213]

Al-Ghazali's (450–505/1058–1111) argument is simple and straightforward. Human beings need each other to fulfill their diverse needs. This gives birth to societies. Maintaining order and justice in society requires a social structure based on the division of labor. Al-Ghazali identifies three categories of social *classes* that include those who are engaged in production of food, animal husbandry, and crafts, then the soldiers, and finally those who run the affairs of the government such as tax collectors, administrators, and governors.[214] Given al-Ghazali's status as the most eminent jurist and theologian of his time, it is interesting to note that he said jurisprudence and theology alone cannot inspire true religion. Man's basic needs must be fulfilled, and this can

210 Abu Nasr al-Farabi, *On the Perfect State*, Revised text with Introduction, Translation, and Commentary by Richard Walzer (Oxford University Press: 1985), Reprinted in Chicago: Kazi Publications, 1998, 229, 233.

211 Antony Black, *The History of Islamic Political Thought* (New York: Routledge, 2001), 73.

212 Mohsen Kadivar, *Falsafeh-ye siyasi ye-ibn Sina*, Website, accessed June 13, 2021.

213 Antony Black, *History of Islamic Political Thought*, 75.

214 Abu Hamid Muhammad al-Ghazali, *Ihya 'ulum al-din* (*The Revification of Religious Sciences*) as quoted in Antony Black, *History of Islamic Political Thought*, 102.

be achieved through collaboration of different social groups because all classes are economically interdependent. At the same time he emphasized the significance of spiritual brotherhood among different classes. This was an important principle in shaping the ethics of *class* relationship in society for centuries to come.[215]

Ibn Rushd (520–595/1126–1198) added another principle to the ideas of his predecessors by emphasizing the necessity of specialization in professional work force. "The employment of man in more than one art is either impossible, or if it is possible, it is not the best way. Every man in the city should do the work that is in his nature and do it the best way that he possibly can."[216] His other important contribution was to initiate a discussion on the necessity of bringing in women into professional life.

Of particular interest and relevance in any discussion of social classes are the views of Ikhwan al-safa who appeared sometime in third/ninth century Basrah and compiled the *Epistles* (*Rasa'il*), an encyclopedic work that is devoted to all fields of knowledge of its time.[217] Their ideas on the necessity of formation of society and cooperation, love and friendship among its members, division of labor and benefits of specialization in one field of economic activity are similar to those of other philosophers discussed before.[218] Ikhwan also discussed the classification of some professions like agriculture as noble professions because they fulfil society's basic needs. Some professions like cloth making and dyeing and selling herbs are superior to some others, and professions like making tools for astronomy are very valuable, but some seemingly low professions like street sweeping are superior to others because of the useful service it provides to society.[219]

One issue of utmost importance that is absent in other discussions and Ikhwan pays particular attention to is the existence of poverty in society. In their analysis of poverty, the Ikhwan present three causes for poverty; they are natural, human, and metaphysical. While each of these causes have a part in the existence of poverty, their interpretation indicates that the main cause is

215 Antony Black, *History of Islamic Political Thought*, 101.

216 Nearly three centuries before ibn Rushd, Abu Bakr Razi (d. 313/925) wrote, "By cooperating as specialists in diverse things, all humans could be servants and served alike; everyone, however lowly, benefited from other people's labour in some respects." Crone, *God's Rule*, 341.

217 On Ikhwan al-Safa, see Seyyed Hossein Nasr, *An Introduction to Islamic Cosmological Doctrines: Conceptions of nature and methods used for its study by the Ikhwan Al-Safa, Al-Biruni, and Ibn Sina* (Cambridge: Harvard University Press, 1964); Ian Richard Netton, *Muslim Neoplatonists: An Introduction to the Thought of the Brethren of Purity*, 1st ed. (Edinburgh: Edinburgh University Press, 1991); and, Nader El-Bizri, *Epistles of the Brethren of Purity. Ikhwan al-Safa and their Rasa'il*, 1st ed. (Oxford University Press, 2008). *See also*, Muhammad Taqi Daneshpazhuh and Iraj Afshar, *Majma' al-hikmah: tarjumah gooneh-i as rasa'il ikhwan al-safa* (An Abridged Persian Translation of Ikhwan al-safa) (Tehran: 1996).

218 "Know that the felicity in this world and the Hereafter is not attainable except through cooperation of people and love and friendship among them." Rajabi et al., *The Rasa'il*, vol. 1, 270–272, in *Tarikh-i tafakkur-i ijtima 'i dar islam* (Tehran: 2012), 77.

219 Rajabi et al., *Rasa'il*, 83.

human, that is, the violation of the rights of the deprived and the greed of the wealthy.[220]

Ikhwan al-Safa present three different classifications on social stratification. One is intellectual, based on the degree of intellect (*'aql*) each class possesses and its effects on its faith and social behavior. These include:

1. Prophets who introduce divine law to the people.
2. Protectors and defenders of religion and religious rituals.
3. Philosophers and people of wisdom (*hikmah*) and scholarship.
4. Government employees including the king and all his representatives and subordinates.
5. Professionals in the service of the public such as architects and farmers.
6. Craftsmen, industrialists, and repairmen.
7. Merchants and importers of goods.
8. Daily workers.
9. The urban poor and the handicapped.

The second category is based on professional affiliation and is composed of six classes:

1. The people of the sword, i.e. the military men.
2. Professional politicians, ministers, scribes, secretaries, physicians, and tax collectors.
3. Architects, builders, and farmers.
4. The judges, the jurists, and scholars of religion (the 'ulama').
5. Merchants and craftsmen.
6. Treasurers, government envoys, security guards, servants and workers of the court who are the king's confidants.

Finally the third category is based on status and power and includes:

1. The upper class that includes the king and members of the ruling elite.
2. The middle class that is composed of the wealthy merchants and craftsmen.
3. The lower class that includes the urban poor.

Each class is in need of a leader who is superior to others in intellect, power, or wealth and his followers must obey him at all times.[221]

It was this framework of discussion and the legacies of those thinkers that inspired Tusi to write *Nasirian Ethics* and present the most comprehensive discussion of social *classes* that was not only theoretically sound but also proved its efficiency and applicability in practice. Interestingly his classification of social groupings was welcomed and adopted more in the Sunni world of the

220 Rajabi et al., *Rasa'il*, 84.
221 Rajabi et al., *Rasa'il*, 85–88.

Ottoman and Mughal empires than in the Shi'a world where only in the sixteenth century it attracted the attention of the Safavid state in Persia.

The Nasirian Ethics[222]

Tusi's views on politics and social classes are discussed in *Nasirian Ethics*. He wrote this book at the request of Nasir al-Din 'Abd al-Rahim ibn Mansur, the Isma'ili ruler of Quhistan and presented it to him. Although influenced by the views of thinkers such as ibn Muskuyah, al-Farabi, and ibn Sina, Tusi presented some original theories about politics and ethics, social systems, division of labor, characteristics of social classes, and class relationships.

The book consists of three parts. In part one, Tusi discusses ethics and its connection to politics. In part two, he examines domestic politics (*tadbir-i manzil*). The third part is on politics and is divided into eight sections.[223] The main theme of the book is the formation of a civil society that is attainable through cooperation among social classes. There are similarities with and continuity in Tusi's views and earlier philosophers on the necessity of formation of society, priority of public interest over individual's, collective as well as individual responsibilities, division of labor, specialization of professional work force, and the necessity of cooperation among social classes.

The central principle in Tusi's discussion of society is religion for he regards religion as the foundation of the state and the state as the support of religion. A government without religion is doomed to fail and a religion without a government would not be efficacious and useful for it is said, "Religion and state are like twin brothers, one would not be perfect without the other."[224] According to Tusi, every society has its own peculiar order and laws. Perfection of the people is possible through religion and discovering the minute details of the law (the Shari'ah) and putting them into practice. Through cooperation and the implementation of the law a society will be able to protect its interests

222 Tusi's life and adventures have been studied extensively in recent years. For a detailed account of his life and contributions see, Hamid Dabbashi, "Khwajah Nasir al-Din Tusi: The Philosopher/vizier and the intellectual climate of his time," in *History of Islamic Philosophy*, Part 1, ed. Seyyed Hossein Nasr and Oliver Leman (London, 1991). See also, Ishaq Husayni Koohsari, *Tarikh-i falsafah islami* (Tehran: 1993), 177–184; Gholam Husayn Ibrahimi Dinani, *Nasir al-Din Tusi, filsoof-I goftego* (Tehran: 1997); and, Antony Black, *History of Islamic Political Thought*, chapter 15. For his association with the Isma'ili rulers see Dabbashi, in Nasr and Leaman, *History of Islamic Philosophy*, 535–536. See also Mahmud Rajabi et al., *Tarikh-i tafakkur-i ijtima'i dar islam*, 141.

223 *Akhlaq-i Nasri* (Tehran: 'Ilmiyyah Islamiyyah Publishers, n.d.). See the introduction, pp. 3–4. A translation of the book appeared in 1964. See, *The Nasirian Ethics*, trans. G.M. Wickens (London: Allen & Unwin, 1964).

224 الدین و الملک توامان لا یتم احدهما الا بالآخر. The statement is often cited as a hadith. However, its authenticity as a hadith has been questioned. This was originally a part of the Testament of Ardashir, the Sassanid king, compiled for his successor and ibn Muskuyah translated that into Arabic and cited in his *Tajarib al-umam*. See, "Ibn Miskawayh," in *Encyclopaedia of Islam*, 2nd ed., ed. P. Bearman, T. Bianquis, C.E. Bosworth, E. van Donzel, and W.P. Heinrichs. First published online: 2012, accessed August 10, 2021. See also, "tajarib al-umam" in *Lughat nameh* by Dehkhoda.

and attain public welfare. The welfare and interests of a society are not merely in providing material well-being and fulfilling physical pleasure. Rather, the interest of the society is in moving towards true perfection that [in Islamic society] is meaningful only in relation to the principles of Islam. Without social cooperation it is not possible to protect public interest.[225]

Thus, public interest does not include providing the material needs of the people alone, but in moving towards true perfection (*kamal*), it must include observing the injunctions of religion. This is the science that Tusi calls practical wisdom or practical philosophy (*hikmat-i 'amali*) defined as a field of knowledge that deals with universal laws that protect the interest of the people and is the leading science among all other sciences. *Hikmat 'amali* is concerned with individual and collective domains. Its objective is to enable man to attain perfection, but this is possible only in the perfection of all members of society. It is a science that addresses man's worldly pursuits as well as his station in the Hereafter. Therefore, man's effort to make a living is tied up with ethics and spiritual life.[226]

Nowhere else is this connection more visible than in the creation of guilds in Islamic societies. Guilds were association of professionals who were engaged in the same field of economic activity. Every major field of economic activity, from production to distribution to sales as well as services was organized into guilds. Every profession had its own guild, and every major bazaar was divided into quarters in accordance with the type of economic activities guilds performed. Affiliation with a guild was an important part of the individual's identity. The duties of the guild included safeguarding the secrets of the profession, protecting the interest of its members, preventing hoarding and other unethical practices. The significance of guilds in the social fabric of Islamic society becomes even clearer if one realizes that they were not isolated associations but rather had close connection to other social institutions. What made the guilds in the Muslim world especially powerful was their close affiliation with Sufism and Sufi orders, and their adoption of the principles of *futuwwah* (spiritual chivalry) as ethical and moral code of conduct. Therefore, a guild was not just an economic organization composed of members of a profession, but an institution that took moral and spiritual character of its members seriously. Such affiliation was the reason for cultivating virtues and ethical values through extensive spiritual training. The close identification with guilds and concept of spiritual chivalry established firmly the idea of nobility and virtuous nature of work. It created an ambience within which work was considered a sacred task. Hence Tusi described the economic activity of each class as its virtue.[227]

225 Ibid., 210.

226 *Akhlaq-i Nasri*, 9.

227 There are numerous treatises available on the concept and institution of *futuwwah* in Arabic and

A profession unto itself did not enjoy any particular status or prestige. Rather, its worth and value was determined by the degree of usefulness of the service to the society and its reputation depended on the nobility of character of those engaged in that profession.[228] The *futuwwah* organizations integrated the economic activities of members of guilds into their religious-spiritual lives.[229] Thus, man's character and virtues gave nobility to work and sanctified it. It is this contemplative ambience that helps explain the fact that practically every guild identified a particular prophet or saint as being its patron, thus endowing the craft with something of the sacred character of the personage: material work and holy significance were in this manner never allowed to diverge, the sacred was manifested outwardly in the work, and the work was ennobled by the inward presence of the sacred. For example, the carpenters took as their patron the Prophet Noah having built the ark. The Virgin Mary was adopted by the weavers as their patroness. The Persian companion of the Prophet, Salman Farsi was the patron of the barber's guild.[230]

Tusi's Views on Division of Labor

For Tusi, society is an integrated whole composed of complementary parts in which each component performs a specific function. Harmony between these components guarantees order, efficiency, and perfection of the whole. In his discussion the footnote he uses terms such as the "system" (*nizam*), "systematic" (*nizammand*), "moderation" and "harmony" (*i'tidal, ta'dil*), "equilibrium and balance" (*ta'adul*), "justice" (*ma'dalat*), "conformity in application of the law, unity in the objectives of work" (*wahdat-i karkard*) and the like. Many of these terms were in fact applicable to Islamic political discourse.

Tusi argues that not all men can attain the same degree of perfection. As there are profound differences between various types of plants and animals, such differences exist in more pronounced ways among human beings. For example, some men may have qualities unique to them, and some may be the noblest of all. Every man attains perfection in accordance with his talents and capabilities.[231] That is the reason not every man can be a minister or adviser

---

Persian. See for example, Husayn Va'iz Kashifi, *futuwwat nameh-ye sultani,* with an introduction by Mohammad Ja 'far Mahjub, Tehran, 1969, and, Mir Sayyid 'Ali Hamadani, *Futuwwaat Nameh*, ed. Muhammad Riyad (Tehran, 2001).

228 Qur'an, 53:40: "*and that a man shall have to his account only as he has laboured, and that his labouring shall surely be seen, then he shall be recompensed for it with the fullest recompense.*"

"*Prayer is composed of ten parts, and nine parts of it is to work for a* [*lawful*] *living*"; and "*He who works to provide for his household is like the one who fights for Allah's Cause, or like him who performs prayers all the night and fasts all the day.*" (Hadith)

229 Seyyed Hossein Nasr, "Spiritual Chivalry," 310, and Titus Burckhardt, "The Spirituality of Islamic Art," in *Islamic Spirituality: Manifestations,* ed. Seyyed Hossein Nasr, 526–527. (N.Y.: 1991).

230 Yusuf Ibish, "Traditional Guilds in the Ottoman Empire: An Evaluation of their Spiritual Role and Social Function," in Turkey: The Pendulum Swings Back, *Islamic World Report* (London, 1988).

231 Ibish, "Traditional Guilds," 70.

to the king, for such a position requires much patience that many men may lack. "No position can be more difficult than that of a minister to the Sultan because many rivals would constantly challenge him, many would be jealous of him and have an eye on his position waiting for a proper moment to stab him in the back. No virtue is more important for a minister than patience and tolerance."[232]

Tusi then presents an extensive discussion on the division of labor based on the expertise of the individual in one craft. This is necessary for the survival and growth of the society. In his ideal society, the individual must realize that he is working to fulfill the needs of others and other people work to meet his needs.

As men of wisdom (i.e. the philosophers) have said, a thousand working men are needed so that a man can feed himself. Since the fulfillment of man's needs is contingent upon group cooperation and because cooperation is possible only when men rise to fulfill each other's needs in a just and equitable manner, multiplicity of professions is therefore an indispensable requirement of the social system.[233]

Every man should have the freedom to concentrate on one specific profession and skill and avoid the multiplicity of occupation because each man can be useful and productive only in a single craft. Such a choice must be made in consideration with his constitution and nature given to man by God. Each man's nature has its own qualities different from another man. Not every man's nature can excel in crafts that he wishes. In other words, each man has a special talent by nature to excel in one craft. By concentrating on a single craft man attains excellence in that field. Conversely, man's preoccupation with more than one profession will result in the imperfection of all. One can excel in one craft in the course of time. If he divides his talent and time in multiple crafts, he will not be able to excel in any of them.[234]

Class Differences

While the term *class* as a social unit and as defined in modern Western discourse is absent in social and political discussion in traditional Islamic society, this does not mean that the concept of social class did not exist. In fact, Muslim thinkers were aware of the necessity of the existence of *class* except that its definition, behavior, and relationship were different from what the term denotes in modern Western social and political discourse.

232 Ibish, "Traditional Guilds," 275.
233 *Akhlaq-i Nasri*, 250–251.
و در عبارت حکما همین معنی باشد بر این وجه: که هزار شخص کارکن بباید تا یک شخص لقمه ای در دهان نهاد. و چون مدار کار انسان به معاونت یکدیگر است و معاونت بر آن وجه صورت می بندد که به مهمات یکدیگر بتکافی و تساوی قیام نماید. پس اختلاف صنایع که ازاختلاف عزائم صادرشود مقتضی نظام بود.
234 *Akhlaq-i Nasri*, 288.

Tusi examines issues related to class and society from the perspective of civil or social philosophy (*hikmat-i madani*). He explains the lifestyle that can lead to true felicity and perfection. His view on class relationship, notwithstanding differences in intellect, wealth and power is egalitarian. This does not mean that he believed that all men are equal economically or socially. He finds equality of all men impossible as people are different in nature. Some men may be superior to others in wisdom and insight, some in power and majesty, some others in capabilities, while some may lack wisdom and intellect. As it has been said, "If all people were equal, all of them would perish."[235] Diversity in occupation results in the diversity of production of wealth. In the process some people get rich while some get poor. This results naturally in the emergence of class and the acceptance of stratification on the basis of wealth. However, he argues that since it is God's will that people enter into different occupations where some get rich and some remain poor, there is therefore no particular privilege or prestige to any given class. The poor and the rich each in fact fulfills God's will and are equal before Him. Thus, Tusi is aware of the inevitability of hierarchy and class differences but does not believe that one's economic standing alone defines his status in the society, but also one's ethical, intellectual, and spiritual constitution are even more important factors. God in His wisdom ordained occupational divisions in order for members of the society to fulfill each other's needs. Therefore, every occupation in its own right is sanctified by His command. If some occupations produce less wealth than some others, it is so by God's will because if everybody wished to follow a particular profession of his own liking, other needs of the society would not be fulfilled and the society would collapse. However, he is quick to mention that no man's social standing and class is permanent. Social mobility is possible through individual effort and education. Every man must assess his situation in consideration with members of other classes. If the individual finds his status lower than others, he must use his utmost effort to improve and elevate his situation through hard work and education. If he finds himself on the same level as the majority, he should try to perfect his qualities and elevate his rank. However, if he finds himself above others, he must be humble and attempt to maintain his standing.[236]

Social Classes: The Role of the State

Tusi examines the role of the state in leading society towards perfection. Even though man is a social being by nature (*al-insan madaniyun bi'l tab'*) and has to cooperate with others to fulfill his needs, every man's aspirations, intentions, interests, and behaviors are different from another and are often

235 *Akhlaq-i Nasri*, 209.
236 *Akhlaq-i Nasri*, 291.

individualistic. If people are left alone to do what they wish, they will quarrel with one another, injustice will spread, and the economic life of society will be threatened. To prevent this, society needs the law and a capable leader who can implement it, one who is superior to others by virtue of being endowed with divine inspiration so that others would obey him.[237] Such a leader is like a physician who knows the ills and imperfections of the society and is able to cure them, for "the king is the physician of the world." [238] Therefore, it is his duty to establish and preserve harmony between different classes. To achieve this end the king must establish justice and equality between members of all social classes. "It is incumbent upon the king to pay close attention to the condition of his subjects and use utmost effort to maintain justice among them, for the survival of the kingdom depends on justice."[239]

The king must meet three conditions to be able to establish justice: The first condition to establish justice is to create and maintain a balance between classes. As the balance between four natural elements guarantees the health of nature, so does the balance between classes guarantees the health of the society. To establish justice is to maintain and protect the complementarity of relationship between classes, like nature whose equilibrium is maintained by keeping its four natures in balance. Justice demands that the king should keep each class in its proper place and does not allow it to step beyond its boundaries.[240]

The second condition to establish justice in society is for the king to observe the behavior of the people of the kingdom and allot each class its fair share in consideration with its needs and qualifications.[241] The third condition is to treat them equally in terms of giving each class of the bounties of the kingdom and take into consideration the needs and merits of each class. Giving each class a share of the bounties of the kingdom guarantees the health of the society, for there is no virtue greater than generosity.[242] The king must also be superior in God-given qualities so that others would be obedient to him. He should be able to heal the society when it is hit by illness, for "the king is the physician of the world."[243]

Tusi also examines the role of the government as the agency responsible to bring about harmony and love among classes through establishing economic justice,[244] which according to him is to "take [wealth] from some and give it to

237 *Akhlaq-i Nasri*, 253.
238 *Akhlaq-i Nasri*, 259.
239 *Akhlaq-i Nasri*, 266.
240 *Akhlaq-i Nasri*, 262.
241 *Akhlaq-i Nasri*, 262.
242 *Akhlaq-i Nasri*, 264–265.
243 *Akhlaq-i Nasri*, 259.
244 و چون مردم مدنی بالطبع است و معیشت او جز به تعاون ممکن نه... و تعاون موقوف بود بر آنکه بعضی خدمت کنند و از بعضی ستانند و به به بعضی دهند تا مکافات و مساوات و مناسبت مرتفع نشود.

some others [i.e. the poor] so that equality and fairness would not disappear." Indeed the survival and growth of the state depends on the degree of its success in creating a spirit of fairness, cooperation and love among diverse classes and groups. Otherwise, anarchy will prevail, and the social order will collapse.[245] Cooperation of members of society is possible only through participation in the economic life of the society. Cooperation means that people serve one another and fulfill each other's needs. None of these can be achieved unless two essential factors are present. One is cohesion that is based on the cooperation among all classes and the other is love and friendship (*ulfat, ta'alluf*) among them. Without cooperation among people of all classes love cannot be established in the society and in the absence of love the establishment of civil society will be impossible to attain.

With these considerations in mind, Tusi then presents two types of classification of the social classes. One is based on faith and religious knowledge rather than wealth and power because religious knowledge and moral qualities of leadership matter most for the people. This classification was perhaps influenced by his association with the Isma'ili community while he was in the service of Nasir al-Din 'Abd al-Rahim ibn Mansur, the Isma'ili ruler of Quhistan.[246] This classification includes four groups.

The first is composed of those who possess intellect and true consciousness. They are the most learned and virtuous among the philosophers (*afadil-i hukama*). The second group is composed of men who do not have access to true consciousness and in observing the commands [of religion] are conscious of their life in the world and the Day of Judgment. They are inclined towards issues that are concerned with their material life and corporeal being. These men are called the people of faith (*ahl-i iman*). The third group includes those men who are in a lower station, do not possess intellectual imagination but are concerned with conjecture. Their understanding of [human] felicity, his origin, and the final Return (*ma'ad*) is in physical and material terms. They acknowledge the superiority of the first two groups. These are men of submission (*ahl-i taslim*). Finally, the fourth group is ordinary believers who are conscious of and content with the outward (*ahl-i zahir*). They are the downtrodden (*mustad'afan*) and acknowledge the superiority and knowledge of the first three groups. [247]

Tusi's second and more important classification of the society is based on economic and professional function each class performs. He assigns various degrees of honor and nobility to each profession in proportion to its service and usefulness to the society. For example, a profession like medicine is more useful in his opinion than tanning dead animal skin because medicine's purpose is to

245 *Akhlaq-i Nasri*, 252.
246 Crone, *God's Rule*, 337.
247 Crone, *God's Rule*, 239–241.

improve the health of human being. Therefore, a profession whose goal is to save the life of the noblest of creation is the noblest of all professions in principle. Still, what makes that profession noble is the dignity and the character of the man who is engaged in that profession. In other words, it is the man who gives nobility to the profession. When every member of each class sets to fulfill his duties, the society finds order and stability and people prosper. This is a fact upon which all philosophers are in consensus.[248] With this explanation, Tusi divided the society into four distinctive classes, in addition to the king and his entourage, as follows,

1. Men of Pen: This group consists of several sub-groups that include the artists, scientists, astronomers, physicians, philosophers, and religious scholars (the 'ulama'). The duty of this group is to show the straight path of God to believers and protect it with their teachings, explain the mysteries of life, and promote honesty and integrity in society. Their function prevents people from forgetting ethical values and guidelines. Preservation of the world and protection of religion depends on them. They correspond to water in nature that is needed for survival of human beings.
2. Men of Sword: These men oversee the protection of the foundation of the state, establishing order and security of the kingdom. They also protect the borders and guard the boundaries of the kingdom. The order and peace in the world depend on their presence. They must possess four qualities. They must be honest and sincere with the king, be obedient to him alone, be kind to one another, and must possess mastery in the art of war. The king in turn must observe four conditions in dealing with the men of sword. He has the duty to provide weapons, clothing, good horses, and provisions for them and divide the spoils of war among them. He must appoint every one of them to positions in consideration with their capabilities. Their temperament corresponds to fire in nature.
3. Men of trade and crafts: The craftsmen are those who produce tools for the industry and the farmers while men of trade transfer wealth from one place to another. Their services are essential for the prosperity of the individual and the society and without their collaboration industries cannot produce and people will be unable to earn a living. Their nature corresponds to air without which life cannot sustain.
4. Men of Soil: Finally, the farmers and food producers without whose work people will not survive. Their nature corresponds to that of soil. They are the most beloved class in the eye of God for by producing

248 *Akhlaq-i Nasiri*, 69–70.

> food and feeding people they are in a sense participating in God's quality of the Supreme Provider and the Giver of Sustenance.[249]

In performing the assigned function, Tusi concludes, each class in fact attains virtues and perfection. The degree of virtuosity and perfection of man depends on the perfection of performing the assigned function.

As philosophers and wise men have said [before us], the virtue of the farmers is cooperation to work and produce, the virtue of merchants is cooperation with their wealth, the virtue of the king is cooperation in politics, and the virtue of scholars [of religion] is rule in accordance with the truth. Together they can cooperate to build the kingdom on goodness and virtue.[250]

As we can see Tusi classifies social classes in correspondence with the laws of nature. The four classes in his opinion correspond to the four elements, water, air, fire, and soil that also constitute human nature. As the balance between the four natural elements guarantee the balance and health of the body, the harmony and balance between the four classes ensures order, stability, and health of the society. If one element dominates the others, the health of the body will be compromised. Similarly, if one class dominates the others the health of the society will be harmed and chaos and anarchy will prevail.[251]

In classical Sufi texts we find explanations of the proper conduct of each occupational group. For example, Najm al-Din Razi (573–654/1177–1247) in *Mirsdad al-'ibad* describes the proper manner of behavior of members of each class. He mentions that People of the Pen,

> must use their knowledge to attain felicity in the Hereafter, and those who use knowledge to accumulate wealth or attain power, are in fact ignorant and not a scholar.[252] Merchants and craftsmen must be aware that wealth can be a ladder to ascend heaven or fall in hell. They must use their wealth to earn paradise. Some merchants trade for the sake of the world and that is condemned. Some trade for

---

249 It is reported that a certain Harun Wasit, a close disciple of Ja'far al-Sadiq once asked him about the virtues of farming and the status of farmers before God. He said, "They are God's treasures on earth and there is no action loved by God more than farming. Were not every prophet sent by God as a farmer, except Idris who was a tailor and made clothing for the farmers?" As quoted in *Tahdhib al-ahkam*, vol. 6, 384.

«سَأَلْتُ جَعْفَرَبْنَ مُحَمَّدٍ عليهاالسلام عَنِ الْفَلَّاحِينَ» «فَقَالَ هُمُ الزَّارِعُونَ كُنُوزُ اللهِ فِي أَرْضِهِ وَ مَا فِي الْأَعْمَالِ شَئْ ءٌ أَحَبَّ إِلَى اللهِ مِنَ الزِّرَاعَةِ وَ مَا بَعَثَ اللهُ نَبِيّاً إِلَّا زَارِعاً إِلَّا إِدْرِيسَ عَلَيهِ السَّلامُ فَإِنَّهُ كَانَ خَيَّاطاً للفلاحين»

250 *Akhlaq-i Nasri*, 261–264.

و از الفاظ حکما در این معنی آمده است که "فظیلة الفلاحین هو التعاون با لاعمال، و فضلة التجار التعاون بالاموال، و الملوک هو التعاون بالارا و السیاسة و فضیلة الالاهیون هو التعاون بالحکم الحقیقة—ثم جمیعا یتعاونون علی عمارة المدن بالخیرات و الفضایل.

251 *Akhlaq-i Nasri*, 304–305.

و چنانکه ازغلبه یک عنصر بر دیگرعناصر انحراف مزاج از اعتدال و انحلال ترکیب لازم آید غلبه یک صنف از این اصناف برسه دیگرانحراف امور اجتاع از اعتدال و فساد نوع لازم آید.

252 Najm al-Din Razi, *Mirsdad al-'ibad*, ed. Muhammad Amin Riyahi (Tehran: 'Ilmi Publishers, 1994), 265–268. See also Abulqasim 'Abd al-Karim al-Qushayri, *Risalah Qushayriyah*, Persian edition, ed. Badi' al-zama Furuzanfar, 3rd ed. (Tehran, 1988), 355–365.
Mirsad al-'ibad, 245–253.

> the reward in the Hereafter and in the process, they gain worldly rewards as well. They must know that the real possessor of their wealth is God. Therefore, they must take a fair share enough to support their family and leave the rest for people and God's needy servants. They must prove trustworthy and honest, and avoid usury. They must not buy and sell slaves. If they travel, they should visit scholars and saintly people, and their tombs. Landlords and people who own properties must not be attached to their property and turn proud. They are not to belittle or look down at their helpers and peasants. They should give them their proper dues and fair share, performing their function as part of servanthood towards God.[253] Craftsmen must know that it is the Supreme Creator that gives existentiation to crafts. When a craftsman realizes this, the beauty of God's art and His artistic qualities are revealed. It is then that he could understand that his work is to serve God's servants and for His pleasure.[254]
>
> Farmers must consider themselves deputies of God. They should recognize that it is in fact God who allows them to plant, He wills the seeds to grow and the land to remain fertile and produce.[255] They are the most beloved class in the eye of God for by producing food and feeding people they are in a sense participating in God's quality of the Supreme Provider and the Giver of Sustenance (*al-Razzaq*). [256]

The most important outcome of this classification, as it can be seen, is a horizontal model of class relation in which classes are dependent on one another. A horizontal relationship guarantees that no single class dominates other classes or is seen as superior but classes are connected to one another by virtue of performing a specific function that is needed to guarantee the health of the entire society. Since class relationship is marked by interdependence of all classes to one another, the prosperity of one class results in the prosperity of all classes. The king is responsible for the maintenance of order and justice. The farmer must produce food to feed people and along with merchants and craftsmen pay taxes to enable the king to maintain an army which then defends the kingdom. Therefore, common interest and collective welfare results in collaboration among all classes and this in turn leads to the creation of a collective consciousness that results in further cooperation between classes rather than in conflicting interest, hostility, and constant class struggle, hence, the complementarity of classes.

To guarantee the working of this system and prevent class hostility, a spirit of cooperation, friendship and respect must be promoted among classes. Cooperation results in unity of purpose in such a way that through cooperation as specialists in diverse fields, each class would feel that it is the servant and served alike; everyone, however lowly, benefits from other people's labor in

253 *Mirsad al-'ibad*, 263–268.
254 *Mirsad al-'ibad*, 269–272.
255 *Mirsad al-'ibad*, 255–259.
256 See footnote 250.

some respects as some philosophers have said.[257] What makes cooperation even more effective and productive is the factor of love (*mahabbah*) that in Tusi's opinion is an important factor in creating social cohesion and solidarity.

Tusi emphasizes the role of love in creating cohesion, a spirit of cooperation and solidarity in society. He calls love, friendship, and honesty the greatest virtues and nurturing and promoting those virtues the most important of affairs. Indeed love is a quest for honor and perfection. He who longs to attain these virtues is eager for perfection and it is easier for him to achieve it. The reason the *shari'ah* gives priority to communal prayer over individual is that when people gather in one place, they become intimate, engage in transactions and that would most likely result in friendship. Thus, love works as the glue that connects diverse populations and classes to one another.[258]

Some early philosophers talked about love in an exaggerated manner to the extent that the existence of all beings depended on love and that no being can sustain without love. By the same token, the absence of love is an indication of weakness and imperfection.[259] One observer likens Tusi's definition of *mahhabbah* (group sentiments) to Ibn Khaldun's conception of *'asabiyyah*, translated as "group feeling" and to Emile Durkheim's "collective conscience." [260]

In Tusi's opinion, there is also a connection between love among members of each society and justice. Love leads to unity and enables the society to function naturally. In such a situation justice will prevail in a natural way. However, since people have diverse natures and some may violate other people's rights, the state has to intervene to establish justice. It is the duty of the state (i.e. the king) to assure that the rule of law and justice are observed. According to Tusi, justice is to treat people fairly and this is only possible when the authorities maintain constant contact with subjects.[261] "Justice rests the order of the heaven and earth," as the Prophet said.[262]

Tusi mentions three conditions for the king to establish justice. The first condition that enables the king to establish harmony and equilibrium among diverse classes is to persuade his subjects through wisdom and education to respect the laws of justice. As nature derives its harmony from the four elements that constitute its existence, society achieves its stability and harmony through justice that establishes balance and harmony between the four classes mentioned above. As it has been said, The King must demand his subjects to respect the laws of justice. No other virtue is nobler that the virtue of justice and no honor is more exalted than establishing equality in society.[263]

257 Abu Bakr Razi (d. 313/925), as quoted in Crone, *God's Rule*, 341.
258 *Akhlaq-i-Nasri*, 222.
259 *Akhlaq-i-Nasri*, 217, 218, 222, 291.
260 Dabbashi, in Nasr and Leaman, *History of Islamic Philosophy*, 567, 574.
261 *Akhlaq-i-Nasri*, 216.
262 *Akhlaq-i-Nasri*, 111.
263 *Akhlaq-i-Nasri*, 95, 266.

The second condition for establishing justice is for the king to observe the situation of his subjects carefully, and be aware of their psychological and spiritual needs and grant each class the rights and status in accordance with its qualifications and rank. Finally, the third condition is that once the government succeeds in the establishing the first two conditions, it must distribute wealth and other privileges among them in an equal manner in consideration with their merits and qualities, as it has been said, providing for the common good is the source of the health of the society.[264] When the king takes away wealth from some classes and gives it to some others moderation and balance will be established and a dyer (*sabbagh*) will be equal to a prominent merchant or a physician. This is the meaning of civil justice (*'adl-i madani*) and the world will prosper by it.[265]

In contrast to Ibn Rushd and considering Tusi's scholarly standing, it is surprising that he does not discuss the place of women in the social system but examines their role as mothers and wives. In that context Dabbashi states that Tusi's attitude towards women is "liberal" but his "liberality" must not be overestimated.[266] His position on women is in a sense reflective of the prevailing attitude of the society. On some issues however, his views are different and sometimes in conflict with the views of other scholars and jurists in the sense that he advises against polygamy, supports the wife's right to represent her husband in his absence, and her partnership in husband's wealth. The best wife however, is the one who is pious, fertile, has good manners and is capable of raising good children, and most of all obedient to her husband.[267] He strongly rejects educating young girls, consulting with women, exposing one's wife to strangers, and expressing love and sentiments to her. [268]

Conclusion

Nasirian Ethics is one of the most important examples of advice literature that deals with the concept of class and social stratification within the framework of traditional Islamic political thought. Heavily influenced by the pre-Islamic Persian notion of governance, it is expressed through Islamic terms and vocabularies. It presents a different pattern of relationship between the state and the people as well as among social classes, with emphasis on the centrality of justice, protection of religion, and welfare of the population.

Whether Tusi's ideals were put into practice is a different issue with which we are not concerned here. Even though Tusi was a Shi'a scholar and statesman, and worked and taught in the Persian speaking world, his fame and intellectual

264 *Akhlaq-i-Nasri,* 261–264. For more detail see 257–271.
265 *Akhlaq-i-Nasri*, 99.
266 Dabbashi in Nasr and Leaman, *History of Islamic Philosophy,* 572.
267 *Akhlaq-i-Nasri,* 175–183.
268 *Akhlaq-i-Nasri*, 190.

influence transcended geographical boundaries and sectarian considerations. *Nasirian Ethics* was read widely in India and in the Ottoman intellectual and political circles especially during the sixteenth to eighteenth centuries when the Ottoman Empire went through a series of political and military crises and as a result the advice literature received renewed attention. Ottoman intellectuals and statesmen like Tursun Bey (d. 1491), Kinalizadeh (d. 1572), Kocu Bey (d. 1650), Katip Celebi (d. 1657), Kupurlu Muhammad Pasha (d. 1661), and his son Kupurlu 'Abdullah Pasha (d. 1736) were greatly influenced by Tusi's writings especially *Nasirian Ethics*. In fact, Kinalizadeh's book title *'Ala'i Ethics* (*akhlaq-i 'ala'i*) is an abridged version of Tusi's book in Turkish in which he uses Tusi's model of social classes. In the Persian speaking world, the Safavid Empire also adopted Tusi's classification with some modifications. As a result of the establishment of the new dynasty that declared Shi'ism as the official religion of the state, traditional clergy paid more attention to Tusi's writing on theology and jurisprudence than his works on ethics, Sufism, and philosophy.

In recent times *Nasirian Ethics* has received renewed attention. After its translation into English by G. M. Wickens, published in London in 1964, several new critical editions of the book have been published in Persian with commentaries and annotations and are under translation into several European languages. There are still lessons that can be learned from *Nasirian Ethics*, especially the necessity of connection between politics and ethics at a time when modern politics and politicians have turned their back on ethics and ethical values in the realm of politics.

Bibliography

"Ibn Miskawayh." In *Encyclopaedia of Islam, Second Edition,* edited by P. Bearman, T. Bianquis, C.E. Bosworth, E. van Donzel, and W.P. Heinrichs. http://dx.doi.org/10.1163/1573-3912_islam_SIM_5235

al-Farabi, Abu Nasr. *On the Perfect State.* Revised text with Introduction, Translation, and Commentary by Richard Walzer. Oxford University Press: 1985, Reprinted in Chicago: Kazi Publications, 1998.

al-Qushayri, Abulqasim 'Abd al-Karim. *Risalah Qushayriyah,* edited by Badi' al-zama Furuzanfar, Persian edition. 3rd ed. Tehran, 1988.

Black, Antony. *The History of Islamic Political Thought.* New York: Routledge, 2001.

Burckhardt, Titus. "The Spirituality of Islamic Art." In *Islamic Spirituality: Manifestations,* edited by Seyyed Hossein Nasr, 526–527. New York: 1991.

Crone, Patricia. *God's Rule: Government and Islam.* New York: Columbia University Press, 2004.

Dabbashi, Hamid. "Khwajah Nasir al-Din Tusi: The Philosopher/Vizier and the Intellectual Climate of His Time." In *History of Islamic Philosophy,* Part 1, edited by Seyyed Hossein Nasr and Oliver Leaman. London, 1991.

Daneshpazhuh, Muhammad Taqi, and Iraj Afshar. *Majma' al-hikmah: tarjumah gooneh-i as rasa'il ikhwan al-safa* (*An Abridged Persian Translation of Ikhwan al-Safa*). Tehran: 1996.

Dinani, Gholam Husayn Ibrahimi. *Nasir al-Din Tusi, filsoof-I goftego.* Tehran: 1997.

El-Bizri, Nader. *Epistles of the Brethren of Purity. Ikhwan al-Safa and their Rasa'il.* 1st ed. Oxford University Press, 2008.

Feuer, Lewis S. "Marx and the Intellectuals." *Encyclopedia Britannica.* Accessed June 10, 2021.

Hamadani, Mir Sayyid 'Ali. *Futuwwaat Nameh,* edited by Muhammad Riyad. Tehran, 2001.

Ibish, Yusuf. "Traditional Guilds in the Ottoman Empire: An Evaluation of their Spiritual Role and Social Function." In *Turkey: The Pendulum Swings Back.* London: Islamic World Report, 1988.

Jeong, Ho-Won, and Eleftherios Michael. "Theories of Conflict." In *Encyclopedia of Violence, Peace, & Conflict,* vol. 3. 2nd ed. New York & Oxford: ELSEVIER, 2008.

Kadivar, Mohsen. *Falsafeh-ye siyasi ye-ibn Sina.* Accessed June 13, 2021.

Kashifi, Husayn Va'iz. *Futuwwat nameh-ye sultani.* Tehran, 1969.
Koohsari, Ishaq Husayni. *Tarikh-i falsafah islami.* Tehran: 1993.
Mahmud Rajabi et al. *Tarikh-i tafakkur-i ijtima 'i dar islam.* Tehran: 2012.
Nasr, Seyyed Hossein. *An Introduction to Islamic Cosmological Doctrines: Conceptions of Nature and Methods used for its Study by the Ikhwan Al-Safa, Al-Biruni, and Ibn Sina.* Cambridge: Harvard University Press, 1964.
Netton, Ian Richard. *Muslim Neoplatonists: An Introduction to the Thought of the Brethren of Purity.* 1st ed. Edinburgh: Edinburgh University Press, 1991.
Razi, Najm al-Din. *Mirsdad al-'ibad,* edited Muhammad Amin Riyahi. Tehran: 'Ilmi Publishers, 1994.
Tusi, Nasir al-Din. *Aklaq-i Nasri.* Tehran: 'Ilmiyyah Islamiyyah Publishers, n.d.
Tusi, Nasir al-Din. *The Nasirian Ethics.* Translated by G.M. Wickens. London: Allen & Unwin, 1964.
Zarrinkoob, Abdulhossein. *Karnameh-yi islam.* 5th ed. Tehran: 1998.

Chapter 7

Synergy of Knowledge in the Formation of Islamic Jurisprudence The Five Categories of Legal Rulings (*Aḥkām*) from 'Abd al-Jabbār to al-Ghazālī

Yasushi Kosugi

Professor and Director of Asia-Japan Research Institute,
Ritsumeikan University, Japan

The *Sharī'a*, often misleadingly translated as Islamic Law, is far wider than any law in non-Islamic societies in its function for the lives of Muslims. One important observation for any student of Muslim societies in the last five decades or so is that the *Sharī'a* was defined mostly as statute law in Muslim countries under the dominance of modernity but it remains as a spiritual and societal force. It remains very vivid in the hearts of the adherents of Islam. The so-called Islamic revival was made possible in the twentieth century when Islam as a social force and the *Sharī'a* as a legal and ethical framework returned to the public spheres. Previously, the secularization thesis presumed that the state and religion would be separated as societies embrace modernity. Religion would no longer assert a strong influence over political, social, and economic domains as they had in the premodern era.

When I started studying Muslim societies and the history of Islamic thought a half century ago, I realized that the internal force of the *Sharī'a* was vivid in the daily lives of Muslims, and not merely as the legal norms backed by state power. This has remained so in the history of Islamic thought since the premodern era till contemporary times. For this reason, the divides between the historical and the contemporary in the study of the Islamic world can be sometimes erroneous because researchers may not obtain the sense of continuity in society and the living forces in it.

It is well-known that the Islamic world was once a shining seat of world civilizations. The flourishing of the Islamic civilization from the eighth to the fifteenth centuries has been well-recorded, with its contributions to various fields of sciences and technologies. Its contributions to the European Renaissance and modernity are among the favored topics of many historians. However, its decline came in the eighteenth century, and ever since the dawn of modernity, various important initiatives have been activated by Muslim intellectuals and leaders for civilizational renewal and revival. As Osman Bakar observes, given the decay of modern civilization and its attendant global problems, the renewal of the Islamic civilization "is ultimately congruent with civilizational renewal for humanity as a whole."[269]

On the other hand, the technology of what I would term as "social management" as embodied in the *Sharīʿa* has not declined. It has been providing guidelines to a vast majority of Muslims who constitute a quarter of mankind (as of 2020), with varying degrees, from creed and cosmology to religious and spiritual acts to societal and economic behaviors, and to legitimization of governance as well as providing a moral basis to criticize rulers. The practical applications of the *Sharīʿa* may need certain reforms to adapt to contemporary conditions. Still, it has a stronger basis in societies and in the minds of Muslims than its political and economic decline may imply.

Five Categories of Islamic Legal Rulings

Figure 1

Divine Command		
	Order	Prohibition
Demanding Decisively	Obligatory to do = Forbidden to neglect it (Doer will be rewarded by God and neglecter will be punished)	Forbidden to do = Obligatory to avoid it (Avoider will be rewarded by God and doer won't be punished)
Demanding Indecisively	Recommended = Reprehensive to neglect it (Doer will be rewarded by God, but neglecter won't be punished)	Reprehensive = Recommended to avoid it (Avoider will be rewarded by God, but doer will not be punished)
Granting Options	Free to choose	

Source: By the author

Having described the wider context of the discussion, this chapter attempts to clarify one of the most fundamental systemic elements in the *Sharīʿa*, namely, *al-aḥkām al-khamsa*, or the five categories of legal rulings of *Sharīʿa* on human activities. Through these categories, the Islamic jurists define each and

269 Osman Bakar, *Islamic Civilisation and the Modern World: Thematic Essays* (Brunei Darussalam: UBD Press, 2014), 305.

every human action to one of these five categories, namely, 1) obligatory, 2) recommended, 3) permitted (therefore, free for human choice), 4) reprehensible (recommended not to do), and 5) forbidden. The obligatory is also what is forbidden to neglect, and the forbidden is what is obligatory to avoid. The same can be said of "recommended" and "reprehensible." Figure 1 shows the five categories in a plain diagram.

The jurists throughout history have been issuing legal interpretations whenever a new issue arises by interpreting the fundamental texts. There were many new issues in the early periods of the Islamic history when the empires expanded rapidly from the Arabian Peninsula in the seventh and eighth centuries. Muslims encountered things and issues unknown to them before. In those days, the jurists were seeking practical solutions to society's needs. They were called *fuqahā'* (jurists) and, through them, the science of fiqh started to manifest. In those days, they did not concern themselves yet with the integrity of *Sharī'a* since it was taken for granted by the very foundation of divine guidance. The intellectual need for systematization and the construction of *Uṣūl al-Fiqh* only came later.

Early jurists used more nuanced expressions to deliver legal rulings. The "early master jurists would usually say, 'I don't like this,' 'It should not be so,' 'I don't see it as fitting,' ... 'It is not permissible,' and 'This is reprehensible because there is nothing good in it' to express a prohibition. They used to say, 'Nothing is wrong with that' and 'I hope to make it clear that there is nothing wrong with that' to reflect their permission."[270] Even al-Shāfi'ī did not employ a clear categorization of rulings, though he was often credited as being the initiator of *Uṣūl al-Fiqh* or the "first scholar to write on the subject."[271]

Once established, the five categories served Muslim societies' need for *Sharī'a* guidance. In the modern era, new issues increased in light of innovations from the West. By providing legal rulings to all these new issues, or by being able to do so, the jurists have successfully informed ordinary Muslims that the *Sharī'a* can be valid and useful in any time.[272]

For ordinary Muslims, this means that the Islamic teachings come to them as instructions in these five categories. Any serious Muslim must ask him/herself if the action he/she is going to do is permissible or at least reprehensible which means that though it is not recommended, it does not constitute a sin or an error. If he/she does not know, he/she may like to ask someone with knowledge. Such clear categorizations of any action served as an effective instrument

270 Labeeb Ahmed Bsoul, *Formation of the Islamic Jurisprudence: From the Time of the Prophet Muhammad to the 4th Century* (Basingstoke: Palgrave Macmillan, 2016), 163.

271 Ibn Khaldūn, *The Muqaddimah: An Introduction to History*, 3 vols., trans. Franz Rosenthal (London: Routledge and Kegan Paul, 1958), 28.

272 Unanimity of the interpretation or of the resultant ruling is not required. An ordinary Muslim can follow any judgment of a qualified scholar. The integrity of the framework of five categories is what matters.

for the implementation of the *Sharīʿa*. It was part of the technology of social management to teach Muslims how to seek Islamic guidance in their lives.

Now we may ask from where this categorization appeared. Looking into the verses of the Qur'an, the first source of the *Sharīʿa*, and the Ḥadīth collections which contain the sayings and actions of the Prophet Muhammad, that is, the second source of the *Sharīʿa*, we find no direct references to the five categories. It is the result of human endeavors at a later date, not from the Prophetic period or in immediately subsequent periods. This leads to a question: By who, how, and why, was the categorization made? This chapter will answer this question and clarify how this categorization was developed. I look at the creation of the science of Islamic Jurisprudence, or *ʿIlm Uṣūl al-Fiqh* and how it gave birth to the Islamic value system which has endured to our day. During the formulation of this Islamic value system, a synergy of Islamic and Greek knowledge occurred through contributions by those Muslim scholars who excelled and dared to employ what was originally foreign for the benefit of the Muslims.

An Inquiry in the Twentieth Century *Usūlī* Works

The word *Sharīʿa* in the Qur'an, coming from the root verb sh-r-ʿ which implies "paths leading to drinking spots,"[273] refers to the divinely inspired Islamic way of life as a whole. In an arid land such as the Arabian Peninsula which constitutes the context of the Qur'anic revelation, paths leading to drinking spots are indispensable for any human life for one's own survival, so the foundational meaning of *Sharīʿa* is clear. The Qur'an says: "Then We [Allah] have set you [Muhammad] upon a clear path [*Sharīʿa*] from the [divine] command, so follow it" (45:18). The word of Fiqh, coming from the root verb f-q-h, implying "to understand, to learn, to acquire knowledge; comprehension" occurs in two forms of verb in the Qur'an.[274] So, in the Qur'anic sense, *Sharīʿa* is the fundamental guidance and fiqh is the understanding of the *Sharīʿa* to be implemented in all domains of life.

However, as scholarly knowledge accumulated, a division of subjects occurred. Fiqh was confined to the domain of human actions, separating it from the creed. Hence, the Fiqh rulings are about what Muslims should do or should not do in actions and behaviors and the rulings in creed are about what Muslims should or should not believe in their hearts. In later eras, including ours, the word Fiqh is sometimes equated with the *Sharīʿa*, as the "College of *Sharīʿa*" in Islamic universities may well indicate. This is a matter of convenience, since the Qur'anic definition of the comprehensive *Sharīʿa* continues to be in force.

273 Elsaid M. Badawi and M. Abdel Haleem, *Arabic-English Dictionary of Qur'anic Usage* (Leiden: Brill, 2010), 481.

274 Badawi and Abdel Haleem, *Arabic-English Dictionary*, 719–720.

Having said so, we now turn to authorities on *Uṣūl al-fiqh* in the twentieth century and see how they explain these legal terms. Muḥammad Abū Zahra (1898–1994) was quite influential in the middle of the twentieth century as an authority on the *Sharīʿa*. He was "an Egyptian legal scholar and one of the leading Muslim jurists of the twentieth century. He left behind a distinctive body of scholarship that gained him international acclaim during his lifetime."[275] One of his important contributions for the contemporary revival of Fiqh was initiating the Fiqh compendium to comprehend all legal issues across the eight existing legal schools.[276] The ambitious plan of the compendium he initiated is still in progress.[277]

In his *Uṣūl al-Fiqh*, Abū Zahra defines *Fiqh* as the "knowledge of every and each [legal] issue with detailed evidences [for its ruling]" and *Uṣūl al-Fiqh* as the "methodology which defines and clarifies the path that jurists must take when extracting the rulings from their sources."[278] He likens the latter's position to the former as "like [the relationship of] logic to the rest of the philosophical knowledge."[279] As for the legal rulings, he states, quoting al-Ghazali, that the knowledge of legal ruling (*ḥukm sharʿī*) is "the fruits of both sciences of *Fiqh* and *Uṣūl*, defining the legal rulings of what is related to the actions of the responsible [Muslims], while the *Uṣūl* deals with the methodology of its [ruling's] precision and sources, and the *Fiqh* deals with the actual findings of the rulings within the circle described by the *Uṣūl*."[280] He divides the rulings into two fundamental categories, namely, the impositional rulings, or defining rulings (*ḥakm taklīfī*) which is the "five categories" of our discussion, and the compositional rulings, or declaratory rulings (*ḥukm waḍʿī*) which are supplementary to the rulings of imposition, such as conditions, components of validity or lack of it for a ruling, and elements of nullification. However, he does not specify the historical process in which the legal rulings were systematized.

Prior to this work, he contributed to the re-publication of *Uṣūl al-Fiqh* by ʿAbd al-Wahhāb Khallāf. The book was originally published in 1942. Abū Zahra and his colleagues decided to republish it to commemorate the author after his death in 1956. Khallāf's work[281] is written in modern prose that is easy to read and systematically arranged in chapters and sections. It has been

275 M. Hashim Kamali, "Abū Zahra, Muḥammad," in *Encyclopaedia of Islam, Three* (online), 2008.

276 These eights schools are five Sunni schools, namely, the four major schools of law existent today, Hanafi, Maliki, Shafii, and Hanbali schools, and Zahiri school, not practiced today but existent as knowledge; two Shiite schools, namely, Ja'fari and Zaydi schools; and Ibadi school, a moderate Khawarij school.

277 The Egyptian project was a pioneering one when it was started in 1966. In terms of circulation, the Fiqh encyclopedia published by the Kuwaiti ministry of religious affairs (Wizāra al-Awqāf wa al-Shu'ūn al-Islāmīya 1980–2006) is rendered useful by both specialists and general readers.

278 M. Abū Zahra, *Uṣūl al-Fiqh* (Cairo: Dār al-Fikr al-ʿArabī, 1958).

279 Abū Zahra, *Uṣūl al-Fiqh*, 4–6.

280 Abū Zahra, *Uṣūl al-Fiqh*, 23.

281 ʿAbd al-Wahhāb Khallāf. *ʿIlm Uṣūl al-Fiqh* (Cairo: Dār al-Ḥadīth, 2002).

widely circulated in the Islamic world. It is noteworthy that this was the first Arabic book on the subject to be translated into Japanese by Kojiro Nakamura in 1984.[282] As for the legal rulings, Khallāf also does not inform us much about the historical formation of its categories.

Another important work is *Uṣūl al-Fiqh: Tārīkhuhu wa Rijāluhu* by Sha'bān Muḥammad Ismā'īl published in 1981. Its subtitle, "its History and its Authors," invites our curiosity. However, again, the author is comfortable in not explaining what we are looking for. This work was well-received partly because it cites all major authorities in the history of *Uṣūl al-Fiqh*. The vast majority of its more than 600 pages are devoted to 379 authors and their works, 22 of whom lived in the first half of the twentieth century. Khallāf is one of them. More recent works by the established authorities in Muslim countries also follow a similar style of writing.[283]

A Vacuum of History of the Five Categories in Modern Studies in English

In recent decades, two authors writing in English are prominent in the study of *Fiqh*. One of them is Mohammad Hashim Kamali who has been very active in elaborating various aspects of the *Sharī'a* and Uṣūl al-Fiqh.[284] Aside from writing a comprehensive work on *Uṣūl al-Fiqh* as a legal science, he has also spent much ink on the halal/haram issues, employing *Uṣūl* arguments in many places. The halal/haram issues have been pivotal since dietary rulings are one of the most important issues for the everyday life of Muslims. Based on observation of actual Muslim lives for nearly five decades, I have found that daily food and family affairs (marriage, divorce, subsistence and inheritance) are the two most important arenas. These two domains are apparently where secular statute law has failed to encroach on the *Sharī'a*.

However, Kamali's works are the English equivalent of the Arabic sources which I cited in the previous section, namely works which are more concerned with *Uṣūl al-Fiqh* as an established legal science and not so much with its historical formation. It illustrates this science as it was finally systematized and formulated in history. It includes in its scope the contemporary revitalization of this science and its prospects for the future. While these works are extremely useful for any student to learn *Sharī'a*, they rarely focus much on how this systematization actually happened.

---

282 Kojiro Nakamura (1936–) was instrumental to establishment of Department of Islamic Studies in the University of Tokyo and served there from its inception in 1982 for 15 years. While he is known for his studies on al-Ghazali, he translated this legal work after he was impressed by actuality of *Sharī'a* he observed in Saudi Arabia.

283 'Alī Jum'a, *Tārīkh Uṣūl al-Fiqh* (Cairo: Dār al-Muqaṭṭam, 2015).

284 M. Hashim Kamali, *Principles of Islamic Jurisprudence* (Cambridge: Islamic Text Society, 2003); *Sharī'ah Law: An Introduction* (Oxford: One World, 2008); *Sharī'a and the Halal Industry* (Oxford: Oxford University Press, 2021).

Meanwhile, Hallaq (1997) published a history of the Sunni *Uṣūl al-Fiqh*, that is, the majority branch of Islam. Although it is full of elaborate discussions, it does not provide information of the systematization of the five categories. Instead, it simply tells us: Islamic legal theory after al-Shāfiʿī came to recognize five values with which all legal acts must be labeled. In other words, when the jurist arrives at a legal solution for a new case of law, his decision must fall into one of five categories; the obligatory (*wājib*), the recommended (*mandūb*), the permissible (*mubāḥ*), the prohibited (*ḥarām*), or the reprehensible (*makrūh*).[285]

As I will clarify later, the systematization of the five categories took its final form from the fifth to early sixth century AH/eleventh to the early twelfth century CE. There is a period of nearly three centuries between the death of al-Shāfiʿī (150–204 AH/767–820 CE) and the systematization. So, Hallaq's description is too sketchy an account.

The recent rise of interest in the *Sharīʿa* in the West brought a number of reference works on Islamic law. An investigation into them, however, discloses again a lack of focus on the five categories. *The Oxford Handbook of Islamic Law*,[286] for example, has a chapter on *Uṣūl al-fiqh*.[287] Yet, it does not discuss the construction of the five categories, which are "the fruits of both sciences of *Fiqh* and *Uṣūl*."[288] After reading this excellent Western exposition on the subject, one wonders whether there is a lack of interest in discovering the inner logic of the making of *Sharīʿa* rulings.

Arguments on *Taklīf* (Assigning Responsibility) in Speculative Theology as a Basis for the Five Categories

The five categories are called the impositional rulings, or defining rulings (*ḥukm taklīfī*), because they impose some hardship on Muslims by ordering this or that and forbidding this or that. The verbal form of *taklīf* is *kallafa*, whose meaning in the Qur'an is "to burden someone with (a task)."[289] A Qur'anic verse says: "We [Allah] do not burden any soul with more than it can bear" (23:62). So, these are rulings coming from the communication of Divine Commands, which burden human beings with certain tasks to test them.

These rulings apply to men and women who are Muslims, having reason and sound senses, and are matured. Non-Muslims are not bound by *Sharīʿa*. Minors are not responsible. Insane persons will not be held responsible. So, the one in a responsible position is *mukallaf* (one who is burdened or charged). The five categories are the categorization of actions by such a *mukallaf* person.

285 Wael B. Hallaq, *A History of Islamic Legal Theories: An Introduction to Sunni Usul al-Fiqh* (Cambridge: Cambridge University Press, 1997), 40.
286 Anver M. Emon and Rumee Ahmed, eds., *The Oxford Handbook of Islamic Law* (Oxford: Oxford University Press).
287 Youcef Soufi, "The Historiography of Sunni Usul al-Fiqh," in *The Oxford Handbook of Islamic Law*, 249–270.
288 Abū Zahra, *Uṣūl al-Fiqh*, 23.
289 Badawi and Abdel-Haleem, *Arabic-English Dictionary*, 816.

Any specialist on Islamic creed quickly finds links between the Muʿtazilī school of speculative theology and the concept of *taklīf.* Indeed, contemporary authorities on *Uṣūl al-Fiqh* most often cite al-Qāḍī ʿAbd al-Jabbār, a major theologian of the later Muʿtazilī school, as one of first pivotal contributors to the making of *Uṣūl al-Fiqh*. He was born between 320 and 325 AH/932 and 937 CE and died around 415 AH/1024 CE. Known as al-Qāḍī (Judge), he served as the chief judge in Rayy, leading the Shāfiʿī school of law, while as a theologian he was the leader of the Muʿtazilīs. In those days, there was fierce competition between the Muʿtazilīs and the Ashʿarīs. The Sunni theological position was not yet defined by the victory of the latter.[290]

ʿAbd al-Jabbār wrote a major work on *Uṣūl al-Fiqh*, named *al-ʿUmad* ("Pillars" or "Supports"). Unfortunately, this work no longer exists, although we can learn some of his *Uṣūl* thought from a portion of his voluminous theological work, *al-Mughnī fī Abwāb al-Tawḥīd wa al-ʿAdl.* His disciple, Abū Ḥusayn al-Baṣrī al-Muʿtazilī (d. 436/1044), after studying with his mentor, wrote his Uṣūl work, *al-Muʿtamad fī Uṣūl al-Fiqh* ("What is supported" in *Uṣūl al-Fiqh),*[291] though unlike his mentor, al-Baṣrī was a Ḥanafī jurist. We can appreciate the actual contents of Muʿtazilī *Uṣūl* thought from it to a great extent.

Al-Basrī speaks of the five categories, addressing the reader:

> Know that actions of a *mukallaf* [one in charge of one's actions] in a rational state are of two kinds, namely, evil [*qabīḥ*] and good [*ḥasan*]. The evil are such as injustice, ignorance, lies, ungratefulness and the like. The good are of two kinds. One of them is what is considered better to do than to abstain from. The other kind is what is not considered better to do than to abstain from. The first kind includes what is proper to do such as virtue (*iḥsān*) and generosity. It also includes what one has to do, and this is obligatory, such as moral correctness and appreciation of grace. What is not considered better to do than to abstain from is something permissible, such as benefiting from foods and drinks.[292]

We can see a prototype for the categorization of the rulings here, but not clearly elaborated as we know them today.

In the foundation, there was the Muʿtazilī position of *Naẓarīya al-Ḥasan wa al-Qabīḥ al-ʿAqlīyayn* (Theory of the goodness and the repugnant in the rational discernment), which was based on the doctrine of al-ʿAdl al-Ilāhī (Divine Justice).[293] The Muʿtazilīs were firm in their rationalism, saying that good and evil can be determined by reason. Abū al-Ḥasan al-Ashʿarī (d. 324

290 The other branch of "orthodox" theology, al-Māturīdīs, is mostly intertwined with Ḥanafī school of law so it is not part of this chapter's discussion.

291 al-Baṣrī, *Kitāb al-Muʿtamad fī Uṣūl al-Fiqh*, 2 vols., ed. M. Ḥamīd Allāh (Damascus: al-Maʿhad al-ʿIlmī al-Faransī li-l-Dirāsāt al-ʿArabīya, 1964).

292 al-Baṣrī, *Kitāb al-Muʿtamad fī Uṣūl al-Fiqh,* vol. 2, 868.

293 Malīka Khathīrī, *al-Fikr al-Uṣūlī ʿinda al-Muʿtazila: Rijāluhum wa Turāthuhum* (Beirut: Dār al-Kutub al-ʿIlmīya, 2018), 211.

AH/935–6 CE) was once a Muʿtazilī but broke away to form his own position. Whether reason can determine what is good and what is evil in *Sharīʿa* or not became a bone of theological, and subsequently legal, contention between the two schools.

Abū Bakr al-Bāqillānī, a contemporary of ʿAbd al-Jabbār, was also a judge and both himself and Abd al-Jabbar are often referred as al-Qāḍiyān (Two Judges). This expresses well the high esteem they enjoyed and the rivalry between them. Al-Bāqillānī was the "venerable judge, diplomat, and theologian, considered the first great systematizer of Ashʿarī thought,"[294] leading the second generation of Ashʿarīs. He was also "given honorary titles such as 'Lisān al-Umma' ('Speaker of the community') and 'Shaykh al-Sunna' ('master of the prophetic sunna')."[295]

He composed three versions of *Uṣūl al-fiqh* work all with the same name, namely, *al-Taqrīb wa al-Irshād* ("Access and Guidance"), Large, Medium, and Short. Of them, the Short still exists today, though this "short" version is over 1,200 pages in today's printed edition. In it, Al-Bāqillānī speaks in it of the five categories as follows:

> We have already said that all actions of the *mukallaf* [responsible Muslim] are either he can do them or not. Then, all of them are divided into just three categories, where the fourth doesn't exist, namely, what is ordered, what is prohibited, and what is permitted.
>
> What is ordered is divided to two kinds, obligatory and recommended. The obligatory is what is attributed as obligatory [upon a Muslim] to do. The recommended is attributed to be better and preferred to do.
>
> The prohibited is also of two kinds; the first is what is forbidden and banned to which it is attributed that it must be abstained and avoided. Some [scholars] say that it is obligatory not to do it, without referring to abstaining and avoiding it, on the assumption of deeming the human creation of act and abstention permissible. This position [of the Muʿtazilīs] is wrong.
>
> The second kind of the prohibited is prohibited in the sense of recommendation and preference, not in the sense of forbidding and ordering to abstain from it. This kind is attributed to be what is better and preferred not to do, and the better and preferred [as human action] is to abstain from it and avoid it.
>
> The permissible is a category different from the above two. It is what is permitted to which it is not attributed that one must do it, or it is better and preferred to do, or one must not to do, or it is better and preferred to do, since doing it and abstaining from it are the same. There is no action of a *mukallaf* outside of these categories.[296]

294 David R. Vishanoff, *The Formation of Islamic Hermeneutics: How Sunni Legal Theorists Imagined a Revealed Law* (Hew Haven: American Oriental Society, 2011), 152.

295 Hassan Ansari, "al-Bāqillānī, Abū Bakr," translated by Matthew Melvin-Koushuki, in *Encyclopaedia Islamica*, 2013.

296 al-Bāqillānī, *al-Taqrīb wa al-Irshād (al-Ṣaghīr)*, ed. ʿAbd al-Ḥamīd b. ʿAlī Abū Zunayd (Beirut: Mu'assasa al-Risāla, 1998), vol. 1, 286–287.

Al-Bāqillānī employed a categorization into three kinds, subdividing two of them into two kinds each, resulting in five categories consequently, but he did not say "five." Al-Isfarā'īnī was another great *Uṣūl* scholar, who was one of the co-students of al-Bāqillānī under the same master. Al-Juwaynī inherited *Uṣūl* thought from both al-Isfarā'īnī and al-Bāqillānī. Al-Juwaynī is known by an honorific title, Imām al-Ḥaramayn (Imam of the two sacred cities, Makka and Madina), stemming from his being once the teacher in both cities. In his major *Uṣūl* work called *al-Burhān* ("Evidence"), he clearly cited five categories of what he called *al-Aḥkām al-Shar'īya* (*Sharī'a* rulings): What is related to [Divine] orders and prohibitions comprehends obligation, prohibition, recommendation, reprehension and permission.[297]

He also clarifies the difference between the Mu'tazilīs and the Ash'arīs: As for the obligatory, some [Mu'tazilīs] said that the legally obligatory is that for which a *mukallaf* deserves to be punished if he neglects to do it. This is [an opinion] far from the school of the People of the Truth on the [Divine] reward and punishment. We [Ash'arīs] don't see that Allah needs "deserving" because the Lord [Allah] punishes and gives grace to whoever He wishes.[298]

Final Categorization by al-Ghazali and the Synergy of Primordial and Adopted Knowledges

When al-Juwayni was teaching in Nishapur in a college built for him, a young al-Ghazali became one of his students. Muḥammad b. Muḥammad al-Ghazālī, or Abū Ḥāmid al-Ghazālī, was born in a place near Tūs in northeast Iran and so he was called al-Ṭūsī. Later, "widely known as the Proof of Islam (*Ḥujjat al-Islām*), Ghazālī left his imprint on intellectual traditions both inside and outside of Islamdom."[299] He was a great polymath in Islamic knowledge, including our subject, *Uṣūl al-fiqh*. He was once considered a philosopher in the West, known as Algazel, since his exposition of Greek philosophical ideas (*Maqāṣid al-falāsifah* or *the Aims of the Philosophers*) was superb and fair so that the Western philosophers found it as the best introduction to the subject for many centuries. His severe criticism of the philosophers did not reach them until much later. This episode informs us that he was well-versed in the Greek sciences.

In *Uṣūl al-fiqh*, he studied with al-Juwayni at the Nizamiyya College in Nishapur and later became a professor at Nizamiyya College in Baghdad. After resigning from this prestigious learning center, he wandered to Syria and other parts of the Islamic East in the pursuit of spiritual enlightenment, and

297 al-Juwaynī, *al-Burhān fī Uṣūl al-Fiqh*, 6th ed., 2 vols., ed. 'Abd al-'Aẓīm Maḥmūd al-Dīb (Maṣūra: Dār al-Wafā', 2017), 193.

298 al-Juwaynī, *al-Burhān fī Uṣūl al-Fiqh*, 193.

299 Ebrahim Moosa, "Abū Ḥāmid al-Ghazālī (d. 505/1111)," in *Islamic Legal Thought: A Compendium of Muslim Jurists*, ed. Arabi, Powers, and Spectorsky (Leiden and Boston: Brill, 2013), 261.

then returned to teach at the first college he studied at. He wrote a summary of what he learned from al-Juwaynī entitled *al-Mankhūl min Taʿlīqāt al-Uṣūl* (the "Screened" of the Commentaries on the Sources)[300] when he was young. When he returned to teaching, he composed a quite different work as his own masterpiece *al-Muṣṭasfā min Uṣūl al-Fiqh* (the "Refined" of *Uṣūl al-Fiqh*)[301] shortly before his death.

The first part of the book is dedicated to logic and systemic thinking as a necessary introduction to precise definitions and clear categorization in *Uṣūl al-fiqh*. "Al-Ghazzālī consistently maintained the view that logic is one of the philosophical sciences."[302] He was not hesitant to utilize what is useful for knowledge. It is very clear that he employed the knowledge adopted from Greek sciences, absorbed already in the form of speculative theology, and integrated them into the body of *Uṣūl al-fiqh*. As we have examined above, this process started with the Muʿtazilīs, and continued under the Ashʿarī endeavors, culminating with al-Ghazālī himself. On the five categories, he says:

> .... the categories of rules established for actions of the loci of obligations are five: Obligatory [*wājib*], prohibited [*maḥẓūr*], allowed [*mubāḥ*], recommended [*mandūb*], and reprehensible [*makrūh*]. The reason for this categorization is that the *Sharīʿa* address comes either requiring *doing, not doing*, or the option between doing or not doing. Therefore, if it comes requiring action, it is then a command, and it is either associated with a notification of punishment for its abandonment—therefore becoming obligatory—or not associated [with punishment]—thus becoming recommended. As for that which comes requiring abandonment, if it indicates punishment for doing it, it is then a prohibition; otherwise, it is reprehensible. But if it comes as an option, it is allowed.[303]

We found here a clear final statement of "five" categories.

Thanks to the Muʿtazilīs, who employed the concept of *taklīf* as a basis of Islamic understanding of the Divine Commands, and thanks to the Ashʿarīs, who were able to situate them in the Qur'anic context, derived from the rationalist determination of good and evil by reason. But then, why does the category of permissible which is left to humans' freedom of choice belong to this set of *taklīf* rulings as al-Ghazālī had it? Doesn't *taklīf* involve hardship to which the Divine orders and prohibitions pertain?

Actually, there were arguments on this question during the process of the categorization. Al-Juwaini states:

---

300 al-Ghazālī, *al-Mankhūl min Taʿlīqāt al-Uṣūl*, ed. Muḥammad Ḥasan Ḥaytū (Damascus: Dār al-Fikr, n.d.

301 al-Ghazālī, *al-Muṣṭasfā min ʿIlm al-Uṣūl* (Beirut: Dār al-Nafāʾis, 2011).

302 Osman Bakar, *Classification of Knowledge in Islam* (Kuala Lumpur: Islamic Book Trust, 2019), 220.

303 al-Ghazālī, *Al Mustasfa Min Ilm Al Usul*, tr. by Ahmad Zaki Masur Hammad (Dar Ul Thaqafah, 2018),Vol.1,55. (The italics are by the translator. The translation is slightly modified. For the original in Arabic, see: al-Ghazālī 2011: vol. 1, 193–194).

> As for *taklīf*, al-Qāḍī Abū Bakr [al-Bāqillānī] said that it is a command which contains hardship, and a prohibition which contains hardship. If both are combined, I would say: It is an invitation to what contains hardship, so the order includes recommendation, and the prohibition includes reprehension from [meaning of] *taklīf*. .... As for permission [*ibāḥa*], it doesn't contain the meaning of *taklīf*. The Professor [al-Isfarā'īnī] said that it is part of *taklīf*, but it is a clear mistake [it doesn't contain hardship]. He justified his opinion by saying that it is obligatory to believe [its being] permission .... If asked "Is permission counted within the *Sharī'a*?" we say "Yes, it is," on the assumption that the *Sharī'a* brought it.[304]

Ṣalāḥ Zaydān, an Egyptian jurist, says that, while some Mu'tazilīs took a position that what is permissible is an original state of affairs, the Sunni scholars take the position that the category of permission is included in the five categories because of its *Sharī'a* basis, though they agree that permission does not contain any hardship.[305] According to Aḥmad al-Ḥājjī al-Kurdī, a Syrian jurist, al-Ka'bī (d. 319/931), a Mu'tazilī, equated practising the permissible with avoiding the prohibited and argued that therefore permission is part of *taklīf*.[306] Another justification for including permission in the categories of rulings is to understand the linguistic usage of naming something with the dominant.[307] This is quite applaudable as the reason for naming but it does not explain why permission should be included in the first place.

The following statement by al-Baqillani provides the answer: "... all the actions of the *mukallaf* [responsible Muslim] are either things he can do or things he cannot do. Then, all of them are divided into just three categories, and there is no fourth; namely, what is ordered, what is prohibited, and what is permitted."[308] "There is no action of a *mukallaf* outside of these categories."[309]

This categorization was made for the sake of guidance for human life, not categorization for the sake of categorization. Thus the category of non-*taklīf*, the permission, is necessary if the rest of the categories comprehend *taklīf* issues and human responsibilities towards them. A *mukallaf* will be left without certainty if the categories have a void where he/she doesn't know what the ruling is for this action or that action. There ought to be a category where no Divine order or prohibition exists so that a Muslim can be relieved that he/she accomplishes his/her responsibility without any omission in this area too.

---

304 al-Juwaynī, *al-Burhān fī Uṣūl al-Fiqh*, vol. 1, 83.

305 Ṣalāḥ Zaydān, *al-Ḥukm al-Shar'ī al-Taklīfī* (Cairo: Dār al-Ṣaḥwa, 1987), 157–158.

306 Aḥmad al-Ḥājjī al-Kurdī, *Buḥūth fī 'Ilm Uṣūl al-Fiqh: Maṣādir al-Tashrī' al-Islāmī al-Aṣlīya wa al-Taba'īya wa Mabāḥith al-Ḥukm* (Beirut: Dār al-Bashā'ir al-Islāmīya, 2004), 259–260.

307 Muḥammad 'Abd al-'Āṭī Muḥammad 'Alī, *al-Taklīf al-Shar'ī wa Mā Yat'allaqu bi-hi min Aḥkām* (Cairo: Dār al-Ḥadīth, 2007), 27.

308 al-Bāqillānī, *al-Taqrīb wa al-Irshād*, 286.

309 al-Bāqillānī, *al-Taqrīb wa al-Irshād*, 287.

Was *Uṣūl al-Fiqh* a Later Invention?

This chapter has demonstrated that the five categories of legal rulings were firmly established through systematization by those who were speculative theologians and specialists of jurisprudence at the same time. They combined primordially Islamic knowledges and rational knowledges of "foreign" origins, though the latter was already absorbed into theology through the medium of the Arabic language. Because of their contributions, this trend of *Uṣūl al-Fiqh* is called the Path of Mutakallimūn (speculative theologians). When we consider the *Sharī'a* as primordially Islamic as well as Arabic (since all sources are in Arabic), the synergy of the two branches of knowledges may cast a serious doubt as to the origin of *Uṣūl al-fiqh*. Even without this question, the later making of this science calls for an explanation: If *Uṣūl al-fiqh* is to be seen as the foundational science of *Sharī'a*, why did it come into existence at such a late date as the fifth and sixth centuries AH?

In this regard, we should look at the other trend, namely, what is called the Path of *Fuqahā'* (Jurists). It is basically the method taken by the Hanafi jurists.[310] They did not start systemizing the methodologies of interpretation. Abū al-Ḥusayn al-Baṣrī al-Mu'tazilī, the above mentioned, was an exception to this, being a Mu'tazilī theologian and a Ḥanafī jurist at the same time. In the Path of Jurists, at first accumulation of legal reasoning and judgments occurred through interpretations by their pioneering precursors. They composed works containing actual rulings but did not compose works on the methodologies. Later scholars extracted the methodologies from these judgments through induction. *Uṣūl al-Fiqh* employs, on the other hand, deduction. It is based on deduction from the roots (*uṣūl*) to reach the branches (*furū'*) and built the methodologies of interpretations from the sources to the final rulings.

What was induced in the Path of Jurists from the preceding cases of their great imams were the "Legal Principles" (*al-Qawā'id al-Fiqhīya*). These principles can be applied to new cases, so that they now serve as a basis for legal interpretation. One important example of such principles is that "the norm in regard to things is that of permissibility."[311] Therefore, all food is permissible to eat for Muslims unless there are clear texts that forbid it (or that make it reprehensible to eat). Since this principle is contained in Qur'anic verses, *Uṣūl* methodologies can deduce the same conclusion. Here both trends meet.

On the difference between the two Paths, or between deduction and induction, 'Alī Jum'a (1952–), a contemporary *Uṣūlī* authority and a former Mufti of Egypt, sums this up by saying "Uṣūl al-Fiqh is before Fiqh, and the

310 'Abd al-Ra'ūf Mufḍī Kharābisha, *Manhaj al-Mutakallimīn fī Istinbāṭ al-Aḥkām al-Shar'īya: Dirāsāt Uṣūlīya Muqārana fī Mabāḥith al-Alfāẓ wa Dalālātihā 'alā al-Aḥkām* (Beirut: Dār Ibn Ḥazm, 2005), 56–72; 'Alī Jum'a, *al-Ḥukm al-Shar'ī 'inda al-Uṣūlīyīn*, 3rd ed. (Cairo: Dar al-Salām, 2013), 29–32.

311 Kamali, *Shari'ah Law*, 146.

Legal Principles are after Fiqh" in reply to a question directed to him.[312] Al-Sa'īdī qualified the former as theoretical and the latter as practical.[313] Now in the Path of the Jurists, it is easy to argue that the methodologies were there from the very beginning. They just needed to be extracted later.

Can we say the same for the Path of Theologian-Jurists? I have just employed an expression of "theologian-jurists" because calling them theologians can be misleading. They were specialists of jurisprudence who utilized the systemic thinking developed in the theology, thus "theologian-jurists" is a clearer term. Al-Ḥasanāt argues that *Uṣūl al-Fiqh* was there from the beginning, since all jurists were exercising their interpretations and it is inconceivable that they did so without methodologies.[314] We can agree with this argument only if we mean these methodologies in potentiality, but not necessarily manifest, or as "tacit knowledge." Such knowledge ought to be articulated and systematized to become an independent knowledge as in the case of *Uṣūl al-fiqh*. This chapter has demonstrated that the process took some centuries and evolved through a synergy of knowledges.

Different Significances of *Ḥukm* in Fiqh and *Uṣūl al-Fiqh*

It seems apparent that the systematization of *Uṣūl al-Fiqh* was possible only after the actual rulings were accumulated and in fact the *Uṣūl al-Fiqh* was composed later. However, it claimed to be superior to the Fiqh because it contains the roots while the Fiqh contains the branches. It goes without saying that there are no branches nor a tree as a whole without having roots at the base. They seem to meet at their fruits, that is, the legal rulings with the five categories.

We have to pay attention, however, to the different meanings and significance of a ruling (*ḥukm*) between the two branches of Islamic legal knowledge. *Uṣūl al-Fiqh* defines it as "Allah's addresses [*khiṭāb Allah*] related to the actions of *mukallafs* [responsible Muslims] with requirement or granting options."[315] Requirement (*iqtiḍā'*) is either by asking for an action or an abstention, either decisively or not. We have seen that asking for an action decisively is an order and asking indecisively is a recommendation, and that asking for an abstention decisively is a prohibition and asking indecisively is reprehension. Granting options (*takhyīr*) is giving freedom of choice to human beings. These five comprehend all human actions.

On the other hand, Fiqh defines a ruling (*ḥukm*) as "a consequence of Allah's addresses related to the actions of *mukallafs* with requirement or granting

312 'Alī Jum'a, *al-Kalim al-Ṭayyib: Fatāwā 'Aṣrīya* (Cairo: Dār al-Salām, 2005), 244.

313 'Abd al-Malik b. 'Abd al-Raḥmān al-Sa'dī, *Dalālāt al-Alfāẓ fī Tafsīr al-Nuṣūṣ al-Shar'īya wa Atharuhā fī al-Istinbāṭ* (Amman: Dār al-Nūr al-Mubīn, 2018), 14–15.

314 Aḥmad al-Ḥasanāt, *Taṭawwur al-Fikr al-Uṣūlī 'inda al-Mutakallimīn* (Amman: Dār al-Nūr al-Mubīn, 2015), 45–47.

315 Jum'a, *al-Ḥukm al-Shar'ī 'inda al-Uṣūlīyīn*, 47.

options."[316] The only difference between the two is whether it is an address or a consequence of one. Regarding the Qur'anic verse saying, "And establish the prayers" (2:43), *Uṣūl al-Fiqh* says that it is a Divine ruling and it is obligatory upon a Muslim to establish the prayers, while Fiqh says that the ruling of an obligation to establish the prayers is the *consequence* of this address. The reason for the difference must be clear for our readers. *Uṣūlī* scholars concern themselves with the sources so that they always endeavor to clarify the nature of the Divine command contained in the source through proper methodologies. For ordinary jurists and Muslims, the consequent rulings matter.

Wahba al-Zaḥaylī (1932–2015), another *Uṣūlī* authority from Syria, preferred the Fiqh way of using the term *ḥukm*: "Although this difference brings no actual benefit since the two technical terms are compatible, I prefer the Fiqh terminology, because it separates the Sharia ruling and its evidence in the Qur'an and the Sunna from other sources."[317] His argument is again convincing speaking as he were as an *Uṣūlī* who concerns himself with the interpretive methodologies.

Conclusion

The *Sharī'a* started to develop from the very early Islamic era and later two branches of its knowledge became manifest. The first branch, the science of Fiqh, was separated from creed and became crucial to Muslims' lives as it provided indispensable guidance. The second branch, the science of *Uṣūl al-Fiqh,* developed later as a foundation to Fiqh since it provides methodologies of legal interpretation. The most important fruit of both sciences is the five categories of legal rulings, which has sustained the *Sharī'a* consciousness of Muslims and contributed greatly to the Islamic revival in the twentieth century. Since the *Sharī'a* provides the technology of social management within the Islamic civilization, its survival and resurgence in modern conditions was of great importance for Islam and global society as a whole.

The five categories of legal rulings are instrumental to this technology of social management, and its process of historical systematization was analyzed in this chapter. It was articulated and systematized by the theologian-jurists in the fifth to sixth centuries AH/tenth to eleventh centuries CE, from al-Qāḍī 'Abd al-Jabbār to al-Ghazālī, through a synergy of knowledge inherent in Islam and Greek-originated knowledge. In this period, *Uṣūl al-Fiqh* was firmly constructed through an amalgamation of the Arabic language, Greek-originated logic and the principles of Islamic law making.

To end, if we ask ourselves what can be learnt from this process of synergy for our tasks of civilizational renewal in the current context, I would venture to suggest that we must move beyond looking through Islamic eyes but instead be global in our vision.

---

316 Jum'a, *al-Ḥukm al-Sharʿī ʿinda al-Uṣūlīyīn*, 50.

317 Wahba al-Zuḥaylī, *Uṣūl al-Fiqh al-Islāmī*, (Damascus: Dār al-Fikr, 1986), Vol 1., 41.

Bibliography

Abū Zahra, Muḥammad. *Uṣūl al-Fiqh*. Cairo: Dār al-Fikr al-'Arabī, 1958.

Al-Ghazali, *Al Mustasfa Min Ilm Al Usul: On Legal Theory of Muslim Jurisprudence,* tr. by Ahmad Zaki Masur Hammad, Vol.1, Dar Ul Thaqafah, 2018.

'Alī, Muḥammad 'Abd al-'Āṭī Muḥammad. *al-Taklīf al-Shar'ī wa Mā Yat'allaqu bi-hi min Aḥkām*. Cairo: Dār al-Ḥadīth, 2007.

Ansari, Hassan. "al-Bāqillānī, Abū Bakr." Translated by Matthew Melvin-Koushuki. *Encyclopaedia Islamica.* 2013.

Badawi, Elsaid M., and Muhammad Abdel Haleem. *Arabic-English Dictionary of Qur'anic Usage*. Leiden: Brill, 2010.

al-Bāqillānī, Abū Bakr, Muḥammad b. al-Ṭayyib. *al-Taqrīb wa al-Irshād (al-Ṣaghīr)*. 2nd expanded ed., 2 vols., edited by 'Abd al-Ḥamīd b. 'Alī Abū Zunayd. Beirut: Mu'assasa al-Risāla, 1998.

al-Baṣrī, Abū al-Ḥusayn Muḥammad b. 'Alī b. al-Ṭayyib, al-Mu'tazilī. *Kitāb al-Mu'tamad fī Uṣūl al-Fiqh*. 2 vols., edited by Muḥammad Ḥamīd Allāh. Damascus: al-Ma'had al-'Ilmī al-Faransī li-l-Dirāsāt al-'Arabīya, 1964.

Bsoul, Labeeb Ahmed. Formation of the Islamic Jurisprudence: From the Time of the Prophet Muhammad to the 4th Century. Basingstoke: Palgrave Macmillan, 2016.

Emon, Anver M., and Rumee Ahmed, eds. *The Oxford Handbook of Islamic Law.* Oxford: Oxford University Press.

al-Ghazālī, Abū Ḥāmid Muḥammad b. Muḥammad. *al- Muṣṭasfā min 'Ilm al-Uṣūl,* edited by Muḥammad 'Abd al-Raḥmān al-Mar'ashī, 2 vols. Beirut: Dār al-Nafā'is, 2011.

al-Ghazālī, Abū Ḥāmid Muḥammad b. Muḥammad. *al-Mankhūl min Ta'līqāt al-Uṣūl,* edited by Muḥammad Ḥasan Ḥaytū, Damascus: Dār al-Fikr, n.d.

al-Ḥasanāt, Aḥmad. *Taṭawwur al-Fikr al-Uṣūlī 'inda al-Mutakallimīn*. Amman: Dār al-Nūr al-Mubīn, 2015.

Hallaq, Wael B. *A History of Islamic Legal Theories: An Introduction to Sunni Usul al-Fiqh*. Cambridge: Cambridge University Press, 1997.

Ibn Khaldūn. *The Muqaddimah: An Introduction to History*. 3 vols. Translated by Franz Rosenthal. London: Routledge and Kegan Paul, 1958.

Ismā'īl, Sha'bān Muḥammad. *Uṣūl al-Fiqh: Tārkhuhu wa Rijāluhu*. Riyadh: Dār al-Murīkh, 1981.

al-Juwaynī, Abū al-Ma'ālī 'Abd al-Malik b. 'Abdullāh Yūsuf. *al-Burhān fī Uṣūl al-Fiqh.* 6th ed., 2 vols., edited by 'Abd al-'Aẓīm Maḥmūd al-Dīb. Maṣūra: Dār al-Wafā', 2017
Jum'a, 'Alī. *al-Kalim al-Ṭayyib: Fatāwā 'Aṣrīya.* Cairo: Dār al-Salām, 2005.
Jum'a, 'Alī. *al-Ḥukm al-Shar'ī 'inda al-Uṣūlīyīn.* 3rd ed. Cairo: Dar al-Salām, 2013.
Jum'a, 'Alī. *Tārīkh Uṣūl al-Fiqh.* Cairo: Dār al-Muqaṭṭam, 2015.
Kamali, Mohammad Hashim. *Principles of Islamic Jurisprudence.* Cambridge: Islamic Text Society, 2003.
Kamali, Mohammad Hashim. "Abū Zahra, Muḥammad." In *Encyclopaedia of Islam, Three* (online). 2008.
Kamali, Mohammad Hashim. *Shari'ah Law: An Introduction.* Oxford: One World, 2008.
Kamali, Mohammad Hashim. *Sharī'a and the Halal Industry.* Oxford: Oxford University Press, 2021.
Khallāf, 'Abd al-Wahhāb. *'Ilm Uṣūl al-Fiqh.* Cairo' Dār al-Ḥadīth, 2002.
Kharābisha, 'Abd al-Ra'ūf Mufḍī. *Manhaj al-Mutakallimīn fī Istinbāṭ al-Aḥkām al-Shar'īya: Dirāsāt Uṣūlīya Muqārana fī Mabāḥith al-Alfāẓ wa Dalālātihā 'alā al-Aḥkām.* Beirut: Dār Ibn Ḥazm, 2005.
Khathīrī, Malīka. *al-Fikr al-Uṣūlī 'inda al-Mu'tazila: Rijāluhum wa Turāthuhum.* Beirut: Dār al-Kutub al-'Ilmīya, 2018.
al-Kurdī, Aḥmad al-Ḥājjī. *Buḥūth fī 'Ilm Uṣūl al-Fiqh: Maṣādir al-Tashrī' al-Islāmī al-Aṣlīya wa al-Taba'īya wa Mabāḥith al-Ḥukm.* Beirut: Dār al-Bashā'ir al-Islāmīya, 2004.
Moosa, Ebrahim. "Abū Ḥāmid al-Ghazālī (d. 505/1111)." *Islamic Legal Thought: A Compendium of Muslim Jurists,* edited by Oussama Arabi, David Powers, and Susan Spectorsky, 261–293. Leiden and Boston: Brill, 2013.
Osman Bakar. *Islamic Civilisation and the Modern World: Thematic Essays.* Brunei Darussalam: UBD Press, 2014.
Osman Bakar. *Classification of Knowledge in Islam: A Study in Islamic Schools of Epistemology.* Kuala Lumpur: Islamic Book Trust, 2019.
al-Sa'dī, 'Abd al-Malik b, 'Abd al-Raḥmān. *Dalālāt al-Alfāẓ fī Tafsīr al-Nuṣūṣ al-Shar'īya wa Atharuhā fī al-Istinbāṭ.* Amman: Dār al-Nūr al-Mubīn, 2018.
Soufi, Youcef. "The Historiography of Sunni Usul al-Fiqh." In *The Oxford Handbook of Islamic Law,* edited by Anver M. Emon and Rumee Ahmed, 249–270. Oxford: Oxford University Press, 2018.
Vishanoff, David R. *The Formation of Islamic Hermeneutics: How Sunni Legal Theorists Imagined a Revealed Law.* Hew Haven: American Oriental Society, 2011.

Wizāra al-Awqāf wa al-Shu'ūn al-Islāmīya, ed. *al-Mawsū'a al-Fiqhīya*. 45 vols. Kuwait: Wizāra al-Awqāf wa al-Shu'ūn al-Islāmīya, 1980–2006.
Zaydān, Ṣalāḥ. *al-Ḥukm al-Shar'ī al-Taklīfī*. Cairo: Dār al-Ṣaḥwa, 1987.
al-Zuḥaylī, Wahba. *Uṣūl al-Fiqh al-Islāmī*. 2 vols. Damascus: Dār al-Fikr, 1986.

Chapter 8

Religion and Science: Selected Views of Iqbal and Bohm

Muhammad Suheyl Umar

Professor and former Director of Iqbal Academy Pakistan

Religion and science are permanent fixtures in history. The obvious question is how they are to get along. Alfred North Whitehead was of the opinion that, more than any other single factor, the future of humanity depends on the way these two most powerful forces in history interact with each other. Osman Bakar agrees with this point of view and calls for the recovery of religion in the making of modern science. To be sure, revelation has shaped human history more than any other force besides technology. The periodic incursions —explosions, we might call them—of this power in history are what created the world's great religions, and by extension, the civilizations they have embodied. Its dynamite is its news of another world. Revelation invariably tells us of a separate though not removed order of existence that simultaneously relativizes and exalts the one we normally know. It relativizes the everyday world by showing it to be less than the "all" that we unthinkingly take it to be, and that demotion turns out to be exhilarating. By placing the quotidian world in a vastly more meaningful context, revelation dignifies it the way a worthy setting enhances the beauty of a precious stone.

People respond to this news of life's larger meaning because they hear in it the final warrant for their existence. It was Peter Berger who, expanding on his famous dictum "Homo Sapiens have always been homo religiousus" had alerted us to the fact that "If anything characterizes modernity it is the loss of the sense of transcendence—of a reality that exceeds and encompasses our everyday affairs" and "a human existence bereft of transcendence is an impoverished and finally untenable condition."[318] It is modern science, or to be more correct, the *scientistic* worldview of the Enlightenment project bequeathed to modernity, which tries to maintain this "impoverished and finally untenable condition."

318 Peter L. Berger, "Secularism in Retreat," *The National Interest* 46 (1996): 3–12.

Religious triumphalism died a century or two ago, and its scientistic counterpart seems now to be following suit.[319] It seems clear that both science and religion are here to stay, and they have to enter into a healthy relationship, one that is mutually enriching and based on a wise "division of labour." What could then be a viable model for a splice between science and religion? David Bohm's ideas provide us with one such model.

"Reality *has a physical and a metaphysical aspect.*" This statement could be considered as the epitome of David Bohm's findings endorsed by his research in frontier physics that spanned well over five decades. Bohm, physicist and close colleague of both Oppenheimer and Einstein, was a theorist whose work was an advance on Einstein's theory and greatly impacted the scientific worldview, opening new vistas that led towards a viable model for a splice between science and religion. Bohm was making such interesting claims about the nature of reality. One could not think of anyone whose theories had deeper ramifications for religion and philosophy, an unexpected ally in the fight against dogmatic, scientistic, materialism that had prevailed in the academy and was responsible for the colonizing effects of science on humanities.[320] William C. Chittick has masterfully summarised this "colonizing disease":

In order to understand the nature of the disease, we need to remember that practically all of us suffer from it, whether or not we are aware of it. The reason for this is that it is a characteristic of modernity (and of "post-modernity" as well). The disease is co-extensive with the worldview that informs modern thought. It is very difficult to characterize the modem worldview with a single label. One word that has often been suggested is "scientism." I understand this word to designate the notion that the scientific method and scientific findings are the sole criterion for truth. So defined, scientism is a belief-system. Like most belief-systems, it has become second nature to its believers. They do not recognize it as a belief system, because they think it is self-evident truth.

Scientism is a basic characteristic of the modem worldview and the contemporary *zeitgeist.* People see the world and their own psyches in terms of what they have learned in schools, universities, and television documentaries.

319 Here and there diehards turn up – Richard Dawkins, who likens belief in God to belief in fairies, and Daniel Dennett, with his claim that John Locke's belief that mind must precede matter was born of the kind of conceptual paralysis that is now as obsolete as the quill pen – but these echoes of Julian Huxley's pronouncement around mid-century that "it will soon be as impossible for an intelligent or educated man or woman to believe in God as it is now to believe that the earth is flat" are now pretty much recognized as polemical bluster.

320 The scientific method, says Iqbal, has created an economic, political and educational system that values facts over curiosity, financial gains over social contributions, precision over insights. This was the cause of our spiritual crisis. It joined other crises as we entered the new century – the environmental crisis, the population explosion, the widening gulf between the rich and the poor. Muhammad Iqbal, *Bāl i Jibrīl,* in *Kulliyāt i Iqbāl* (Collected Poetical Works=CPW), Urdu (Lahore: Iqbal Academy Pakistan, 2007), 434/35.

It is taken for granted that the universe as described by science is the real universe. As for religious teachings, these are understood to pertain to ritual and morality, but not to the "real world," since we have been taught to see the world only with scientistic eyes.[321]

That is Iqbal's view as well.[322] According to him, the modern era is characterized by a loss of faith in transcendence, in God as an objective reality. It is the age of eclipse of transcendence. No socio-cultural environment in the pre-modern times had turned its back on Transcendence in the systematic way that characterized modernity.[323] In Iqbal's perspective, Transcendence means that there is another reality that is more real, more powerful, and better than this mundane order. The eclipse of transcendence impacted our way of looking at the world, that is, forming a worldview. In his view there is a Big Picture and his writings give us to understand that the postmodern view of the self and its world is in no way nobler than the ones that the world's religions proclaim. Postmodernists yield to their dilapidated views, not because they like them, but because they think that reason and human historicity now force them upon us. Iqbal would argue that it is not necessarily the case and the present predicament is the result of a tunnel vision that we have adopted but which really is not the only option for us. Here is Iqbal's depiction of the conceptual shift that the enlightenment project and modernity's worldview had brought in human thought, the damage that it had done to academia. Cultures and their worldviews are ruled by their mandarins, the intellectuals and they, as well as their institutions that shape the minds that rule the modern world are unreservedly secular. Iqbal addressed them in this poem:

> *The Schoolman is an architect/The artefact he shapes and moulds is the human soul;*
> *Something remarkable for you to ponder/ Has been left by the Sage, Qā'ānī;*
> *Do not raise a wall in the face of the illuminating Sun/If you wish the courtyard of your house to be filled with light.*[324]

---

321 William C. Chittick, "Traditional Islamic Thought and the Challenge of Scientism" *Spektrum Iran*, 2004, 48.

322 "We must not forget that what is called science is ... a mass of sectional views of Reality ... The various natural sciences are like so many vultures falling on the dead body of Nature, and each running away with a piece of its flesh. Nature as the subject of science is a highly artificial affair, and this artificiality is the result of that selective process to which science must subject her in the interests of precision." Muhammad Iqbal, *The Reconstruction of Religious Thought in Islam* (Lahore: Iqbal Academy, 1986), 33–34.

323 Martin Lings while speaking of the Arabs forgetting that all human character traits were rooted in God, hence ignoring transcendence, had remarked: "No socio-cultural environment in the pre-Modern times had turned its back on Transcendence in the systematic way that characterized Modernity." See his *Mecca: From Before Genesis Until Now* (London: Archetype, 2004), 5

324 Iqbal, "Shaykh i Maktab," in *Bāl i Jibrīl, Kulliyāt i Iqbāl* (CPW), 494/170.

The issue of "Reductionism" and lack of "Transcendence" that riddled the discourse of modernity and, later on bequeathed to postmodernism, was a problem of the greatest magnitude in Iqbal's opinion. He was convinced that whatever transpires in other domains of life—politics, living standards, environmental conditions, interpersonal relationships, the arts—was ultimately dependent on our presiding world view. He captures the issue in these poems:

This Gathering is dying for the vision of the metaphorical
The object of thy gaze is the secluded abode of mysteries
Every heart is drunk with the inebriety of the wine of the imaginary
The present day "Kalīms" have a very different Ṭūr (The Burning Bush) for themselves. [325]
Modern knowledge is based on the sensory (the physical, corporeal, palpable)
The glass of belief has been broken into smithereens in this age. [326]
Don't be an ardent admirer of the "Unseen," be mad for the witnessed, the corporeal
Now the impact of the "present" Deity has taken hold of the peoples. [327]

This is what was wrong with the presiding paradigm or worldview that his age had come to espouse.[328] In his view, modern Westerners, forsaking clear thinking, allowed themselves to become so obsessed with life's material underpinnings that they had written science a blank cheque; a blank cheque for science's claims concerning what constituted Reality, knowledge and justified belief.[329] No one knew this better than Nietzsche who in *Thus Spake Zarathustra*, with his poetic and metaphoric description of the assassination of God—the mad man crying [in fact, lamenting] in the streets, "God is dead"[330]—has caused so much confusion in these matters. In *The Twilight of Idols*, Nietzsche clarifies the confusion himself and tells us what the word "God" meant in *Zarathustra*. It is merely a symbol for the supersensual realm as understood by metaphysics; he now uses instead of "God" the words "true world" and says:

325 *Kalīm* (lit: whom God addressed), a metaphor for Moses and Ṭūr (Mount Sinai) for the self-disclosure of God, the Beyond, the Transcendent.

326 Iqbal, *Bāng i Darā, in Kulliyāt i Iqbāl* (CPW), 275–6/260–1.

327 Iqbal, *Bāng i Darā*, 272/256.

328 Iqbal had termed it as the "crisis of the present age من، روان، فتنۂ عصرِ به دورِ فتنۂ عصرِ روان." (I redress the crisis of the present age). Iqbal, *Armaghān i Ḥijāz*, in *Kulliyāt i Iqbāl* (CPW), Persian, 803/51.

"*Like Rūmī I made the prayer-call in the Sanctuary (the Muslim Community);*
And learned from him the secrets of the soul.
He was meant to take up the challenge of the past age;
I am meant to take up the challenge of this age.

329 [*my age has been enamoured by "water and clay"/ The folk of the Real are in trouble after trouble]*

M. Iqbal, *Pas Cheh Bāyad Kard* in CPW, Persian, (Lahore: Iqbal Academy Pakistan, 1994), 736/60.

330 Iqbal says:

آدمی یزدان کشی آدم پرست　　آدمِ او صورتِ ماہی بہ شست

Its Adam entrapped in the net like a fish/ He has killed God and worships man.

> *"We have abolished the true world. What has remained? The apparent one perhaps? Oh no! With the true world we have also abolished the apparent one."*[331]

In the inimitable words of Rūmī:

> *Reason claims that six dimensions are the limit and there is no way out of these confines*
> *Love says, no, there is a way and often have I gone that way!*

And in Iqbal's words,

> *Western thought has fallen into prostration (i.e., collapsed into abject submission) in front of the metaphorical (sensory, apparent, physical)*
> *Seeing yet blind and enraptured by this play of colours and scent!*
> *East laid waste and the West even more severely ruined.*
> *The world is dead, through and through, and without a penchant for search and inquiry.*[332]

Iqbal continued to honour science for what it tells us about nature, but as that is not all that exists, science cannot provide us with a worldview—not a valid one. The most it can show us is half of the world, but as emphasized by Huston Smith,[333] the other half pertaining to normative and intrinsic values, existential and ultimate meanings, teleology, qualities, immaterial realities, and beings that are superior to us do not appear.

Empiricism and mechanism being ill-suited to deal with transcendence and the unseen, the Promethean epistemology necessarily conjures for us a naturalistic world. Hannah Arendt stressed this towards the close of her life. "What has come to an end," she wrote, "is the distinction between the sensual and the supersensual, together with the notion, at least as old as Parmenides, that whatever is not given to the senses... is more real, more truthful, more meaningful than what appears; that it is not just beyond sense perception but above the world of the senses."[334] Emphasizing that "what is 'dead' is not only the localization of... 'eternal truths' but the [temporal/eternal, sensual/supersensual] distinction itself" Arendt further argues that once the supersensual realm is discarded, its opposite, the world of appearances as understood for so many centuries, is also annihilated. The sensual, as still understood by the positivists, cannot survive the death of the supersensual.[335]

In all the metaphysical doctrines of the East and premodern West, there is the premise that the physical world, the realm of change and impermanence,

331 Hannah Arendt, "Thinking and Moral Consideration," *Social Research* 38 (Autumn 1971): 240.

332 Note xxi.

333 Smith argues that despite its power, six things slip through the controlled experiments of science. These are values, meanings, final causes, invisibles, qualities, and our superiors. See Huston Smith, *Why Religion Matters*, (Harper, 2001), 194–200.

334 Arendt, "Thinking and Moral Consideration," 240.

335 Arendt, "Thinking and Moral Consideration," 240.

rises out of an unmanifest reality, and that Reality itself is also non-local. Bohm was arguing,[336] that all of reality is interrelational,[337] and it is to be noted that Bohm did not leave the phenomenon of consciousness out of his theory regarding this interconnectedness.[338] Reality merely comprises varying densities of one infinitely self-referential and all-inclusive phenomenon. Iqbal's parallel with Bohm's formulation, which he termed as the "ultimate *ground of all experience"* [read*: phenomenon, physical patterns and events*], despite Bohm's non-theological scientific terminology, would not have been lost on the readers! Where Newtonians and strict materialists had argued that consciousness is an epiphenomenon of matter (consciousness having developed slowly as a by-product of increasingly sophisticated stages of biological evolution), Bohm wondered if it might not be the other way around—perhaps material creation is actually an epiphenomenon of consciousness. He was arguing that there is a facet of reality that science cannot see. Like Schrodinger, Bohm was saying that the best understanding of the universe necessitated the acceptance of the view that reality has a metaphysical aspect, an aspect that could never be directly quantified or measured, though its effects in the realm of time and space could be. And this is precisely what Iqbal had proposed with reference to the Qur'ānic verse "*He is the First (Al-Awwal) and the last (Al-Ākhir) and the Outward (Al-Ẓāhir) and the Inward (Al-Bāṭin),*[339] a line of thinking which later thinkers also took up in their deliberations.

It was ironic that at this time when metaphysics had been barred from philosophy and psychology and was not taken seriously in the academic study of religion, it was being legitimately considered in the discipline of physics, the hardest of the hard sciences. Einstein had suggested changes in Newton's view of a three-dimensional universe floating in linear time with a four-dimensional space-time continuum where matter and energy are transposable. [340] History shows that even though the Newtonian worldview may be spurious—indeed a "myth" in the pejorative sense of this equivocal term—it has nonetheless functioned brilliantly as a scientific paradigm. It appears that error, too, has its use![341] Suffice it to say that the Newtonian scheme had extended its sway

336 In accord with *Advaita* ('non-dual,' or even 'non-local') Vedanta.

337 A differentiation must be made between interconnectedness and interrelatedness. Suffices to say here that while interconnectedness relates to the subtle though corporeal domain, interrelational signifies the unmanifest and the metaphysical aspect of reality.

338 In fact, Bohm had devoted two full chapters of his book to a discussion of the nature of consciousness, arguing that as matter and energy were once treated as separate entities, along with space and time, perhaps nothing, including consciousness and matter, is ultimately separate from anything else.

339 Iqbal, "The Philosophic Test of the Revelations of Religious Experience," Lecture 2, in *Reconstruction*, 26.

340 One of the three "presiding paradigms" the Newtonian, upheld the notion of a mechanical world or clockwork universe. What exists, supposedly, is "bare matter," the parts of which interact through forces of attraction or repulsion, so that the movement of the whole is determined by the disposition of the parts.

341 Science in the modern sense would never have "gotten off the ground" without the benefit of a worldview which is drastically oversimplified. The success of this dubious paradigm has been spectacular

beyond the bounds of mechanics, as commonly understood, to include electromagnetism, which, as it turns out, cannot be pictured in grossly mechanical terms.[342] However, the luck of the Newtonian paradigm began to run out with the advent of quantum mechanics, which strictly speaking is not a mechanics at all. The whole, it now turns out, is no longer reducible to its infinitesimal parts. At the same time, and indeed as a consequence of this irreducibility, the new so-called mechanics proves not to be deterministic: the rather odd and philosophically difficult notion of probability has now entered the picture in a fundamental and irreplaceable way.[343] This is not to say that our present ideas about physics will prove to be the last word; but whatever the future may bring, it is safe to conclude that a return to mechanism is not on the cards.

Quantum mechanics had suggested that the universe isn't built out of atoms or any other absolute or indivisible particles, but rather is a complex interaction of energetic processes arising from pure potentiality (the "storehouses" [*khazā'in*)]of the Qur'ān, the Hidden Treasure of Hadith, the Divine Ground of Being, the Brahma[344] and, "the ultimate ground of all experience" [read physical patterns and events]"[345] of Iqbal). The universe, composed of interrelational vibratory events, is more like a cosmic interference pattern than a structure comprising discrete material objects. In fact, with reference to objects, quantum physics was—*and is*—entirely undermining the materialists' viewpoint, and so Bohm was simply adding support to this position. Even he came to see that his views had a definite resonance with certain ancient viewpoints.[346]

---

and unprecedented. From the publication of Newton's Principia in 1687 to the beginning of the 20th century, it was regarded, not simply as a paradigm, but indeed as the master key which in principle unlocks all the secrets of Nature, from the motion of the stars and planets to the functioning of her minutest parts.

342 Yet even here, in this "aetherial" domain, the notion of a whole rigorously reducible to its infinitesimal parts has proved once again to be the key: the famous Maxwell field equations testify to this fact. What is more, even the revolutionary proposals of Albert Einstein, which did break with some of the basic Newtonian conceptions, have left the foundational paradigm intact: here too, in this sophisticated post-Newtonian physics, we are left with a physical universe which can in principle be described with perfect accuracy in terms of a system of differential equations. In a vastly extended sense, the Einsteinian universe is still mechanical. It is mechanical, in fact, precisely because it conforms to what we have termed the Newtonian paradigm, which captures the very essence of mechanism.

343 It is no wonder that Albert Einstein – the greatest and loftiest among the advocates of mechanism – was profoundly dismayed, and staunchly refused to accept quantum theory as the fundamental physics. Yet everything we know today does point to that conclusion. For an interesting overview of Einstein's attitude see Wolfgang Smith: https://youtu.be/71i22w5G9KE.

344 In order to avoid all confusion, it should be observed that the word *Brahma,* without an accent, is neuter while the word *Brahma* is masculine; the use, current among orientalists, of the single form *Brahman,* which is common to both genders, has the serious disadvantage of obscuring this essential distinction, which is sometimes further marked by expressions such as *Pāra-Brahma* or the "Supreme Brahma," and *Apāra-Brahma or* the "non-supreme; Brahma."

345 As we shall see in due course, Iqbal has used the word "*experience*" in his *Reconstruction* interchangeably for "events," "phenomenon" or "entified existence."

346 And later in his life he would discuss these similarities with mystics of several traditions, most notably with Jiddu Krishnamurti, the Indian holy man.

Iqbal was the sage who, while reformulating the classical perspective of the Islamic tradition on the nature of reality, both in his prose and poetry, offered fresh insights about how religion and science are to get along. "Science can prove nothing about God, because God lies outside its province. But ... its resources for deepening religious insights and enriching religious thinking are inexhaustible."[347] This remark from Huston Smith would accurately describe Iqbal's methodology, in his *The Reconstruction of Religious Thought in Islam* in particular, on the issue of the relationship between religion and science. And we hasten to add here another warning from Huston Smith: "We must be careful here, for science cannot take a single step toward proving transcendence. But what it proves in its own domain in the way of unity, inter-relatedness, the 'immaterial,' and the awesome makes it one of the most powerful symbols of transcendence our age affords."[348]

Iqbal was a man whose thought was focused on God, intensely engaged with life of the Spirit. His entire project, in broad terms, related to the task of restoring God to the public and the private sphere. Through his first-hand encounter with the paradigm of modernity in the West, especially at Cambridge, he had developed a deep insight into the worldview of modernity and the overarching perspective that governed this important conceptual shift brought about in human thought, refusing to fall prey to the colonizing effects of his western education and the intellectual hegemony of the militantly secular post-Enlightenment paradigm that was the hallmark of late high modernity. He also had a tremendous capability of bringing different, even conflicting, perspectives into conversation. He was keenly aware of the ills of modernity and, in a sense, presaged the debates that took centre stage after the advent of postmodernism and are even ardently pursued in present-day academia in the context of the human sciences as well as their relationship to religion and science. A large part of his poetical and prose works is focused on the deficiencies and shortcomings of the worldview of modernity and its radical departure from the "human collectivity" with regard to the view of reality of which we can speak for the entire premodern world in the singular and may claim that a common metaphysical "spine" underlies the differences in the worldviews, the theologies of the classical languages of the human soul, the world's great religions or wisdom traditions. He was also sensitive to and clearly conscious of the limitations of the sources of wisdom at the disposal of the worldview of modernity and its inadequacy to map certain regions of reality, to register certain types/modes of knowledge and to successfully deal with and provide guidance for certain aspects of human life. Iqbal had something to offer to philosophy, he had something to offer to science and he has something to

347 Smith, *Why Religion Matters*, 137.
348 Huston Smith, *Beyond the Post-Modern Mind* (Quest Books, 1989), 100.

offer to religion, that is, to repair the ills in their respective domains by taping at the sources of wisdom offered by tradition. He articulated the best Muslim response to modernity in the twentieth century Islamic world. His response has two dimensions:

- A creative engagement with the conceptual paradigm of modernism at a sophisticated philosophical level through his prose writings, mainly his *The Reconstruction of Religious Thought in Islam* which presents his basic philosophic insights.
- His Urdu and Persian poetry which is the best embodiment of poetically mediated thought, squarely in the traditional continuity of Islamic literature and perhaps the finest flowering of wisdom poetry, or contemplative poetry or inspired poetry in the modern times.

Bohm's views, developed through his laboratory experiments spanned over a period of thirty years, supported the theory that the universe has a metaphysical aspect. In fact, Bohm described a transcendent level of reality that sounded almost identical—*if not identical*—to Eckhart's and Aldous Huxley's "Divine Ground of Being," as well as Hinduism's *Brahma* and, to our astonishment, to the Iqbalian "…..*the ultimate ground of all experience*"[349] the Immanent-Infinite (Iqbal's Model of the Ultimate Reality).[350] We would have occasion to say more about it later but let us first have a look at what Bohm had to say about the matter.

Bohm published his landmark book, *Wholeness and the Implicate Order*, in 1980, in which he presented a distillation of a theory he had been working on for more than thirty years. He had been nudged towards his revolutionary views by the unusual behaviour of quantum entities called photons. In brief, the aspect that intrigued Bohm was this: if two related photons of light (related because they result from the splitting of the same *positron,* which is a larger quantum entity) are traveling in opposite directions, they somehow maintain the same angles of polarization (basically, the same orientation in space relative to their point of origin) no matter how far apart they travel in space, or even if one of them is affected by an outside force along the way. For example, if a scientist changes the orientation of one of the photons, the other one will instantaneously be found to have the same new angle of polarization.[351]

349 Iqbal, *Reconstruction*, 50. Iqbal has used the word "*experience*" in his *Reconstruction* interchangeably for "events," "phenomenon" or "entified existence" as in the quote given at note 44.

350 "In fact, the logical understanding is incapable of seeing this multiplicity as a coherent universe. Its only method is generalization based on resemblances, but its generalizations are only fictitious unities which do not affect the reality of concrete things. In its deeper movement, however, thought is capable of reaching an immanent Infinite in whose self-unfolding movement the various finite concepts are merely moments." Iqbal, *Reconstruction*, 5.

351 For this game-changing concept, see Jean Borella and Wolfgang Smith, *Rediscovering the Integral Cosmos, Physics, Metaphysics, and Vertical Causality* (Angelico Press, 2018), *passim*.

This phenomenon was proven conclusively by experiment two years later, in 1982, at the Institute of Optics at the University of Paris. It had already been accepted as most likely even at the beginning of Bohm's career, and what drew Bohm's attention—and everyone else's—was that it seemed to present a contradiction to Einstein's theory that nothing could travel faster than the speed of light. This idea of one photon changing its orientation in summary with another seemed to suggest a sort of instantaneous communication between two distant objects. Instantaneous occurs outside the realm of speed altogether, let alone faster than the speed of light. For Bohm, who agreed with Einstein that nothing was likely to break light speed, this phenomenon of the "communicating" photons suggested that quantum theory must somehow be incomplete (almost the same as what Iqbal had said in 1929),[352] that perhaps a better theory could resolve or explain away what appeared to be a contradiction from inside the current view. Maybe nothing could travel faster than light but instantaneous communication is somehow also possible.

Bohm began to draft a new and broader perspective, and after more than two decades finally arrived at his theory, arguing that quantum reality is based on what he termed an "implicate order." His view was that there is a fundamental but *unobservable* level of order in the universe that gives rise to all observable phenomena, including not only light photons but, at higher magnitudes of reality, humans, trees and inanimate matter, which Rūmī had termed as "Dust and wind, water and fire, are servants; dead for you and me, but alive with the Real" [353] and which Iqbal had versified in myriad ways:

> *It is Thine glimpse that manifests in the moon, the sun, the star*
> *It is Your luminous radiance that clearly appears in the lightning, the fire, the spark.*[354]

The underlying level, which he termed the "enfolded order" (synonymous with what others have termed the "quantum potential"), sometimes "unfolds" into discrete quantum moments of physical being. However, Bohm believed that on the "enfolded" level, where nothing is manifest as an observable entity, all things are really part of one thing—though this thing is not a thing at all, at least not in the Newtonian sense.[355] Bohm described it as an "implicate order" that underlies the "explicate order" of the physical universe. He theorized that as various quanta emerge from it, they retain some characteristics of their implicate and infinitely interconnected original state. The beauty of this theory for the problem of those pesky photons that seem to instantaneously

352 Iqbal's critique of Einstein in: *Reconstruction*, 31–32; 106.

353 خاک و باد و آب و آتش بنده اند با من و تو مرده ، با حق زنده اند *Mathnawī* (Nicholson edition), book III, 30.

354 Iqbal, *Reconstruction of Religious Thought.*

355 Known in the language of Far Eastern metaphysic as the distinction between "Non-Being" and "Being" or, nearer home, as "Being" and "Beyond Being."

communicate with each other was that it allowed for the photons to exist as discrete particles on one level of their being (as they moved away from each other in the explicate order) but explained how they could also change their orientation simultaneously. On the explicate level, the photons were in cahoots simply because they still retained characteristics of the implicate level from which they had emerged. They were not communicating across a vast distance at a speed greater than light; they were simply behaving as the one thing they fundamentally were on the implicate level of existence.

This summary is a redacted explanation of Bohm's theory in his *Wholeness and the Implicate Order* and intends to illustrate the components of Bohm's work that are in sync with Iqbal's views that he expounded with reference to the Qur'ānic verse "He is the First (*Al-Awwal*) and the last (*Al-Ākhir*) and the Outward (*Al-Ẓāhir*) and the Inward (*Al-Bāṭin*)."[356] First and foremost, it contains the premise that there is a level of things that transcends physical reality and this level of quantum potentiality not only exists but is the foundation for all existence, a view which sounds very much like the doctrines from Vedanta, Christian Mystical Theology, Kabbalah, Islamic Metaphysics, the Far Eastern Doctrines, Muslim sages, Sufis and mystics and Iqbal who had combined in himself the characteristics of a mystic and a metaphysician. Though the presence of the implicate order is strongly suggested by the behaviour of quantum entities like split photons, it cannot, because of its implicit and unmanifest nature, be quantified directly by scientific methods, since there is nothing to "see" with the tools of science. This concept also chimes with the claims of mystics, (in Iqbal's words: "religious experts in all ages and countries."[357]) who had written that the purest level of Being exists beyond both time and space. No creature is identifiable with "God-the-Outward," who in Himself is Existence, Life and Consciousness. He is also space, time, form, number, matter and their positive contents, the perceptible reflections of the Divine Qualities.[358] *Al-Ẓāhir* assumes forms, life and other contingencies without becoming confused with this or that; that is to say that He is all that exists, but nothing in particular; we see Him, because He is "the Outward," while yet not seeing Him, because He is God "the Outward."

If one tries to fathom Bohm's view of Reality more deeply, the points of resonance with the traditional/religious views keep mounting. For example, Bohm's theory supported and expressed the notion that the universe, at least at its quantum level, is *non-local,* meaning, in the jargon of physics,[359] that

356 Qur'ān, 41:53.

357 Iqbal, *Reconstruction of Religious Thought*, 146.

358 Excepting the Prophets–whence the testimony 'He who has seen me has seen God' (*Al-Ḥaqq*, 'the Truth' or 'the Reality')– and the sacred symbols such as the letters and sounds of the Divine Names, or the great phenomena of nature or some of them, depending on the Revelation or traditional perspective involved.

359 Also argued earlier by John Stewart Bell.

the events and entities we encounter in the explicate order are not ultimately autonomous or disconnected. Bohm argued that at the implicate level, all knowledge of the universe is stored as pure potentiality in a state of "dynamic vacuum," ("the infinite inner possibilities of the infinity of the Ultimate Ego" in Iqbal's formulation[360] and "immutable entities" of Ibn 'Arabī[361]) and at that level, where there are no observable phenomena, reality is entirely non-local and non-temporal. On that enfolded level, it is Oneness—or None-ness' (since it's difficult to speak of a singularity from which nothing can be separate, including a place from which to observe its oneness)—that then unfolds into physical patterns and events. The closer we get to the subtlest and most implicate level of Reality, events express themselves with increasing degrees of profoundly interconnected, self-referential, and therefore "non-local" behaviour.

The idea of pure potentiality, which Bohm attributed to the level of the "implicate order" is in fact a shared metaphysical idea of all civilizations and traditional theologies of the world religions. In Iqbal's words, ".....the ultimate ground of all experience"[362] about which he had said, "Like pearls do we live and move and have our being in the perpetual flow of Divine life."[363] The striking parallel with the Upanishads will not be lost on the readers! "Upon me, these worlds are held/Like pearls strung on a thread" and "The world, in all its details, from the mechanical movement of what we call the atom of matter to the free movement of thought in the human ego, is the self-revelation of the 'Great I am.'"[364]

Ibn 'Arabī's formulation deserves attention here as it is the basis on which Iqbal built his mystical theology. Here is a brief account.

Those things that are "existent" can be "found" in the outside world through our senses. But those things that are "non-existents" cannot be found.

---

360 One of the Iqbal's remarks reads as follows: "The infinity of the Ultimate Ego consists in the infinite inner possibilities of His creative activity of which the universe, as known to us, is only a partial expression. In one word God's infinity is intensive, not extensive. It involves an infinite series, but is not that series." Iqbal, *Reconstruction*, 52.

361 One of the more common and probably best-known terms that Ibn al-'Arabī employs for the nonexistent objects of God's knowledge is "immutable entity" (*'ayn thābita*). Entity with him is synonymous with "thing" (*shay'*), and "thing," as should be apparent from the way he employs the term all along, is "one of the most indefinite of the indefinites" (*min ankar al-nakirāt*), since it can be applied to anything whatsoever, existent or nonexistent (though it is not normally applied to God as Being). The "existent things" are the creatures of the cosmos (though never ceasing to be nonexistent objects of God's knowledge). The "nonexistent things" are objects of knowledge, also called the "immutable entities."

362 Iqbal, *Reconstruction*, 50.

363 Underlying the human self and animating it is a reservoir of being that never dies, is never exhausted, and is unrestricted in consciousness and bliss. This infinite centre of every life, this hidden self, is no less than the Godhead. Body, personality, and this infinite centre– a human self is not completely accounted for until all three are noted. That was not only Iqbal's fundamental position, as reflected in this quatrain, but the shared "anthropocosmic" vision of all wisdom traditions of the world.

364 This is reference to Qur'ān, 20:14. The statement continues: "Every atom of Divine energy, however low in the scale of existence, is an ego. But there are degrees in the expression of egohood." Iqbal, *Reconstruction*, 57–58.

However, they are not pure nothingness, since "nonexistence" is an ambiguous category, not too much different from existence. The nonexistence of the things is clearly a relative (*iḍāfī*) matter. For example, a person may claim that galaxies are non-existent, and in relationship to his understanding, this may be a true statement. On another level, your fantasies are non-existent for me, existent for you. On the cosmic level, any creature which can be found in the outside world is existent if it continues to be found there. But when it is destroyed or dies or decays, it ceases to be found in its original form, so it is non-existent. Any creature that God has not yet brought into existence is also non-existent, though it certainly exists in some mode, since it is an object of God's knowledge. It is "found" with God. He knows that He will bring it into the cosmos at a certain time and place, so it exists with Him, but is non-existent in the cosmos. Ibn 'Arabī employs the term "objects of [God's] knowledge" (*ma'lūmāt*) synonymously with the term "non-existent things." Both terms denote things or creatures as found with God "before" or "after" they have existed in the cosmos. However, it needs to be kept in mind that these things never "leave" God's knowledge, so everything existent in the cosmos at this moment is also a "non-existent object of knowledge." Here again its situation is ambiguous. هو / الهو — He / Not He.

> *Don't take the kneading of my clay to be done with, in all eternity;*
> *Because we are as yet the khayāl*[365] *in the hidden core of Being.*

Only Being—the Necessary Being—is absolutely unquestionable and unambiguous. But since It is utterly free of every limitation that can be applied to anything else, we can only know It by negating from It all the ambiguities of "that which is other than Being." Things, immutable entities, existent entities, acts, creatures, existents, non-existents, possible things, and anything else we can name are in themselves "Not He." This is what might be called God's radical transcendence, His utter and absolute incomparability. From this point of view, true knowledge of God can only come through negation. This is the classical position of much of Islamic theology, but, however essential and true, it must be complemented—in Ibn al-'Arabī's view—with the acknowledgment that the acts do possess a certain derivative actuality and existence, all the more so since we are situated in their midst and cannot ignore them. Everything other than God is Not He, which means that everything other than God is not Reality, not Being, not Finding, not Knowledge, not Power, etc. Nevertheless, we do "find" the effects of these attributes in the existent things, and this lets

365 This is the Iqbalian formulation of the Sufi metaphysical idea of the projection of the Principle towards manifestation presented through the quasi standard trope of all Persian wisdom poetry, according to which "all entified existence is nothing but the existentiated objects of God's eternal knowledge (*khayāl*), receiving His self-disclosures through the dispersal of His Divine Names." For *khayāl* and its various shades of meaning in Ibn 'Arabī and the larger Islamic tradition see, William C. Chittick, *The Sufi Path of Knowledge, Ibn Al-'Arabī's Metaphysics of Imagination* (State University of New York Press, 1989).

us know that He is present. "We are nearer to [man] than the jugular vein" (Qur'ān 50:16). "Whithersoever you turn, there is the Face of God" (2:115).[366]

One of the formulations of Ibn ʿArabī for the non-existent objects of God's knowledge is "immutable entity" (*ʿayn thābita*). Entity with him is synonymous with "thing" (*shay'*), and "thing," as should be apparent from the way he employs the term all along, is "one of the most indefinite of the indefinites" (*min ankar al-nakirāt*), since it can be applied to anything whatsoever, existent or non-existent (though it is not normally applied to God as Being). The "existent things" are the creatures of the cosmos (though never ceasing to be non-existent objects of God's knowledge). The "non-existent things" are objects of knowledge, also called the "immutable entities." These things or entities are immutable because they never change, just as God's knowledge never changes. He knows them for all eternity. This point is crucial so I detail it here.

God's Being is Necessary Being. Therefore, all other entities, in their *faqr wujūdī*[367] or *iftiqār wujūdī* "ontological indigence,"[368] depend on Him for their existence,[369] or all the things in the created order have some form of existence, which is, in a way, "borrowed" from God.[370] But how, exactly, does God's Being differ from that of the rest of the created order? Ibn ʿArabī tells us that God's existence has two aspects: non-manifest Being and manifest Being: God reported about Himself that He possesses two relationships: a relationship with the cosmos through the Divine Names which affirm the entities of the cosmos, and the relationship of His independence from the cosmos. In respect of His relationship of independence, He knows Himself and we know Him not.[371]

All that we can say about God's non-manifest Being is that it "is" God's Essence (*dhāt*). Ibn ʿArabī calls it "most indefinite of the indefinites" (*ankar al-nakirāt*).[372] In other words, God's non-manifest Being is only known to Him and, as in the case of the *Tao* that transcends speech, cannot be spoken of in any determinate fashion whatsoever. The cosmos, on the other hand, is brought about by God's manifestation through His Divine Names. It is God's manifest Being (*Al-Ẓāhir:* the Outward) that brings about existence, not His Absolute, non-manifest Being (*Al-Bāṭin*: the Inward). On the other hand, things that can never come into any type of existence are the exact opposite

---

366 Chittick, *Sufi Path of Knowledge*, 11–12.

367 Qur'ān, 35:15.

368 Muḥyi 'l-Dīn Ibn al-ʿArabī, *al-Futuḥāt al-Makkiyyah*, trans. Claude Addas, in *The Voyage of No Return*, trans. David Streight (Cambridge University Press, 2000), 29.

369 "He is petitioned by those who are in the heavens and on earth: every day bringeth He things to pass." Qur'ān, 55:29.

370 William C. Chittick, *The Self-Disclosure of God: Principles of Ibn al-ʿArabī's Cosmology* (State University of New York Press, 1998), 12–13.

371 Ibn al-ʿArabī, *Futuḥāt*, 2:533.4, trans. Chittick, in *Sufi Path*, 64.

372 Ibn al-ʿArabī, *Fuṣūṣ al-Ḥikam*, 188, trans. Toshihiko Izutsu in *Sufism and Taoism*, 2nd edition (Berkeley: University of California Press, 1983), 23. At 36n1 Izutsu notes that in another passage on the same page of the Fuṣūṣ, the Shaykh also uses this expression to refer to the word "thing."

of God's non-manifest Being. What lies between Absolute Being and absolute non-being is possible being, which is the realm of the possible existents or possible things. For Ibn al-ʿArabī, the possible things are equivalent to the cosmos or "everything other than God."[373] That is, the possible things, including the "human realm," are in an intermediate state, an isthmus (*barzakh*) between necessary and impossible existence; the situation earlier described as هو / لاهو—He/Not He.

For Ibn ʿArabī, God's knowledge of the cosmos is the same as His knowledge of Himself.[374] This is because nothing, whether it has already existed, is existing, or will exist, can be outside of God's knowledge. Those entities in God's knowledge before they are existentiated, are known as the *al-ʿayn thābita* (the immutable entities).[375] Thus, the things in existence are known to God before they actually exist, since they have always been objects of His knowledge in their fixity. It must be noted that the immutable entities are not the same things as the Platonic forms.[376] The immutable entities are the "things" forever fixed in God's knowledge, whereas Plato's forms act as ontological archetypes for everything (be they concepts or physically existing things) in existence.[377]

It should also be noted that the immutable entities, like the actual existent possible things, are always in a state of possibility and, thus, are relatively non-existent.[378] But, when they become entified, they take on relative existence.[379] When God wants to existentiate them, He orders them to become through the divine *fiat* expressed in the Qurʾān: *Be!* (35:7). This is an act of kindness since the possible things begged (petitioned)[380] God for existence: "They ask the Necessary Being with the tongue of their immutability to bring their entities into existence, so that their knowledge may become tasting. Hence He brings them into existence for themselves, not for Himself."[381] But, if as Ibn ʿArabī tells us, there is nothing in being but God's Being, and the things are existentiated by the divine *fiat*, what is the difference between their state in their immutability and their "existing" as entities? In terms of their fixity, there is no difference. However, each immutable entity, when existentiated, acts as a locus (*maẓhar*) for God's manifestation (*ẓuhūr*) or self-disclosure (*tajallī*) as Ibn ʿArabī himself explains in the *Futuḥāt*.[382]

373 Ibn al-ʿArabī, *Futuḥāt*, 2:248.24, trans. Chittick, in *Sufi Path*, 87.
374 Ibn al-ʿArabī, *Futuḥāt*, 1:90.23, trans. Chittick, in *Sufi Path*, 84.
375 Chittick, in *Sufi Path of Knowledge*, 83–84.
376 Chittick, in *Sufi Path of Knowledge*, 84.
377 Chittick, in *Sufi Path of Knowledge*, 84.
378 Izutsu, *Sufism and Taoism*, 161.
379 Addas, *Voyage of No Return*, 88.
380 "He is petitioned by those who are in the heavens and on earth: every day bringeth He things to pass." Qurʾān, 55:29.
381 Ibn al-ʿArabī, *Futuḥāt*, 3:306.19, trans. Chittick, in *Sufi Path*, 86.
382 "The existence of the possible thing is necessary through Him, since it is His locus of manifestation, and He is manifest within it. The possible entity is concealed (*mastūr*) by the Manifest within it. So,

Although there are many loci of manifestation, it is God's *wujūd* that permeates all of them. Along with this, Ibn 'Arabī upholds the idea put forth before his time, that the divine self-disclosure never repeats itself. Because of His Divine Vastness, God continually creates, perpetually permeating the cosmos with His *wujūd.* This is why Ibn 'Arabī speaks of creation as being in a state of perpetual renewal (*tajdīd al-khalq*). Iqbal has faithfully followed Ibn 'Arabī in this regard.[383]

manifestation and the Manifest become qualified by possibility." Ibn al-'Arabī, *Futuḥāt*, 2:56.16, trans. Chittick, in *Sufi Path*, 90.

383 Also see his *Reconstruction* where he has a lot more to say on the point: "From another point of view, the process of creation, lasting through thousands of years, is a single indivisible act, "*swift as the twinkling of an eye*" (54:49–50).

Bibliography

Arendt, Hannah. “Thinking and Moral Consideration.” *Social Research* 38 (1971): 417–446.

Berger, Peter L. “Secularism in Retreat.” *The National Interest* 46 (1996): 3–12.

Bohm, David. *Wholeness and the Implicate Order.* London: Routledge, 1980.

Borella, Jean, and Wolfgang Smith. *Rediscovering the Integral Cosmos, Physics, Metaphysics, and Vertical Causality.* Brooklyn, NY: Angelico Press, 2018.

Chittick, William C. “Traditional Islamic Thought and the Challenge of Scientism.” *Spektrum Iran* (2004).

Chittick, William C. *The Self-Disclosure of God: Principles of Ibn al-ʿArabī's Cosmology.* State University of New York Press, 1998.

Chittick, William C. *The Sufi Path of Knowledge, Ibn Al-ʿArabī's Metaphysics of Imagination.* State University of New York Press, 1989.

Ibn al-ʿArabī, Muḥyi ʾl-Dīn. *al-Futuḥāt al-Makkiyyah*, translated by Claude Addas. In *The Voyage of No Return*, translated by David Streight. Cambridge University Press, 2000.

Ibn al-ʿArabī, Muḥyi ʾl-Dīn. *Fuṣūṣ al-Ḥikam*. In *Sufism and Taoism* by Toshihiko Izutsu. 2nd ed. Berkeley: University of California Press, 1983.

Iqbal, Muhammad. *Kulliyāt i Iqbāl* (Collected Poetical Works=CPW), Urdu. Lahore: Iqbal Academy Pakistan, 2007.

Iqbal, Muhammad. *Kulliyāt i Iqbāl* (Collected Poetical Works=CPW), Persian. Lahore: Iqbal Academy Pakistan, 1994.

Iqbal, Muhammad. *The Reconstruction of Religious Thought in Islam.* Lahore: Iqbal Academy, 1986.

Smith, Huston. *Beyond the Post-Modern Mind.* Wheaton, IL: Quest Books, 1989.

Smith, Huston. *Why Religion Matters.* New York: Harper, 2001.

Chapter 9

Osman Bakar and the Dialogue with Chinese Civilization and Philosophies

Nevad Kahteran

Faculty of Philosophy, University of Sarajevo,
Bosnia and Herzegovina

Part I

A quick search in www.academia.edu shows 13,202 papers making references to Osman Bakar's works. His own website, "A Voyage Into The Realm Of The Intellect (The Website Of Osman Bakar),"[384] testifies to his deep immersion in academic life since the publication of his doctoral thesis.[385] Osman's call for dialogue and cooperation between civilizations has gained him global recognition. His works have up to now been translated into Arabic, French, Indonesian, Spanish, Bosnian and Urdu. He was honored with the title Dato' in 1994 by the Sultan of Pahang and then the title Datuk by HM the King of Malaysia in 2000. This was a token of gratitude for his service to Islam in the Malay world, which is the gate of Asia, and his own great scientific endeavors and achievements.[386]

I first met Osman when he was the Malaysia Chair of Islam in Southeast Asia at the Center for Muslim-Christian Understanding, Georgetown

---

384 https://obbakar.wordpress.com/about/; as well as https://ubd.academia.edu/OsmanBakar.

385 His doctoral dissertation entitled 'Classification of the Sciences in Islamic Intellectual History' under the supervision of Seyyed Hossein Nasr was presented to Temple University, Philadelphia in 1987,, and it was published under the title: Classification of Knowledge in Islam.

386 See his own website: https://obbakar.wordpress.com/about/, accessed June 6, 2021.

Also see: Osman Bakar, "Towards a Postmodern Synthesis of Islamic Science and Modern Science: The Epistemological Groundwork," in *The Muslim 500: The World's 500 Most Influential Muslims*, 2020 (Amman, Jordan: The Royal Islamic Strategic Studies Centre, 2019), 197–201; "Dialogue for the Future between Japan and the Islamic World," *ICR Journal* 3, no. 4 (2012); "Eighth Annual Seminar on 'Dialogue of Civilisation' Between Japan and the Islamic World," *ICR Journal* 1, no. 4 (2010); "Cultural Pluralism in a Globalised World: Challenges to Peaceful Coexistence," *ICR Journal* 1, no. 3 (2010); "Islam and the Challenge of Diversity and Pluralism: Must Islam Reform Itself?" *ICR Journal* 1, no. 1 (2009); "The Spirit of Islamic Science in Hokkaido Science Symposium," *IAIS Journal of Civilisation Studies* 1, no. 1 (2008): 203–207.

University in Washington. This was upon an invitation I received from Professor John L. Esposito in 2003 to deliver a lecture on Bosnian thought and multicultural relations, which was expanded into a book.[387] I found out that Osman studied under the supervision of our *ustaz-muhtaram* (esteemed professor), Seyyed Hossein Nasr, whose thought permeates Bakar's work and serves as a connecting point between us. I learnt from the works of Osman that dialogue between civilizations is possible through science.[388] The chief aim of Islamic philosophy of science in the modern period, of which Bakar is one of the best proponents and in line with Nasr's philosophy, is to bridge the gaps between Islam and the rest of humankind.[389]

As the pioneering proponent of comparative philosophy in Bosnia and an admirer of Osman, I find it necessary to establish a critical discourse between different philosophical systems to broaden our philosophical horizons and expand the possibilities for better understanding to establish international peace. Multicultural communities like Bosnia and Malaysia are in dire need of inter-traditional, intercultural, inter-system, integrative and global studies, beyond the prevalent cult of the nation with the idea of the philosophical resonance and complementarity of different philosophical positions at its core. Such a discourse will encourage the dialectics of intercultural logos.

Osman's stature as one of the foremost contemporary Muslim philosophers of science and how he used science as a vehicle for inter-civilizational dialogue has been examined by Katherine Nielsen. She looked at Osman's attempts at promoting an inter-civilizational dialogue between two cultural blocs: Islamic and Chinese. Indeed, Osman sees the Muslim world as a land bridge between Europe, Asia, and Africa which makes it an ideal mediator of inter-civilizational dialogue. Osman employs philosophical schools of thought from other civilizations, namely the Greek, Chinese, Indian, and Islamic traditions, to develop his own brand of philosophy of science. He agrees with Nasr's position on the desecularization of Western science and the recovery of all that is sacred in nature.

Here, I wish to focus on a specific example of inter-civilizational dialogue which Osman delved into in an edited book titled *Islam and Confucianism*.[390] For me personally, from the Islamic point of view, this is one of the most important books alongside with Tu Weiming's *The Sage Learning of Liu Zhi:*

387 Nevad Kahteran, *Situating the Bosnian Paradigm: The Bosnian Experience of Multicultural Relations* (New York: Global Scholarly Publications, 2008).

388 See: Katherine Nielsen, "The Philosophy of Osman bin Bakar," *International Studies in the Philosophy of Science* 22, no. 1 (2008): 81–95.

389 See: *The Philosophy of Seyyed Hossein Nasr*, vol. 28 (Chicago: Open Court, 2001), and Osman Bakar, "Nature as a Sacred Book: A Core Element of Seyyed Hossein Nasr's Philosophical Teachings," *Sacred Web* 40 (2017): 75–101.

390 Cheng Gek Nai and Osman Bakar, eds., *Islam and Confucianism: A Civilizational Dialogue* (Kuala Lumpur: ISTAC-IIUM Publications, 2019, New Edition).

Islamic Thought in Confucian Terms[391] and Sachiko Murata's magnificent opus in this field of Sino-Islamic scholarship.[392] In the Indian context, we have Fathullah Mujtabai's (2007) *Hindu-Muslim Cultural Relations,*[393] and Reza Shah Kazemi's (2010) *Common Ground Between Islam and Buddhism.*[394] Like these scholars, Osman explores the history, contributions, and potentials of different civilizations in fostering dialogue and cultural renaissance.

As the Bosnian pioneer in the field of Eastern and Comparative philosophy, I too promote the cultivation of a new philosophy that cuts across the classical borders and that promotes universality and openness to a multitude of cultural and intellectual histories. Inspired by Osman's ground-breaking work, *Islam and Confucianism* which I have translated into Bosnian,[395] I wish to underline here the importance of studying Chinese philosophy and Chinese Muslim contributions to Islamic thought. This will pave the way for the establishment of an Islamic-Confucian-Daoist dialogue in the Balkans, for the region to join hands with what has already been done by the Islamic community from the easternmost Islamic frontier, or Malay-Indonesian world.[396] Broadening philosophical horizons will heighten intercultural exchange between senior and younger researchers in the two regions.

To be sure, Professors Osman and Tu Weiming once visited Ljubljana on behalf of the UN to enhance civilizational dialogue in the aftermath of the war in former Yugoslavia, almost thirty years ago. Unfortunately, the tunnel-vision of our nationalist leaders prevented any kind of peaceful solution for the ex-YU countries. Later in April 2016, a project known as *Islam-Confucian Dialogue in the Balkans and the Malay-Indonesian World: Comparative Philosophical Perspectives* was proposed with SOASCIS as a follow-up to an earlier publication on the topic.[397] I was supposed to be affiliated at UBD as a visiting profes-

---

391 Harvard-Yenching Institute monograph series 65 (2009).

392 See: *The Tao of Islam: A Sourcebook on Gender Relationships in Islamic Thought* (SUNY Press, 1992); *Chinese Gleams of Sufi Light: Wang Tai-yü's Great Learning of the Pure and Real and Liu Chih's Displaying the Concealment of the Real Realm* (SUNY Press, 2000); and with the collaboration of William C. Chittick and Tu Weiming, *The Sage Learning of Liu Zhi: Islamic Thought in Confucian Terms* (Harvard University Press, 2009).

393 *HINDUSKO-MUSLIMANSKE kulturne relacije,* trans. Nevad Kahteran (Filozofski fakultet UNSA, Sarajevo, 2020), 154, http://www.ff-eizdavastvo.ba/Books/HINDUSKO-MUSLIMANSKE_kulturne_relacije.pdf.

394 Reza Shah-Kazemi, *Common Ground Between Islam and Buddhism* (Verlag: Fons Vitae, 2010).

395 See Bosnian Translation of *Islam and Confucianism: A Civilizational Dialogue*: Osman Bakar and Cheng Gek Nai, eds., *Islam i konfucijanstvo: civilizacijski dijalog* 伊斯兰教与儒家：不同文明之间的对话, trans. Nevad Kahteran (Sarajevo: El-Kalem, 2018), 318, http://www.elkalem.ba/Islam%20i%20konfucijanstvo.

396 Nevad Kahteran, *Platforma za islamsko-konfucijansko-daoistički dijalog na Balkanu* ("伊斯兰教一儒家一道家在巴尔干国家中的对话讲坛" (A Platform for Islamic-Confucian-Daoist Dialogue in the Balkans), (Sarajevo: ITD Sedam, 2010), 155.

397 See: Osman Bakar, "Balkan Islam and Malay Islam as Branches of Islamic Civilization: An Introductory Discussion of Their Similarities and Differences," in *Islam in Southeast Europe*, ed. Mesut Idriz and Osman Bakar, 1–6 (Bandar Seri Begawan: UBD Press, 2014).

sor at the SOASCIS even though the plan did not materialise due to Osman's health at that time. The project was a continuation of Nasr's observation that:

> Bosnia lies at the heart of the European continent, at once a witness to the reality of Islam, a bridge between the Islamic world and the West and for most of its history a living example of religious accord and harmony between the followers of the Abrahamic religions. Today in a world so much in need of mutual religious and cultural understanding, Bosnia can play an important role far beyond the extent of its geographic size or population, provided it remains faithful to its own universal vision of Islam threatened nowadays by forces both within and outside its borders.[398]

As a matter of retrospection, Osman was planning to have the SOASCIS Annual Conference (SICON 5) in the third week of April 2016 under the theme: "Tradition, Innovation and Entrepreneurship in Islamic Studies in the 21st Century: Issues and Responses." My participation in the conference was supposed to be part of that visit. Even though the event did not take place, I hope that SOASCIS or ISTAC-IIUM would organise a whole series of public lectures that would inevitably stimulate intercultural thinking among Bosnians to bring about a transformation in the study of comparative philosophy in the contemporary world. This would deepen the ongoing Islamic-Confucian dialogue and result in more publications like the one I produced through a Fulbright grant.[399] Osman, in turn, continued to write about Islam and Chinese thought.[400] He explained the sinicization agenda in China as nothing more than the state's attempt at controlling and suppressing religions in China.

The reasons for both of us writing on these topics are straightforward enough. Both Osman and myself believe that the dialogue of various cultures and traditions in the global world is a prerequisite for their survival. These traditions include not just the Abrahamic faiths that are central to the making of Europe, but other theistic and non-theistic belief systems. As of 2010, at least 80% of the 6.7 billion world's population then humans belonged to four of the world's main religions. Four out of five people on earth are either Christians (32%), Muslim (23%), Hindu (14%), or Buddhist (12%). Dialogue, cross-cultural exchange, and mutual understanding has become more important world-wide. As I once noted: "Tolerance is necessary, but not sufficient. Dialogue is not a panacea either, but, unlike tolerance, at least it provides a prospect for development."[401]

398 S.H. Nasr in his Preface to our Bosnian translation of his *The Heart of Islam: Enduring Values for Humanity / Srce islama: trajne vrijednosti za čovječanstvo* (Sarajevo: El-Kalem, 2002).

399 Kahteran, *Situating the Bosnian Paradigm*.

400 See: Osman Bakar, "Islam in China and the Challenge of Sinicization of Religion: Past and Present," in *The Muslim 500: The World's 500 Most Influential Muslims*, 2021 (Amman: The Royal Islamic Strategic Studies Centre, 2020), 233–237.

401 Nevad Kahteran, "Recognizing a model of postmodern pluralism through looking at Islam from the standpoint of Far Eastern traditions: A Dialogue between Islam, Hinduism, Buddhism, and Confucianism," *SYNTHESIS PHILOSOPHICA* 62, no. 2 (2016): 434.

The above mentioned reflection provides more reasons why scholars must join hands to enhance and deepen our cross-cultural understanding in this increasingly interdependent world. Unfortunately, very few dialogues between Japanese, Chinese, Indian and Islamic traditions have been made. The Truth is one, even if the wise describe it in rather different ways. This idea of the truth is not confined only to our own Abrahamic philosophical and theological traditions but is also promoted by many traditions today, thanks to the rise of postmodern pluralism.[402]

Part II

Islamic and Chinese civilizations have consistently intersected since over a millennium ago. Muslim minorities live in China and Chinese minorities live in Muslim countries such as Malaysia. For Osman, this is why civilizational dialogue is so important. The papers published in his mentioned book were presented at a larger international seminar hosted by the University of Malaya in 1995, for the purposes of civilizational dialogue between Islam and Confucianism. The goals of this seminar, as well as Bakar's own position in relation to civilizational dialogue, were defined as follows:

1. To foster greater mutual understanding among the major world civilizations in general and between Chinese and Islamic cultures and civilizations in particular;
2. To contribute towards a better understanding of the nature and extent of past and present encounters and interactions between the two civilizations;
3. To identify "problem areas" in the contemporary encounter and interaction between Confucianism and Islam, and
4. To suggest ways and means that can be pursued as part of an overall attempt to resolve these contemporary problems.[403]

This framework is in some way a continuation of the efforts of *Han Kitāb* (*Han ketabu* 汉克塔布), authors[404] who led the making of Sino Muslim identity. These published materials offer a vista onto the world of Chinese Muslim literati who produced a collection of over one hundred texts of canonical status. The *Han Kitāb* has been the the basic curriculum within the Chinese Muslim learned community and their own education. This corpus presents the essence of the Chinese form of Islamic knowledge, the rise of the intellectual

402 Kahteran, "Recognizing a Model of Postmodern Pluralism," 437. Also see: Md. Yousuf Ali and Osman Bakar, "Issues of Hindu-Muslim Relations in the Works of Syed Ahmad Khan," *Al-Shajarah* 25, no. 2 (2020): 315–333.

403 Bakar 1997d, 4.

404 This term "Sino Muslim" has a historical relevance of more than 1,300 years in China for a Sinophone Muslim population, upon which a body of Islamic literature written in Chinese three hundred years ago, known as *Han Kitab*.

current in China, which was done through successful "Sinicization" and accommodation. It is our hope that these materials will help to generate a new interest among the people of Bosnia and Herzegovina and the Malay world in the comparative study of Islam and Confucianism. They would be useful in our quest for a new Asia as points of convergence that recognize religious pluralism and multiculturalism and the urgent need for sharable, common values and arguments for pluralism rather than exclusivism, especially among our academic and scholarly community.[405]

Osman argues for the complementariness and acceptability of Confucian ideals within Islamic philosophy. He proposes that this goal can be achieved through the discipline of comparative religion, in which specialists research into both traditions and then present their findings to the general public.[406] He sees the works of "Muslim Confucians" in history as foundational to this dialogue because they lived with both cultures and saw no conflict between them.[407] After introducing Confucianism and its major tenets, Osman concludes with a discussion on whether Confucius was a prophet of Islam. It is believed within the Islamic tradition that Allah sent prophets to many cultures *wa li kulli qawmin resūl* (For every people there is a messenger),[408] *wa li kulli qawmin hādin* (and to every people a guide),[409] and Osman views Confucius potentially as one of these prophets, sent to the Chinese civilization, as he brought codified laws.[410] We are speaking about one fifth of Chinese in the world at one side, and one fifth of Muslims which represents another portion of the world population. The rest of the world have to be engaged in the constructive engagement through cross-cultural and cross-civilizational dialogue without premeditated plans.

In this regard, Osman's insistence on the renewal of *Tawhidic* Epistemology[411] is crucial. He propagates the birth of a new scientific culture that is in conformity with the Islamic world-view and value system. This naturally entails the creation of a new synthesis of modern scientific knowledge and traditional scientific principles embodied in the teachings of Islam, especially in its cosmology.[412] Urging Malay and Bosnian scholars in this direction is also

405 Osman Bakar, "Towards a New Science of Civilization: A Synthetic Study of the Philosophical Views of al-Farabi, Ibn Khaldun, Arnold Toynbee, and Samuel Huntington," *Synthesis Philosophica* 62, no. 2 (2016): 313–333, https://doi.org/10.21464/sp31206.

406 Bakar 1997e, 62.

407 Bakar, 1997e, 63.

408 Qur'an 10:47, trans. Yusuf Ali, 1934, http://sacred-texts.com.

409 Qur'an 13:7, trans. Yusuf Ali.

410 Bakar, 1997e, 72.

411 See, for instance, "The Identity Crisis of the Contemporary Muslim Ummah: the Loss of *Tawhidic* Epistemology as Its Root Cause," *ICR Journal* 3, no. 4 (2012); "The Qur'anic Identity of the Muslim Ummah: *Tawhidic* Epistemology as Its Foundation and Sustainer," *ICR Journal* 3, no. 3 (2012); and "Islamic Science, Modern Science, and Post-Modernity: Towards a New Synthesis through a *Tawhidic* Epistemology," *Revelation and Science* 1, no. 3 (2011).

412 See: *Qur'anic Pictures of the Universe: The Scriptural Foundation of Islamic Cosmology* (Islamic Book

especially meaningful as it would enable new horizons to emerge on the fruitful crossroads of many different histories, cultures, ideologies and religions. Osman's ongoing dialogue with Confucian religions and social theories, as well as his strong emphasis on inter-cultural, inter-religious, inter-disciplinary, and inter-civilizational dialogue, which is one of the defining features of his undertakings, ought to be further developed.[413]

Indeed, Osman's belief that dialogue can transcend the borders of ethnicity, religion and ideology, and that it is certainly the best and surest method to achieve a peaceful solution to any problem, since it includes a continuous discussion with various world leaders and others, representing various cultural, educational, and religious organizations. In this regard, he takes into account the twenty-first century Chinese era that would be actively pursuing a dialogue and peace culture, interpersonal and intercultural exchanges based on respect of differences, openness and tolerance as well as the reforms they offer to the modern world.

Cultural diversity demands the art of listening and the cultivation of respect which might require years and even decades. This is the first step in realization of a true dialogue and the building of a culture of peace in the present radically complex world of conflicting hatreds, contradictory interests and conflicts. In it, at least in the opinion of this thinker, the most significant bilateral relationship in constructing a healthy world order is the Sino-American connection, whereas the view that China is only a threat truly and significantly hinders such efforts.[414]

The tendency towards the desecularization of society, and a discussion of how the spiritual resources which religions possess must be activated to revitalize today's civilization and the philosophical and theological bases for the building of a harmonious society of peaceful coexistence, great harmony (*datong* 大同) or the harmony of differences, with the aim of achieving and building a society on a more hopeful basis of dialogical civilization as advocated by Osman.[415]

Trust, 2014); "Cosmology and Models of the Cosmos" in *The Oxford Encyclopaedia of Philosophy, Science, and Technology in Islam*, vol. 1, ed. Ibrahim Kalin, 156–163 (Oxford University Press).

413 Prof. Osman was also the founder of the university's Center for Civilizational Dialogue (1996).

414 See Nevad Kahteran, *Philosophizing at the Big Fault Line: The Role of Comparative Philosophy* (Cambridge Scholars Publishing, 2021), chap. 2. Also, the Malaysian Chinese people, also known as Chinese Malaysians, are Malaysian citizens of Han Chinese ethnicity and formed almost one quarter of Malaysian population. See: https://en.wikipedia.org/wiki/Malaysian_Chinese (accessed June 7, 2021).

415 As presented in The Spirit of Islamic Science in Hokkaido Science Symposium by Osman Bakar, in *IAIS Journal of Civilisation Studies* 1, no. 1 (2008): 203–207, and "From Secular Science to Sacred Science: The Need for a Transformation" by Osman Bakar.

Part III

Unfortunately, such a dialogical civilization is no longer present in the so called Islamic world, because we do not want to be part of an established network and an indispensable cooperative conversation, although it is an imperative of a deeper understanding. We are witnessing conflicts and wars but we are not willing to completely acknowledge the value of openness and cultural diversity.

Following this line of Osman Bakar's thinking, Islamic traditions assume a distinctive contemporary relevance and may be a force for challenging and a peaceful changing of the international order and constantly reminds us that all philosophy should be truly comparative.[416] For me personally as a philosopher-comparativist, it is extremely important to see his insistence and opening debate on the pluralization of Islamic societies in a globalized world, which is longstanding procedure in front of all of us.[417]

Osman also drew attention to the importance of Tianfang Trilogy as a paradigm in his co-editorial, which is crucial in this Sino-Muslim relationship anyway. Chinese Muslims (*Huihui*, or Sinophone Muslims: Chinese: *Huizu* 回族) developed their unique tradition of Islamic teachings during the mid-seventh century as Islam was introduced in China. Over twenty-three million Muslims are living in China today. There are over 35,000 mosques in China, 40,000 Islamic religious leaders (imams), more than 400 Islamic associations in the entire country, and thirteen Islamic institutes today. More than 90% of Chinese Muslims are Sunni, while only 1.3% of them are Shiah. Islam in China maintains good relationships with other religions, and among the fifteen Chinese minorities in China there are ten observing Islam, namely the Hui, Uyghur, Kazak, Khalkhas, Uzbek, Tajik, Tatar, Dongxiang, Sala and Baoan, mainly inhabiting the northwest provinces of Xijiang, Ningxia, Gansu, and Qinghai, and the southwest province of Yunnan. Many other Muslims live almost in every city in the country. The Islamic presence in China is as old as Islam itself, and with over 1,400 years of Sino-Islamic relations, ranging from the early efforts of the Prophet's companion, Saʿd ibn Abī Waqqās (who died 674 AD in Guangzhou, China), to the pioneering journeys of the greatest naval commander in Chinese history, Admiral Zheng He (鄭和; 1371–1433 or 1435). Islam and Chinese Muslims have made significant contributions to China and Chinese civilisation, and vice versa, and without doubt we can say that Muslims have a rich and unique relationship with China.[418]

416 See Osman Bakar, "Towards a Postmodern Synthesis of Islamic Science and Modern Science: The Epistemological Groundwork," in *The Muslim 500: The World's 500 Most Influential Muslims*, 2020. https://themuslim500.com.

417 See: "Cultural Pluralism in a Globalised World: Challenges to Peaceful Coexistence," *Islam and Civilisational Renewal* 1, no. 3 (2010).

418 Kahteran, *Philosophizing at the Big Fault Line.*

Understanding the distinctive traditions of Chinese Muslims and the Islamic heritage in China, as well as its relevance to understanding both the evolution of Chinese history and culture, and appreciating the complex, multi-ethnic influences on modern China, is imperative. This multifaceted cultural heritage continues to the present day. Muslims in China have adapted to the local cultural circumstances, while continually adhering to their Islamic traditions.[419]

Or, as Chung-Ying Cheng himself points out: "We need to ponder whether Confucian culture and Islamic culture could indeed form a union, on the one hand to meet the challenges of Western domination and on the other to foster a greater mutual understanding, thereby presenting a model of postmodern pluralistic form of intercultural and international life."[420]

Taking into account that in recent years there has been an increased academic interest in the long history of Islam in China, as well as its interaction with Chinese culture and civilization, the study of Islam and Muslims in China has to be promoted from a cross-disciplinary approach with the understanding that the interlinking of these traditions would be very helpful to scholars interested in this field. As mentioned earlier, the Han Kitāb itself is the product of a remarkable, centuries-long period of intense intellectual interaction between Islam and Confucianism. This is the very reason why Professor Tu Weiming is convinced that it is a major contribution to Neo-Confucian thought from a comparative philosophical perspective,[421] as well as that those acquainted with these issues will find a wealth of possibilities that will help bridge the gap between the Islamic and Confucian conceptual universes "to interpret the thought of Islam through Confucianism," "to make a supplement to Confucianism by Islam" and "to achieve flourished development of both Islam and Confucianism." [422]

Some preliminary efforts in these directions have been made with Osman Bakar and others, but, for the moment, perhaps on a smaller scale, much remains to be done, because the very notion of philosophy has to be interpreted in a wider sense when applied to the Islamic context and Sino-Muslim intellectual evolution from the time of the *Han Kitāb* until today. Apparently, there has been a plurality of philosophical approaches in the Islamic world and, in consequence, in the Chinese context too.[423]

---

419 See: Osman Bakar, "Islam in China."

420 Chung-ying Cheng, "Confucianism and Islam as Two Major Postmodern Resources of Humanity and Cohumanity" in *Islam and Confucianism: A Civilizational Dialogue,* 121.

421 In his "Epilogue" to *The Sage Learning of Liu Zhi,* ed. Murata et al., 598.

422 Chinese term for Confucianism is "scholarly tradition" (*rujia*), which is primarily intended to mean the school as a philosophical movement of thought with regard to humanism. See Bo Mou, *Chinese Philosophy A-Z* (Edinburgh: Edinburgh University Press, 2009), 31.

423 Raji C. Steineck, Ralph Weber, Robert Gassmann, and Elena Lange, eds., *Concepts of Philosophy in Asia and the Islamic World* (Leiden, Boston: Brill, 2018); Kristian Petersen, "Understanding the Sources

Part IV

I hope this chapter is a clear indication that a new vision of Chineseness from a pluralistic, tolerant, and dialogical perspective is possible, especially with the inclusion of the Chinese-Muslim heritage in Osman's intellectual deliberations and investigations. Among other distinguished scholars, he expressed full recognition of the value of openness, cultural diversity, and self-reflexivity He revitalizes the Confucian and Sino-Muslim discourse through his collaborative work with the patriarchs in this field. It is crucial to stress the emergence of a "common awareness" (*gongshi*) among Chinese intellectuals throughout the world who are hoping to build a transnational network for an understanding of being Chinese within a global context. For Tu Weiming, the meaning of being Chinese is not a political but a human concern, rich with ethical-religious implications. Finally, I will end with a quote from Tu Weiming about a major contribution to Neo-Confucian thought from a comparative philosophical perspective, considering Liu Zhi's approach as presenting Islam in Neo-Confucian terms:

"This is, so far as I know, a significant event even in Islamic theology. It has often been assumed that Arabic and the languages that employed the Arabic script—Persian, Turkish, and Urdu—were the languages for expounding original Islamic thinking before the nineteenth century. If classical Chinese could also facilitate such a subtle and sophisticated task in the seventeenth and eighteenth centuries, it means that Islam is more than a regional phenomenon in philosophy. It also means that the classical Chinese can extend its scholarly community beyond the so-called Confucian cultural area...."[424] Above all, I would recall Oliver Leaman's words in the preface of my new book: "Let's see what philosophical ideas resonate throughout the world and examine them critically. That is comparative philosophy at its best."[425]

---

of the Sino-Islamic Intellectual Tradition: A Review Essay on The Sage Learning of Liu Zhi: Islamic Thought in Confucian Terms, by Sachiko Murata, William C. Chittick, and Tu Weiming, and Recent Chinese Literary Treasuries," *Philosophy East and West* 61, no. 3 (2011): 546–559.

424 Murata et al., *The Sage Learning of Liu Zhi*, 589–590.

425 Kahteran, "Preface," in *Philosophizing at the Big Fault Line*.

Bibliography

Ali, Md. Yousuf, and Osman Bakar. "Issues of Hindu-Muslim relations in the works of Syed Ahmad Khan." *Al-Shajarah* 25, no. 2 (2020): 315–333.

Ali, Yusuf, trans. *The Holy Qur'ān*. 1934. http://sacred-texts.com.

Ben-Dor Benite, Zvi. "Afterword." In *Platforma za islamsko-konfucijansko-daoistički dijalog na Balkanu / A Platform for Islamic-Confucian-Daoist Dialogue in the Balkans,* edited by Nevad Kahteran. Sarajevo: ITD Sedam, 2010.

Ben-Dor Benite, Zvi. *The Dao of Muhammad: A Cultural History of Muslims in Late Imperial China.* Cambridge: Harvard University Press, 2005.

Kahteran, Nevad, and Bo Mou. *Nove granice kineske filozofije / New Frontiers of Chinese Philosophy* 中國哲學新探索. Sarajevo: El-Kalem, 2018. http://www.elkalem.ba/Islam%20i%20konfucijanstvo.

Kahteran, Nevad, and Daniel Bučan. "Islamic and Comparative Philosophy – A Special Issue of Synthesis Philosophica." *Synthesis Philosophica* 31, no. 2 (2016): 227-482.

Kahteran, Nevad. "Recognizing a Model of Postmodern Pluralism through Looking at Islam from the Standpoint of Far Eastern Traditions." *Synthesis Philosophica* 31, no. 2 (2016): 433–450.

Kahteran, Nevad. *Philosophizing at the Big Fault Line: The Role of Comparative Philosophy.* Cambridge Scholars Publishing, 2021.

Kahteran, Nevad. *Platforma za islamsko-konfucijansko-daoistički dijalog na Balkanu ("伊斯兰教一儒家一道家在巴尔干国家中的对话讲坛"/ A Platform for Islamic-Confucian-Daoist Dialogue in the Balkans).* Sarajevo: ITD Sedam, 2010.

Kahteran, Nevad. *Situating the Bosnian Paradigm: The Bosnian Experience of Multicultural Relations.* New York: Global Scholarly Publication, 2008.

Mou, Bo. "On Constructive-Engagement Strategy of Comparative Philosophy." *Comparative Philosophy* 1, no. 1 (2010): 1–32. https://scholarworks.sjsu.edu/comparativephilosophy/

Mou, Bo. *Chinese Philosophy A-Z.* Edinburgh: Edinburgh University Press, 2009.

Mujtabai, Fathullah. *Hindu-Muslim Cultural Relations / Hindusko-muslimanske kulturne relacije.* Translated by Nevad Kahteran. Sarajevo: Filozofski fakultet UNSA, 2020. http://www.ff-eizdavastvo.ba/Books/HINDUSKO-MUSLIMANSKE_kulturne_relacije.pdf.

Murata, Sachiko, William C. Chittick, and Tu Weiming. *The Sage Learning of Liu Zhi: Islamic Thought in Confucian Terms.* Cambridge, MA: Harvard

University Asia Center and Harvard University Press, 2009.
Nielsen, Katherine. "The Philosophy of Osman Bin Bakar." *International Studies in the Philosophy of Science* 22, no. 1 (2008): 81–95.
Osman Bakar and Cheng Gek Nai. *Islam i konfucijanstvo / Islam and Confucianism* 伊斯兰教与儒家：不同文明之间的对话. Bosnian translation. Sarajevo: El-Kalem, 2018.
Osman Bakar. "Cultural Symbiosis and the Role of Religion in the Contemporary World: An Islamic Perspective." *KATHA – The Official Journal of the Centre for Civilisational Dialogue* 4 (2008): 31–58. Osman Bakar. "From Secular Science to Sacred Science: The Need for a Transformation." *Sacred Web* 33 (Summer 2014): 25–49.
Osman Bakar. "Islam in China and the Challenge of Sinicization of Religion: Past and Present." In *The Muslim 500: The World's 500 Most Influential Muslims, 2021*. Amman: The Royal Islamic Strategic Studies Centre, 2020. https://themuslim500.com.
Osman Bakar. "Nature as a Sacred Book: A Core Element of Seyyed Hossein Nasr's Philosophical Teachings." *Sacred Web* 40 (Winter 2017): 75–101.
Osman Bakar. "Towards a Postmodern Synthesis of Islamic Science and Modern Science: The Epistemological Groundwork." In *The Muslim 500: The World's 500 Most Influential Muslims, 2020*. Amman: The Royal Islamic Strategic Studies Centre, 2019. https://themuslim500.com.
Osman Bakar. *Classification of Knowledge in Islam*. Institute for Policy Studies, 1992, 1st ed.; Cambridge: Islamic Texts Society, 1998, 2nd ed.
Osman Bakar. *Islam in Southeast Europe: Past Reflections and Future Prospects*, edited by Mesut Idriz and Osman Bakar. Bandar Seri Begawan: UBD Press, 2014.
Osman Bakar. *Qur'anic Pictures of the Universe: The Scriptural Foundation of Islamic Cosmology*. Kuala Lumpur: Islamic Book Trust, 2016.
Petersen, Kristian. "Understanding the Sources of the Sino-Islamic Intellectual Tradition: A Review Essay on *The Sage Learning of Liu Zhi: Islamic Thought in Confucian Terms* by Sachiko Murata, William C. Chittick, and Tu Weiming, and Recent Chinese Literary Treasuries." *Philosophy East and West* 61, no. 3 (2011): 546–559.
Rošker, Jana. "On the Tiny Bridge of Understanding: Chinese Philosophy, Western Discourse and Fusion of New Horizons." In *Nove granice kineske filozofije - 中國哲學新探索 - New Frontiers of Chinese Philosophy*, edited by Nevad Kahteran and Bo Mou 牟博. Sarajevo: El-Kalem, 2018.
Shah-Kazemi, Reza. *Common Ground Between Islam and Buddhism: Spiritual and Ethical Affinities*. Fons Vitae, 2010.
Steineck, Raji C., Ralph Weber, Robert Gassmann, and Elena Lange, eds. *Concepts of Philosophy in Asia and the Islamic World*. Leiden, Boston: Brill, 2018.

Chapter 10

The Making of a Korean-Islamic Tradition

Hee Soo Lee

Professor in the Department of Cultural Anthropology of Hanyang University, South Korea

Among the many themes that defined Professor Osman Bakar's scholarly career was the interactions between civilizations, especially between Confucianist-based civilizations in East Asia with the Islamic world. In this chapter, I broach this theme through a historical analysis of Islam's arrival and spread in Korea from the earliest times up till the present. I show the ways in which Islamic ideals, precepts, rituals, ceremonies, and science interacted with and left an indelible impact on generations of ethnic Koreans, bringing about the creation of a Korean-Islamic tradition. According to Arabic and Persian manuscripts, Muslims entered the Korean Peninsula around 845 AD. The connection and exchange between the two worlds have actually taken place as early as the Unified Silla Period (676–935) based on evidence from archaeological relics and written documents. It can be said then that the Korean Peninsula and Muslim world had extensive transnational trade and cultural exchanges that stretched for 1200 years. Under the assimilation policy of the Joseon Dynasty (1392–1910), Muslim culture and traditions were prohibited and regarded as alien by a strict royal decree passed in 1427. Muslim settlers in Korea gradually shed their native attire, customs, and rituals.

Islamic activities in Korea were revived by 200 Russian Turks who sought political asylum in the 1920s after escaping the suppression of the Russian Bolshevik regime. The Turkic population settled in Korea and maintained their ethnic and Islamic identity under Japanese protection. However, they were pressured to emigrate to other countries due to the political turmoil in Korea after its independence in 1945 and the outbreak of the Korean War in 1950.[426] The participation of Turkish soldiers during the Korean War (1950–53) and the *da'wah* (missionary) activities of the *imams* (prayer leaders) of the Turkish

426 Hee Soo Lee, *Korea and the Muslim World: A Historical Account* (Istanbul: IRCICA, 2020), 20–23.

Brigade opened a new era for Islam in Korea. Today, there are about 200,000 Muslims, 40,000 of which are ethnically Korean. Although we have no reliable records, it is estimated that there are more than twenty-five mosques and 150 *musallahs* (prayer halls) opened in major cities..[427]

Historical Background of Korea-Muslim World Relations

The exact date at which Muslims first came to Korea remains inconclusive but it is believed that they came to Korea via China during the Unified Silla Kingdom (661–935). China had close commercial relations with Arab and Persian Muslims who traveled to T'ang China (618–907) mostly along sea-routes of the Indian Ocean. Archaeological excavations, anthropological materials, folklore, and oral traditions provide reliable evidence for cultural exchanges between ancient Korea and Western Asia. The trade goods between the two regions include Roman and Persian-type glassware and clay busts and have been excavated from Silla royal tombs. Aside from that, Persian carpets were recorded in the *Sam Guk Sa Gi* (*Chronicles of Three Kingdoms,* herein referred to as "SGSG"). Stone statues resembling Central Asian or Persian people, as well as symmetrical patterns and designs of trees and birds in Gyeong-ju, the capital of Korean kingdom have been found.[428] An ancient Persian epic entitled *"Kushnâmâ"* which deals with a love story between the Sassanid Persian prince and the Silla princess in the mid-seventh century has recently also been discovered and researched. The epic attests to the cultural and historical encounters and exchanges between Korean and Western Asia.[429] Clearly, Western Asian culture has long been flowing into the Korean Peninsula even before the advent of Islam. It would have taken within ten months to travel the Silk Road from Constantinople to Gyeong-ju in the eighth and ninth centuries based on the distance and the speed of the camels which were used as a means of transnational transportation. Therefore, it can be said that the Korean Peninsula and Arab-Muslim world were already living in the "*simultaneous fashion era"* for over 1,200 years.

At the height of its prosperity, Korea forged strong political, economic and cultural relations with the T'ang Dynasty. There were regular voyage routes that took only a few days from the western part of Korea to various southern and eastern ports in China, where large Muslim communities were found. It is very likely that Silla people came into contact with Muslims in China through such business transactions, diplomatic exchanges, the dispatch of students,

427 Hee Soo Lee, "The Silk Road and Korea-Middle East Cultural Connections," *Acta Koreana* 21, no.1 (June 2018): 8.

428 Lee, "The Silk Road and Korea-Middle East Cultural Connections," 5.

429 Hee Soo Lee, "Evaluation of Kushnama as a Historical Source in Regard to Description of Basila," *Acta Koreana* 21, no.1 (June 2018): 15–16.

and roving Buddhist monks.[430] From the Muslim manuals of navigation that have come down to us, it is clear that Muslim navigators were quite at home in the south-eastern sea of China and had established their own colonies called *Fan Fang* as early as the eighth century. According to some Arab travelers who visited China in the mid-ninth century such as Sulaimān al-Tājir and Abu Zaid, there were more than 100,000 Muslims in the south-eastern coast of China. Direct encounters between two different cultural representatives in the Korean peninsula were recorded, and more than sixty Arabic and Persian references to Silla were found in the writings by thirty-one Muslim historians or geographers such as Ibn Khurdādbih, Sulaimān al-Tājir and Masʿūdī, who wrote their accounts between the ninth to fifteenth centuries. Ibn Khurdādbih was the first Arab to be informed of Muslim colonies in Silla, Korea.[431]

In addition to Islamic sources, the *SGSG* gives us a list of trade goods including frankincense and Persian carpets transacted mainly by Muslim merchants. The descriptions showed clearly that such trade goods had already found their way into Korea. The first Korean historical document on the relations with Muslims was *Goryeo-sa* (herein referred to as *GS*), the official chronicle of the Goryeo Dynasty (918–1392). According to *GS*, a *Tashi* (Arab) group of 100 members headed by Al-Razi came to Korea for trade in 1024. Later, several Muslim trade groups headed by Hassan, Razi, and Abu Nahab continued to trade in Korea with their native products. They were treated as important guests and returned with Korean products given by the king.[432]

When the Mongol Yüan Dynasty (1270–1368) controlled Korea from 1270 to 1356, many Muslims who rose up the ranks of the Mongol government came to Korea. During the thirteenth to fifteenth centuries, many Muslims settled down permanently and assimilated into Korean society, thanks to the preferential treatment and profitable economic advantages.[433] Muslims in Korea formed their own communities in Gae-seong (the capital of the Goryeo dynasty) and its outskirts. They practised their own cultural customs, traditions, as well as religious occasions. They owned shops that sold native products in Gae-seong. They built mosques called "*Yegung.*" Religious leaders were chosen in the Muslim communities to ensure that acts of worship were in accordance with Islamic law and customs. From time to time, the Muslim leaders were honoured with special invitations to attend court ceremonies

430 Lee, *Korea and the Muslim World*, 21.

431 See more detailed information. Lee, *Korea and the Muslim World*, 96–115./ Kei Won Chung and George F. Hourani, "Arab Geographers on Korea," *Journal of the American Oriental Society* 58, no. 4 (1938): 658–661./ Mohammed Bagher Vosoughi and Hee Soo Lee, *Ancient Korea in the Arabic and Persian Manuscripts* (Samarkand: IICAS Publication, 2020), 26–27.

432 Hee Soo Lee, "Islam in the Far East," in *The Different Aspects of Islamic Culture, Volume Three The Spread of Islam through the World*, ed. Idris El Hareir and El Hadji Ravane M' Baye (Paris: UNESCO Publishing, 2011), 768.

433 Lee, *Korea and the Muslim World*, 151–156.

where they recited the Holy Qur'an and prayed for the king and the prosperity of the country.[434]

The assimilation policy of new Joseon Dynasty (1392–1910) obliterated most of the traces of the Islamic presence in old Korea. Nevertheless, the imprint of Islam lingered. According to *Joseon Wangjo Silok* (JWS: official chronicles of the Joseon Dynasty), the Korean lunar calendar system, which was widely used during the Joseon Dynasty was based on Islamic astronomical-lunar calendar system. The invention of various scientific instruments in Korea in the mid-fifteenth century, such as the celestial globe, water clock, sundial, astronomic clock, and rainfall gauge must have been derived from local acquaintance with Islamic science.[435] The Joseon Dynasty which soon adopted Neo-Confucianism as a national ideology became more conservative and less receptive towards Islam. In 1427, a Royal Decree prohibited the practice of Muslim culture and rituals which effectively brought an end to the spread of Islam in Korea. The commercial dominance of western maritime powers such as the Portuguese, Spanish and Dutch in East Asia in the later centuries further discouraged Muslims from maintaining their presence and activities in the Korean peninsula. Since the fifteenth century up until the early twentieth century, no historical documents registered the presence of Muslims in Korea.[436]

Islamic activities in East Asia became vigorous again with the coming of religious missionaries who were dispatched officially or secretly to China and Japan as a part of the Pan-Islamic policy of Ottoman Sultan Abdulhamid II.[437] Abdurreshid Ibrahim Efendi, for example, came to Korea to disseminate Islam. A patriotic Pan-Islamist and Russian Turk, his efforts were however not successful because of the restrictions he encountered from the Japanese authorities. His poor grasp of the Korean language limited his contacts and collection of accurate information from the Koreans. Nevertheless, his travel account *Alem-i Islam (Islam in the World)* is regarded as a valuable resource for the study of modern Korea for the period before Japan annexation in 1910, albeit from the Muslims' point of view.[438]

With the coming of Russian Turks in the 1920s who escaped from the suppression of the Russian Bolshevik regime, Islamic activities saw a period of resurgence. Around 200 Russian Muslim Turks, mostly Kazans, settled permanently in Korea. The Turkic group established their own national and religious federation (Millî ve dinî cemiyet). They enjoyed the profitable regional trade

---

434 Ibid., 177–178.

435 For the detailed discussion on the influence of Islamic culture in Joseon society, see Lee, *Korea and the Muslim World*, 183–199.

436 Lee, *Korea and the Muslim World*, 182.

437 Hee Soo Lee, *Islam ve Turk Kulturunun Uzak Dogu'ya Yayilmasi* (Ankara: Turkiye Diyanet Vakfi, 1988), 181–182.

438 Lee, *Korea and the Muslim World*, 271–272./ Lee, *Islam ve Turk Kulturunun Uzak Dogu'ya Yayilmais*, 234.

between Manchuria, Korea, and Japan and obtained a high social position under the protection of the Japanese Government-General. After Korean independence in 1945 and the Korean war of 1950–53, however, they were forced to emigrate to Turkey and elsewhere.[439] Nonetheless, these Muslim Turks introduced elements of Islamic and Turkic culture and made the Qur'an known to Korean society. Some Koreans embraced Islam under the guidance of these Muslim Turks and are regarded as the earliest Korean Muslims. Another community of Muslim Turks who had participated in the Korean War settled in the country in 1955. These Turkish soldiers propagated their religion and opened a new era for Islam in Korea.

Contemporary Muslim Community in South Korea: Da'wah Methodologies of Islamic Movements and Their Rapid Expansion

Islam started to spread in Korea but in utmost slowness since 1955 with the establishment of the Korea Islamic Society. The Society survived for almost a decade until 1964 and made remarkable efforts in propagating Islam and managing the welfare of orphaned children. Many transnational Islamic organizations and institutions showed great interest in the growing Korean Muslim population due to the work of the Society. Until the 1960s, however, only Muslim-majority countries such as Malaysia and Pakistan extended support. The then Malaysian Prime Minister Tunku Abdul Rahman financed the building of a Mosque in Seoul but the project was cut short due to insufficient funds. Another important figure to be mentioned here is Maulana Sayyid Muhammad Jamil, then president of the Qur'an Society of Pakistan. He visited Korea frequently and mesmerized the Koreans through his excellent speeches. He was best remembered as a humble Muslim.

In 1965, a group of devoted Korean Muslims formed a committee through which a temporary mosque came into existence and gathered scattered Muslims under the motto of "unity and mutual encouragement." Two years later, the Korea Islamic Foundation was officially registered and recognized as the new representative of the Muslim community in Korea. It emerged as a unique legal integration body for Islamic Da'wah in Korea. The foundation's efforts gained more momentum from the 1970s onwards. Under the Foundation, the Korea Muslim Federation was set up as an administrative organization that managed the Student Association, Youth Association, Women Association, and Foreign Muslim Association as its sub-organizations. There were ten to fifteen branches in major provinces and big cities doing local level Islamic activities. In addition, several committees were established to look into matters of *Sharī'a* (Islamic legal code), *da'wah*, halal certification, Qur'an translation,

439 Lee, "Islam in the Far East," 778.

and publications. Although it has not yet been officially approved by the Korean Office of Education, since the 1990s, the KMF has established a kindergarten and elementary school-level *madrasa* (Islamic school) named Sultan Bin Abdul Aziz, where foreign Muslim children including some Korean kids were given the opportunity to learn the Arabic and English languages and Islamic culture.[440]

The KMF took into consideration the *da'wah* methodology in spreading Islam in Korea. It placed its focus first on correcting the distorted information on Islam in school textbooks, on giving reliable information and sources on Islam and the Muslim world to mass-media and academic circles, and published beautifully designed Islamic literature by Korean scholars. Towards that end, the KMF translated a series of Islamic works, organized regular Islamic seminars and conferences for non-Muslims, conducted Arabic language courses free of charge, offered training programs for Muslim leaders, held Islamic cultural exhibitions, operated a free clinic for foreign workers, sent Muslim students to pursue their studies in Islamic institutes overseas, and published periodicals such as *Weekly Newsletter*, *Al-Masjid*, and *Al-Islam*, among many others.[441]

The KMF also commissioned an in-depth study on Korean tradition and culture to ensure a harmonious coexistence with Islamic principles as part of its Islamic propagation strategy. The exemplary conduct shown by foreign Muslims who are active in the KMF impressed upon local Koreans the Muslim way of life. The continuous social contribution by Korean Muslims has had a positive influence on Korean society. In a word, the KMF's main methodology was to create a non-hostile atmosphere towards Muslims, to make Korea a place where local Muslims can live freely and advance in society without any discrimination or disadvantage.

By the mid-1970s, the Korean government saw the importance of establishing close ties with Islamic countries, particularly with the advent of the Oil Crisis. A new era of rapid spread of Islam begun in Korea, especially when many Arab and Islamic countries extended their whole-hearted assistance to Korean Muslims. The Seoul Central Mosque and Islamic Center was built in 1976 as a symbol of cooperation between Korea and the Muslim World. The number of Muslims in Korea increased from 5,000 in 1975 to 10,000 in 1979. In the meantime, two mosques were built in cities of Busan and Gwangju. Another two mosques were constructed between 1986 and 1987 to address the increasing number of Muslims. The seeds of a Korean-Islamic tradition were firmly planted from then on.

Islam in Korea experienced a major change since 1994 when Muslim foreign workers from Indonesia, Pakistan, Bangladesh, and Uzbekistan were

440 Korea Muslim Federation, *Islam in Korea* (Seoul: Korea Muslim Federation Publication, 2008), 21–22.
441 Ibid., 25–30.

permitted to enter the country. Some inter-married with local Koreans. As of 2021, there are about 200,000 Muslims, including about 5,000 married immigrants and 40,000 Korean converts that are congregants of the twenty-five mosques and 150 prayer halls in major cities. The Pew Research Center estimated that there were 3,000 Muslims in North Korea in 2010, an increase from the 1,000 Muslims since 1990.[442] There is one mosque which is within the compound of the Iranian embassy in Pyongyang called Ar-Rahman Mosque. The mosque was likely built for the embassy staff, but is open to outsiders.[443]

Even though Muslim minority community in Korea is faced with certain obstacles like Islamophobia and pressures against the Muslim way of life such as the demands for halal food and *sukuk* (sharia-compliant securities), it has adopted *da'wah* strategies to enhance its development and value through promoting relations with the Muslim world and by maintaining friendly relations with the Korean government.

Socio-Economic Conditions of Korean Muslims

The economic status of Korean Muslims in general is good and in sync with economic development in Korea. Most Korean Muslims are in the position to help others through their donations to a host of Muslim causes. The KMF reported that its funds were mostly from income gained through its activities and charity. They still rely on donations from foreign charity foundations in the Muslim world. During my interviews with the leaders of the KMF, they mentioned that they have laid the foundations for the long-term *da'wah*, and will continue to receive full support from Islamic charity foundations.

The social position of Muslims is less advantageous due to basic difficulties they have to handle. Every Korean can embrace Islam with ease through the declaration of Shahada. The average number of annual converts have reached about 1,000 people in the 1970s, and since the 1980s, the number has been estimated to be around 250 people. As for daily prayers, most new converts cannot fulfil this obligation due to the negative working environment. Muslim men can however participate in the *Juma'ah* (Friday) prayers.[444]

Fasting during the month of Ramadhan is equally challenging. Most Korean Muslims try to perform a few days of fasting. If Ramadhan falls on the vacation period, many young Muslims would fast and attend *i'tikaf* (remaining in worship) at the mosques. *Zakat* (compulsory tax) is scarcely paid. This is caused by Muslims' ignorance of the importance of *Zakat* or by the lack of an established system to collect the *zakat*. The number of Korean Muslims

442 Pew Research Center, "Table: Muslim Population by Country," January 27, 2011.

443 Chad O'Carroll, "Iran Builds Pyongyang's First Mosque," *NK News*, January 22, 2013, https://www.nknews.org/2013/01/iran-buillds-pyongyangs-first-mosque.

444 Lee, *Korea and the Muslim World*, 293.

performing *hajj* (pilgrimage to Makkah) is not many. In the 1970s, they were able to organize an annual *hajj* team of several hundred people. Around twenty people from Korea and other Koreans who were working in Arab countries joined the pilgrimage to Makkah. Since the 1990s, however, the annual number of Korean pilgrims has decreased to several people.[445]

Apart from the five pillars of Islam, Korean Muslims are also faced with difficulties in fulfilling other religious obligations in their daily life. In avoiding things that are considered *haram* (prohibition) in Islam, new converts stop eating pork, while they continue to drink alcohol for a certain period as drinking is an essential part of social gatherings in Korea. But halal food has been on the rise since more halal butcher shops in the Seoul Islamic Center have been established since 1983. Now Muslims can find sufficient shops and markets supplying halal materials and foods in every big city, or through on-line purchase.

Marriage between Muslims is very rare in Korea. Most Korean Muslim bridegrooms choose non-Muslim Korean partners on the condition that the bride will convert to Islam someday. In the case of Muslim women, it is more difficult to invite non-Muslim husbands to Islam. Therefore, pious Korean Muslim women tend to get married to foreign Muslims. The number of foreign Muslim laborers from Pakistan and Bangladesh married to Korean women has increased in recent years. The weddings of Korean Muslims are usually celebrated twice, once in the mosques in the Islamic way, and then in the wedding ceremonial hall in the Korean-western style.

Many Korean Muslims conduct funeral ceremonies according to Korean traditions, which are slightly different from the Islamic style. The absence of Muslim cemeteries is another difficulty the Muslim community is faced with. Of course, the matter of how to fulfill Islamic teachings completely relies on the Muslim's personal intention and faith (*iman*). In order to upgrade the standard of Muslim's way of life based on pure Islamic commandment, the Muslim community should make its utmost effort in creating a positive environment for Islam in Korean society.

Political Strategies and Relations with Korean governments to protect the Muslim Ummah

In Korea, freedom of religion is guaranteed by the constitution. It can be said that the Korean government is not negative towards Korean Muslims and their contribution to the national interest. From the viewpoint of national interest, Korea needs friendly relations with Muslim countries, including oil-rich Arab nations. At the same time, Korea Muslim Federation, the sole registered non-profit organization, always adopts a survival strategy to contribute to

445 Lee, *Korea and the Muslim World*, 293–294.

Korean society by maintaining friendly relations with the Korean government and bridging relations between Korea and the Muslim World.

After the first oil crisis in the early 1970s, the Korean government wanted good relations with Arab oil-producing countries. The KMF played a significant role in bridging Korea and Muslim countries. In the late 1970s, the Korean government advocated pro-Arab policy and endorsed the existence of the PLO. This atmosphere led to the Korean government's active cooperation with KMF in securing the land for Central Mosque in Seoul in 1976. During the second oil crisis in 1979, the KMF sent a special joint public-private delegation to ten Arab oil-producing countries to appeal for crude oil on behalf of Korea. The then Crown Prince Fahd Bin Abdulaziz of Saudi Arabia accepted the appeal of Korean Muslims and sent a letter to KMF that he would provide oil to the country. In order to meet with the active role and dedication of Korean Muslims, the Korean government has stepped up efforts to cooperate and secure the site for the establishment of the Korea Islamic University, a long-cherished hope of Korean Muslims. Although the Islamic University project was not completed, it remains in the memory of Muslims as a symbolic project of strategic cooperation between the Korean government and the KMF at the time. In the 1980s and 1990s, Korean Muslim leaders also played a positive role in expanding economic exchanges and establishing diplomatic relations with Muslim socialist countries such as Egypt, Libya, and Algeria. In addition, more than one million Korean workers worked in the Arab-Iran construction markets. KMF was in charge of ensuring that these workers were given a full understanding of Islam. KMF also managed new converts, and until recently, under MOU with local government, provided Korean translation and notarization of Arabic Driving Licenses, and Halal Certification services. Of course, the political orientation and support for any political party are the individual Muslim's choice, but KMF has maintained friendly relations with the government regardless of its conservative or liberal stance.

Islamophobia and Current Understanding of Koreans about Islam

The greatest difficulty and obstacle for Muslims in Korea is a widespread misconception about Islam by western mass-media. According to a recent survey, the most common image about Arabs and Islam for most Koreans was terror, war, conflict zones.[446] Another survey showed that 44.7% Koreans viewed refugees negatively, 66.6% were negative towards Muslim refugees specifically.[447] Similarly, a survey conducted by *The Asian Institute for Policy*

446 Suwan Kim, "Koreans' Perception on Image of Arab, Islam in the Media in Korea" (Korean), *Korean Journal of Middle Eastern Studies* 37, no.1 (2016): 205.

447 Seong Woon Yu, "Refugees can be accepted, but not Muslim Refugees-Islamophobia in Korea" (Korean), *Joongang Daily*, August 5, 2018, https://news.joins.com/article/22860819.

Studies Institute on 4–24 December 2019 showed that 70.9% Koreans had negative perceptions about Middle Eastern immigrants when compared to other regions.[448] In August 2018, when around 550 Yemeni asylum seekers landed on the resort island of Jeju using the visa-free entry system, there was a strong public reaction. 714,875 Koreans posted on the online petition of the Presidential Office against Yemeni refugees entering the country. This was the largest petition ever posted on the website.[449] Even if the Koreans change their negative stance on the influx of new foreigners, it takes a relatively positive stance towards immigrants who are already in the country for years and who fillthe job shortages in South Korean companies.

The distorted images on Islam and Islamophobia are mostly reproduced by the media, Christian groups, and western-oriented academics. Islamophobia became more prevalent in the 2000s after the 9/11 attacks and a series of terrorist attacks by the armed group, ISIL (Islamic State in the Levant, or in Korea more well-known as IS). Perceptions of Islam as a religion of violence and terrorism is widespread, particularly in conservative and xenophobic Korean Christian circles.[450] During the eighteenth Presidential Elections, in 2012, the 2016 General Elections and again for the 2022 Presidential Election, the Protestant parties spread Islamophobia and combined anti-homosexuality and anti-Islamism as part of their party slogans.[451] Islamophobic perceptions in Korean society hinder efforts to cultivate and nurture a "Korean-Islamic Tradition" which could transform Korea into an attractive place for Muslim tourists.[452]

The issue of hate speech and discrimination against Islam and Muslim migrants which is spreading through social media has serious implications. Compared to European societies, public awareness of the severity of Islamophobia remains at ground level in Korea.[453] In this sense, it is necessary to legislate as soon as possible a "no discrimination law" which will remove some of the negative effects of hate speech or discrimination towards Muslims in Korea.

---

448 Survey on Islamophobia in Korea by Joongang Daily conducted by one of the major daily newspapers (conducted on August 1st and 2nd 2018). Compared to the negative responses about Middle Eastern migrants, negative responses towards European and North American migrants were very low as around 20%, and it shows the dual racism within Korean society.

449 Jeeyun Kwon, "South Korea's Yemeni Refugee Problem," *Essay of MEI* (Middle East Institute), April 23, 2019, https://www.mei.edu/publications/south-koreas-yemeni-refugee-problem.

450 Farrah Sheikh, " Exploring "Korean Islam" in a Climate of Exclusion and Islamophobia," *International Journal of Diaspora & Cultural Criticism* 9, no. 22 (2019): 206.

451 In 2015 March, President Pak Ken-Hye signed a memorandum of understanding for halal food cooperation at a meeting with the Crown Prince of the UAE, which paved the way for Korean companies to enter the halal food market. In the cooperation, it was decided to create a 'Halal Food Theme Park' in Iksan in Jeonrabuk-do Province, Korea.

452 Farrah Sheikh, "Exploring "Korean Islam"," 204.

453 Gi Yeon Koo, "Islamophobia and the Politics of Representation of Islam in Korea," *Journal of Korean Religions* 9, no. 1 (April 2018): 186.

Foreign Muslim Migrants in Korea

The foreign Korean Muslim community has experienced wide changes since the mid-1990s. Foreign workers have been accepted since 1994 to cover the shortage of workers in the labour markets. A large number of Southeast Asians entered the country as wage earners, and they include Muslim workers from Indonesia, Bangladesh, Pakistan, and Uzbekistan. Furthermore, since the 2000s, the number of foreign Muslims in Korea has soared to the point where the number of Muslim tourists and international students have surpassed that of local Korean Muslims, due to the influence of the "Korean Wave." Fortunately, foreign Muslims in Korea contribute greatly to the growth and development of the Korean Muslim community as they generally get along well with local Muslims. The 2020 statistics estimate that the number of foreign Muslims in Korea was about 150,000 people. In 2021, the number of Muslim immigrants decreased significantly due to the Covid-19 pandemic.

When asked about their overall life in South Korea by a survey done on foreign Muslims in Korea, over 80% of respondents answered that they were either satisfied or very satisfied.[454] High wages and good working conditions, safety, stable social order, and good amenities were cited as reasons as to why they were happy with life in South Korea. The residence-oriented multiculturalism in Europe is fundamentally different from Korean cases, as labor migrants in Korea are granted temporary stay rather than permanent residence. Among more than 150,000 Muslim migrants, about 5,000 married immigrant couples are settlement groups, while others are wage earners, international students, diplomats, and senior citizens. Most immigrant would return home or move to other countries after a certain period of time.

Challenges and Future Prospects

The greatest difficulty and obstacle in Islamic *da'wah* in Korea, like other Western society, seem to be a wide-spread misconception and negativity about Islam. The media has distorted the image of Islam into a faith that promotes polygamy, the abuse of women's rights, terrorism, and medievalism.[455] Aside from that, *da'wah* activities lack funding. There is also a dearth of readable Islamic literature written by qualified Korean scholars based on well-designed methodology and erudition that would be appealing to the Korean general public. An Islamic Research Institute or Islamic College which can train

454 Hee Soo Lee and Young Joo Jo, "A Survey of Muslim Immigrants in Korea – Focused on adaptation to Korean Life-style and Religious Observation," *Korea Journal of Middle Eastern Studies* 33, no. 1 (2012). Hee Soo Lee, "A Survey Report On Halal Food Consumption Among Muslim Students And Housewives In Korea," *Institute of Asian Muslim Studies Waseda Universty*, https://www.waseda.jp/inst/ias/assets/uploads/2017/03/Muslims-in-Korea-Waseda-Survey-Report_revised_2016-Mother-26-Student-2.27.pdf, 103.

455 Lee, "Islam in the Far East," 782.

Muslim experts to conduct professional and systematic research on various Islamic subjects and promote Islamic understanding is by far non-existent.

The KMF has always shown a high degree of willingness to contribute to Korean society as the non-official bridge to connect between Korea and the Muslim World whenever such relations face undesirable deadlocks. But their efforts are often restricted by prejudice shown by many Christian evangelicals that display a provocative attitude towards Islam and Muslims.

I would like to propose for Muslims in Korea to concentrate on the following efforts so as to enhance the Muslim community as well as resolve certain issues facing Muslim society:

1. Cultivate young Muslim leaders by sponsoring them to pursue higher education in Muslim countries and encourage them to explain about Islam to Korean society.
2. Publish Korean translations of the Qur'an, Islamic literature that harmonize Islamic principles and Korean culture, and other resources that showcase beautiful aspects of Islam to highly educated Koreans.
3. Educate Muslim women leaders who will lead social reforms in Korea through the reinterpretation of gender equality in Islam. Through this, the existing image of Muslim women as suppressed and passive entities will be drastically changed.
4. Establish an Islamic research institute and Islamic college to produce qualified young Muslim leaders with specialties in various Islamic subjects.
5. Expand and revitalize online *da'wah* works by cooperating with power bloggers and YouTubers on social networking platforms. Currently, the YouTube channels of Daud Kim and Ayana Moon are gaining millions of followers in Korea and South-east Asia.

In spite of certain obstacles at the present moment, the future of Islam in Korea seems to be bright due to several reasons such as its *Tawhid* (Oneness of God). In fact, Koreans who have converted from Christianity to Islam are receptive to the message of *Tawhid* that Islam propagates. Korea's economic interests, which are inevitably intertwined with the Muslim world, would make Koreans more willing to learn about Islamic culture and have friendly relations with the Muslim world. Korea has never experienced uncomfortable conflicts with the Muslim world due to its historical friendship, and it is a historical partnership that has survived for 1200 years. This is a pivotal factor that Koreans need to be sensitized to for them to look at the Muslim world differently and move away from Western-oriented history.

Korean traditional ideas rooted in Confucian teachings are in agreement with Islamic basic principles. Although the values of the new generation are changing rapidly, family relationships, filial piety to parents, respect and courtesy for elders and seniors, consideration for the weak and women, and community spirit which are all part of the Korean tradition are in line with the spirit and morality of Islam.[456] Therefore, if Islamophobia is removed and Islam's true message is known, Islam can grow rapidly in Korea just as Christianity had within only a century since its arrival on Korea's shores. Islam will no longer be a new religion. It will be the open and true religion that Koreans have and will continue to forge relationship with for the longest time.

Moreover, many Koreans are in search of a new spirituality to substitute the western value system. Under these circumstances, the universal messages in Islam would be appealing to Koreans. The Korean Muslim community has developed a strong solidarity through the work of the KMF and has good collaboration with several dozens of foreign Muslim groups, which enables Korean Muslims to overcome obstacles in *da'wah*. Korean Muslims must enthusiastically keep their religious tenets which cannot be compromised with Korean traditions and customs. They must assist Muslim immigrants who aspire for integration within mainstream Korean society, while underscoring their distinctiveness. To conclude, the increasing inflow of foreign Muslim workers, marriage immigrants, and students into Korean society could be a valuable resource for Islam to grow. These Muslims can play a pivotal role as a bridge between Korea and the Muslim world of two billion, and become part of the already emerging Korean-Islamic tradition.

456 Ibid.

Bibliography

Al-Idrīsī. *Nuzhat al-mushtāq fi khtirāq al-āfāq*. Leiden, 1970.

Al-Masʿūdī. *Kitāb al-tanbīh wa-l-ishrāf.* Baghdad, 1938.

Chung, Ki Won, and F. George Hourani. "Arab Geographers on Korea." *Journal of the American Oriental Society* 58, no. 4 (1938).

Ferrand, Gabriel. *Relations de voyages et textes géographiques arabes, persans et turks relatifs à l'extreme-orient du VIII au XVIII siècles*. Paris, 1913.

Ibn Khurdādhbih. *Kitāb al-masālik wa-l-mamālik*, edited by M. J. de Goeje. Leiden, 1889.

Koo, Gi Yeon. "Islamophobia and the Politics of Representation of Islam in Korea." *Journal of Korean Religions* 9, no.1 (April 2018).

Korea Muslim Federation. *Islam in Korea*. Seoul: Korea Muslim Federation Publication, 2008.

Kwon, Jeeyun. "South Korea's Yemeni Refugee Problem." Essay of MEI (Middle East Institute). April 23, 2019. https://www.mei.edu/publications/south-koreas-yemeni-refugee-problem.

Langlois, John S., ed. *China under Mongol rule*. New Jersey: 1981.

Lee, Hee Soo. *Korea and the Muslim World: A Historical Account.* Istanbul: IRCICA, 2020.

Lee, Hee-Soo. *Kushnameh (Korean)*. Seoul: Cheong-A Publication, 2014.

Lee, Hee Soo. "Evaluation of Kushnama as a Historical Source in Related to Description of Basilla. *Acta Koreana* 21, no. 1 (June 2018).

Lee, Hee Soo. *Islam Turk Kulturunun Uzak Dogu'ya Yayilmasi.* Ankara: Turkiye Diyanet Vakfi, 1988.

Lee, Hee Soo. "Islam in Far East." In *The Spread of Islam through the World,* edited by Idris El Hareir and El Hadji Ravane M' Baye, 759–783. Paris: UNESCO Publishing: 2011.

Lee, Hee Soo, and Young Joo Jo. "A Survey of Muslim Immigrants in Korea – Focused on adaptation to Korean Life-style and Religious Observation. *Korea Journal of Middle Eastern Studies* 33, no. 1 (2012).

Sheikh, Farrah. " Exploring "Korean Islam" in a Climate of Exclusion and Islamophobia." *International Journal of Diaspora & Cultural Criticism* 9, no. 22 (2019).

al-Tājir, Sulaymān. *Akhbār al-Ṣīn wa-l-Hind,* edited and translated by J. Savagat. Paris, 1948.

Vosoughi, Mohammed Bagher, and Hee Soo Lee. *Ancient Korea in the Arabic and Persian Manuscripts*. Samarkand: IICAS Publication, 2020.

Chapter 11

The Muslim Art of Management: Zheng He (1371–1433) and his Maritime Expeditions

LEE Cheuk Yin

Senior Professor of East Asian Studies, Institute of Asian Studies, Universiti Brunei Darussalam

About 600 years ago, a huge fleet with more than 27,000 men set sail from the Liujia harbour in Nanjing to begin China's first-ever large-scale oceanic journey, marking a brilliant chapter in the maritime history of mankind. The expeditions were the largest naval expedition during that period of time as it comprised of as many as 300 ships of various sizes (including 62 large treasure ships).[457] In a span of twenty-eight years, from 1405 to 1433, seven expeditions were made to Southeast Asia, the Indian Ocean, the Red Sea, and the east coast of Africa, covering more than thirty countries and regions that include Annam, Champa, Cambodia, Malacca, Siam, Java, Ryukyu, Palembang, Brunei, Sumatra, Bengal, Ceylon, Cochin, Hormuz, Dhufar, Aden along the Red Sea, and Mogadishu on the east coast of Africa. The person who commanded the expeditions was the Muslim diplomat Zheng He 郑和 (1371–1433).

Zheng He was born to a Muslim family in 1371 at Kunyang in Yunnan province, China. His original surname at birth was Ma, a very common surname among Muslims in China. In 1382, the Ming army defeated the Mongols in Yunnan, and Ma He was captured and brought to the imperial capital where he was made a eunuch and assigned to service in the palace of the Prince of Yan. He served the prince faithfully and distinguished himself when the prince usurped the throne in 1403 and became Emperor Yongle. He was gradually promoted to the rank of grand eunuch and honoured with the surname Zheng. In 1405, to publicize the Ming dynasty's wealth and supremacy to countries in Southeast Asia and beyond, Emperor Yongle ordered Zheng

457 Louise Levathes, *When China Ruled the Seas: The Treasure Fleet of the Dragon Throne, 1405-1433* (New York: Oxford University Press, 1997), 87.

He to head the first maritime expedition overseas. From 1405 to 1433, Zheng He led seven maritime expeditions to the "western oceans."[458] He was praised by historians as a navigator, discoverer, and diplomat of the Ming dynasty.[459]

Dates and Places of Visit of Zheng He's Seven Voyages[460]

Year	Places of Visit
1405–1407	Visited Champa, Java, Palembang, Malacca and Aden, Captured pirate leader Chen Zuyi in Palembang.
1407–1409	Visited Brunei, Siam, Cambodia, and Calicut.
1409–1411	Visited Champa, Siam, Java, Malacca, Aru, Sumatra, Lambri, Ceylon, Quilon, Cochin, Calicut and Cambay.
1413–1415	Visited most of the countries in Southeast Asia, and as far as eastern coast of Africa.
1417–1419	Visited more than 19 countries, as far as Hormuz and Mogadishu.
1421–1422	Visited Siam, Sumatra, Dhofar, Aden, and Mogadishu.
1431–1433	Visited Champa, Malacca, Java, Palembang, Sumatra, Ceylon, Calicut, Hormuz.

The main motivation behind the expeditions has always been a controversial subject. During the Ming Dynasty, the Chinese showed much interest in the neighboring countries and specifically, what they could offer them economically. Historians such as Edward Dreyer and Roderich Ptak have described the expeditions as diplomatic and commercial. These voyages expanded China's trade route and improved overseas trade of goods such as silk and porcelain with exploring neighbouring countries.[461] Edward Dreyer argued that the voyages were rather peaceful ones, having no interest in "conquering or looting the countries reached by his fleet, but rather in exploring and expanding commerce and diplomatic relations within the tribute system."[462] Dreyer also stated that "the naval expeditions formed the main channel for the promotion of

458 Western Oceans is an expression used to denote places west of Malacca during the Ming dynasty.
459 Refer to Chiu Ling-yeong, "Zheng He: Navigator, Discoverer and Diplomat," *Wu Teh Yao Memorial Lectures 2000* (Singapore: UniPress, 2001).
460 Details of dates and places of visit refer to Edward L. Dreyer, *Zheng He: China and the Oceans in the Early Ming Dynasty, 1405–1433* (New York: Pearson Longman, 2007); Cheuk Yin Lee, ed., *Zheng He and Maritime Asia* (Singapore: National Library Board, 2005).
461 Roderich Ptak, *China and the Asian Seas: Trade, Travel, and Visions of the Other (1400–1750)* (Aldershot: Ashgate, 1998), 23.
462 Edward L. Dreyer, *Early Ming China: A Political History 1355–1435* (Stanford: Stanford University Press, 1982), 195.

trade with countries of the south."[463] This was shared by Louise Levathes who claimed that the main purpose of the voyages was to expand their trade route for foreign goods.[464] Zheng He's expeditions were more for a commercial purpose rather than political. Other historians such as Chiu Ling-Yeong of the University of Hong Kong argues that the significance of the voyages was to demonstrate China's military superiority and conciliatory diplomacy.

Works that have been done on the expeditions attest to their historical and economical implications, as well as diplomatic and cultural contributions. However, expeditions of such a large scale involved detailed planning, organising, meticulous management, and operation. Zheng He's wisdom in managing these unparalleled operations has however not been fully studied. Treating the expedition team as a gigantic organization and Zheng He as its leader, this chapter attempts to examine this enormous achievement from a different perspective. I focus on the management traits that we can learn from Zheng He.

Effective Leadership and Human Resources Management

According to Han Fei Zi (born around 280–233 BC), who is regarded as the founder of the Legalist School and the advocator of law and punishment that contributed to the unification of China by Emperor Qin Shihuang in 221 BC, a good ruler and leader should have the following qualities:

> The ruler must not reveal his desire; for if he reveals his desires his ministers will put on the mask that pleases him. He must not reveal his will; for if he does so his ministers will show a different face. So, it is said: Discard likes and dislikes and the ministers will show their true form; discard wisdom and wile and the ministers will watch their step. Hence, though the ruler is wise, he hatches no schemes from his wisdom, but causes all men to know their place. Though he is worth, he does not display it in his deeds, but observes the motives of his ministers. Though he is brave, he does not flaunt his bravery in shows of indignation but allows his subordinates to display their valor to the full... When the ministers stick to their posts, the hundred officials have their regular duties, and the ruler employs each according to his particular ability, this is known as the state of manifold constancy.[465]

Effective leadership is an important factor in determining the success of an operation or organization. Zheng He was personally selected by the emperor to lead the expeditions. He was chosen because of his bravery in assisting the emperor to ascend to the throne during a military coup. He demonstrated the ability of an effective leader with his good sense of management, living up

463 Ibid.

464 Levathes, *When China Ruled the Seas*, 88.

465 See Burton Watson, *Han Fei Tzu*, Section 5, "The Way of the Ruler," (Columbia University Press, 1964), 16.

to Emperor Yongle wise judgement in identifying an accomplished person to achieve his vision.

As leader of the operations, Zheng He was efficacious in building up his team of senior administrators to support him. According to historical records, he was able to identify many capable talents as assistants, such as senior eunuchs Wang Jinghong 王景弘 , Hou Xian 侯显, Li Xing 李兴, Zhu Liang 朱良, Yang Zhen 杨珍, Hong Bao 洪保, Zhou Man 周满, Zhang Da 张达, and Wu Zhong 吴忠. Some of them are experienced diplomats with official experiences to the western seas or other countries in present central Asia. His team of experts also included talented scholars Ma Huan 马欢, Fei Xin 费信, and Gong Zhen 巩珍. They served as record-keepers and interpreters and compiled very detailed travelogues of the countries they visited after they returned to China. Some examples that could be cited here are: the *Yengyai Shenglan* 瀛涯胜览 (Wonderful Scenery of the Boundless Oceans) by Ma Huan, the *Xingcha Shenglan* 星槎胜览 (Wonderful Scenery of the Starry Travels) by Fei Xin, and the *Xiyang fanguo zhi* 西洋番国志 (Record of the Foreign States in the Western Oceans) by Gong Zhen. Their first-hand accounts of the scenery and culture of the foreign lands enhanced Chinese understanding of the western countries and re-shaped their worldview.

The expeditions also demonstrated Zheng He's well-planned allocation and placement of human resources. During the first expedition in 1405, Zheng He brought along 27,800 men, which included seven imperial eunuchs serving as envoys, ten proctors as deputy envoys, ten junior eunuchs, fifty-three eunuch-chamberlains, two regional military commissioners, ninety-three guard commanders, 104 battalion commanders, 403 company commanders, one Ministry of Revenue director, two officers from Ministry of Rites, two drafters, one instructor, one official astrologer and four assistants, ten interpreters, 108 medical officers and medical assistants, and 26,803 military officers, chosen officers, soldiers, cooks, and clerks.[466] The division of labour and assembling a team of talents in accordance with their aptitude, contributed to the smooth implementation of the unpredictable visits and the success of the operation.

It takes vision to be a leader. Zheng He's determination and hard work should be credited for the success of the large-scale and extensive expeditions. From 1405 to 1433, Zheng He made seven voyages to the western oceans. Within the time span of twenty-eight years, he was travelling consecutively and spent most of his time at sea. Many of the places he visited had no previous contact with China, which made the trips full of uncertainty and danger. Besides, one trip, back and forth and waiting time for the monsoons, usually took almost two years. Between the expeditions, Zheng He was back in

466 *Zheng He Jiapu* 郑和家谱, see Chiu Ling-yeong, *Zheng He: Navigator, Discoverer and Diplomat*, 10.

Nanjing only for a few months to repair his ships and replenish his supplies. Some of his entourage and sailors would also be replaced so that they could stay with their families and rest, but not Zheng He, who exemplified the indomitable spirit of a leader.

Rigorous Coordination and Communication Strategy

According to the classical work *The Art of War* by Sun Zi (Sun Wu, 545–470 BC), "There is no difference between administering many troops and few troops, a large army or small army. It is a matter of organization and communication respectively."[467] Besides acting as a strategist, an effective leader should also be a good organizer. It is important for a leader to have a clear and efficient organizational structure with properly defined authority and responsibility, reporting relationships and structure of communication. A good organization structure will clarify the flow of command. Organization structure resembles the backbone or skeleton of a human being. The skeleton supports the human body, it provides the framework of the body and holds the internal organs in place. Without it, the human body will not be able to stand and move. Similarly, in an organization, it is important to have a properly defined structure and chain of command, an unbroken line of authority that flows from the topmost level to the lowest. The structure of Zheng He's high sea fleet demonstrates his organizational capability.

China's ship building industry was making rapid progress even before the Ming dynasty. When the founding emperor of the Ming dynasty Emperor Hungwu unified China, he defeated his rivals Chen Youliang and Zhang Shicheng in river battles with galleon fleets and later incorporated their navy into his own forces. This laid the foundation for the maritime expeditions about 50 years later. To prepare for the expeditions, Zheng He spent more than two years to build his ships at the Longjiang shipyard in Nanjing. The ships, according to the *Xiyang Ji* 西洋记 (Records of Western Oceans) by Luo Maodeng in 1697, can be classified into five types:

1. Treasure ship with 9 masts, 44.4 zhang long and 18 zhang broad.
2. Horse ship with 8 masts, 37 zhang long and 15 zhang broad.
3. Supply ship with 7 masts, 28 zhang long and 12 zhang broad.
4. Billet ship with 6 masts, 24 zhang long and 9.4 zhang broad.
5. Battleship with 5 masts, 18 zhang long and 6.8 zhang broad.

Based on the measurement of the Ming dynasty, one *zhang* 丈 is made up of ten "*chi*" or "Chinese feet." Although the exact length of a *zhang* and *chi* has varied over time, the Ming *chi* was probably about 12.2 inches (31.1

467 For a detailed discussion, see Lionel Giles, *Sun Tzu: The Art of War*, "Critical Notes and Commentaries" (Hong Kong: Tuttle Publishing, 2008).

centimeters) according to the research by Edward Dreyer. Incredibly, the largest ships in the fleet (called "treasure ships") were likely between 440 and 538 feet long by 210 feet wide. The 4-decked treasure ship had an estimated displacement of 20–30,000 tons, roughly 1/3 to 1/2 the displacement of modern American aircraft carriers. Each had nine masts on its deck, rigged with square sails that could be adjusted in series to maximize efficiency in different wind conditions. Emperor Yongle ordered the construction of an amazing sixty-two or sixty-three such treasure ships for Zheng He's first voyage in 1405. Extant records show that another forty-eight were ordered in 1408, plus forty-one more in 1419, along with 185 smaller ships throughout that time. Along with dozens of treasure ships, each armada included hundreds of smaller ships. The eight-masted ships, called "horse ships," were about 2/3 the size of the treasure ships measuring approximately 340 feet by 138 feet. As indicated by the name, it carried horses along with timber for repairs and tribute goods, whereas the seven-masted grain ships or supply ships carried rice and other food for the crew and soldiers in the fleet. A supply ship was about 257 feet by 115 feet in size. The next ships in descending order of size were the Billet ships, at 220 by 84 feet, with each transport ship having six masts. Finally, the small, five-masted battleships, each about 165 feet long, were designed to be maneuverable in battle.

However, coordinating 27,000 people separated in more than 200 ships, needs an efficient and effective communication system. How did Zheng He command and move his fleet and people? Without the benefit of today's technologies, how did Zheng He communicate with his fleet and crew throughout his voyages?

Zheng He made use of an elaborate system of sight and sound signals to communicate among the various ships of his unprecedented epic fleet when they were out in the open seas.[468] All his ships carried with them one large flag, some signal bells, five banners, one large drum, gongs, and ten lanterns. Sound signals were activated when commands needed to be issued on board a ship, while gongs and drums were used to create audible signals between ships so as, for example, to issue a warning for the fleet to take shelter in a safe harbour when a storm was imminent, or to communicate during war, or even bad weather. Each of Zheng He's ships was also identified by its special colour and a black flag with a large white character that indicated which squadron it belonged to. During the day, flag signals were used for communication. In the darkness of night, and in bad weather, lanterns were used to convey signals that were visible over some distances. Carrier pigeons were used for longer-range communication.

468 Levathes, *When China Ruled the Seas*, 83.

Apparently to support this system of sight and sound communication, Zheng He also carefully sailed with a fleet formation called "Flying Swallow Formation" that looked like a flying swallow with its two wings spread out.[469] In the middle would be the large treasure ships that carried the imperial gifts and Zheng He and his senior associates; then surrounding these would command ships which functioned as the navigational operations centre; then the supplies ships (carrying grains and water supplies) would be positioned to the front, back, left and right; and all these were guarded by the battle ships. With Zheng He's Commander-in-Chief Ship right in the centre of the formation, he could more easily oversee and communicate and hence command the entire fleet. This unique communication system and formation enabled Zheng He to command and communicate with his associates and crew effectively and readily.

Winning the Hearts is to Win the World

In the *Loulin* 娄离 chapter of the *Book of Mencius*, Mencius said: "One who wins the people wins the world." To win the world, you must win people's heart; to win people's heart, it starts with your own heart. Thus, in the *Analects*, Confucius said: "If you want to rule the country, first put your house in order; if you want to cultivate your morality, first put your heart right. To put your heart right, you must be sincere." By extension of this understanding, Confucius advocates: "A man of benevolence, wishing himself to be established, sees that others are established; wishing himself to be successful, sees that others are successful." To be able to mobilize 27,000 people to seek after the vision of such an adventurous expedition, Zheng He not only had to win the heart and trust of his team but also that of the people along the way.

The maritime expedition was Ming China's attempt to restore the existing tributary relations with foreign countries. The Chinese tributary system had been in practice since the Zhou dynasty. However, if we are to use institutional organization as a criterion, a "formal" "system" of tributary relations dated no earlier than the Ming. It was an integral part of the traditional Chinese World Order that China is the "Middle Kingdom," the emperor was the "Son of Heaven," and thus "All-under-Heaven" are imperial territories.[470] Under this relationship, the vassal states pay tribute to China and, in return, they received generous gifts and protection from the suzerain.[471] Ming China interacted with its tributaries in an arrangement combining both ceremonial vassalage

469 Tan Ta Sen, *Cheng Ho and Malacca* (Singapore: International Zheng He Society, 2005), 16–17.
470 For a discussion on the Chinese World Order, refer to John King Fairbank, ed., *The Chinese World Order: Traditional Foreign Relations* (Cambridge: Harvard University Press, 1968), "A Preliminary Framework," 1–19.
471 Tan Ta Sen, *Admiral Zheng He and Southeast Asia* (Singapore: Institute of Southeast Asian Studies, 2005), 53.

and gift exchanges. The arrangement was reciprocal in the sense that non-Chinese tributaries submitted to the Chinese emperor, who in turn rewarded displays of compliance and loyalty with benevolence, usually in the form of generous gifts and trade concessions.

Zheng He's seven maritime expeditions demonstrated the financial and military strength of Ming China during the Yongle reign, aiming to establish tributary relations between the Chinese court and foreign territories. Thus, it can be inferred that Emperor Yongle, who had a passion for undertaking monumental projects, saw the re-establishment of the tributary system as a driving force for the Ming dynasty in seeking recognition from neighbouring countries and legitimization of his ascension to the throne. As the *Official History of the Ming Dynasty* has mentioned, the expeditions were political and diplomatic. Emperor Yongle wanted to "display his soldiers in strange lands in order to make manifest the wealth and power of the Middle Kingdom." [472] Therefore, it can be deduced that the expansion of the trade route or promotion of trade was not entirely a goal that Emperor Yongle had in mind. In retrospect, the tributary system was often plainly a "thin cover for trade." [473] Emperor Yongle ordered the fleet simply to "display his power and for them to comply with Chinese tributary system." [474] In sum, the expeditions focused less on trade, but more emphasis was placed on re-enforcing the tributary system that was inactive during the time of Emperor Hongwu. In conjunction, it was also aimed at strengthening the diplomatic relations with neighboring states.

However, in his contact with foreign countries, though accompanied by more than 15,000 soldiers, Zheng He tried his best to win the hearts of the people he encountered and adopted a policy of peaceful collaboration rather than military confrontation. Whenever he arrived at a country, Zheng He would communicate the Ming emperor-decreed mission to others and sought to reassure the locals and rulers by having the imperial decree read out in public. This would also include the reading of imperial appointments which represented the Ming emperor's endorsement and respect for the authority of the local rulers.[475] An example of the imperial decree issued by the Emperor Yongle in 1409 read:

> I, the emperor, send my words to the kings and chieftains of foreign states in the far west, that I follow heaven's order to rule the world, to execute heaven's will to grant blessings and virtues. It is my wish that in all lands covered with sunshine and showered with moonlight, and moistened by frost and dew, its people,

472 Zhang Tingyu et al., eds., *Ming Shi* (Official History of the Ming Dynasty), 304:7766.
473 Dreyer, *Zheng He: China and the Oceans in the Early Ming Dynasty, 1405–1433*, 34.
474 Ibid., 26.
475 Tan Ta Sen and Chia Lin Sien, eds., *The Zheng He Epic*, 1st edition in Chinese edited by Zhou Wenlin et al. (Kunming, Yunnan, China: Yunnan's Publishing House, Yunnan Fine Arts Publishing House, Auora Publishing House, 2006), 316.

> regardless of age, may be granted a stable livelihood, and a safe shelter. Today, I send Zheng He to spread my message. All must obey heaven's will and follow my words and know your limits. Do not bully the minority. Do not attack the weak. All should share in the prosperity of peaceful times. If you wish to pay tribute to my court, you will be bestowed with gifts of goodwill. I send my edict to let you know my message.[476]

The imperial decree demonstrated the Ming government's intention to share blessings and goodwill, and that all peoples should live in peace and be able to have a stable livelihood. There was also a call for all to follow heaven's will and not to bully or attack others, especially the weak. By announcing the Ming Court's vision of peace and stability and his maritime mission undertaken to achieve that vision, Zheng He was able to give the locals the peace of mind that his large fleet's visit was not a threat. The visits reconfirmed Emperor Yongle's vision that if there were peace and friendly ties amongst nations, trade would prosper, and all peoples would benefit.

Hum Sin Hoon in his study of the expeditions, categorized Zheng He's strategies as "Art of Collaboration" and regarded it as an alternative model to Sun Zi's "Art of War" for the approach towards achieving a goal. Instead of using aggression, antagonism and colonization to help China prosper and rule the waves and hence the world, Zheng He used a softer approach and collaborated with other countries for mutual benefit. In contrast to the more well-known Sun Zi's *Art of War* which sees and seeks to overcome others as competitors and enemies, the lesser-known Zheng He's *Art of Collaboration* seeks to work with others as friendly neighbours and peaceful partners. This alternative worldview and mindset embodied in the Zheng He's *Art of Collaboration* is a major implication for our consideration and adoption in today's world.[477]

Besides highlighting the importance of peaceful co-existence, the maritime expeditions also manifested China's recognition of cultural and religious diversity. During one of Zheng He's expeditions, a trilingual inscription tablet written in Chinese, Persian, and Tamil was installed in Sri Lanka around 1411–1412. While the Chinese text of the inscription pays homage to the Buddha and Buddhist relics on the island, the Persian text invokes Allah, and the Tamil version offers reverence to the deity Tenavarai-nāyanār, an incarnation of the Brahmanical god Vishnu. The inscription, which is now in the National Museum in Colombo, is a unique and important artefact that demonstrates Ming China's awareness of the presence of different peoples on the island, as well as their respective faiths and languages; it is also a symbol of connectivity in the

476 《郑和家谱》*Zheng He Jiapu* (Genealogy of Zheng He), 〈敕谕海外诸番条〉 in《郑和下西洋资料汇编》*Zheng He xiaxiyang ziliao huibian* (Compilation of Resources on Zheng He's Voyages to the Western Oceans), Volume 1 (Shanghai: Ocean Press, 2005), 531.

477 Hum Sin Hoon, *Zheng He's Art of Collaboration: Understanding the Legendary Chinese Admiral from Management Perspective* (Singapore: Institute of Southeast Asian Studies, 2012), 50.

Indian Ocean that Sri Lanka is a hub for itinerant merchant groups, shipping networks, and strategic interests.[478] As a diplomat of the Chinese government, respecting the faith and culture of the people in the Western Oceans contributed to Zheng He's success in winning the hearts of the people along the way. His inclusiveness and peaceful collaboration marked the characteristics of his management values that still have a role to play in our modern world.

Conclusion

The *Art of War* said: "When the general is weak and lacks authority; when his instructions are not clear and distinct; when there are no consistent duties assigned to officers and men, and the ranks are slovenly formed, the result is utter disorganization."[479] The statement strongly emphasizes the importance of leadership. In fact, leadership has always been recognized as the most important factor contributing towards organizational effectiveness and success. Zheng He's maritime expeditions demonstrated his extraordinary leadership ability and served as an interesting case study for multi-cultural interactions.

Wang Daiyu 王岱舆 (a. 1580–1658), the first Muslim thinker to write in Chinese to explain the teachings of the Qur'ān, wrote in his momentous work *Zhengjiao Zhenquan* 正教真铨 (The Real Commentary on the True Teaching) about leadership: "The Sage said: You all have to show sympathy for your subordinates. We all are the creation of the True Lord. Our body and fate are the same, happiness and anger are naturally no different. Thus, what we do not accept, we should not lay on others. Otherwise, on the judgment day, the True Lord and myself will be the witness."[480] As a Chinese Muslim, Zheng He is well versed in both Islam and Chinese values. He was guided by Islam principles and the Chinese wisdom of human relationships. His emphasis on harmonizing the ideals of Islam and that of other civilizations form the core of Osman Bakar's lifetime works which we are celebrating in this volume. As Osman has emphasized, Chinese-Confucian values stress the importance of human relationships and seniority. For example, in the core value of "benevolence" (ren 仁) in Confucianism, the Chinese character for "ren" is a combination of the "person" radical and the "two" ideogram, which denotes the relationships of two persons and the importance of human relations in ancient Chinese thought. This is in line with the Islamic emphasis on

478 See Tansen Sen, "Serendipitous Connections: The Chinese Engagements with Sri Lanka," in *Connectivity in Motion: Island Hubs in the Indian Ocean World*, eds. Burkhard Schnepel & Edward Alpers (New York: Palgrave Macmillan, 2018).

479 Sun Zi, *The Art of War*, 10/18. Translation of the passage refer to Lionel Giles, *Sun Tzu: The Art of War*, 44, with modification.

480 Wang Daiyu, *Zhengjiao Zhenquan* (Yinchuan: Ningxia People's Press, 1988), 97. For a discussion on Wang Daiyu, see Lee Cheuk Yin, "Islamic Values in Confucian Terms: Wang Daiyu and His *Zhengjiao Zhenquan*," in *Islam and Confucianism: A Civilizational Dialogue*, ed. Osman Bakar (ISTAC-IIUM Publications, 2019), 87–106.

respect towards all in society. For the same reason, Zheng He's Islamic heritage and acquired Chinese values enable him to manoeuvre between two cultures. Management is about human relationships and how we deal with people. To win the hearts of the people and accomplish his task, Zheng He's leadership traits and policy of respect and collaboration made the expeditions a great success.

Zheng He was entrusted by the emperor with the fundamental mission of pursuing a maritime diplomacy by spreading China's supremacy and forging tributary ties between China and countries in Asia and Africa. He was to lead the voyages to the west to spread goodwill, and in the process, network and build bridges for trade and collaboration, so that everyone would coexist harmoniously as they were ruled in accordance with the ways of heaven, and in this way, do justice to the grandeur and splendour of the Ming Imperial Court.[481] It was the lofty visions of these expeditions that stimulated trade relations between China and countries in Southeast Asia, South Asia, and the Middle East. It was also these expeditions which demonstrated China's maritime superiority in the fifteenth century,[482] and the eventual establishment of the so-called Maritime Silk Road, because of such an enormous task. The impact of such expeditions is immense and everlasting. To a certain extent, we may say that the current Belt and Road Initiative (BRI) is a continuation of Zheng He's peaceful diplomacy and international trade.

481 Hum Sin Hoon, *Zheng He's Art of Collaboration*, 9–10.

482 Chiu Ling-yeong, *Zheng He: Navigator, Discoverer and Diplomat*, 5.

Bibliography

Chia, Lin Sien, and Sally Church, eds. *Zheng He and the Afro-Asian World.* Malaysia: Perbadanan Muzium Melaka (PERZIM), 2012.

Chiu, Ling-Yeong. *Zheng He: Navigator, Discoverer and Diplomat.* Singapore: Unipress, the Centre of the Arts, National University of Singapore, 2001.

Dreyer, Edward L. *Early Ming China, A Political History 1355–1435.* Stanford: Stanford University Press, 1982.

Dreyer, Edward L. *Zheng He: China and the Oceans in the Early Ming Dynasty, 1405–1433.* New York: Pearson Longman, 2007.

Fairbank, John King, ed., *The Chinese World Order: Traditional Foreign Relations.* Cambridge: Harvard University Press, 1968.

Fang, Zhong Fu, and Li Erhe. *Peace Missions on a Grand Scale.* Beijing: Foreign Language Press, 2005.

Giles, Lionel. *Sun Tzu: The Art of War.* Hong Kong: Tuttle Publishing, 2008.

Hum, Sin Hoon. *Zheng He's Art of Collaboration: Understanding the Legendary Chinese Admiral from Management Perspective.* Singapore: Institute of Southeast Asian Studies, 2012.

Lee, Cheuk Yin, ed. *Zheng He and Maritime Asia.* Singapore: National Library Board, 2005.

Levathes, Louise. *When China Ruled the Seas: The Treasure Fleet of the Dragon Throne, 1405–1433.* New York: Oxford University Press, 1997.

Osman Bakar and Cheng Gek Nai, eds. *Islam and Confucianism: A Civilizational Dialogue.* Kuala Lumpur: ISTAC-IIUM Publications, 2019.

Ptak, Roderich. *China and the Asian Seas: Trade, Travel, and Visions of the Other (1400–1750).* Aldershot: Ashgate, 1998.

Ptak, Roderich. *China's Seaborne Trade with South and Southeast Asia, 1200–1750.* Aldershot: Ashgate, 1999.

Tan, Ta Sen. *Admiral Zheng He and Southeast Asia.* Singapore: Institute of Southeast Asian Studies, 2005.

Wade, Geoff, and Sun Laichen, ed. *Southeast Asia in the Fifteenth Century: The Ming Factor.* Singapore: NUS Press, 2010.

Wang, Gungwu. *China and the Chinese Overseas.* Singapore: Times Academic Press, 1991.

Su, Ming-Yang. *Seven Epic Voyages of Zheng He in Ming China, 1405–1433: Facts, Fiction and Fabrication.* California: Torrance, 2005.

Zhang, Tingyu et al., eds. *Ming Shi* (Official History of the Ming Dynasty). Beijing: Zhonghua Book Store, 1974.

Part 2

Civilizational Unity and Renewal

Chapter 12

Knowledge of Unity and the Thrust of the Esoteric in Religion

Patrick Laude

Professor at the School of Foreign Service (Qatar), Georgetown University

The following essay builds on the bedrock of Osman Bakar's intellectual contribution: the relationship between knowledge and Divine Unity, and the process of "unification" of human knowledge that this relationship involves. Osman's perspective on Islamic knowledge is predicated on the principle of synthetic inclusion and harmonization that he sees as inherent to Qur'ānic *tawḥīd*. He articulated it as follows: "The essence of Qur'anic *tawḥīd* is the first article of faith, namely the belief in one God, which, metaphysically speaking, contains all the other articles of faith (*arkān al-īmān*)."[483] The "first article of faith" is the witnessing of Divine Unity (*lā ilāha ill'Allāh*: No god but God).[484] Readers familiar with Islam will also recognize "all the other articles of faith" mentioned in the previous statement as "God's angels, His books, His messengers, and the Last Day, and that you affirm the Decree [predestination], the good of it and the bad of it" according to the *ḥadīth* of Gabriel (*Muslim*). Osman Bakar essentially argues that the belief in one God, as understood theologically in reference to the exclusive unity of the Divinity, translates metaphysically as including all components of the faith. This implies a crucial distinction between the concept of Unity and its metaphysical grasp.

To be sure, if *theology* is about God (ο Θεός, *o théos*), then Islamic theology can be simply defined by the principle that God is One, since the elementary basis of religion amounts to rejecting of any divine plurality. When Islam emerged in the seventh century of the Christian era, it primarily affirmed itself in opposition to the worship of the Arabian idols. However, this "numerical" dimension of Qur'ānic teachings is only the most basic stake. Metaphysically,

483 Osman Bakar, *Islamic Civilisation and the Modern World: Thematic Essays* (Brunei Darussalam: UBD Press, 2014), 49.

484 The second article of faith is a soteriological complement of the first: *Muhammad Rasūl Allāh* (Muhammad is the Messenger of God).

this same statement actually refers to Being, and not merely to number; to say that God is One means that He is *the* One Being (*wujūd).* Metaphysically, the God without associates cannot but be, in the last analysis, the only Reality, the One without any second: "Everything perishes but the Face of God." (Qur'ān, 28:88) Thus, a metaphysical understanding of Unity implies that multiplicity finds reality and meaning only through "unification" (*tawhīd*) or the "making one" of the (apparently) many. All the components of faith retrace aspects of this unification, the major ways in which multiplicity is "re-integrated" into Unity. The Angels, the Books and the Messengers are the holy mediators by which Unity is "brought into" multiplicity, whereas the Last Day and the Decree crystallize the ways in which multiplicity is brought back to Unity. In other words, the soteriological and the eschatological are essentially included in the metaphysical, and they unfold from it, or rather they are various modes of its very unfolding.

This essay starts from the premise that "the belief in one God," metaphysically speaking, contains all the other articles of faith. It is, in itself, an *esoteric* statement, which amounts to saying, as we will explain further on, that it is metaphysical, and not merely theological. The adjective "esoteric" may mean different things to different people, conjuring up the lures of the mysterious, or unease with the hidden. The Greek word *esoterikon* was originally associated with Ancient Greek philosophy and Mysteries religions.[485] It referred to teachings deemed to be relatively private and exclusive by contrast with public ones, which would be considered *exoteric.*[486] This is, needless to say, an extrinsic consideration, since the previous distinction does not tell us anything about the actual *content* of the respective teachings. We are just left with the assumption that esoteric teachings are either not accessible, or not acceptable, to all. The association of the esoteric with the metaphysical takes us deeper, however, than such an extrinsic consideration. It flows from our earlier definition of metaphysics as knowledge of the Unity that transcends multiplicity while embracing it.

Our contention is that the exoteric never reaches the ultimate consequences of such a consideration of Unity. It remains intrinsically formal, indirect, and "symbolic" (in a sense we will elaborate upon further on). By exoteric we mean, therefore, a religious perspective that sees knowledge as universally

485 Leo Strauss has referred to this distinction in terms of the Platonic contrast between "opinion" and "knowledge" and has seen philosophy as a discipline that considers the two levels, the exoteric out of respect for dogmatic conventions and the esoteric out of a search for the truth.

486 For instance, it has been referred to Plato's esoteric teachings: "(...) the word esoteric (...) is frequently applied to Platonic studies. In one common use, the idea of the esoteric suggests doctrines that circulated within the Academy (...) [i.e] 'unwritten doctrines,' a term that is borrowed initially from Aristotle's *Physics,* where Aristotle mentions certain principles of Plato's metaphysics revealed in his 'so-called unwritten doctrines.'" Sara Ahbel-Rappe, *Socratic Ignorance and Platonic Knowledge in the Dialogues of Plato* (Albany: SUNY Press, 2018), ix.

"mediated" and "transmitted," exclusively identified with specific forms, whether they be theological, juridical, moral and ritual, and, therefore, a point of view from which the relationship with Divine Reality pertains to "representation" rather than "presentation." By representation, I mean a mode of cognition that remains at a distance from its object and envisages it only indirectly, a vantage point whose limited horizon precludes the very possibility of bridging the ontological and epistemological gap that it absolutizes. This impossibility lies inherently with the exoteric point of view itself, as well as the mentalities and sensibilities it informs, and it follows from its formal and analytical scope. The exoteric scope envisages religious forms and practices *in reference to,* or *in response to,* a Divine Unity that is approached either as a superlative entity or as a rational principle: the One is never contemplated as the only Reality—such a point of view being incompatible with the very nature of the exclusively religious outlook. Exoteric perspectives are not in a position to address religious realities in terms of essential or synthetic inclusion, in terms of plurality being *contained* within Unity. By contrast, the argument of this essay is that knowledge is not only about Unity, but also from Unity, and ultimately Unity itself, the "esoteric" being none other than the most consistent orientation of the quest for knowledge. In this regard, knowledge of Unity, whether in Islam or elsewhere, cannot but have, in its most rigorous and consistent demands, an esoteric bent.

We live in a world in which multiplicity is celebrated as a measure, a condition, or even a guarantee of freedom and creativeness. Although a unity of purpose and action is often called for in response to collective objectives, the metaphysical affirmation of Unity tends to be seen, in our day and age, as reductive, if not oppressive, although there are many extenuating circumstances for this perception, particularly with respect to historical Islam. By contrast, multiplicity must remain multiple to abide by the cultural demands of the postmodern *Weltanschauung*. It must manifest, epistemologically, in an irreducible diversity of discrete modes of knowledge.[487] In this context, the "truth" is always relative to particular fields or experiences, and so-called doctrinal "narratives" fail to subsume this multiplicity under a unity of knowledge. Against such a dispersing deconstruction of knowledge, one of the main arguments presented by Osman Bakar is that knowledge, in Islam, has been unified by its Ultimate and Unique Object, hence a classification of knowledge that is totalizing, hierarchized and integrated.

While rooted in Divine Unity, the tawhīdic apprehension of reality is in no way uniform and leveled down. A comprehensive knowledge of Unity must involve, from a human point of view, a multiplicity that is unified, and

487 "Postmodern novels... openly assert that there are only truths in the plural, and never one Truth; and thee is rarely falseness *per se,* just others' truths." Charles D. Sabatos, *Frontier Orientalism and the Turkish Image in Central European Literature* (Lanham, Maryland: Lexington Books, 2020), 130.

therefore different degrees and modes in the way of this unification. In other words, *tawhīd*, whether in terms of being or knowing, means that the relationship to Unity needs to be considered at different stages in the process of "making one." This is so, first of all, because Unity is reflected, and refracted, in countless ways, the whole of the manifold being none other than the manifestation of the One. The ambiguity of this manifold reality—the theatre of our experiences—is highlighted by the tension between the negativity attached to centrifugal motion and the positivity inherent in Manifestation as Divine Reality, as implied by the Divine Name the Outer, *az-Zāhir*. The esoteric thrust of knowledge lies, precisely, in the centripetal quest that is the response to the onto-cosmic unfolding; the power of knowledge is re-integrating. It is akin to an inward motion through layers of reality in the direction of the principle of Unity. While the inward journey towards Reality may involve innumerable steps as knowledge moves, in various modes, from the periphery to the core Essence, it can in a way be synthesized as embracing three main moments: theoretical or abstract for the first, speculative for the second, and realizational by identity for the third. It is within the context of the second that the esoteric unfolds, while it is also true that the esoteric finds its *raison d'être* in the third and ultimate kind of knowledge, which, as we will suggest, both perfects and annuls it *as* esoteric.

These three ways of knowing—or not knowing depending on the vantage point—parallel Ibn 'Arabī's categorization in his *Bezels of Wisdom,* of the "knower," the "non-knower," and the "ignorant." "He who sees the Reality from His standpoint, in Him by Him is a gnostic [a 'knower' (*'ārif*)]. He who sees the Reality from His standpoint, in Him, but with himself as the seer, is not a gnostic ['non-knower' or 'other than a knower' (*ghayr 'ārif*)]. He who does not see the Reality in this way, but expects to see Him by himself, is ignorant (*jāhil*)." [488]

The current essay is an examination of some of the main implications of this distinction, and it develops reflections on the ways they bear upon the esoteric dimension of knowledge.

Ibn 'Arabī's Epistemological Tripartition

Ibn 'Arabī's categorization is based on the principle that any knowledge is ultimately a self-knowledge, meaning God's knowledge of Himself, in conformity with the sacred prophetic tradition: "I was a Hidden Treasure and I wanted to be known so I created the world." The world is the mirror in which

488 Ibn 'Arabī, *The Bezels of Wisdom*, trans. R.W.J. Austin (Mahwah, New Jersey: Paulist Press, 1980), 135–136. Caner Dagli's translation (*Ringstones of Wisdom*, Chicago: Kazi Publications, 2004, 115) is more precise in rendering the Arabic by "waiting to see Him with his own eye," which Izutsu (*Sufism and Taoism*, Berkeley: University of California Press, 2016, 253) renders even more explicitly as referring to a vision in the Hereafter, "to see the Absolute (in the Hereafter) by his own self."

God projects His unfathomable and infinite wealth of being. Ibn 'Arabī's understanding of this tradition encompasses all modes and degrees of being as knowledge, which means that any creature crystallizes an instantiation of Divine Self-knowledge. Knowledge is not just of the mind or the intellect. In epistemological terms, any cognition can be envisaged either as a mere instantiation within the fold of God's Self-knowledge, or as Self-knowledge itself. When considered from a human point of view, the two perceptions can be respectively designated as ignorance and knowledge, even though ignorance itself must paradoxically, and ultimately, be recognized as a mode of God's Self-knowledge. Ignorance is, in that sense, an "abstraction" of the cognized existent from the essential *Wujūd*, as it is also an "abstraction" of the cognizing agent from Divine Consciousness, *ash-Shuhūd*. While ignorance is a form of abstraction, a way of "detaching" the part from the Whole, knowledge is always "concrete," in the sense that it tends to integrate the part into the Whole. Thus, in typical fashion, Ibn 'Arabī identifies ignorance both as the illusion of a distance from the Real, and as an individual limitation on the real. It entails both not knowing in God, therefore outside of Unity, and knowing Him from the point of view of one's limitation and "by way of" this limitation, as "god of belief," therefore within a delimited form that falls short of His Reality.

Ultimately, however, this is a function of the Divine Jealousy whereby God hides the secret of His Unity—meaning that He is none other than His Creation, behind the veil of the ego and its limited belief. In such a context, the Hereafter, as object of the expectation or "waiting for" the vision of God, becomes a symbol of an incapacity to perceive the Real in the now of creation, *khalq al-jadīd*, that is as Unity of Essence. The unbridgeable and "forbidden" limit or partition, *hijran mahjuran* (25:53), eschatologically speaking, behind this world and the next, is a most suggestive expression of this otherness. The ignorance of the *jāhil*, whose encounter with the Real is both limited by his own form, and deferred in time, is ignorance from the point of view of true knowledge, that is metaphysical *tawhīd*, but it is no doubt an indirect and "symbolic" way of knowing, since it is oriented towards the Real. The Arabic word *jāhil* is akin to the noun *jāhiliyyah*, which refers to the "time of ignorance," the time of polytheism. Now, metaphysically, *jāhiliyyah* is nothing else than the negation of the Unity of Being, *wahdat al-wujūd*, or in other words the negation of Oneness.

The traditional Sufi distinction between *sharī'ah*, *tarīqah* and *haqīqah* corresponds, by and large, to Ibn 'Arabī's three epistemological categories. These are respectively the Law as periphery of the circle of knowledge, the Path as radius between the periphery and the center of knowledge, and the Truth as core reality of knowledge. This triadic arrangement is also aligned, with slightly different inflections, with another classic Sufi tripartition, that of *'ilm al-yaqīn*, *'ayn al-yaqīn* and *haqq al-yaqīn*, or the "science of certitude" or hearing about the fire, "the eye of certitude" or seeing the fire, and "the truth of certitude" or burning in the fire.[489] It is widely known, in Sufi lore, that these three modes of knowing correspond to stages having to do with reception, contemplation, and realization. In other words, hearing about the Truth means being receptive to its reality short of any direct contact with it. Seeing the truth, by contrast, is a form of *théôria* in the etymological sense of a contemplative perception of the Real. Finally, being consumed is none other than being That which one knows, or knowledge as disappearance (*fanā'*) and permanence (*baqā'*) in the One. By contrast with the *sharī'ah* and *'ilm al-yaqīn*, the *haqīqah*, or *haqq al-yaqīn*, is pure Unity and pure Identity. It annuls any distance, any difference, any other, through pure metaphysical *tawhīd*. As we have seen, it alone deserves the name of knowledge since this knowledge entails no "ignorance," all "others" having been consumed in the Fire of Unity. This is the essence of knowledge, and Ibn 'Arabī's very definition of the *'ārif bi-Llāh*, the knower "by God."

Knowledge by Identity

In his *Paths to Transcendence*, Reza Shah-Kazemi has convincingly shown that the highest knowledge of God that is envisaged by Ibn 'Arabī cannot be attributed to the individual as such, but can only be the Self-knowledge of the Divine Ipseity. Commenting upon Ibn 'Arabī's point that "*wujūd* [Being] is finding the Real in ecstasy" Shah-Kazemi notes that "here, the emphasis is placed upon the fact that the true nature of being is revealed only when it is absolutely identical with consciousness ("finding"); the inner content of this experience being the supreme beatitude proper to the Absolute. However, this transcendent level strictly excludes the individual (...)"[490] Ecstasy is not, as all-too often assumed, an individual experience of enthusiasm, transcendence or "otherness." In fact, what could be called "ecstatic knowledge" in its truest sense has rigorously nothing individual about it, even though some consequences of this knowledge might manifest extrinsically. This amounts to saying that this knowledge knows of no relativity. It is pure "savoring" of the Absolute, *al-Haqq*, by Itself. Although one can refer to this self-knowledge as "absolutely esoteric" on account of its identification with the pure *Bātin*, the Divine Inner, by contrast with "theophanic" modes of knowledge that are centered on the *Zāhir*, the Exterior, it is also evident that the adjective esoteric, inasmuch as it implies relativity, i.e. an exoteric domain, falls short of expressing that which is beyond all relativities, contrasts and relationships.

489 "The Divine Truth is symbolised by the element fire. The three degrees, in ascending order, are the Lore of Certainty (*'ilm al-yaqīn*), the Eye of Certainty (*'ayn al-yaqīn*) and the Truth of Certainty (*haqq al-yaqīn*). The Lore is the certainty that comes from hearing the fire described; the Eye is the certainty that comes from seeing its flames; the Truth is the certainty which comes from being consumed in it." Martin Lings, *What is Sufism?* (Berkeley: University of California Press, 1999), 61.

490 Reza Shah-Kazemi, *Paths to Transcendence* (Bloomington, Indiana: World Wisdom, 2006), 92.

Actually, such Self-knowledge annuls any difference and duality, hence the very distinction between an outer and an inner, an exoteric and an esoteric, as is couched, for example, in a passage from the *Fusūṣ* in the chapter "The Word of Enoch," "Naught is except the Essence, which is Elevated in Itself, its elevation being unrelated to any other."[491] The very notion of an "elevation in itself," with its oxymoronic implications, parallels the paradoxical status of Supreme Knowledge, sometimes approached as a Holy Ignorance, since the individual *qua* individual, therefore within the field of duality, cannot appropriate it in any real way: "The Divinity is beyond 'knowledge' insofar as this implies a subject and an object; for this reason the divine Essence is 'unknowable.'"[492]

As a prolongation of Ibn 'Arabī's distinctions, it is fruitful to consider Frithjof Schuon's meditation on the "conceptual dimensions" of knowledge in his *Transcendent Unity of Religions*. As we will further develop in this essay, Schuon distinguishes a two-dimensional knowledge, a three-dimensional knowledge, and a third epistemological dimension, which is none other than the perfection of knowledge. Leaving aside for now the first two modes, to which we shall return, "perfect knowledge" pertains to being, so to a dimension that transcends the merely conceptual. According to Schuon, this "perfect knowledge of (...) [the integral nature of the object] would be nothing else than identity with it." [493] It goes without saying that such an identity is utterly impossible on the formal plane, since the latter entails distinction and precludes identity. Identity presupposes an essential Unity that is of an altogether different order, indeed an incommensurable one. This order is unambiguously contemplated in Hindu *Advaita* in the form of a radical non-dualism that excludes any individual affirmation, any scission and any distance, being predicated as it is on the notion of *ajāta*, or non-creation. Creation is only metaphorical, it *is* not; Reality is What it is and That Thou Art, *Tat Tvam Asi*.

Ignorance of the Essence

Returning to the correspondence between the status of *jāhil* and the perspective of the *sharī'ah*, connections of the Law with "ignorance" run the risk of inducing potential misunderstandings, and the peril of unsettling conventional perceptions. It must be acknowledged, at any rate, that the main function of the Law is, in the first place, to palliate ignorance. The Law is like "the knowledge of ignorance," if such a paradoxical expression may be allowed. It is not strictly speaking a mode of knowledge, but a manner of participating indirectly and "symbolically" in it. It involves reception of, and obedience to, injunctions from the Real *qua* transcendent and relational Reality. Moreover, the

491 Ibn 'Arabī, *Bezels*, 85.
492 Frithjof Schuon, *Spiritual Perspectives and Human Facts* (Bloomington, Indiana: World Wisdom, 2007), 173.
493 Frithjof Schuon, *The Transcendent Unity of Religions* (Wheaton, Illinois, Chennai, India, 1984), 4.

Law is "abstract" inasmuch as it is a holy multiplicity in view of Divine Unity, not Unity itself. Indeed, the plurality of the sacred laws or *Sharīʿa*, that Islam acknowledges, is the very evidence that the legal sphere is "external" to Unity, and that it always entails a margin of ignorance, if only in what it excludes. Moreover, the Law emphasizes transcendence and *tanzīh*, Divine abstraction and incomparability. It is exoteric in that it considers forms of action not as participation in a higher reality—a concept it hardly grasps and considers with suspicion—but as imperative human responses to God's legal commands.

As for the "realizational" dimension of knowledge, the Law does not produce of itself transformation and union; it merely provides an external framework for it. Any given practice, like praying or fasting, traces the formal, symbolic contours of mere reflections of an internal reality, or even a given aspect of the Divine nature. Analogously ʿArabī's *jāhil,* although essentially "ignorant," is not utterly bereft of "knowledge," since the expectation of "seeing" God in the thereafter is an indirect apprehension of the Divine within the soteriological scope of the Law. As for the concept of *ʿilm al-yaqīn,* it is most often connected to "hearing about the truth," and there is little doubt that the verb "hearing," and its semantic kin "listening," corresponds to the Law since it evokes command, receptivity and obedience. In this regard, legal and eschatological realities belong to the same formal sphere of merits and rewards. To sum it up, all of these modes of "knowing ignorance" involve ontological and epistemological distance in ways that are unbridgeable on their own level. They bear the hallmark of an irreducibly dualistic outlook that is metaphysically lacking in regard to the most consistent *tawḥīd.* Notwithstanding, these formal realities provide indirect means of access to knowledge, which implies that they cannot be called "ignorance" without reservations, or without an allusive esoteric intent. In other words, the exoteric is not only a system in itself, it is also potentially a formal key of access to the esoteric, thus to Reality itself.

Now, what can be said of the Law in the realm of action can also be said, *mutatis mutandis*, of doctrine in the domain of thought. This is true both with regard to theological dogmas and metaphysical teachings.[494] In this respect, Frithjof Schuon[495] highlights that a merely "theoretical notion" is akin to the fixed and static vision of an object, and is therefore limited both with regard to the position of the seer and that of the seen object. It is therefore exclusive

494 The first is the theological fixation of a particular outlook that functions as the constraining and exclusive foundation of a religious creed. The second is the conceptual crystallization of a speculative approach to Reality. The difference between the two is that the first is fixed objectively, collectively and functionally, as it were, whereas the second is fixed only subjectively and "accidentally," since it is in principle a mere symbolic crystallization that points beyond its own limitations, as it were: "the ideas formulated in esoterism and in metaphysical doctrines generally may in turn be understood according to the dogmatic or theoristic tendency, and the case is then analogous to that of the religious dogmatism (...)" Schuon, *Transcendent Unity of Religions,* 2.
495 Schuon, *Transcendent Unity of Religions,* 4.

of any diversity of viewpoints and any plurality of facets. Being incapable of "reveal[ing] all possible aspects" of the object, it is also unable to grasp its "integral nature." Schuon refers, in this context, to the well-known Jain apologue of the blind men and the elephant. Each and every blind man has a limited view of the elephant not only because he is unable to see the animal, but also because his sensory identification with a given part of the animal prevents him from shifting his vantage point. The "theoristic" understanding of metaphysical ideas suffers from an analogous deficiency inasmuch as it replaces the symbolic understanding of metaphysical teachings with the mere "formal homogeneity of the doctrine." It follows that the issue is not with conceptual formulations as such, but rather with the ways in which they may be reductively envisaged.

We can see in *Advaita Vedānta* how a theoristic apprehension of the doctrine, far from being an intrinsic character of conceptual expression, is in fact an aberration of its nature and function, in a way that is analogous to the distinction between the legal and the legalistic, the formal and the formalistic. The traditional Advaitin training generally entails four stages, which can in a way be reduced to three. These are "listening," "reflecting," "meditating" and "realizing," or *śravana*, *manana*, *nididhyāsana* and *moksha*. The first two may be deemed to correspond to the formal and theoretical dimension. In Hindu *Advaita,* scripture and "mental meditation" provide the "exoteric" framework, as it were, even though the term "exoteric" is arguably ill-suited to be applied to a non-religious perspective.[496] Now, the hearing of scriptures and meditation upon them—or rather upon the doctrinal hermeneutics that is applied to them, correspond respectively to the passive and active poles of an elementary, two-dimensional apprehension of Reality. The second aspect, active mental meditation, is akin to what Schuon refers to as a "savor[ing] of the formal homogeneity of the doctrine,"[497] even though the implications of this "savoring" are indeed positive in *Advaita*, and in no way connected to self-indulgent intellectualism, by contrast with the theoristic tendency Schuon has in view. In *Advaita*, pondering, or *manana,* is a way to fathom the formal homogeneity of the teachings in order to establish solid grounds for spiritual realization. The latter comes forth with the stages of *nididhyāsana* and *moksha* or *nirvikalpa samādhi.* Hence, it is said: "Know meditation [*manana*]) to be a hundred times (superior) to listening [*śravaka*], assimilation [*nididhyāsana*], to be hundred thousand times (superior) to meditation [*manana*], and *nirvikalpa samādhi* to

496 This appears in full light when considering that scriptures can be understood "conventionally," therefore "exoterically," or "ultimately," therefore "esoterically," the first type of hermeneutics being dualistic (as entailing a distinction between *Brahman* and *jagat*) and the second consistently non-dualistic.

497 Actually Schuon uses this expression in the negative context of an understanding that is "merely conceptual and fixed as it were in one dimension" and therefore amounts to "an essential incomprehension." Schuon, *Spiritual Perspectives*, 80. It may be applied, however, more generally to any merely theoretical apprehension of metaphysical teachings.

be infinitely (superior) to assimilation." [498] Significantly, the adverb "infinitely" is only used in reference to the last stage, thereby highlighting the incommensurability between any formal component of the spiritual path and its goal.

Speculative and Esoteric Knowledge

Returning to Ibn Arabī's distinction between the *'ārif* and the *ghayr 'ārif*, it must be stressed that the only "otherness" entailed by the latter lies in the interposition of the human self. As the *'ārif*, the *ghayr ārif* knows God "in God" and "from God," but in contrast to the former, he merely knows Him "*by* himself." There is no difference between the metaphysical origin, "space" and content of knowledge and "other-than-knowledge" except with regard to the agent of knowledge. In other words, the non-knower is a *'ārif* that is "other" (*ghayr*) than his knowledge; which amounts to an intrusion of duality within knowledge. Notwithstanding the sharp contrast intended by Ibn 'Arabī in order to highlight the *pure* reality of knowledge, the epistemological status of *ghayr 'ārif* echoes the main thrust of speculative knowledge. In the latter indeed, Reality is reflected onto the human self, or perceived by the human eye as in a mirror, *speculum*. While the term "speculative" has become pejorative in contemporary parlance, since it connotes a lack of foundation and a want of reality, it retains positive denotations in traditional metaphysics as a symbolic allusion to the unhampered functioning of the human intellect.

In this regard, the most relevant elements of classic Sufi lore are the *tarīqah* and, with different inflections, *'ayn al-yaqīn*. As we have seen, the *tarīqah* is mediation between the *haqīqah* and the *sharī'ah*, the center and the periphery. It pertains to identity in difference, thus to a reflection of the Divine within the human. It also denotes motion upon the path, therefore a displacement of perspective. As for *'ayn al-yaqīn*, its symbolic field is that of vision, and it regards, as such, theophany, thus the speculative in the highest sense, since God is mirrored within His creation. This is the province of the esoteric as "contemplative interiorization" of phenomena and concepts. As the entire universe is none other than the Divine Self-disclosure, Ibn 'Arabī sees human perfection as a permanent receptivity to the countless ways in which the Ultimate makes Himself Manifest. In fact, the only way in which the human being *qua* human being may know God is as theophany, *tajalliyāt,* as in Ibn 'Arabī's famous verses from his *Tarjumān al-Ashwāq*, *The Interpreter of Desire:* "My heart has become capable of every form: it is a pasture for gazelles and a convent for Christian monks, and a temple for idols and the pilgrim's Ka'aba and the tables of the Tora and the book of the Koran."[499] This way is "esoteric"

498 Rājarāma Tukārāma Tātyā, *A Compendium of the Raja Yoga Philosophy: Comprising the Principal Treatises of Shrimat Shankaracharya and Other Renowned Authors* (Bombay: Bombay Theosophical Publication Fund, 1901), 149.

499 Muhyi'ddīn Ibn al-'Arabī, *The Tarjumān al-Ashwāq, A Collection of Mystical Odes,* trans. Reynold A.

to the extent that it is distinct from the "exoteric" perspective of Islam, which emphasizes transcendence: it entails an inner reading of the signs of God (*āyāt*) in the world, the Book and the soul. While the general economy of Islam emphasizes transcendence, thereby parrying idolatry, the esoteric reading of the world stresses Divine immanence, a perspective that is much less accessible than the former, and fraught with difficulties and challenges within the climate of Abrahamic monotheism.

As we have mentioned earlier, the "otherness" of speculative knowledge as seen in Ibn 'Arabī's "non-knowledge" presupposes a duality upon which unity is mirrored. Knowledge is unity, ignorance is duality, "other-than-knowledge" is unity reflected in multiplicity. There is, therefore, in the very nature of "other-than-knowledge" a relativity in the apprehension of the Absolute, since its perspective is *a priori* steeped in the manifold. This is the key to the pluriperspectival nature of knowledge *as* esoteric. We already quoted Schuon's point that "the perfect knowledge of (…) [the integral nature of the object] would be nothing else than identity with it." It goes without saying that such an identity is impossible on formal planes, since the latter entail distinction and preclude identity. Identity presupposes a unity of Essence that is incommensurable with any relative standpoint. There is, however, short of identity as such, "a certain mode of identity" that is accessible on the conceptual level, one that Schuon refers to as characteristic of the "dimensions of space": "a speculative and herefore intellectually unlimited conception (...) may be compared to the sum of all possible views of the object (...), views that presuppose in the subject a power of displacement or an ability to alter his viewpoint, hence a certain mode of identity with the dimensions of space, which themselves effectually reveal the integral nature of the object (...)."[500] This is the speculative dimension of knowledge; it is still contained within the domain of form, but it is free from the exclusive limitations of the latter to the extent that is possible within the formal order. There lie limitless conceptual modalities in response to the infinite aspects of the truth. The conceptual symbol is thereby open on both sides, that of the symbolizer and that of the symbolized.

The speculative and esoteric dimension of knowledge that has been sketched is akin, in some major respects, to the Advaitin *nididhyāsana*. The term, which refers to the third stage of Advaitin training, denotes "deep and repeated consideration, thinking of or recalling repeatedly."[501] There is, therefore, both a spatial and a temporal dimension to *nididhyāsana*. It involves an inward motion, a search within the dimension of inner depth, as well as a repetitive prodding in time, in succession. The term "consideration" is much more appropriate than "meditation" to refer to an activity that evokes, symbolically

Nicholson (Madras and Wheaton, Illinois: Theosophical Publishing House, 1978), 67.

500 Schuon, *Transcendent Unity*, 5.

501 H.H. Wilson, *A Dictionary of Sanscrit and English* (Calcutta: Education Press,1832), 467.

at least, contemplative intuition. According to Swami Satchidānandendra, *nididhyāsana* "means fixing the mental gaze on the principle of reality to determine its true nature, like one examining a jewel."[502] It is, therefore, nothing less than a relentless Self-examination. Thus, Michael James identifies *nididhyāsana* with the *Ātma-vichāra*, or Self-inquiry, of Ramana Maharshi. [503]

The Maharshi himself compares this investigation to the wooden stick that is used to push the corpse into the fire of the pyre.[504] This inquiry entails a gazing, a motion, a transformation and, ultimately a disappearance. It is a methodical means that is expedient, or instrumental, and destined to vanish into Unity. Inasmuch as it is situated at the meeting point, as it were, of assimilation as a process and assimilation as an outcome, *nididhayāsana* has been referred to as an "immediate intuition" identifiable with *vijñana*, "intuitive discerning knowledge." Indeed, this identification practically blurs the distinction between *nididhyāsana* and *moksha*: "All that has to be effected by immediate intuition is the practical negation of our Ignorance that we are the universal Self. Liberation is in no way distinct from immediate intuition of the Self.[505] Thus, Sureśvara does not hesitate to set *nididhyāsana* on the side of Self-realization, by contrast with a strict emphasis on its methodical aspect.[506] At any rate, the ambivalence of *nididhyāsana* is not without echoing our earlier reflections upon the two possible identifications of the esoteric with the *tarīqah* and the *haqīqah*, the first emphasizing its relativity, the second its quasi-identification with the Absolute itself. By contrast with *Advaita*, Ibn 'Arabi tends to stress the gap between "knowledge" and "other-than-knowledge," the gap between "speculative" knowledge and "Self-knowledge of the Absolute" remaining with him unbridgeable, in conformity with the religious determinations of the Islamic tradition.

It flows from what precedes that the full range of the knowledge of Unity embraces contemplative vision, or *théôria* in the Platonic sense, an ability to displace one's angle of consideration and contemplation, and a transformative assimilation of the Object that opens onto essential identification. The esoteric nature of knowledge lies in its moving from the propedeutic fixity

---

502 Sri Swami Satchidānandendra, *The Method of the Vedānta - A Critical Account of the Advaita Tradition*, 147.

503 "Therefore, if we truly wish to understand Sri Ramana's teachings clearly and correctly, merely reading them will not be sufficient, nor even will *manana* or deep meditation upon their meaning, unless our *śravana* and *manana* are accompanied by actual *nididhyāsana* — practice of *Ātma-vichāra*, Self-enquiry, Self-investigation, Self-scrutiny or keen Self-attentiveness." Michael James, https://happinessofbeing.blogspot.com/2008/06/self-enquiry-underlying-philosophy-can.html

504 "By the inquiry 'Who am I?' the thought 'Who am I?' will destroy all other thoughts, and like the stick used for stirring the burning pyre, it will itself in the end get destroyed." Gabriele Ebert, *Ramana Maharshi: His Life* (Norderstedt, BoD Books, 2015), 190.

505 Satchidānandendra, *Method of Vedānta*, 365.

506 "[Sureśvara] denies that *nididhyāsana* is a mental act and affirms that it, being identical with *vijñāna*, has liberation as its direct and unavoidable result and exists for itself (...)" Alexander Pereverzev, *Danubius* 37 (2019): 407.

of conceptual forms to the infinite, all-encompassing possibility of the One through the mediations of attentive contemplation, speculative ductility and unifying transmutation. Knowledge is esoteric insofar as it informs the human aspiration to realize its inherent Divinity.

Bibliography

Ahbel-Rappe, Sara. *Socratic Ignorance and Platonic Knowledge in the Dialogues of Plato*. Albany: SUNY Press, 2018.

Ebert, Gabriele. *Ramana Maharshi: His Life*. Norderstedt, BoD Books, 2015.

Ibn 'Arabī. *The Bezels of Wisdom*. Translated by R.W.J. Austin. Mahwah, New Jersey: Paulist Press, 1980.

Ibn 'Arabi. *Ringstones of Wisdom*. Translated by Caner Dagli. Chicago: Kazi Publications, 2004.

Ibn al-'Arabī, Muhyi'ddīn. *The Tarjumān al-Ashwāq, A Collection of Mystical Odes*. Translated by Reynold A. Nicholson. Madras and Wheaton, Illinois: Theosophical Publishing House, 1978.

Izutsu, Toshihiko. *Sufism and Taoism*. Berkeley: University of California Press, 2016.

James, Michael. "Self-enquiry: the underlying philosophy can be clearly understood only by putting it into practice." June 17, 2008, https://happinessofbeing.blogspot.com/2008/06/self-enquiry-underlying-philosophy-can.html

Lings, Martin. *What is Sufism?* Berkeley: University of California Press, 1999.

Osman Bakar. *Islamic Civilization and the Modern World: Thematic Essays*. Brunei Darussalam: UBD Press, 2014.

Pereverzev, Alexander. "Sureśvara as a Commentator of the Advaita Vedānta Tradition." *Danubius* 37 (2019): 381–415.

Rājarāma Tukārāma Tātyā. *A Compendium of the Raja Yoga Philosophy: Comprising the Principal Treatises of Shrimat Shankaracharya and Other Renowned Authors*. Bombay: Bombay Theosophical Publication Fund, 1901.

Sabatos, Charles D. Frontier Orientalism and the Turkish Image in Central European Literature. Lanham, Maryland: Lexington Books, 2020.

Satchidānandendra, Sri Swami. *The Method of the Vedānta – A Critical Account of the Advaita Tradition*. 1997.

Schuon, Frithjof. *Spiritual Perspectives and Human Facts*. Bloomington, Indiana: World Wisdom, 2007.

Schuon, Frithjof. *The Transcendent Unity of Religions*. Madras and Wheaton, Illinois: Theosophical Publishing House, 1984.

Shah-Kazemi, Reza. *Paths to Transcendence*. Bloomington, Indiana: World Wisdom, 2006.

Wilson, H.H. *A Dictionary of Sanscrit and English*. Calcutta: Education Press, 1832.

Chapter 13

Tajdid (Renewal), Reform (*Islah*), and *Ijtihad* in Islamic Civilisation

Mohammad Hashim Kamali

Professor and a Founding Chairman and CEO of the International Institute of Advanced Islamic Studies (IAIS), Malaysia

Linguistically, *tajdid* means renewal, or something that is made to become new. This process takes place when its original state has changed over time due to neglect. When something is restored to its essence or initial condition, that is *tajdid*.[507] Still, to engage in *tajdid* is to first recognize the original state of the subject to which renewal is applied. The existence of a valid precedent, a principle, or body of principles that fell prey to distortion and neglect must not be taken for granted and restoring their purity is what *tajdid* seeks to achieve.

Another closely-related Arabic word to *tajdid* is *ihya'* (revival), which means restoring the status quo ante without necessarily any attempt to improve or reform it. Some authors have however used *ihya'* in a generic sense that did not preclude renewal and reform. This may be said of Imam al-Ghazali's (d. 1111) renowned work, *Ihya' 'Ulum al-Din* (Revival of the Religious Sciences). On the other hand, the prominent Indian author, Wahiduddin Khan's choice of *Tajdid 'Ulum al-Din* (Renewal of the Religious Sciences) for his well-known book convey the notion of revival (*ihya'*) rather than that of *tajdid.* Jalal al-Din al-Suyuti has used *tajdid* in his writings to refer mainly to *ijtihad* (independent reasoning). Two well-known works of twentieth century origin on *tajdid* that may be mentioned are that of the Egyptian 'Abd al-Muatta'al al-Sa'idi's *Al-Mujaddidin fi'l-Islam* (The Renewers of the Religion in Islam), and Muhammad Iqbal's *The Reconstruction of Religious Thought in Islam,* both looked at the various aspects of *tajdid.*[508] Other authors who have contributed to the

507 Ibn Manzur al-Ifriqi, *Lisan al-'Arab*, vol. 3 (Beirut: Dar Sadir, 1414H), 111; and Muhammad ibn Abu Bakar al-Razi, *Mukhtar al-Sihah*, 95 – as quoted in 'Adnan Muhammad Imamah, *al-Tajdid fi'l-Fikr al-Islami* (Beirut: Dar Ibn al-Jawzi, 2001), 19.

508 See for details 'Abd al-Sattar al-Sayyid, "al-Tajdid fi'l-Fikr al-Islami: Mashru'iyyatuh wa Dawabituh," in *Tajdid al-Fikr al-Islami*, ed. Mahmud Hamdi Zaqzuq (Cairo: Wizarat al-Awqaf, 1430H/2009), 364f.

tajdid discourse in recent times include, Muhammad 'Abduh and his disciple Muhammad Rashid Rida, Yusuf al-Qaradawi, Muhammad al-Ghazali, Abu'l A'la Maududi, Isma'il Raji al-Faruqi, Hasan al-Turabi, Taha Jabir al-'Alwani, Abdullah bin Bayyah, Fazlur Rahman and many others. While one would hesitate to identify them as *mujaddidin* in the traditional sense, their substantive contribution of ideas to the revivalist discourse in Islam and Islamic civilisation is beyond doubt. With the advent of globalisation, newly emerging technologies and science, and consequent socio-political changes that came with these developments, the conventional notion of *tajdid* itself changed as scholars took into account new ideas.[509]

A brief mention may also be made of two other allied expressions to *tajdid*, namely *al-nahdah,* and *al-sahwah* (awakening, resurgence), both of which signify movement and a demand for change. Some movements are using these words in their call for a total revival of the Islamic heritage. Others are utterly critical of modernity and Westernisation, and there exists a third group that takes a more balanced view of *tajdid.*[510]

All groups acknowledge that *tajdid* is not necessarily concerned with new beginnings and new principles. The task of renewal and *tajdid* does not lend itself to overly restrictive applications, nor to a mere revival of past precedent. At a certain stage of its development, a given Muslim community's touch with the original impulse and premises of Islam may have been weakened, or even lost, under the strain of challenging conditions—such as *taqlid*, colonialism, rampant secularism, liberal capitalism, and globalisation. The recourse to *tajdid* is contingent on such existing norms and praxes and the renewers would usually prioritize which aspects require immediate attention and be restored to their original states. *Tajdid* in the modern world is therefore likely to acquire different and even unpredictable dimensions.

Definition of *Tajdid*

Muslim scholars have recorded a variety of definitions for *tajdid*, some of which are closely tied to precedent whereas others are more open-ended. The earliest definition on record of *tajdid* was that of Ibn Shihab al-Zuhri (d. 124H/741–742) who wrote that *tajdid* in the hadith "means revival (*ihya'*) of that which has disappeared or died out due to neglect of the Qur'an and Sunnah and their requirements."[511] Ibn al-Athir's (d. 630H/1233) definition of

509 Cf., Abu Bakr al-Rafiq, 'Al-Tajdid wa Ahammiyyatuh fi'l-'Asr al-Hadith,' in *Tajdid al-Fikr al-Islami*, ed. Zaqzuq, 603.

510 Cf., 'Ammar al-Talibi, "al-Tajdid fi'l-Fikr al-Malik Bin Nabi," in *Tajdid al-Fikr al-Islami*, ed. Zaqzuq, 863.

511 Ibn Hajar al-'Asqalani, *Tawali al-Ta'sis li-ma'ali Muhammad ibn Idris* – as quoted in Abd al-Rahman al-Haaj Ibrahim, "Al-Tajdid: Min al-Nass 'ala'l-Khitab: Bahth fi Tarikhiyat al-Mafhum al-Tajdid," *al-Tajdid* 3, no. 61420 (1999): 100.

tajdid reflected the scholastic developments of his time. *Tajdid* was accordingly equated with the revival (*ihya'*) of the legacy of the leading *madhahib*. The *mujaddid*, or the carrier of *tajdid*, is thus described as "a prominent leader who emerges at the head of every century to revive the religion for the ummah and preserve the *madhhabs* of their following under the leadership of their respective imams."[512] On a broader note, al-Suyuti (d. 911/1505) wrote that "*tajdid* in religion means renewal of its guidance, explanation of its truth, as well as eradication of pernicious innovation (*bid'ah*), of extremism (*al-ghuluw*) or laxity in religion." He went on to add that *tajdid* involves "observance of people's benefits, societal traditions and the norms of civilisation and *Sharī'a*."[513]

Writing in the late twentieth century, Yusuf al-Qaradawi understood *tajdid* as "combining the beneficial old with the appropriate new," and being "open to the outside world without melting into it." He juxtaposed *tajdid* with *ijtihad* and added that *ijtihad* captures the intellectual and knowledge dimensions of *tajdid*. But *tajdid* is wider in the sense that it also encapsulates the psychological and practical dimensions of revival.[514] Hence *ijtihad* and *tajdid* are the same on the intellectual plane, but *tajdid* has an emotive component manifested in collective activism and movement. Hasan al-Turabi, for example, was critical of those who confined *tajdid* to the revival of the spirit of religiosity and theological doctrines only. For him, *tajdid* consists of individual or collective *ijtihad* in theoretical and practical matters. It can be used to visualise a new prototype that unites the timeless guidelines of *Sharī'a* with new realities and circumstances.[515] Turabi added further that religious *tajdid* has two aspects, one that looks at the *Sharī'a* from within and consists essentially of its revival (*ihya'*), whereas the other stretches its perimeters by bringing in new elements that may bring about a diversification of the resources of religion (*tatwir li'l-din*).

Clearly, *tajdid* and what it meant to commentators were influenced by various factors, prominent among which were challenges faced by people and societies in different historical periods and circumstances. They tended to interpret *tajdid* in light of their own experiences and conditions. Another factor is the interpreter's viewpoint and specialisation. A jurist may understand *tajdid* differently from a historian or a sociologist. The prevalence of imitation or *taqlid* over many centuries is yet another factor affecting the understanding of *tajdid*.[516] The time factor is evidently important for *tajdid*. Reading the views

512 Jalal al-Din al-Suyuti, "al-Jami' al-Saghir" – as quoted in Imamah, *al-Tajdid fi'l-Fikr al-Islami*, 19.

513 Al-Mubarak bin Muhammad al-Jazari Ibn al-Athir, *Jami' al-Usul li-Ahadith al-Rasul*, ed. Abd al-Qadir al-Arnaut, 3rd ed., vol. 11 (Beirut: Dar al-Fikr, 1983), 321.

514 Yusuf al-Qaradawi, *Liqa'at wa Hiwarat Hawl Qadaya al-Islam wa'l-'Asr* (Cairo: Maktabah Wahbah, 1992), 85–6.

515 Hasan al-Turabi, *Tajdid al-Fikr al-Islami*, 2nd ed. (Jeddah: al-Dar al-Su'udiyah lil-Nashr, 1978), 176, also 32.

516 Ibid., 103.

of a 20th century scholar or *faqih* may well provide a different vision of *tajdid* compared to his earlier counterparts. This is partly because *tajdid* is inherently dynamic and multi-dimensional, and may be derived from many other ideas and principles. *Tajdid* is also likely to go beyond a strictly theological framework and touch on issues concerning the renewal of Islamic society and civilization.[517] In Muhammad 'Imarah's view, since the ummah is faced with a crisis in its encounter with modernity, the work of *tajdid* must include a reading of scriptures in conjunction with new realities through the lenses of rationality and *ijtihad*.[518]

Islam's long history has undoubtedly witnessed instances of a nexus between rejuvenating *tajdid* and deadening *taqlid*. Under the weight of unwarranted *taqlid*, Muslim scholars even declared, at some point, that the door of creative thinking and *ijtihad* was closed. Inspiring thinkers and *mujaddids* went against such intellectual stagnancy. Among the luminaries of *tajdid* were Abu Hamid al-Ghazali, Ibrahim al-Shatibi (d. 1388) with his innovative contributions on the higher purposes of the *Sharīʿa* (or *maqasid*); Taqi al-Din Ibn Taymiyyah (d. 1328), the harbinger of political revival; the polymaths of civilisational renewal, 'Abd al-Rahman Ibn Khaldun (d. 1406) and Shah Wali Allaah Dihlawi (d. 1762), and many more.

Textual Origins

Tajdid originates in the authority of a renowned hadith that provides: "God will raise for this *ummah*, at the head of each century, someone who will rejuvenate for them their religion: *inna'Llaha yab'athu li-hadhihi'l-ummati 'ala ra'si kulli mi'ati sanathin man yujaddid laha dinaha*."[519] This hadith clearly indicates that *tajdid* is theo-centric, for it begins with the reference that "God will send to this ummah…." *Tajdid* here is primarily concerned with the religion. Furthermore, even though *tajdid* is theo-centric in the symbolic sense, it is carried and constructed by a renewer (*mujaddid*) for the benefit of the ummah. The hadith also makes clear that *tajdid* is an essential part of Islam but does not articulate what it consists of. The task of the *mujaddid* is to construct an understanding of *tajdid* in the context of his time and the prevailing conditions of his society and the ummah. The fact that the hadith specifies a certain time frame, namely a century, for *tajdid* implies that it is time-bound and

517 Usman Muhammad Bugagie, "Concept of Revitalisation in Islam," (Unpublished PhD thesis), 5.

518 Muhammad 'Imarah, *Azmat al-Fikr al-Islami al-Mu'asir* (Cairo: Dar al-Shuruq al-Awsat, 1990), 83–5.

519 'Abd Allah al- Khatib al-Tabrizi, *Mishkat al-Masabih*, ed. Muhammad Nasir al-Din al-Albani, 2nd ed. vol. 1 (Beirut: Al-Maktab al-Islami, 1399H/1979) *hadith* no. 247. This is a collection of verified *hadiths* from the six major books of *hadith*, known as *Al-Kutub al-Sittah*. See also for an analysis of this *hadith* and its significance for civilisational renewal: Mohammad Hashim Kamali, *Civilisational Renewal: Revisiting the Islam Hadhari Approach*, 2nd ed. (Kuala Lumpur: International Institute of Advanced Islamic Studies, 2009), 51ff.

infrequent. It is not confined to the period of the Companions, the Successors and others but becomes necessary at any era in response to the changing conditions and experience of a specific generation of Muslims. The only specification of time and place is when the religion has fallen victim to neglect and, during such a landmark moment, a qualified *mujaddid* will emerge. These are some of the salient features of the hadith of *tajdid*. But almost every aspect of *tajdid* has invoked responses from commentators which I will review below.

Commentators have pointed out that the message of this hadith goes beyond its literal meaning. It accentuates the need for renewal, interpretation, and *ijtihad* on unprecedented issues and developments that the ummah may encounter over time.[520] The hadith is also grounded in the idea of continuous renewal throughout the ages and that Islam must move along with the changing conditions and realities of the ummah. The principal actor of this sustained renewal—the *mujaddid*—is the product of his time and generation. His task is to contextualise and integrate contextual changes in line with the general principles of Islam. Should the change in question be of a juridical kind, then he is likely to be engaged in *ijtihad*. The *mujaddid* is therefore a qualified *mujtahid*.

It must be noted here that, in intellectual and juridical matters, *tajdid* is akin to *ijtihad* and should therefore be regulated by the methodological guidelines of *ijtihad*.[521] It is widely acknowledged that *ijtihad* is Islam's principal tool of constructive regeneration and renewal and may well include *tajdid*. Yet the two terms technically differ in that *ijtihad* proceeds mainly in conjunction with practical *fiqhi* matters, legal and juridical issues, whereas *tajdid* extends to all aspects of the religion, indeed to the life of the ummah, its ethos, lifestyle, and civilisation. Muhammad 'Imarah observed that *tajdid* propels the growth of Islamic jurisprudence in accordance with its distinctive methods and characteristics. *Tajdid* greatly influences the interface between Islamic thought and the on-going march of the vibrant Muslim civilisation towards self-renewal.[522]

The hadith under review also means that Islam will not die nor become redundant. God Most High will help this ummah to reconnect with the original messages of Islam. The hadith conveys a message of hope and assurance that God will guide this ummah to be on the right path and assist in a quest to restore its past heritage to face new challenges.[523]

---

520 Sufi Abu Talib, "Al-Tajdid wa Darurat al-Tawazun," conference paper presented to the Third International Forum of al-Azhar Alumni, Kuala Lumpur, 16 February 2008, 5.

521 Cf., Ra'id Nasri Abu Mu'nis, "Ishkaliyyat al-Nass wa'l-*Ijtihad* bi'l-Ra'y fi'l-'Asr al-Hadith," *Islamiyyat al-Ma'rifah* 96 (1440H/2019): 84.

522 Muhammad 'Imarah, 'Ma'alim al-Manhaj al-Islami,' *Majallah Islamiyyat al-Ma'rifah* 1 (1995): 95.

523 Muhammad Mas'ad Yaqut, 'Nazarat fi Hadith al-Tajdid: Fi Haza'l-Qarn Na'tajula Harakah Tajdidiyah Shamilah Mustanirah,' *Said al-Fawa'id*, accessed August 26, 2012, http://saaid.net/aldawlah/359.htm.

The fact that the hadith of *tajdid* refers to *mujaddid* in the singular, does not necessarily mean only one *mujaddid* will emerge at any given place or century. This is because the Arabic pronoun "*man*" therein can refer to one person or to a multitude. *Tajdid* may accordingly be attempted by one person or a group of persons, party, or movement. Notwithstanding the emergence of individual *mujaddids* that featured prominently in the writings of early commentators, modern interpretators of *tajdid* favour collective *tajdid* undertaken by groups of ulama, specialists, and scholars in various disciplines. One *mujaddid* may be a jurist, another a political scientist, yet another an economist, and so forth.

Muhammad 'Abid al-Jabiri commented that the renewal of religious affairs in the hadith includes temporal affairs since Islam essentially does not separate the two. He also noted that the requirements of *tajdid* are changeable. *Tajdid* is thus applicable in matters of worship (*'ibadat*), matrimonial law and also socio-economic and political affairs, all that which call for new diagnoses and solutions that could not be found in the past. *Tajdid* is thus the Islamic invitation to progress in tandem with the march of modernity and civilisation.[524]

Tajdid and Civilisational Renewal

The civilisational thrust of Islam is founded in the Qur'anic principle of the vicegerency of humankind in the earth, to be fulfilled through developing the earth and establishing a social order grounded in moral uprightness, human dignity (*karamah*), justice (*'adl*) and beneficence (*ihsan*). The Qur'an also commits the faithful to the promotion of what is fair and the prevention of what is unfair and rejected (*amr bi'l-ma'ruf wa nahy 'an al-munkar*), and upholding the common good (*maslahah*) of the people. It places emphasis on the maintenance of the ties of kinship, honouring one's neighbours, rigorous pursuit of knowledge, earning of one's living through lawful work, and helping the needy. If *maslahah* brings about *ihsan* (good) then renewal/*tajdid* brings about *jamal* (beauty). The principle of Divine Oneness (*tawhid*) is a unitarian vision of humanity that forbids discrimination of any kind as moral excellence is the only criterion of distinction in the eyes of God Most High. Mutual recognition (*ta'aruf*) among nations, cooperation in good works, and fraternity (*ta'awun, ukhuwwah*) constitute the conceptual framework of the vicegerency of humans in the earth.

Fathi Malkawi and the *Islamiyyat al-Ma'rifah* editorial team espoused a culture of renewal (*thaqafat al-tajdid*) for the ummah of today and maintain that this is integral to the overall vision of the Qur'an and Sunnah. These sacred sources call to attention the exercise of reason, acquisition of knowledge,

524 Muhammad 'Abid al-Jabiri, *Al-Din wa'l-Dawlah wa Tatbiq al-Sharia* (Beirut: Markaz Dirasat al-Wahda al-'Arabiyya, 1996), 130–2.

dedication to truth and justice, and ultimately to the building of a just society and civilisation in the earth. This is further endorsed by the fact, Malkawi notes, that God Most High sent Messengers to remind people to advocate the truth and be vigilant to change their condition for the better when they have departed from the right path. Malkawi added that the Prophet Muhammad spoke of renewal in every century by qualified *mujaddids*. A culture of *tajdid* must be nurtured for renewal to be realised.[525]

I would add that *tajdid* must be driven by *tazkiyah* and *falah* (purity and spiritual attainment) and a battle against all forms of corruption (cf., Q. Fatir, 35:18; al-A'la, 87:14). This driving forces of *tajdid* is often invoked in daily prayers by the faithful which are taken from the Qur'an: "O God! grant us good in this world and good in the hereafter" (al-Baqarah, 2:201). Indeed, Islam is also a religion of action. The fourth caliph, 'Ali b. Abu Talib drove this point home when he said that Islam enjoins the believer to "strive in your worldly affairs as if you will live forever, and strive in your affairs of the hereafter as if you will die tomorrow."[526] All of these prompted the early Muslims to manifest their role as God's vicegerents through establishing a good government and developing a culture of civility in the widest sense. Muslims are deeply convinced that what happens in this life is of lasting religious and civilisational significance. The material manifestations of Islamic civilisation are, according to Muslim beliefs, inseparable from its religious and ethical callings.

To be able to fulfil his role as God's vicegerent, the *mujaddid* must possess a number of qualifications: 1) a clear understanding and ability to differentiate between the changeable and the unchangeable (*thawabit wa mutaghayyirat*) aspects of Islam. The unchangeable in Islam refers to the essentials of belief, worship and morality, as well as its decisive scriptural injunctions. Islamic principles that pertain to civil transactions (*mu'amalat*) are, on the other hand, open to interpretation and adjustment and therefore changeable; 2) Knowledge of the normal and concessionary (*'azimah*, and *rukhsah*) rulings that pertain to normal and exceptional circumstances respectively; 3) Knowledge of the place of rationality and ratiocination (*ta'lil*) in the understanding of the scripture; 4) Due regard for the common good (*maslahah*) and people's legitimate interests; 5) Due observance of the approved customs of society.[527]

525 "Editorial article," *Islamiyyat al-Ma'rifah* 20, no. 78 (Autumn 1435H/2014): 5.

526 There have been several opinions regarding the names of the companions who said this. At least 3 names are suggested to be the origin of this phrase; 1) 'Ali b. Abu Talib, 2) Abdullah bin Amru, and 3) Abdullah ibn 'Umar. Syaikh Bin Baz is among those who supported that these are the words of Ali b. Abu Talib. See for more details, Abdul 'Aziz bin Baz, "Ma Sihhah Qawl: I'mal li Dunyaka kaanaka Ta'ish Abada?" Official Website of Al-Imam Ibn Baz, accessed December 15, 2021, https://binbaz.org.sa/fatwas/.

527 With reference to the changeable-and-unchangeable in Islam, it is of interest to note that there is a half–century old movement in Indonesia that constructed an 'Indonesian Madhhab' and reshaped the laws of inheritance by reinterpreting the Qur'an and hadith so they will no longer be bound by the patriarchal customs of the Arab society. The purpose was to reflect instead the matriarchal customs of Indonesia and abandon the 'two for one' principle. In support of this argument that the patriarchal model did not reflect

It is probably due to its inherent dynamism that *tajdid* has not been subjected to a pre-determined methodology and framework, which would explain, to some extent, why Muslim scholars have frequently underlined their concern over the Islamic authenticity of what can be rightly subsumed under *tajdid*. "The true *mujaddid* is," according to al-Qaradawi, "one who rejuvenates religion through the religion itself. *Tajdid* through syncretism and implantation of anything that has no basis in the religion does not qualify as *tajdid*."[528] Yet al-Qaradawi also refutes the assertion by some that the religion, its tenets and principles are not open to *tajdid*. He argued that Islam has been open to *tajdid* in all areas by the authority of sacred texts, but it would be incorrect to change the essential pillars and beliefs of Islam in the name of *tajdid*.[529]

Civilisation *(Hadarah)* in Islamic History

The English word *civilisation* is derived from *civitas*, a Latin term by origin which means "pertaining to the citizen" or "state," also implying a transformation from nomadism to urbanity and settlement. The Muslim philosopher Abu Nasr al-Farabi (d. 950 CE) drew on the Arabic word for city (*medina*) in his writings and spoke of advanced urban society as *tamaddun*. He also authored a book titled *al-Medina al-Fadila*. In a similar vein, the renowned North African polymath, 'Abd al-Rahman Ibn Khaldun (d. 1406) used *hadarah* (civilisation) in the sense of transformation from nomadism to *'umran*, signifying an urban milieu inhabited by settled populations and societies. Being the antonym of *badawah* (nomadism), *hadarah* signifies the interaction between man and his environment, and has its genesis in man's quest to harness the existential world around him in pursuit of worthy objectives. Humankind's mission as God's vicegerent places upon them the responsibility to "build the earth" in a manner that befits their status as the most honoured of God's creatures.

Malik Bennabi (d. 1973) characterized civilisation as the sum-total of the moral and the material that enable a society to provide each of its members with all the social support needed by him to progress. Civilisation is not merely a matter of economic and technical progress. It is the product of dynamic, integrated and concrete elements, the most important of which according to Bennabi, is the moral, which is anchored in the structure of values provided by the religion.

---

the only possible interpretation of the Qur'an, a reference was also made to differences between the Sunni and Shia inheritance rules, which granted greater rights to female blood lines. Islamic law was adapted to the demands of the nation state. This has revived aspects of modern *ijtihad*, and if successful, could further advance the ideals of equality and justice in the *Sharī'a*. See Mohamad Tahir El-Messawi, ed., *Maqasid al-Sharī'a*, 159–60 – taken from Mark E. Cammack, 'Islam and Nationalism in Modern Indonesia: Forging an Indonesian Madhhab,' in *The Islamic School of Law: Evolution, Devolution and Progress*, ed. Peri Bearman, Rudolph Peters, and Frank E. Vogel (Cambridge, MA: Harvard University Press, 2006). See also Imamah, *al-Tajdid fi'l-Fikr al-Islami*, 26f.

528 Yusuf al-Qaradawi, *Hawl Qadaya al-Islam wa'l-'Asr*, 3rd ed. (Cairo: Maktabah Wahbah, 1427H/2006), 89.

529 Ibid., 85.

Comparing the "realm of objects" with the 'realm of ideas,' Bennabi considered it historically proven that when a society possessed a good balance of ideas, objects, and commodities, a civilisation could easily be created. For example, Germany's infrastructure was totally destroyed during the Second World War and its people had lost their "realm of objects." However, because they were still in control of their "realm of ideas," they reconstructed and restored their leadership in Europe.

Civilisation cannot be borrowed, it can only grow from within. This is because, Bennabi observes, "accumulating the products of one civilisation could never create a civilisation for another society." Bennabi added that "civilisation cannot sell its spirit, ideas, intimate wealth, tastes ... and notion of meaning." Muslims in the postcolonial Third World made the mistake of promoting an object-based civilisation (*hadarah shay'iyyah*) based on the accumulation of objects and importing of material commodities. For this reason, they were unable to create ideas and produce objects for themselves. Another reason why Muslims were unable to regain their self-image and standing in the world community was their failure to reconnect with their civilisation and ideational wealth they accumulated before the colonial onslaught. Even if they had the knowledge base, they were overwhelmed by Western ideas and institutions. Western educated Muslim elites were moulded to view their own distinctive heritage and mode of leadership in disdain.

Islamic Revivalism, Modernity and *Tajdid*

Expressions such as "Islamic modernism," "Islamic revivalism," and "Islamic reform" are often attributed to Jamaluddin al-Afghani, Muhammad 'Abduh and Muhammad Rashid Rida. These and other thinkers sought to reconcile modern values such as constitutionalism, scientific investigation, modern methods of education, women's rights, and cultural revival with the tenets and principles of Islam. Islamic revivalism of the latter part of the twentieth century strengthened the affinity between *tajdid* and the guidelines laid down in Islamic scriptures. Muhammad Iqbal's seminal work, *The Reconstruction of Religious Thought in Islam*, was translated into Arabic by Abbas Mahmud al-Aqqad in 1955, and 'Abd al-Mutta'al Sa'idi's work, *al-Mujaddidin fi'l-Islam – min al-Qarn al-Awwal ila'l-Rabi' 'Ashar* (Renewers of Religion in Islam, From the First to the Fourteenth Century) was published in the same year. Both expatiated on the scope and space that Islamic sources provide for regeneration and renewal. Amin al-Khuli's title, *al-Tajdid fil-Din* (Renewal in Religion), initially published as an article, and later as book, also reflected on similar themes.

Al-Sa'idi's previous book, published in the early 1950s, *Tarikh al-Islah fi'l-Azhar* (History of Reform in Azhar) focused more on the concept of *islah* initiating in the meantime a call for a revolutionary reformer (*al-muslih al-tha'ir*).

But, he was almost totally silent on *tajdid*, which then became the central theme of his subsequent book in 1955.[530] The main reason for this change of focus was the realisation that Western modernity had begun to penetrate and derail *islah* with currents of opinion that were not Islamically credible. The spread of nationalism and secular ideologies during the post-colonial period that consisted mainly of political mottos made things worse. Added to this were Arab defeats during the wars with Israel, and the tussle that followed between Islamic movements and governments in power in many Muslim countries. A climate of crisis prevailed and the ideology of *islah* began to give way to *tajdid* because the latter clearer grounding in the scripture.

Fazlur Rahman (d. 1988) praised 'Abduh for recognising the need for reform, just as he commended Hasan al-Banna (d. 1949) and Abul A'la Mawdudi (d. 1979) for countering the excesses of Islamic modernism and defending Islam against secularism. But he criticised them for not having a clear methodology of revival and reform and largely ad hoc nature of the solutions they proposed to major issues confronting Muslims. Rahman tried, in turn, to articulate a new Islamic methodology as he believed that traditional methods had fallen short of developing an intellectual framework that is suited for the modern age. He focused his attention on the Qur'an and on modern methods of interpretation. Rahman's mission may be summed up as an endeavour to retrieve the moral elan of the Qur'an in order to formulate a Qur'an-centred ethic. For he believed that without an explicitly formulated ethical system, one can hardly do justice to Islam.[531]

Fazlur Rahman criticised the "atomistic approach" of traditional scholarship. The methodology of the jurists was also lacking of a systematically broad socio-ethical theory that he believed should underlie law-making. Indeed, the jurists, in their quest to develop a highly structured legal system, missed out the importance of fluidity in thought.[532] Rahman expounded as to how the Qur'anic guidance was intimately connected with the religious, political, economic and cultural life of the people of Hijaz, and more broadly the people of Arabia. However, this close connection was later disrupted by the lengthy disputations over Islamic theology and law and created an ever-widening gap in thought. Revelation came to be seen as ahistorical and transcendent beyond the reach of humankind. The occasions of revelation (*asbab al-nuzul*) that played a vital role in explicating certain texts were marginalised and the link between tafsir, fiqh, theology, and everyday lives of Muslims was further weakened.[533] It is remarkable to note also that Muslim writings on ethics were

530 Al-Haaj Ibrahim, "al-Tajdid: Min al-Nass," 109.

531 Abdullah Saeed, "Fazlur Rahman: A Framework for Interpreting the Ethico-Legal Content of the Qur'an," in *Modern Muslim Intellectuals and the Qur'an*, ed. Suha Taji Farouki (London: OUP and The Institute of Ismaili Studies, 2004), 42–3.

532 Ibid., 44.

533 Ibid., 48.

mainly developed outside the framework of the *Sharīʿa*. They were explicitly based on Greek and Persian sources. Fazlur Rahman has made a reference, in turn, to Majid Fakhry's *Ethical Theories* (1991) and the latter to A.J. Arberry (1955)—all of whom concur that writers on Islamic ethical theories have mostly relied on Greek and Persian sources but also that Islamic ethical theories bore the influence of Islamic jurisprudence and fiqh.[534]

In his writings on *tajdid* in fiqh, Jamal al-Din Atiyah raised several issues that called for a review and renewal of fiqh in many areas. Beginning with devotional matters (*ʿibadat*), Atiyah noted that too much emphasis is placed on rituals at the expense of the spiritual component of *ʿibadat*. Whereas psychologists have spoken of the many psychological and character building benefits of prayer and fasting, this was totally absent in fiqh. With regards to marriage, the Qur'an characterized it as "friendship and compassion—*mawaddah wa rahmah*," which the fiqh scholars have reduced to a contract resembling that of ownership (*ʿaqd al-tamlik*), marking a total departure from the original Qur'anic spirit.[535] The emphasis on both *ʿibadat* and contracts falls instead on formalities, pillars, and conditions (*arkan wa shurut*) in highly structured formulations that often compromise the essence and spirit of the subject.[536] Then again, Islam is a religion of unity (*tawhid*), whereas the divisive impact of the schools of jurisprudence, or *madhhabs,* on Muslim unity is disconcerting. The schools of jurisprudence were a manifestation of latitude in scholarly inquiry and *ijtihad*, but which lost focus and became an instrument of fanaticism and disunity among Muslims. In a similar vein, Islamic jurisprudence in the era of *taqlid* became focused on details and took an atomistic approach to law at the expense of developing general theories and comprehensive guidelines. There was also a certain disconnect between fiqh with that of the beliefs and ethical norms of Islam and how these forms of knowledge relate to governance.[537]

Related to the above, I wish to recount here what Atiyah heard from al-Qaradawi as a youth in his early years in Egypt. He attended the Ramadan lessons at the local mosque in late evenings between the *maghrib* and *ʿishaʾ* prayers. The lessons were on ablution and cleanliness. Al-Qaradawi humorously remarked that "all the thirty nights we did not move beyond that one subject." Compare this with the approach the Prophet (pbuh) took when a Bedouin came and asked him how to perform the salah, and the Prophet simply said to him: "Pray the way you see me praying."[538]

534 Ibid., 52. See also Majid Fakhry, *Ethical Theories in Islam* (Leiden: E.J Brill, 1991), 2–8, and A.J. Arberry, "The Nicomachean Ethics in Arabic," *Bulletin of the School of Oriental and African Studies* 17 (1955): 1–9.

535 Jamal al-Din ʿAtiyah and Wahbah al-Zuhaili, *Tajdid al-Fiqh al-Islami* (Beirut: Dar al-Fikr, 1422/2002), 31–2.

536 Ibid., 35.

537 Ibid.

538 Ibid., 46.

In his book *al-Fiqh al-Islami fi Tariq al-Tajdid* (Islamic Jurisprudence in the Path of Renewal),[539] Muhamed Salim el-Awa speaks of the stagnation of fiqh due to longstanding *taqlid*, and highlight that innovative responses are wanting. He also noted that political jurisprudence (*al-fiqh al-siyasi,* also *al-siyasah al-shar'iyah*) had failed to integrate the Qur'anic principles of *shura* (consensus) and accountability. El-Awa maintains that limiting the tenure of office of the head of state is no longer an option but a necessity, and that in many other areas, fiqh needs to be developed through comprehensive *ijtihad* to provide relevant responses to issues of citizenship, freedom of association, political parties in the context of nation state, and peaceful relations with other states. He further added that the woman's right of participation in the political life of the community, her entitlement to act as judge and witness, and absolute equality in her right of life as expounded in some scholastic works were patently discriminatory especially with reference to the issue of blood money or *diyah*. Similar questions arise over equality in respect of the fundamental rights of non-Muslims and fiqh formulations over the imposition of poll tax (*jizyah*), and Islam's position on art and music. Important as well are issues in criminal law concerning apostasy and the law of evidence, especially methods of proof that necessitate modern and more reliable scientific means of establishing facts.

El-Awa started his afore-mentioned book with a review of Jamal al-Banna's book, entitled *Nahw Fiqh Jadid* (Towards a New Fiqh), and found commonalities in their respective approaches to aspects of the renewal of fiqh. El-Awa commented, however, on a point of difference between him and al-Banna. Whereas al-Banna seems to depart from the established methodologies on renewal and reform, el-Awa thought that most issues can be addressed through the accepted Islamic methodologies of *ijtihad*.[540]

The foregoing presents a fairly long list of issues that involve a healthy dose of self-criticism among Muslim scholars within the ambit of renewal and *tajdid*. Some progress has also been made in the realm of family law through reforms in legislation and scholarship, although progress is uneven in various countries and generally eclectic. Many of the authors I discussed have not only posed searching questions but have also addressed them and deliberated over prospective solutions. Space does not permit me to go into more detail but I have elsewhere attempted to provide a fuller picture of twentieth century Islamic law reforms through statutory legislation, juristic doctrine and research.[541] Twentieth century "Islamic resurgence" witnessed aspects of

---

539 Muhammad Salim al-Awa, *al-Fiqh al-Islami fi Tariq al-Tajdid*, 2nd ed. (Cairo: al-Maktab al-Islami, 1998), 272.
540 Ibid., 200–22.
541 Mohammad Hashim Kamali, *Shari'ah Law: An Introduction* (Oxford: Oneworld Publications, 2008), ch. 12, Adaptation and Reform, 246–62.

revivalism that included both the *salafiyyah* type of revivalism, and that of modern reform in statutory legislations. However, one area that did not see tangible *tajdid*-based improvement was constitutional laws. The Arab Spring that began in 2010 generated some political reforms when revivalist Islamic thinkers pointed to comprehensive changes to state of democracy and human rights in the Middle East. The Arab dictators and monarchies dug their heels and the Arab Spring was halted. But the movement it created, according to some commentators, may regain more momentum in the near future.

The Relevance of *Maqasid*

The renewed interest in *maqasid shari'ah* (the higher purposes of Islamic law) in Islamic thought and scholarship of recent decades is a partial response to the textualist overtones of scholastic methodologies of interpretation and *ijtihad*. *Maqasid* has now become an accepted term of reference and the framework for Islamic reformist ideas and initiatives. Whenever *tajdid* introduces an initiative, plan, or purpose which can be subsumed under the five essential *maqasid* (i.e. the *daruriyyat*),[542] its authenticity is most likely verified in that context. In the event, however, where an instance of *tajdid* cannot be related to any of the recognised *maqasid*, one may apply a "negative test," which is to say that *tajdid* is valid if it does not contravene any of the immutable norms and principles of Islam and its higher purposes. In this case, one would not need to produce affirmative evidence from Islamic sources to prove the acceptability of *tajdid*. The application of *tajdid* to the dogma and basic pillars (*arkan*) of Islam is apparently limited. But since *tajdid* means engaging in matters outside this sphere, covering issues of concern to human relations and *mu'amalat* with greater flexibility; it has wide relevance to address the concerns of modernity and civilisational renewal.

Linking the *maqasid* to *tajdid* may be visualised with reference to fighting poverty through economic development and the realisation of equitable distribution of wealth. Al-Ghazali and al-Shatibi were of the view that Islamic thought must concern itself with the broader objectives of our religion and not solely with its prohibitive aspects, or to exclusively literalist interpretations.[543] This vision can best be achieved by drawing attention to the *maqasid* that are entirely goal-oriented, broader in scope, and capable of rising above particularities that can sometimes run in different directions and need to be made coherent in the light of *maqasid*.

Looked at from another angle, the *maqasid* themselves can be developed through *tajdid*. Some aspects of the *maqasid* that have remained underdeveloped

542 The five essential *maqasid* are protection of life, religion, human intellect, property and family. A sixth item added to this list is personal dignity or honour. See for further detail on *maqasid*, Kamali, *Shari'ah Law: An Introduction*, ch. 6, 123–40.
543 Ibid., 40–1.

could thus be developed through *tajdid*-oriented research. This may be said of the role of rationality (*'aql*) in the identification of *maqasid*, and whether or not the scope of the conventional enumeration of the essential *maqasid*, or *daruriyyat*, can be widened to include other values and objectives that are clearly upheld in the scriptural sources. In a similar vein, two other categories of *maqasid*, namely the complementary (*hajiyyat*) and embellishments (*tahsiniyyat*) may be better indicators and methodological refinements to minimise arbitrariness in their identification. I have discussed this subject in fuller detail elsewhere.[544] Suffice it to say here there is a dire need to forge a closer nexus between the scriptural injunctions (*nusus*) and the *maqasid*. It is no longer enough, therefore, to extract a ruling (*hukm*) of *Sharī'a* from a text in total isolation and neglect of its purposes and objective.[545]

A Critique of *Tajdid*

The climate of crisis that dominated the post-colonial Muslim world also began to erode the credibility of *tajdid*. Public opinion grew increasingly critical of the *tajdid* movements in Turkey, for example, after the collapse of the Ottoman caliphate. Rashid Rida later called the rise of questionable *tajdid*-cum-*islah* groups, such as that of Ataturk with his Westernised and secularist overtones, as imitative *tajdid* infected by Western models. *Tajdid* was no longer seen asgrounded in the Prophetic hadith but in Western modernity and thus of doubtful authenticity. Some even began to equate *tajdid* with secularism, and others with pernicious innovation (*bid'ah*) in the guise of Islam.[546]

Twentieth century developments in the *tajdid* discourse may be summarised into four clusters as follows:

1. Precedent-oriented tajdid (*al-ijtihad al-turath*) that mainly sought to address new issues through *ijtihad*. The advocates of this position linked tajdid to past precedent, which mirrored the methodology of the Salafiyah movement. Precedent is here understood not only to consist of text and scripture but also of schools, learned personalities, and imams of the past, which evidently brought it closer to imitation and *taqlid*, except that the advocates of this current of opinion remained open to *ijtihad*, albeit a restrictive and well-regulated *ijtihad*. Rashid Rida, Sa'id Ramadan al-Buti, and Mahmud al-Tahhan belonged to this strand.[547]

544 Cf., Ibid., Chapter six on 'History and Methodology of Maqasid.' See also idem, *Maqasid, Ijtihad and Civilisational Renewal* (London & Kuala Lumpur: IIIT and IAIS Malaysia, 2012). See also 'Ali Jum'ah, "Tajdid Usul al-Fiqh," in *Tajdid al-Fikr*, ed. Zaqzuq, 357f.

545 Cf., Isam al-Bashir, "al-Tajdid fi'l-Fikr al-Islami," in *Tajdid al-Fikr*, ed. Zaqzuq, 94.

546 Ibid., 111–2.

547 Ibid., 113–4.

2. Advocacy of open *ijtihad* (*al-ijtihad al-maftuh*) that reads scripture and rationality side by side. Muhammad Iqbal, Abd al-Mutta'al Sa'idi, Amin al-Khuli, Yusuf al-Qaradawi, Abdullah bin Bayyah, Fazlur Rahman, and Saleem el-Awa are within this current in their call for the liberation of Islamic thought, advocacy of *Sharī'a*, and *ijtihad* in tandem with modern realities and developments.
3. Islamisation of knowledge (*islamiyyat al-ma'rifah*) and the epistemological reform movement that sought to address a perceived crisis of civilisation (*azmat al-hadarah*) through methodological innovation and reform. This current of opinion is manifested by the Virginia-based International Institute of Islamic Thought since its inception in 1981. The Institute and its founders are critical of taqlid and attempt to overcome the challenges of modernity through a creative employment of Western ideas. Tajdid to the advocates of this current means reforming the methodologies of thought (*islah manahij al-fikr*), which consist of two readings, namely reading of the scripture (*qira'at al-nass*), and reading the existential reality (*qira'at al-kawn*) side by side in light of Islamic values. The focus is evidently on tools and methodologies more than on subject matter and content. Abdul Hamid Abu Sulayman, Taha Jabir Alalwani, 'Imad al-Din Khalil, Muhammad Kamal Hassan, and others sit well within this current of opinion.[548]
4. Tajdid-cum-globalisation (*tajdid wal-'awlamah*), which proposes a much wider understanding of tajdid that is not tied to any particular methodology or framework but seeks to address the challenges of modernity in their own context. Globalisation has posed the Muslim world with challenges of civilisational proportions, hence efforts at renewal and tajdid should accordingly be informed by its wide scope and dimensions. The advocates of this current include Muhammad 'Abid al-Jabiri, Abul-Qasim Haaj Ahmad, Abd al-Rahman al-Kawakibi, Muhammad al-Talbi, Hasan al-Turabi and others who maintain that tajdid movements of the past have failed to realise their objectives due mainly to their eclectic and insufficiently developed approaches to past heritage and modern developments.

Muslim reformist movements, according to Malik Bennabi (d. 1973), have suffered from poor planning and lack of direction. The result was confusion among the two schools of thought, namely the modernists and the reformists. The first lost its way while journeying to the West searching for ready-made solutions to local problems, while the second remained servile to

548 Abdul Hamid Abu Sulayman, *Azmat al-'Aql al-Muslim*, 3rd ed. (Virginia: al-Ma'had al-'Alami li'l-Fikr al-Islami, 1994), 40; Taha Jabir al-'Alwani, *Islah al-Fikr al-Islami: Madkhal ila Nizam al-Khitab al-Islami al-Mu'asir*, 3rd ed. (Virginia: al-Ma'had al-'Alami li'l-Fikr al-Islami, 1995), 72–3.

past glories, faithful to the *status quo*, and unable to penetrate the very causes of the malaise.[549] Another observer noted that Islam fell victim to parochialism and became reduced to a set of ritualistic performances that suppressed its broader civilisational objectives. Unfortunately, purely non-civilisational issues have occupied the agendas of many Islamic revivalist movements.[550] In a 2005 Cairo University conference on Dialogue of Civilisations (*Hiwar al-Hadarat*) Tariq al-Bishri observed that, *mu'asarah* (modernism) in the Muslim usage of the post-colonial period has on the whole been premised on Western modernity and Western civilisation. Muslims looked at themselves through the Western lens. Another commentator on the same event, Ibrahim al-Bayyumi, noted that "the modernity discourse among Islamic movements has largely consisted of approximation and comparison with the Western model. The liberal secularist movements have uncritically taken that model for their own agendas."[551] This is illustrated in the works of Qassim Amin, who advocated gender equality under the influence of 'Abduh's ideas, but it soon succumbed to the currents of Western modernity such that its Islamic credentials became increasingly overshadowed by Western thought.

Conclusion

Islamic civilisation has not lost its vitality but it has certainly been suppressed in the post-colonial period up till now in the era of globalisation. *Tajdid* is necessary under these circumstances and may reflect on the following:

1. *Tajdid* must rely on the internal resources of Islam and avoid the pitfalls of syncretism and reliance on the resources of alien civilisations especially the West. This has not been possible in the colonial and post-colonial periods and becomes challenging in the era of globalisation especially for the weaker Muslim countries and economies. Yet, it is possible to reduce and gradually minimise reliance on Western sources and ideas.
2. The possibilities of beneficial cooperation (*ta'awun*) and exchange among Muslim countries are extensive in the spheres particularly of traditional and modern science, technology and commerce, environmental care, education and campaign against terrorism and violence.
3. The Qur'anic guideline that "Good and bad can never be equal. Respond to evil in a way that is better, then the one who was a foe will become as if he were an intimate friend" (Fussilat, 41:34) is an

549 Fawzia Barium, *Malik Bennabi: His Life and Theory of Civilisation* (Kuala Lumpur: Budaya Ilmu, 1993), 163–4.
550 Maimul Ahsan Khan, *Human Rights in the Muslim World* (Durham, NC: Carolina Academic Press, 2003), 58.
551 Ibid.

excellent guideline for peaceful coexistence and cooperation in mutually beneficial ways.[552]

4. Recognition and advocacy of pluralism in the political, economic, and technical spheres of civilisation should be informed by the Qur'anic declaration "To each of you We have assigned a law and an open way. If God had so willed, He would have made you a single nation, but His plan is to test you in what you have been given. So vie with one another in pursuit of virtues" (al-Ma'idah, 5:48; al-Hujurat, 49:13).
5. Civilisational renewal must pay attention to art and culture and the beauty-enhancement values (*al-qiyam al-jamaliyyah*) of Islam. References abound in the Qur'an to earth's unlimited potential for beautification. Instructive in this regard are also these two renowned hadiths: "God is beautiful and He loves beauty;" and "Truly God has inscribed beauty upon everything."
6. Protection and advancement of people's basic freedoms, equality, human rights, gender justice, and protection of the human dignity of women.[553]
7. A resolute commitment to make the elimination of sectarian conflict among the Sunnis and Shi'ites by living up to the Qur'anic call: "Verily the believers are brethren; so make peace among your brothers," (al-Hujurat, 49:10) a reality of relations among all Muslim communities and nations.

I wish to end this chapter with a note in passing about the Kuala Lumpur-based International Institute of Advanced Islamic Studies (IAIS) Malaysia that works on civilisational renewal (*tajdid hadari*) as its main agenda. Professor Osman Bakar whom we are honouring in this Festschrift is an active member and contributor to the IAIS's vision and mission for civilisational renewal in Islam. The Institute has endeavoured to widen the scope of the late twentieth century revivalist discourse from its narrow focus on fiqh issues, to pay greater attention to wider issues of concern to civilisation including justice and good governance, poverty eradication, science, technology, environment and Islam's relation with other civilisations.[554]

---

552 Ibid.

553 Ibid., 95–6.

554 The Institute also publishes a refereed journal titled *Islam and Civilisational Renewal*. See for details IAIS Malaysia website at www.iais.org.my. IAIS has published about 600 publications since its inception in 2008.

Bibliography

Abu Mu'nis, Ra'id Nasri. "Ishkaliyyat al-Nass wa'l-*Ijtihad* bi'l-Ra'y fi'l-'Asr al-Hadith." *Islamiyyat al-Ma'rifah* 96 (1440H/2019).

Abu Sulayman, Abdul Hamid. *Azmat al-'Aql al-Muslim*. 3rd ed. Virginia: al-Ma'had al-'Alami li'l-Fikr al-Islami, 1994.

Abu Talib, Sufi. "Al-Tajdid wa Darurat al-Tawazun." Conference paper presented to the Third International Forum of al-Azhar Alumni, Kuala Lumpur, 16 February 2008.

Al-'Alwani, Taha Jabir. *Islah al-Fikr al-Islami: Madkhal ila Nizam al-Khitab al-Islami al-Mu'asir.* 3rd ed. Virginia: al-Ma'had al-'Alami li'l-Fikr al-Islami, 1995.

Al-Awa, Muhammad Salim. *Al-Fiqh al-Islami fi Tariq al-Tajdid.* 2nd ed. Cairo: al-Maktab al-Islami, 1998.

Al-Bashir, Isam. "Al-Tajdid fi'l-Fikr al-Islami." In *Tajdid al-Fikr al-Islami*, edited by Mahmud Hamdi Zaqzuq. Cairo: Wizarat al-Awqaf, 1430H/2009.

Al-Ifriqi, Ibn Manzur. *Lisan al-'Arab*. Vol. 3. Beirut: Dar Sadir, 1414H.

Al-Jabiri, Muhammad 'Abid. *Al-Din wa'l-Dawlah wa Tatbiq al-Sharia.* Beirut: Markaz Dirasat al-Wahda al-'Arabiyya, 1996.

Al-Qaradawi, Yusuf. *Hawl Qadaya al-Islam wa'l-'Asr.* 3rd ed. Cairo: Maktabah Wahbah, 1427H/2006.

______. *Liqa'at wa Hiwarat Hawl Qadaya al-Islam wa'l-'Asr.* Cairo: Maktabah Wahbah, 1992.

Al-Rafiq, Abu Bakr. "Al-Tajdid wa Ahammiyyatuh fi'l-'Asr al-Hadith." In Zaqzuq, *Tajdid al-Fikr al-Islami.*

Al-Sayyid, 'Abd al-Sattar. "Al-Tajdid fi'l-Fikr al-Islami: Mashru'iyyatuh wa Dawabituh." In Zaqzuq, *Tajdid al-Fikr al-Islami.*

Al-Tabrizi, Abd Allah al-Khatib. *Mishkat al-Masabih*, edited by Muhammad Nasir al-Din al-Albani. 2nd ed. Vol. 1. Beirut: Al-Maktab al-Islami, 1399H/1979.

Al-Talibi, 'Ammar. "Al-Tajdid fi'l-Fikr al-Malik Bin Nabi." In Zaqzuq, *Tajdid al-Fikr al-Islami.*

Al-Turabi, Hasan. *Tajdid al-Fikr al-Islami.* 2nd ed. Jeddah: al-Dar al-Su'udiyah lil-Nashr, 1978.

'Atiyah, Jamal al-Din, and Wahbah al-Zuhaili. *Tajdid al-Fiqh al-Islami.* Beirut: Dar al-Fikr, 1422/2002.

Barium, Fawzia. *Malik Bennabi: His Life and Theory of Civilisation.* Kuala Lumpur: Budaya Ilmu, 1993.

Bugagie, Usman Muhammad. "Concept of Revitalisation in Islam." Unpublished PhD thesis.

Cammak, Mark E. "Islam and Nationalism in Modern Indonesia: Forging an Indonesian Madhhab." In *The Islamic School of Law: Evolution, Devolution and Progress,* edited by Peri Bearman, Rudolph Peters and Frank E. Vogel. Cambridge, MA: Harvard University Press, 2006.

"Editorial article." *Islamiyyat al-Ma'rifah* 20, no. 78 (Autumn 1435H/2014): 5.

Ibn al-Athir, Al-Mubarak bin Muhammad al-Jazari. *Jami' al-Usul li-Ahadith al-Rasul*, edited by Abd al-Qadir al-Arnaut. 3rd ed. Vol. 11. Beirut: Dar al-Fikr, 1983.

Ibrahim, Abd al-Rahman al-Haaj. "Al-Tajdid: Min al-Nass 'ala'l-Khitab: Bahth fi Tarikhiyat al-Mafhum al-Tajdid." *Al-Tajdid* 3, no. 61420 (1999).

Imamah, Adnan Muhammad. *Al-Tajdid fi'l-Fikr al-Islami.* Beirut: Dar Ibn al-Jawzi, 2001.

'Imarah, Muhammad. "Ma'alim al-Manhaj al-Islami." *Majallah Islamiyyat al-Ma'rifah* 1 (1995).

______. *Azmat al-Fikr al-Islami al-Mu'asir.* Cairo: Dar al-Shuruq al-Awsat, 1990.

Kamali, Mohammad Hashim. *Civilisational Renewal: Revisiting the Islam Hadhari Approach.* 2nd ed. Kuala Lumpur: International Institute of Advanced Islamic Studies, 2009.

______. *Maqasid, Ijtihad and Civilisational Renewal.* London & Kuala Lumpur: IIIT and IAIS Malaysia, 2012.

______. *Shari'ah Law: An Introduction.* Oxford: Oneworld Publications, 2008.

Khan, Maimul Ahsan. *Human Rights in the Muslim World.* Durham, NC: Carolina Academic Press, 2003.

Saeed, Abdullah. "Fazlur Rahman: A Framework for Interpreting the Ethico-Legal Content of the Qur'an." In *Modern Muslim Intellectuals and the Qur'an,* edited by Suha Taji Farouki. London: OUP and The Institute of Ismaili Studies, 2004.

Yaqut, Muhammad Mas'ad. "Nazarat fi Hadith al-Tajdid: Fi Haza'l-Qarn Na'tajula Harakah Tajdidiyah Shamilah Mustanirah." *Said al-Fawa'id.* http://saaid.net/aldawlah/359.htm.

Chapter 14

Sufism in Indonesian Islam: A Brief History and a New Typology

Azyumardi Azra

Professor at the Syarif Hidayatullah State Islamic University Jakarta

Professor Osman Bakar, a scholar who has contributed significantly to many aspects of Islamic knowledge and beyond, is deserving of both tribute and utmost respect. He has published a long list of books, papers as well as essays, and honoured with illustrious positions such as the Malaysia Chair of Islam in Southeast Asia at Georgetown University, Chair Professor and Director of Sultan Omar Ali Saifuddien Centre for Islamic Studies (SOASCIS) at the University of Brunei Darussalam, and the most recent being The Ghazali Chair at the International Institute of Islamic Thought and Civilization (ISTAC), International Islamic University of Malaysia (IIUM). I present this article on Sufism in Indonesia as a note of *tahniah* (congratulations) to Professor Bakar whose works I constantly turn to for inspiration.

In this chapter, I further his contributions to esoteric knowledge through an exposition of the career of Sufism in Indonesian Islam, with a particular attention paid to transformations of Sufism in contemporary Indonesian Islam. As is well-known, Sufism has played an instrumental role in the massive spread of Islam in the Malay-Indonesian archipelago from the late eleventh and early thirteenth centuries onwards. It was and still is responsible for the consolidation and intensification of Islamicity, if not orthodoxy, of many Malay-Indonesian Muslims. Sufi peripatetic teachers traversed to the furthest parts of the archipelago, preaching Islam in a very accommodative way. The spread of Sufism in the archipelago was not without challenges as Sufis were met with opposition from Muslims and non-Muslims in the archipelago. Some Sufis therefore tolerated syncretism between Islam with that of local beliefs and practices.

This chapter focuses on the period when Sufism in Indonesia underwent a period of internal renewal and reform in the seventeenth century right up to the contemporary period.[555] The rise of Islamic modernism or reformism since the early nineteenth century brought new challenges to Sufism, particularly the strand that was practised collectively by the *tariqahs*. Sufi teachers and their deputies (*murshids*, *khalifahs*) and *murids* (disciples) were targeted by Muslim modernists or reformists in their critiques of the factors that led to the decline of Islam in Indonesia which ushered in European colonialism. In post-independent Indonesia from the early 1970s onwards, rapid economic developments and social engineering launched by President Soeharto was the most depressing phase for Sufism and *tariqahs*. They were regarded by many as incompatible to modern life and irrelevant to a rapidly growing Muslim population that placed more attention on material progress. Still, far from forgotten, Sufism and *tariqahs* continue to influence the lives of Muslims and non-Muslims from almost all walks of life. In the final part of this chapter, I propose a new typology that would aid in our understanding of contemporary Sufism in Indonesia and, perhaps also, elsewhere in the world.

Sufism in Indonesian Islam and the Return to Orthodoxy

The return to orthodoxy of Sufism in the archipelago had a lot to do with the transnational networks of `*ulama*' centered in seventeenth century Mecca and Medina (the Haramayn). A good number of Malay-Indonesian students, known in Arabic sources of the time as '*ashab al-Jawiyyin*' (Malay-Indonesian fellows), were part of these networks. Having studied in the Haramayn, most—if not all—of the '*ashab al-Jawiyyin*,' returned to the archipelago. They played an instrumental role in the reform and renewal of Indonesian Islam. The most important among them throughout the seventeenth and eighteenth centuries were Nur al-Din al-Raniri, `Abd al-Ra'uf al-Sinkili, Muhammad Yusuf al-Maqassari, `Abd al-Shamad al-Palimbani, Muhammad Arshad al-Banjari, Muhammad Nafis al-Banjari, and Daud ibn `Abd Allah al-Patani.[556]

These Malay-Indonesian `*ulama*' (scholars) were experts in *shari`ah* and well-versed in Sufism. They wrote many works that touched on *ilmu-ilmu zahir* (exoteric) sciences such as *fiqh* (jurisprudence), *tafsir* (exegesis) and *hadith* (prophetic traditions), and *ilmu-ilmu batin* (esoteric) sciences, such as *tasawwuf* and *kalam* (speculative theology). Nuruddin Al-Raniri was the first scholar who wrote a book on *fiqh al-`ibadah* (jurisprudence of worship) in the Malay language entitled *al-Sirat al-Mustaqim* (The Straight Path). Abdul Rauf al-Sinkili was the first scholar who wrote a *fiqh al-mu`amalah* (jurisprudence

555 Azyumardi Azra, "The Opposition to Sufism in the 17th and 18th Centuries," in *Islam in the Indonesian World: An Account of Institutional Formation* (Bandung: Mizan, 2007); Martin van Bruinessen, "Saints, Politicians and Sufi Bureaucrats: Mysticism and Politics in Indonesia's New Order," in *Sufism and the 'Modern' in Islam*, eds. J.D. Howell and Martin van Bruinessen (London: IB Tauris, 2007), 92–112.
556 Azyumardi Azra, *The Origins of Islamic Reformism in Southeast Asia: Networks of Malay-Indonesian and Middle Eastern 'Ulama' in the 17th and 18th Centuries* (Canberra: AAAS & Allen-Unwin, 2004).

of transactions) book, entitled *Mir'at al-Tullab* (Mirror of Seekers), as well as a *tafsir*, entitled *Tarjuman al-Mustafid* (The Interpreter That Gives Benefit) in Malay.

These *`ulama'* also produced a good number of works on Sufism written mostly in Arabic. Such works were intended for the *khawas* (religious specialists) and not for the *awwam* (common people) who could only read Malay texts written in Jawi scripts. Many of these scholars were also *khalifah* (deputy of Sufi masters) of *tariqah*s who were responsible for introducing and disseminating the Qadiriyyah, Naqshbandiyyah, Sammaniyah, Khalwatiyah and many others Sufi brotherhoods to the Muslims. Thanks to their networks of students in the archipelago, the *tariqah*s soon gained momentum, which in turn became important vehicles in confronting European colonialism in the region.

The most important theme found in the works of the Malay-Indonesian `ulama' mentioned above was the reconciliation between *shari`ah* (Islamic legal and ethical code) and *tasawwuf*. As early as the seventeenth century, there were bitter controversies among them on the doctrine of *wahdat al-wujud* (unity of existence) proposed by the Great Shaikh Ibn `Arabi and elaborated further by `Abd al-Karim al-Jili and Muhammad ibn Fadl Allah al-Burhanpuri. There was also fierce opposition against Hamzah al-Fansuri and Shams al-Din al-Sumatrani, who were regarded as having been heretical by al-Raniri, for instance, for their concept of *wujudiyyah*, a Malay-Indonesian version of Ibn `Arabi's *wahdat al-wujud*. Al-Raniri made a distinction between what he called as '*wujudiyyah mulhid*' (heretical *wujudiyah*) to which al-Fansuri and al-Sumatrani belonged and *wujudiyyah muwahhid* (*Tawhidic wujudiyyah*), that is in line with the Unity of God to which al-Raniri belonged to.

In retrospect, the controversies therefore basically originated from their different emphasis on certain aspects of *wahdat al-wujud*. On the one hand, al-Fansuri and al-Sumatrani put a strong emphasis on the *tashbih* (immanency) aspect of God. al-Raniri and al-Sinkili, in turn, emphasized the *tanzih* (transcendence) aspect of God. Despite their differences and controversies, they were all proponents of the *wahdat al-wujud*.[557]

Sufism that was introduced by the Malay-Indonesian `ulama' in the seventeenth and eighteenth centuries can be categorized as "neo-Sufism." There has been some discussion among scholars on the term of "neo-Sufism" itself. The brand of neo-Sufism among the Malay-Indonesian `ulama' was one that emphasized social activism and socio-moral reconstruction and transformation of Muslim society. They were exemplary figures of activism in the archipelago and were involved not only in religious but also social and political affairs. Al-Fansuri, al-Sumatrani, al-Raniri, and al-Sinkili rose to become the highest

557 Azra, "The Opposition to Sufism in the 17th and 18th Centuries."

dignitaries of the Acehnese Sultanate. Al-Maqassari was one of the most important leaders of the Bantenese Sultanate and led wars against the Dutch. Therefore, it is wrong to assert that the Sufism they introduced was escapist and pacifist, or otherwise, "antinomian Sufism."

In fact, strong exclusivist and radicalist tendencies since the mid-eighteenth century developed within the *tariqah*s in the archipelago. The "membership" of the *tariqah*s became more strict and restricted. Sufis were now expected to subscribe to one single rather than multiple *tariqahs* of their own choosing which was acceptable in the earlier period. At the same time, the discourse on *jihad* became more pronounced in the archipelago. Al-Palimbangi was responsible for appealing to Malay-Indonesian Muslims to wage *jihad* against the Dutch as they encroached deeper into the political-economy of the archipelago. While in Mecca, he wrote a book on *jihad*, entitled the *Fada'il al-Jihad* (Virtues of *Jihad*), and sent several letters to the Mataram Sultan of Java to wage *jihad* against the Dutch. Another stage of transformation of Sufism and *tariqah*s in the archipelago became discernible. Sufism inspired many rebellions throughout the nineteenth century such as the Diponegoro war in Java, the *beratib beramal* (recite and act) rebellion in South Kalimantan, and the peasant rebellions of Banten.

The transnational networks of Sufism and *tariqah*s existed among the Acehnese, Palembanese, Bantenese, Banjarese, Patanis, and the Javanese. Several recent studies, particularly done by Merle C. Ricklefs, have shown that the "ulama" in seventeenth and eighteenth centuries Aceh, Palembang, and Banjarmasin were influenced by religious tendencies in Java which called for the reconciliation of *shari`ah* and *tasawwuf.* This paved the way for increased orthodoxy.[558] In the early nineteenth century, a number of *ashab al-Jawiyyin* (companions of the people from Jawah) in Mecca such as Ahmad Rifai of Kalisalak (Pekalongan), Muhammad Saleh Darat al-Samarani (Semarang), Muhammad Mahfuz al-Termasi (from Termas, East Java) and Nawawi al-Banteni returned to Java island. They pioneered the *pesantren* tradition that gained momentum in the nineteenth century. And soon enough, *pesantren*s became not only centers of Islamic learning, but also of Sufism and *tariqah*s.

By the end of the nineteenth century, however, there appeared again increased criticism of certain `*ulama*' on the *tariqah*s. This time, as one might expect, the criticism came also from Malay-Indonesian `*ulama*' who lived in Mecca for some decades and developed transnational connections. Prominent among them were Nawawi al-Banteni and Ahmad Khatib al-Minangkabawi. Another scholar in this period who was very critical of *tariqah*s was Sayyid `Uthman of Batavia. He was of Arab-Hadrami origin.

558 M.C. Ricklefs, *Mystic Synthesis in Java: A History of Islamization from the 14th to the Early 19th Centuries* (Norwalk, CT: East Bridge, 2006); M.C. Ricklefs, *The Seen and Unseen in Java, 1726–1749: History, Literature and Islam in the Court of Pakubuwana II* (St Leonards, NSW & Honolulu: Asian Studies Association of Australia & Allen-Unwin & University of Hawaii Press, 1998).

Despite their criticism of *tariqahs*, both al-Banteni and al-Minangkabawi did not oppose *tasawwuf* in totality but took aim at certain practices of Sufi shaykhs that, in their opinion, ran contrary to the *shari`ah*. They castigated popular Sufism that was mixed with un-Islamic practices. Noteworthy in this regard was Sayyid `Uthman's fierce criticisms of the *tariqahs* which were in part colored by his defense and support of Dutch colonialism in the archipelago.[559] Sufis during this period were divided between those who opposed colonialism wholeheartedly and those who endorsed it for pragmatic and strategic reasons.

Sufism and Islamic Modernism

The rise of Islamic modernism in Indonesia in the early decades of the twentieth century under the influence of such modernist scholars as Muhammad `Abduh and Muhammad Rashid Rida placed Sufism and *tariqahs* under heavy criticism especially by movements such as the Muhammadiyah and Persis (Persatuan Islam).[560] For 'Abduh, Rida, and the movements that followed their ideas, both Sufism and *tariqahs* were responsible for the decline and backwardness of Muslims since the post-Baghdad period. Sufism and *tariqahs* led Muslims towards passivism, withdrawal from worldly life (*uzlah*), and to excessive practice of ascetic life (*zuhud*). That is why the modernists maintained that Muslims must discard of Sufistic practices and abandon *tariqahs* to progress.

There are other reasons why the reformists were opposed to Sufism and the *tariqahs*. First, they found Sufism to be overly philosophical and speculative regarding the essence of God. Such discussions did not address the challenges which modern Muslims faced. Second, the reformists perceived that both Sufism and *tariqahs* contained only unwarranted innovations (*bid`ah*), delusions (*khurafat*), and superstitions (*takhayyul*) that brought Muslims into irrationality. Motivated by the puritanical ideology of Salafism, the reformists hoped to cleanse the religious practices of Muslims in the path to make them more attuned to the demands of the authentic scriptures and ever-changing contexts.

Third, the reformists viewed Sufism and *tariqahs* as being excessively absorbed in rituals, particularly *dhikr* (remembrance of God). This led to neglect of worldly life. Concepts in Sufism such as *zuhd* (austere life), *uzlah* (withdrawal), and the like were, to the reformists, no more than escapism and passivism which the Sufis embraced in their pursuit of the hereafter. Above all,

559 Azyumardi Azra, "The Opposition to Sufism in the 17th and 18th Centuries"; and Azyumardi Azra, "Sayyid Uthman: Preliminary Study," *Studia Islamika: Indonesian Journal of Islamic Studies* 1, no. 1 (1994).

560 Alfian, *Muhammadiyah: The Political Behavior of a Muslim Modernist Organization under Dutch Colonialism* (Yogyakarta: Gadjah Mada University Press, 1989); Deliar Noer, *The Modernist Muslim Movement in Indonesia 1900–1942* (Kuala Lumpur: Oxford University Press, 1973); Mitsuo Nakamura, *The Crescent arises over the Banyan Tree: A Study of the Muhammadiyah Movement in a Central Javanese Town* (Yogyakarta: Gadjah Mada University Press, 1983).

the reformists criticized blind obedience towards Sufi shaykhs, *murshids* (Sufi master), and *khalifahs* (deputy of Sufi masters). In fact, there is a principle in *tariqahs* that the disciples of *tariqahs* should be like "dead bodies in the hands of their washers." This principle leaves no room for the *tariqah*'s followers to question, let alone to oppose, the Sufi masters. Sufi disciples regarded their masters as *wasilah* (intercessors) between them and God. This principle runs contrary to the teachings of the reformists in that Muslims should exercise their own reason (*ijtihad*) and act accordingly rather than following anyone blindly, be it Sufi masters or the "*ulama*" in general.

Despite their opposition to Sufi masters and *tariqahs*, certain reformist circles accept a brand of Sufism that was stripped of speculative or philosophical discourses and that was free from excessive rituals and uncontested veneration of Sufi masters. A leading Muhammadiyah scholar of modern Indonesia, Haji Abdul Malik Abdul Karim Amrullah (or more popularly known as "Hamka," for instance, introduced what he called as "*tasawuf moderen*" (modern Sufism/*tasawwuf*).[561] Deriving from Imam al-Ghazali's *tasawwuf akhlaqi* (ethical Sufism), this was a kind of *tasawwuf* that puts strong emphasis on good morality and ethics (*al-akhlaq al-karimah*). When practised devotedly, Muslims could attain a higher degree (*maqam*/*maqamat*) of spiritual enjoyment.

Most, if not all, Indonesian reformists, however, despised Sufism and prevented Muslims from being pulled into any *tariqahs*. Some followed the footsteps of Hamka by practising *tasawwuf* without *tariqahs*. *Tasawwuf* for these circles was simply one of the means to improve their *al-akhlaq al-karimah* (morality and ethics) rather than to achieve a unity with God.

The rapid religious and social changes in Indonesia in the last three decades made way for religious convergence between the reformists represented by Muhammadiyah, and the traditionalists represented by the Nahdlatul Ulama (NU). More and more reformists adopt religious practices conventionally associated with the *tasawwuf*, particularly the *tasawwuf akhlaqi* (ethical Sufism). Thus, despite the reformists' criticism and attacks against Sufism and *tariqahs*, Sufism and *tariqahs* have survived and regained their influence in recent years. I find this unsurprising because Sufism and *tariqahs* have become part and parcel of Islam since the eleventh century, when Imam al-Ghazali successfully reconciled two opposing strong tendencies in Islam: the *Sharī'a*-oriented Islam and the Sufistic-oriented. Sufism became an integral part of the Islamic orthodoxy or tradition.

Having been under constant attack by the reformists, Sufism and *tariqahs* in Indonesia initially regained their strength with the foundation of the Nahdlatul Ulama (NU) in 1926. Usually regarded as a "traditionalist" Muslim organization, the religious ideology of the NU was called "Aswaja" (Ahl al-Sunnah

561 Hamka, *Tasawuf Moderen* (Jakarta: Pustaka Panjimas, 1939/1990).

wa al-Jamaah) which consists of the following: the theology of 'Asy'ariyyah, the Shafi'i school of Islamic law, and the Ghazalian *tasawwuf* and recognized *tariqahs*. The NU follows what it believes as the tradition of Islam throughout history.

NU's ideology is different from Muhammadiyah despite the fact that this organization saw itself also as Ahl al-Sunnah wa al-Jamaah. As a reformist organization, Muhammadiyah follow the Islamic tradition strictly, even though it is moderate, modern, urban-oriented, and very critical of Sufism and *tariqahs*, much like the Salafis. On the other hand, most of the NU *kiyais* were also leaders of *tariqahs* based mostly in the *pesantren* and rural areas. Many, if not, most senior teachers of *pesantrens* were disciples of *tariqahs*. As a rule, *pesantren* students are not involved in the *tariqahs*. The NU later consolidated *tasawwuf* and *tariqahs* through the establishment of the Jam`iyyah Tarekat Mu`tabarah (Association of Recognized Tariqahs) that exists up until today despite internal conflicts resulting from the involvement of certain NU leaders in politics, particularly during the Soeharto period.

Contemporary Indonesian Sufism and A New Typology

Rapid political, economic, social, and cultural changes during the New Order modernization in the 1970s led to the revival of Sufism, along with new discourses and practices among Sufistic and *tariqah* circles. The revival of Sufism and *tariqahs* in contemporary Indonesia, no doubt, owed to many factors following the economic policies of the Soeharto regime. For better or worse, such authoritarian-based economic policies brought about rapid political, social, and cultural changes, that in effect, created disruption and disorientation among Muslims.

Rapid dislocation particularly among youth, the increased use of drugs and other juvenile delinquencies created a lot of concerns among Sufistic and *tariqah* circles. A lot discussions involving some leaders of the Jam`iyyah Tarekat Mu`tabarah were held on how Sufis could use their networks and resources to address social problems. This led to the foundation of the Inabah Drug Rehabilitation Centers by Abah Anom of Tarekat Qadiriyyah Nasybandiyyah (TQN) to rehabilitate drug users. Abah Anom employs certain methods of *dhikr*, other Sufistic rituals, and utilized transnational networks in Southeast Asia. Through such dynamic involvement, Sufistic ideas and practices such as those propagated by the TQN continue to flourish among many Indonesian Muslims.

Because of the complexity of the current development of Indonesian Islam, particularly of Indonesian Sufism, I can only give a broad typology of contemporary Indonesian Sufism. This proposed typology could help us grasp the complexities of Indonesian Sufism. I divide the typology into "collectivist

Sufism," individualist Sufism," "philosophist Sufism," "transnationalist Sufism," "televangelicalist Sufism," and "perennialist Sufism."

The core of current Indonesian Sufism is no doubt "collectivist Sufism," which is expressed in the form of the *tariqah.* Against all skepticism, *tariqahs* are still going strong in Indonesia. The old *tariqahs,* like the Shattariyyah in West Sumatra, have now gained new strength. More and more disciples of the *tariqahs* flock to their conventional places of gathering, which often are located nearby the tombs of Sufi masters. Furthermore, the associations of the recognised *tariqahs* continue to exist and exert strong influence among the populace. As mentioned earlier, one of the most important among them is the Jam'iyyah Ahl al-Thariqah al-Mu'tabarah Indonesia (JATMI, the Association of Indonesian Recognised Tariqahs). Most leaders and disciples of *tariqahs* in the association are affiliated to the NU. From time to time, the associations have been pulled into party politics. That *tariqah* leaders have been regarded by some people as living saints provided them with political leverage. They acted as spiritual advisers to the political elite of the country and have been consulted by leaders of the political parties, particularly during election time.[562]

The second typology of Sufism in contemporary Indonesia is the one that is practised individually or, in other words, "individualist Sufism." This is the Hamka or Muhammadiyah model of *tasawwuf* (cf. Hamka 1939/1990) which is a Sufism without *tariqahs.* Such an approach to Sufism comes as no surprise since the Muhammadiyah rejects *taqlid* (blind obedience) to *ulama,* let alone to Sufi shaykhs. In the Muhammadiyah circles, individualistic Sufism is thus practised through living a devout lifestyle based on the principles of modesty, humility, self-restraint, repentance, and constant remembrance of God. The practice of Sufism without *tasawwuf* is of course not limited to Muhammadiyah members. Many middle class Muslims who have busy schedules prefer to practise *tasawwuf* individually. In some instances, they form small congregations that read *dhikr* in their houses or in certain designated places.

There is also another tendency of Sufistic practices among middle class Muslims which I term as "philosophist Sufism." This tendency is intellectual in nature and includes devoting time to discuss various aspects of Islam and Sufism. They come in the form of institutions as the Lembaga Studi Agama dan Filsafat (LSAF) and Yayasan Wakaf Paramadina in Jakarta. They provide special classes devoted to studying *tasawwuf* and are attended by enthusiastic audiences. As a rule, these *tasawwuf* courses must remain "theoretical," "philosophical," and "academic" in nature and downplay the importance of rituals and recitation of litanies. The increased demand for "practical Sufism" within these groups eventually led to the formation of "*dhikr* groups" founded by non-*tariqah* scholars such as Jalaluddin Rahmat and others.

562 van Bruinessen, "Saints, Politicians and Sufi Bureaucrats."

There exists as well "transnationalist Sufism" in contemporary Indonesia, among which was the Darul Arqam, originally founded in the 1970s in Malaysia. Strongly colored by Sufistic revivalist ideology, the movement and its economic enterprises soon spread to Indonesia. The Darul Arqam Sufistic tendencies have attracted some Muhammadiyah members and this brought strong condemnation by the movement leaders. They appealed to the Indonesian government to ban the Darul Arqam in light of Mahathir Mohamad government's shutting down the Sufi tariqah in 1994.

The Arqam was however not banned in Indonesia, because of NU's strong opposition and appeals to the Indonesian government. One of the reasons why the NU defended the Darul Arqam was because its Sufistic practices were similar to NU. Despite that, the Darul Arqam in Indonesia declined considerably. After the fall of President Soeharto in 1998, the movement was revived under a new name, "Rufaqa."

Another tendency of Sufistic practices is what one can call "televangelicalist Sufism" popularized by such preachers as Abdullah Gymnastiar (otherwise known as "Aa' Gym"), Arifin Ilham and some other lesser-known figures. They conducted massive *dhikr* along with long and emotional prayers seeking for God's forgiveness. Leaders of this massive televangelicalist Sufism rise and fall within a matter of a few years and are dependent on television channels that broadcast their activities and lectures. Still, televangelical Sufism continues to survive, albeit with declining support and followers. The transformation of Sufism from collectivist *tariqah*s to individualist and then to televangelicalist is worth further research.

Last within the typology of Indonesian Sufism is "perennialist Sufism." This is basically "new age" movements that were popular in many parts of the Western world. Inspired to a large extent by "perennial philosophy," these Sufi groups are a mixture of various kinds of spiritual tradition. The followers of these groups, as one might expect, consist of people who see themselves as belonging to different religions at once.[563]

Conclusion

To conclude, the seismic changes in Indonesia since the last four centuries have contributed a great deal to the making of various tendencies in Sufism in Indonesia today. Even so, the religious convergence that has been taking place in Indonesia, particularly among the members of traditional NU and of reformist Muhammadiyah, has made it possible for Sufism to widen its seemingly lost appeal. With the continued dynamism of religious life in Indonesia, one can expect Sufism and other kinds of spirituality to continue to flourish

563 Julia Day Howell, "Modernity and Islamic Spirituality in Indonesia's New Sufi Network," in *Sufism and the 'Modern' in Islam*, 237.

in Indonesia. Conflicting trends and tendencies arising from rapid religious, economic, social, cultural, and political changes, would lead many believers to search for stronger and deeper religious experience that is provided by Sufism regardless of the kinds of expression. Sufism is, therefore, far from having lost its ground in the heyday of economic, social, and cultural modernization of the country. It will continue to be an inalienable part of Indonesian Islam.

Bibliography

Alfian. *Muhammadiyah: The Political Behavior of a Muslim Modernist Organization under Dutch Colonialism*. Yogyakarta: Gadjah Mada University Press, 1989.

Azra, Azyumardi. *The Origins of Islamic Reformism in Southeast Asia: Networks of Malay-Indonesian and Middle Eastern 'Ulama' in the 17th and 18th Centuries*. Canberra: AAAS & Allen-Unwin, 2004.

Azra, Azyumardi. "The Opposition to Sufism in the 17th and 18th Centuries." In *Islam in the Indonesian World: An Account of Institutional Formation*. Bandung: Mizan, 2007; originally published in *Islamic Mysticism Contested: Thirteen Centuries of Controversies and Polemics*, edited by Frederick de Jong and Berndt Radtke. Leiden: Brill, 1999.

Azra, Azyumardi. "Sayyid Uthman: Preliminary Study." In *Islam in the Indonesian World: An Account of Institutional Formation*. Bandung: Mizan; originally published in *Studia Islamika: Indonesian Journal of Islamic Studies* 1, no. 1 (1994).

Barton, Greg, and Greg Fealy, eds. *Nahdlatul Ulama: Traditional Islam and Modernity in Indonesia*. Clayton: Monash Asia Institute, 1996.

Bruinessen, Martin van. "Saints, Politicians and Sufi Bureaucrats: Mysticism and Politics in Indonesia's New Order." In *Sufism and the 'Modern' in Islam*, edited by J.D. Howell and Martin van Bruinessen, 92–112. London: IB Tauris, 2007.

Bruinessen, Martin van. "Controversies and Polemics Involving the Sufi Orders in Twentieth-Century Indonesia." In *Islamic Mysticism Contested: Thirteen Centuries of Controversies and Polemics*, edited by Frederick de Jong and Bernd Radtke, 705–28. Leiden: E.J. Brill, 1999.

Bruinessen, Martin van. "The Origins and Development of Sufi Orders (Tarekat) in Southeast Asia." *Studia Islamika: Indonesian Journal for Islamic Studies* 1, no. 1 (1994): 1–23.

Bruinessen, Martin van. *Tareket Naqsyabandiyah di Indonesia: Survei Historis, Geografis dan Sosiologis*. Bandung: Mizan, 1992.

Bruinessen, Martin van. "The Origins and Development of the Naqshbandi Order in Indonesia." *Der Islam* 67 (1990): 150–79.

Elizar, Giora. "The Islamic Reformist Movement in the Malay-Indonesian World in the First Four Decades of the 20th Century: Insights Gained from a Comparative Look at Egypt." *Studia Islamika*: Indonesian Journal for Islamic Studies 9, no. 1, (2002).

Gilsenan, Michael. "Trajectories of Contemporary Sufism." In *Islamic Dilemmas: Reformers, Nationalists and Industrialization*, edited by Ernest Gellner, 187–98. Amsterdam: Mouton, 1985.

Gilsenan, Michael. *Saint and Sufi in Modern Egypt: An Essay in the Sociology of Religion*. Oxford: Oxford University Press, 1973.

Gilsenan, Michael. "Some Factors in the Decline of Sufi Orders in Modern Egypt." *The Muslim World* 57 (1967): 11–57.

Hamka. *Tasawuf Moderen*. Jakarta: Pustaka Panjimas, 1939/1990.

Heelas, Paul, and Linda Woodhead. *The Spiritual Revolution: Why Religion is Going Way to Spirituality*. Oxford: Blackwell, 2005.

Howell, Julia Day, and Martin van Bruinessen. "Sufism and the 'Modern' in Islam." In *Sufism and the 'Modern' in Islam*, edited by J.D. Howell and Martin van Bruinessen, 3–18. London: IB Tauris, 2007.

Howell, Julia Day. "Modernity and Islamic Spirituality in Indonesia's New Sufi Network." In *Sufism and the 'Modern' in Islam*, edited by J.D. Howell and Martin van Bruinessen, 217–40. London: IB Tauris, 2007.

Howell, Julia Day. "Muslims, the New Age and Marginal Religions in Indonesia: Changing Meanings of Religious Pluralism." *Social Compass* 52, no. 4 (2005): 473–93.

Howell, Julia Day. "Sufism and the Indonesian Islamic Revival." *Journal of Asian Studies* 60, no. 3 (2001): 701–29.

Howell, Julia Day, Subandi, and Peter L. Nelson. "New Faces of Indonesian Sufism: A Demographic Profile of Tarekat Qodiriyyah-Naqsyabandiyyah, Pesantren Suryalaya, in the 1990s." *Review of Indonesian and Malaysian Affairs* 35, no. 2 (2001): 33–60.

Howell, Julia Day. "Indonesia's Urban Sufis: Challenging Stereotypes of Islamic Revival." *ISIM—International Institute for the Study of Islam in the Modern World—Newsletter* 6, no. 17 (2000).

Howell, Julia Day, Subandi, and Peter. L Nelson. "Indonesian Sufism: Sign of Resurgence." In *New Trends and Development in the World of Islam*, edited by Peter B. Clarke, 277–98. London: Luzac Oriental, 1998.

Johansen, Julian. *Sufism and Islamic Reform in Egypt: The Battle for Islamic Tradition*. Oxford: Clarendon Press, 1996.

Laffan, Michael. "National Crisis and the Representation of Traditional Sufism in Indonesia: The Periodicals *Salafy* and *Sufi*." In *Sufism and the 'Modern' in Islam*, edited by J.D. Howell and Martin van Bruinessen, 149–171. London: IB Tauris, 2007.

Laffan, Michael. *Islamic Nationhood and Colonial Indonesia: The Umma below the Winds*. London: RoutledgeCurzon, 2003.

Lombard, Denys. "Les Tarekat en Insulinde." In *Les Ordres Mystiques en Islam*, edited by Alexandre Popovic and Gilles Veinstein, 139–63. Paris: EHESS, 1985.

Nakamura, Mitsuo. *The Crescent arises over the Banyan Tree: A Study of the Muhammadiyah Movement in a Central Javanese Town*. Yogyakarta: Gadjah Mada University Press, 1983.

Noer, Deliar. *The Modernist Muslim Movement in Indonesia 1900–1942*. Kuala Lumpur: Oxford University Press, 1973.

Rahman, Fazlur. *Islam: Second Edition*. Chicago: University of Chicago Press, 1979.

Ricklefs, M.C. *Mystic Synthesis in Java: A History of Islamization from the 14th to the Early 19th Centuries*. Norwalk, CT: East Bridge, 2006.

Ricklefs, M.C. *The Seen and Unseen in Java, 1726–1749: History, Literature and Islam in the Court of Pakubuwana II*. St Leonards, NSW & Honolulu: Asian Studies Association of Australia & Allen-Unwin & University of Hawaii Press, 1998.

Sila, Muhammad Adlin. *Tasawuf Perkotaan: Kasus Pusat Kajian Tasawuf (PKT) Tazkiyah Sejati Jakarta*. Jakarta: Badan Penelitian dan Pengembangan Agama, 2000.

Sirriyeh, Elizabeth. *Sufis and Anti-Sufis: The Defence, Rethinking and Rejection of Sufism in the Modern World*. London: Curson, 1999.

Soebardi, Soebakin. "The Pesantren Tarikat of Surialaya in West Java." In *Spectrum: Essays Presented to ST Alisjahbana*, edited by S. Udin, 215–36. Jakarta: Dian Rakyat, 1978.

Stange, Paul. "Legitimate Mysticism in Java." *Review of Indonesian and Malaysian Affairs* 20, no. 2 (1986): 76–117.

Voll, John O. "Contemporary Sufism and Current Social Theory." In *Sufism and the 'Modern' in Islam*, edited by J.D. Howell and Martin van Bruinessen, 281–98. London: IB Tauris, 2007.

Chapter 15

What Makes a Family and Its Values: A Critical Response to Professor Osman Bakar's Thoughts

Zaleha Kamaruddin

Professor of Law and Deputy Director-General of the Institute for Islamic Understanding Malaysia (IKIM)

Professor Emeritus Dato' Dr. Osman Bakar is an indispensable source of reference for those studying philosophy, civilization and Islam. His scholarship has guided and influenced the thinking of former and current students over the last four decades and as a colleague, I am no exception. Although my work has been on Comparative Family Laws since the last thirty-six years, I have personally benefited from Osman's writings. Among the works that have influenced me is, "Family Values, the Family Institution, and the Challenges of the Twenty First Century; An Islamic Perspective" (2011). This chapter critically analyses that essay in light of my own scholarly pursuits.

To give some context to my engagement with Osman's article, sometime near the end of 2020, I remember telling Professor Osman briefly over a meeting, that I was struggling to find literatures during the Covid-19 lockdown as access to ISTAC's library was very limited. I was then writing an essay on mapping the trends of the family institution from a comparative literature review perspective. He was very kind and thoughtful in his response and sent me his article the following day.

My initial reaction upon reading his article was our contrasting approach to the subject matter of family law. He uses the lens of civilization to study the family institution and focuses on the formation of family through marriages which are sacred in nature. He stresses the importance of traditional marriages and relates it to religion. These are terms which I am familiar with but paid less attention to because, as a person trained in law, I was mostly working from the opposite end of the family institution, i.e. divorce and ancillary matters. The justification for me using this approach is the large number of failed marriages ending up in court. And, even when dealing with the subject of marriage from the legal perspective, the usual focus would be from its technical aspects such as assessing the validity of the said marriage from legal or *Sharī'a* perspectives or any other matters that fall under those categories. My "fire-fighting" approach to the said issues seems unending, unsatisfying, and ineffective in curbing the problems. His approach through logical reasoning, as well as synthesizing and countering arguments is based on his good theoretical grounding and has successfully convinced me to agree with his key ideas. Focusing on marriage from a different angle has been truly beneficial for me in augmenting the scope of my research. One of the many important lessons that I learnt from him is to work and challenge ourselves to progress beyond our comfort zones, in my case, substantive law. It is very intellectually rewarding because it opens up more avenues to understand the subject matter holistically.

The nature of our disciplines may be different; however, we share some important conclusions, including the inference that the family is indeed the basic unit that makes up civilization and has been faced by many added factors that have challenged the institution itself. Osman identifies key elements and loopholes and connected many important "big dots" in relation to the family. To strengthen the institution of the family and to prevent crises, he advocates the need to preserve and protect the traditional family values. He relates it to a bigger picture of which, in his own words, "the perennial relevance of traditional family values to the survival of human civilisation and to the sustainable development of society."[564]

Overall, I realise that reading the article alone is inadequate to fully appreciate his worldview and one needs to supplement it with his other works to comprehend the greater context. Attending his lectures also assists us to understand why he has chosen the faith-based approach. Had I known him earlier when Professor Osman was the Deputy Vice Chancellor (Academic and Research) at the University of Malaya from 1995–2000, perhaps I would have appreciated his writing differently. Knowing the author personally is an added advantage.

The little history behind this needs to be mentioned because it did not come easily. It started with the opportunity to know him personally at the end of 2018, where I went to his office in the beautiful ISTAC campus in Kuala Lumpur in his capacity as *Shaykhul Kulliyyah* to discuss the possibility of working with ISTAC on Islam and Gender Equity. Soon after that, I attended his evening classes for a semester to learn, understand, and later appreciate philosophy, civilization, and Islam. The classes were extrapolated from his magnum opus, *The Classification of Knowledge in Islam* (1998).

564 Osman Bakar, "Family Values, the Family Institution, and the Challenges of the Twenty-First Century: An Islamic Perspective," *Islam and Civilisational Renewal Journal* 2, no. 2 (2011): 32.

After my smooth transfer from Ahmad Ibrahim Kulliyyah of Laws to ISTAC, I knew him further as a colleague, and found that his approach to knowledge is very unconventional and inspiring. He is in fact very instrumental to ISTAC. Students around the world flocked to him to benefit from his ideas, and it is not surprising as he is a renowned Malay-Muslim philosopher. I could attest to this because when I was assigned to guide doctoral students to prepare research proposals, a majority of these students would propose him to be their supervisor. Their main reason, understandably, is that Professor Osman is recognized as among the world's influential Muslim thinkers, but most importantly, he rarely turns down students who wish to work under his wing. He is very busy as the second holder of the Al-Ghazali Chair at ISTAC and it is remarkable that he can give time to all his supervisees and attend to their intellectual requests. Indeed, he is a scholar with a big heart.

His collegial commitment should also be emulated by the new generation of younger scholars. His passion and wisdom is reflected not only in his works but also through many other ways, among others are, his readiness to contribute to ISTAC's programs, his sharp insight in our faculty's meetings, and our frequent informal WhatsApp ISTAC Academic group's discussions, and his willingness to contribute and share his knowledge through many webinars. As its Editor-in-Chief of the Al-Shajarah journal, he demonstrates intellectual leadership and unfailing drive towards ensuring high quality of publications. He does not negotiate on his principles. It is only apt that Osman is regarded as one of 500 influential Muslims in the world since 2009 till now.

The Meaning of Family in Islam and its Place in Modernity

The article entitled "Family Values, the Family Institution, and the Challenges of the Twenty-First Century: An Islamic Perspective" was primarily based on a conference paper which was presented at the International Conference on Family as a Value in Religion, Tradition and Modernity in Antalya, Turkey in November, 2010. It was later revised for another conference along the same theme: The International Conference on Family Values and the Family Institution in the Twenty-First Century in Kuala Lumpur on the 13–14th December the same year at the International Institute of Advanced Islamic Studies (IAIS). The article was published by the *Journal of Islam and Civilisational Renewal* (ICR) in 2011. From the title, it is clear that he had opted to embrace a faith-based approach and would use insights from Islamic scriptures and other works to support his points.

Osman begins with a short overview of the main aims which are basically two-fold. It "is to discuss the concept of family and its values and its place and role as a multi-dimensional institution from the Islamic perspective."[565]

565 Osman Bakar, "Family Values," 12.

In this, he focuses on three major issues which are, first, the concept and types of families and values therein, second, dissecting the roles of the family as a multi-dimensional institution from the Islamic perspective, and third, analysing proposals to address this string of challenges.

Osman then proceeds to defining key terms and relies heavily on the Qur'an which, according to him, justifies the necessity of definitions as conceptual tools for explanation. It should be mentioned here that Osman finds that by emphasizing on definitions as a background to analyse issues, it would facilitate further discussions. This matter was also highlighted during his deliberations in ISTAC's first Writing.lab @ ISTAC series. He guides us to understand that good definitions are valuable assets. In doing so, it allows us to assess situations better, and teaches us to make better decisions. It quickly brings the reader onto the same page as the author, which allows them to traverse the proceeding discussions together, with minimal misunderstandings.

Since the focal point of his article rests upon the ideas of "family," "family values," and "the family institution" from the Islamic perspective, Osman finds it pertinent to deliberate on what a family is. He draws on the English dictionary that gives seven different meanings of the word "family," namely:[566]

1. all the people living in the same house; household;
   (a) a social unit consisting of parents and the children they rear;
   (b) the children of the same parents;
   (c) one's husband (or wife) and children;
2. a group of people related by ancestry or marriage; relatives;
3. all those claiming descent from a common ancestor; tribe or clan; lineage;
4. a criminal syndicate under a single leader such as a Mafia family;
5. a commune living in one household, especially under one head;
6. a group of things having a common source or similar features.

Osman argues that these definitions are based mainly on the various types of families in modern and post-modern Western societies. A new categorization is needed and he offers his own as follows:[567]

1. the immediate or the household family;
2. the extended family;
3. the nuclear family;
4. the tribal family;
5. the human family; and
6. the political family.

566 Michael Agnes, ed., *Webster's New World College Dictionary* (New York: Macmillan USA, 1997), 512.

567 Osman Bakar, "Family Values," 15.

Osman then synthesizes all these meanings of family and offers his own definition in light of the Qur'anic perspective. One of the words used in the Qur'an for family is *ahl*, which has many meanings. One example of the usage of this term is in reference to the People of the Book (*ahl al-kitāb)* in the following verse. Say: "O People of the Book (*ahl al-kitāb*)! Come to common terms as between us and you: that we worship none but God; and that we shall not ascribe divinity to aught beside Him; and that we shall not take human beings for our lords and patrons beside God." And if they turn away, then say: "Bear witness that it is we who have surrendered ourselves unto Him" (Qur'an 3:64). He highlights this verse because it has become exceptionally distinctive in recent years among the Christians and the Muslims following the so-called "Common Word" dialogue. This discourse was between the leading representatives of the two major religious groups of the world on the basis of common spiritual duties.

The term *ahl* in this verse signifies the owners of property and titles of respect or those who are entitled to be duly regarded or to be given trust and responsibility (Qur'an 4:58). Some classical Arabic lexicologists' distinguish between the meanings of *ahl* and *āl* both in reference to family. *Ahl* refers to blood relations in general, whereas *āl* specifically to blood relations that have followers. Osman argues that although the term can take more general meanings to also denote people who share similarities such as one's larger family circles (*al-aqrabūn*), one's race, religion, and occupation, as well as "dependants" in the most comprehensive manner, as pointed out by many classical commentators of the Qur'an, it is the believer's immediate family that this verse seeks to emphasise.[568]

The classical Arabic lexicology, according to him, conveys the specific meaning of "a man's nearer, or nearest relations on his father's side" and the slightly wider meaning of "a man's near kinsmen."[569] He relates it to modern and contemporary Arabic which retains the term *usrah* in its second classical meaning when referring to the immediate household family. He then brought in another useful term: *ahl al-bayt* which may be observed to include the wider family network and its support system. A verse in the Qur'an (33:33) was also cited to show clearly that it refers to the Prophet Muḥammad's family. Semantically then, the idea of the family household plays the pivotal role as a dynamo for ideas and meanings of family and familial relations at all levels and in all their aspects and dimensions. Osman states that, "it would be enough of a basis to justify the claim that, socially and institutionally, the family household is the most fundamental human social institution to ensure order and stability in society."[570]

568 Muhammad Asad, *The Message of the Qur'an* (Gibraltar: Dar Al-Andalus, 1980), 876.
569 Edward William Lane, *Arabic-English Lexicon* (Cambridge: Islamic Texts Society, 1984), 1:58.
570 Osman Bakar, "Family Values," 24.

He also relates that to the term *āl* which is of special significance in the context of the discussion on family values and the family institution. This is so when it is examined from the point of view of the role of divinely "chosen families" in the spiritual and religious history of mankind. He supports it with reference to several verses of the Qur'an, and sums up at that point that, the Qur'anic *ahl* implies and conveys the idea of familial relationships at various levels on the basis of blood relations.

Osman emphasises that "blood is thicker than water" and explains why familial relations through blood are prioritised over marriage. To further support his arguments, he cites the verse in the Qur'an (4:36) which refers to the moral obligation of the believers to be good and to serve what is good to near relatives. He rightly identifies the roles of near relatives which are unfortunately considered unimportant in contemporary society. The near relatives (*al-aqrabun)* have an important role to play in the family institution and in the strengthening of the social structure. Furthermore, the Qur'an (2:180) emplaces a social structure where grandparents could still have a role to play in assisting to preserve and enhance family values and the family institution.

Osman is not only concerned with the linguistic meaning of families. He was attentive to the string of challenges faced by families. He identified the severe crises in the family institution of modern times with the fault of the so-called "modern man." The concept of "modern man" which he further elaborates in this section is quite thought-provoking. According to him, the "modern man" has a radically conflicting perception about his origin and his identity, which fundamentally contradicts the values of the traditional religious family. Since the nineteenth century, the modern theories of cultural evolution have left a severe destructive impact on the modern man's attitudes towards the family institution. Consequently, it disrupts the main values propounded by the traditional religions. He rightly points out that it is pertinent to understand this "ideological challenge" to the traditional family institution to comprehend the prime cause why the institution is in a dire predicament in modern times. The uncovering of this fact is very pertinent because in treating the disease that befalls the family, one should treat the root cause of the problem not the symptoms.

Osman cites the Qur'anic verse (5:27–34) that tells the story of the murder with the view of sending home a universal moral message to humanity on the meaning and consequences of taking an innocent human life to support his contention. Modernity has murdered the family institution. He further delves into the historical origin of the first human couple as cited in the Qur'an (2:30–9): the story of Adam and Eve. Both of them were bonded in a sacred marriage as husband and wife and later raised their own offspring. They were the first family from whom all human beings descended.

Based on this fact, he goes back to his main premise and reiterates that "the traditional family institution is anchored on the principle of sacred marriage." This concept is not new as he mentions that it has been prescribed by religion. The traditional family has been nurtured over time by a series of divine revelations. The current disruption threatens the family institution. Professor Osman positively assures in his article that if we were to hold on to traditional families as a religious entity and on divine law, the Islamic family would have a brighter future.

For this to happen, modern families must manifest the spirit of the Qur'an. To Osman, the family institution is divinely sanctioned and plays a multi-dimensional function. He relates it to the concept of unitary, which is based on the principle of *al-tawhid* (principles of unity) and cites several verses that explains that God has ordained marriage and created favourable conditions as well as revealed adequate guidance for the realisation of a stable and healthy marriage. He explains further that Allah establishes relationships of lineage (*nasab*) and marriage, and desires marriage to be one of His signs, particularly of His wisdom and power. This sign is to be shown through the attainment of rest and tranquillity (*sakīnah*) and love and mercy (*mawaddah wa raḥmah*) in the relationship between husband and wife (Qur'an 30:21).

He reasserts and relates the fundamental religious role of the family to create a harmonious balance for spiritual and moral development and focuses on the achievement of the twin goals of existence, i.e. servitude to God (*ubudiyyah*) and the fulfilment of societal roles as *khalifah* on earth. These two goals are fulfilled through man's relationship with Allah (*hablun min Allah)* and man's relationship with fellow men (*hablun min al nas*). He explains this in-depth through the support of verses from the Qur'an and highlights on divinely "chosen families" in human history from Prophet Abraham, the family of Al-Imran, and Prophet Muhammad (pbuh) as models for us to emulate.

Based on these, he argues the importance of relating it to the role of near relatives and cites the verse from the Qur'an to confirm this contention. In this sense, we could discern that the Qur'an (4:36) provides due recognition to the role of the near relatives (*dhī 'l-qurbā*) in assisting to buttress marriage and family relationships. In this, he emphasises another interesting fact that those with blood relations have closer personal ties in the decree of Allah than the brotherhood of believers and the emigrants (*al-muhājirūn*). Osman also cites another verse in the Qur'an (30:21) to further strengthen his statement that the creation of males and females are for the purpose of procreation and are aligned with *fitrah* which is instrumental to the inculcation of *sakinah* and *mawaddah wa rahmah* between husband and wife within a lawful marriage.

In explaining the role of the family as a place for spiritual and moral upliftment, he fused the discussions under the role of the family as a divine institution instead of a separate section because they are so closely intertwined. Osman stresses on the role of family members to assist each other towards salvation in accordance with Islamic teachings. He stresses the importance of early education (*fard al-'ayn*) by parents as their children's first school and later their continuous guidance when teachers and parents join hands to educate the child. With a good educational foundation, young adults are set to learn what is right from society.

He sums up that Islam provides further avenues to economic health and spiritual development for both the family and the community through many ways, including through its faith-based economic institutions. He then goes back to reiterate his main thesis on the fundamental religious role of the family, i.e. to create a human environment conducive for family health to prosper based on three important roles; religious, educational and economic. He re-emphasizes that marriage in the traditional Islamic sense is to regulate human life with the view of attaining success and prosperity in this life and in the Hereafter (Qur'an 23:6). He also fortifies the role of marriage in religious and spiritual life by referring to a saying of Prophet Muḥammad (pbuh) that "marriage is half of religion."

The Family Institution in Crisis and Osman's Proposed Solutions

Like all other traditional family institutions, Osman sees the traditional Islamic family as confronted with many different forms of challenges due to globalisation, modernisation, and secularisation. In his analysis of the socio-economic role of the family, Osman acknowledges research that has shown that whenever there is a major financial crisis, the average family's economic well-being will be unfavourably affected. Consequently, conflicts and divorces happen. He referred to the research findings from the onset of the recent Covid-19 pandemic in 2020 and 2021.

Cumulatively, as a result of all these threats and challenges, he concludes that the traditional family is facing its worst crisis in the history of human civilisation. In response, he focuses instead on initiatives to protect the traditional family by proposing effective measures as well as the need to provide a far-reaching appraisal of ideologies and philosophies of life that are detrimental to the traditional family both as a social value and as a social institution.

In this context, he acknowledges the various studies that have shown that there are numerous societal "push" and "pull" factors that are gradually eroding traditional family values. Osman also observes that at the level of ideas and beliefs, many modern ideologies and philosophies of life are currently bombarding the traditional family institution and values. He also put forward initiatives that are considered urgent, which includes the need to reassert the wisdom and the contemporary relevance of traditional family values and its institution.

After analysing all these factors, he observes that at each level, the nature of these challenges to the traditional family is different. Therefore, he suggests that the approach should also vary according to the challenge faced. Consequently, the response proposed by him also focuses on practical measures that would seek to protect and strengthen traditional family values and its institution and that would concurrently seek to minimise negative external influences which can have the effect of weakening traditional family values.

He also registers his major concerns on a more worrying trend that is confronting traditional marriage and traditional family values, i.e. same-sex marriages which are on the increase and have been normalised in some countries as an acceptable practice. These various anti-family ideologies and philosophies of life are seen by him as a connivance to denigrate the traditional family in particular and intentionally done to portray that the traditional family structure is outdated.

On addressing how to confront challenges from an Islamic perspective, Professor Osman concludes his article with something different. To him, the strongest defenders of the traditional family are from the faithful followers of the traditional religions. The future of the traditional family depends on the strengths of the traditional religions and the followers of different religions should join hands in confronting those threats. But more studies and research is required to be undertaken on contemporary challenges faced by the family institution. A national research institute is proposed to dedicate its main objectives to the pursuit of intensive study on Islam and family values and the family institution.

Socio-economic policy-makers need to be more sensitive in safeguarding family values and the virtues of the family institution in their pursuit of socio-economic development. He further adds that since family health and household governance are closely intertwined, it is pertinent that policy makers in all fields of community and national developments are made aware of the importance of good household governance (*tadbir al-manzil*) to a healthy family life. Finally, for the purpose of effective problem solving, he urges Muslim groups to have more dialogues with non-Muslim groups on the common challenges confronting family values and the family institution.

Conclusion

Osman's main contribution is his civilizational approach that opens more avenues for interesting discussions on other major concerns relating to the family institution and has created a more holistic perspective. His article also provides a unique example of innovative study of the concepts of families, including its values and role as a multi-dimensional institution from the Islamic perspective. His emphasis is a refreshing approach based on protecting and giving emphasis on the traditional family which, according to him, could play a key role in strengthening the family institution.

Osman walks the extra mile to illustrate alternative methods to solve the crisis that confronts the family institution. While his article may appear to be philosophical to the general audience, it is this approach that is needed because, in doing so, he proposes the integration of reason and revealed knowledge to recover the multi-functional role of the family. This perspective allows us to appreciate the relationship of important factors that make up a family and its values.

I would like to end by expressing my gratefulness for having been invited to write an essay in this festschrift to honour his lifetime commitment and contributions. It is a great honour on my part as it gives me the opportunity to reflect on Osman as a renowned academic and a mentor.

Bibliography

Agnes, Michael, ed. *Webster's New World College Dictionary.* New York: Macmillan USA, 1997.

Asad, Muhammad. *The Message of the Qur'an.* Gibraltar: Dar Al-Andalus, 1980.

Lane, Edward William. *Arabic-English Lexicon.* Cambridge: Islamic Texts Society, 1984.

Osman Bakar. "Family Values, the Family Institution, and the Challenges of the Twenty-First Century: An Islamic Perspective." *Islam and Civilisational Renewal Journal* 2, no. 2 (2011): 12–36.

Osman Bakar. *Classification of Knowledge in Islam.* Cambridge: Islamic Texts Society, 1998.

Chapter 16

Spiritual Knowledge and Humanities as a Foundation for National Development and Peaceful Existence

Md. Salleh Yaapar

Professor at the School of Humanities, University Sains Malaysia

The unity of scientific and spiritual knowledge is realized when each of the particular sciences is organically related to the supreme knowledge of *al-Tawhid.*
Osman Bakar, *Tawhid and Science* (2008)

"Science alone cannot get to the heart of what makes us human, which is why the humanities and social sciences matter so much."
Editorial, *Times Higher Education Supplement* (March 17th 2011)

The quotations above seem to point out that the humanities and spiritual knowledge matter so much in the success of industries, nations or countries, regions, and human life in general. In fact, as a cluster of academic disciplines which generally deals with all things human, it should be considered and used as a foundation for nation building and human development in general. Yet, the humanities are not appreciated, if not, totally ignored or forsaken. Many assume that humanities have had no positive impact in daily life. The consequence of this is the lack of integrity and ethics in politics, business, and financial matters across many societies and countries issues. Development projects are hampered by dearth of funds because of malpractices such as favoritism, bribery, and even outright robbery of government coffers. This has led to economic crises, social unrest, and political turmoil, all of which could be seen in Malaysia. Take for examples, the classic case of the 1MDB financial scandals and the mismanagement of the Tabung Haji funds.

This chapter argues that the humanities and spiritual knowledge are necessary as a foundation for a nation's development and peaceful existence. Unfortunately, they have been prevented from performing their rightful role. The question is: Why are the humanities prevented from playing their role as a positive force in human development. To answer this, we must take a close look at modern history of education.

Humanities in Modern Education

In the history of modern education, knowledge has unfortunately for a long time been marked by a problematic dichotomy. This comes in the form of the separation of Arts and STEM (Science, Technology, Engineering and Math) subjects. Prominent in the Arts group is the cluster of disciplines referred to as the humanities. Conventionally, these disciplines include Language, Literature, Geography, History, Culture, Religious Studies, Philosophy, and Civilizational Studies. All disciplines within the humanities have human beings' multi-faceted earthly endeavor as their objects of study. Science and other STEM subjects, on the contrary, focus mainly on the natural phenomena and processes. The humanities use methods that are primarily critical, theoretical, and speculative, as opposed to STEM which basically employs the empirical and rational methods.

STEM is well-lodged within this context of the academic dichotomy. It is considered the royal road to progress. This is not the case with the humanities which sit on the margins, with their relevance always in question. In fact, recent economic downturns and rapid development in technology has led to decreased enrollment in the humanities in most universities globally. The current situation in Malaysia have made things even more depressing for the humanities. Political instability, economic stagnancy, and the rise in the cost of living meant that universities suffer from severe budget cutbacks and increase in fees.

As indicated above, it is commonly thought that humanities are irrelevant and do not contribute to the progress of nations. This is a simplistic way of looking at this very fundamental and significant branch of knowledge. As a cluster of knowledge, the humanities are capable of performing their function as a foundation for a nation's development, especially in the present age of reverence for technology and quantification where human values and spiritual aspirations are not accorded due attention. As I will show that there is dire need to reposition the humanities for it to be accepted as the main foundation to a nation's progress and development as well as to life in general. Let us begin with what could be referred to as the rumblings in the academia in the Euro-American world.

Rumblings In Academia

America and Europe

According to Humanities Indicators Prototype, a database of the American Academy of Arts and Sciences, the heyday of the humanities in the USA was the mid-to-late 1960s. By 2009, their share of college degrees was less than half of what it was before.[571] *The New York Times* noted: "In the last three months at least two dozen colleges have canceled or postponed faculty searches in religion and philosophy…The Modern Language Association's end-of-the-year job listings in English, literature and foreign languages dropped 21 percent for 2008–09 from the previous year, the biggest decline in 34 years."

Until early 2016 nothing changed. Thus in March the same academy reported that: The number of bachelor's degrees conferred in what the academy considers core humanities disciplines (English language and literature, history, languages and literatures other than English, linguistics, classical studies, and philosophy) declined 8.7 percent from 2012 to 2014, falling to the smallest number of degrees conferred since 2003: 106,869.[572] According to a report in *Inside Higher Ed*:[573] "The sharpest drops in majors occurred in the core humanities departments: art history, English, history and philosophy."

In Great Britain, the story is more or less the same. Disturbed by the continuous negative developments in the humanities, on Sunday 28th February 2010, major directors of institutions of the arts and a number of university vice-chancellors, headed by Prof Geoffrey Crossick of the University of London, published an open letter in *The Observer.* They pleaded relevant authorities in Britain not to simply ditch the humanities funding in favor of STEM. Due to the lop-sided system of education, Glasgow University in turn proposed significant cuts to a number of Arts and Humanities programs early 2011. The reason given was they "do not fit into the University's 'academic shape.'" Thus, the university's School of Modern Languages and Cultures was downsized.[574] Later, Malcolm Gillies (the Vice-Chancellor of London Metropolitan University), announced that the university had decided to close a number of subjects/programs. This included: i) History, (ii) Philosophy, (iii) Caribbean Studies, (iv) Theatre Studies, (v) Dance, (vi) parts of Multimedia and (vii) Performing Arts.[575] In 2013, the university launched a new strategy with the hope that the institution would eventually fare better.[576] It is obvious that the humanities are really under threat.

571 Patricia Cohen, "In Tough Times, the Humanities Must Justify Their Worth," *New York Times*, February 24, 2009.

572 Scott Jaschik, "The Shrinking Humanities Major," *Inside Higher Ed*, March 14, 2016.

573 Steven Mintz, "Reimagining the Humanities for the 21st Century," *Inside Higher Ed*, October 15, 2020.

574 *Humanities Matter*, March 20, 2011.

575 Harriet Swain, "London Metropolitan University eliminates history, philosophy, and performing arts from degree courses," *The Guardian*, May 3, 2011.

576 Anna Fazackerley, "London Met launches survival strategy," *The Guardian*, April 15, 2013.

Malaysia

The lop-sided system of education as presented above is not exclusive to the Euro- American regions. Within the Malaysian educational, STEM subjects too occupy center stage, while the humanities, especially Islamic Studies (Pengajian Islam), sit precariously at the margins. Like in other Southeast Asian countries, it has been commonly thought that the humanities do not matter in Malaysia, and do not contribute to the progress and wellbeing of the nation. Thus Malaysian students are separated into streams. "Bright" kids admitted to the science stream, especially the prestigious Sekolah Menengah Sains (Science Secondary Schools), while the lesser ones are sent to the Arts Stream. In the Arts Stream schools, some humanities subjects are not accorded proper places. Kesusasteraan Melayu (Malay Literature), for example, is not part of the secondary school curriculum for decades and are considered as insignificant. Instead, only rudiments of Malay Literature are made available to students through the Malay Language subject aside from "KOMSAS," the acronym for Komponen Sastera (Literary Component).

In "KOMSAS" classes only average literary works are introduced to students. Malay literary master pieces such as *Sulalat al-Salatin* (Malay Annals)[577] and *Hikayat Hang Tuah* (The Tale of Hang Tuah)[578] and great works by Malaysian National Laureates are not taught as they are considered difficult. Malaysian secondary school students are generally oblivious of the literary canons that represent the high culture within the Malay literary tradition. At the university level, the dichotomy and lop-sidedness are clear. Heavily funded programs (such as Medicine, Engineering, Pure Sciences, Computer Science etc.) are meant for "bright" students. The humanities usually get "weaker" candidates and always the last choice.

Generally, background courses such as "Philosophy of Science" and "History of Science" are not taught as compulsory subjects. Fortunately, there are some compulsory university level courses, such as "Tamadun Islam dan Tamadun Asia" (Islamic and Asian Civilization) or TITAS and "Hubungan Etnik" (Ethnic Relations) that are shared by students on both sides of the academic divide. TITAS is however slowly disappearing now.

In terms of research, in 2011, the Ministry of Higher Education Malaysia introduced the Long Term Research Grant Scheme (LRGS). For a few early years the scheme for the Top-Down Category were dedicated to 7 niche areas, all in the domain of STEM. The Niche Areas for the Top-Down Category were:

577 A.Samad Ahmad, ed., *Sulalatus Salatin* (Kuala Lumpur: Dewan Bahasa dan Pustaka, 2008).
578 Kassim Ahmad, ed. *Hikayat Hang Tuah*. Kuala Lumpur: Yayasan Karyawan dan Dewan Bahasa dan Pustaka, 1997.

1. Global Warming
2. Infectious Diseases
3. Tropical Medicine
4. Energy and Water Safety
5. Food Security
6. Advanced Manufacturing
7. Information Communication Technology

Clearly, the humanities were neglected and scholars in those disciplines were marginalized. Generally, they were seen as not qualified to participate in the top-down LRGS. Those few who were fortunate were allowed to help out only with the social aspect of each of the seven niche areas. Obviously moral-religious and socio-cultural issues were not considered important by the education bureaucrats. Whereas in reality these issues were pertinent as evidenced in rural and urban poverty, "hell riding," drug abuse, free sex, and baby dumping, involving mostly Malay youngsters. These have for a long time been the number one social ills in the country. Alas, there was not even one Top-Down LRGS allocated to them.

The Top-Down LRGS did not last long. It was soon erased and all applicants for Long Term Research Grant Scheme (LRGS), Fundamental Research Grant Scheme (FRGS) as well as other related schemes, could then choose from the newly introduced research domains. Introduced since 2019, the domains are: Pure and Applied Science, Technology and Engineering, Social Science, Information and Communication Technology, Clinical and Health Science, Arts and Applied Arts, and Natural and Cultural Heritage.

The Humanities Matter

Now it is time to go back to the efforts in the West to strengthen the humanities and integrate it with STEM. Alarmed with the above-mentioned situation, many academics heeded the historic open letter to *The Observer* by Prof Geoffrey Crossick and his colleagues who pleaded authorities not to ditch humanities in favor of STEM. A landmark symposium on "The Future of the Humanities" was held at Johns Hopkins University, Baltimore, on 29th March 2011.

At the symposium current challenges of the time as well as the way ahead for humanities, and its integration with STEM, were seriously discussed. The symposium was not the only initiative taken to strengthen the Humanities. Slightly earlier, the Commission on the Humanities and Social Sciences was assigned to come up with concrete and actionable plans for those in government, education and philanthropy to enhance teaching and research in the

Humanities.[579] Next was the Stanford Campaign carried out by Stanford University, Stanford, California. This relates to the "Admit Weekend" event, titled "Creativity and the Human Condition: Humanities Research and Arts Endeavors at Stanford." The event was held on 30th April, 2011[580]. The main aim of the campaign was to persuade students to register for the humanities.

In addition to the above, in early 2011, a concerned group in the United Kingdom chaired by Nicola Miller, Professor of Latin American History, University College London, started the "Humanities Matter Campaign." The group organized humanities advocacy projects and supported world-leading humanities and social science teaching and research in United Kingdom universities. Its members believed in higher education that is informed by research that clearly engages with the human societies.

The Humanities Matter Campaign had a positive response. For example, in a strong editorial on 17 March, 2011, the *Times Higher Education Supplement* clearly endorsed it, saying that: "Science alone cannot get to the heart of what makes us human, which is why the humanities and social sciences matter so much." This is very much in tune with the view expressed later by Prof. Deborah Fitzgerald, Dean of the MIT School of Humanities, Arts and Social Sciences. In a short write-up in *The Boston Globe* dated 30th April, 2014, the Professor of the History of Technology clearly stated: "Some may be surprised, and I hope, reassured to learn that here at MIT—a bastion of STEM education—we view the humanities, arts, and social sciences as essential, both for educating great engineers and scientists, and for sustaining our capacity for innovation." Prof. Fitzgerald went on to say that:

> ...the Institute's mission is to advance knowledge and educate students who are prepared to help solve the world's most challenging problems. To do this our graduates naturally need advanced technical skills. But the world's problems are never tidily confined to the laboratory or spreadsheet... the challenges of our age are unwaveringly human in nature and scale, and engineering and science issues are always embedded in broader human realities, from deeply felt cultural traditions to building codes to political tensions... So our students also need an in-depth understanding of human complexities—the political, cultural, and economic realities that shape our existence—as well as fluency in the powerful forms of thinking and creativity cultivated by the humanities, arts, and social sciences.

True to Fitzgerald's statement, generally MIT students are required to take a minimum of eight Humanities or Social Sciences courses, thus dedicating about 25% of their studies to non-STEM materials. Properly considered, this is an ideal arrangement for it will allow students to cultivate multiple-skills

579 Dan Berrett, "Humanities, For Sake Of Humanity," *Inside Higher Ed*, March 30, 2011.

580 Samantha McGirr, "Stanford launches effort to increase study of humanities," *The Stanford Daily*, April 19, 2011.

and intercultural competencies, much needed for national development for all countries, including Malaysia. It is not surprising that many other universities in the USA are now slowly emphasizing the significance of Humanities, some by approving joint-majors.

In spite of the new attraction to the humanities, skepticism lingers. Many are oblivious of the fact that humanities and the arts are capable of imparting real meanings to life and even protecting it from catastrophes.

At this juncture it is fruitful to highlight Fitzgerald's observation that "… Engineering and Science issues are always embedded in broader human realities." Very much in line with the observation, it is important to remember the above *Times Higher Education Supplement's* editorial which upholds that: "Science alone cannot get to the heart of what makes us human, which is why the humanities and social sciences matter so much." Here, one may want to add that while STEM subjects concentrate on nature, humanities subjects are dedicated to the study of mankind, the best of Allah's creation. Indeed, without the humanities—with their emphasis on values, ethics, the spiritual dimension of life and man-nature-divine relationship—STEM subjects can only produce humanoids, not humans!

In a world of advanced technology like ours, the possibility of losing our human nature is even greater. As John Naisbitt at the turn of the millennium correctly reminded us in his highly celebrated book, *High Tech, High Touch* (1999), day in and day out we are all wired with i-phones, i-pads, laptops, pagers, tweeters etc. Indeed, we have recklessly positioned ourselves in a "Technologically Intoxicated Zone." This is a highly dangerous zone where human beings are bombarded not only by technological stimuli but also with endless radiation. Socially, the gadgets have also turned them into creatures who are always distracted, physically close, but socially and spiritually distanced from one another.

It is in the above context that the humanities would be of great help. Very much in line with the message in *High Tech, High Touch*, it will assist us in giving a break to the machines and gadgets and spend more time with our fellow humans and the natural as well as divine environments. More so in the case of Muslim educational system where unity of knowledge is upheld, with the supreme knowledge of *al-Tawhid* always at the top. Within this contact, everything is based on Islamic *Tasawwur* (Islamic Worldview), anchored on the cardinal principle of *al-Tawhid* itself. As rightly expressed by Osman Bakar: "The unity of scientific and spiritual knowledge is realized when each of the particular sciences is organically related to the supreme knowledge of *al-Tawhid.*[581]

---

581 Osman Bakar, *Tawhid and Science* (Kuala Lumpur: Arah Publications, 2008), 72.

Transforming the Humanities

Indeed, to get to the heart of what makes us human we need the humanities. But how should they be presented to scholars, university students and the public at large? Are humanities subjects generally a luxury or a necessity? Are they detached? Should they be connected to other subjects? Should the humanities be transformed? As it is now, humanities subjects do not seem to prepare students for a specific vocation. They are merely prerequisites for personal growth and participation in society, regardless of career choice. As Patricia Cohen once stated, the study of the humanities evolved during the twentieth century, "to focus almost entirely on personal intellectual development."[582] Its central and sacred mission is to explore "what it means to be a human being."

To a certain extent this is fine. However, according to Richard M. Freeland, the Massachusetts Commissioner of Higher Education, "But what we haven't paid a lot of attention to is how students can put those abilities effectively to use in the world. We've created a disjunction between the liberal arts and sciences and our role as citizens and professionals."[583] The Association of American Colleges and Universities suggested that the Humanities should abandon the "old Ivory Tower view of liberal education" and instead emphasize its practical and economic values.

A useful article to be discussed here is Auburn Rutledge's, "A Crumbling Ivory Tower: Are the Humanities Becoming Irrelevant?" published in 2009. He writes: And here I finally return to my metaphor of the Childlike Empress in her tower. The outdated model of the study of humanities is like the Empress of the film, locked in her tower, a distant, mysterious and disconnected creature. She is the main element of the plot and yet she feels irrelevant—the very problem that students and their families, college administrators, and even professors themselves are finding with humanities today."[584]

Like the message in the story of the Childlike Empress, the article say: to be relevant Humanities must innovate and transform. It must force "its way into the world, to adapt its curriculum, to tie classroom lessons in with real job opportunities, and to make the world understand why there must be a necessary unity between the arts and the sciences."

Based on the above discussion, it is clear that the humanities should be quickly transformed. To start with, the Humanities subjects should be properly positioned in the 2020s so that it is no longer marginalized. Basically, it should no longer be a luxury but a necessity, including for STEM students. Such an effort to reposition the humanities can be seen in 2011 when the School of Humanities, Universiti Sains Malaysia organized a national seminar

582 Cohen, "In Tough Times."

583 Cohen, "In Tough Times."

584 Auburn Rutledge, "A Crumbling Ivory Tower: Are the Humanities Becoming Irrelevant?" *Greenleaf Book Group LLC*, February, 27, 2009.

on Malay Language and Literature Studies. The main idea then was for Malay Language and Literature Studies, as part of humanities, to remain relevant and win more students as well as the university's support. For this they must transform themselves, relate strongly to other disciplines (e.g. New Media, Film, ICT, Science, Environmental Studies etc.), and address contemporary realities. Interdisciplinarity was seen as a must. It was thought that, as disciplines within the Humanities, Malay Language and Literature Studies should be transformed. They should be less exclusive, less detached, and more tangible. They should teach students "what it means to be human beings" as well as "how to succeed skillfully in a profitable vocation."

This is the reason why the Literature Section at the School of Humanities, Universiti Sains Malaysia, has since then added Media, Digital, Creative and Entrepreneurial components, as well as Industrial Training, to its literary curriculum. In fact, members of the section now are of the opinion that interdisciplinarity is the only way forward for literary studies. The Literature Section is now looking deeper into the relationship between literature and computer science. In this regard, the section derives its inspiration from writers such as Peter Swirski. In his book, *From Literature to Biterature* (2013), Swirski indicates that computer will be a creative creature. It will be able to create literary works of art, such as poetry, novels, short stories, and dramas. In 2016, *The Day a Computer Writes a Novel*, a prose "written" by a robot (AI software) from Future University Hakodate managed to pass through the first round of the Nikkei Shinichi Hoshi Literary Award ceremony in Japan. Indeed, this might be the ultimate future of creative writings, with contributions coming not only from human authors, but also from *computhors* or robots. Of course, as Allah's creations, human beings especially Muslims, should always be careful not to leave everything to *computhors* or other forms of robots. These creatures have artificial intelligence, but no souls.

The discussion on the relationship between literature and computer, literary futurology and *computhors* finally brings us to digital humanities. Digital humanities is a new field of scholarly activities and studies. It is situated at the intersection of Computer Science and the various disciplines of Humanities. It involves a range of activities, from the practical, such as digitizing ancient documents, to the creative, such as writing digital poems, and the reflective, such as analysing the philosophical works of Plato, Ibn Tufayl, Tagore and Lao Tze.

Digital Humanities provides opportunities for the intersection between science, engineering, and humanities. It can help bring together scholars and students from different backgrounds and reduce academic dichotomy. It can also prepare humanities students for a wide range of job opportunities and for fruitful involvement with communities especially the B40 group. Digital humanities and other forms of interdisciplinary or/and multidisciplinary activities might be able to make humanities more relevant to STEM and actual life situations. Together with spiritual knowledge, they can prepare students for a better and brighter future, especially as leaders of nations. They can aid all scholars and students to appreciate the Millennium Development Goals (MDGs) and post-MDG agenda to sustain human population and the natural environments towards a more peaceful existence.

Epilogue

The above discussion has pointed out the significance of the humanities as a foundation for national development, human progress and peaceful existence. I began with a short look at the modern history of education, followed by the rumblings in the academia, particularly regarding the marginal position of the humanities.

For the Humanities to be really significant, it must first be strengthened and transformed. To strengthen the Humanities, there must be a paradigm shift in the education system, including in Malaysia. The dichotomy and imbalance between STEM and non-STEM subjects must be corrected. Some form of unity or fusion between the two must be established. Also, scholars of humanities must seriously look into their respective disciplines. They need to embrace interdisciplinary orientation. In short, they need to transform the Humanities. They must engage STEM professors and convince them that the humanities do not assume detached postures, that they are not elitist, insubstantial and intangible.

Finally, scholars of humanities themselves must convince their stakeholders that humanities subjects enrich the thinking faculty and illuminate the human condition. Through this, they pave the way towards the making of true humans, servants and vicegerents of Allah who are truly useful for the peaceful development of nations and mankind at large.

Bibliography

A Samad Ahmad, ed. *Sulalatus Salatin*. Kuala Lumpur: Dewan Bahasa dan Pustaka, 2008.

Battershill, Claire, and Shawna Ross. Using Digital Humanities in the Classroom Practical Introduction for Teachers, Lecturers, and Students. Bloomsbury: Bloomsbury Academic, 2017.

Berrett, Dan. "Humanities, For Sake Of Humanity." *Inside Higher Ed*, March 30, 2011.

Braginsky, V. *The Heritage of Traditional Malay Literature: A Historical Survey of Genres, Writings and Literary Views*. Leiden: KITLV Press, 2004.

Cohen, Patricia. "In Tough Times, the Humanities Must Justify Their Worth." *New York Times*, February 24, 2009.

Collins, J. T. *Malay, World Language of the Ages: A Sketch of its History*. Kuala Lumpur: Dewan Bahasa dan Pustaka, 1998.

Eagleton, Terry. "AC Grayling's private university is odious." *The Guardian*, June 6, 2011.

"Editorial." *Times Higher Ed*, March 17, 2011.

Fazackerley, Anna. "London Met launches survival strategy." *The Guardian*, April 15, 2013

Fitzgerald, Deborah K. "At MIT, the Humanities are just as important as STEM." *Boston Globe*, April 30, 2014.

Harpham, Geoffrey Galt. The Humanities and the Dream of America. Chicago: University of Chicago Press, 2011.

Jaschik, Scott. "The Shrinking Humanities Major." *Inside Higher Ed*, March 14, 2016.

Kassim Ahmad, ed. *Hikayat Hang Tuah*. Kuala Lumpur: Yayasan Karyawan dan Dewan Bahasa dan Pustaka, 1997.

McGirr, Samantha. "Stanford launches effort to increase study of humanities." *The Stanford Daily*, April 19, 2011.

Md. Salleh Yaapar. "The Relevance of Literature to Life: A Reiteration at the Moment of Reckoning." In *Knowledge Is Light: Essays in Honor of Seyyed Hossein Nasr*, edited by Zailan Morris. Chicago: ABC International Group Inc, 1999.

Md. Salleh Yaapar. "From Tolerance to Celebration in Nurturing World Peace: Lessons from Literature." In *Islam and Knowledge: al Faruqi's Concept of Religion in Islamic Thought*, edited by Imtiyaz Yusuf, 177–93. London: I. B. Tauris, 2012.

Mintz, Steven. "Reimagining the Humanities for the 21st Century." *Inside Higher Ed*, October 15, 2020.

Naisbitt, John. *High Tech, High Touch: Technology and Our Search for Meaning.* New York: Broadway Books, 1999.

Nield, David. "A Novel Written by AI Passes the First Round in a Japanese Literary Competition." *Science Alert*, March 24, 2016.

Osman Bakar. *Tawhid and Science: Islamic Perspectives on Religion and Science.* Kuala Lumpur: Arah Publications, 2008.

Osman Bakar. *The History and Philosophy of Islamic Science.* Cambridge: The Islamic Texts Society, 2000.

Osman Bakar. *Classification of Knowledge in Islam.* Kuala Lumpur: Institute for Policy Research, 1992.

Swain, Harriet. "London Metropolitan University eliminates history, philosophy, and performing arts from degree courses." *The Guardian,* May 3, 2011.

Swirski, Peter. *From Literature to Biterature.* Montreal: McGill-Queen's University Press, 2013.

Chapter 17

Bridging Religious Studies and Sustainable Development Goals via the Idea of Guardianship of the Environment

Azizan Baharuddin

Professor and Director Centre for Civilisational Dialogue, University of Malaya

The essay argues for the need to reinvigorate the roles of religious studies and philosophy in sustainable development, and for these two domains to be the ethical bases of other disciplines such as science, economics, and law. We begin from the premise that, just as the physical basis for any society is its bricks and mortar, so too in the human and social dimension of life there is a need to strengthen beliefs and values.[585] Guardianship (*khalifah)* in Islam, which is one of the pillars of the *Maqasid Shari'ah* (objectives of *Shari'ah*), is a value or belief that should be put to action to achieve the seventeen goals of sustainable development, as explicated in Table 1.[586]

Principles of the United Nation Sustainable Development Goals (SDG) (2015)

1. No Poverty – End poverty in all its forms everywhere.
    - Extreme poverty has been cut by more than half since 1990; however, more than 1 in 5 people live on less than USD 1.25 a day.
    - Poverty is more than a lack of income or resources; it includes lack of basic services, such as education, hunger, social discrimination and exclusion, as well as lack of participation in decision making.

585 See Azizan Baharuddin, "Guardianship of the Environment: An Islamic Perspective in the Context of Religious Studies, Theology, and Sustainable Development," in *Humanity: Texts and Contexts: Christian and Muslim Perspectives*, eds. M. Ipgrave and D. Marshall (Washington: Georgetown University Press, 2011), 41–49.

586 17 Principles of the United Nation Sustainable Development Goals (SDG) (2015), adopted from https://en.wikipedia.org/wiki/Sustainable_Development_Goals.

- Gender injustices plays a large role in the perpetuation of poverty and its risks. Through poverty women face potentially life-threatening risks from possible forced early pregnancy by which they lose hope for an education and a better life for example.
- Age groups are affected differently when struck with poverty; its most devastating effects are on children, to whom it poses a great threat. It affects their education, health, nutrition, and security. It also negatively affects the emotional and spiritual development of children through the environment it creates.

2. Zero Hunger – End hunger, achieve food security and improve nutrition and promote sustainable agriculture.

    - Globally, 1 in 9 people are undernourished, the vast majority of these people live in developing (and most probably Muslim) countries.
    - Agriculture is the single largest employer in the world, providing livelihoods for 40% of today's global population. It is the largest source of income and jobs for poor rural households. Women comprise on average 43% of the agricultural labor force in developing countries, and over 50% in parts of Asia and Africa, yet they only own 20% of the land.
    - Poor nutrition causes nearly half (45%) of deaths in children under five – 3.1 million children each year.

3. Good Health and Well-being – Ensure healthy lives and promote well-being for all at all ages.

    - Significant strides have been made in increasing life expectancy and reducing some of the common killers associated with child and maternal mortality, and major progress has been made on increasing access to clean water and sanitation, reducing malaria, tuberculosis, polio and the spread of HIV/AIDS.
    - Only half of the women in developing countries have received the health care they need; more than 225 million women have an unmet need for contraception.
    - An important target is to substantially reduce the number of deaths and illnesses from pollution-related diseases.
    - Quality Education – Ensure inclusive and equitable quality education and promote lifelong learning opportunities for all.
    - Major progress has been made for access to education, specifically at the primary school level, for both boys and girls; however access does not always mean quality or completion of education. Currently, 103

million youths worldwide still lack basic literacy skills, and more than 60% of them are women.
- "By 2030, it is targeted that all girls and boys will be able to obtain free, equitable and quality primary and secondary education leading to relevant and effective learning outcomes."

4. Gender Equality (or for Muslims "gender justice") so as to empower women and girls.

    - Providing women and girls with equal access to education, health care, decent work, and representation in political and economic decision-making processes will positively influence sustainable economies and benefit societies and humanity at large.

5. Clean Water and Sanitation – Ensure availability and sustainable management of water and sanitation for all.
6. Affordable and Clean Energy – Ensure access to affordable, reliable, sustainable and modern energy for all.
7. Decent Work and Economic Growth – Promote sustained, inclusive and sustainable economic growth, full and productive employment as well as decent work for all.
8. Industry, Innovation and Infrastructure – Build resilient infrastructure, promote inclusive and sustainable industrialization as well as foster innovation.
9. Reduced Inequalities – Reduce income inequality within and among countries.
10. Sustainable Cities and Communities – Make cities and human settlements inclusive, safe, resilient and sustainable.
11. Responsible Consumption and Production—Ensure sustainable consumption and production patterns.
12. Climate Action – Take urgent action to combat climate change and its impacts by regulating emissions and promoting developments in renewable energy.
13. Life Below Water – Conserve and sustainably use the oceans, seas and marine resources for sustainable development.
14. Life on Land – Protect, restore and promote sustainable use of terrestrial ecosystems, sustainably manage forests, combat desertification, halt and reverse land degradation as well as halt biodiversity loss.
15. Peace, Justice and Strong Institutions – Promote peaceful and inclusive societies for sustainable development, provide access to justice for all and build effective, accountable and inclusive institutions at all levels.
16. Partnerships for the Goals – Strengthen the means of implementation and revitalize local land and global partnerships for sustainable development.

The Role of Philosophy

Philosophy can be used in two ways: as the subject or as an intellectual tool.[587] Philosophy is critical because it questions whether religious studies (the guardianship of nature among one important dimension of religion) can contribute to the concept of sustainable development, the most recent expression being in the form of the 17 Sustainable Development Goals (SDG) elaborated above and The Earth Charter (2000).[588] Philosophy can help explicate the ethical principles for sustainable development. It can also help us infuse into religious studies the very idea of sustainable development, which is now promoted by the Malaysian religious authorities as in line with the principles of *Maqasid Sharī'a*.[589] The idea of the guardianship of nature can also be argued to be the basis of the Earth Charter, as well as the sustainable development goals which, in turn can all be an important constituent of religious instruction. Examples of questions that philosophy poses are: What do we mean? What are our reasons? What lies behind? What are the implications? Such questions help construct a much-needed dialogue that leads to the mutual understanding and mutual borrowing that is needed between the various disciplines (the economic, scientific, environmental, and socio-cultural) currently understood as being embraced by sustainable development,[590] and by the same token various branches within Islamic studies. Such mutual borrowing or transdisciplinarity, as described by Basarab Nicolescu, can lead to a fusion of horizons between religion and science, religion and economics, as well as religion and other fields.[591]

Although the term "philosophy" is derived from the Greek *philo-sophia*, in Islam, it is often understood as the love of wisdom or *hikma* or, more accurately, knowledge of the proper place for everything. The quest for wisdom, which cannot be divorced from the truth—*Haqq*, one of the names of Allah—is at the heart of Islam. Humanity has forever been looking beyond itself to find answers about itself: Where have we come from? Where are we going? How should we live? While philosophy asks the big questions, religion provides us with the grand narratives as answers, or at least clues, if not the details. Philosophy also has to ask probing, critical, and analytical questions, and so the search

587 See, for example, Douglas Pratt, "Philosophy of Religion," Seminar on Philosophy and Civilisational Dialogue, Centre for Civilisational Dialogue, June 26–27, 2007.

588 "The Earth Charter," www.earthcharterinaction.org/content/pages/Read-the-Charter.html.

589 The Profile of *Maqasid Sharī'a* in State Governance published by Department of Islamic Development Malaysia 2018, www.islam.gov.my. See also Azizan Baharuddin, *Konsep Rahmah dalam Pengurusan Alam Sekitar* (Putrajaya: Jabatan Kemajuan Islam Malaysia (JAKIM), 2009), 1–3.

590 Thomas Davis, "What Is Sustainable Development?" Sustainable Development Institute, College of Menominee Nation, www.menominee.edu/sdi/whatis.htm.

591 Basarab Nicolescu, "Transdisciplinarity as Methodological Framework for Going beyond the Science and Religion Debate," The Global Spiral, Metanexus Institute, May 24, 2007, www.metanexus.net/magazine/tabid/68/id/10013/Default.aspx.

for wisdom leads to the realm of empirical and experimental investigation and the rise of the sciences. In the Islamic perspective, philosophy (speculative) and science (empirical) are necessary for the believer to reach, explain, understand and manifest religiosity. In fact, the two are subsumable under religion, which in Islam is called *din*, a total way of life consisting of the physical, mental, social, and spiritual. This idea is expressed by the poet philosopher, Muhammad Iqbal (1877–1938), in his description of the four phases of religiosity: blind following, questioning, exploration and experience, witness and acceptance.[592]

The evolution of religious consciousness requires the believer to have deep knowledge and experience of nature and life. Such a holistic approach to religion, and the comprehensive solutions and guidance it offers can make teachers and practitioners of religious studies today aware of the gap between the ideal and reality in understanding, manifesting, and practicing of religion.[593] To give two examples, in explaining the relevance of religion in today's world, many Muslim believers may not really understand, or are not able to articulate, the significance either the finality of the prophethood of their prophet or the actual "contemporariness" of their religion as implied by the concept of the Islamic city (*Madīna*). These statements are not meant to be apologetic but can be linked to the most recent discourses about the nature of reality currently actively pursued in the Western "modern," postmodern and now "post post-modern" world.[594]

It is critical to begin with such a discussion for several reasons. To many in the West, such ways of thinking may be seen to represent a non-modern worldview. However, the fact that the Islamic civilization did play a critical role in the development of the West itself and that the heritage of the modern West was not merely the Greco-Roman shows that Islam and the West share similar pasts.[595] The perceived difference between the Islamic and Western worlds should not be seen as an insurmountable obstacle to fruitful dialogue on the principle of the guardianship of the environment. It should be seen to move towards a philosophy of science for a sustainable planet. Dialogue between people of different faith groups is also imperative because there is a gap in the understanding of the relationship between man and nature. This vital understanding lies at the very heart of the religious worldview. Sharing his views on

592 Azizan Baharuddin, *Science and Religion: Discourses on New Perceptions* (Institut Kajian Dasar: Kuala Lumpur, 1994), 21–82. See also Muhammad Iqbal, *The Reconstruction of Religious Thought in Islam* (Batu Caves, Selangor: Masterpiece Publication Sdn. Bhd., 2016), 1–25.

593 Hazizan Noor, "Islamic Studies in Malaysian Universities: Review and Prospect," in *Islamic Studies and Civilisational Dialogue: A Transdisciplinary Approach for Sustainability*, eds. Azizan Baharuddin et al., 11–19 (Kuala Lumpur: Centre for Civilisational Dialogue, University of Malaya, 2013).

594 See for example: Oswald Spangler, *The Decline of the West: Form and Actuality*, trans. Francis Atkinson Charles, 6th print (New York: Alfred A. Knoff Inc., 1927). See for example https://slife.org/postmodernism/.

595 See Carl Ernst, *Following Muhammad: Rethinking Islam in the Contemporary World* (Chapel Hill: University of North Carolina Press, 2003).

this theme, Fazlun Khalid a leading Muslim environmentalist analyses how modernity has imposed itself on the world, peripheralizing traditional ways of life and causing them to weaken.

This disruption has destroyed the balance within the Earth's natural ecosystem while turning promises of progress into mere illusions. The 'process' of achieving the so-called progress through industrialization and unlimited economic growth had also led unfortunately to over consumerism fed by a human-centered worldview. Such a worldview has it that man exists apart from nature instead of actually being a part of nature. In his recent book *Signs on the Earth: Islam, Modernity and the Climate Crisis*, Fazlun Khalid calls for a radical reconsideration of prevailing models of development that should draw inspiration from the revealed text or "realm of the sacred."[596]

What needs to be promoted today especially amongst Muslims who make up about 25% of the world's population is the Islamic ethos that integrate belief with ethics as well as a code of conduct which pays attention to the environment. Fazlun Khalid emphasizes this idea when he says that Islam prescribes a way of life that goes beyond the performance of rituals, that is, it provides a holistic approach to existence.[597] Indeed, Islam does not demarcate nor separate the world of mankind from nature.[598] In Chapter 40 verse 57, the Qur'an says "*the creation of the heavens and the Earth is far greater than the creation of humankind. But most humankinds do not know it.*"

The question is, however, is this message clear to the experts and policy makers? Especially when religious studies curricula is not yet sufficiently enriched and to initiate wider changes. At the same time, a dialogical frame of mind also need to be developed in order to recognize that other faith and non-faith traditions also bear the collective responsibility for the creation as well as the overcoming of the crisis. Here, it is hoped that philosophy can be a bridging factor.

Moving towards this end, most recently the United Nations Environment Program (UNEP) Faith for Earth Division assembled a team to prepare the document called "*Al-Mizan*: A Covenant for the Earth" which aspires to be a comprehensive Islamic view on the environment which will then be presented to the Islamic Council of Environment Ministers and the United Nations (UN).[599] An earlier document was in the form of "The Islamic Declaration for Climate Change" initiated by the Islamic Relief Worldwide (IRW), The Islamic Foundation for Ecology and Environmental Sciences (IFEES), and

596 Fazlun Khalid, *Signs on the Earth: Islam Modernity and the Climate Crisis* (UK: Kube Publishing Ltd., 2019), ix–xi.

597 Fazlun, xv.

598 Fazlun, xv.

599 United Nations Environment Program (UNEP), "Faith for Earth Initiative," https://www.unep.org/about-un-environment/faith-earth-initiative.

The Climate Action Network (CAN) which was launched in 2015 as well as presented at the Conference of Parties (COP) 21 in Paris in 2016.[600]

The Earth Charter: Unity of Humanity and Its Relationship with Nature

At the heart of the environmental crisis is humanity's spiritual crisis.[601] It is high time now that, despite the successes of materialistic science, we build a unity of knowledge and understanding as the basis of a more holistic (incorporating science, religion, and philosophy) worldview and plan of action. This is what the Earth Charter is asking us to do for the sake of our future. It clearly sends out a message to the fragmented components of our lost humanity when it says:

> We stand at a critical moment in Earth's history, a time when humanity must choose its future. As the world becomes increasingly interdependent and fragile, the future at once holds great peril and great promise. To move forward we must recognize that in the midst of a magnificent diversity of cultures and life forms we are one human family and one Earth community with a common destiny. We must join together to bring forth a sustainable global society founded on respect of nature, universal human rights, economic justice and a culture of peace. Towards this end, it is imperative that we, the people of Earth, declare our responsibility to one another, to the greater community of life and to future generations.[602]

And this responsibility, as we have mentioned, can be nurtured via the religious principle of guardianship. The charter also reminds us of "our responsibility to one another." In regard to the diversity of human beings, the Qur'an tells us: "*O mankind! Lo! We have created you male and female, and have made you nations and tribes that ye may know one another. Lo! The noblest of you in the sight of Allah, is the best in conduct. Lo! Allah is Knower, Aware*" (49:13). Other faith communities should be able to agree that religious studies is crucial to imbibe morality and practical expression to ethical values, both of which are psychological movers of sustainable development today.

The Challenges Ahead

The Earth Charter describes the challenge that lies ahead as:

> The choice is ours: form a global partnership to care for Earth and one another or risk the destruction of ourselves and the diversity of life. Fundamental changes

600 This writer was one of the drafters of this declaration. See https://en.wikipedia.org/wiki/The_Islamic_Declaration_on_Global_Climate_Change.

601 S. H. Nasr, *The Encounter of Man and Nature: The Spiritual Crisis of the Man* (London: George, Allen Unwind, 1968).

602 "Preamble Earth Charter," http://erdcharta.de/1/the-earth-charter/the text/preamble/. We are aware that Muslims would want the phrase "universal human rights" not to include ideas and practices that are against the Qur'an or Hadith. However, the overall spirit of the Charter should not be an issue.

are needed in our values, institutions, and ways of living. We must realize that when basic needs have been met, human development is primarily about being more, not having more. We have the knowledge and technology to provide for all and to reduce our impacts on the environment. The emergence of a global civil society is creating new opportunities to build a democratic and humane world. Our environmental, economic, political, social, and spiritual challenges are interconnected, and together we can forge inclusive solutions.[603]

In Malaysia, the concept of a civil society, or *Masyarakat Madani*, was actively debated and was already pursued in the 1990s. Today the trend continues with the policy of *Maqasid Shari'ah* and i-MaqSD,[604] which strives to harmonize religion and development as espoused by the Qur'an (62:10): "*Seek the bounty of Allah and celebrate the praises of Allah often; that ye may prosper.*"

Gratitude for the Gift of Life

The guardianship of the environment can be concretized in our thinking through the foundational notion of the gratitude for the gift of life. In this context, Prof. S. M. N. al-Attas explains the concept of religion (*dīn*) in Islam as actually connoting indebtedness, submissiveness, judicious power, and natural inclination or tendency.[605] *Dāyana*, derived from *dīn*, gives the meaning of being indebted. When we are in a state of debt, we have to follow the laws and ordinances governing the debt that we owe. A person in debt is also under obligation to a ruler or governor, a *dayyan* (Mighty Ruler). *Dīn* is also connected to *maddana*, which means opening or to build cities; to civilize, humanize, refine. From *maddana* in turn arise the concepts of *madīna*, the city, and *tamaddun*, civilization.[606]

In the context of guardianship of nature and sustainable development, the concept of *dīn* implies that humans are indebted to the Creator for their existence to begin with, and that they already acknowledged Allah as their Creator the moment their souls were created. Al-Attas explains that the nature of this debt of creation and existence is so total that "at the instance he is created and given existence, man is in a state of utter dependence because 'he' really possesses nothing himself; which means everything in him, from him, and about him is what the creator, the *Rabb* (who owns everything) owns. This also means that mankind is totally dependent for his sustenance on the sustainer

603 Earth Charter Initiative Germany, "Preamble," https://erdcharta.de/1/the-earth-charter/the-text/praeambel/.
604 See www.islam.gov.my; i-maqSD stands for a program initiated by the religious authorities to harmonise SDG's with the *Maqasid Sharī'a* in the development plans of the nation. Also see footnote 6.
605 S. M. N. al-Attas, *Islam, the Concept of Religion and the Foundations of Ethics* (Kuala Lumpur: Dewan Bahasa dan Pustaka and Ministry of Education, 1992), 1–3.
606 Al-Attas, *Islam, the Concept of Religion*, 1–3. See also '*dāyana*' at https://en.bab.la/dictionary/arabic-english/.

of Life Himself."[607] This is explained further in the Qur'an (7:17): "When thy Lord drew forth from the children of Adam—from their loins—their descendants, and made them testify concerning themselves (saying): 'Am I not your Lord?'—They said— 'Yes! We do testify."

Because he owns nothing, man can only repay his debt with the only thing that is his, namely his consciousness. It is through this consciousness that he "returns" himself to the Creator, who owns him absolutely. This is why in Islam *dhikr*, or "remembrance," is so crucial. It is the means for "returning," and hence for attaining *hikma* – "wisdom." *Hikma* underlies man's thoughts, intentions, decisions, and actions, the sum total of which is *'ibāda*, service or good works—the original reason for man's creation.

To be of service or do good works (*'ibāda*), man needs nature or the environment; the Qur'an explains that this (nature) has been made malleable or *tashkīr* for him. The environment is the theatre for his *'ibāda*. For example, to perform the *zakat* (tithe),[608] man needs to work on and with the environment around him and achieve this he must possess scientific and technological knowledge and skills for the "what" and "how" of his use of nature. Nature does not belong to him but is given to him only for his sustenance, comfort, and entertainment as a trust (*amāna*).[609] His relationship to nature is in the capacity of *khalīfah* or vicegerent.

This state of being in which man gives back to Allah does not mean that man is unhappy as a slave. It is in submission that man realizes what his inherent nature truly is. In submitting, man returns to his true nature in which he finds peace and happiness (*salām*). His "returning" is in fact a gain. This is the state of being of the *khalīfa*, the "slave" who is also vicegerent of the Almighty on earth. He who enslaves himself gains. "*Who is he that will loan to Allah a beautiful loan, which Allah will double unto his credit and multiply many times?*" (Qur'an 2:245).

In the Islamic context at least, one of the basic challenges for religious studies is to show the contemporary relevance of the position of man as slave of Allah and yet also His vicegerent (guardian of nature). Nature is made malleable for him (*taskhīr*), yet he must not transgress the boundaries of what is good (*ḥalāl*) and harmful (*haram*), what is just (*'adl*) and unjust (*zulm*). These and other values are all part of *maqasid Sharī'a*, the "beneficial objectives" of the *Sharī'a*, regulations prescribed by revelation.

607 Al-Attas, *Islam, the Concept of Religion,* 1–3. Al-Attas' gender-specific language is retained in these paragraphs to make clear the personal connections drawn between contemporary humans and Adam.

608 *Zakat* is the giving out of a certain percentage of one's wealth that has been accumulated over a certain period.

609 See I. R. al-Faruqi and L. L. al-Faruqi, *Cultural Atlas of Islam* (Kuala Lumpur: Dewan Bahasa dan Pustaka, 1992), 334–36.

The "*halal-ness*" or "*haram-ness*" of a thing or act is explicable from the components and processes of nature or society and societal life studied through the natural and human sciences. As such, the ethics underlying sustainable development need to be explained through both science (including humanities and the social sciences) and religion, with philosophy providing tools for connecting the two and articulating the arguments and principles arising out of their harmonization. This exercise of explaining revelation by using scientific facts is also called "theology of nature" which can be part of the new philosophy of science for a sustainable planet. It is a kind of dialogue between science and religion.

In using the environment and the resources it offers in ways that ensure balance, peace, and sustainability, humans enslave themselves to God in order to fulfill his commands and ordinances as "debtors," as the somber religious language describes it, to fulfill their guardianship of nature. God has created the environment, nature, and the universe not only for Him to be known but also to enable humans to do good works (*ibadah*) which mean submission. In submitting to the divine, humans intrinsically becomes "environmentally ethical," being "best in conduct." Through this "enslavement," which means being ethical and respectful of nature's ways, humans operationalize their God-given powers judiciously. Through guardianship, humanity attains to great heights of civilizational achievement: And He it is who created the heavens and the earth . . . and His throne was upon the water that He might try you, which of you is best in conduct (Qur'an 11:7). Lo! We have placed all that is in the Earth as an ornament thereof that we may try them: which of them is best in conduct (Qur'an 18:7).

Misconceptions Regarding the Idea of *Khalifah*

Lynn White Jr. once wrote that the concept of the vicegerency or stewardship of humanity in the Christian worldview and possibly, the Islamic worldview as well, was responsible for the anthropocentric attitude to nature that gave rise to the environmental crisis.[610] Muslims would disagree with White's claim. In the Islamic tradition, as mentioned earlier, nature has indeed been made malleable (*taskhīr*) for humanity:[611]

> See ye not how Allah hath made serviceable unto you whatsoever is in the skies and whatsoever is in the earth and hath loaded you with His favours both without and within? Yet of mankind is he who disputeth concerning Allah, without knowledge or guidance or a Scripture giving light (Qur'an 31:20).

610 Lynn White, "The Historical Roots of Our Ecologic Crisis," *Science* 155 (1967): 1203–1207.

611 See al-Faruqi and al-Faruqi, *Cultural Atlas of Islam*, 334–36.

> Hast thou not seen how Allah hath made all that is in the earth subservient unto you? And the ship runneth upon the sea by His command, and He holdeth back the heaven from falling on the earth unless by His leave. Lo! Allah is, for mankind, Full of Pity, Merciful (Qur'an 22:65).

The subservience of nature is only in the context of the Creator having willed it so and despite the "power" they yield, human beings should not transgress boundaries nor abuse nature. To behave in an ethical manner towards the environment is in a sense what guardianship means. In the Islamic perspective, it also means that humans are fulfilling the purpose of their existence, which is to serve their Creator. In so doing, they achieve happiness, as they are naturally inclined to do. This natural inclination—connected to man's natural human habits, dispositions, customs, ethics, *dīn*—is also called *fitra*, the pattern of God's way (*sunnat Allah*) of creating things. This "way" is indeed what is alluded to the *Sharī'a* of God. Behaving in accordance with *fitra* via the *Sharī'a* results in harmony. It leads to the realization of what is actually intrinsically in one's true nature. *Sharī'a* is cosmos (order) as opposed to chaos, justice as opposed to injustice; justice exists when something is where it belongs.[612] Could sustainable development ultimately mean, then, that humans will discover their true states and beings as well as nature's true state and being, and that humans will live in accordance with this knowledge? Hazel Henderson and Daisaku Ikeda, both champions of the Earth Charter, may agree when they express their hope for the fostering of leaders for the creative coexistence of nature and humanity through education.[613]

Fitra and justice intrinsically reside in human nature, and scientific pursuits fortifies this fact. Muhammad Iqbal said that in his studying of nature, the scientist is actually in a state of contemplation and worship.[614] In this regard we are reminded of the Qur'anic verses that allude to all creatures as "glorifying God in their own ways" according to their own natures. Exegetes have taken this to mean spiritual acts of glorifying (*tasbīh*), praising (*tahmīd*), prostrating (*sujud*) and praying (*ṣalāh*) to Him.[615] As such, before environmental ethics can be clearly expounded, ecological knowledge can be grasped through scientific observation, which the Qur'an encourages. Observing nature to understand creation and thence the revelation of God is part of the theology of nature. God "*hath created the seven heavens in harmony. Thou canst see no fault in the Beneficent One's creation; then look again: Canst thou see any rifts?*" (Qur'an 67:3).

This is also part of the meaning of submission (*islām*). Submission does not mean the loss of freedom because in fact it is freedom to live according

612 Al-Attas, *Islam, the Concept of Religion*, 12–13.

613 Hazel Henderson and Daisaku Ikeda, *Planetary Citizenship* (Chicago: Middleway Press, 2004), 152.

614 Muhammad Iqbal, "A Plea for Deeper Studies," *Islamic Culture* 3, no. 2 (1929): 201–209.

615 Osman Bakar, *Environmental Wisdom*, 63. See also Qur'ān, an-Nur: 41.

to the demands of one's true nature. To be at one with life, which has no beginning, no end, and it encompasses the seen (*zahīr*) and the unseen (*batīn*). Through submission, human beings can distinguish truth from falsehood, right from wrong, and to set out a clear ethics, the realization of which can be seen as sustainable development as enjoined by God: "*And we created not the heavens and the earth, and all that is between them in play. We created them not save with truth; but most of them know not*" (Qur'an 44:38–39).

Sources Regarding the Environment

The Qur'an for Muslims is the most important source regarding the environment. It speaks about the cosmos, humanity, and the world of nature, all together participating in the process of revelation that is ongoing. It points to the cosmos as God's revelation, taking place in the form of the phenomena of nature including the processes in leaves, the faces of mountains, the features of animals, and the sounds of winds and flowing rivers. Every natural phenomenon even events in the soul, is a sign (*'āyah*) of God.[616]

Other sources and teachings on the environment include the *ḥādīth* (sayings and acts of the Prophet) regarding treatment of the environment. The injunctions made concerning the environment pertaining to water, soil, animals, and plants; and texts on Islamic ethics that touch upon human passions and conduct that can affect the environment. Moreover, Islamic philosophy and theology of nature are expressed in art, architecture, landscaping, and urban design. Forms of Islamic literature such as poetry also played an important role, for example among the intellectual elite of the so-called Golden Age in Andalusia (ninth to eleventh centuries).[617] In this context, Seyyed Hossein Nasr quotes the famous Sufi poet Sa'di:

I am joyous in the world of nature
For the world of nature is joyous through Him,
I am in love with the whole cosmos
For the whole cosmos comes from Him.[618]

Likewise, various literatures of Muslims ranging from the Arab, Malay, and Persian to Bengali, Swahili and others contain a vast wealth of material on the Islamic view of the relationship between man and the environment. In our own Malay-Muslim community, environmental wisdom is embodied in proverbs and poetic rhymes articulating principles, instructions, and guidance influenced by a religious ethics (*adab*).[619] By drawing analogies with the

616 R. C. Foltz, F. M. Denny, and A. Baharuddin, eds., *Islam and Ecology: A Bestowed Trust* (Cambridge: Harvard University Press, 2003), 85–107.

617 S. H. Nasr, *The Need for a Sacred Science* (Albany: State University of New York Press, 1993), 129.

618 Nasr, *Need for a Sacred Science*, 129.

619 Azizan Baharuddin, "Science in the Malay World,' (in Malay), at Seminar Sains dan Tamadun Melayu [Science and Malay Civilisation], December 20–21, 2006.

perceived behavior of nature's flora and fauna, these proverbs express an ethics (*adab*) pertaining to different situations in life faced by the individual, and they teach lessons to be learned. In the Malay Archipelago, for example, such proverbs include *Berani-berani lalat* ("Brave like a fly"): This proverb explains the situation of someone who is not really as brave as he tries to portray himself to be. *Seperti rusa masuk kampung* ("Like the deer entering the village"): This explains the condition or behavior of someone who is a stranger in a new place. *Seperti kerbau dicucuk hidung* ("Like the buffalo being led by the nose"): This is the condition of someone who is being bullied by someone else. *Sarang tebuan jangan dijolok* ("Do not poke the bee-hive"): This warns against "disturbing" someone or something that may be volatile. *Burung terbang dipipiskan lada* ("Whilst the bird still flies, the chili is pounded"): This proverb teaches against making preparations for the enjoyment of something that has not yet been properly obtained.

Applying Religion for Sustainable Development: Examples of Dialogue between Religion and Conventional Knowledge (Science, Environment, and Economics)

A Case Study in the Context of Economics

The writings of Umer Chapra show creative interpretations of religious injunctions that can further studies of environmental science and sustainable development. Chapra has been economic adviser to the government of several Muslim countries and has written extensively on Islamic economics and finance. His most important work is "Towards a Just Monetary System: A Discussion of Money, Banking, and Monetary Policy in the Light of Islamic Teachings."[620] He is a Muslim economist who is confident in what Islam has to offer, to be able to explain at length how economics, development, and religion might interact. His ideas are also set out in a work titled *Islam and the Economic Challenge*,[621] although written almost 30 years ago, in the context of today's economic uncertainties, Chapra appeals to Muslim countries to consider the goals of the *Sharīʿa* (*Maqasid Sharīʿa*) as a means of avoiding economic disintegration. One example of this was the currency and debt crises in the 1990s that ravaged many economies in Asia. Many who became poor and jobless demanded removal of their leaders through mass demonstrations. Observing the huge disparities in wealth between the various sectors of society, many were disillusioned with their corrupt leaders, whom they feel have forgotten their duties as vicegerents (*khalifah*) of God.

---

620 See Umar Chapra, *Islam and the Economic Challenge* (Leicester: The Islamic Foundation, 1992); Osman Bakar, *Environmental Wisdom*.

621 See Azizan Baharuddin, "Rediscovering The Resources of Religion," in *The Lab, the Temple & the Market: Reflection at the Intersection of Science, Religion & Development*, ed. Sharon Harper (Ottawa: International Development Research Centre, 2000), 140–142.

The goals of the *Sharī'a* are, first, human well-being (*falah*) and the good life (*hayat tayyiba*). To Chapra, the *Sharī'a* is the basis of the development because it places emphasis on socioeconomic justice. It aims to satisfy both the spiritual and material needs of human beings. Chapra derives inspiration from al-Ghazali, whom he quotes as saying that "the very objective of the *Sharī'a* is to promote the welfare of the people, which lies in safeguarding their faith, their life, their intellect, their posterity and their wealth. Whatever ensures the safeguarding of these five serves public interest and is desirable."[622]

Chapra also agrees with al-Ghazali in putting faith at the top of the pillars of the *maqasid*. It is the most crucial ingredient because, through faith, human relations are placed on a proper foundation, enabling human beings to interact in a balanced and mutually caring manner for the well-being of all. Faith also acts as a moral filter to keep the allocation and distribution of resources in line with requirements for unity and socioeconomic justice. Without the element of faith in human economic decisions—in the household, the corporate boardroom, the market—we cannot possibly realize efficiency and equity or avoid macroeconomic imbalances, economic instability, crime, conflict, and the many symptoms of anomie or the lack of social and ethical standards.

Chapra emphasizes that if we are to achieve equilibrium between scarce resources and the various claims on those resources, we need to focus on human beings rather than on the market or the state. It is imperative, therefore, to reinstate the human being as the foundation of the economic system. Humans must be motivated to pursue self-interest within the constraint facing the world. Truly believing in the possibility of a just and sane economic system, Chapra sets out the various stages for achieving such a system.

Like others, Chapra begins with a critique of the present situation followed by a reevaluation of principles embedded in the religious metaphysics of Islam. Using the three fundamental principles of *tawhid* (unity), *khalifah* (vicegerency, trusteeship), and *'adl* or *'adala* (justice), he describes a strategy for a more enlightened economic system. In his treatment, he deals with all the details and complexities of the modern economic system and integrated religious principles and the best from the conventional economics throughout.

Chapra speaks of *tawhid*, *khalifah*, and *'adala* as connected with and translatable into ideas about fellowship, resources as a trust, humble lifestyles (*zuhd*), human dignity, needs fulfillment, and equitable distribution of income and wealth, growth, and stability (and sustainable development). He suggests the revival of systems laid out in the Qur'an, such as the *zakat* (tithe) system, and other principles pertaining to wealth. He deals clearly with an entire complex of ideas, starting with the role of the *ulama* (clergy), the restructuring of policies, land and labor reforms, education and training, access to finance, and

622 Azizan, "Rediscovering The Resources of Religion," 140–142.

the size of land holdings, and moving then to the restructuring of the financial and investment systems, just and efficient taxation, tariffs and import substitution, and priorities in spending.

Chapra concludes his treatise by reiterating that imbuing economics with religious values would imply a serious effort at raising the spiritual and material well-being of all people. On the spiritual side, inner happiness can be achieved only by drawing nearer to God. On the material side, Islamisation requires the just and efficient allocation of resources so that the good life (*hayat tayyiba*) can be achieved. Islamisation is not necessarily against liberalization; rather, it involves passing public—and private—sector economic decisions through the filter of moral values before they influence the market. Without the integration of science, religion, and development, it would be impossible for Muslim countries to achieve development that is sustainable. Chapra observes, however, that policymakers have yet to be convinced to translate Islam's economic ideals into development policies.[623] This is an urgent and arduous task.

Conclusion

There cannot be a better example on the issue of guardianship of our environment than the Prophet. He was and is still *Rahmatan lil-Alamin,* mercy to the world: *"We sent you not but as a mercy for all the world"* (Qur'an 21:101). The Prophet declared that removing an obstacle in the path of others can lead one to Paradise; and the act of tying a cat and depriving it of water and food can take one to Hell. Muslims must try to emulate such mercy especially when so much misrepresentation of Islam exists today. In the context of sustainable development, Muslims need to live up to the demands of their religion.

Scientific calculations have shown that the existence of the universe is based on the contingency principle which means that its running in an orderly manner is according to laws of causality which if not disturbed, results in a state of balance or *mizan* and beauty. However, as we all know due to our failures in truly understanding, respecting, and complying with these principles, the balance we have in the last 300 years or so dwindled and culminated in sustainability crisis and climate change. For Muslims, this is pointed out in Surah ar-Rum (30:49) "*mischief (fasad or corruption) has appeared on land and sea because of that which man's hands have earned, that He may make them taste a part of that which they have done, so that they may return to Allah (take heed and return to the right path),*" and in Surah ar-Rahman (55:13), after explaining the gifts of livelihood He has given to mankind and the order that He has established in Nature, the Creator asks the question "*So which of the favors of your Lord would you deny?*"

623 Azizan, "Rediscovering The Resources of Religion," 140–142.

We think, to reflect upon this question which is repeated 31 times in the Surah is a major imperative that we cannot neglect; it is a cue for us to take action. This is because, as implied in verse 41 of Surah ar-Rum earlier on, the *Ar-Rahman* and *Ar-Rahim,* Allah has not abandoned us.[624] He has merely allowed us to taste some of the effects of our failures (as verified by scientific data) to live in harmony with the rest of creation who has submitted fully to the Creator (Qur'an 41:9–12).

Nature's fate now in fact lies in our hands. We are the vicegerents, the *khalifah*, the guardians of the planet with its myriads of organisms and bountiful resources. Muslims need to know that they are the conduits of the Creator's love and mercy (*Rahmah*). They should not let the flow of this love and *rahmah,* which is the driver for balance, to stop. They should join efforts with others to correct the misuse of the Earth's resources and work within its limits.[625]

It is imperative that religious studies work together with scientific and philosophical studies and the humanities in general to help promote the ideals of sustainable development. Through dialogue between these and other disciplines, the outcome of which can be described to be the new philosophy of science for a sustainable planet. Earth-sustaining principles can be shared and worked on so that all disciplines can be better taught to embrace the new philosophy of sustainability.

624 *Ar-Rahman* refers to the vastness of Allah's mercy. *Ar-Rahim* refers specifically to His mercy He bestows on His creation.

625 Azizan Baharuddin, "Compassion for People and the Planet," Conference Alliance of World Religion (AWR), October 17–18, 2021.

Bibliography

Al-Attas, S. M. N. *Islam, the Concept of Religion and the Foundations of Ethics.* Kuala Lumpur: Dewan Bahasa dan Pustaka and Ministry of Education, 1992.

Al-Faruqi, I. R., and L. L. al-Faruqi. *Cultural Atlas of Islam.* Kuala Lumpur: Dewan Bahasa dan Pustaka, 1992.

Azizan Baharuddin. "Guardianship of the Environment: An Islamic Perspective in the Context of Religious Studies, Theology, and Sustainable Development." In *Humanity: Texts and Contexts: Christian and Muslim Perspectives,* edited by Michael Ipgrave and David Marshall, 41–49. Washington, DC: Georgetown University Press, 2011.

Azizan Baharuddin. "Rediscovering The Resources of Religion." In *The Lab, the Temple, and the Market: Reflection at the Intersection of Science, Religion, and Development,* edited by Sharon Harper, 140–142. Ottawa: International Development Research Centre, 2000.

Azizan Baharuddin. *Konsep Rahmah dalam Pengurusan Alam Sekitar.* Putrajaya: Jabatan Kemajuan Islam Malaysia (JAKIM), 2009.

Azizan Baharuddin. *Science and Religion: Discourses on New Perceptions.* Institut Kajian Dasar: Kuala Lumpur, 1994.

Chapra, Umar. *Islam and the Economic Challenge.* Leicester: The Islamic Foundation, 1992.

Davis, Thomas. "What Is Sustainable Development?" Sustainable Development Institute, College of Menominee Nation, www.menominee.edu/sdi/whatis.htm.

Earth Charter Initiative Germany. "Preamble." https://erdcharta.de/1/the-earth-charter/the-text/praeambel/.

Earth Charter International. "The Earth Charter." https://earthcharter.org.

Ernst, Carl. *Following Muhammad: Rethinking Islam in the Contemporary World.* Chapel Hill: University of North Carolina Press, 2003.

Foltz, Richard C., Frederick M. Denny, and Azizan Baharuddin, eds. *Islam and Ecology: A Bestowed Trust.* Cambridge: Harvard University Press, 2003.

Hazizan Noor. "Islamic Studies in Malaysian Universities: Review and Prospect." In *Islamic Studies and Civilisational Dialogue: A Transdisciplinary Approach for Sustainability,* edited by Azizan Baharuddin, Amran Muhammad, Ibrahim Ismail, Raihanah Abdullah, and Zuraidah Abdullah, 11–19. Kuala Lumpur: Centre for Civilisational Dialogue, University of Malaya, 2013.

Henderson, Hazel, and Daisaku Ikeda. *Planetary Citizenship.* Chicago: Middleway Press, 2004.

Iqbal, Muhammad. "A Plea for Deeper Studies." *Islamic Culture* 3, no. 2 (1929): 201–209.

Iqbal, Muhammad. *The Reconstruction of Religious Thought in Islam.* Batu Caves, Selangor: Masterpiece Publication Sdn. Bhd., 2016.

Khalid, Fazlun. *Signs on the Earth: Islam Modernity and the Climate Crisis.* UK: Kube Publishing Ltd., 2019.

Nasr, Seyyed Hossein. *The Encounter of Man and Nature: The Spiritual Crisis of the Man.* London: George, Allen Unwind, 1968.

Nasr, Seyyed Hossein. *The Need for a Sacred Science.* Albany: State University of New York Press, 1993.

Nicolescu, Basarab. "Transdisciplinarity as Methodological Framework for Going beyond the Science and Religion Debate." The Global Spiral, Metanexus Institute, May 24, 2007, www.metanexus.net/magazine/tabid/68/id/10013/Default.aspx.

Spangler, Oswald. *The Decline of the West: Form and Actuality.* Translated by Francis Atkinson Charles, 6th print. New York: Alfred A. Knoff Inc., 1927.

Steffen, W., W. Broadgate, L. Deutsch, O. Gaffney, and C. Ludwig. "The Trajectory of the Anthropocene: The Great Acceleration." *The Anthropocene Review* 2, no. 1 (2015): 81–98.

United Nations Environment Program (UNEP). "Faith for Earth Initiative." https://www.unep.org/about-un-environment/faith-earth-initiative.

White, Lynn. "The Historical Roots of Our Ecologic Crisis." *Science* 155 (1967): 1203–1207.

Chapter 18

Reclaiming Philosophical Sciences in Muslim Education

Rosnani Hashim

Adjunct Professor of Educational Foundations at the Faculty of Education, International Islamic University Malaysia (IIUM)

The Islamic civilization is a knowledge-based civilization with the Qur'an as the epitome of knowledge and the Prophet Muhammad exemplifying it. The wife of the prophet, Aishah (may peace be upon her) once described him as the "walking Qur'an." The companions of the Prophet considered the Qur'an as the message revealed by God to His Prophet and the Prophet Muhammad as the living embodiment. When not clearly understood, the companions would seek further elaboration or clarification from the Prophet on the intended meanings of revelation. They often asked the Prophet if the message was a revelation or the product of his thought. There was an understanding that if it was from God, then early Muslims would submit to the commandments but if it was from the Prophet, it became a matter of discussion in pursuit of the prophetic wisdom.

The Qur'an is the major source of knowledge that addresses many areas of life such as human psychology and sociology, history of mankind, God's creations in the universe or the physical and natural sciences as well as matters of faith. One of the most important tasks set in the Qur'an is for the readers to reflect on the signs of God in the world of nature. Thus, it is embedded in the Qur'an (88:17–20) the notion that human beings can know God and the Way (Shari'ah) from the verses on beliefs especially through the teachings of the Prophet and they can know God from His Signs which have been laid out in His creation. This is why the Qur'an states that everything has been created for the purpose of facilitating man's living. "Indeed in the creation of the heavens and earth and the alternation of the night and the day are signs for those of understanding, who remember Allah while standing or sitting or [lying] on their sides and give thought to the creation of the heavens and the earth, [saying], "Our Lord, You did not create this aimlessly; exalted are

You [above such a thing]; then protect us from the punishment of the Fire" (Qur'an, 3:189–90).[626]

In the light of these verses, Osman formulates what he describes as "*Tawhidic* Sciences" guiding human beings towards the belief in the One God. He sees a unity of purpose in both the '*aqliyy* and the *naqliyy* (revealed) knowledge or sciences, which are the terms used by al-Ghazali in his classification of knowledge to denote its sources. These two terms are sometimes also referred to as the *fard kifayah* and *fard 'ayn* respectively when discussed in the context of its obligatory nature with respect to the community and the individual.

The purposes of these sciences were well understood by the early Muslim scholars in the ninth till the thirteenth century. They employed their knowledge to many domains of life such as in determining the direction of Makkah as the *qiblat* (focal point) for prayer. The result of this was the discovery of the trigonometric ratios, compass, and the astrolabe. They delved and formulated theories on the blood circulatory system and surgery, developed mathematical formulas such as algebra for the division of inheritance as spelled in the Qur'an, devised astronomical calculations of the days and years, and wrote philosophical treatises leading to founding of the science of *kalam* (speculative theology), and so on. Most of the Muslim scientists were also well-versed in the Qur'an and the religious sciences. Ibn Sina was a *hafiz* (one who memorized the entire Qur'an) and some like Ibn Rushd and Ibn Khaldun were *fuqaha* (jurists) and *qadi* (judges). As early as ninth century, Muslim philosophers corrected theories that separate knowledge from action and theory from practice. These separations originated from Greek classical philosophy that held thought and knowledge in high regard, but a low opinion of practice and action. Separate systems of education for the elites and the masses were developed as a result of this philosophical position. In uniting knowledge and action, Muslim scholars brought about the reflowering of experimental science and the flourishing of scientific thought and knowledge. In this respect, Muslim scholars preceded John Dewey, who attempted to dissolve the dichotomy between thought and practice in his *The Quest for Certainty*.[627]

Decline happened when Muslims prioritised religious sciences over the acquired sciences beginning with al-Ghazali's criticism of the philosophers in *Tahafut al-Falasifah* (The Incoherence of the Philosophers). Although Ibn Rushd provided a response, in *Tahafut at-Tahafut* (The Incoherence of the Incoherence) and attempted a synthesis between the two sciences through his *Fasal al-Maqal* (On the Harmony of Religion and Philosophy) and Ibn Tufayl through *Hayy Ibn Yaqzan*, the damaged has been done. Consequently, the bifurcation of religious sciences and *Tawhidic* sciences emerged which finally led to the

626 See also: The Qur'an, 45:13.

627 John Dewey, *The Quest for Certainty* (Gifford Lectures, 1929).

decline of the acquired sciences in the Muslim world. This continued until the nineteenth century when reformers such as Afghani and Abduh attempted to resuscitate the incorporation of science in Muslim education.

Muslim educational crisis and attempted reform in the twentieth century

By the eighteenth century, Muslim lands were mostly colonized by Western powers. Afghani called for the reform of Muslim minds through the return to the Qur'an and Sunnah and criticism of *taqlid* (blind imitation) encouraged by the *ulama*. He refuted the French philosopher, Ernest Renan who argued that Islam and science were incompatible. His legacy, his disciple, Muhammad Abduh, took the path of educational reform. Abduh tried to introduce the philosophical sciences into al-Azhar University's curriculum but his idea was rejected. Although there were minimal changes in the university curriculum by the time of his death in 1905, his ideas live on through his students such as Mahmud Yunus and Syaikh Ahmad al-Hadi from the Malay Archipelago.

By the beginning of the twentieth century, the colonial masters had introduced another system of education based on the utilitarian philosophy to serve their exploitative needs. This led to the dualistic education system as the colonial education ran parallel to the Islamic religious education. Rosnani argues that this dualistic system left a big negative impact on Muslims due to the contradicting philosophies underlying both. It is evident that each system was half-baked in terms of its epistemology, metaphysics, and values. Consequently, the system produced two groups of graduates—the secular and religious, in opposition to each other and this is manifested in the legal system, in the civil service, economic sector, and also the political system.[628]

Muslim thinkers were aware of the importance of a proper educational system. Many attempts were made by Muslim reformers to reform Muslim education in the early twentieth century such as Sir Ahmad Khan in India, Mahmud Yunus and Imam Zarkasyi in Indonesia, Za'ba and Shaikh Ahmad al-Hadi in Malaya. They hoped to integrate the philosophies and curriculums of the two systems.[629] Upon independence, each country devised its own education system which followed colonial characteristics thus retaining the dualism. According to Osman, the 1970s proved an important phase in the history of Muslim education. One of the most important events was the First World Conference on Muslim Education held in Makkah in 1977.[630] Three scholars,

628 Rosnani Hashim, *Educational Dualism in Malaysia* (London: Oxford University Press, 1996).

629 Rosnani Hashim, *Reclaiming the Conversation: Islamic Intellectual Tradition in the Malay Archipelago* (Kuala Lumpur: The Other Press, 2010).

630 Osman Bakar, "The Identity Crisis of the Contemporary Muslim Ummah: The Loss of *Tawhidic* Epistemology as its Root Cause," *Islam and Civilisational Renewal Journal* 3, no. 4 (2012): 637–53. https://doi.org/10.52282/icr.v3i4.509

Naquib al-Attas, Ismail al-Faruqi and Seyyed Hossein Nasr, who had a great influence on Osman attended this conference and headed different committees. Among the important resolutions that emerged from the conference were formulation of the Islamic philosophy of education, the need for Islamization of knowledge, the establishment of Islamic schools and universities, and the revision of the curriculum of Muslim educational institutions. The philosophy of education highlighted the holistic, balanced and integrated individual as its goal and his obligation as the steward of God and His servant. Meanwhile, Islamization of knowledge aims at remolding Western sciences that are secular, and Islamic schools and universities implied a change in philosophy and curriculum.

The three scholars analyzed and evaluated crises in the Muslim world and they agreed that epistemology was the core of the problem and Islamization of knowledge as an antidote. They founded institutions devoted to this mission. Al-Attas founded the International Institute of Islamic Thought and Civilization (ISTAC) in Kuala Lumpur in 1987 while al-Faruqi founded the International Institute of Islamic Thought (IIIT) in Herndon, Virginia in 1981. Al-Attas identified the problems of erroneous knowledge, loss of adab, and false leaders with the root cause being secularism.[631] Meanwhile, al-Faruqi traced the problem to educational dualism, loss of the Islamic vision, and the crisis of the ummatic identity. Like al-Attas, he blamed secularism as the main cause for the degeneration of Muslim social life.[632] They both agreed that knowledge is not value neutral but was indeed value-laden. Al-Attas emphasized the Islamic worldview as his framework while al-Faruqi emphasized *Tawhid.* Al-Attas' goal was to produce the good man or a scholar with Islamic personality which is manifested socially in the adabic order. The resolution for al-Attas was to imbibe the Islamic Worldview and a program that provided the intellectual foundation for a comprehensive understanding of Islamic and Western Philosophies, The Qur'an and Hadith and Arabic Language. On the other hand, al-Faruqi aimed at a critical analysis and synthesis between the Islamic traditional sciences and the Western philosophical sciences and then to Islamize modern disciplines and modernize Islamic traditional sciences based on the principle of unity (Unity of God, of Truth, of Mankind, of Prophet, Knowledge). He envisioned the production of Islamized textbooks towards the creation of the ummatic order. Like the two previous scholars, Nasr diagnosed the problem to the loss of sacredness in modern science.[633] He thus championed the revitalization

631 S.M.N. Al-Attas, *Islam and Secularism* (Kuala Lumpur: Muslim Youth Movement of Malaysia, 1978).

632 Ismail R. Al-Faruqi, *Islamization of Knowledge* (Herndon, VA: IIIT, 1982).

633 Nasr is a historian and philosopher of science. He has written a lot on Islamic science, civilization, the crisis of man and nature as seen from his works. See Nasr's work: *Science and Civilization in Islam,* 2nd ed. (Cambridge: Islamic Text Society, 1987), *Knowledge and the Sacred* (NY: SUNY Press, 1989), *Islam and the Plight of Modern Man* (London: Islamic Texts Society, 2002), *In Quest of the Sacred: The Modern*

of Islamic and philosophical sciences and called for the teaching of philosophy in Muslim higher educational institutions. He considered this a sacred duty to enhance Muslim thinking, creativity, and wisdom.

Osman's diagnosis of the Muslim crisis

Osman stands midway between these three intellectual giants and offers fresh ideas on intellectual reform. He agrees with al-Attas and al-Faruqi' on Islamization of Knowledge as to resolve an epistemological crisis besieging Muslims. He was however more influenced by Nasr in his advocacy for the revitalization of Islamic Science as evidenced in his doctoral studies and later on in his role as the President of the Academy of Islamic Science in Malaysia (ASASI).

Osman argues that the Muslim *ummah* (community) was faced with a knowledge—and identity—crisis, thus combining al-Attas' and Faruqi's insights. He explains that the *Tawhidic* epistemology is the foundation and sustainer to the identity of the Muslim Ummah.[634] The Qur'anic theory of multi-religious identities, according to him, is rooted in a common identity structure for all revealed religions and their respective communities.[635] This is based on the verse: "To each among you, We have prescribed a Law (*shari'ah*) and a spiritual Way (*minhaj*). If God had so willed, He would have made you a single people, but (His Plan is) to test you in what He had given you: so strive as in a race in all virtues. The goal of you all is to God; it is He that will show you the truth of the matters in which you dispute" (Qur'an 5:48). He argues further that the essence of the Muslim ummah is its distinctive knowledge-culture founded on Qur'anic *Tawhid* and the Muhammadan Shari'ah. The *Tawhidic* vision of knowledge is one that affirms "all true human knowledge ought to be ultimately related to the unity of God, since all things are ontologically related to their Divine Origin"[636]. He asserts that Muslims today "no longer possess the whole of *Tawhidic* epistemology along with its accompanying exemplary thinking culture. This has resulted in deviations from established norms rooted in traditional Islamic intellectual culture."

Osman argues that Muslim modern education based on secular epistemologies accelerated the decline of *Tawhidic* epistemology which made it unable to respond effectively to the challenges posed by modern epistemologies. This

World in the Light of Tradition (Lahore: Suhail Academy, 2001), *Islamic Science: an Illustrated Study* (London: World of Islam Festival Publishing, 1976), *Man and Nature: the Spiritual Crisis in Modern Man* (Chicago: ABC International, 1997), *Religion and the Order of Nature 1996, Traditional Islam in the Modern World* (London: Kegan Paul International,1994).

634 Osman Bakar, "Identity Crisis of the Contemporary Muslim Ummah."

635 Osman Bakar, "The Qur'anic Identity of the Muslim Ummah: *Tawhidic* Epistemology as its Foundation and Sustainer," Islam and Civilisational Renewal Journal 3, no. 3 (2012): 438–54. https://doi.org/10.52282/icr.v3i3.531.

636 Osman Bakar, Qur'anic Identity of the Muslim Ummah, 438.

unresolved intellectual conflict between the surviving elements of *Tawhidic* epistemology and modern epistemology led to the epistemological crisis that is devastating to Muslim life and thought. From his perspective, "only a sound epistemological order exemplified in *Tawhidic* epistemology may guarantee a healthy thinking and knowledge-culture on which alone the strength of the Muslim ummatic identity depends. "[637] A renewal (*tajdid*) of *Tawhidic* epistemology is much needed.

Universal and modern science

Osman cements the role of sciences in contemporary society. He argues that science was used in the Islamic tradition 'to reaffirm such perennial truths as Divine Unity and the consequent principles of the Unicity of Nature.'[638] As a result, it can be seen that all 'traditional sciences share not only common goals but also a hierarchic picture of the universe and common epistemological principles.'[639] Osman's idea of science is not the same as 'modern' science of the present-day period. For him, modern science is built on the assumptions and conclusions that expunge religious and philosophical influences.[640] Osman argues that the myth of the neutrality of science in relation to cultural values has long been shattered by numerous excellent works on the history and philosophy of science. Scientific and technological developments are influenced by beliefs, be it religious, anti-religious, philosophical, or ideological, and by cultural and socioeconomic factors. Therefore, there is a need to make a careful distinction between universal values and virtues as against those that are unique to a particular religion, culture, or ideology.[641] This reflects Nasr's position on Western science which is secular and an anti-thesis of all that is sacred in nature.

Osman states that the early Muslim philosopher-scientists were interested in classifying the sciences within a hierarchy of knowledge while, at the same time, developing and creating new knowledge.[642] Science, for Osman, is not simply the observation and experimentation, but also involves logical thinking, mathematical analysis, and the rational interpretation of sacred books.[643] There are, therefore, many sources of knowledge, which can be approached through a variety of methodologies. Science is done not for its own sake, but for the betterment of life and understanding of the world. Hence, it is 'useful

637 Osman Bakar, Qur'anic Identity of the Muslim Ummah, 438.

638 Osman Bakar, *Islam and Civilizational Dialogue: The Quest for a Truly Universal Civilization.* (Kuala Lumpur: University of Malaya Press, 1997), 92.

639 Osman Bakar, *Islam and Civilizational Dialogue*, 94.

640 Osman Bakar, *Islam and Civilizational Dialogue*, 93.

641 Osman Bakar, "Civilizational Dialogue in Philosophy," in *Islam and Civilizational Dialogue*, 109.

642 Osman Bakar, "Science," in *History of Islamic Philosophy: Part II*, ed. Seyyed Hossein Nasr and Oliver Leaman (New York: Routledge, 1996), 930.

643 Osman Bakar, "Science," 941.

in the quest for the perfection of the soul, which is a necessary condition for happiness in this world and in the life hereafter.'[644] Therefore, it is obligatory for every human being to engage in science, at least on some level, in order to develop their soul and gain happiness. He draws on Nasr's view: The truth descends upon the mind ... it gushes forth and inundates the mind like a deep well which has suddenly burst forth into a spring ... the sapiential nature of what the human being receives through spiritual experience is not the result of man's mental faculty but issues from the nature of that experience itself. Man can know through intuition and revelation ... because knowledge is being.[645] The ultimate goal, then, is becoming full human beings that seek to understand the world and their place in it.[646]

Religious consciousness and the scientific spirit in Islamic tradition

Osman argues that there is a strong connection between religious consciousness and the scientific spirit in the Islamic tradition. Islam deals not only with what man must and must not do. Islam is both a way of acting and a way of knowing. Islam looks upon knowledge as the way to salvation and to the attainment of human happiness in this life and in the hereafter. He asserts that *Tawhid* (Divine Unity) is the source of the scientific spirit and that Muslim philosophers studied the world through an understanding of this Unity.[647] The cosmos is made up of many levels of reality, not just the physical. But it constitutes a unity because it must manifest the oneness of its metaphysical source and origin. The Qur'an strongly argues that cosmic unity is a clear proof of Divine Unity (21:22). Through understanding *Tawhid*, one can 'affirm the truth that God is One in His Essence, in His Attributes and Qualities, and in His Works.'[648]

The scientific spirit in Islam was first demonstrated in the religious sciences. Osman explains that "the passion for truth and objectivity, the general respect for fully corroborated empirical evidence and a mind skilled in the classification of things were some of the most outstanding features of early Muslim religious scholarship as can be seen in their studies of jurisprudence and the prophetic traditions."[649] A love for definitions and conceptual or semantic analysis with great emphasis on logical clarity and precision was also very much evident in Qur'anic exegesis. Logic was never conceived as being

644 Osman Bakar, "Science," 943.

645 Nasr, 2007, 131.

646 Katherine Nielsen, "The Philosophy of Osman Bakar," *International Studies in the Philosophy of Science* 22, no. 1 (March 2008): 88.

647 Osman Bakar, *Tawhid and Science* (Kuala Lumpur: Secretariat for Islamic Philosophy and Science, 1991), 1.

648 Osman Bakar, *Tawhid and Science*, 2.

649 Osman Bakar, *Tawhid and Science*, 2.

opposed to religious faith, but rather an indispensable tool of scientific thinking. Muslim philosophers and scientists viewed logic as a form of *hikmah* (wisdom), a form of knowledge which is extolled by the Qur'ān. They were aware that logic can serve both truth and error. But they were concerned with clarity and consistency as with truth and certitude. They developed logic within the framework of a religious consciousness of the Transcendent.

In their view, logic, when used correctly and by an intellect that is not corrupted by the lower passions, may lead one to the Transcendent itself.[650] Some philosophers-scientists such as al-Farabi and religious scholars such as al-Ghazali wrote works which sought to demonstrate that Aristotelian logic found strong scriptural support in the Qur'ān and hadith. "*Mantiq* in its Islamic home became an important tool not only of the philosophical sciences but also for the religious sciences. According to al-Ghazali, the term *al-Mizan* in the Qur'an is translated as the balance, refers among other things to logic which is the balance with which man weighs ideas and opinions to arrive at the correct measurement or judgment."[651] It was further argued that "the extensive use of logic in Islam did not lead to the kind of rationalism and logicism one finds in the modern West precisely because the use of reason was never cut off from faith in divine revelation."[652]

Similarly, the importance attached to logical thinking did not stifle the spirit of experimentation among Muslim scientists who were all noted for their observational powers and experimental tendencies. Their studies of the natural sciences did not lead them to regard sensual experiences as the source of all knowledge.[653] The traditional Islamic epistemology provides all the necessary safeguards against such kinds of philosophical deviations. Islamic science is also influenced by the conception of *i'tidal* (equilibrium). All paths to developing knowledge and understanding are to be valued, and function together to develop a clear and complete vision of the universe.[654] There are, however, degrees and gradations of truth, and of ways of coming to that truth. Some techniques are better than others for understanding the absolute truth (*al-Haqq*) of both the world and of God. Science is a legitimate and valued technique to learning about *tawhid* because it employs all five senses, as well as other faculties of human beings, such as memory, imagination, rational intellect, and spiritual faculties.[655] Therefore, while science in the West was inspired by skepticism in religion, at least in part, Islamic science was inspired by religion.

650 Frithjof Schuon, *The Transcendent Unity of Religions* (Wheatson, IL: Theosophical), quoted in Osman Bakar, *Tawhid and Science*, 3.
651 Osman Bakar, *Tawhid and Science*, 4.
652 Osman Bakar, *Tawhid and Science*, 4.
653 Osman Bakar, *Tawhid and Science*, 4.
654 Osman Bakar, *Tawhid and Science*, 5.
655 Osman Bakar, *Tawhid and Science*, 6.

Osman asserts that the quest for objectivity is not unique to modern civilization. In the Islamic perspective, this quest is not only legitimate and desirable but it is also rooted in man's inner nature. It has a profound religious significance and objectivity is essential to the process of Islamic science. It is both impartial and public in that anyone can seek to verify claims.[656] Verifiability is not, however, the absolute proof of correctness of conclusions, as there may be other discoveries in the future that may disprove, or call into question, the objective, empirical knowledge gathered up to now. According to Osman, this attempt to cultivate objectivity is a result of man's desire to emulate God since humans were created in God's image, they have the potential to emulate all of God's divine qualities.[657] In Islamic tradition, the sense of objectivity refers to impartiality, disinterestedness, and justice in the domain of knowledge which is inseparable from the religious consciousness of Tawhid. This is totally different from the modern world where religion is regarded as the greatest impediment in the realization of impartiality and justice. It is also different from modern scholarship where objectivity is confined to empirical or experimental domain whereas in Islamic tradition objectivity is also the concern of the higher planes of human consciousness (Ibid: 8–10). Humans are therefore capable of objectivity because God endowed them with this nature, hence humans are called 'rational animals.'[658]

In summary, *tawhid* is the source of the scientific spirit in all domains of knowledge. The Islamic intellectual tradition does not entertain the idea of the natural sciences as being more scientific than the other sciences. Similarly, the idea of objectivity is inseparable from religious consciousness and spirituality.

Resolving the Ummatic Crisis

Osman argues that there is a need for a real *tajdīd* (renewal) in epistemology in the twenty-first century to create a new epistemology for the Muslim ummah and humanity by a synthesis of traditional Islamic epistemology and the best of modern and postmodern epistemologies. In the pursuit of this objective, he recommended the following courses of actions:

1. More studies need to be done on the epistemological roots of the ummah's knowledge crisis in modern times and the implications of this crisis for the ummah's identity. Centres of Islamic studies need to intensify research on the issue given its importance to the health and dignity of the ummah.
2. Existing research centres and groups dedicated to the rediscovery and recovery of classical Islamic ideas of perennial value that have been lost

656 Osman Bakar, *Tawhid and Science*, 8.
657 Osman Bakar, *Tawhid and Science*, 10.
658 Osman Bakar, *Tawhid and Science*, 28.

or forgotten need to be further strengthened with material and moral support.

3. *Tawhidic* epistemology needs to be made better known to the present generation of Muslim scholars because of the important role that it can play in overcoming the ummah's knowledge crisis and contributing to the development of a healthy knowledge culture. There is a need to reformulate and intellectually 'repackage' this epistemology in contemporary language so that they would be easily understood, digested and internalised by the present generation of Muslims.
4. There should be more teaching and research programs on epistemology from the Islamic perspectives in the Muslim world that will result in much needed publications on the subject;
5. Islam's knowledge and thinking-culture needs to be better understood and cultivated by the Muslims with the view of strengthening the ummatic identity. [659]

Osman laid out his theoretical framework by drawing from the Islamic philosophical, religious and scientific traditions, the Qur'an and Prophetic Traditions, and also the current modern scientific thoughts and practices. Based on this framework, he had attempted to put his ideas into practice. He was the principal founder of the Islamic Academy of Science (ASASI) in 1977, and served as its first Secretary-General (1977–1981), and later became the President (1987–1992).[660] Among the aims of the Academy is to promote the study and research of religion and science, particularly from an Islamic point of view. During this period, Osman and his group from ASASI popularized "Islamic science" and contributed to advancing cross-cultural studies, as well as the history and philosophy of science. He was also the chief editor of the Academy's bilingual biannual journal *Kesturi.* Osman also founded the Institute of Islamic Sciences (*Institut Pengajian Ilmu-Ilmu Islam),* under ABIM (Muslim Youth Movement of Malaysia) in 1989 (now known as the Darul Hikmah College) where he introduced and designed a course on Islamic Philosophy of Science which was made compulsory for the Institute's Diploma Programme. This was the first full course on Islamic philosophy of science ever to be taught in Malaysia.

Osman took to translating his ideas more seriously as a faculty member of the Faculty of Science in University Malaya (UM) where he later became its Deputy Dean and held the Chair of Philosophy of Science. He was later appointed as the Deputy Vice-Chancellor of the same university. He initiated many courses on Philosophy and History of Science, Logic and also Religion in the university, mainly for the undergraduates in the Faculty of Science. Later, several faculties in the university began to offer a course on the philosophy

659 Osman Bakar, "Qur'anic Identity," and "Identity Crisis of the Contemporary Muslim Ummah."
660 Osman Bakar, "Qur'anic Identity," and "Identity Crisis of the Contemporary Muslim Ummah."

of the discipline such as Philosophy of Education and Philosophy of Psychology. A course on Science and Religion was introduced in the Islamic Studies Academy (APIUM). Osman also introduced some of these philosophical sciences in other universities in the country and abroad. He has been credited for introducing forty-one different courses in several universities in Malaysia and Brunei in the last forty-five years (1973–2018) a few among which are shown in Table 1.

Table 1 Selected list of courses initiated by Osman between 1973–2018

1. Introduction to Philosophy (University Malaya, UM)
2. Introduction to Science and Technology Studies (UM)
3. Religion and Philosophy of Science (Universiti Kebangsaan Malaysia, UKM)
4. History of Islamic Science (UM; International Inst of Islamic Thought & Civ., ISTAC)
5. Philosophy of Islamic Science (UKM; UM; Universiti Putra Malaysia, UPM)
6. History of Traditional Chinese Science (UM)
7. History of Traditional Indian Science (UM)
8. Philosophy of Mathematical Sciences (UM)
9. Logic and Scientific Method (UM)
10. History of Modern Science (UM)
11. Introduction to Epistemology (UM; Universiti Malaysia Sabah, UNIMAS)
12. Epistemology and Research Methodology (UM)
13. Introduction to Islamic Philosophy (UM; Universiti Brunei Darussalam, UBD)
14. Philosophy of Science in Management Science (UM)
15. Environmental Ethics and Sustainable Development (UM)
16. The Meaning of Civilization (UM): graduate course
17. Contributions of Islamic Civilization to Science (UKM; UM; Universiti Teknologi MARA, UiTM)
18. Philosophy of Cognitive Science (UNIMAS)
19. Philosophy of Psychology (UPM)
20. Philosophy of Education (UPM)
21. Professional Ethics (UM; Universiti Utara Malaysia, UUM)
22. Qur'ānic Foundation of Islamic Science (ISTAC, IIUM)
23. History of Islamic Science (ISTAC, IIUM)
24. Issues in Islamization of Knowledge (ISTAC, IIUM)
25. Religion and Science in Contemporary Islam (Georgetown University, GU)
26. Contemporary Islamic Thought and Movements in Southeast Asia (GU)

His efforts at increasing courses on epistemology from the Islamic perspective in higher education is consistent with his vision of the revival of the Islamic scientific spirit. Osman also helped to set up the new Department of Science and Technology Studies in the Faculty of Science which offers a program on History and Philosophy of Science. Many doctoral candidates have become lecturers in this area and continues the seeds of a new *Tawhidic* epistemology he had planted many years ago.

Discussion and Conclusion

It is clear that Osman had diagnosed the problem of the Muslim ummah to that of identity and lack of epistemological vision. He revitalized the discourse on Islamic intellectual sciences by recovering the soul to this body of knowledge so that it will achieve its goal of Divine Unity, balance and harmony. In practical terms, Osman's strategy was in developing courses and programs in higher education on history and philosophy of Islamic science, religion and science, philosophy of each discipline from the Islamic perspective in the various faculties. He did not establish institutions like al-Attas or al-Faruqi but was a thought leader in many established universities in Southeast Asia and the United States. One setback that Osman faced was that no dedicated departments dealing with the philosophy of science and religion had ever been established. Without a department, there will not be a proper center to train local students to really deepen their knowledge of the various philosophies and their problems.

In a sense, what Osman has done is similar to al-Attas which is Islamization of knowledge. However, Osman's approach is more focus on the natural and applied sciences in contrast to al-Attas who focuses on the social sciences and humanities. Another difference is al-Attas' focus on the individual personality while Osman focuses on the ummatic identity. Osman leans closer to al-Faruqi in that he diagnosed the crisis of the ummah as stemming from epistemological problems and loss of identity. The two men differed in terms of methodology. Al-Faruqi was concerned with scholars who are experts of modern disciplines and are, at the same time, competent and knowledgeable in Islamic traditional knowledge. Meanwhile Osman is focused on transforming the minds of undergraduate and graduate students in the natural and applied sciences towards having a holistic and Islamic view of their fields. In this sense, he continues the intellectual tradition of Nasr.

It has been almost forty-five years since the epistemological crisis was identified and addressed but has the Muslim Ummah made any progress? According to Osman, Muslims have failed to present a lasting solution to the crisis because "they do not have in their hands a total Islamic epistemology that comprehends the inadequacy of their current understanding of Islamic epistemology as well as the limitations and dangers inherent in the prevailing Western-originated secular epistemologies. They have not decisively settled which vision of knowledge they need to guide them in societal life and civilization-making."[661] The importance of logic to sharpen the mind has risen to the fore again in Malaysia when the Ministry of Higher Education replaced the existing two required core courses on Asian and Islamic civilizations (TITAS) for undergraduates in all Malaysian universities with two courses, namely Philosophy and Current Issues, and Appreciation of Ethics and Civilization in 2020. The first is an introductory course on philosophy and its applications in analyzing current issues and the second discusses ethics from the perspective of major civilizations which retained some features of the former TITAS courses. Will this initiate a change?

The lack of planning and of lecturers specializing in philosophy and philosophical methods may result in a failure of this project. Students will be made to memorize facts rather than engage in philosophical inquiry. Departments of philosophy should be established in some universities to cater for a new generation of philosophy lecturers. In University of Malaya (UM) where Osman was the Deputy Vice-Chancellor in charge of academic affairs, there was no department of philosophy but he managed to set up a graduate program for philosophy of science in the Department of Science and Technology. The IIUM had a department of philosophy but it was closed due to the lack of undergraduates specializing in it and instead some of its courses were transferred and taught under the Department of Usuluddin. Only later ISTAC was established to offer the philosophical sciences for postgraduate students only.

Osman must be credited for introducing the philosophy of education and also philosophy of science courses to the Bachelor of Science with Education degree program for school teachers in the UM. Would-be teachers can relate to the students spiritual elements in science. However, this integration between science and religion will not be complete if the students from the faculty of Islamic Studies which also produces the religious teachers are not exposed to philosophy of science. So the course, Religion and Science that is offered in the Islamic Studies Academy UM is very relevant in producing a new breed of teachers. This is something new because even in IIUM which champions the Islamization of Knowledge, its students from the Kulliyyah of Islamic Revealed Knowledge are not exposed to the philosophy or history of science. But this integrated program between Religious Sciences and Natural or Philosophical Sciences for the Bachelor of Education students is crucial because without the proper knowledge they will not be able to convince their young students of the

661 Osman Bakar, "Identity Crisis," 650.

unity of knowledge. In this regard, Rosnani,[662] Naji and Rosnani,[663] and Wan Yusoff and Rosnani[664] have asserted the necessity of introducing the Hikmah (Wisdom) Pedagogy of philosophical inquiry in Muslim education curriculum in schools and the universities based on the results of their research and practices in these institutions since 2006, when the Center for Philosophical Inquiry in Education was founded.

My final observation is on the philosophical mind. One major indicator for the philosophical mind is the love of inquiry or asking questions. But there are other cognitive behavioral indicators too such as deliberation through discussion, giving reasons, justifying positions, providing arguments or evidence to support proposition, listening before speaking out, taking turn, self-corrections, using criteria and considering all possible alternatives for making decision, more mutual respect, and open-mindedness regardless of differences of opinions. Are the classes becoming more community centered, that is, both students and teachers are questioning and probing or is it still the teacher as the sage on the stage? Have all these courses been able to produce such students and classes? If so, then we can say that the project is successful. In addition, will this new package of the *Tawhidic* intellectual natural sciences motivate Muslim and non-Muslim students to take up natural sciences as a specialization at the higher level since interest in this area is waning in the university? Or will the philosophical inquiry approach to the subject be a catalyst? Definitely, more studies on these are needed.

662 Rosnani Hashim, *Hikmah (Wisdom) Pedagogy for Critical, Creative, Caring, and Collaborative Thinking: A Guide for Teachers* (Kuala Lumpur: Centre for Teaching Thinking, IIUM, 2016), and *Revitalizing Philosophy and Philosophical Inquiry in Muslim Education* (Kuala Lumpur: Kulliyyah of Education, 2017).

663 Saeed Naji and Rosnani Hashim, *History, Theory and Practice of Philosophy for Children: International Perspectives* (London: Routledge, 2017).

664 Wan Mazwati Wan Yusoff and Rosnani Hashim, *Enhancing Thinking Through Doing Philosophy* (Kuala Lumpur: IIUM Press, 2017).

Bibliography

Al-Attas, Syed Muhammad Naquib. *Islam and Secularism*. Kuala Lumpur: Muslim Youth Movement of Malaysia, 1978.

Al-Faruqi, Ismail Raji. *Islamization of Knowledge*. Herndon, VA: IIIT, 1982.

Dewey, John. *The Quest for Certainty: A Study of the Relation of Knowledge and Action* (Gifford Lectures 1929). New York: Putnam, 1960.

Nasr, Seyyed Hossein. *Traditional Islam in the Modern World.* London: KPI, 1987.

Nielsen, Katherine. "The Philosophy of Osman Bakar." *International Studies in the Philosophy of Science* 22, no. 1 (March 2008): 81–95.

Osman Bakar. *Tawhid and Science.* Kuala Lumpur: Secretariat for Islamic Philosophy and Science, 1991.

Osman Bakar. "Science." In *History of Islamic Philosophy: Part II,* edited by Seyyed Hossein Nasr and Oliver Leaman. New York: Routledge, 1996.

Osman Bakar. *Islam and Civilizational Dialogue: The Quest for a Truly Universal Civilization.* Kuala Lumpur: University of Malaya Press, 1997.

Osman Bakar. "The Qur'anic Identity of the Muslim Ummah: *Tawhidic* Epistemology as its Foundation and Sustainer." *Islam and Civilisational Renewal Journal* 3, no. 3 (2012): 438–54. https://doi.org/10.52282/icr.v3i3.531.

Osman Bakar. "The Identity Crisis of the Contemporary Muslim Ummah: The Loss of *Tawhidic* Epistomology as its Root Cause." *Islam and Civilisational Renewal Journal* 3, no. 4 (2012): 637–53. https://doi.org/10.52282/icr.v3i4.509.

Rosnani Hashim. *Educational Dualism in Malaysia*. London: Oxford University Press, 1996.

Rosnani Hashim. *Reclaiming the Conversation: Islamic Intellectual Tradition in the Malay Archipelago.* Kuala Lumpur: The Other Press, 2010.

Rosnani Hashim. *Hikmah (Wisdom) Pedagogy for Critical, Creative, Caring, and Collaborative Thinking: A Guide for Teachers.* Kuala Lumpur: Centre for Teaching Thinking, IIUM, 2016.

Rosnani Hashim. *Revitalizing Philosophy and Philosophical Inquiry in Muslim Education.* Kuala Lumpur: Kulliyyah of Education, 2017.

Saeed Naji and Rosnani Hashim. *History, Theory and Practice of Philosophy for Children: International Perspectives.* London: Routledge, 2017.

Schuon, Frithjof. *Transcendent Unity of Religions*. Wheatson, IL: Theosophical, 1975.

Wan Mazwati Wan Yusoff and Rosnani Hashim. *Enhancing Thinking Through Doing Philosophy.* Kuala Lumpur: IIUM Press, 2017.

Chapter 19

Ars Sine Scientia? Integral Aesthetics and Islamic Metaphysics

Reza Shah-Kazemi

Research Associate at the Institute of Ismaili Studies, London

I would like to begin this chapter by situating it within the context of the contemporary quest for Islamic authenticity and integrity, sometimes called the 'Islamisation of knowledge'—a quest to which Osman Bakar has devoted his fruitful professional life. There can be no doubt that Muslims certainly need to be aware of the extent to which modern and post-modern epistemology imposes upon the traditional Islamic modes of knowledge its own, often distorting, categories. Let us start by noting that knowledge (*'ilm*) traditionally comprised both the physical and the intellectual sciences, and that the latter embraced art, understood in its widest sense. Art, therefore, should be seen as an integral expression of the creative spirit of the intellect, and not as something divorced from knowledge and the intellect, something irrational, sentimental, and purely subjective. When the intellect functions in accordance with its God-given nature, it intuits the relationship between beauty and divinity. It is this intuition that allows the artist to produce works of art which are, properly speaking, inspiring. They satisfy, at one and the same time, aesthetic sensibility and objective intellectuality. This understanding of the true nature of beauty in the light of the dimensions of ultimate reality is well expressed by Frithjof Schuon, in an essay appropriately entitled 'Foundations of an Integral Aesthetics': "In reflecting the Absolute, beauty realizes a mode of regularity, and in reflecting the Infinite, it realizes a mode of mystery. Beauty, being perfection, is regularity and mystery; it is through these two qualities that it stimulates and at the same time appeases the intelligence and also a sensibility which is in conformity with the intelligence."[665]

---

665 Frithjof Schuon, "Foundations of an Integral Aesthetics," in *Esoterism as Principle and as Way*, trans. William Stoddart (Bedfont: Perennial Books, 1990), 177. Although my main arguments are based on reflections on verses of the Qur'ān and sayings of the Prophet—together with the commentaries thereon

This statement by Schuon helps us to see how the principle of *tawḥīd* (Oneness of God) integrates art and beauty within intelligence and divinity. For the reason, I did not entitle this chapter 'The Philosophy of Art in Islam,' and chose instead the terms 'metaphysics' and 'aesthetics.' Both terms, 'philosophy' and 'art,' are used in our times in ways which undermine the principle of *tawḥīd*. On the one hand, philosophy is deemed to be a purely logical or mental exercise, and on the other, art is seen as something unconnected with 'real life.' In other words, art is deemed in our times to be something luxurious or extraneous in relation to the realities—both the most exalted and the most commonplace—of everyday life. Putting the two terms together, as 'philosophy of art,' one arrives at a notion which no traditional artist or craftsman, in Islam or any other tradition, would recognise as having anything to do with either the ultimate or the immediate significance of what they are doing. For traditional Muslim artists who lived, worked, and thought in a spiritual ambience governed, to some degree or another, by the worldview of *tawḥīd*, there was no compartmentalisation of thought and life. There was no artificial separation between the inner significance of things and their practical utility.

As for the term 'metaphysics,' this term better conveys the all-encompassing implication of *tawḥīd*, conceived as a supple, unifying spiritual principle and 'energetic' process, as opposed to a rigid theological tenet. Theologically, *tawḥīd* is all too often reduced to the idea that God is a single being or an absolute Being. No doubt but God is also an entity among other entities within the same category, a being residing 'up there' in Heaven, alone, and with no other divinity alongside Him. Understood metaphysically, or spiritually, however, *tawḥīd* opens up an understanding of the oneness of reality, and also leads to a vision of the innumerable ways in which everything in the cosmos is subtly inter-dependent. It is this vision that explains why in the Islamic tradition all spheres of existence be it science and art, thought and being, prayer and work, ethics and metaphysics were woven within a civilizational texture that enrobed the whole of life.[666]

---

by sages and saints within the Islamic mystical tradition—the impetus for my reflections come from this, and other seminal writings by Schuon, on the spiritual dimensions of beauty; and also from the writings of two of the most profound sages of sacred art in Islam in recent times, Titus Burckhardt and Martin Lings, both of whom applied to the Islamic artistic tradition the metaphysical insights of Schuon and the other two 'founders' of what has been termed the Sophia Perennis, René Guénon and Ananda Coomaraswamy. As regards the latter, see especially his *Figures of Speech or Figures of Thought? The Traditional View of Art*, ed. William Wroth (Bloomington: World Wisdom Books, 2007). See also the book of selected writings of Schuon on art, which graphically reveals the distinction between traditional and modern art with the use of appropriate illustrations, *Art—from the Sacred to the Profane, East and West*, ed. Catherine Schuon (Bloomington: World Wisdom Books, 2007).

666 One must refer here to the vast corpus of Seyyed Hossein Nasr: a stunning array of writings which manifest in myriad ways how the principle of *tawḥīd* was articulated in this civilizational manner. See, for example, his *Science and Civilization in Islam* (Cambridge: Islamic Texts Society, 1987); *Introduction to Islamic Cosmological Doctrines* (London: Thames & Hudson, 1978); *Islamic Science: An Illustrated Study* (London: World of Islam Festival Publishing Company, 1976); and *Islamic Art and Spirituality* (Ipswich:

At first sight, it might appear that aesthetics and metaphysics are poles apart. Aesthetics is all about appreciating forms, while metaphysics is all about going beyond forms. A look at their etymology would confirm this appearance: the word 'aesthetic' is derived from the Greek *aisthetikos*, from *aistheta*: 'things perceptible by the senses.' As for the word 'metaphysics,' this literally means 'that which is after or beyond nature,' *meta-physis*. In other words, aesthetics pertains to outward forms, perceived by the senses. Metaphysics pertains to inner essences, transcending form, that is, to truths, realities and principles that are intelligible but not sensible. But in the light cast by the principle of *tawḥīd*, it is possible to discern a significant relationship between aesthetics, grasped as the spiritual intuition of beauty, and metaphysics, the science of ultimate reality.

Seen in that light, I intend to make two complementary arguments in this chapter. The first is *tawḥīd*, understood both as the oneness of Reality and as a metaphysical vision of the unifying power of the One, enables one to plumb the spiritual significance of beauty. Secondly, the spiritual assimilation of beauty deepens one's intuition of the intrinsic nature of Reality. It opens our eyes to the truth expressed by the prophetic utterance: 'Truly God is Beautiful and He loves beauty.'[667]

Let us begin with the following introductory remarks on this prophetic saying. God as the absolutely Real is absolutely beautiful, and He[668] loves His own beauty both inwardly and outwardly; that is, He loves the beauty that He is *per se*, in His own Essence, and He loves the beauty of His creation. Creation, understood metaphysically, constitutes the divine self-projection into relativity, and from this self-projection there arises the manifestation of divine beauty in relative mode. Because God is beautiful by essence, that which He creates or manifests must likewise be essentially beautiful; this essential beauty resides in the very bosom of relativity. To speak of relativity is to speak of contrasts and veilings, as well as manifestations and revelations. God 'loves' all of that which, within the domain of the relative, bears witness to His own beauty. It is the task of the human being to discriminate between what is beautiful and what is ugly, and then to identify with beauty, inward and outward; and, conversely, to disengage from ugliness, inward and outward.[669]

Golgonooza Press, 1987).

667 *Ṣaḥīḥ Muslim*, vol. 1, p. 53, saying no. 275. *Encyclopaedia of Ḥadīth* (Liechtenstein: Thesaurus Islamicus Foundation, 2001). The saying is also found in the collections of al-Tirmidhī and Aḥmad b. Ḥanbal.

668 Let it be noted that, in Arabic, when one refers to Allah, one uses the masculine, He; but when referring to the Essence of Allah (*dhāt Allāh*), one uses the feminine, She.

669 'Come not close to shameful deeds, whether openly manifested (*mā ẓahara minhā*) or inwardly concealed (*mā baṭana*)' (Q 6:151); the same idea is found expressed at Q 7:33. The translations given here are based on the now 'classic' translation of Muhammad Marmaduke Pickthall, with certain modifications; the translations of M.A.S. Abdel Haleem (Oxford: Oxford University Press, 2005), 'Ali Quli Qara'i (London: Islamic College for Advanced Studies, 2004), and Muhammad Asad (Bristol: The Book

To the extent that this identification with beauty is complete, it is tantamount to loving God, source of all beauty. To love God, while conforming to His beauty is to be loved by God. The Prophet, *Ḥabīb Allāh*, 'beloved of God'—and thus supremely beautiful by definition—is told to say to the believers: 'If you love God, follow me; God will love you' (3:31). The Prophet as the beautiful exemplar (*uswa ḥasana*) (33:21) resides at the very heart of all art worthy of the designation 'Islamic.'

Qurʾān as *Ḥaqīqa*

Titus Burckhardt writes: "The most profound link between Islamic art and the Qurʾān lies not in the form of the Qurʾān but in its *ḥaqīqa*, its formless essence, and more particularly in the notion of *tawḥīd*, unity or union, with its contemplative implications; Islamic art ... is essentially the projection into the visual order of certain aspects or dimensions of Divine Unity."[670]

Two questions follow from this acute observation by Titus Burckhardt. What are the 'contemplative implications' of *tawḥīd*? How can contemplation—the ultimate basis of all true art—be related to the Qurʾān's *ḥaqīqa*, a spiritual reality defined by Burckhardt as an essence which is formless? In other words, how can one contemplate that which has no form?

We cannot hope to do justice here to such vast questions, but let us try and at least suggest a few spiritual principles by which some answers to these questions might be articulated or intuited. First, it might be said, very summarily, that the traditions of Islamic art and spirituality, taken together, provide the answer to the question regarding the contemplative implications of *tawḥīd*. Traditionally, artists and craftsmen were not just pious, they were also deeply spiritual—this explains why the majority of artists in the medieval and premodern Muslim world were members of Sufi orders. Their art was an expression of their spirituality, and their spirituality was the creative source of their art.[671]

The contemplative implication of *tawḥīd* is clear: traditional art was an expression of the artist's ability to contemplate the beauty of divine unity and a translation of intuition of divine beauty into a visible, audible or material form. This traditional art can be qualified as 'sacred' in the measure that God Himself is the true agent of the art. The human artist is, to one degree or another, effaced before the creativity of God, which, as it were, passes through the human agent, and this explains why so many traditional artists preferred to remain anonymous. As we shall see below, the artist's self-effacement before

---

Foundation, 2003), were also consulted.

670 Titus Burckhardt, *Art of Islam: Language and Meaning*, trans. J. Peter Hobson (London: World of Islam Festival Publishing Company, 1976), 46.

671 See the fine chapter in this volume by Dr Shoaib Ahmad, '*Khush navīsī aur Taṭhīr-i Zāt*' ('Calligraphy and the purification of oneself').

the art which manifests through him or her finds its contemplative archetype in the state called *fanā'*, extinction.

The spiritual vision of the artist is organically related to the *ḥaqīqa*, or spiritual essence, of the Qur'ān. This leads us directly to what we might call 'the art of Qur'anic worship,' a form of worship which transforms the very substance of the worshipper: the soul itself becomes fashioned by worship into a beautiful work of art, in accordance with the blessings, the *baraka*, emanating from both the spiritual essence and the sonoral form of the Qur'ān.[672] This transformation comes about through the miraculous power of the Qur'ān. The uncreated Word of God is transmitted by the Qur'ān, such that what the Qur'ān *is* takes precedence over what it *says*, just as what God *is* ontologically precedes what God *says*. The Qur'ān, as Speech of God, conveys and constitutes the very presence of God, and this presence in turn imparts truth; it is thus, properly speaking, a theurgy, a means by which the presence of God makes itself available to those who engage with it with *their* presence, that is, with their heart and soul and not just their tongue and mind.[673]

As regards the relationship between the Qur'ān and sacred art in general, let us also take careful note of the following penetrating insight of Titus Burckhardt: 'The revealed Word reverberates in the musical order, and this is most assuredly the firmest possible link between rite and art.'[674] The revealed 'music' of the Divine Speech (*kalām Allāh*) might be seen as the archetype of all musicality, and this is one of the most tangible and transformative modes of beauty in creation, being a kind of descent of supra-formal, celestial melodies within the field of audible, terrestrial sound. The Shaykh al-'Alawī, makes a remark that is most pertinent here: 'Music is not crippled with the dry bones

672 'God's Work in the universe is poetic and musical. In everything He does, He superbly combines function with beauty. This is nowhere more clearly reflected than in His book and final religion, the Koran and Islam. The Koran, in its own inimitable way, is a poetical and musical text, its meaning conveyed in a lyric style which is to be chanted in the distinctive harmonic mode known as *Tajwīd*. Five daily prayers reflect this poetic and musical dimension of Islam: the believer is enjoined to recite the poetic text of the Koran with the best possible voice he can summon. This develops his sensitivity towards beauty and yields a particular kind of subtle excellence in every aspect of his life. It also teaches that one's speech and actions not only the content but also the form and the way it is presented must be nothing less than the best.' Recep Şentürk, preface to *The Mantle Adorned: Imam Busiri's Burda*, trans. Abdal Hakim Murad (London: The Quilliam Press, 2009), 4.

673 If, to begin with, the theurgic presence demands the engagement of the human presence, ultimately, it demands effacement of the human presence: 'the theurgical, as universal and divine, is the opposite of anything particular and individualistic, anything based on one's subjective whims and egocentric drives. Without the fundamental realization of our own nothingness (*sunaisthesis ten peri heauton oudeneias* [quoting Iamblichus:] *De myster.* 47.13–14), no one can be saved.' Algis Uždavinys, *Philosophy and Theurgy in Late Antiquity* (San Rafael: Sophia Perennis, 2010), 83. What Iamblichus says, in accordance with the Platonic tradition generally, about theurgy applies, *mutatis mutandis*, to the Qur'ān, as Uždavinys notes; see ibid., 81. See also the remarkable observations by Uždavinys on the theurgic power of the Qur'ān and of the Torah in his comparative work, *Ascent to Heaven: In Islamic and Jewish Mysticism* (London: The Matheson Trust, 2011), 69–74; 138–140.

674 Titus Burckhardt, *Art of Islam*, 83.

of words. Liquid and flowing like a stream, it carries us into the Presence of God.'[675] This in turn might be seen as a comment on the saying of the Prophet: amongst the greatest of the beauties of creation is 'the fine intonation of a beautiful voice (*naghmata'l-ṣawt al-ḥasan*).'[676] Such statements help us to understand that the melodic recitation of the Qur'ān can be seen as an intrinsic dimension of Islamic 'art,' both in itself and in its effects: generating that sense of profound peace, harmony and happiness which is a crucial component of aesthetic sensibility and artistic creativity. This joyous state of soul does not exclude, but rather is deepened by, extreme sobriety and lucidity. As Burckhardt writes: 'The diapason of the Qur'ān never fails to join intoxicating nostalgia to extreme sobriety: it is a radiation of the divine Sun on the human desert.' He rightly stresses that the state of inner harmony brought into being by the recitation of the Qur'ān 'is situated on quite another plane than, for example, perfect poetry... it is both comforting and purifying, like a rainstorm. Purely human art does not possess this virtue.'[677]

This underlines the importance of the relationship between the creativity of the Muslim artist and the witnessing of Divine unity. For the artist in Islam is, first and foremost, one who witnesses the evidence of God's oneness and beauty in the 'handiwork,' the *ṣun'* of God, a term used in verse 27:88, which allows us to refer to God as *al-Ṣāni'*, literally, 'The Artisan.' Moses is 'fashioned' by God for God's own Self, we are told, in verse 41 of the Sūra Ṭā Hā (no.20) (*wa'ṣtana'tuka li-nafsī*). This means that every Messenger of God is a supreme work of art produced by *al-Ṣāni'*. Here, it should be stressed that contemplative affinity for the unitive (*tawḥīdī*) dimension of divine beauty lies at the basis of all true artistic creativity. For without a sense of the unique—the one and only—source of creation, there can be no intuition of the ontological root of the harmony embedded in creation, and thus no sense in which the sap flowing from this root penetrates and unites the whole of creation; and without this intuition of the unitive source of the harmony of the created order, there can be no sense of the beauty of God's creation—still less, any possibility of producing, oneself, a work of art which conforms to the divine archetypes or principles of beauty. Only this kind of art, reflecting the work of the divine 'Artisan,' can be called art in the strict sense. The modern tenet, 'art for the sake of art' is to be rejected in favour of the principle: 'art for the sake of the divine Artisan.' Art is therefore true to itself in proportion to its degree of conformity with principles that transcend the human order and are directly related to the divine nature. It is thus objective and is not to be seen as the handmaiden of subjective whims, tastes, and passions. In other words, true art has nothing

675 Martin Lings, *A Sufi Saint*, 115.
676 See for discussion, *Spiritual Quest*, 7.
677 Titus Burckhardt, *Art of Islam*, 46.

to do with the subjectivist reductionism expressed by that other shibboleth of modern art: 'beauty is in the eye of the beholder.'[678]

Let us note also, in passing, that in the Islamic spiritual tradition, this appreciation of the Word of God revealed through scripture is universal. It is not confined to the Qur'ān alone. Several verses of the Qur'ān itself attest to this universality of revelation,[679] but suffice to quote here the vision of one totally attuned to this Qur'anic universality, Rūzbihān Baqlī (d. 606/1209), about whose doctrines we shall hear more presently: he writes that he was given a vision of all of the prophets, and that 'Moses made me taste the Torah, Jesus made me taste the Gospels, David made me taste the Psalms and Muḥammad made me taste the Qur'ān.'[680]

We should constantly bear in mind the importance of this idea of 'tasting,' especially when we turn to certain aspects of contemplation articulated in the Qur'ān. For these doctrines and perspectives call out to be 'tasted'—that is, intuited in a concrete manner, not merely thought about in the abstract—failing which the aesthetic dimension of the Qur'ān will be lost on us. We observe in the Qur'ān that the mode of *tawḥīd* just described—the conjunction of human love and Divine beauty—is rendered quite explicit. For the fundamental message which the Qur'ān imparts to us concerning the intrinsic nature of reality is articulated in terms of the names and qualities of God—all of which are described not only as beautiful, but as 'most beautiful.' All of these names and qualities can be grasped metaphysically as aspects of Being. But Being itself is qualified, as a totality, in terms of beauty, *ḥusn*. Some of the names of God are wrathful and fierce—such as *al-Qahhār*, the All-Conquering, and *al-Muntaqim*, the Avenger—while others are gentle and loving—such as *al-Laṭīf*, the Loving-Kind, and *al-Raḥmān*, the infinitely Compassionate. Nonetheless, their categorical definition is given in terms of beauty. They are *al-asmā' al-ḥusnā*: 'the Most Beautiful Names.'

'Abd al-Karīm al-Jīlī (d. 832/1428), a renowned authority in the school of Ibn al-'Arabī, asserts that there is in truth nothing in being except beauty. For the whole of creation is constituted by the theophanic manifestation (*tajallī*) of the divine Names and Qualities. Since these are all beautiful, everything in creation is beautiful. From this point of view, ugliness (*al-qubḥ*) does not cease to be ugly. Rather, it is seen as that which distorts or corrupts a pre-existing

678 Although this saying, understood in Platonic terms, expresses an undeniable truth: only that 'eye' in which beauty already resides will be able to 'see' beauty, just as according to Plato it is only that 'eye' which is already luminous that can see light. See for discussion my 'Divine Beatitude: Supreme Archetype of Aesthetic Experience,' in Barry McDonald (ed.), *Seeing God Everywhere: Essays on Nature and the Sacred* (Bloomington: World Wisdom Books, 2003).

679 See for discussion my The Other in the Light of the One: The Universality of the Qur'an and Interfaith Dialogue (Cambridge: Islamic Texts Society, 2006).

680 Cited by Henry Corbin, En Islam iranien: Aspects spirituels et philosophiques (Paris: Editions Gallimard, 1972), vol.3, p. 46.

beauty: it is beauty which, alone, has an ontological essence, or archetype, rooted in true Being, which is divine Reality—thus it is beauty which is real, as it is a manifestation of the Real; whilst ugliness is unreal, inasmuch as it does not possess an ontological essence, it has no root in true Being. 'Ugliness cannot be found in the cosmos except by way of relationship [with what can be found, namely, beauty], so that which is ugly has no property of absoluteness (or non-delimitation, *iṭlāq*). Nothing then remains in being except absolute (or non-delimited) beauty (*al-ḥusn al-muṭlaq*).'[681] The principle here in question is graphically illustrated by the following image in the Qur'ān:

He sends down water from the sky, so that valleys flow according to their measure, and the flood carries scum on its surface—such as also arises from that metal they smelt in fire to make ornaments and tools; thus does God strike [similitudes for the sake of distinguishing] the true and the false (*al-ḥaqq wa al-bāṭil*). As for the scum, it passes away as dross; but that which is of benefit to mankind, it abides on earth. Thus does God strike similitudes (13:17).

Just as one does not confuse the scum for the water, so one does not confuse the ugly for the beautiful, or the true for the false. The scum is, as it were, generated by the water from which it is inseparable, and from which it derives its very substance; but, as a disfiguration of that substance, it will 'pass away.' The water—and, in this similitude, the ornaments and tools—remains; this symbolises the beauty of Reality, which is eternal; in contrast, that which disfigures it, and which is like scum on its surface—ugliness—is doomed to transience. The verse immediately following this description of the scum brings home the relationship of this similitude to the reality of beauty: 'For those who answered God's call is that which is most beautiful (*ḥusnā*)... (13:18).'[682] We are given essentially the same message in this passage:

The similitude of the life of the world is only as water which We send down from the sky, then the earth's growth of that which men and cattle eat mingles with it till, when the earth has taken on her ornaments and is embellished, and her people deem that they are her masters, Our commandment comes by night or by day, and We make it as reaped corn as if it had not flourished yesterday. Thus do We expound the revelations for people who reflect. And God summons to the abode of peace, and guides whom He will to a straight path. *For those who make beautiful is that which is most beautiful,* and yet more. Neither dust nor ignominy blights their faces. Such are rightful owners of the Garden; they will abide therein (10:24–26; emphasis added).

---

681 *Al-Insān al-kāmil* (Cairo: al-Maktaba al-Tawfīqiyya, n.d.), p. 101.

682 The word, *ḥusnā*, in certain contexts means Paradise, as discussed below. It is interesting to note that, in his translation, Muhammad Asad joins the end of verse 17 to the beginning of verse 18, so that the similitude or parable in question is all about 'those who answered God's call.' His translation reads as follows: '... In this way does God set forth the parables of [i.e., describing] those who have responded to their Sustainer [i.e., Lord, *Rabb*] with a goodly response.'

To say, then, that God alone subsists, all ugliness being ephemeral, is to say that beauty is alone real, and ugliness does not truly exist. 'Wherever you turn, there is the Face of God' (2:115): the Face of God is infinite Beauty, so even in the face of apparent ugliness, this Face is the abiding reality. In this light, the following verses should be meditated upon as expressions of the inspiring principle—at once metaphysical and aesthetic—that beauty is alone real or true (*ḥaqq*), and ugliness is unreal (*bāṭil*):

- Everything on earth is vanishing (*fān*); and there abides (*yabqā*) only the Face of your Lord, owner of Majesty and Honour (55:26–27).
- Everything is perishing (*hālik*) except His Face (28:88).
- Say: the Truth (*al-Ḥaqq*) has come and falsehood (*al-bāṭil*) has passed away; indeed falsehood is ever passing away (17:81).

The manifestation of beauty is therefore the manifestation of a reality which is eternal, being rooted in the eternity of the infinitely beautiful 'Face' of God. By contrast, the appearance of ugliness is the transient 'scum' on the face of beauty: it is governed by that nothingness to which it is doomed, and which it therefore *is:* ugliness is nothing, even when it appears to exist—such is the metaphysical import of Jīlī's assertion that ugliness does not really exist, and that there is 'nothing in being except absolute beauty (*al-ḥusn al-muṭlaq*).' The relative phenomena manifesting beauty may themselves pass out of being *qua* phenomena; but the principle they manifest is absolute, or nondelimited, this principle being the very Face of God, eternally real, infinitely beautiful. To spiritually perceive this Face of God through all phenomena is to have what Schuon aptly refers to as the sense of the 'metaphysical transparency of phenomena.'[683] That is, to see through phenomena to the archetypes which they manifest; these celestial archetypes are nothing other than configurations of divine qualities, hence, so many aspects or expressions of the Face of God. To see the archetypes through phenomena is thus to see the Face of God wherever one turns. In the following verse, these celestial archetypes are referred to as paradisal 'fruits': 'Each time they [the people of Paradise] are given to eat from its fruits, they say: "This is what we were given to eat before." And they were given the like thereof' (2:25). All positive phenomena on earth are therefore at once projections and prefigurations of heavenly archetypes; while all negative phenomena are corruptions or negations of the archetypes, thus negations of divine reality; they are, by 'ontological definition,' non-existent.

683 Commenting on the ḥadīth 'God is beautiful and He loves beauty,' Schuon writes: 'this is the doctrine of the metaphysical transparency of phenomena. This notion of beauty or harmony, with all the subtle rhythms and symmetries which it implies, has in Islam the widest possible significance: "to God belong the most beautiful Names," says the Qur'an more than once, and the virtues are called "beautiful things."' *Dimensions of Islam*, trans. Peter Townsend (London: George Allen & Unwin, 1969), p. 129.

So, when it is said in the Qur'ān (5:54), that 'God loves them'—His creatures—this means, according to Abū Ḥamid al-Ghazālī (d. 505 /1111) in his book on love in the *Iḥyā' 'ulūm al-dīn*, that He loves only Himself. In other words, He loves nothing other than the theophanies of His own beauty, for 'there is nothing in being except His Essence and His acts ... so in reality He loves nothing other than Himself, in the sense that He is the totality [of being], and there is nothing in being apart from Him.'[684] To the extent that we see the creation through the vision of God—a possibility we discuss below—the whole of creation will be seen as beautiful. In this light one can understand better the meaning of the verse: 'He made beautiful everything He created (*aḥsana kulla shay'in khalaqahu*)' (32: 7).

Iḥsān: Making beautiful

If God loves what is beautiful, and He has made beautiful everything He created, it follows that the definitive aspect of God's relationship with His creatures is love of beauty.[685] 'I was a hidden treasure,' we are told in a Divine utterance much commented upon in the Sufi tradition, 'so I created the world.' The treasure, *kanz*, is a treasure on account of its priceless beauty. It is this hidden, inner beauty—His own absolute, infinite perfection—which God *loved*, not just wished or desired, to render 'known,' He loved to make this beauty known to 'another.' This apparent 'other' is the human being, *al-insān*, a word which means not only man, in a non-gender-specific sense, but also 'pupil of the eye,' as Ibn al-'Arabī stresses in the first chapter of his *Fuṣūṣ al-ḥikam*,[686] addressing the wisdom of Adam, a chapter to which we shall return below.

It is interesting to note here that, although the divine utterance pertaining to the 'hidden treasure' is not considered sound by the scholars of Ḥadīth in terms of its chain of transmission (*isnād*), its meaning is nonetheless accepted by most of these same scholars, as it is completely in accordance with this verse of the Qur'ān: 'I only created the Jinn and mankind in order that they might worship Me' (51:56). The standard interpretation of the phrase 'that they might worship Me' is 'that they might know Me':[687] coming to know God—fulfilling the purpose of creation—is the fruit of worship; the combination of knowledge and worship is a mode of contemplation; and this contemplation is nothing other than the human heart gazing lovingly at the beauty

684 Al-Ghazzālī cites the saying of Shaykh Sa'īd al-Mayhinī here. *Iḥyā' 'ulūm al-dīn* (Beirut: Dār al-Jīl, 1992), book 6, part 4, vol. 5, p. 221. See the forthcoming translation of the book of love by Eric Ormsby.

685 See the pioneering work of Prince Ghazi bin Muhammad, *Love in the Holy Qur'an* (Chicago: Kazi Publications, 2012).

686 See Caner Dagli, *The Ringstones of Wisdom*—Fuṣūṣ al-ḥikam (Chicago: Kazi Publications, 2004), p. 6.

687 Many exoteric scholars cite this interpretation, on the authority of Ibn 'Abbās. See, for example, Fakhr al-Dīn al-Rāzī, who cites the saying of the 'hidden treasure' at the end of his commentary on 51:56. *Tafsīr al-kabīr* (Beirut: Dār Iḥyā' al-Turāth al-'Arabī, 2001), vol. 10, p. 194.

of God—or at that aspect of the 'hidden treasure' which can be made known through divine Self-disclosure.

It is man, alone who can 'see' in all its fullness the manifestation of the Divine beauty, for man, alone, is made in the very image of that Beauty: 'Truly God made Adam according to His own image,'[688] the Prophet tells us, in a saying echoing the words of Genesis, 1:27. The very means by which we as human beings come to *know* God, therefore, is inextricably tied to the process by which we come to *love* God; that is, to engage in the loving contemplation of Divine beauty, and to conform ourselves totally to that beauty. We cannot love God without acquiring knowledge of Him, and conversely, we cannot know God without, as it were, falling in love with Him.

Let us approach this theme from another angle by focusing a little on the root of the word, *aḥsana*. The notions of goodness and beauty are inextricably intertwined in this root, *ḥā/sīn/nūn*. The verb *ḥasuna* means to be good, fine, excellent, fair, beautiful; when the Qur'ān speaks of one who 'believes in *al-ḥusnā*' (92:6), 'the most beautiful,' we are told by the commentators that the reference here is to the paradisal Garden;[689] and the crucial term, *iḥsān*, often weakly translated into English as 'kindness' or simply 'doing good,' should be translated as 'making beautiful.'[690] The cluster of ideas around this key principle thus comes to include beauty, virtue, excellence, and Paradise, the latter being intuited as the inherent substance of beauty and the fruit of goodness, as noted above: 'Each time they [the people of Paradise] are given to eat from its fruits, they say: "This is what we were given to eat before." And they were given the like thereof' (2:25).

This understanding of *iḥsān* radically transforms our perception of the import of the hundreds of verses in which the root of this word appears in the Qur'ān, particularly as regards the description of the *muḥsinūn*, who can be understood as those who are virtuous, being those who 'do what is beautiful,' and those whose virtues evoke the perfumes of Paradise. The *muḥsin*, therefore, is a person whose virtue has a radiance at once celestial and 'aesthetic.' In other words, the *muḥsin* is a kind of 'artist,' his own soul being his work of art. As Ananda Coomaraswamy puts it: 'The artist is not a special kind of person, but every man is a special kind of artist.'[691]

---

688 This saying is found in various collections; for example, the *Ṣaḥīḥ* of Muslim, vol.2, p. 1108, no.6821; and Ibn Ḥanbal's *Musnad*, vol.3, p.1544, no.7441. Both references are to the edition of *Encyclopaedia of Ḥadīth*, op. cit.

689 According to Ibn Manẓūr's classical Arabic lexicon, *Lisān al-'Arab* (Cairo: Dār al-Ma'ārif, n.d.), p. 877.

690 See the excellent discussion by Sachiko Murata and William Chittick in their introduction to Islam, *The Vision of Islam* (State University of New York, 1994), pp. xxxii, 267–273.

691 See Brian Keeble's fine collection of essays inspired by this saying, *Every Man an Artist: Readings in the Traditional Philosophy of Art* (Bloomington: World Wisdom Books, 2005).

In the Islamic ethical tradition, good and evil are simply described in terms of the polarity *ḥusn wa qubḥ*, beauty and ugliness. It could then be said that aesthetics is the heart of ethics in Islam; and aesthetics, in turn, is both a key to understanding metaphysics, while being itself a fundamental expression of the principle of *tawḥīd.* The key link binding together the domains of ethics, aesthetics and metaphysics is given in the prophetic definition of *iḥsān*. This comes in the famous answer to one of the questions posed by Gabriel to the Prophet. The latter informed us that Gabriel came 'to teach you your religion,' by means of these questions and their answers.

According to this narrative, Gabriel, in the form of a man, asked the Prophet what is *islām*, what is *īmān*, and what is *iḥsān*. To the first question, the Prophet replied with mention of the five pillars: what one must do, in terms of the Law, in order to enter the formal religion is to make the double testimony, observe the daily prayers, fast during the month of Ramadan, pay one's alms-tax (*zakāt*), and to perform the Hajj. To the second, pertaining to faith, *īmān*, his reply focused on what one must believe, in terms of doctrine: God, His angels, His scriptures, His prophets, and the divine fore-ordainment of all things. In response to the third question, what is *iḥsān*, the Prophet appeared to repeat what he had already mentioned, for the answer is all about worship—and the prayer, *al-ṣalāt*, had already been mentioned. But the worship in question here, in relation to *iḥsān*, is of a more all-encompassing nature: '*Al-iḥsān*,' he replied, 'is that you should worship God as if you could see Him, and if you see Him not, He nonetheless sees you.'[692] Permanent, contemplative awareness of God is the very core and summit of *iḥsān*, or 'making beautiful.' It is from consciousness of the divine source of Beauty that one becomes *muḥsin*, understanding the *muḥsin* not just as one who does good outwardly, but one who 'makes beautiful,' inwardly: virtue being grasped here as inward beauty, and beauty as outward virtue, in the felicitous formulation of Frithjof Schuon.[693]

Imam 'Alī helps us to see the way in which the two synonymous terms for beauty, *ḥusn* and *jamāl*, intertwine, doing so in a remarkably revealing statement about the 'aesthetic' dimension of the intellect. He tells us that the beauty or excellence (*ḥusn*) of the intellect lies in its capacity to see the beauty (*jamāl*) of things both outwardly apparent and inwardly hidden (*ḥusn al-'aql jamāl al-ẓawāhir wa'l-bawāṭin*).[694] He likewise stresses the role of love in the process by which the intellect comes to fruition: 'The beginning of [the actualisation of] the intellect is the manifestation and assimilation of love (*awwal al-'aql al-tawaddud*).'[695]

692 See for the full text in English and Arabic, *ḥadīth* no.2 of *An-Nawawī's Forty Hadith*, tr. E. Ibrahim and D. Johnson-Davies (Damascus, 1976), pp. 28–33 (our translation is slightly modified).

693 *Esoterism as Principle and as Way*, op. cit., p. 239.

694 See *Justice and Remembrance*, op. cit., p. 47, for discussion.

695 Ibid, pp. 47–48.

Returning to the Ḥadīth Jibrīl, it is important to note that the angel did not ask: what is *tawḥīd?* We might suggest, somewhat speculatively, that this is because all three answers, integrated as one, themselves constitute an implicit answer. The key element by which the acts manifesting *islām*, and the beliefs comprised within *īmān* are calibrated and deepened is *iḥsān*, a mode of intrinsic being, as opposed to outward action and formal thought. For, to the extent that worship encompasses one's whole life, one's innermost being will be perpetually inspired by consciousness of God—by 'seeing God'; and this unification of being and consciousness is the perfect reflection, on the human plane, of Divine unity. Hence we find Imam 'Alī telling us: 'He who knows God integrates himself (*man 'arafa'Llāha tawaḥḥada*).'[696] As regards the idea of worshipping God as if one could see Him, it is important to grasp this not only as a possibility but also as an actuality: for, the Prophet claimed: 'I saw my Lord in the most beautiful form (*ra'aytu Rabbī fī aḥsani ṣūratin*).'[697] This vision of God can also be understood as a witnessing of the Divine 'Face,' that Face by which one is always confronted, wherever one may look—as noted above (2:115)

Through the Prophet, we are invited to participate in this adoration that is rooted in spiritual vision, and we do so chiefly by means of the devotions prescribed to us by God. It is this which explains why it is that God says, in a famous *ḥadīth qudsī*, that He loves nothing *more* than the legal prescriptions of worship He has ordained: 'My servant draws close to Me by nothing which I love more than that which I have made incumbent upon him.'[698] We shall look at the second part of this utterance below. But here we wish to stress the implication of this first part: If God loves nothing more than the legal obligations, the *farā'iḍ* of Islam, this can only mean that these obligations are intrinsically beautiful. We appreciate the beauty of these legal obligations found in the Qur'an—bearing witness to God and His messenger; praying; fasting; paying the *zakāt*; performing the Hajj—when we focus on the cornerstone of these obligations: prayer, the substance of which is derived from the Qur'anic revelation.[699] We thus return to the invitation to engage in loving communion, to gaze upon God as our Beloved, as if we could see Him. In this light, the

696 Ibid, p. 42. Cf. the acute observation by James Morris, which resonates deeply with the idea of self-integration through knowledge of divine beauty: 'inspired awareness of divine Beauty ... must be transformed through spiritual seeing and inspired insight into our uniquely personal, creative manifestations of right and beautiful action (*iḥsān*)—that active culmination of spiritual life eventually leading on to the realization of the beatific Vision of God.' *The Reflective Heart: Discovering Spiritual Intelligence in Ibn 'Arabī's Meccan Illuminations* (Louisville: Fons Vitae, 2005), p. 7.

697 *Sunan al-Tirmidhī*, vol. 2, pp. 87–88, saying no.3043; in *Encyclopaedia of Hadith*, op. cit.

698 *Ṣaḥīḥ al-Bukhārī* (Summarised) trans. M. M. Khan (Riyadh: Maktaba Dar-us-Salam, 1994), p. 992, no. 2117 (translation modified).

699 It should be noted that the foremost thing made obligatory for the Prophet, and by extension all Muslims, is the Qur'an itself: 'He who made the Qur'an incumbent upon you, He will bring you back [to Him]' (28:85).

movements of the prayer are transformed into a dance to the Beloved, and the words recited during prayer, a song to the Beloved.[700] The daily prayer is thus far from mere lip-service and mechanical obedience to a set of arbitrary rules dictated by the inscrutable will of an inaccessibly remote Deity. Rather, it is an inseparable part of that 'alchemy of worship' by which the soul is itself fashioned as a work of art by the divine Artisan, *al-Ṣāniʿ*.[701]

The Prophet as *Ḥabīb Allāh*

The Prophet was the perfect lover of God, seeing the divine beauty through all the veils of existence. As mentioned above, he said: 'I saw my Lord in the most beautiful form.'[702] We would venture the opinion that no mystic has given a more inspiring commentary on this saying, combining the mysteries of *tawḥīd* with those of aesthetics, than Rūzbihān Baqlī. In one of the many places throughout his corpus where he cites and comments on this saying, we read the following. This is from his most famous work in the domain of what one might call 'the metaphysics of aesthetics,' *'Abhar al-'āshiqīn* ('Jasmin of the Lovers'), written in Persian. He is speaking about 'principial beauty (*ḥusn-i aṣlī*)' or that beauty which pertains to the 'root' of reality, as expressed by the Prophet, described by Rūzbihān as 'the Revealer of the religious Law and the Founder of the mystical Path':

He speaks from the state disclosing the meaning of *iltibās*,[703] unveiling it as pure love, and showing that the mystery of the Real (*sirr-i Ḥaqq*) is in the self-disclosing theophany of beauty (*tajallī-yi ḥusn*). The souls of the lovers perceive in the beauty of primordial human nature (*ḥusn-i fiṭrī*) the reflection of eternal beauty, finding in this symbol the key to the science which was [hitherto] unknown. The Prophet said: 'I saw my Lord in the most beautiful form.'[704]

As we shall see further below, this vision of the beauty of God is directly and inextricably related to aesthetics as well as ethics in the prophetic paradigm.

---

700 See our essay, 'The Metaphysics of Oneness and the Consummation of Love in Islamic Mysticism,' in *Jewish, Christian and Islamic Perspectives on the Love of God*, ed. Sheelah Trefle-Hidden (New York, 2014), pp.73–102.

701 'Man prays and prayer fashions man. The saint has himself become prayer, the meeting-place of earth and Heaven; he thereby contains the universe, and the universe prays with him. He is everywhere where nature prays, and he prays with her and in her: in the peaks, which touch the void and eternity; in a flower, which scatters its scent; in the carefree song of a bird. He who lives in prayer has not lived in vain.' Frithjof Schuon, *Spiritual Perspectives and Human Facts*, ed. James S. Cutsinger (Bloomington: World Wisdom Books, 2007, p. 228.

702 *Sunan al-Tirmidhī*, vol. 2, pp. 87–88, saying no.3043; in *Encyclopaedia of Hadith*, op. cit.

703 This key term in Rūzbihān's mystical lexicon can be translated as 'enrobement,' that is, the enrobing of creaturely form by divine beauty. Corbin translates it into French as 'amphibolie'; see his illuminating exposition of this concept in *En Islam iranien*, op. cit., pp. 57 ff. See below, the section entitled 'Sanctity and Creativity,' for further discussion of *iltibās*.

704 Rūzbihān Baqlī, *'Abhar al-'āshiqīn* , eds. Henry Corbin and Muḥammad Mu'īn (Tehran: Intishārāt-i Manūchehrī, 1383 Sh./2004), p. 31. See Corbin's magisterial elucidation of Rūzbihān's perspective in *En Islam iranien*: op. cit., 'Rūzbihān Baqlī Shīrāzī et le Soufisme des Fidèles d'Amour,' pp. 9–146.

But before proceeding with this line of inquiry, it would be helpful to continue with Rūzbihān's perspective on the relationship between beauty and love in relation to the Prophet. The following comes from the introduction to another work by Rūzbihān, written in Arabic, *Lawāmiʿ al-tawḥīd* ('Flashes of *tawḥīd*'):

God disclosed to the Prophet the lights of contemplation, bringing him into proximity to Him, by Him, from Him; causing him to be brought into the divine Presence. He lifted the veil of His divinity (*ilāhiyatihi*) for him, causing him to hear the harmonious sounds of union (*aṣwāt al-wuṣla*)... He extinguished him from himself, then gave him to taste the sweetness of the wine of hope from the cup of expansiveness, and then made him intimate with the fragrance of the rose of purity. He bestowed upon him the robe of subsistence (*qabā' al-baqā'*); coronated him with the crown of spiritual knowledge (*tāj al-maʿrifa*); invested him with the adornment of love (*ḥilyat al-maḥabba*); served him the wine of passionate desire (*sharāb al-shawq*); and caused him to rejoice in the delights of love (*ladhā'idh al-ʿishq*). He seated him on the carpet of joyous exaltation (*bisāṭ al-inbisāṭ*); whelmed him with the lights of the divine qualities; and showed him the beauty of the majesty of the Essence (*arāhu jamāla jalāli'l-Dhāt*).[705]

The last part of this remarkable passage is of particular importance. For it is one thing to be made to see the beauty of God, and it is this vision which makes one, to whatever degree, participate in the love of God perfectly consummated in *Ḥabīb Allāh*; it is quite another to be rendered capable of witnessing the beauty of the *majesty* of God. For this majestic aspect of God relates to the transcendent dimension of the divine nature, and thus reduces all manifestation to nothing. In his chapter on *Jalāl* in *Al-Insān al-Kāmil* (ch. 24), 'Abd al-Karīm Jīlī gives a list of the Names of Majesty (*al-asmā' al-jalāliyya*) which includes the following: a*l-Qābiḍ* (He who contracts), *al-Mumīt* (the Slayer), *al-Wārith* (the Inheritor). In the words of Martin Lings:

Just as the Divine Beauty, being the Archetype of expansion, presides over all outward manifestation, the Divine Majesty presides over the inverse process of contraction, that is, of the reabsorption of all created things in the Essence ... The Divine Beauty displays the world as symbol of God, whereas the Divine Majesty reveals the limitations of the world inasmuch as it is *merely* a symbol [emphasis added] ... It is in this sense that all imperfections, all decay, all sufferings, all evils, which are simply phases of a gradual demonstration that 'there is no he but He,' may be said to come from the Majesty.[706]

In order to integrate even the grievous aspects of existence within the quality of divine beauty and gentleness requires the vision proper to *Ḥabīb Allāh*, the Beloved of God, whose love is such that he sees the beauty of the Beloved

705 *Lawāmiʿ al-tawḥid*, pp. 92–93. See, for a French translation of this important work, Paul Ballanfat, 'Les eclosions etc..... in L'Ennuagement ...

706 *A Sufi Saint*, op. cit., pp. 142–143.

even under the aspect of severity, a vision that is difficult to conceive of, let alone realize. It is, however, precisely the Prophet's vision of the all-encompassing nature of the divine beauty and love that explains why it is that al-Ghazālī, in his commentary on the Divine Names, *al-Maqṣad al-asnā*, gives the following incident as an illustration of the meaning of the Divine Name, *al-Wadūd*, 'The Loving': 'The Messenger of God said, when his teeth were broken and his beard was smeared with blood, "Lord, guide my people, for they do not know."'[707]

Al-Ghazālī's juxtaposition of the divine quality of love with this merciful reaction of the Prophet to injury and insult allows us to understand the love of God as an *infinite* principle, that is, a principle which is not limited or conditional, but which flows forth from the divine nature eternally, perfectly and beautifully. We may come to experience something other than beauty and love on earth, but we have the capacity to transform any outward trial into a demonstration of the all-encompassing nature of divine love if, like the Prophet, our spiritual reaction to the trial is 'beautiful.' The particular illustration of this principle—having a beautiful reaction to adversity—is here a prayer for those inflicting the adversity. But the principle is not restricted to this one kind of reaction. The Prophet transformed an outwardly negative situation—his being grievously wounded by his own people—into an eminently positive one: an occasion for reflecting the infinite love of God as *al-Wadūd* through his own unconditional compassion.[708] This principle, at once 'Muhammadan' and 'Christic,' or *'Īsawī*—'Father, forgive them, for they know not what they do' (Luke, 23:34)—was also expressed by Ḥusayn b. Manṣūr al-Ḥallāj (d. 309/922), who prayed that his killers be not only forgiven, but also rewarded.[709]

The key principle here is not simply *ṣabr*, patient fortitude in the face of adversity, it is what Jacob refers to in the Qur'ān as 'beautiful' (*ṣabrun jamīl*) (12:18), the kind of patience which qualifies those who manifest the 'beautiful withdrawal,' from mockers and persecutors, such as is referred to in the Sūrat al-Muzzammil (73:10). It is also the kind of patience that allows one to see

---

707 *Allāhumma'hdi qawmī fa-innahum lā ya'lamūn.* Al-Ghazālī, *Al-Maqṣad al-asnā fī sharḥ asmā' Allāh al-ḥusnā* (Arabic text), ed. Fadlou A. Shehadi (Beirut: Dar El-Machreq, 1971), p. 119. See the English translation, *The Ninety-Nine Beautiful Names of God (al-Maqṣad al-asnā fī sharḥ asmā' Allāh al-ḥusnā)* (tr. David B. Burrell, N. Daher) (Cambridge: Islamic Texts Society, 1999), p. 119.

708 'To accept a trial,' writes Frithjof Schuon, liberates us from bitterness; if it does not do so, this means that our acceptance is not sufficient.' He continues: 'To accept a trial is to thank God for it, with the understanding that it permits us a victory: a detachment with relation to the world and with relation to the ego, which imprisons us therein. To let oneself be overcome by resentment is "hypocrisy," for it amounts to not accepting the appeasing [peace-giving] Truth of God, save on condition that so-and-so behave well; now without appeasement, there is no sincerity of faith.' Unpublished text.

709 See Louis Massignon, *La Passion de Husayn ibn Mansûr Hallâj* (Paris: Gallimard, 1975), vol. 1, p. 332; and our forthcoming book, *Muslim Perspectives on Christian Mysteries: Trinity, Incarnation, Crucifixion* (Green Knight Multimedia, 2021).

beauty even in the midst of the most appalling trial: 'I saw nothing but beauty (*wa mā ra'aytu illā jamīlan*),' said Hazrat Zaynab,[710] sister of Imam Ḥusayn, in her passionate speech denouncing the murderers of her brother and the martyrs of Karbalā'. Despite the outward appearance of suffering, the inner reality of their sacrifice was pure beauty: they were bearing witness not just to the reality of God and the Afterlife, but also to the infinite beauty of that reality to which they were testifying with their life-blood. Only a metaphysical vision of beauty allows us to comprehend this permanent capacity to view the beauty of God under all circumstances. It is a vision in which beauty and majesty come together in perfection: *jamāl* and *jalāl* are synthesised within *kamāl*. What is in question here is a beauty transcending the conventional aesthetic distinction between beauty and ugliness, and the equally conventional theological distinction between divine mercy and divine vengeance. Imam 'Alī alludes to this transcendent beauty in the following enigmatic statement: God is described as being 'He whose vengeance against His enemies is intense in the very vastness of His mercy; and whose mercy towards His friends is vast in the very intensity of His vengeance.'[711]

In this statement, the 'friends' of God—that is, the saints—are those who are never blinded from the 'vastness' of divine mercy, even when witnessing the 'intensity' of divine vengeance or retribution. This 'retribution' can be understood in ontological rather than moral terms, that is, as a description of the process by which the inevitable disequilibria of phenomenal existence are brought into harmony with the immutable equilibrium of the essence of Being. The ineluctable return of all things to God entails two processes, one which is empirically destructive, the other metaphysically constructive. First, in the process of return, phenomena are destroyed, or more precisely, the return to God entails the destruction of whatever is 'other than God' within phenomena. This process—morally and theologically termed 'vengeance'—derives from the metaphysical 'enactment' of the divine quality of 'majesty' *al-Jalāl*. Second, in the process of return, phenomena are reintegrated; or, more precisely: the return to God entails the reintegration within Reality of the element of divinity—or metaphysical beauty—by which phenomena, all phenomena, subsist. This process—morally and theologically termed 'mercy'—derives from the metaphysical 'enactment' of the divine quality of 'beauty,' *al-Jamāl*.

Understanding the Prophet as both *Ḥabīb Allāh*, and *'Abd Allāh* helps us to observe some deeper aspects of the traditional invocation of blessing upon

710 Cited in 'Abd Allāh Jawādī Āmulī, *Ḥamāsah wa 'irfān* (Qum: Isra Publication Centre, 1378 Sh./1999), p. 256. Imam Ḥusayn himself is reported as having said, prior to his martyrdom: 'Let the believers yearn for the meeting with his Lord in truth; for I see in death nothing but felicity (*sa'āda*).' In similar vein, Imam 'Alī, some twenty years earlier, when hearing of the name of Karbala as he and his troops were marching past it, said: this is the plain of the lovers and the witnesses (*'ushshāq* and *shuhadā'*). Cited in ibid, pp. 267, 229.

711 *Nahj al-Balāgha*, ed. Muḥammad 'Abduh (Beirut: Maktabat al-Ma'ārif, 1996), sermon 88, p. 235.

the Prophet, *al-ṣalāt ʿalāʾl-Nabī*. Grasping the Prophet as the Beloved of God also helps us to appreciate more fully why the Prophet plays such a fundamental role in all the Islamic arts, and particularly, in the Ottoman calligraphic art of the inscription of his *ḥilya*,[712] or ornamental description, and what is known more generally as the *shamāʾil* literature, depicting his beautiful qualities.[713] If God loves beauty, according to our opening *ḥadīth*, then the Prophet, as the Beloved of God, must be beautiful; to invoke blessings upon the Prophet is therefore to invoke blessings—along with God and His angels—upon this perfect manifestation of beauty; to invoke this beauty is, potentially or actually, to receive oneself a tenfold blessing, according to the Prophet himself—a blessing which opens one up to the inward assimilation of that beauty: beauty of character, first and foremost, but also beauty as such. In turn, beauty as such is at one with reality, so here, again, the crucial link between the cultivation of beauty and the realization of *tawḥīd* is affirmed. To assimilate beauty—to become inwardly beautiful oneself—is, by definition and inescapably, to become, oneself, beloved of God: for God loves beauty. It is thus that emulating the Prophet as a 'beautiful role-model,' an *uswa ḥasana*, renders us lovable unto God, and this is given in the crucial verse, already noted above, as the very goal that motivates us, or ought to motivate us, as followers of the Prophet: 'If you love God,' the Prophet is told to say to us in the Qurʾān, 'follow me: God will love you' (3:31).

Sanctity and Creativity

This process by which sanctity, or *walāya*, is realized can be seen as the archetype of the artist's self-effacement before the Divine creativity, when truly sacred art emerges through the hands of the artist. For Rūzbihān Baqlī, this effacement is presupposed by what he calls 'vision of the vision': *ʿīyān al-ʿīyān*. This vision pertains to the highest degrees of *tawḥīd*, which in turn is founded upon deciphering the cosmic phenomena, understood by Rūzbihān as so many modes of *iltibās*, 'enrobing.' Within each phenomenon one must discern the beauty of the Divine Self-disclosure, and, as it were, disrobe it of its creaturely limitations. This is what we might call his 'aesthetic' key which unlocks the mysteries of esoteric *tawḥīd*.

The true *muwaḥḥid* not only sees God, he sees his own vision as being the vision of God. This is one of the most profound meanings of witnessing, *shahāda*, and it helps us to appreciate the totality of self-effacement that

712 See Mohamed Zakariyya, 'The Hilye of the Prophet Muhammad,' in *Seasons—Semiannual Journal of the Zaytuna Institute*, vol. 1, no. 2, 2003–2004, pp. 13–22.

713 See Annemarie Schimmel's excellent overview of this literature, taking in the length and breadth of the Muslim world, from the earliest period to our own day, *And Muhammad is His Messenger: The Veneration of the Prophet in Islamic Piety* (Chapel Hill & London: The University of North Carolina Press, 1985).

is metaphysically implied in the heart's vision of Divine beauty, source of all artistic creativity. The true *shāhid*, the true witness, according to Rūzbihān, is also a *shahīd*, a martyr. He is effaced in his own witnessing of the true Witness, *al-Shahīd*, who witnesses His own creation through the witnesses He has created. The human witness thus knows that he is both witness and object of Divine witnessing, contemplator and contemplated, *shāhid* and *mashhūd*. But more than this, he realizes that his act of witnessing is itself a channel by which God witnesses and loves His own creation. As noted earlier, God, alone is 'the Hearer, the Seer,' and therefore 'nothing is like Him,' even if we appear to hear and see. The one who has awakened to this vision of God as both source and substance of all consciousness sees the beauty of God mirrored not only throughout creation, objectively, but also within himself, subjectively. He comes to understand, in a manner that eludes rational comprehension, that God is the true agent in his own acts of cognition, witnessing, and contemplation. This, according to Rūzbihān, is one of the keys to understanding the meaning of the signs 'on the horizons and in their own souls' (41:53).

But none of this can come about without two degrees of negation: the negation of the negation of the soul's self-consciousness. By means of the first negation, *fanā'* in the ordinary sense, the transcendence of the individual is realized—the soul is reduced to nothing through the impact of the vision of the transcendence of the Essence. But by means of the second negation, the *fanā'* of *fanā'*, producing *baqā'* ('subsistence'), the soul returns to self-consciousness, but a mode of consciousness now transfigured, such that the divine Reality is grasped, in accordance with the *ḥadīth qudsī* just cited, as the very substance of one's perceptions, cognitions and actions. Rūzbihān writes as follows in one of his treatises, entitled *Risālat al-Quds*: 'Without yourself, the vision of the vision (*'īyān-i 'īyān*) shines within you; after the double phase of effacement and recovered consciousness, every atom of your being proclaims [that which al-Ḥallāj proclaimed]: "I am the Truth," *ana'l-Ḥaqq*. This is the ... very mystery of *tawḥīd*.'[714]

This resonates deeply with another of al-Ḥallāj's famous verses: 'My extinction was extinguished in my extinction, so in my extinction, You found Yourself (*fa-fī fanā'ī fanā fanā'ī, wa-fī fanā'ī wajadta anta*).'[715] Rūzbihān alludes to this same mystery when he writes, in his *'Abhar al-'Āshiqīn*: 'I am in love with myself, without myself (*man bar man bī-man 'āshiq-am*).'[716] The first stage of becoming liberated from oneself is to purify oneself of all the impurities that contaminate one's love for the manifestations of beauty. Rūzbihān is insistent on this: If the seeker (*murīd*) is purified of the psychic maladies in-

714 Cited by Corbin, *En Islam iranien*, op. cit., p. 132.

715 *Dīwān al-Ḥallāj*, ed. Sa'dī Ḍannāwī (Beirut: Dār Ṣadir, 1998), p. 31.

716 *'Abhar al-'āshiqīn*, eds. Henry Corbin, Muḥammad Mu'īn (Tehran: Editions Manūchehrī, 1987), p. 49.

herent in human love, he will become firm in Divine love. But if there remain in the robe of his soul any stain of concupiscence, he will be thrown off the mount which carries one to the truth in the Divine realm.[717]

For Ruzbihān, the seeker must make a pilgrimage; from human love to spiritual love, and from spiritual love to Divine love. The path of this pilgrimage follows the tracks of beauty to its original source—then, and only then, can one's love of the beauty of outward phenomena be at one with love of God, and this love is a form of union with the Beloved. This union is beautifully expressed by Rūzbihan in another great saying, one in which the aesthetic dimension of the principle of *tawḥīd* is most clearly expressed. He writes as follows, in relation to the verse of Light (24:35): In the measure that the lover perceives in the qualities of the beloved the primordial beauty (*ḥusn-i aṣlī*), his love will increase, for the lamp of love is fed by the oil of eternal Beauty (*miṣbāh-i ʿishq rā rawghan az ḥusn-i qidam ast*).[718]

Such a union of love with beauty only comes about, according to Rūzbihān, when love searches for beauty in that which transcends the human, corporeal dimension. 'The sadness of love washes away with its tears the ephemeral dust from the Face of the eternal Bride,' as Rūzbihān so poetically puts it.[719] And when the heart of the lover is purified of all passion and concupiscence, then one can speak about 'Light upon Light.' For it is God alone who can come to see His own beauty, through the now transparent veil of the human subject. As Ibn al-ʿArabī writes: The object of vision, which is the Real, is light, while that through which the perceiver perceives Him is light. Hence light becomes included within light. It is as if it returns to the root from which it became manifest. So nothing sees Him but He.[720]

Here one might profitably mention the classic love story of Majnūn and Laylā, which, for Rūzbihān, is the perfect illustration of esoteric *tawḥīd* consummated through the purest possible love for Divine beauty. When asked who he is, Majnūn can only say: 'Laylā'; and this is identical to the proclamation that Rūzbihān makes: I am in love with myself without myself. For so complete is Majnūn's extinction in the face of the Divine beauty of which Laylā's physical form is but a transient manifestation, that he turns away from this physical form, for it is now a distraction from the eternal beauty witnessed by Majnūn through Laylā. But he also witnesses this eternal beauty within himself, for both the perception of his own heart and the form of her manifested beauty have now become perfectly polished mirrors of the Divine beauty. Majnūn's witnessing is God's witnessing: God has become the 'eye'

717 Ibid, p. 42.

718 Ibid, p. 46. See also Corbin, *En Islam iranien*, op. cit., p. 135, n. 196.

719 Ibid, p. 56.

720 Cited in William C. Chittick, *The Sufi Path of Knowledge: Ibn al-ʿArabī and the Metaphysics of the Imagination* (State University of New York, 1987), p. 215.

by which Majnūn sees beauty, and this means that Majnūn has become the eye by which God sees His own beauty. The veils—both outward forms and inward cognitions—have been transformed into spotless mirrors. Nothing but God sees, and nothing but God is seen: both that which sees and that which is seen are transparent to divine beauty: 'God is beautiful and He loves beauty.' *Is the reward of making beautiful* (iḥsān) *anything but making beautiful?* (55:60). The light sees itself through nothing other than its own light in this return of beauty to its source, and this return, re-integration, or re-absorption, is the consummation of *tawḥīd*, realized by the saint here and now. The metaphysics of aesthetics stands revealed as the re-integration of beauty within its transcendent source; and the aesthetics of metaphysics stands revealed as the inseparability of beauty from the ultimate realization of oneness.

***

Thinking of the way a mirror 'works' helps us to see that God's most beautiful names and qualities display the 'hidden treasure' in a manner akin to that by which an object is seen in a mirror. It is the mirror that, in a sense, 'produces' the reflection *qua* reflection—the object remains inactive, it remains what it is, it does not have to exert any influence other than that which derives from its *presence*: it simply has to be present before the mirror, and the mirror 'does' the rest. We observe a mode of 'activity' without action—what the Chinese Taoists call *wu-wei*. Nothing is diminished from the object, nothing departs from it. There is no question of incarnation, the substance of the mirror never comes to incorporate within itself anything of the material substance of the object it reflects. The mirror analogy, then, nicely combines the two principles of transcendence and immanence, so central to the integrity of the *tawḥīdī* vision of Divine beauty. The object and the mirror are totally separate, but the image seen in the mirror has no reality other than that of the object. The image is mysteriously identical to the object—its only 'identity' is nothing other than that of the object. But the image is reduced to nothing without the object: its reality is totally dependent upon the object, while the object is totally independent of the image.

To further the mirror analogy, every property of the image is also and inescapably the property of the object, but the image remains what it is and the object remains what it is. The slave remains always the slave, as Ibn al-'Arabī repeatedly insists. This is a point which is made emphatically by the Sufis in order to avoid the accusation of *shirk*, polytheistic idolatry: the beauty of God is somehow 'in' the creature, but only in the sense that an image is 'in' the mirror. There is no question of the glass of the mirror undergoing any material change as a result of the image that is present on its surface, nor is there any question of a material change or physical descent of the object into the mirror.

Thus God remains absolutely transcendent, just as, *mutatis mutandis*, the object remains totally distinct from the mirror.

God is not only beautiful by nature, He is continuously overflowing with beauty, just as the sun ceaselessly radiates and illuminates by its very nature. This beauty is 'cast' into the mirrors of creation, which thereby display the innumerable, kaleidoscopic expressions of this one and only beauty. It is by virtue of the different shapes and forms and colours of these mirrors that the one and only beauty of God assumes myriad forms, apparitions, faces. But whatever be the created form in which beauty resides, it is always, and exclusively, the beauty of God—that 'face' of God that is there, 'wherever you may look' (2:115). As Ibn al-ʿArabī says, in his chapter on *maḥabba* in the *Futūḥāt*: 'For He is the apparent/outward aspect of every beloved thing, apparent as such to the eye of every lover ... If you have loved anything because of its beauty, you have only loved God for He is the Beautiful.'[721]

But there is also the subjective aspect, or rather—to apply the logic of Rūzbihān's double negation—the subjectivity shorn of subjectivity. The slave who is extinguished before the face of his Beloved, he whose heart has been burnished by the remembrance of the Beloved such that it is now a spotless mirror reflecting the face of the Beloved, comprehends that he is himself, *without himself*, the Beloved. He has become *Ḥabīb Allāh* precisely because, and to the extent that, he is the perfect slave of God, *ʿAbd Allāh*, one who owns nothing of his own, has no identity of his own, and is thereby purely identified with that that of which he is an image. The following extraordinary saying of the Prophet deepens the mysteries being touched upon: 'Increase your remembrance to such an extent that they call you mad (*majnūn*).'[722]

The madness in question has nothing to do with ordinary insanity: in the Sūrat al-Qalam, God swears an oath by the Pen and what is written by it, and then tells the Prophet that, by the grace of God, he is certainly not *majnūn*. Rather, he is described as having a tremendous character (*khuluq ʿaẓīm*) (68:1–4). According to esoteric *tawḥīd*, this 'tremendous' nature is not exhausted by its human manifestation: rather, this nature is a perfect reflection of the 'most beautiful Names' of God. These Names, and the Qualities they designate, are reflected in the spotless mirror of the Prophet's heart, and it is this which renders him not only the Messenger of God, but also a dazzlingly beautiful disclosure of the very nature of God. Love of the beauty of the Prophet is therefore not only an indispensable principle in Islamic spirituality, it is also one of the

721 *Al-Futūḥāt*, op. cit., vol. 2, p. 326, lines 19, 25–26. See, for a complete French translation of the book of *maḥabba* in the *Futūḥāt*, Maurice Gloton, *Traité de l'Amour* (Paris: Éditions Albin Michel, 1986).

722 This saying is found in the *Musnad* of Ibn Ḥanbal, vol.5, p. 2445, Hadith no. 11832. For this, and several other traditions of similar import, together with relevant Qur'anic verses relating to the *dhikr*, see the Shaykh al-ʿAlawī's powerful rebuttal of accusations made against the Sufis by 'reformers' in Algeria in the 1920s and 1930s, in Lings, *A Sufi Saint*, op. cit., pp. 93–95.

principal dynamics within the contemplative process by which sacred art is produced in Islam.

Conclusion

We may, in conclusion, summarise the perspective on the aesthetics of metaphysics expounded here in the following adaptation of the double testimony: *lā jamīla illa'l-Jamīl; Muḥammadun mir'āt al-Jamīl.* 'No beauty but that of The Beautiful; Muḥammad is the mirror of The Beautiful.' This is tantamount to the assertion of Rūzbihān: 'the mystery of the Real is in the self-disclosing theophany of beauty.' In this aesthetic vision of reality, the formula 'Muḥammad is the Messenger of God' is equivalent to saying that formal beauty is the revelation of essential reality.[723]

723 This echoes the well-known Platonic dictum, 'Beauty is the splendour of the True,' and also the saying of St Augustine: 'It is in the nature of the sovereign Good to wish to communicate itself.'

Bibliography

Abdel Haleem, M.A.S. (Translated by). *Al-Qur'an.* Oxford: Oxford University Press, 2005.

'Abduh, Muḥammad, ed. *Nahj al-Balāgha.* Beirut: Maktabat al-Ma'ārif, 1996.

Al-Ghazālī. *Al-Maqṣad al-asnā fī sharḥ asmā' Allāh al-ḥusnā* (Arabic text), edited by Fadlou A. Shehadi. Beirut: Dar El-Machreq, 1971.

Al-Ghazālī. *Iḥyā' 'ulūm al-dīn.* Beirut: Dār al-Jīl, 1992.

Al-Ghazālī. *The Ninety-Nine Beautiful Names of God (al-Maqṣad al-asnā fī sharḥ asmā' Allāh al-ḥusnā).* Translated by David B. Burrell and N. Daher. Cambridge: Islamic Texts Society, 1999.

al-Jīlī, 'Abd al-Karīm. *Al-Insān al-kāmil.* Cairo: al-Maktaba al-Tawfiqiyya, n.d.

al-Rāzī, Fakhr al-Dīn. *Tafsīr al-kabīr.* Beirut: Dār Iḥyā' al-Turāth al-'Arabī, 2001.

Āmulī, 'Abd Allāh Jawādī. *Ḥamāsah wa 'irfān.* Qum: Isra Publication Centre, 1999.

Asad, Muhammad (Translated by). *The Message of the Qur'an.* Bristol: The Book Foundation, 2003.

Baqlī, Rūzbihān. *'Abhar al-'āshiqīn*, edited by Henry Corbin and Muḥammad Mu'īn. Tehran: Intishārāt-i Manūchehrī, 2004.

Burckhardt, Titus. *Art of Islam: Language and Meaning.* Translated by J. Peter Hobson. London: World of Islam Festival Publishing Company, 1976.

Chittick, William C. *The Sufi Path of Knowledge: Ibn al-'Arabī and the Metaphysics of the Imagination.* State University of New York, 1987.

Coomaraswamy, Ananda. *Figures of Speech or Figures of Thought? The Traditional View of Art*, edited by William Wroth. Bloomington: World Wisdom Books, 2007.

Corbin, Henry and Muḥammad Mu'īn, eds. *'Abhar al-'āshiqīn.* Tehran: Editions Manūchehrī, 1987.

Corbin, Henry. *En Islam iranien: Aspects spirituels et philosophiques.* 4 vols. Paris: Editions Gallimard, 1972.

Dagli, Caner. *The Ringstones of Wisdom*—Fuṣūṣ al-ḥikam. Chicago: Kazi Publications, 2004.

Ḍannāwī, Sa'dī, ed. *Dīwān al-Ḥallāj.* Beirut: Dār Ṣadir, 1998.

Encyclopaedia of Ḥadīth. Liechtenstein: Thesaurus Islamicus Foundation, 2001.

Gloton, Maurice. *Traité de l'Amour.* Paris: Éditions Albin Michel, 1986.

Ibn Manẓūr. *Lisān al-'Arab.* Cairo: Dār al-Ma'ārif, n.d.

Ibrahim, E., and D. Johnson-Davies (Translated by). *An-Nawawī's Forty*

Hadith. Damascus, 1976.

Keeble, Brian. *Every Man an Artist: Readings in the Traditional Philosophy of Art*. Bloomington: World Wisdom Books, 2005.

Khan, M. M. (Translated by). *Ṣaḥīḥ al-Bukhārī* (Summarised). Riyadh: Maktaba Dar-us-Salam, 1994.

Lings, Martin. *A Sufi Saint of the Twentieth Century: Shaikh Ahmad al-Alawi – His Spiritual Heritage and Legacy*. 2nd ed. Berkeley: University of California Press, 1971.

Massignon, Louis. *La Passion de Husayn ibn Mansûr Hallâj*. Paris: Gallimard, 1975.

Morris, James. *The Reflective Heart: Discovering Spiritual Intelligence in Ibn 'Arabi's Meccan Illuminations*. Louisville: Fons Vitae, 2005.

Murata, Sachiko, and William Chittick. *The Vision of Islam*. State University of New York, 1994.

Nasr, Seyyed Hossein. *Introduction to Islamic Cosmological Doctrines*. London: Thames & Hudson, 1978.

Nasr, Seyyed Hossein. *Islamic Art and Spirituality*. Ipswich: Golgonooza Press, 1987.

Nasr, Seyyed Hossein. *Islamic Science: An Illustrated Study*. London: World of Islam Festival Publishing Company, 1976.

Nasr, Seyyed Hossein. *Science and Civilization in Islam*. Cambridge: Islamic Texts Society, 1987.

Ormsby, Eric (Translated by). *Book of Love, Longing, Intimacy and Contentment: Book XXXVI of the Revival of the Religious Sciences*. Cambridge: Islamic Texts Society, 2011.

Prince Ghazi bin Muhammad. *Love in the Holy Qur'an*. Chicago: Kazi Publications, 2012.

Qara'I, 'Ali Quli (Translated by). *The Qur'an with a Phrase-by-Phrase English Translation*. London: Islamic College for Advanced Studies, 2004.

Schimmel, Annemarie. *And Muhammad is His Messenger: The Veneration of the Prophet in Islamic Piety*. Chapel Hill & London: The University of North Carolina Press, 1985.

Schuon, Frithjof. "Foundations of an Integral Aesthetics." In *Esoterism as Principle and as Way*. Translated by William Stoddart. Bedfont: Perennial Books, 1990.

Schuon, Frithjof. *Art—from the Sacred to the Profane, East and West*, edited by Catherine Schuon. Bloomington: World Wisdom Books, 2007.

Schuon, Frithjof. *Dimensions of Islam*. Translated by Peter Townsend. London: George Allen & Unwin, 1969.

Schuon, Frithjof. *Spiritual Perspectives and Human Facts*, edited by James S. Cutsinger. Bloomington: World Wisdom Books, 2007.

Şentürk, Recep. "Preface." In *The Mantle Adorned: Imam Busiri's Burda.* Translated by Abdal Hakim Murad. London: The Quilliam Press, 2009.

Shah-Kazemi, Reza. "Divine Beatitude: Supreme Archetype of Aesthetic Experience." In *Seeing God Everywhere: Essays on Nature and the Sacred,* edited by Barry McDonald. Bloomington: World Wisdom Books, 2003.

Shah-Kazemi, Reza. "The Metaphysics of Oneness and the Consummation of Love in Islamic Mysticism." In *Jewish, Christian and Islamic Perspectives on the Love of God,* edited by Sheelah Trefle-Hidden, 73–102. New York: Palgrave Macmillan, 2014.

Shah-Kazemi, Reza. *Justice and Remembrance: Introducing the Spirituality of Imam Ali.* I. B. Tauris, 2006.

Shah-Kazemi, Reza. *Muslim Perspectives on Christian Mysteries: Trinity, Incarnation, Crucifixion.* Green Knight Multimedia, forthcoming.

Shah-Kazemi, Reza. *Spiritual Quest: Reflections on Qur'ānic Prayer According to the Teachings of Imam Ali.* London: I.B. Tauris: 2011.

Uždavinys, Algis. *Ascent to Heaven: In Islamic and Jewish Mysticism.* London: The Matheson Trust, 2011.

Uždavinys, Algis. *Philosophy and Theurgy in Late Antiquity.* San Rafael: Sophia Perennis, 2010.

Zakariyya, Mohamed. "The Hilye of the Prophet Muhammad." In *Seasons—Semiannual Journal of the Zaytuna Institute* 1, no. 2 (2003–2004): 13–22.

Chapter 20

Scientific Realism and Islamic Science

Mohd Hazim Shah

Professor at the Universiti Utara Malaysia, Malaysia

Scientific realism has a long history, dating back to the seventeenth century with advent of the Copernican model in astronomy, if not earlier.[724] In the nineteenth century the debate assumed new proportions with the rise of the atomic theory. The protagonists in the debate were mainly philosopher-scientists such as Pierre Duhem, Ernst Mach, and Ludwig Boltzmann. If the earlier debates on realism in astronomy concerned macroscopic bodies, the later debates on scientific realism in the nineteenth century revolved around microscopic entities. This focus on microscopic entities has since characterized debates on scientific realism. Scholars on Islamic Science such as Hossein Nasr, Abdelhamid Sabra, and Osman Bakar, have also referred to the issue of scientific realism in some of their works. In his writings on Islamic Science, Osman Bakar has alluded to the question of the ontological status of scientific concepts or theoretical entities in science, as found for example, in his book *Tawhid and Science: Islamic Perspectives on Religion and Science* (2008).

Here, I wish to unravel the relationship between the development of the natural sciences after the scientific revolution, the discourse on scientific realism in western philosophy of science, and its relationship to the discourse on Islamic science. My contention is that the discourse is not only about whether theoretical entities really exist or not, or whether scientific theories are literally true descriptions about the physical world, but underlying it is the more fundamental question about the cultural role of scientific knowledge in modern society and culture.[725] In other words, can we rely on science for knowledge

---

724 See Karl Popper, *Conjectures and Refutations* (London: Routledge, 1972), in chapter three entitled "Three Views Concerning Human Knowledge," where he alluded to Galileo's realist interpretation of the Copernican model in astronomy. Also see, Peter Barker and Bernard Goldstein, "Realism and Instrumentalism in Sixteenth Century Astronomy," *Perspectives on Science* 6, no. 3 (1998): 232–258.

725 See Joseph Rouse, "Philosophy of Science and the Persistent Narratives of Modernity," *Studies in History and Philosophy of Science* 22, no. 1 (1991): 141–162; and "The Politics of Postmodern Philosophy of Science," *Philosophy of Science* 58, no. 4 (1991): 607–627, for an account of how philosophy of science can be seen as part of the wider discourse on modernity in the West.

about the external physical world, where by knowledge we mean 'a comprehension or understanding of the nature of the physical world' in the way the ancients and the medievals understood it, that is, science as 'episteme' or 'natural philosophy,' rather than as 'techne' or 'instrumentality.'[726] Or alternatively, the broader question: "how should we construe scientific knowledge?" The current battle seems to be fought between those who believe in the traditional role of science as providing true knowledge about the world (realists)—a view held by modernists such as Popper and Gellner, and those who insist that science is a set of successful practices (pragmatists).

In other words, what I am suggesting is that the question about how to view knowledge which has been implicit in scientific realism is itself a consequence of the development of science from its medieval to its modern phase when science finally became 'operationalized.' Thus, this enquiry or venture can also be viewed as an exercise in the sociology of philosophy. The very posing of the question itself is dependent on the nature of knowledge-formation or construction in the seventeenth and eighteenth centuries. The decisive turning point in the history of the development of science occurred with the rise of modern science through the scientific revolution of the seventeenth century and its aftermath. To locate the historical roots of the problem of scientific realism, we have to go back to the seventeenth century and look at how modern science was formed as a result of the integration of natural philosophy, mathematics, and the experimental method. In fact, contemporary debates in the philosophy of science on scientific realism, mirrors or reflects the three components with its divergent tendencies and orientations. Roughly—and at the risk of appearing 'simplistic'—'natural philosophy' corresponds to 'scientific realism,' 'mathematics' to 'structural realism,' and 'experimental method' to pragmatism. As historians of science such as Floris Cohen have shown, modern science arose as result of the integration of hitherto three separate domains in the history of human knowledge, namely natural philosophy, mathematics, and the experimental method.[727] The first two are knowledge in the traditional sense, while the third is method which is linked to knowledge production and now studied in terms of "practices."

But as Cunningham has suggested, the scientific revolution which started in the seventeenth century did not really produce a full-fledged modern science until about the eighteenth or early nineteenth century when it began to

726 To quote Peter Dear, *The Intelligibility of Nature* (Chicago and London: The University of Chicago Press, 2006), 9: "The distinction was rooted in the works of the Greek philosopher Aristotle… Aristotle's Greek terms were *episteme* and *techne,* translated into Latin in the Middle Ages as *scientia* (science) and *ars* (art).The first item in the pair designated logically and empirically demonstrable knowledge of truth, while the latter referred to the skilled practice of manipulating material things (*techne* is a root of the word "technology," just as *ars* is of the word "artificial")."

727 H. Floris Cohen, *How Modern Science Came Into the World* (Amsterdam: University of Amsterdam Press, 2010).

bear fruit and led to empirical successes.[728] It is not surprising then that we find debates on scientific realism in the form we find it today, which developed as late as the nineteenth century with Duhem, Mach and Boltzmann.[729] And it is no accident too that it centred on the atomic theory, which defined the focus of the problem of scientific realism, i.e. the status of microscopic or theoretical entities which are unobservable, until today.

The Transformation of Natural Philosophy, and the New Role of Mathematics and the Experimental Method

Historians of science have given various accounts of the birth of modern science. Among the notable ones are A.R. Hall[730] and Herbert Butterfield[731] in the 1950s, and in the recent past by Stephen Gaukroger,[732] Edward Grant,[733] Peter Dear,[734] and John Henry.[735] The most systematic and cogent analysis of the birth of modern science of late, was by H. Floris Cohen in a 2005 article on "The Onset of the Scientific Revolution." This was a brief summary of a full-fledged book entitled *How Modern Science Came Into the World* (Cohen 2010).[736] According to Cohen, before modern science emerged through the Scientific Revolution of the seventeenth century, three important transformations occurred in the mathematical sciences, natural philosophy, and the experimental method.[737] Cohen describes the transformations as follows:

1. The first transformation involved a continuation of the inherited 'Alexandrian'[738] tradition of mathematical science, by scientists such as Galileo and Kepler in the first half of the seventeenth century. Cohen referred

728 Andrew Cunningham and Perry Williams, "De-Centering the 'Big Picture': 'The Origins of Modern Science' and the Modern Origins of Science," *The British Journal for the History of Science* 26, no. 4 (1993): 407–432.

729 H.W. De Regt, "Scientific Realism in Action. Molecular Models and Boltzmann's *Bildtheorie.*" *Erkenntnis* 63 (2005): 205–230.

730 A.R. Hall, *The Scientific Revolution, 1500–1800: The Formation of the Modern Scientific Attitude* (London: Longmans, 1954).

731 H. Butterfield, *The Origins of Modern Science* (London: G. Bell, 1957).

732 Stephen Gaukroger, *The Emergence of a Scientific Culture* (Cambridge: Cambridge University Press, 2006).

733 E. Grant, *A History of Natural Philosophy: From the Ancient World to the Nineteenth Century* (Cambridge: Cambridge University Press, 2007).

734 P. Dear, *Intelligibility of Nature.*

735 J. Henry, *The Scientific Revolution and the Origins of Modern Science* (Basingstoke, Hampshire: Palgrave MacMillan, 2008).

736 Cohen, *How Modern Science Came Into the World.*

737 H. Floris Cohen, "The Onset of the Scientific Revolution," in *The Science of Nature in the Seventeenth Century*, eds. P. R. Anstey and J. A. Schuster, 9–33 (Dordrecht: Springer, 2005).

738 The distinction between the 'Alexandrian' and 'Athenian' approaches in ancient science is given in Cohen, *How Modern Science Came Into the World.* The 'Athenian' approach derives its name from 'Athens,' where Greek natural philosophy flourished and characterised early Greek science. The 'Alexandrian' approach derives its name from 'Alexandria' [Iskandariah] which is now part of Egypt and was formerly part of the Hellenistic world. This approach reflects more of the 'engineering' tradition in science associated with Archimedes, for example, and is instrumentalist and practical in nature.

to this scientific program as 'realist Mathematical Science.' It was a project of the 'mathematisation of nature' with added methods of observation and experimentation. It was also 'realist' in orientation in that science was about the study of the real structure of the universe. Galileo, for example, believed that the knowledge of nature could be found in the language of mathematics. This feature constitutes another difference with the previous Alexandrian tradition, which was basically 'instrumentalist.'

2. The second transformation refers to a transformation in natural philosophy. Previously, natural philosophy in the ancient and medieval periods were based on the philosophies of the four Athenian schools, namely: (i) Platonism (ii) Aristotelianism (iii) Stoicism, and (iv) Atomism, with Aristotelianism being dominant. There was a revival of the natural philosophy of atomism through the kinetic corpuscularism of Descartes and the atomistic ideas of Gassendi and Boyle. Another novel feature of this updated 'Athenian' approach is the emphasis on motion. Thus, there appear to be a shift from the qualitative—as was the case in Aristotelian natural philosophy—to the quantitative, with the focus on atoms moving in a void, according to specific laws of motion. This feature of the scientific revolution, however, was transient or contingent, unlike the other two, according to Cohen.
3. The third transformation involves what Cohen termed as 'coercive empiricism.' There was an emphasis on accuracy of description and experimentation, in order to manipulate and control nature. Cohen contextualizes this scientific tendency within the broader framework of European history that witnessed European voyages of discovery and a worldly approach towards nature which was sanctioned by Christianity. The concept of 'coercive empiricism' was not only epistemological but also sociological. That is, it was not really aimed at an objective description of nature, but a description that facilitated an effective handling of nature by man so much so that scientific observation became selective and purposive. A spokesman for this renewed empirical approach towards the study of nature was Francis Bacon in seventeenth century England.[739]

The Transformation of Natural Philosophy: From Aristotelianism to Atomism and the Mechanical Philosophy

Let me begin with the second transformation mentioned by Cohen: the transformation in natural philosophy. Aristotelian natural philosophy was already under attack for some time and was eventually replaced by a new natural philosophy in the seventeenth century. The new natural philosophy

739 Gaukroger, *Francis Bacon and the Transformation of Early-Modern Philosophy.*

was integrated with mathematics and the experimental method. Sometimes labeled as the 'mechanical philosophy,' the natural philosophy was associated with a revived form of Atomism and was programmatic in nature. It was crafted by philosophers and scientists such as Rene Descartes, Pierre Gassendi, Robert Boyle, and Isaac Beeckman and was equally comprehensive as Aristotelian natural philosophy. It is a system of explanation of the natural world that encompassed several different fields, ranging from physics to medicine. Yet, its acceptance came *prior* to its fusion with mathematics and the experimental method, which gave rise to the kind of 'operational science' associated with the scientific revolution. Being programmatic, the new natural philosophy did not yet yield empirical results as had Aristotelian natural philosophy.

Given that its acceptance was not based on empirical contribution of the experimental type, the interesting question therefore arises: "what accounted for the growing influence of the new natural philosophy?" Several answers can be given to the above question. Among these are:

1. The decline of Aristotelian natural philosophy beginning in the Middle Ages, and the search for alternatives.
2. The efforts of philosophers such as Gassendi and Boyle to overcome the 'atheistic image' of Atomism.
3. The increasing use of machines and the rise of the mechanistic worldview.
4. The ability of the new natural philosophy to be equally comprehensive in scope and to function effectively as an alternate explanatory system.

Integrated with mathematics and the experimental method, the new natural philosophy now gained added value, because now it is not 'merely explanatory' but equally predictive and functional. This, I believe, accounts for its longevity, because now to dislodge would require an equally comprehensive explanatory system of the world, and one that has new methodological standards that was equally empirical and functional.

The integration of the new natural philosophy with mathematics and the experimental method set the stage for early modern science and provided the model or prototype of the science to come. But apart from its ability to satisfy the Baconian edict that 'scientific truth should bear practical fruits,' it now raises deep epistemological question about the nature of truth, the relationship between theory and practice, thought, and action. It is this new configuration brought about by the amalgamation of natural philosophy, mathematics, and the experimental method, which, I believe, gave rise to the problem of scientific realism. The problem of scientific realism was an epistemological as well as a cultural problem.

On the Role of Mathematics

The role of mathematics in the Scientific Revolution is two-fold, involving 'backward' and 'forward' linkages with natural philosophy and experimentation respectively. Its connection with natural philosophy has sometimes been described in terms of the 'mathematisation of nature' or the 'mathematisation of the world-picture.'[740] By mathematising nature or by making natural philosophy mathematical, we obtain a more precise picture of the natural world—at least conceptually thus rendering it amenable to quantification and measurement. However, not all attempts at mathematisation of natural philosophy or of the mixed sciences such as astronomy and mechanics yielded fruitful results. Three outstanding examples of such lack of empirical fecundity resulting from mathematisation are: (i) Kepler's geometrical model of the universe using the five Platonic or regular solids, (ii) the mathematical approach of the Merton school in mechanics and (iii) Oresme's graphical analysis of motion.[741] Kepler's geometrical model perpetuated the old natural philosophy ideal of arriving at a satisfactory intellectual account of nature, without necessarily having any empirical or predictive value. In fact, it was the mismatch between model and data (i.e. Tycho Brahe's astronomical data), which led Kepler to abandon the geometrical model and moved towards the discovery of the planetary laws of motion.[742]

The mathematical approach adopted by both the Merton school and Nicholas Oresme in mechanics, in turn, did not bear empirical result because no attempt was made towards operationalizing the concept, or linking it to practice. The successful move was only made later by Galileo in the seventeenth century through the inclined-plane experiment.

This brings us to the second role or aspect of mathematisation, that is, its linkage with experimentation. Galileo's linkage between mathematics and the experimental method brought fruitful empirical results. To do so, Galileo had to treat the mathematical variables such as distance (s) and time (t) as abstract mathematical or physical parameters, and more important still, as *quantifiable* and *measurable* quantities. This enabled the linkage with nature and practice. It required not only conceptual finesse, but also the skills of the artisan and the 'mechanic' in the design and execution of the actual experiment. For example, measuring values such as distance travelled or time taken in the inclined-plane experiment was complex. The experiment itself attested to Galileo's ingenuity in measuring distance and time in 'free fall' motion.

740 E. J. Dijksterhuis, *The Mechanization of the World Picture* (Princeton, New Jersey: Princeton University Press, 1986).

741 Edward Grant, *Physical Science in the Middle Ages* (Cambridge: Cambridge University Press, 1977), 55–59.

742 Bernard Cohen, *The Birth of a New Physics* (New York: Penguin Books, 1992), 132–137.

But it could be argued that such an 'operational' science was already found in Alexandrian science of antiquity where there was a link between mathematics and practice, but not with natural philosophy. Admittedly, linking mathematics with natural philosophy was a more daunting task since it was not clear on what basis the connection should be made. Given that the task of ancient and medieval science—in the guise of natural philosophy—was to give a causal explanation of natural phenomena and hence fulfill its cultural role as 'episteme' rather than 'techne,' the use of mathematics which was deemed as non-causal and hence non-explanatory, was therefore not encouraged. It required a significant shift in the content of natural philosophy, through atomism in the seventeenth century, for mathematics to play a role in theory-construction in science. Atomism allows for mathematisation since the motion of the atoms was to be mathematically treated or analyzed through Newton's laws of motion. The revival of atomism therefore allowed mathematics to play a more constructive role. The emphasis on the study of *motion* was made more precise through Newton's (mathematical) laws of motion. Newton himself was aware of this important shift when he titled his work, *The Mathematical Principles of Natural Philosophy.*[743] The central ideas of natural philosophy were given a more precise definition through mathematics. For example, 'force' was not merely a 'quality' without quantitative dimensions, but mathematically defined as F= ma.

By treating atoms in motion mathematically, Newtonians were able to explain macroscopic phenomena in terms of the motion of the microscopic atoms. This program of linking the micro and macro worlds was evidenced in the 'Kinetic Theory of Gases,' which can be regarded as a supreme achievement. Here, the conceptual elegance found in the mathematical analysis of the motion of the gas molecules done at the micro-level, matched with the empirical results in the form of the gas laws at the macro-level. Had it remained mathematically and conceptually elegant but without empirical fruit, it would have remained a 'failed' Cartesian program or remained at the level of 'medieval mechanics.'

The Experimental Method

An important feature which separated seventeenth century science from the science of the previous centuries, was the use of the experimental method. The experimental method was the third and final piece in the jigsaw puzzle, which ultimately led to the birth of modern science which was a science that was conceptual, explanatory, operational, and predictive. It provided a link between the world of ideas and the world of practice, making practice dependent on thought, and likewise, making thought constrained by practice.

743 Grant, *History of Natural Philosophy.*

How was the linkage effected between experiment, mathematics, and the natural philosophy? The linkage was effected through several levels namely,

1. Institutional-social
2. Individual effort, e.g. by Galileo, Boyle, or Bacon
3. Disciplinary development

Although certain individuals such as Pythagoras or Grosseteste had practiced the experimental method in the past, it was not institutionalized. According to Zilsel, with the breakdown of social barriers between the scholars/literati and the artisans in the fifteenth and sixteenth centuries, the experimental method in science became more respectable.[744] The institutionalization of the experimental method took place in the seventeenth century in England through the work of the Royal Society.

At the individual level, the efforts of practitioners like Galileo and Boyle, and philosophers such as Francis Bacon, went a long way towards making the experimental method an essential feature of science. The driving force behind the efforts of these individuals was the desire to effect a link between the world of idea and the world of practice, or between theory and practice. In the case of Galileo, experiment was used as a means of confirming his mathematical model of the motion of objects, and in the case of Robert Boyle it was a means of connecting his corpuscular natural philosophy to experimentally observed nature. For Francis Bacon, who was more of a philosopher rather than a scientific practitioner, the union between theory and practice was seen as a means of attaining mastery over nature through an understanding of the real nature of the natural world.

Despite the desires and efforts of such individuals and the breakdown of social barriers, the experimental method could not have been successfully implemented if certain other pre-conditions were not met. Two of them are:

1. The precise articulation of theory through mathematics.
2. The creation of scientific instruments that made scientific measurement possible.

Experiments can be thought of as being of two kinds, namely: (a) fact finding (b) theory-testing. Fact-finding experiments are generally aimed at finding what happens when nature is put under certain unnatural conditions. This experimental approach need not be guided by an underlying theory. On the other hand, experimentation aimed at testing theories, are guided by established scientific theories. It is this latter kind of experimentation that serves to link thought and practice in a more systematic way. And as we shall see, it is

744 E. Zilsel, "The Sociological Roots of Modern Science," *The American Journal of Sociology* 47, no. 4 (1942): 544–562.

also this kind of experimental activity, which has a bearing on the question of scientific realism, because the experimental results are construed as confirmation of the ontology of the underlying theory.[745]

Mathematics and the Experimental Method in Science

The use of mathematics and the experimental method in science has brought about a radical change in the way scientists *conceptualize* nature. Gone are the days of speculative abstract theorizing which are mostly qualitative in nature backed by rational arguments such as those developed by the ancient Greeks. Instead, with the application of mathematics to the study of the physical world, what we have is a more precise conceptualization of nature, to be verified empirically. Speculate and theorize about nature if you will, but if you cannot meet the mathematical and experimental standards of the scientific community, then those ideas about nature will remain speculative. One might have 'enchanting' and 'symbolically pleasant' ideas about nature, but in the end, it was the mathematical and experimental standards of the scientific community that will determine the survival or otherwise of scientific concepts. Kepler realized this earlier on in the seventeenth century when he tried to propose his 'model of the universe' based on the five Platonic solids.[746] During the Greek period, this would have sufficed and the matter would have ended there. But instead, what happened was that Kepler paid heed to Tycho Brahe's data and acknowledged that the 'non-fit' was serious enough to suspend judgment on the model of the universe. Kepler instead took a different turn, which eventually resulted in his discovery of the three laws of planetary motion. The mathematical approach was retained and used in combination with the empirical approach. We can see here the beginning of the constraint of theory by practice. But Kepler took it in a positive manner, where 'the lesser idol' had to be sacrificed to get at the 'Truth.' In other words, he did not mind abandoning an 'enchanted world picture,' as given by his archetypal model of the Universe based on the five Platonic solids, in exchange for one which fits in with the astronomical data.[747] Subsequent narratives in the history of science repeat this experience of Kepler's. One example is the violation of parity and the disappointment it created in Pauli. The archetype of 'harmony' was proven to be untrue by experimental evidence involving weak interactions.[748]

745 Richard Boyd, "Realism, Underdetermination, and a Causal Theory of Evidence," *Noûs* 7, no. 1 (1973): 1–12.

746 Bernard Cohen, *The Birth of a New Physics*, 134–135.

747 Gerald Holton, *Thematic Origins of Scientific Thought: Kepler to Einstein* (Cambridge: Harvard University Press, 1973), 78–80.

748 Arther Miller, *Deciphering the Cosmic Number: The Strange Friendship of Wolfgang Pauli and Carl Jung* (New York: W.W. Norton & Company, 2010), 237.

The Integration of Natural Philosophy, Mathematics, and the Experimental Method, and Its Philosophico-Cultural Consequences

There are several consequences, which have philosophical and cultural import, resulting from the integration of natural philosophy, mathematics and the scientific method. These consequences can be discussed under the following headings:

1. From paradigmatic pluralism to paradigmatic monism.
2. The adoption of the experimental method and the second disenchantment of nature.
3. The fusion of theory and practice, and the constraint on natural philosophy by practice and empiricism.
4. The unstable alliance between "instrumentality" and "natural philosophy."

First, there was a shift from 'paradigmatic pluralism' to 'paradigmatic monism.' Before the seventeenth century, several different paradigms of nature or several different natural philosophies co-existed. They existed as some version or variant of the four major 'Athenian' natural philosophies, namely: (i) Platonism (ii) Aristotelianism (iii) Stoicism, and (iv) Atomism.[749] Although (i) and (ii) predominated over the rest at different times, their competitors were not completely rejected, to the extent that there were still 'followers' of those natural philosophies or 'cosmologies.' One reason why they were not completely eliminated was because natural philosophy as it existed prior to the seventeenth century was not subjected to experiments and hence did not require empirical 'confirmation' for its acceptance. With the integration of natural philosophy with mathematics and the experimental method, natural philosophies which are not experimentally verified or empirically fruitful, were eliminated regardless of their connection with other areas of human culture. Previously, Ptolemaic astronomy and Aristotelian cosmology were able to sustain itself through its interconnections with other areas of human culture, such as religion, despite encountering difficulties. Thus, in post-seventeenth century science, largely because of the requirement of experimental evidence and empirical fruitfulness, one has no choice over which natural philosophy or cosmology to adopt.

This brings us to our second point, with regards to the philosophic—cultural consequences of the integration. It has to do with what has been labeled as the 'disenchantment' of nature. In fact, it could be more appropriately labeled as 'the second disenchantment of nature,' the first being the banishment of spirits and deities from the physical or natural world, with the coming of

749 S. Sambursky, *The Physical World of the Greeks* (Princeton: Princeton University Press, 1987).

Greek natural philosophy beginning from the sixth century BC, which can be seen as a rational enquiry of the natural world. What the experimental method did was to continue this tendency towards 'disenchantment' by eliminating 'enchanted' views of nature or natural philosophies that do not have experimental or empirical support. Thus, natural philosophies such as the Aristotelian, or the Platonic, which were compatible with some religious worldviews, such as that of Christianity in the Middle Ages, and hence 'enchanting' in some sense, were replaced by the natural philosophy of 'Atomism,' which was previously held as 'materialist' or even 'atheistic.' Thus, an important part of the program of Atomism and the Mechanical philosophy in the seventeenth century was devoted towards overcoming such objections to the image of Atomism.[750]

The third significant consequence of the integration lies in the fusion between theory and practice in post-seventeenth century science, something, which was hitherto absent. This fusion in turn, produced its own radical consequences owing to the coupling between thought and action, theory and praxis. Although the sociologist Jurgen Habermas[751] using the Weberian concept of 'rationalisation' hailed such a move as productive and progressive, the epistemological, philosophical and cultural problems, which arose as a result, cannot be denied, and to which the philosophical responses which emerged, can be located in philosophical discourses on scientific realism. By tying thought to action, theory to practice, man is now no longer free to articulate a world-view which is compatible with other areas of his belief-system, especially the religious, or even the 'humanistic.' Seyyed Hossein Nasr describes this situation as 'the rupture between the two universes of discourse, namely the religious and the scientific.' To quote Nasr:

> It was this common universe of discourse that was rent asunder by the rise of modern science as a result of which the religious view of the order of nature, which is always based on symbolism, was reduced either to irrelevance or to a matter of mere subjective concern, which made the cosmic teachings of religion to appear as unreal and irrelevant. Also, it was through the destruction of the unitary vision of the cosmos that the "laws of nature" became divorced from moral laws and the

---

750 To be fair however, it has to be conceded that in a sense, Atomism and Mechanism was accepted in the seventeenth century prior to it being a full-fledged empirical research program, and was still programmatic in nature so its acceptance cannot be fully explained terms of empirical support. However, its continuity and sustainability can attributed to its empirical success in the following centuries, especially in physics and chemistry.

751 To quote J. Habermas, *The Theory of Communicative Action,* vol.1 (Boston: Beacon Press, 1981), p215, "In this area the uncoupling of theory from the *experiential domains of practice*—particularly from those of social labor—had to be overcome. Theoretical argumentation had to be rejoined above all with those experiential domains accessible from the technical perspective of the craftsman. The solution to this second problem came in the form of the experimental natural sciences. The social carriers of those strands of tradition that were combined amazingly, in modern science –the Scholastics, the Humanists, and above all the engineers and artists of the Renaissance—played a role in releasing for purposes of research practice the potential stored in cognitively rationalized worldviews—a role similar to that played by the Protestant sects in transposing ethically rationalized worldviews into everyday practice."

sciences of nature became divorced at their roots from the foundations of religious ethics. The consequence of this segmentation and separation was the alienation of man from an image of the Universe created by himself but given a purely objective and nonanthropomorphic status and the surrender of nature as a mass without spiritual significance to be analyzed and dissected with impunity on the one hand and plundered and raped with uncontrolled avidity on the other. Thus, it is of the utmost importance to try to understand in depth how the modern scientific view of the order of nature was founded and how it has evolved during the past four centuries to the present day.[752]

This situation arose because thought has been subjected not only to the dictates of 'Reason' but to the requirement of experimental evidence, empirical support, and technological efficacy. Hence, ontology and metaphysics now became subjected to methodology and cannot be framed independently of it, thus disabling enchantment. This subjection of belief to action, thought to practice on both epistemological and pragmatic grounds, enabled action to be more 'productive' thus securing man's mastery over nature. However, it did not come without a price. The price paid can be characterised as some form of 'disenchantment,' or the creation of a 'disjuncture' between on the one hand, one's 'scientific' view of the world, and on the other hand, one's 'religious,' 'metaphysical,' or even 'enchanted' view of the natural world. Alan Macfarlane in his analysis of Gellner's thought on modernity, admirably captured this idea in the following passage:

> ...Yet this 'freedom of thought' is bought at a price. Gellner takes from Kant and Weber, among others, his analysis of the consequences of this disenchantment. The modern world 'provides no warm cosy habitat for man.... The impersonality and regularity.... which makes it knowable are also, at the same time, the very features, which makes it almost.... unadaptable. Our world is 'notoriously a cold, morally indifferent world.' It is notable for its 'icy indifference to values, its failure to console and reassure, its total inability to validate norms and values...' Within the new world 'there also is and can be no room either for magic or for the sacred.' Revelation offers one vision and science offers, not another, but none.'[753]

Yet despite the culturally problematic nature of the new science, Gellner saw no alternative for humanity, but to accept this superior or progressive version of human cognition. Quoting Gellner, Macfarlane continued:

> Yet we cannot go back to innocence. 'The central fact about our world is that, for better or worse, a superior, more effective from of cognition does exist.' Thus the 'world we live in is defined, above all, by existence of a unique, unstable

752 Seyyed Hossein Nasr, *Religion and the Order of Nature* (New York: Oxford University Press, 1996), 129.

753 Alan Macfarlane, "Ernest Gellner on Liberty and Modernity," in *Ernest Gellner and Contemporary Social Thought*, eds. Sinisa Malesevic and Mark Haugard, 31–49. Cambridge: Cambridge University Press, 2007), 39.

and powerful system of knowledge of nature, and its corrosive, unharmonious relationship to the other clusters of ideas ("cultures") in terms of which men live. *This* is our problem. This 'atomized, cognitively unstable world, which does not underwrite the identities and values of those who dwell in it, is neither comfortable nor romantic.' All we can do is realize that it is mistaken to believe that 'the price need not be paid at all, that one can both have one's romantic cake and scientifically eat it.'[754]

Gellner has perceptively addressed the problem arising from the subjugation of thought to practice, in terms of 'disenchantment.' However, a better understanding of the problem can be obtained by looking at Kuhn's close study of science and the scientific community through his idea of 'paradigms.'[755] The chief significance of Kuhn's concept of "paradigms" in helping us understand this unique cultural problem due to the emergence of modern science, lies in his articulation and explication of how paradigms connect theory to practice, thought or belief, to action. The connection is established in such a way that the one reinforces the other. That thought becomes 'real' through action, and how action in turn impinges on, or reinforces belief. Kuhn's concept of "paradigms" does not separate thought from practice, belief from action, but instead showed how the two are inextricably linked. Far from being harmless or innocent, such linkage was to produce major epistemological, philosophical, and cultural consequences.

Fourthly, the integration of 'natural philosophy' and 'instrumentality' in the new science, although it created an operational science, could form a potentially problematic alliance in the epistemological sense because of their different orientations. While 'natural philosophy' is about truth of the natural world, 'instrumentality' is about successful action and practice. Of course, legitimation stories must be told, and it was Bacon who should be credited for incorporating the pragmatic into the epistemic. By linking 'practice' with 'truth,' he retained the old epistemological virtues found in the Greeks and the Medievals, whilst at the same time inaugurating the birth of a new practical and pragmatic science. Thus, the standard of truth and knowledge of nature is now transformed to include the criteria of empirical and experimental evidence.

In the days of old, natural philosophy serves as 'episteme' (understood in the context of the distinction between 'Episteme' and 'Techne') and as cosmology. As such, it is of wider import, serving man's intellectual need to understand the world around him and in the process understands and provides meaning to his own existence. It is this sense that Cunningham's view

754 Macfarlane, "Ernest Gellner on Liberty and Modernity," 39.

755 Thomas Kuhn, *The Structure of Scientific Revolutions*, 2nd ed. (Chicago: University of Chicago Press, 1970).

that natural philosophy is 'all about God and religion,' can be understood.[756] In fact, if we look at the role of natural philosophy during the Greek and Medieval periods, this was indeed the case. Natural philosophy served as a handmaiden to theology in the Latin West. It was better received in Europe than it was in Islam, which had its own cosmology and world-view based on the Qur'an and the teachings of the Prophet Muhammad, and in which the study of Greek natural philosophy was discouraged. But even the rejection of Greek natural philosophy in Islam proves the point about the major cultural role played by natural philosophy. Now given this central cultural role played by natural philosophy in a civilization's worldview, the transformation in natural philosophy and its subsequent integration with mathematics and the experimental method, which ultimately led to modern science, cannot but have grave intellectual and cultural consequences. Edward Grant believed that natural philosophy survived as late as the nineteenth century.[757] Its disappearance being attributed to the rise of modern science. In this, his viewpoint is at odds with Cunningham and Williams who believed that it ended earlier.[758] But I would even go further than Grant and suggest that natural philosophy survived in a new form after the nineteenth century, through the philosophy of scientific realism. Scientific Realism is basically the attempt to re-instate the 'natural philosophy' component in modern science, and have science play its traditional role of providing 'episteme' or true knowledge about the world, rather than being mere instrumentality. Anti-Realism on the other hand can be partly seen as a rejection of this attempt at re-instating 'natural philosophy.' It could be either that the 'natural philosophy' or metaphysics implicit in the current scientific theories are 'unpalatable,' or it could be due to a rejection of metaphysics in science in general, as espoused by the Logical Positivists.

Thus, the battle over scientific realism in contemporary philosophy of science can be traced back to its historical roots, to the process of the emergence of modern science. Although scientific realism has been discussed mostly in the philosophy of science, there has been an attempt to discuss the subject from a historical point of view. This was made by Peter Dear through his analysis of science as instrumentality and science as natural philosophy.[759] Dear saw and seized on the tension existing because of the fusion of 'theory' and 'practice' in science, of science as 'episteme,' and of science as 'techne.' One strand of this fusion pulls towards 'episteme' and 'natural philosophy,' while the other strands pull towards 'techne' and 'instrumentality.' Roughly, the former corresponds with Realism, the latter with Anti-Realism. Given Dear's

756 Cunningham and Williams, "De-Centering the 'Big Picture.'"

757 Grant, *History of Natural Philosophy.*

758 Cunningham and Williams, "De-Centering the 'Big Picture.'"

759 Peter Dear, *Intelligibility of Nature;* and "What Is the History of Science the History *Of*? Early Modern Roots of the Ideology of Modern Science," *Isis* 96 (2005): 390–406.

tendency against scientific realism, an attempt was made in Dear to show that the connection between 'truth' and 'instrumentality' was a contingent and not a necessary matter. Dear tried, to historically deconstruct scientific realism by exposing the historically contingent nature of that belief, or what he termed as 'ideology.' What this attempt by Dear illustrates is that it makes sense to try and contextualize the problem of scientific realism by locating it within its historical context. Although I do not necessarily agree that the philosophical merit of realism or anti-realism is to be determined by historical analysis, I do see the point of understanding the issue within a historical context. This is because the issue of scientific realism is not only a narrow philosophical issue, but also has social and cultural ramifications and implications.[760] Given this broader implication of scientific realism, looking at it in terms other than the purely philosophical, seems to be justified.

A Comparison with Islamic Science

We have looked at how modern science emerged in the West through the Scientific Revolution, the consequences that resulted from it in epistemological and cultural terms, and how the discourse on scientific realism can be considered as a philosophical response to the new science. In order to extend our argument, we will now look at Islamic science, or science in Islamic Civilization because of the interesting fact that although the Muslims were ahead of the West until about the fourteen century, they did not give birth to modern science. Through such a comparison, we will not only be able to understand or suggest why modern science did not emerge from Islamic Civilization, but will also arrive at a better understanding of the relationship between natural philosophy, natural science, and realist philosophies and attitudes to science. I argue that the development of science took a different turn in the West as compared to Islam and that these differences have significant philosophical and cultural implications for both civilizations.[761] I further contend that the character of Islamic science essentially retained the distinction and separation between the 'Athenian' and 'Alexandrian' approaches. The success of Islamic science was mainly due to the development of science in the 'Alexandrian' mode, the non-integration of natural philosophy with mathematics and experimentation, and an instrumentalist approach towards the study of nature. This approach has its limitations, and perhaps reached its highest point in the sixteenth century. As history had proven, the next step in the development of science required the integration of natural philosophy, mathematics and the experimental method, which took place in Europe in the seventeenth century.

760 Richard Rorty, *Philosophy as Cultural Politics* (Cambridge: Cambridge University Press, 2007).

761 Seyyed Hossein Nasr, "Islamic Science, Western Science: Common Heritage, Diverse Destinies," in *The Revenge of Athena Science, Exploitation and the Third World*, ed. Ziaudin Sardar, 239–259 (London and New York: Mansell Publishing Limited, 1998).

Although the scientific revolution did not occur in Islamic civilization, that civilization was spared the kind of philosophico-epistemological cultural crises that affected the West, as witnessed in the Galileo episode. It was only in the twentieth century with the transplant of science to Muslim countries through colonisation that the Muslim world was compelled to provide intellectual or philosophical responses to modern scientific knowledge.[762]

The question of whether Islamic science is realist or instrumentalist, and whether natural philosophy plays a role in its development, is an interesting question because it helps to shed light on some of the issues which we have examined in relation to science in Western culture and civilisation. What were the salient differences between Islamic and modern western science that led to material progress and disenchantment in the case of the latter, but stagnation and non-disenchantment in the case of the former? Here, I would like to highlight two features of Islamic science that would help to answer the question posed. The first relates to the role of natural philosophy in Islamic science, and the second relates to the instrumentalist or non-realist character and orientation of Islamic science.

With regards to the role of natural philosophy, Edward Grant suggests that it was the lack of the development of natural philosophy in Islamic culture which prevented the emergence of modern science in Islamic civilization.[763] This, according to Grant, stands in contrast to the European experience in which natural philosophy was cultivated in the medieval universities and that there existed a class of theologians who gave religious legitimation to the pursuit of natural philosophy, thus enabling its institutionalization in medieval European universities.[764] The link between natural philosophy and modern science, according to him, lies in the fact that further development of the exact sciences was dependent on 'natural philosophy' which was readily available in Europe but not in Islam. However, the Muslim historian of science, Seyyed Hossein Nasr took a different view. He did not mourn over the inability of Islamic science to transform itself to modern science through the incorporation of Greek natural philosophy. If anything, Nasr regarded it as a virtue that Islamic science retained its character. He argued that modern science and its 'vulgar' metaphysics is not a cultural ideal to be emulated. But although Nasr and Grant disagreed on the status of modern science, they both seem to point to metaphysics and natural philosophy as providing the answer to the question

762 Ali Zaidi, "Muslim Reconstructions of Knowledge and the Re-enchantment of Modernity," *Theory, Culture & Society* 23, no. 5 (2006): 69–91; and Maisarah Hasbullah and Mohd Hazim Shah, "The Rise of Modern Science: Islam and the West," *Philosophy East & West* 68, no. 1 (2018): 78–96.

763 Edward Grant, *Science and Religion, 400 BC to 1550 AD* (Baltimore: Johns Hopkins, 2004), 233–243; and "The Fate of Ancient Greek Natural Philosophy in the Middle Ages: Islam and Western Christianity," *The Review of Metaphysics* 61, no. 3 (2008): 503–526.

764 Edward Grant, *The Foundations of Modern Science in the Middle Ages* (Cambridge: Cambridge University Press, 1996), 173–176.

'why did the Scientific Revolution not take place in Islamic civilization?' But what exactly is the role of the so-called 'natural philosophy' in modern science, to the extent that so much seems to hinge on its presence or absence? One possible answer is that its role is to provide a theoretical base or the conceptual resources from which predictions are derived and tested experimentally. But if this is so, then why was there experimentation in Islamic science in the absence of natural philosophy? We have to look more closely at the nature of experimentation in Islamic science and its relationship (if any) to 'theory' to unravel this puzzle.

The second feature of Islamic science, which is relevant to our enquiry is the question of whether Islamic science is realist or instrumentalist. The question of whether Islamic science is realist or instrumentalist is indeed an interesting question. It is also related to the question of the existence of natural philosophy in Islamic science. If natural philosophy is not encouraged, and hence marginal to, the development of the natural sciences in Islamic science, then how could it be realist? This is because natural philosophy purports to describe the reality of the world and hence any (scientific) realist account of the world has to include natural philosophy. If Islamic science is uninfluenced by or devoid of natural philosophy and consists only of mathematics and the experimental method, then it is difficult to see how it could be realist.

Abdelhamid Sabra expounded the 'appropriation thesis' in which Islamic science is basically instrumentalist.[765] It is largely utilitarian and served as a handmaiden to religion. Sabra saw the non-realist nature of Islamic science as being the reason for its stagnation and eventual decline. Muslim scientists did not take the step of conceiving scientific knowledge as being capable of unveiling the ultimate nature of the physical world, which was the ultimate aim of scientific realism. Evidence for such a claim can be found in the Islamic sciences such as astronomy, (applied) mathematics, and optics. But it must also be conceded that even in 'utilitarian' Islamic sciences such as astronomy, debates on the realist status of the astronomical models have indeed occurred. Although there might be evidence to suggest that realist positions (for example in astronomy) have indeed been adopted in Islamic science, this does not necessarily imply that natural philosophy is systematically developed in the construction of Islamic science. George Saliba initially suggested that Muslim astronomers such as Tusi and Ibn Shatir were aware of the need to align geometrical models with a causal account of the physical universe.[766] But what matters in the end seems to be more of a concern in ensuring that the geometrical models are consistent with the astronomical observations, rather

765 Abdelhamid Sabra, "The Appropriation and Subsequent Naturalization of Greek Science in Medieval Islam: A Preliminary Statement," *History of Science* 25 (1987): 223–243.

766 George Saliba, *Islamic Science and the Making of the European Renaissance* (Cambridge, Massachusetts: The MIT Press, 2007), 169–170.

than fulfilling some realist criteria such as consistency with the notion of (real) crystalline spheres.

Nasr has however suggested that Muslim scientists such as Ibn Haytham adopted a realist approach towards science, which laid the basis for future European orientation towards science:[767]

> ...But even more important in the long run for the philosophy of science, was Alhazen's insistence upon the crystalline nature of the spheres. In Greek science, while the Aristotelian insisted that the aim of science was to know the nature of things, the mathematicians and astronomers generally believed that their aim was to 'save the phenomena.' The Ptolemaic spheres were convenient mathematical inventions that aided calculation and had no physical reality. Perhaps the most important heritage that Islamic science bequeathed upon the West was to insist that the role of science, including mathematics, must be the search for knowledge of the reality and being of things. The emphasis upon the crystalline nature of the spheres by Alhazen was precisely a statement of this belief. Physics in Muslim eyes was inseparable from ontology. This quest for the real in mathematical physics and astronomy was so thoroughly adopted in the West that even during the scientific revolution no one doubted that the role of physics was to discover the nature of things. Newton was actually following a philosophy of physics that Alhazen and other Muslim thinkers had bestowed upon all science of nature, not only the Aristotelian but also the mathematical and geometric sciences of Euclid, Ptolemy and their successors. The modern debates between the points of view of Meyerson, Cassirer, Northrop and the positivists and the analysts reveal in retrospect the significance of the realism imported to mathematical physics by Alhazen and certain other Muslim thinkers.

Although the view expressed by Nasr above might suggest that Islamic science is basically realist in nature, it can however be argued that the approach adopted by Alhazen is an isolated case, and not representative of Islamic science. Indeed, Alhazen was unique in his attempt to combine natural philosophy, mathematics, and the experimental method, both in his study of astronomy as well as optics. Nasr was quite correct in suggesting that Alhazen was the precursor of modern science, and that Newton's approach to science is similar to that of Alhazen. However, Nasr in some of his other works took a different position on the question of scientific realism in Islamic science as a whole. Although Nasr might have lauded Alhazen's scientific realism as a precursor to the approach adopted by Newton in particular, and modern science in general, he critiqued the mechanical philosophy of early modern science for robbing the science of nature of its symbolic dimension, and replacing it with a materialist view of the world.[768] Seventeenth century science, especially physics, conceived in a realist sense, would regard the world as essentially

767 Seyyed Hossein Nasr, *Islamic Life and Thought* (Petaling Jaya: Islamic Book Trust, 2010), 70–71.

768 Nasr, *Religion and the Order of Nature*.

materialistic, being made up of matter (i.e. atoms) in motion. Although it might be a laudable aim for Muslim scientists to discover the real nature of things, this according to Nasr in some of his other works, cannot be known through modern science. Nasr's criticism of the 'metaphysics of science' and its inferior status with respect to Islamic or religious metaphysics, have been articulated in his other works such as *Knowledge and the Sacred*.[769]

It is fair to say that overall Nasr's position seems to be against scientific realism, and that the view expressed concerning Alhazen's realist approach to science cannot be representative of Islamic science. One would therefore conclude, as had Sabra, that Islamic science is basically instrumentalist.[770] The instrumentalist nature of Islamic science, and the non-integration of (Greek) natural philosophy with mathematics and experimentation, kept Islamic science immune from the kind of epistemological-cultural crisis that was later to beset the West. Thus, despite its lack of material progress, Islamic science managed to save its soul. The absence of debates on scientific realism among Muslim thinkers after the seventeenth century attests to this, and the belated response of Muslim thinkers in terms of the "Islamization of Science/Knowledge" to the cultural crisis of science illustrates how the different trajectories in the development of science in the two civilizations leads to different intellectual and cultural responses.

Conclusion

I have tried to show how the discourse on scientific realism can be seen within the broader context of the discourse on modernity and the place of modern science in contemporary culture. The problem of scientific realism, as it pertains to scientific knowledge, only makes sense with respect to the 'new' rather than the 'old' science, in which the integration between natural philosophy, mathematics, and the experimental method occurred in the formation of modern science. One crucial feature in the making of the new science was the fusion between 'natural philosophy' and 'instrumentality' which made science not merely intellectual and explanatory, but also efficacious and predictive. It is this combination between thought and practice, belief and action, that created an in-built epistemological tension whose resolution was a philosophical response. The discourse on scientific realism provides the resources for the resolution of this tension. Interestingly, the major philosophical positions taken on the question of scientific realism, highlight either one of the three components mentioned above. Roughly, the scientific realists, by stressing on the role of scientific theories as giving us a true account of the natural world, re-assert the status of science as 'episteme' or 'natural philosophy'—a role which it played in

769 Seyyed Hossein Nasr, *Knowledge and the Sacred* (Edinburgh: Edinburgh University Press, 1981).
770 Sabra, "Appropriation and Subsequent Naturalization of Greek Science."

the ancient and medieval periods. The instrumentalists and pragmatists on the other hand, construed the role of science as a conceptual device which enabled us to deal effectively with nature and emphasized the 'instrumentality' aspect of science and its efficacy through experimentation. The structural realists, on the other hand, whose effort was aimed at salvaging a metaphysical version of scientific realism in the face of the collapse of ontic and convergent realism, appealed to the mathematical component of modern science by giving it a realist interpretation.

In the Islamic world, however, apart from the debates in astronomy in the Middle Ages, the issue of scientific realism in its modern form did not occur because the fusion of natural philosophy with mathematics and experimentation was absent in the Islamic world.[771] However, the pivotal role played by western imperialism and its fusion of science, technology and the economy and later implantation in colonized Muslim states, forced Muslim intellectuals to provide their own belated intellectual responses.[772] One such response is found in the programmatic "Islamisation of Science" discourse beginning in the 1980s, and subsequent attempts to align or contextualise science within an Islamic framework. Osman Bakar was one of the proponents of the Islamization of Science movement. But he has recently suggested that Muslim intellectuals must go beyond such a discourse to looking at how the various forms of knowledge developed by different civilizations could be approached from a universalist perspective and then fused to bring about a new epistemology. This can also be seen as an attempt to 're-enchant' science through Islamic ethics and metaphysics in an effort to contain the damaging cultural impact of a realist construal of science in a modernizing Muslim society.[773]

To conclude, the different trajectories taken by Islamic and European science beginning from the Middle Ages to the Scientific Revolution of the seventeenth century, especially in relation to the role of natural philosophy in the development of science, have brought about different philosophical responses. The integration of natural philosophy, mathematics, and the experimental method in the seventeenth century has brought about a situation in which metaphysics and ontology has been subjected to a secular methodology, thus eliminating culturally enchanting paradigms as no longer intellectually respectable in modern culture. This has evoked philosophical responses both in the West and the Islamic world. In the West, it took the form of the discourse on scientific realism. In the Islamic world, although scientific realism

771 Mohd Hazim Shah, "Rethinking the Needham Question: Why Should Islamic Civilisation Give Rise to the Scientific Revolution?" in *The Bright Dark Ages: Comparative and Connective Perspectives*, eds. Arun Bala and Prasenjit Duara, 217–235 (Leiden: Brill, 2016).

772 Maisarah and Mohd Hazim, "The Rise of Modern Science."

773 Chai Choon Lee, Mohd Hazim Shah, and Maisarah Hasbullah, "The Islamisation of Knowledge as a Response to Societal Rationalisation and Disenchantment in Malaysia," *Southeast Asian Social Science Review* 1 (2016): 70–92; and Zaidi, "Muslim Reconstructions of Knowledge."

was not the main theme through which the intellectual response was made, it nevertheless included it. That response was more broadly articulated within the alternative discourse of the Islamization of Science.

Bibliography

Al-Daffa, Ali A., and John Stroyls. *Studies in the Exact Sciences in Medieval Islam.* Dhahran, Saudi Arabia: University of Petroleum and Minerals, and Chichester: John Wiley & Sons, 1984.

Anstey, Peter R., and John A. Schuster, eds. *The Science of Nature in the Seventeenth Century: Patterns of Change in Early Modern Natural Philosophy.* Dordrecht: Springer, 2005.

Barker, Peter, and Bernard Goldstein. "Realism and Instrumentalism in Sixteenth Century Astronomy." *Perspectives on Science* 6, no. 3 (1998): 232–258.

Blair, Ann. "Natural Philosophy." In *The Cambridge History of Science. Volume 3: Early Modern Science,* edited by Katharine Park and Lorraine Daston, 365–406. Cambridge: Cambridge University Press, 2006.

Boyd, Richard N. "Realism, Underdetermination, and a Causal Theory of Evidence." *Noûs* 7, no. 1 (1973): 1–12.

Butterfield, Herbert. *The Origins of Modern Science.* London: G. Bell, 1957.

Cohen, H. Floris. "The Onset of the Scientific Revolution: Three Near-Simultaneous Transformations." In *The Science of Nature in the Seventeenth Century: Patterns of Change in Early Modern Natural Philosophy*, edited by Peter R. Anstey and John A. Schuster, 9–33. Dordrecht: Springer, 2005.

_____. *How Modern Science Came Into the World.* Amsterdam: University of Amsterdam Press, 2010.

Cohen, I. Bernard. *The Birth of a New Physics.* New York: Penguin Books, 1992.

Cunningham, Andrew, and Perry Williams. "De-Centering the 'Big Picture': "The Origins of Modern Science" and the Modern Origins of Science." *The British Journal for the History of Science* 26, no. 4 (1993): 407–432.

De Regt, H.W. "Scientific Realism in Action. Molecular Models and Boltzmann's *Bildtheorie.*" *Erkenntnis* 63 (2005): 205–230.

Dear, Peter. "The Mathematical Principles of Natural Philosophy: Toward a Heuristic Narrative for the Scientific Revolution." *Configurations* 6, no. 2 (1998): 173–193.

_______. Intelligibility in Science. *Configurations* 11 (2003): 145–161.

_______. "What Is the History of Science the History *Of*? Early Modern Roots of the Ideology of Modern Science." *Isis* 96 (2005): 390–406.

_______. *The Intelligibility of Nature.* Chicago and London: The University of Chicago Press, 2006.

Dijksterhuis, E. J. *The Mechanization of the World Picture.* Princeton, New Jersey: Princeton University Press, 1986.

Gaukroger, Stephen, *The Emergence of a Scientific Culture* (Cambridge: Cambridge University Press, 2006).

_______. *The Emergence of a Scientific Culture.* Cambridge: Cambridge University Press, 2006.

Gellner, E. *The Legitimation of Belief.* Cambridge: Cambridge University Press, 1974.

Grant, Edward. *Physical Science in the Middle Ages.* Cambridge: Cambridge University Press, 1977.

_______. *The Foundations of Modern Science in the Middle Ages.* Cambridge: Cambridge University Press, 1996.

_______. *Science and Religion, 400 BC to 1550 AD.* Baltimore: Johns Hopkins, 2004.

_______. *A History of Natural Philosophy: From the Ancient World to the Nineteenth Century.* Cambridge: Cambridge University Press, 2007.

_______. "The Fate of Ancient Greek Natural Philosophy in the Middle Ages: Islam and Western Christianity." *The Review of Metaphysics* 61, no. 3 (2008): 503–526.

Habermas, J. *The Theory of Communicative Action.* Vol.1. Boston: Beacon Press, 1981.

Hall, A. R. *The Scientific Revolution, 1500–1800: The Formation of the Modern Scientific Attitude.* London: Longmans, 1954.

Henry, John. *The Scientific Revolution and the Origins of Modern Science.* Basingstoke, Hampshire: Palgrave MacMillan, 2008.

Hogendijk, Jan P., and Abdelhamid I. Sabra. *The Enterprise of Science in Islam: New Perspectives.* Cambridge, Massachusetts: The MIT Press, 2003.

Holton, Gerald. *Thematic Origins of Scientific Thought: Kepler to Einstein.* Cambridge, Massachusetts: Harvard University Press, 1973.

Hoodbhoy, Pervez. *Islam and Science: Religious Orthodoxy and the Battle for Rationality.* Kuala Lumpur: S. Abdul Majeed, 1992.

Huff, Toby. *The Rise of Early Modern Science.* Cambridge: Cambridge University Press, 1995.

Iqbal, Muzaffar. *Science and Islam.* Westport, Connecticut and London: Greenwood Press 2007.

Kheirandish, Elaheh. "Organizing Scientific Knowledge: The 'Mixed' Sciences in Early Classifications." In *Organizing Knowledge: Encyclopedic Activities in the Pre-Eighteenth Century Islamic World,* edited by Gerhard Endress, 135–154. Leiden: Brill, 2006.

Kuhn, Thomas. *The Structure of Scientific Revolutions.* Chicago: University of Chicago Press, 1970, 2nd edition.

Lee, Chai Choon, Mohd Hazim Shah, and Maisarah Hasbullah. "The Islamisation of Knowledge as a Response to Societal Rationalisation and Disenchantment in Malaysia." *Southeast Asian Social Science Review* 1 (2016): 70–92.

Macfarlane, Alan. "Ernest Gellner on Liberty and Modernity." In *Ernest Gellner and Contemporary Social Thought*, edited by Sinisa Malesevic and Mark Haugard, 31–49. Cambridge: Cambridge University Press, 2007.

Maisarah Hasbullah and Mohd Hazim Shah. "The Rise of Modern Science: Islam and the West." *Philosophy East & West* 68, no. 1 (2018): 78–96.

Malesevic, Sinisa, and Mark Haugard, eds. *Ernest Gellner and Contemporary Social Thought.* Cambridge: Cambridge University Press, 2007.

Miller, Arthur I. *Deciphering the Cosmic Number: The Strange Friendship of Wolfgang Pauli and Carl Jung.* New York: W.W. Norton & Company, 2010.

Mohd Hazim Shah. "Rethinking the Needham Question: Why Should Islamic Civilisation Give Rise to the Scientific Revolution?" In *The Bright Dark Ages: Comparative and Connective Perspectives*, edited by Arun Bala and Prasenjit Duara, 217–235. Leiden: Brill, 2016.

Nasr, Seyyed Hossein. *Knowledge and the Sacred.* Edinburgh: Edinburgh University Press, 1981.

_________. *Religion and the Order of Nature.* New York: Oxford University Press, 1996.

_________. "Islamic Science, Western Science: Common Heritage, Diverse Destinies." In *The Revenge of Athena Science, Exploitation and the Third World*, edited by Ziaudin Sardar, 239–259. London and New York: Mansell Publishing Limited, 1998.

_________. *Islamic Life and Thought.* Petaling Jaya: Islamic Book Trust, 2010.

Osman Bakar. *Tawhid and Science: Islamic Perspectives on Religion and Science.* Shah Alam: Arah Publications. Second Edition, 2008.

Papineau, David, ed. *The Philosophy of Science.* Oxford: Oxford University Press, 1996.

Popper, Karl. *Conjectures and Refutations.* London: Routledge, 1972.

Psillos, Stathis. *Scientific Realism: How Science Tracks Truth.* Routledge: London and New York, 1999.

Ragep, F. Jamil. "Freeing Astronomy from Philosophy: An Aspect of Islamic Influence on Science." *Osiris* 2nd Series, 16 (2001): 49–64.

Rorty, Richard. *Philosophy as Cultural Politics.* Cambridge: Cambridge University Press, 2007.

Rouse, Joseph. "Philosophy of Science and the Persistent Narratives of Modernity." *Studies in History and Philosophy of Science* 22, no. 1 (1991a): 141–162.

_______. "The Politics of Postmodern Philosophy of Science." *Philosophy of Science* 58, no. 4 (1991b): 607–627.

Sabra, Abdelhamid I. "The Appropriation and Subsequent Naturalization of Greek Science in Medieval Islam: A Preliminary Statement." *History of Science* 25 (1987): 223–243.

Saliba, George. *Islamic Science and the Making of the European Renaissance.* Cambridge, Massachusetts: The MIT Press, 2007.

Sambursky, S. *The Physical World of the Greeks.* Princeton, New Jersey: Princeton University Press, 1987.

Zaidi, Ali. "Muslim Reconstructions of Knowledge and the Re-enchantment of Modernity." *Theory, Culture & Society* 23, no. 5 (2006): 69–91.

_______. *Islam, Modernity, and the Human Sciences.* New York: Palgrave Macmillan, 2011.

Zilsel, E. "The Sociological Roots of Modern Science." *The American Journal of Sociology* 47, no. 4 (1942): 544–562.

Chapter 21

Bridging Civilizational Divides: Osman Bakar's Life-Long Quest for the Middle Ground

Peter T. C. Chang

Senior Lecturer and Deputy Director of the Institute of China Studies, University of Malaya

In 1989, the world heaved a sigh of relief at the sight of the fall of the Berlin Wall. After nearly half a century, the West has prevailed over the Soviet Union, winning the Cold War without an open conflict thus sparing humankind from the dreaded risk of a nuclear catastrophe. This historic moment of triumph for the free world led to Francis Fukuyama's grand declaration of the 'end of history.' Liberal democracy has proven victorious, marking the apex of human political progress. For Samuel Huntington, on the other hand, the Cold War win did not spell the end of human conflict. It merely shifted the contours of hostilities from ideological to religious fault lines. Future fault lines are likely to develop between the world's diverse civilizational blocks. Huntingdon's 'clash of civilization' thesis became the dominant theory, dictating the intellectual discourse on the remaking a post-Cold War new world order.[774]

Then came the fateful September 11, 2001, attacks in New York City. This tragedy turned what was then an academic hypothesis into a historical reality. For many, the collapse of the World Trade Centre twin towers validated the Huntington thesis on the inevitability of the clash of civilizations. Indeed, the horrific assault on mainland America sent the United States into a protracted global war against terrorism, and by extension, an open conflict between "the Christian West" with "the Islamic world." This sets the backdrop of Osman Bakar's expansive body of works on inter-civilization dialogue. Trained in mathematics, Osman's primary scholastic interest was to explore the

774 For background reading on these historical shifts see Francis Fukuyama, *The End of History and the Last Man* (New York: Macmillan, 1992) and Samuel P. Huntington, *The Clash of Civilizations and the Remaking of World Order* (New York, Simon & Schuster, 1996).

nexus between science and Islam. Later, Osman's scholarly inquiry extended into cross-cultural and inter-religious studies. In 1998, he founded the Centre for Inter-Civilizational Dialogue at the University of Malaya and hosted the inaugural Islam and Confucianism conference. In the aftermath of the 9/11 tragedy however, Osman's attention shifted towards addressing the deteriorating trust between Islam and the West. He sought to find points of reconciliation between these two civilizations.

As a bridge-builder, Osman understands that both sides must meet half-way in order to establish common grounds for co-existence. This accommodation would require a delicate management of sets of dialectics: unity versus diversity, orthodoxy versus heterodoxy, the earthly versus the heavenly, among others. Indeed, Osman is particularly mindful of the antithesis between faith and reason. As a man of science, he is cognizant that the convictions of heart, if left unchecked by the illumination of the mind, can lead to inhumane theological dogmas. Still and all, as a man of faith, he is also aware that scientific advancement without the underpinning of spirituality will ultimately yield a hollow material vassal. This chapter will look at Osman's scholastic accomplishments from the perspective of his life-long search for the middle-ground, as he tirelessly seeks to forge the commonalities needed for the worlds diverse civilizations to co-exist peacefully. This study will consist of five sections.

We begin with an overview of the post 9/11 realities and examine Osman's call for critical self-introspection by all sides including the Islamic civilization, as part of the process to heal a traumatized and fractured world. The second section then looks at Osman's analysis of the intra-conflict between the Abrahamic traditions and the pervasive misperception of Islam as immoderate and intolerant. Despite its monotheistic worldview, Islam affirms an inclusive and pluralistic *ummah*. But the failure to consistently live out these ideals, Osman laments, led to the erroneous representation of Islam as incapable of co-existence with others. In calling for self-rectification, Osman extols his fellow Muslims to move beyond mere tolerance into active engagement with other civilizations. The third section will examine Osman's broader definition of 'salvation' and the case made for inter-civilization collaboration with, among others, Confucianism, to advance the fate of humankind at present. In the quest to establish the common good, Osman wrestles with the perennial tension between unity and diversity, reason and faith. Finally, I will consider Osman's enduring search for the middle ground and analyse his criticism of secular modernity and its irreverence for the sacred. The chapter closes with a look at Malaysia, widely considered a moderate and stable multi-racial, multi-religious Muslim country. We will explore two factors underpinning this reputation: the Malay civilization's forbearing temperament and Malaysian's collective willingness to meet half-way for the sake of national unity. I surmise that these judicious disposition and pragmatic acumen are similarly aptly embodied in the life and scholarship of Osman Bakar, the Malay scholar and Muslim intellectual.

The 9/11 Aftermath and Self-Introspection

To some extent, the current geopolitical tussle between United States (USA) and China is an iteration of the earlier ideological driven 'Cold War', as the CPC-PRC (Communist Party of China-People's Republic of China) authoritarian one-party-state continues to rebuff the embrace of liberal democracy. But today's US-Sino superpower rivalry may also be seen as a post-cold war conflict between two distinct civilizational blocks, namely, Christianity and Confucianism. Indeed, these two religious and philosophical traditions represent two very different belief systems, namely, monotheism and polytheism respectively. And in many ways the contentious Asian values debates in the 1990s underscore some of their dissimilarities. The Christian West and Confucian East opposing interpretation of human rights, and differing view of individual liberty in relations to communal responsibility, are cultural dissonances that bear the markings of what Huntington called the 'clash of civilizations.'

Subsisting alongside the present-day estranged US-China relationship is the prevailing tension between the Christian West and Islamic world. The long-history of animosity between these two Abrahamic traditions may be traced back to the medieval crusades. In the modern era, the legacies of colonialism and the intractable Palestine crisis continue to perplex interactions between the two civilizations. Then in 2001, this acrimony came to a climax with the tragic September 11 New York City attack. The collapse of the twin towers was a visually shocking assault on humanity that instantly drew universal condemnation and outpouring of commiseration. As Osman Bakar describes it: "The September 11 attacks evoked widespread sympathy for the US in Southeast Asia. Muslims throughout the region were horrified by the senseless barbarity of the attack, which was carried out in the name of their religion."[775] This senseless violence, Osman asserts, does not represent what Islam stood for. There was solidarity in grief as Muslims around the globe mourned the loss and renounced the inhumanity of radical jihadists.

The Americans' response to the horrific 9/11 attack was immediate and devastating. On the military front, the US retaliated with the invasion of Afghanistan and then Iraq. Across multiple fronts, the 'war on terrorism' that was waged inside and outside of the United States. It fuelled waves of Islamophobic sentiments and violence against the wider Muslim communities. The Americans' harsh and indiscriminate reprisal diluted the Muslim sympathy

---

775 Osman Bakar, "The Impact of the American War on Terror on Malaysian Islam," *Islam and Christian – Muslim Relations* 16, no. 2 (2005): 113.

that came forth in the aftermath of the 9/11 tragedy. The vindictive counter response created resentment that divided the Islamic world. Some Muslims reverted to their defiant stance, accusing the West of bedevilling Islam. Others, including Osman maintain conflicted feelings. What the US has done is damaging and reprehensible but they are mindful that in order to stop the cycle of violence, both sides must step back and take stock of their respective culpabilities. As is the case in every civilizational conflict, none is ever blameless. According to Osman, in the present clash with the West, Muslims must also bear some guilt for the current state of affairs. "Muslims may point to US faults, but are they also looking at their own faults? What is clearly lacking in the post-September 11 Muslim world is self-criticism, an attempt at a self-reflection or self-understanding of its internal problem."[776]

Thus, Osman stressed that it is incumbent upon the Muslim world to undertake a process of self-introspection in the interest of healing wounds and restoring mutual trust. And one area that calls for critical self-reflection is the pervasive misperception of Muslims as intolerant towards others. While the lack of understanding among non-Muslims has resulted in some of these misrepresentations, in Osman's assessment, this is a problem aggravated by the failure among Muslim to measure up to their Islamic inclusive ideals.

The Challenge Within: Actualizing One's Ideals

Why are we here? And what awaits us after the expiration of life in the here and now? Existential angst over human mortality have perplexed the human soul since the beginning of time. And humankind continues to turn to the worlds' diverse religiosity and spiritualities in search for answers into the mysteries of the hereafter. All Abrahamic faiths believe that there is life after death. To attain a place in the paradise, one must live life in conformity with God's divine precepts as revealed in the Holy Scriptures. The Abrahamic belief in the only one true God underpins the monotheistic conviction that the 'Peoples of the Book' are endowed with the special revelation necessary for post-humus spiritual salvation.

But there are points of disagreement among the adherents of the 'Religions of the Book' over who possess the complete corpus of God's sacred pronouncements. This feud lies at the heart of the continuing animosity within the Abrahamic family, with Judaism, Christianity, and Islam, each viewing the other's scripture as insufficient for salvation. For Osman, the sister traditions' disputes over who holds the key to paradise are misguided and inconsistent with the teachings of the Qur'an. The Qur'ān is clear that if the spiritual descendants of Abraham live a life in reverence of the only one true God, then their reward in Heaven is assured. Osman cites the following verse as evidence of this point:

776 Osman Bakar, "The Impact of the American War," 116.

Verily, those who believe [i.e., the Muslims] and those who are Jews and Christians, and Sabians, whoever believes in God and the Last Day and do righteous deeds shall have their reward with their Lord; and then shall be no fear nor shall they grieve.[777]

In the doctrine of the *Dhimmi*, Islam's embrace of non-Muslims actually extends to the non-Abrahamic religions, who were accorded protection and rights that include the freedom to practise their polytheistic beliefs. Granted that the non-Muslim minorities must abide by some Islamic norms, are subjected to certain restrictions, and are not accorded the same rights. Still, to assert that the Islamic world as fundamentally intolerant of those different from themselves is theologically erroneous and historically incorrect. The Islamic Golden Age, for instance, was a period of great inter-civilizational exchange. Muslims flourished through the cross-fertilization of cultural ideas and scientific knowledge with the Greek, India, and Sinic civilizations. Admittedly, the Islamic empires do not always live up to its highest ideals. Some Muslims have persecuted and mistreated religious minorities and contravened the inclusive spirit of Islam. Regrettably, these episodes have led some to the distorted perception and misrepresentation of Islam as inherently intolerant.

Surely, the falling short of one's own standard is not a failure of the entire tradition. Across history, all human civilizations have invariably transgressed against their avowed universal principles and values. To some extent, the reason why the world civilizations had at times come into conflict with each other is because either one or both sides have strayed from their individual moral ideals. Therefore, in order to ensure harmonious co-existence, one crucial step every civilization must undertake is to make certain each stay true to their respective aspirations. For Osman, Muslims have their share of critical self-reflection to do. If Islamic countries and societies have not consistently actualized the Prophet's vision of an inclusive *ummah*, they must henceforth strive harder to sustain an open and pluralistic milieu that is reflective of the twenty-first century globalized reality.

Beyond Tolerance: Engaging Confucianism and the World

In Osman's assessment, one key factor why Muslims tend to succumb to an exclusive worldview is due to the narrow definition of what constitute 'salvation.'

Yet another important understanding of the idea of exclusivity and inclusivity in religious belief and practices, but which is still not well understood by many people, pertains not to salvation in post-humus life but to societal

777 Osman Bakar, "Exclusive and Inclusive Islam in the Qur'ān: Implications for Muslim-Jewish Relations," *Journal of the Interdisciplinary Study of Monotheistic Religions (JISMOR)* 5 (February 2010): 12.

salvation here and now in this earthly life. In this context, what we are having is a broadening of the idea of salvation in relation to the issue of inclusivity and exclusivity. Salvation is usually understood to refer to the post-humus human state. But here the word 'salvation' is used to refer to the terrestrial human life as well.[778]

Osman's broader definition of 'salvation' is important at two levels. First, this is an appeal for a more holistic view of life. Without question, the post-humus spiritual salvation is the ultimate concern but this should not be pursuit at the expense of our terrestrial wellbeing. An excessive preoccupation with the other-worldly to the neglect of the this-worldly is surely incompatible with the Prophet's teaching. The wholesome life is one that meets the demands of both the spiritual and the bodily, the heavenly and the earthly.

The call for a balanced account of the meaning of life is linked to Osman's appeal to a more inclusive view and embrace of the world. To be sure, the Abrahamic traditions retain the exclusive precepts needed for post-humus spiritual salvation. But on matters pertaining to societal salvation, there ought to be room for inter-civilizational collaborations. In other words, even if there are disagreements about the after-life, the different world religions can and should work together to better the fate of humankind in the here and now. The theological basis and justification for the multi-religious cooperation is the doctrine of natural law. In addition to the sacred precepts revealed to the Religion of the Book, God has also revealed a set of moral law in nature that is universally accessible to all humankind. While inadequate for post-humus spiritual salvation, these general revelations serve to govern and advance societal salvation in the present life. For Osman, these shared universal moral principles open the door for Islam to engage with the non-Abrahamic world religions, including with Confucianism, which as a matter of fact, represents a radically different belief system.

Indeed, Islam and Confucianism profess very distinct view of the world. In the Islamic dualistic universe, for example, there is a strict dichotomy between the creator and the created, the sacred and the profane. By contrast in the Confucian organic cosmology, all things including the mundane and the transcendent are seen as ultimately one. On the existential angst over life after death, for instance, the Chinese sages adopted a stoic demeanour, cautioning against an excessive preoccupation with the here-after. The following student-teacher exchange recorded in the *Analects* provides an example:

> Zilu asked how to serve the spirits and gods. The Master said: "You are not yet able to serve men, how could you serve the spirits?"
> Zilu said: "May I ask you about death?" The Master said: "You do not yet know life, how could you know death?"[779]

778 Osman Bakar, "Exclusive and Inclusive Islam in the Qur'ān," 6–7.

779 *Analects*, trans. Burton Watson (New York: Columbia University Press, 2007), 73.

The Confucian agnostic silence on the afterlife needs to be understood within the context of its ties with Daoism and Buddhism. In the Chinese moral landscape, these three separate traditions sustain a complex co-existence to form what is commonly understood as Chinese religiosity. And one way to make sense of their intricate interaction is through the perspective of the division of labour. These variegated traditions complement each other by serving specific functions in the life of the Chinese, as an individual, a community, and a civilization. And this distinction can be broadly divided into the 'this-worldly' and 'other-worldly' spheres. With Confucianism taking the lead in shaping the mundane social political order. And Daoism, Buddhism and other folk religions addressing concerns unanswered by Confucianism, mostly on matters pertaining to life after death, the after-world, and the transcendental.[780]

The Confucian this-worldliness has led to questions whether this ancient Chinese moral tradition is a philosophy or religion. For Osman, the answer could be both. Whether Confucianism's precepts are drawn from general or specific revelation, it is above all, a philosophy. Yet the Confucian tradition bear some semblance of a religion in its recognition of a higher authority, namely, the Heaven. Osman thus postulated that Confucius could in fact be considered as a recipient of divine revelation.

> Confucius may or may not have been a prophet of Islam. But a Muslim does not go against the teachings of his religion if he makes the claim that Confucius was a prophet of Islam. After all, the Qur'ān says divine revelation was a universal phenomenon. There was no nation or tribe that has not received a message from Heaven.[781]

As is the case, the Confucians do believe that the universe is governed by a set of Heavenly Principles (天理). Not unlike the natural law, the Chinese philosophers affirmed that these principles revealed by Heaven are discernible to all humankind, regardless of race and creed. Therefore, fundamental dissimilarities notwithstanding, Confucianism share with theistic religions, such as Islam, some common understanding on the existence of universal norms binding all. For Osman, these shared principles provide the basis and justification for co-existence and collaboration.

> With vast human and natural resources and inspired by a long history of civilization, both China and the Muslim world are likely to play a more assertive and influential role on the international scene in the near future. Fruitful encounters between civilizations encompassing numerous aspects of human

780 For additional reading on Chinese philosophy and religion please refer to the following: Wing-Tsit Chan, *A Source Book in Chinese Philosophy* (Princeton, NJ: Princeton University Press, 1963), and Julia Ching, *Chinese Religions* (Maryknoll, NY: Orbis Books, 1993).

781 Osman Bakar, "Confucius and the Analects in the Light of Islam," in *Islam and Confucianism: A Civilizational Dialogue*, ed. Osman Bakar and Cheng Gek Nai (Kuala Lumpur: University of Malaya Press, 1997), 72.

> life and thought ought to be encouraged. Were Chinese and Islamic cultures to engage in another large-scale creative interaction, we could expect them to make important contribution to the future well-being of humankind. It is a fact that, throughout history, an active encounter and interaction of religions have always resulted in mutual influence and benefits.[782]

Hence, despite differences in the conception of post-humus salvation, the Islamic and Confucian civilizations can and should jointly work to improve the human condition, at the societal level in the here and now. In extolling civilizational interaction Osman urge the Islamic world to move beyond mere tolerance and to open room for active engagement with others in advancing the common good. "The issue that interests us here is to what extent Islam is prepared to provide space and opportunities for others outside the Islamic faith to have an active and meaningful participation in societal salvation."[783]

For Osman, across time and space, the cross-fertilization of ideas had occurred between human civilizations and for the betterment of all, including the Islamic world. To deny the good in others is to contradict history and Islam's own values.

> There is nothing to be ashamed of in these kinds of cultural borrowing. Muslims who repudiate them and slam the door of Islam to what is good from other cultures, only invite charges of ignorance of history including their own and the nature of inter-civilizational encounters and relationships. Far worse, they invite charges of infidelity to the many universal teachings of their own religion.[784]

In Search of the Middle Ground

For the sake of the human family, world civilizations must be prepared to set aside differences to establish the common grounds needed for co-existence. That said, even as unity is pursued, diversity must also be preserved. Shared values notwithstanding, the world's religious and philosophical landscape will stay invariably diverse. For the world's traditions to flourish, each must be allowed to so do from within their respective belief system. In the quest for co-existence, each must learn to embrace the 'other' without diluting one's own distinct identity. Indeed, not all external influences are conducive for one's internal development. This is a fact not lost on Osman. Even in advocating greater openness, Osman is cognizant of the need to strike the right balance between embracing diversity without forsaking and compromising Islamic core values.

782 Osman Bakar and Cheng Gek Nai, ed., *Islam and Confucianism,* 3.
783 Osman Bakar, "Exclusive and Inclusive Islam in the Qur'ān," 10.
784 Osman Bakar, "Islam and the Challenge of Diversity and Pluralism: Must Islam Reform Itself?," *Islam and Civilisational Renewal Journal* 1, no. 1 (2009): 65.

While external forces, including those coming from the West, can inspire and even shape reforms in Muslim societies, ultimately what proves to be decisive in determining the lasting efficacy of these reforms would be the factor of their compatibility with Islamic teachings. This means that, for example, democratic reforms and the cultivation of democratic values in Muslim societies have to be sustained and nourished by their Islamic roots, although their external forms may be borrowed from the modern Western democratic traditions.[785]

For Osman, it is imperative to remain grounded in one's roots even when adopting and adapting the wisdom of others. Osman's borrowing of some ideas derived from Western liberal democracy while retaining the spirit of Islam is reminiscent of the Confucian world own encounter with the West. In seeking to modernize Imperial China the late nineteenth century Qing reformist Zhang Zhidong proposed the strategy of "Chinese learning as substance, Western Learning for Application" (中学为体，西学为用 Zhongxue Wei Ti, Xixué Wei Yong), to retain the essence of Chinese civilization while transforming China into a modern state.[786]

As it turned out, premodern China had a tumultuous transition into modernity. Ancient Chinese traditions, including Confucianism, were blamed for Imperial China's backwardness vis-à-vis the modern West. In the rush to embrace modernity, the Chinese chose to discard its traditional religiosities in favour of science and Marxism. As a consequence, the mainland turned wholly secularized, stripped of any traces and remnants of its sacred heritages. The twentieth century was, by all counts, a dark era in the long history of the Sinic civilization. This period of self-inflicted harm culminated in the 1960s cultural revolution when a disenchanted China violently renounced its ancient philosophical and religious legacies. Today, there is growing admission on the part of the Peoples Republic of China's leaders and scholars that modern China's treatment of its premodern past may have been an overreaction. A rebalancing is underway, as religiosity regains a new lease of life in mainland China, with temples and monastery, shrines and pagodas, once more dotting the landscape.

Traumatic transitions like those experienced in China informed and shaped Osman's own perception of Islam's encounter with modernity. Indeed, Osman's openness to civilization exchanges is not without qualification. Critical selection of what is good and appropriate for one's own development and watchful tentativeness came to define Osman's life-long search for the middle ground. His approach is one that accommodates the dissimilar without undermining one's core values, that reconciles the tension between orthodoxy and

785 Osman Bakar, "Islam and the Challenge of Diversity and Pluralism," 61.

786 For further information on Zhang Zhidong, please refer to Adam Chang, "Reappraising Zhang Zhidong: Forgotten Continuities During China's Self-Strengthening, 1884–1901," *West Point Research Papers* 26 (2017).

heterodoxy, the old and the new. This delicate balancing act is captured in Osman's criticism of secular modernity. As a mathematician, Osman recognizes the efficacy of science in advancing human material progress. Yet as a man of faith, he is also acutely mindful of the limits of reason in nourishing the spiritual dimension of humanity.

> Contemporary human civilisation is rich and advanced in scientific and technical knowledge, but poor and backwards in moral and spiritual knowledge and wisdom. Consequently, we are superb at solving even the most complex of scientific and technological problems and extremely successful in controlling the forces of the natural world that is external to us. But we are utterly hopeless when it comes to solving the most basic of human problems, and we fail miserably in the task of social engineering, that is, in ordering and controlling human behaviours and the inner forces of human nature which govern them.[787]

Secular modernity and its unbridled pursuit of material wealth is detrimental to the spiritual wellbeing of the human condition. The root cause for this lopsided development, according to Osman, can be traced to that particular moment in Western history when the God-centric worldview was abandoned in favour of the man-centric worldview, where the vision of the whole man has been lost.[788]

> The present crisis has also a lot to do with the fact that Western civilization has no religiously sanctioned law comparable to the *Sharī'a* of Islam or to the law of the Jews. As a consequence, in its long history it has never really known and experienced balance and equilibrium in the true sense of the words. Instead, it has been oscillating from one extreme to the other.[789]

But Osman warned that the Islamic milieu is not immune from this partiality and excess. "Today, the Muslims too have lost their vision of wholeness and their civilizational renewal agenda must seek to recover this wholeness or *Tawhidic* vision."[790] Extremism is a real and present danger, hence his recurring exhortation to stay firmly grounded in the middle and "to remember that the raison d'etre of the *Sharī'a* is to maintain equilibrium in society." [791]

The Malaysia Lesson: To Meet Halfway

All politics is local and one may add that the practise of theology is similarly shaped by contextual forces. Osman's scholastic endeavour is no exception, informed and moulded by his home country, Malaysia. This brings us to the unique place Malaysia holds in history of civilizational encounters.

787 Osman Bakar, "The Place and Role of Maqasid Al-*Sharī'a* in the Ummah's 21st century Civilizational Renewal," *Islam and Civilisational Renewal Journal* 2, no. 2 (2011): 291.

788 Osman Bakar, "Place and Role of Maqasid Al-*Sharī'a*," 297.

789 Osman Bakar, "Place and Role of Maqasid Al-*Sharī'a*," 298.

790 Osman Bakar, "Place and Role of Maqasid Al-*Sharī'a*," 298.

791 Osman Bakar, "Place and Role of Maqasid Al-*Sharī'a*," 298.

Situated in the great waterways of Southeast Asia, the Malay Archipelago was the crossroad of multiple civilizational streams: the Malay, South Asians, Persian-Arabian, East Asians, and Europeans, among others. Today, Malaysia is widely regarded as a modern, moderate Muslim state. There are tensions to be sure yet Malaysia's multi-racial and multi-religious constituents have, by and large, maintained a peaceable co-existence. Malaysia's reputation as a relatively stable, pluralistic Muslim majority country, is in no small part a testament to some distinctive traits of the Malay civilization.

A universal faith, Islam as practised on the ground, does bear contextual variations. Indeed, theology has a dialectically relationship with the host-culture in which it is embedded. The former can have a transformative effect on the latter but this is by no means a one-way dynamic. Indigenous beliefs and folklore can similarly impact how religious ethos are formulated and enforced. This is true of Islam's interaction with the Malay milieu which has a rich pre-Islamic substratum derived from extensive encounters with the Hindu and Buddhist civilizations. Thus, the Malays' conversion to Islam entailed the complex process of re-evaluating their pre-Islamic heritage and establishing an ethical-legal system and socio-political order in the light of the new religion, and creating a new cultural synthesis.[792] And this synthesized co-existence requires the delicate process of reconciling old customs and the new norms.

The validity of other religious laws and pre-Islamic local customary laws was accepted as long as these are not opposed to the teachings of the Qur'ān. For example, in the Malay-Indonesian world, native customs known in Malay as *adat* (from Arabic *'adah*) were accepted as an important source of Islamic law, although, admittedly, tension has always existed between certain elements in the *adat* and the *Sharī'a.*[793]

> Not all *adat* are admissible and strain persists between the old and the new. Overtime and through the ethnic genius of the Malays and the spiritual genius of Islam, these two living entities forged a Malay-Islamic identity that clearly distinguishes it from both the pre-Islamic Malay civilizational identity and other branches of the global Islamic civilization.[794]

Indeed, Islam in Malaysia is imbued with distinctive Malay characteristics. Among other virtues, the Malay communal ethos and spirit of forbearance is credited for engendering a more inclusive Islamic ummah. One historic expression of this was during the declaration of Malaysian independence when the Malay majority accepted the non-Malay minorities as part of the newly independent country. The Malays "notwithstanding their shortcomings as an

792 Osman Bakar, "Islam and the Malay Civilizational Identity: Tension and Harmony between Ethnicity and Religiosity," *Jurnal Peradaban Melayu* 1 (2003): 118–9.
793 Osman Bakar, "Islam and the Challenge of Diversity and Pluralism: Must Islam Reform Itself?," *Islam and Civilisational Renewal Journal* 1, no. 1 (2009): 69.
794 Osman Bakar, "Islam and the Malay Civilizational Identity," 121.

ethnic and religious community…set a historical precedent in modern times when they collectively agreed to accept the granting of full citizenship en masse to more than a million immigrants of ethnic Chinese and ethnic Indian origins from China and India respectively. In so doing, especially in the context of the time, they demonstrated the rare example of 'ethnic grace' ever to be shown by an indigenous population toward their foreign 'guests,' …"[795]

The magnanimity displayed on the part of the Malays spared Malaysia the strife that afflicted other multi-racial, multi-religious countries as they struggled to forge a new post-colonial national identity. The framing of country's constitution was another concession made to ensure the viability of a pluralistic Malaysia. The founding fathers ruled out the possibility of an Islamic theocracy and at the same time did not accept unmitigated Western secularism. Thus, an alternative pathway was pursuit, straddling between the two. "In speaking of the need for a national policy on interreligious relations, we are actually affirming our strong belief that, as far as Malaysia is concerned, there is a better alternative to ideological secularism or religious exclusivism as a response to the issue of religion in the public space."[796]

In this compromised formulation, Islam is institutionalized as an 'official' religion, granting it priority without the excluding the rights of others. This trade-off is part of the negotiated 'social contract,' whereby each constituent must sacrifice some rights for the good of the whole.

> In a religiously plural society, no religion can hope to enjoy a total freedom of public expression of its beliefs and practices as some or all of its followers wish. In Malaysia, many Muslims feel that as the sole official religion, Islam should be fully practised and implemented by the community as well as by the state but in reality, this is not the case much to the dismay of many Muslims. Similarly, many non-Muslims feel strongly that the Constitution entitles them to a complete freedom to practise and develop their respective religions without any impediment or constraint from the authorities. Again, the reality is different and much to their dismay.[797]

Without question, Malaysia's ability to hold together as a pluralistic society is due to the demand imposed by the country's founding fathers, upon all, Muslims and non-Muslims alike, to meet half way in order to secure the public space needed for co-existence. This self-constraint on the part of the Muslim majority underscores the Malay civilization's fortitude and judicious temperament. Traits that have, in no small measure, helped sustained Malaysia as a uniquely diverse and moderate Muslim country. In many ways, this same

795 Osman Bakar, "Multiculturalism: A Malaysia Perspective" in *Multiculturalism in Asia: Peace and Harmony*, ed. Imtiyaz Yusuf (Bangkok: CRS, Mahidol University, 2018), 92.

796 Osman Bakar, "The Evolving Face of Religious Tolerance in Post-Colonial Malaysia: Understanding its Shaping Factors," *Islam and Civilisational Renewal Journal* 2, no. 4 (2011): 623.

797 Osman Bakar, "The Evolving Face of Religious Tolerance," 636.

Malay ethos is manifestly displayed in the private and public persona of Osman Bakar the Muslim intellectual, exuding a distinct empathy for the other and curiosity for the wider world of ideas.

Conclusion

The September 11 tragedy plunged the Islamic world and the Christian West into the first 'post-Cold War' conflict of the 'clash of civilizations' era. In the past decades, China's rise has compounded tensions, turning it into multipolar contention between civilizations. These adverse developments set the backdrop to Osman Bakar's life-long commitment to civilizational dialogue. For Osman, the foreboding clash is not inevitable, the world's civilizations can and should co-exist. But the process must begin from within, with each religious and philosophical traditions living up their respective ideals. He exhorted this fellow Muslims to move beyond mere tolerance and to actively engaged with others, so as to advance the fate of humanity in the here and now. Even as he extols civilizational collaboration, Osman is mindful of the imperative to reconcile the tension between the orthodoxy and heterodoxy, reason and faith, earthly and heavenly. In order to achieve harmonious co-existence, every member in our invariably diverse human family must be prepared to meet halfway for the good of the whole, as was the case with Malaysia.

Introspective yet inquisitive, Osman understood the need to embrace the universal and, at the same time, remain grounded in the particularity of his Malay and Islamic roots. This acumen for the middle ground defined Osman's life and scholarship, and drove his ceaseless pursuit of a unified yet diversified civilizational co-existence. As a scholar of civilizational studies, he has kept alive a long and revered Islamic legacy of mutual enrichment and learning with the outside world. Today, as we stand at a critical juncture in human history where the 'clash of civilization' dominates the global narrative, Osman's commitment to inter-civilizational engagement is vital in reshaping the current discourse, from one encumbered with enmity and animosity, into one fill with mutual respect and constructive possibilities.

Bibliography

Analects. Translated by Burton Watson. New York: Columbia University Press, 2007.

Chan, Wing-Tsit. *A Source Book in Chinese Philosophy.* Princeton, NJ: Princeton University Press, 1963.

Chang, Adam. "Reappraising Zhang Zhidong: Forgotten Continuities During China's Self-Strengthening, 1884–1901." *West Point Research Papers* 26 (2017).

Ching, Julia. *Chinese Religions.* Maryknoll, NY: Orbis Books, 1993.

Fukuyama, Francis. *The End of History and the Last Man.* New York: Macmillan, 1992.

Huntington, Samuel P. *The Clash of Civilizations and the Remaking of World Order.* New York: Simon & Schuster, 1996.

Osman Bakar and Cheng Gek Nai, eds. *Islam and Confucianism: A Civilizational Dialogue.* Kuala Lumpur: University of Malaya Press, 1997.

Osman Bakar. "Confucius and the Analects in the Light of Islam." In *Islam and Confucianism: A Civilizational Dialogue,* edited by Osman Bakar and Cheng Gek Nai, 61–74. Kuala Lumpur: University of Malaya Press, 1997.

Osman Bakar. "Multiculturalism: A Malaysia Perspective." In *Multiculturalism in Asia: Peace and Harmony,* edited by Imtiyaz Yusuf, 88–108. Bangkok: CRS, Mahidol University, 2018.

Osman Bakar. "The Place and Role of Maqasid Al-*Sharīʿa* in the Ummah's 21st Century Civilizational Renewal." *Islam and Civilisational Renewal Journal* 2, no. 2 (2011): 285–301.

Osman Bakar. "The Evolving Face of Religious Tolerance in Post-Colonial Malaysia: Understanding its Shaping Factors." *Islam and Civilisational Renewal Journal* 2, no. 4 (2011): 621–38.

Osman Bakar. "Exclusive and Inclusive Islam in the Qur'ān: Implications for Muslim-Jewish Relations." *Journal of the Interdisciplinary Study of Monotheistic Religions (JISMOR)* 5 (February 2010): 4–15, http://www.cismor.jp.

Osman Bakar. "The Impact of the American War on Terror on Malaysian Islam." *Islam and Christian – Muslim Relations* 16, no. 2 (2005): 107–127.

Osman Bakar. "Islam and the Challenge of Diversity and Pluralism: Must Islam Reform Itself?" *Islam and Civilisational Renewal Journal* 1, no. 1 (2009): 55–73.

Osman Bakar. "Islam and the Malay Civilizational Identity Tension and Harmony between Ethnicity and Religiosity." *Jurnal Peradaban Melayu* 1 (2003): 107–122.

Chapter 22

Islamic Science, Epistemology, and the Space for Religion

Oliver Leaman

Professor of Philosophy and Zantker Professor of Judaic studies at the University of Kentucky, USA

Osman Bakar has played a significant role in bringing the idea of Islamic science back into the modern discussions of what science should be and how it relates to broader issues such as faith. The clarity of his approach has been very helpful in explaining the intricacies of a protracted debate. What role can religion play in a world that can be explained scientifically? This was a question that arose at every stage in the history of science and Osman's response has not been different from earlier scientists who resoundingly answered that they found no difficulty with reconciling their belief in God and their adherence to science. Previously, religion explained what was not understood scientifically but as our knowledge of the world increased, the room for religion seemed to diminish. Still, many scientists who remained as genuine believers and refused to accept that God was marginalized by their activities. Yet they often left very little for Him to do. The occasionalist strategy was sometimes popular, insisting as it does that God is behind everything that happens, so that it only appears to take place due to physical causes. The Qur'an refers to this when it talks about a human being throwing (8:17), which is obviously possible, but is better described as God carrying out the action, since He is the ultimate cause of everything. This approach has a venerable role in Islam, reaching back as we can see to the Qur'an, to the *kalam*, and to thinkers such as al-Ghazali. Occasionalism is entirely unaffected by the progress of science, since whatever explanation we accept for how things work in the world, we just see divine agency as the ultimate cause. It does not fill in the gaps in our knowledge. It provides another level of explanation, one that is perfectly compatible with whatever scientific theory we adopt.

Taqwa and science

The trouble with occasionalism is that it seems to be superfluous. There are a whole range of causes we could refer to when seeking to explain why something happens, Aristotle provides some very sophisticated examples. But essentially we tend to know why something happened and any deeper explanation is possible, and even desirable, but does not do very much to help us understand what took place. Occasionalism sometimes looks like the thesis that God could have prevented what normally happens from happening, and so in that sense it is all down to Him. We would not generally say that someone who exercised a veto plays a determining role in what happens, the role is mainly that of a spoiler. The idea that everything happens only because God makes it happen, that everything is in short a miracle, diminishes the status of miracles as contraventions of the normal run of things. On the other hand, it does emphasize the significance of God, and as books like the Qur'an and the Torah suggest. This is something that human beings are all ready to forget. It is easy to forget something that is not always in front of us, despite its significance and the central Islamic virtue of *taqwa* refers to this. *Taqwa* or piety means orienting ourselves towards God in the sense of thinking of Him and being prepared to respond to Him in what we do and think. This is the central problem, finding a role for God when He seems so much in the background, and it is not especially a problem for science. It is an issue for all human activity. We obscure the situation if we hark back to the glorious past of Islamic science and assume that in the past scientists were really motivated to carry out their work by what they saw as their religious obligations, or that the way they did science was informed by their religious views.

We need to be sophisticated in how we see the link between religion and human behavior. Take a Jewish example, where many Jews who are concerned with how social justice relate it to the principle of *tikkun olam*, repairing the world, which is indeed a central idea in Jewish ethical thought. In reality, the the notion comes from the kabbalah and another type of thinking altogether. Yes, social justice does have a role in trying to make things better and so could be conceived of as repairing those parts of the world that require treatment, but the idea that it is the Jewish principle that motivated people in this regard is fanciful. More plausibly they wished to carry out those meretricious actions and then looked for some religious label to bring them under. There is nothing wrong with doing that, or with that label, but the idea that the religious formula was what motivated them is not compelling. Perhaps it did and yet the evidence often suggests it did not, since the other parts of their lives do not seem to be especially tied up with their religion.

The same principle operates in Islam where Muslims claim some religious motivation that looks implausible. Do Muslims become doctors because they value life in accordance with the ways in which the Qur'an says we should or is it peer or parental pressure? Is it the desire for a well-paying job and an interesting career? There is no need to be cynical here and deny the possibility of a religious motive. Surely, people often act out of such motives, but the fact that there could be such a motive does not mean that there necessarily is one. This is something well understood in the Qur'an as coming under the description of hypocrisy (*nifaq*) and this is to appear to believe in the principles of Islam while in reality not doing so at all. This is common in religion, and is not necessarily devious and intentional, although the Qur'an suggests it often is. It is where someone asserts his or her belief in something but they really do not and that emerges in the way they act. This is a real problem in religion. It is easy to say one believes in something yet be insincere. A good example is believing that it is really God who is behind what I am doing now, since He is the ultimate cause of everything, and yet not really acting as though this were true. In fact, I may think and act as though I am the cause and only give lip service, a wonderful expression, to the idea that really it is God who is doing it. We cannot see Him do it so we forget His role, while still respecting it formally. It is a bit like the situation of a monarch in a constitutional government, law is made when the monarch signs a document but the monarch has to sign every document put in front of him and her, if it has been passed in the right sort of way by the local parliament.

The role of *tawhid*

This might seem to be taking us a long way away from the idea of Muslim science, After all, God as the creator of the world invites us to understand that creation, and presumably that means that we need to understand what He did if we are to be proper scientists. We need to see the world as more than just a materialist entity, not because this is what we should do morally but because epistemologically this is going to be our route to understanding it. The world is more than its matter, and we need to understand its spiritual foundation and design. Also, we should appreciate the *tawhid*, the unity, that underlies it, and is embodied in the unity of its creator. The Qur'an often pokes fun at the idea of there being more than one god, since everything exhibits unity, and this would be otherwise were there to be many gods, or so we are told. Scientists do often try to bring the phenomena together in a theory that exhibits some degree of unity, and seeing patterns and regularities are familiar aspects here. It is not clear though how a religious sensibility helps us in this quest since a scientist could see such unity as both a desideratum of his or her inquiry and yet at the same time a natural phenomenon. It would just be how the scientist thinks how things are and the scientific task to unravel the appearance to get at the reality is not to go from the material to the spiritual, but from the material to the material.

Scientists often do admire what they discover in their inquiries yet without assigning any particular spiritual meaning to it beyond the aesthetic. This may but need not have a religious basis, and what we are talking about here is not so much whether scientists claim a religious underpinning to the universe and to their work, but whether they really operate in accordance with such a principle. Are they being hypocrites? This is in no way to criticize them as Muslims since they may believe that their faith has nothing to do with their work as scientists. It may have something to do with what, as scientists, they should and should not investigate, but not with how they carry out their work. To give an example, a religious person should be a careful and patient driver, but it is possible to be a good driver without being religious. It is even possible to be a careful and patient driver without being religious. Yet we are constantly told that a major difference between Islam and other religions is that the former, unlike the latter, insists on a total attitude based on religion to everything. There is no secular space, as it were, for Muslims. It certainly is true that in the postmodern world Muslims often seem to be far more serious about religion than those in other faiths. Yet all religions nibble at what might be called secular space, in fact an example has just been produced here of how Reform Jews use the concept of *tikkun olam* to represent the secular notion of social justice. No religion says that its participants have religious duties but can do whatever they like in the rest of their lives. In fact, Islam is quite mild in the demands it makes on its adherents, compared to the dietary laws for observant Jews, for example, or the length of prayer services for Orthodox Christians. It sees itself as defining some moderate space between religious extremes, and so there should be no essential difficulty in the existence of some area of life that is not touched by religion.

Reviving religion in science

There is a hadith according to which every century will see someone setting out to revive Islam (*mujaddid*). This is a phenomenon with which we are familiar from a variety of religions, the idea that over time religions, like other social arrangements, become stale and need to be reinvigorated. What is worth noticing about this is that there is no doubt about the value of the central practice, in this case religion, but it could be marriage, sport, fiction and so on. The practice is worth preserving but the delivery is found to be lacking, it fails to attract adherents or does not enthuse them in the way it did in the past. Of course, over time what we do changes and develops in different ways, some of which we welcome. An old and well-established relationship between people, for example, is not the same as when the relationship started, and yet the familiarity that, at the end of a long period, becomes prevalent may not be at all unwelcome or lead to contempt. In religion, the familiar rites and practices may became stale, the participants do not find them effective in linking them with God any more or even with other believers, and yet they may continue with them. They have become part and parcel of their normal activities and this is part of the problem. They no longer mark opportunities to think about important topics or to resolve problems. There is nothing wrong with the institution, the suggestion goes, just how it is presented to its adherents. Perhaps times have changed and what was effective in the past no longer works so well. Or perhaps the presentation of the institution is just too well known and needs to be livened up a bit in order to resonate with its audience. We are focusing on religion here but it could really be anything, a type of candy or a newspaper.

It might be asked why something that is perfect needs to be changed. This is something that is often said when comparing divine with human law. Obviously, the latter changes but the former, established as it is by God on what He knows about the sorts of world He created, is immutable. When God says that Islam is perfect and He has chosen it for the believers (5:3) the idea presumably is that it need not change, it is fine as it is. Some believers do refer to such a point when dealing with proposed changes, which they then reject with contempt. On the other hand, it might be said that since we are ourselves not perfect changes in how things are done might be a good idea, since they would fit in with our changing and malleable characters. This is also something God knows when He created us and He expects us to take appropriate steps accordingly. A reasonable analogy here might be our physical bodies which also require care and attention, and indeed a changing regime as they change. We should not say that God has made our bodies perfect. Satan responds to the biblical Job's equanimity when things go wrong by suggesting that if he is personally afflicted then there might be a very different outcome (*Job* 2: 4). Job is then covered with boils to test his faith, anything material is going to have problems at some stage and those have to be addressed and rectified over time. Our religious practices are not dissimilar. They call for a very physical response and these are subject to the familiar physical vagaries of lack of attention, boredom, negligence and so on.

Forgetting God

We should remind ourselves of the language of the Bible and the Qur'an, which often use quite mild terms like forgetting to describe the ways in which religious observance declines. Originally, a covenant was made between humanity and God, and we are capable of forgetting this, hence the need for prophets to serve as reminders. Moses warns the Jews in the desert "Take care lest you forget the Lord your God by not keeping his commandments and his rules and his statutes, which I command you today" (Deut. 8:11). Of course during their sojourn in the desert they constantly forgot God and especially the first and second commandments and made a god for themselves that they could see (Ex. 32:1–5). As God put it to Jeremiah, "But my people have forgotten me; they make offerings to false gods" (Jer. 18:15a). The deliberate forgetting of God developed into a trust in false gods, a worship of false gods "even as their fathers forgot my name for Baal" (23:27). The idea is that something as minor as forgetting can lead to huge consequences, it is not just a matter of a little absent mindedness making life a bit more inefficient. Here, forgetting is a major source of moral decline, in Islam a refusal to acknowledge the original covenant with God and something that necessitates divine intervention in the form of the sending of prophets to remind people of what they have forgotten. 45:34 makes clear that in just the same way people forget God, so He will forget them when they are consigned to the fire at the end of their lives, a rather more active notion of what it is to forget something. Here, the idea is not that He is negligent, but rather that they are not entitled to expect Him to respond to their wishes at this late stage of their lives.

It might seem ridiculous to use the idea of forgetting when talking about our creator and the source of our entire being, as though one had just forgotten a bus pass. Yet we do forget important things, especially in personal relationships. To take a more parochial example, we owe our lives to our parents in a more immediate manner than to God, and we may be unpleasant or disrespectful to our parents, frequently this happens, yet we know what our relationship is to them. We do not forget that they are our parents but what the implications of that are, and this is a useful idea, since what is important about forgetting is not what we are thinking about on a particular occasion, but more what the implications are of what we should be thinking about. There is a tradition in Islamic ethics of what is called *adab*, which is often translated as manners or etiquette and it seems to be quite a minor aspect of what we normally call morality. After all, what does politeness and habits associated with it, have to do with how we treat people on the broader level of ethical action? For one thing, we can be very polite and polished in our behavior and totally insincere. We are reminded of the Qur'anic notion of hypocrisy already discussed. On the other hand, there is the expression in English which is quite useful here of forgetting one's place. This can refer to something quite minor, like forgetting that you should let certain sorts of people leave an elevator before you, such as older people or people who require more time and space to do things like that. It can mean not getting out before people to whom we ought to defer because they are socially superior to us, and that is of course more dubious from a moral point of view, since differences of rank might not be things we wish to note, given notions of equality. Knowing your place has a moral aspect to it of acknowledging the differences that exist between people and the implications this has for what we do, a mixing of the epistemological and the moral. If we know our place in a universe created by God then we take account in what we do of our complementary roles, and we take account of what we should do. One of the things we should do is acknowledge where we are with respect to Him and think about what that means for our behavior. The question is moral in the sense of asking ourselves how we should act, and epistemological because that question is based on what we know about where we stand in relationship to the creator. Both these questions are very relevant to what we might mean by Islamic science.

Knowing your metaphysical place

Scientists who do not acknowledge the role of God in the universe do not know their place, in the sense discussed here. They do not know the place that the universe has in the divine plan, and so they fail to take account of God in their work. Yet the question to raise is what do they then lose? What difference does it make to anything? It certainly makes no difference to the actual science, since it is clear that religious affiliation has nothing to do with scientific skill. Scientists are of every and no religion. Yet many scientists do link their professional with their faith lives, and clearly they are sincere in what they are saying. It could be that they are just wrong. This is certainly the case for many artists, who speak at length about why they constructed their art in a particular way and often they are obviously misguided. In fact, the very same issue arises when discussing what is often called Islamic art. There are references to *tawhid*, to the hiddenness of God, to the alleged problems with representation and so on, yet these usually turn out to be irrelevant. In any case the intentions of the artist often have a very marginal relationship to the meaning of the work itself, although the cultural background explains the iconography. The artist who made a beautiful vase or building may be a Muslim, and they may include some obvious Islamic or Arabic symbols, yet this is just as relevant to the assessment of the work as whether it was done on a Monday or a Thursday.

As far as science is concerned, it is surprising that more people do not claim some spiritual background to their work. Many of the scientists working on CRSPR research have Islamic names yet few, if any say, anything about the significance of their research to help the sick, or preserve life, or extend our knowledge as though this were a religious task. It is like the acknowledgements and dedications we often see in books to many people, relations, agents, copyeditors and of course to God. Did they all really play a part in the book, or did the author just sit down and write it? He or she no doubt had friends and colleagues with whom they discussed it, but was this important in the writing or the framing of the text? Maybe but one suspects often not, one just thanks people it is useful or pleasant to mention, what the Americans call "recognizing" someone, and it really says very little about how the book came about, what it is about and what its value might be. These are just superfluous flourishes that are traditionally applied and actually contribute very little to our knowledge of the book itself.

The question to ask about acknowledgements is, who made a difference.?Whose comments, ideas, encouragement and so on helped? Does God help scientists find things out? Well, ultimately of course he does, in the sense that He has created a world that can be understood, hence its regularities, and with people in it who can do the understanding. At this level of generality though we cannot point to any specific help that He has provided to a scientist trying to work something out. Even if we look at the literature dealing with renewal it is difficult to discern any specific difference that God makes. The aim seems to be more bringing a focus back on Him and making His presence more alive to us, as opposed to outlining any new discovery that thinking about the divine role in science can offer.

Al-Ghazali goes in the direction of Sufism when trying to revive Islam since this is an approach that is designed to establish a more tangible sense of God in our world. Sufis talk about *dhawq,* taste, in their methods and the *dhikr* methods of prayer that are used are directly oriented towards remembrance of God. This is not supposed to be a formal remembrance where we just think about someone but something much more dramatic and powerful. God's presence is supposed to dominate our consciousness and we feel ourselves putty in His hands. It is worth emphasizing that what is at stake here is not so much an intellectual idea, that God is in charge, but its emotional equivalent, that we are in a deep relationship with Him. Whatever happens is up to Him and we are completely dependent on Him. As is often rightly said, it is easy to say this but not easy to live as though it were true. The point of reviving religion is to import enthusiasm and passion into what might have become clogged up with tradition and ritual. We need to see ourselves as making the original covenant between us and God, not a long-distant past event, and this is the purpose of the sort of dramatic reworking of the religious material undertaken by al-Ghazali and the orientation towards Sufism.

The role of experience

According to Jewish tradition, a Roman emperor wished to find out why the food in Jewish households tasted so good on the Sabbath (*Shabat* 119a). He arranged for the same food to be cooked in the same way, to be prepared for him and when he came to eat it he was disappointed and accused the Jews of misleading him over the precise ingredients. They replied that what was missing was the Sabbath itself, the Sabbath spice, the fact that for Jews this food was being eaten in celebration of a special day and occasion. That is what gave it its flavor and it is something that could not be replicated by the emperor.

We often have in mind some special contribution that a religion makes to an activity, like a special ingredient in food, which makes all the difference. It is difficult to say what it is though. For Islam, there are angels and jinn as part of the world and they intervene in what takes place, just as God does, but their actions are not perceptible to the naked eye. Here, they differ from the Sabbath spice. The emperor noticed the difference or so the story goes. We are reminded of the immediacy of *dhawq* or taste and the fact that it impinges on our senses in a way that cannot be questioned. Al-Ghazali wants our relationship to God to be like that, but how would that work for science where success is based on experiments and theories, not on feelings and experiences?

The significance of direct experience is something that religions talk about a good deal. The aural quality of the Qur'an is very significant, this is a text designed to be heard rather than read. There is a well-known hadith according to which some listeners, who did not understand Arabic, immediately became Muslims when they heard the Qur'an being recited. The early Muslims included people who remembered and then recited the text and as one can imagine the immediacy of that instilled a good deal of authenticity into the transmission of the message. As they died and perhaps disputes arose as to which version of the Book was the authentic one, it came to be necessary to record the text in writing, which indeed preserved it but what went was that direct connection with the past and those who had been *hafiz* or memorizers in the past.

To give another example of this, with the destruction of the Temple and the exile of the Jews, it was no longer possible for the oral tradition to remain entirely oral. The living link had to be discontinued, despite the fact that according to the Talmud the law should not be written down (*Gittin* 60b). The Oral Law was to be passed down from teacher to student and accordingly an oral tradition is vibrant, dynamic and interactive. By contrast with talking with someone, book based learning is based on a text that is fixed and lacks a personal touch. In religion we do not just get a text but also a messenger, prophet and a whole series of events that provide the context within which the text operates. This notion of personal contact is important in any attempt at reviving faith, since it is often said that it is the absence of that relationship which is part of the process of a religion going stale. The importance of the personal is something that came into the fore during the Covid period, when a lot of person to person teaching came to an end and the substitution of teaching at a distance really did not have the same effect for many participants.

Islam and knowledge

The Qur'ān uses the idea of history by placing the reader or listener in the text when it refers to past events with the phrase "remember" (33:7). One can see the lack of linear structure in the Book as an attack on the idea of putting things in compartments, and we might conclude that following the sort of pattern we find in the Bibles is not essential to a religious text, especially one designed to be heard or recited. The text is embodied as it is recited, it is part of an experience that brings together the physical and the spiritual in a unique manner. The thesis that the Book is untranslatable might mean that it rejects any authority outside of itself to pin it down. It requires, according to Asad, both to be read and to be lived. He suggests "the nontranslatability of the Qur'an in a liturgical context makes it difficult for political as well as ecclesiastical authority to control Qur'anic meaning. The original is always present, generating unlimited possibilities of meaning."[798] This can be taken in a number of different ways. One is that the text cannot be domesticated, made to fit easily, into demanding that it be interpreted in particular ways. Then the representatives of religious authority, insisting as they may do on certain interpretations, can be passed over since they are in favor of only one when many exist. There is another way of looking at it though, since if there are many ways of approaching the text, we would surely need guidance on which was right, or at least more feasible, as compared with the others. One way of limiting meaning is, as Asad shows in his book by living with the text, and those who do this soon discover that certain meanings work while others do not. The Qur'an is a guide to action and the reading and hearing is supposed to go along with an acting and doing, and that combination soon enlightens us on what could work and what looks improbable. It looks like experience again is going to be important.

When considering the Qur'an, some commentators make a firm distinction between the historical accuracy of its contents and their aesthetic qualities. They suggest that the point of the text is admonition (*'ihra*) and exhortation (*'iza*) and not history. Historical accuracy is besides the point. As Abu Zayd says, this looks like it is arguing that the Book is neither accurate nor true, but that is not the claim. The claim is that the Book is not about history but about how people should live their lives. It is difficult to see how to get from there to science.[799] The latter is all about *'ilm al-husuli*, knowledge that is conceptual and which we build up through experiment and experience. The more personal *'ilm al-huduri* is of course incorrigible but for that very reason unsuitable for the construction of natural science. There are certainly many references in the Qur'an to how the world works but it is misleading to see these as some sort of nascent scientific investigation. To think of religious texts as scientific is what philosophers used to call a category mistake, it is just not what they are about. It impresses the more naïve believer but does not withstand serious scrutiny.

798 Talal Asad, *Secular Translations: Nation-State, Modern Self, and Calculative Reason* (New York: Columbia University Press, 2018), 60–61.
799 Nasr Abu Zayd, Rethinking the Qur'ān: Towards a Humanistic Hermeneutics (Utrecht: Humanistics University Press, 2004).

Bibliography

Abu Zayd, Nasr. *Rethinking the Qur'ān: Towards a Humanistic Hermeneutics.* Utrecht: Humanistics University Press, 2004.

Abu Zayd, Nasr. *Reformation of Islamic Thought: A Critical Historical Analysis.* Amsterdam: Amsterdam University Press, 2006.

Asad, Talal. *Secular Translations: Nation-State, Modern Self, and Calculative Reason.* New York: Columbia University Press, 2018.

Campanini, Massimo. Philosophical Perspectives on Modern Qur'anic Exegesis: Key Paradigms and Concepts. Sheffield: Equinox, 2016.

Leaman, Oliver. *The Qur'an: A Philosophical Guide.* London: Bloomsbury, 2016.

Afterword

Osman Bakar and Islamic Thought

John L. Esposito

University Professor at the Alwaleed bin Talal Centre for Muslim-Christian Understanding (ACMCU), Georgetown University, USA

I have been fortunate and blessed to have known Professor Osman Bakar for many years. Osman held the Malaysia Chair for the Study of Islam in Southeast Asia in the Center for Muslim-Christian Understanding for five years from 2000–2005. During these landmark years, he was a coeditor and one of the authors of *Asian Islam in the 21st Century* (Oxford University Press). At Georgetown University, he not only taught and did research but also responded to invitations from the Muslim community. Osman was significantly involved in projects and programs of the International Institute for Islamic Thought (IIIT) which was co-founded by Anwar Ibrahim (former Deputy Prime Minister of Malaysia) and Professor Ismail R. al-Faruqi at Temple University with whom both Osman and I studied.

Osman Bakar is one of the leading Muslim scholars of the late twentieth and early twenty-first century. He diagnosed and advocated the critical need for Islamic renewal (*tajdid*) and reform (*islah*), and promoted interfaith relations. Like Muhammad Iqbal, Sayyid Ahmad Khan, Seyyed Hossein Nasr, Ismail Al-Faruqi, Syed Muhammad Naquib al-Attas, and Hamka (Abdul Malik Karim Amrullah), to name a few prominent Muslim scholars and reformers in the modern Muslim world, Osman Bakar recognized the need for Islamic renewal. This, according to him, would enable Muslims—however different nationally, ethnically, and culturally—to live in a faith-based society and civilization. The process would be a bold reconstruction, rooted in reclaiming the legacy of Islamic philosophy, theology, and science and deeply informed by the best of relevant modern Islamic and Western scholarship.

Throughout his life, scholarship, and career, Osman mastered multiple areas of knowledge and published prolifically. Equally important, he worked to implement his reformist vision as a scholar, teacher, and university administrator. His range of scholarship—rare among most scholars today—is reflected in his astounding number of published books, book chapters, and articles and also in the remarkable number of courses (forty-two) that he has taught in his career.

A selection of Osman Bakar's publications reveals the broad scope and trajectory of his thought: *The History and Philosophy of Islamic Science*; *Al-Farabi: Life, Works and Significance, Ibn Khaldun's Legacy and Its Significance, Tawhid and Science: Islamic Perspectives on Religion and Science. Islam and Civilizational Dialogue: Quest for a Truly Universal Civilization, Islamic Civilization and the Modern World, Contemporary Higher Education in Muslim Countries: Defining the Role of Islam in 21st Century Higher Education, Environmental Wisdom for the Planet Earth: The Islamic Heritage, The Qur'an and Interfaith and Inter-civilization Dialogue: Interpreting a Divine Message for Twenty-first Century Humanity, Islam and Confucianism: A Civilizational Dialogue and Islam and Contemporary Scientific Thought.* The corpus of this scholarship has been informed by his experience of teaching and engaging with an astonishing number of undergraduate and graduate students in Malaysia, Brunei, the US, and Japan as well as the many public lectures he has given throughout his career and tireless participation in interfaith and inter-civilizational dialogues.

Somehow, amidst a lifetime of writing, publishing, and teaching, Osman Bakar also held prominent administrative positions in academia as a Deputy Vice Chancellor and Professor and as the Founding Director of the Sultan Omar Ali Saifuddin Centre for Islamic Studies at the Universiti Brunei Darussalam from 2013–2017.

Most appropriately, Osman Bakar's distinguished career has been recognized by his inclusion in *The Muslim 500* which is a directory of the World's 500 Most Influential Muslims. And now, quite appropriately, his lifetime achievements are discussed in this Festschrift which includes many established scholars. A friend and colleague to many who shares his interests in various facets of the Islamic civilization, I am honored to have been his colleague and hope that our friendship will remain strong in the many years to come!

The Works of Professor Osman Bakar

PUBLICATIONS

Books

2022: *Environmental Wisdom for Planet Earth: The Islamic Heritage* (Kuala Lumpur: The University of Malaya and IBT. Second Edition.

2020: (co-ed with Ahmad Murad Merican and Wan Ali Wan Mamat), *Colonialism in the Malay Archipelago: Civilisational Encounters* (Kuala Lumpur: ISTAC-IIUM Publications and Persatuan Sejarah Malaysia).

2019: (co-ed with Cheng Gek Nai), *Islam and Confucianism: A Civilizational Dialogue* (Kuala Lumpur: ISTAC-IIUM Publications). New Edition.

2019: *Al-Ghazali Chair of Islamic Thought Inaugural Lecture: Advancing Comparative Epistemology and Civilisational and Futures Studies* (Kuala Lumpur: ISTAC-IIUM Publications)

2019: *Islamic Civilization and the Modern World* (Turkish Translation) (Istanbul: Insan Yayilari)

2018: *Al-Farabi: Life, Works and Significance* (Kuala Lumpur: IBT), second edition

2018: (co-ed with Cheng Gek Nai), *Islam and Confucianism: A Civilizational Dialogue* (Bosnian Translation) (Sarajevo: El-Kalem)

2017: *Tawhid and Science: Islamic Perspectives on Religion and Science* (Bengali Translation) (Dacca: Bangladesh IIIT)

2016: *Qur'ānic Pictures of the Universe: The Scriptural Foundation of Islamic Cosmology* (Kuala Lumpur: UBD PRESS and IBT)

2016: (co-ed with Hashim Kamali, Daud Batchelor, Rugayah Hashim), *Islamic Perspectives on Science and Technology: Selected Conference Papers* (Singapore: Springer)

2014: (co-ed with Mesut Idris), *Islam in Southeast Europe: Past Reflections and Future Prospects* (Brunei Darussalam: UBD PRESS)

2014: *Islamic Civilization and the Modern World* (Brunei Darussalam: UBD PRESS)

2012: *Islam Dusuncesinde Ilimlerin Tasnifi* (Turkish translation of *Classification of Knowledge in Islam*) (Istanbul: Insan Yayinlari)

2012: *Islam Bilim Tarihi ve Felsefesi* (Second Turkish translation of *History and Philosophy of Islamic Science*) (Istanbul: Insan Yayinlari)

2012 (co-ed with Airulamri Amran), *The Empowerment of Muslim Communities in Private Higher Education* (Kuala Lumpur: IAIS Malaysia & IKIP International College)

2011 (co-ed with Eric Winkel, and Airulamri Amran), *Contemporary Higher Education in Muslim Countries: Defining the Role of Islam in 21st Century Higher Education* (Kuala Lumpur: IAIS Malaysia & IKIP International College)

2010 (co-translator with Baharudin Ahmad), Seyyed Hossein Nasr, *Pengenalan Doktrin Kosmologi Islam*, Dewan Bahasa dan Pustaka, Kuala Lumpur, 2nd edition

2009 (co-ed with Azizan Baharuddin and Zaid Ahmad), *Modul Pengajian Tamadun Islam dan Tamadun Asia*, University of Malaya Press, Kuala Lumpur

2009 (co-ed. with Baharudin Ahmad), *Ibn Khaldun's Legacy and Its Significance*, ISTAC, Kuala Lumpur

2009 *Tauhid dan Sains: Perspektif Islam tentang Agama dan Sains* (Indonesian translation), Pustaka Hidayah, Bandung, Indonesia, 2nd edition

2008. *Tawhid and Science: Islamic Perspectives on Religion and Science.* Arah Publications, Kuala Lumpur. New (2nd) edition.

2007 (co-ed. with John Esposito and John Voll). *Asian Islam in the Twenty-First Century.* Oxford University Press, New York

2007. *Environmental Wisdom for the Planet Earth: The Islamic Heritage.* University of Malaya, Kuala Lumpur

2006. *The Qur'an and Interfaith and Inter-civilization Dialogue: Interpreting a Divine Message for Twenty-first Century Humanity* (Kuala Lumpur: IIITM & ISUGU)

2006. *The History and Philosophy of Islamic Science* (Persian translation), Mashhad, Iran

2005. *Islam and Civilizational Dialogue* (Indonesian translation), Bandung.

2003. *The History and Philosophy of Islamic Science* (Turkish translation), Istanbul, Turkey

2002. *Classification of Knowledge in Islam* (Persian translation), Mashhad, Iran.

1999. *The History and Philosophy of Islamic Science.* Islamic Texts Society, Cambridge (UK); 1991 edition published by Secretariat for Islamic Philosophy and Science, Science University of Penang and Nurin Enterprise, Kuala Lumpur under the title *Tawhid and Science.*

1998. *Classification of Knowledge in Islam.* Islamic Texts Society, Cambridge (UK); 1992 edition published by Institute for Policy Research, Kuala Lumpur.

1997. *Islam and Civilizational Dialogue: Quest for a Truly Universal Civilization.* University of Malaya Press, Kuala Lumpur.

1997. (ed.). *Islam and Confucianism: A Civilizational Dialogue.* University of Malaya Press, Kuala Lumpur.

1995. *Islamic Art: A Malaysian Perspective.* National Art Gallery, Kuala Lumpur. (in Malay and co-author with Ruzaika Omar Basaree)

1992. (ed.). *Science, Technology, and Art in Human Civilizations.* University of Malaya Press, Kuala Lumpur. (in Malay)

1992. *Bibliography of Islamic Manuscripts at Islamic Museum, Malaysia.* Islamic Affairs Division, Prime Minister's Department and The Academy of Malay Studies, University of Malaya, Kuala Lumpur.

1992. *Classification of Knowledge in Islam.* Institute for Policy Research. Kuala Lumpur.

1991. *Tawhid and Science: Essays on History and Philosophy of Science.* Kuala Lumpur-Penang: Nurin Enterprise and Secretariat of Philosophy of Science, USM.

1989. (ed.). *Islam and Contemporary Scientific Thought.* Islamic Academy of Science, Kuala Lumpur. (in Malay)

1987. (ed.). *Critique of Evolutionary Theory: A Collection of Essays.* Islamic Academy of Science and Nurin Enterprise, Kuala Lumpur.

1987. *Al-Farabi: Life, Works, and Significance.* Islamic Academy of Science, Kuala Lumpur.

Chapters of books (Sole Author unless otherwise stated)

2022: "Kata Pengantar," Seyyed Hossein Nasr, *Manusia dan Alam Tabii: Kemelut Ruhani*, Malay translation, Khairul Anam (Kuala Lumpur: IBDE), pp. xiii–xx.

2021: "Kata Pengantar," *Tao Te Ching, Lao Tzu*, Malay translation by Hazman Baharom (Kuala Lumpur: The Biblio Press Enterprise, 2021), pp. iii–x.

2021: "The concept of human microcosm: Exploring possibilities for a synthesis of traditional and modern biomedicine," in Aasim Padela and Afifi Al-Akiti, eds., *Islam and Biomedicine* (Springer International Publishing), Philosophy and Medicine Series, No. 137, 63–74.

2020: "The Civilisational History of the Malay Archipelago: Arguing for a New Narrative." Introduction to Osman Bakar, Ahmad Murad Merican and Wan Ali Wan Mamat, eds., *Colonialism in the Malay Archipelago: Civilisational Encounters* (Kuala Lumpur: ISTAC-IIUM Publications and Persatuan Sejarah Malaysia), pp. ix–xx.

2020: "Portugal, Malacca, and the Spice Monopoly: The Manueline Imperial Policy as Background." In Osman Bakar, Ahmad Murad Merican and Wan Ali Wan Mamat, eds. *Colonialism in the Malay Archipelago: Civilisational Encounters* (Kuala Lumpur: ISTAC-IIUM Publications and Persatuan Sejarah Malaysia), pp. 1–32.

2020: "Prakata," in *Hikmah Toleransi: Falsafah Kepemurahan dan Keamanan*, terjemahan Md. Sidin Ahmad Ishak (Kuala Lumpur: ISTAC-IIUM Publications), pp. iii–v.

2019: "Aspek Kesejagatan dan Peradaban Falsafah Pendidikan Kebangsaan," in Dzulkifli Abdul Razak & Rosnani Hashim, eds., *Pentafsiran Baharu Falsafah Pendidikan Kebangsaan dan Pelaksanaannya Pasca 2020* (Kuala Lumpur: IIUM Press), pp. 34–51.

2019: "Kata Pengantar," in Rohaiza Rokis, M. Fakhrurrazi Ahmad & Mohd Khairul Ridhwan Adhha Akhiar, eds., *Laskar Alam:Modul Pembudayaan Kelestarian Alam* (Kuala Lumpur: International Institute of Advanced Islamic Studies (IAIS) Malaysia), pp. vi–ix.

2019: "Kata Pengantar," in Shaykh Abdul Rahman al-Kawawibi, *Tabiat Kediktatoran dan Keruduman Perhambaan*, terjemahan Marwan Bukhari A. Hamid (Kuala Lumpur: Maqasid Institute Malaysia), pp. vii–xiv.

2019: "Introduction to New 2019 Edition," in Osman Bakar & Cheng Gek Nai, eds., *Islam and Confucianism: A Civilizational Dialogue* (Kuala Lumpur: ISTAC-IIUM Publications), New Edition, pp. 1–12.

2019: "Enhancing Dialogue between Religious Traditions: An Islamic Perspective," in Mohamad Nawab, ed., *Pathways in Contemporary Islam* (Amsterdam: Amsterdam University Press), pp. 215–234.

2018: "Foreword," in Michelle Kimball, *Shaykh Ahmadou Bamba: A Peacemaker for Our Time* (Kuala Lumpur: The Other Press), pp.

2018: "Multiculturalism: A Malaysian Perspective," in Imtiyaz Yusuf, ed., *Multiculturalism in Asia: Peace and Harmony* (Bangkok: College of Religious Studies, Mahidol University & Konrad Adenauer Stiftung), pp. 88 – 108.

2016: "Understanding the Challenge of Global Warming in the Light of the Qur'ānic Idea of Earth as Our Only Planetary Home," Imtiyaz Yusuf, ed. *A Planetary and Global Ethics for Climate Change and Sustainable Energy* (Bangkok: Konrad-Adenauer-Stiftung and College of Religious Studies, Mahidol University), pp. 117–141.

2016: (with Norhazlin Pg Muhammad, and Ariffin Abu Bakar), "Empowerment of Women and Girls in Muslim Southeast Asia," UNESCO, *A Better World: Actions and Commitments to the Sustainable Development Goals* (London: Tudor Rose), pp. 86–89.

2016: "Agama dan Sains Dalam Perspektif Islam," Syamsuddin Arif, ed., *Islamic Science: Paradigma, Fakta dan Agenda* (Jakarta: Institute for the Study of Islamic Thought and Civilizations), pp. 26–42.

2016: "Spiritual and Intellectual Empowerment of Contemporary Youth: Defining Strategies and Methods," Senad Mrahorovic, ed., *Spirituality and Intellectual Safety in the Light of Religious Doctrines: Proceedings of the 12th Doha Interfaith Conference* (Doha: DICID), pp. 233–242.

2016: "Science and Technology for Mankind's Benefit: Islamic Theories and Practices – Past, Present and Future," M. Hashim Kamali, Osman Bakar, Daud Abdul-Fattah Batchelor, and Rogayah Hashim, eds. *Islamic Perspectives on Science and Technology: Selected Conference Papers* (Singapore: Springer), pp. 19–36.

2016: (with Mohammad Hilmy Baihaqy bin Yussof), "Positing a Spiritual Dimension for Science Education: Brunei Darussalam's Experience," M. Hashim Kamali, Osman Bakar, Daud Abdul-Fattah Bachelor, and Rogayah Hashim, eds., *Islamic Perspectives on Science and Technology: Selected Conference Papers* (Singapore: Springer), pp. 339–345.

2016: (with Daud Abdul-Fattah Batchelor), "Introduction," M. Hashim Kamali, Osman Bakar, Daud Batchelor, and Rogayah Hashim, eds., *Islamic Perspectives on Science and Technology* (Singapore: Springer), pp. 3–12.

2015: (with Jabal Buaben, Norhazlin Pg Muhammad & M. Azmi Mohamad), "An Intercultural Dialogue from within Muslim Communities: A Global Overview," UNESCO, *Agree to Differ* (London: Tudor Rose), pp. 91–96.

2015: "In Search of the Right Synergy between Technology and the Sharia for the Sake of a Healthy Umma," *The Muslim 500: The World's 500 Most Influential Muslims* (Amman: The Royal Islamic Strategic Studies Centre), pp. 192–195.

2015: "Konsep dan Prinsip-Prinsip Wasatiah," *Prosiding Seminar Majlis Ilmu 2015* (Bandar Seri Begawan: Urusetia Seminar Majlis Ilmu), pp. 65–73.

2014: "Balkan Islam and Malay Islam as Branches of Islamic Civilization: An Introductory Discussion of Their Similarities and Differences," Mesut Idriz and Osman Bakar, eds. *Islam in Southeast Europe: Past Reflections and Future Prospects* (Bandar Seri Begawan: UBD PRESS), pp. 1–6.

2012: "The Importance of al-Ghazali and Ibn Rushd in the History of Islamic Discourse on Religion and Science," David Marshall, ed., *Science and Religion: Christian and Muslim Perspectives* (Washington DC: Georgetown University Press, pp. 102–110.

2012: "The Empowerment of Muslim Communities in Private Higher

Education: An Ummatic Agenda," Osman Bakar & Airulamri Amran, eds., *The Empowerment of Muslim Communities in Private Higher Education* (Kuala Lumpur: IAIS Malaysia & IKIP International College), pp. 82–87.

2011. "Islamic Leadership in the Changing ASEAN: Fostering Peace and Development," *Proceedings of Conference on Islamic Leadership in the Changing ASEAN* (Manila: Asian Institute of Management), pp. 38–55.

2011. "The Role of Islam in Higher Educational Policies of Muslim Countries," *Contemporary Higher Education Needs in Muslim Countries: Defining the Role of Islam in 21st Century Higher Education* (Kuala Lumpur: IAIS Malaysia and IKIP International College), pp. 21 – 38.

2010. "Report on Issue of Religious Tolerance: National Dialogue on Islam and Democracy," Ibrahim m. Zein, ed., *Islam and Democracy in Malaysia: Findings from a National Dialogue* (Kuala Lumpur: ISTAC), pp. 118–132.

2010. "Environmental Health and Welfare as an Important Aspect of Civilizational Islam," Mohamed Ajmal bin Abdul Razak al-Aidrus, ed., *Islam Hadhari: Bridging Tradition and Modernity* (Kuala Lumpur: ISTAC), pp. 139–159.

2009. "Religious Reform and the Controversy Surrounding Islamization in Malaysia," Syed Farid al-Atas, ed., *Muslim Reform in Southeast Asia: Perspectives from Malaysia, Indonesia, and Singapore* (Singapore: MUIS), pp. 31–45.

2009. "Konsep Tamadun Malaysia: Kesatuan Dalam Kepelbagaian," Hashim Ismail and Raihanah Abdullah, eds., *Permuafakatan dan Kerukunan: Teras Peradaban Malaysia* (Kuala Lumpur: Akademi Pengajian Melayu and Center for Civilizational Dialogue, University of Malaya), pp. 1–9.

2009. "Islam dalam jati diri tamadun Melayu: konflik dan keharmonian antara tuntutan keetnikan dan keagamaan," Kalthum Ibrahim, Farid Mat Zain, Nasruddin Yunos dan Ezad Azraai Jamsari, eds., *Dunia Melayu dan Islam* (Bangi: ATMA, UKM), pp. 389–398.

2009. "Traditional Muslim Classifications of the Sciences: Comparative Notes on Qutb al-Din al-Shirazi and Ibn Khaldun," Osman Bakar & Baharudin Ahmad, eds., *Ibn Khaldun's Legacy and Its Significance* (Kuala Lumpur: ISTAC), pp. 209–216.

2008. "Challenges to Dialogues of Civilizations and Ways of Overcoming Them," Thomas W. Simon and Azizan Baharuddin, eds., *Dialogue of Civilizations and the Construction of Peace* (Kuala Lumpur: Center for Civilizational Dialogue, University of Malaya), pp. 23–39.

2007. "Islam and the Future of Interreligious Peace in Asia," Imtiyaz Yusuf, ed. *The Role of Religions and Philosophical Traditions in Promoting World Peace: An Asian Perspective* (Singapore: Konrad-Adenauer-Stiftung), pp. 105–116

2007. "Malaysian Islam in the Twenty-first Century," John Esposito, John Voll and Osman Bakar, eds., *Asian Islam in the Twenty-first Century* (New York: Oxford University Press, 2007), pp. 81–108.

2007. "Islam and the Malay Civilizational Identity: Tension and Harmony between Ethnicity and Religiosity," John Donohue and John Esposito, eds., *Islam in Transition: Muslim Perspectives* (New York-Oxford: Oxford University Press, 2007), pp. 480–487.

2006. "Islam, Ethnicity, Pluralism and Democracy: Malaysia's Unique Experience," M. A. Muqtedar Khan, ed., *Islamic Democratic Discourse: Theory, Debates, and Philosophical Perspectives* (Lanham: Lexington Books, 2005), pp. 63–83.

2005. "Competing Visions of Islam in Southeast Asia: American Muslim Scholarship as a Shaping Factor," Philippa Strum, ed., *Muslims in the United States: Identity, Influence, Innovation* (Washington, DC: Woodrow Wilson International Center for Scholars, 2005), pp. 103–120.0

2005. "Malaysia's Path to Modernization and Democratization," Shireen T. Hunter and Huma Malik (eds.), *Modernization, Democracy and Islam* (Westport: Praeger Publishers, 2005), pp. 235–252.

2005. "The Impact of the War on Terror on Malaysia," Shahram Akbarzadeh and Samina Yasmeen (eds.), *Islam and the West: Reflections from Australia* (Sydney: University of New South Wales Press, 2005), pp. 93–113.

2005. "Science and the Idea of the Sacred," Zainal Abidin Bagir, ed., *Science and Religion in a Post-Colonial World: Interfaith Perspectives* (Adelaide: ATF Press, 2005), pp. 103–112.

2004. "Pluralism and the "People of the Book": An Islamic Faith Perspective," Robert A. Seiple ad Dennis R. Hoover, eds., *Religion and Security: The New Nexus in International Relations*, Rowman & Littlefield, pp. 99–112.

2004. "Relations between Malaysia and Islam in America," Abdul Razak Baginda, ed., *Malaysia and the Islamic World*, Malaysia Strategic Research Center, Kuala Lumpur, pp. 225–250.

2003: "Civilizational Dialogue on Environmental Philosophy: Nasr's "Man and Nature" Revisited," Mohammad H. Faghfoory, ed., *Beacon of Knowledge: Essays in Honor of Seyyed Hossein Nasr* (Louisville, KY: Fons Vitae), pp. 291 – 303.

2003. "The Intellectual Impact of American Muslim Scholars on the Muslim world with Special Reference to Southeast Asia" in Philippa Strum and Danielle Tarantolo, eds., *Muslims in the United States* (Washington DC: Woodrow Wilson Center for International Scholars), pp. 151–169.

2003: "Islam and Political Legitimacy in Malaysia," Shahram Akbarzadeh & Abdullah Saeed, eds., *Islam and Political Legitimacy*, Curzon Press, London, pp. 127–149.

2003. "Traditional Malay Thought and Globalization," in Asmah Hj Omar, ed., *The Genius of Malay Civilisation* (Papers and proceedings of the First International Conference on Malay Civilisation, organized by the Institute of Malay Civilisation, Universiti Pendidikan Sultan Idris and held Oct. 1–3, 2002 in Tanjong Malim, Perak).

2001. "Intercivilizational Dialogue: Theory and Practice in Islam" in M. Nakamura, S. Siddique, and O.F. Bajunid, (eds.), *Islam and Civil Society in Southeast Asia*, Institute of Southeast Asian Studies, Singapore, pp. 164–176.

1997. "The Importance of Cosmology in the Cultivation of the Arts," in Wan Abdul Kadir & Hashim Awang (eds.), *Art and Cosmology: Islamic Cosmology and Malay Art*, Academy of Malay Studies, Kuala Lumpur, pp. 1–6.

1996. "Science (as a Branch of Philosophy)" in S.H. Nasr & O. Leaman (eds.), *History of Islamic Philosophy*, Routledge History of World Philosophies, vol. II, chapter 53, pp. 926–958.

1994. "Knowledge of Divine Unity (tawhid) on the Basis of Scientific Knowledge," Ismail Ibrahim & Mohd Sahri Abdul Rahman (eds.), *Knowledge and Excellence in Islamic Perspective*, Institute of Islamic Understanding (IKIM), Kuala Lumpur, pp. 1–9.

1993. "Science in Islamic Perspective," in Azizan Baharuddin (ed.), *Malay Students and Science Education*, Academy of Malay Studies Monograph (Cendekia), University of Malaya, Kuala Lumpur, no. 2, pp. 8–24. (in Malay)

1991. "The Unity of Science and Spiritual Knowledge: The Islamic Experience," in R. Ravindra (ed.), *Science and Spirit*, International Cultural Foundation, New York, pp. 87–101.

1991. "Spiritual Traditions and Science and Technology," in ALIRAN, *The Human Being: Perspectives from Different Spiritual Traditions*, ALIRAN, Kuala Lumpur, pp. 140–155.

1984. "The Question of Methodology in Islamic Science," in Rais Ahmad & S. Naseem Ahmad (eds.), *Quest for New Science: Selected Papers of a Seminar*, Center for Studies on Science, Aligarh (India), pp. 91–109.

1979. "The Role of Science Education in the Spiritual Development of Man," in *PKPIM Collection: Symposium on Islamic Education*, National Union of Muslim Students of Malaysia (PKPIM), Kuala Lumpur, pp. 119–135.

Journals (selected)

2022: "Religious Authority, Ifta' Culture, and Sectarianism in Modern Pakistan: The Impact of its Intra-Islamic Pluralism," *Al-Shajarah*, vol. 27, no. 1, pp. 53–75. (Co-authored with Muhammad Kalim Ullah Khan).

2022: "Book Review of Thupten Jinpa, ed., *Science and Philosophy in the Indian Buddhist Classics, Vol 2: The Mind,"* Al-Shajarah, vol. 27, no. 1, pp. 200–204.

2021: "Coronavirus in the Light of Traditional Integral Ecology." *The Muslim 500: The World's 500 Most Influential Muslims 2022* (Amman: The Royal Islamic Strategic Studies Centre), pp. 209–213.

2021: "Book Review of Thupten Jinpa, ed., *Science and Philosophy in the Indian Buddhist Classics,*" *Al-Shajarah*, vol. 26, no. 1 (2021), pp. 136–140.

2021: Md. Yusuf Ali & Osman Bakar, 'Syed Ahmad Khan's twin objectives of educational reforms in British India,' *Al-Shajarah*, vol. 26, no. 1 (2021), pp. 49–70.

2020: Md. Yusuf Ali & Osman Bakar, 'Issues of Hindu-Muslim relations in the works of Syed Ahmad Khan,' *Al-Shajarah*, vol. 25, no. 2 (2020), pp. 315–333.

2020: 'The link between Coronavirus and Darwin according to Pervez Hoodbhoy: A critical response," *Intellectual Discourse*, vol. 28, no. 2 (2020), pp. 365–386.

2020: "Islam in China and the challenge of Sinicization of religion: Past and present." *The Muslim 500: The World's 500 Most Influential Muslims 2021* (Amman: The Royal Islamic Strategic Studies Centre), pp. 233–237.

2019: 'Towards a Postmodern Synthesis of Islamic Science and Modern Science: The Epistemological Groundwork,' *The Muslim 500: The World's 500 Most Influential Muslims 2020* (Amman: The Royal Islamic Strategic Studies Centre), pp. 197–201.

2018: 'The Poverty of Knowledge Synthesis in the Modern Muslim University: Implications for the Future Muslim Mind,' *The Muslim 500: The World's 500 Most Influential Muslims 2019* (Amman: The Royal Islamic Strategic Studies Centre), pp. 112–114.

2017: 'Nature as a sacred book: A core element of Seyyed Hossein Nasr's philosophical teachings,' *Sacred Web*, vol. 40 (2017), pp. 75–101.

2017: (with Amy Young, Pg Norhazlin Pg Muhammad, Patrick O'Leary & Mohamad Abdalla), 'Children in Brunei Darussalam: Their educational, legal and social protections,' *International Journal of Islamic Thought*, vol. 11: (June) 2017, pp. 6–16.

2016: 'Towards a new science of civilization: A synthetic study of the philosophical views of al-Farabi, Ibn Khaldun, Arnold Toynbee, and Samuel Huntington,' *Synthesis Philosophica*, 62 (2/2016), pp. 313–333.

2014: 'From secular science to sacred science: the need for a transformation,' *Sacred Web*, vol. 33 (2014), Vancouver, Canada, pp. 25–49.

2013: (with Norhazlin Muhammad & Basil Mustafa), 'Implementation of the 'Integrated Education System' in Brunei Darussalam: issues and challenges,' *Journal of Middle Eastern and Islamic Studies (in Asia)*, vol.7, no. 4, December 2013.

2013. 'Islamic civilisation as a global presence with special reference to its knowledge culture,' *Islam and Civilisational Renewal*, vol. 4, no. 4 (October 2013), pp. 512–528.

2012. 'The identity crisis of the contemporary Muslim ummah: the loss of *Tawhidic* epistemology as its root cause,' *Islam and Civilizational Renewal*, vol. 3, no. 4 (July 2012), pp. 638–654.

2012. 'The Arab Spring: Malaysian responses,' *Islam and Civilizational Renewal*, vol. 3, no. 4 (July 2012), pp. 744–748.

2012. 'The Qur'anic identity of the Muslim ummah: *Tawhidic* epistemology as its foundation and sustainer,' *Islam and Civilizational Renewal*, vol. 3, no. 3 (April 2012), pp. 438–454.

2011. 'Family values, the family institution, and the challenges of the twenty-first century,' *Islam and Civilizational Renewal*, vol. 3, no. 1 (October 2011), pp. 12–36.

2011. 'Islamic science, modern science, and post-modernity: towards a new synthesis through a *Tawhidic* epistemology,' *Revelation and Science*, vol. 1, no. 3 (1433/2011), pp. 13–20

2011. 'The evolving face of religious tolerance in post-colonial Malaysia: understanding its shaping factors," *Islam and Civilizational Renewal*, vol. 2, no. 4 (July 2011), pp. 621–638.

2011. 'Malaysia's need for an enlightened national policy on interreligious peace: a dictate of *Maqasid al-Shari'ah*,' *Islam and Civilizational Renewal*, vol. 2, no. 2 (January 2011), pp. 388–392.

2011. 'The place and role of *maqasid al-shari'ah* in the *ummah*'s 21st century civilizational renewal,' *Islam and Civilizational Renewal*, vol. 2, no. 2 (January 2011), pp. 285–301.

2010. 'Why issues of Islamic leadership are important to ASEAN,' *Islamic Civilizational Renewal*, vol. 2, no. 1 (October 2010), pp. 180–183.

2010. 'Interfaith dialogue as a new approach in Islamic education,' *Islamic Civilizational Renewal*, vol. 1, no. 4 (July 2010), pp. 700–704.

2010. 'Islam and the three waves of globalization: The Southeast Asian experience,' *Islam and Civilizational Renewal*, vol. 1, no. 4 (July 2010), pp. 666–684

2010. 'Cultural pluralism in a globalized world: challenges to peaceful coexistence,' *Islam and Civilizational Renewal*, vol. 1, no. 3 (April 2010), pp. 528–531.

2010. 'Economics as a science: insights from classical Muslim classifications of the sciences," *Islam and Civilizational Renewal*, vol. 1, no. 3 (April 2010), pp. 426–444.

2009. 'Exclusive and inclusive Islam in the Qur'an: Implications for Muslim-Jewish relations,' *JISMOR, Journal of the Interdisciplinary Study of Monotheistic Religions*, 5th issue 2009, pp. 4–15. [The Japanese translation of this article appears in the Japanese version of this Journal which is published by CISMOR (Center for Interdisciplinary Study of Monotheistic Religions), Doshisha University, Kyoto, Japan]

2009. 'Islam and the challenge of diversity and pluralism: Must Islam reform itself?' *Islam and Civilizational Renewal*, vol. 1, no. 1 (October 2009), pp. 55–73.

2008. 'The spirit of Islamic science in the Hokkaido Science Symposium,' *IAIS Journal of Civilization Studies*, vol. 1, no. 1 (October 2008), pp. 203–207.

2008. 'The spiritual and ethical foundation of science and technology in Islamic civilization," *IAIS Journal of Civilization Studies*, vol. 1, no. 1 (October 2008), pp. 87–112.

2008. 'Islam and the problem of cultural symbiosis,' *Al-Shajarah, Journal of ISTAC*, vol. 13, No. 1 (2008), pp. 1–21.

2008. 'Pengaruh globalisasi terhadap peradaban,' *Jurnal Peradaban*, vol. 1 (2008), pp. 75–97.

2005. 'The impact of the American war on terror on Malaysian Islam,' *Journal of Islam and Christian-Muslim Relations*, Vol. 16, No. 2 (April 2005), pp. 107–128

2005. 'Gulen on religion and science: A theological perspective,' *The Muslim World*, Vol. 95, Issue 3 (2005), pp. 359–372

2003. 'Reformulating a comprehensive relationship between religion and science: An Islamic perspective,' *Islam and Science Journal*, vol. 1, no. 1, pp. 29–44.

2003. 'Islam and the Malay civilizational identity: Tension and harmony between ethnicity and religiosity,' *Journal of Malay Civilization*, Issue 2003, pp. 107–122.

2000. 'El destino del Islam: Puente civilizacional entre el Este y el Oeste,' *Relaciones Internacionales*, no. 18, 2000, pp. 35–40.

1996. 'Truth and wisdom in a holistic concept of knowledge,' *Pemikir*, no. 3, Jan–March 1996, pp. 100–112. (in Malay)

1994. 'The common philosophical foundation of traditional medicines,' *Sophia*, Winter 1994, no. 6, pp. 1–4.

1993. 'Symbol and archetype: A study of the meaning of existence: A review article,' *Studies in Tradition*, 2:1(Jan–March 1993), pp. 62–78.

1991. 'Atomistic conception of nature in Ash'arite theology,' *Iqbal Review*, 32:3 (October 1991), pp. 19–44.

1990. 'The philosophy of Islamic medicine and its relevance to the modern world,' *MAAS Journal of Islamic Science*, 6:1 (Jan–June 1990), pp. 39–58.

1990. 'Designing a sound syllabus for courses on philosophy of applied and engineering sciences in a 21st century Islamic university,' *Muslim Education Quarterly*, 7:3 (Spring 1990), pp. 19–25.

1988. 'The influence of Islamic science on medieval Christian conceptions of nature,' *MAAS Journal of Islamic Science*, 4:1 (Jan–June 1988), pp. 25–43.

1986. 'Islam and bioethics,' *Greek Orthodox Theological Review*, 3:2 (1986), pp. 157–179.

1986. 'The meaning and significance of doubt in al-Ghazali's philosophy,' *The Islamic Quarterly*, 30:1 (1986), pp. 20–31.

1985. 'Umar Khayyam's criticism of Euclid's theory of parallels,' *MAAS Journal of Islamic Science*, 1:2 (July 1985), pp. 9–18.

1984. 'The question of methodology in Islamic science,' *Muslim Education Quarterly*, 2:1 (Autumn 1984), pp. 16–30.

1984. 'Ibn Sina's methodological approach toward the study of nature in his Oriental Philosophy,' *Hamdard Islamicus*, vol. VII, no. 2 (Summer 1984), pp. 33–49.

In Encyclopedias

"Interreligious Dialogues in Malaysia," *Oxford Islamic Studies Online*, 2020.

"Religion, Science, and Technology: Islamic Bioethics" in *The Oxford Encyclopedia of Islamic Bioethics.* Ayman Shabana (ed.), Oxford University Press, Doha, 2017.

"Philosophy of Science," *The Oxford Encyclopedia of Islamic Bioethics*, Oxford University Press, 2017.

"Cosmology and Models of the Cosmos" in *The Oxford Encyclopaedia of Philosophy, Science, and Technology in Islam,* 2014, vol. 1, pp. 156–163. Ibrahim Kalin (ed.), Oxford University Press, 2 vols.

"Islam: Science, Technology, and Ethics from an Islamic Perspective," *Encyclopedia of Science, Technology and Ethics*, Macmillan Reference USA, 2014 (revised edition), vol. 1, pp. 605–611.

"Malaysia" (with Kamal Hassan) in John Esposito, ed., *Oxford Encyclopedia of the Modern Islamic World.* New edition, 2007.

"Islam: Science, Technology, and Ethics from an Islamic Perspective," *Encyclopedia of Science, Technology and Ethics*, Macmillan Reference USA, 2005.

"Islam" in *Encyclopedia of Science and Religion*, Macmillan Reference USA, 2002.

"Cosmology" in John L. Esposito (ed.), *Oxford Encyclopedia of the Modern Islamic World*, vol. 1(1995), pp. 322–328.

"Abortion: Islamic Perspectives" in Warren Thomas Reich (ed.), *Encyclopedia of Bioethics*, rev. edition, vol. 1(1995), pp. 38–42.

"Sufism in the Malay-Indonesian World" in S. H. Nasr (ed.), *Islamic Spirituality: Manifestations*, vol. 20 of *World Spirituality: An Encyclopedic History of the Religious Quest*, Routledge & Kegan Paul, London and The Crossroad Publishing Co., New York (1990), pp. 159–189.

Index

A

Abrahamic faiths 166, 364
aesthetics 75, 309, 310, 311, 320, 322, 329, 331,
Al-Farabi 5, 30, 57, 58, 59, 64, 108,
Al-Ghazali 9, 30, 32, 48, 108, 131, 132, 136, 217, 218, 220, 242, 288, 294, 300, 375, 382,
Anglo-Burmese Wars 102
Arab 68, 69, 72, 75, 88, 89, 90, 91, 92, 93, 94, 95, 97, 98, 99, 100, 101, 102,, 176, 177, 180, 182, 183, 217, 223, 226, 229, 234, 240, 286, 319, 332, 400
archipelago 91, 93, 96, 97, 98, 237, 238, 239, 240, 241
Aristotle 58, 59, 60, 204, 336, 376
Asharite 60
astronomy 62, 109, 335, 340, 344, 351, 352, 354
atomic theory 335, 337

B

Badawi, Abdullah 24
Bohm, David 5, 145, 146, 150, 151, 153, 154, 155, 156,
Bolshevik 175, 178
Buddhism 6, 23, 97, 165, 166, 177, 197, 367, 371, 398
Burckhardt, Titus 27, 113,, 310, 312, 313, 314,

C

capitalism 63, 73, 76, 77, 82, 87, 88, 91, 97, 98, 99, 100, 101, 102, 218
Chinese civilization 168, 369
Chinese Muslims 165, 167, 170, 171, 198
Chinese philosophy 165
Chinese thought 5, 6, 166, 198
Chinese tributary system 195, 196
Chittick, William 146, 147, 157, 158, 159, 160, 165, 172, 319, 328,
Christianity 26, 101, 155, 164, 184, 186, 203, 212, 275, 284, 322, 324,, 361, 363, 373,
citizenship 228, 372
civilizational dialogue 50, 164, 165, 167, 168, 169, 373
civilizational studies 2, 19, 53, 373
civil justice 122
Classification of Knowledge
  according to al-Farabi 58
  according to Ibn Khaldun 61
  according to Ibn Sina 60

contemporary 61
in Greek thought 58
Classification of Knowledge in Islam 1, 5, 31, 32,, 48,, 57, 137, 163, 252,, 274,
climate change 46, 146, 277 280 281, 284, 289
Cold War 41, 361, 363, 373
colonial-capitalism 76, 82, 87, 88, 91, 97, 98, 99, 100, 101, 102
colonialism 2 4, 11, 63, 67, 70, 74, 99, 102, 218, 238, 239, 241, 363
comparative philosophy 164, 166, 172
Confucianism 5, 6, 165, 166, 168, 169, 171, 172, 186, 195, 198, 363, 366, 367, 368, 369,
Neo-Confucianism 178
consciousness 74, 106, 117, 120, 141, 150, 156, 208, 279, 283, 299, 300, 301, 320, 321, 327, 382
Covid 24, 55, 185, 251, 258, 383
Crawfurd, John 88, 89, 90, 93, 95, 96, 97, 98, 99, 100, 101, 102,

D

Darwin, Charles 47, 399
diversity 9, 96, 115, 169, 170, 172, 197, 205, 211, 281, 362, 368,
Divine Unity 203, 205, 210, 298, 299, 304, 312,
division of labour 146, 192, 367
Durkheim, Emile 121

E

education system 39, 58, 272, 295
in Islam 53
in Malaysia 39
Einstein, Albert 146, 150, 151, 154, 343, 357
empiricism 45, 338, 344
engaged scholarship 2, 21, 22, 24, 25, 26, 35
Enlightenment 7, 40, 145, 152
ethics 5, 7, 9, 59, 60, 64, 67, 109, 111, 112, 123, 226, 242, 263, 269, 280, 284, 285, 286, 287, 305, 310, 320, 322, 346, 354, 380
extremism 219, 370

F

family values 252, 254, 256, 258, 259
feudal system 106
Foucault, Michel 70
futurology 53, 54, 271

G

globalisation 2, 218, 231, 232, 258

H

hadith 61, 62, 111, 113, 151, 218, 220, 221, 222, 223, 230, 238, 281, 296, 300, 320, 321, 322, 330, 378, 383
Hanafi 131, 139
health care 276, 277
hegemony 7, 70, 78, 79, 152
higher education 10, 20, 21, 36, 38, 186, 263, 266, 268, 269, 270, 304, 305,
Hinduism 153, 165, 166, 167, 209, 211, 371
humanities 9, 10, 11, 62, 146, 263, 264, 265, 266, 267, 268, 269, 270, 271, 272, 284, 290, 304
human resources 192
human rights 229, 233, 281, 363

I

Ibn Rushd 60, 109, 122, 294,
Ibn Sina 5, 30, 57, 60, 108, 109, 125, 294, 402
Ibn Arabī 156, 157, 158, 159, 160
imperialism 4, 7, 70, 77, 78, 354
Industrial Revolution 40, 47, 49, 106
Iqbal, Muhammad 5, 12, 146, 147, 148, 149 150, 151, 152 153, 154, 155, 156, 160, 217, 225, 231, 279, 285, 387
Islamic art 310, 312, 313, 326, 331, 381
Islamic civilization 7, 8, 9, 10, 15, 28, 44, 52, 53, 56, 127, 128, 141, 143, 203, 217, 279, 293, 350, 351, 354, 358, 362, 371, 388, 401
Islamic cosmology 27
Islamic history 10, 106, 129
Islamic law ,5, 59, 60, 61, 62, 127, 129, 130, 131, 132, 133, 134, 135, 136, 137, 138, 139, 140, 141, 142, 143, 144, 177, 221, 224, 226, 227, 228, 229, 230, 233, 234, 238, 243, 371
Islamic philosophy 2, 5, 19, 25, 30, 33, 43, 54, 58, 59, 164, 168, 224, 253, 286, 296, 298, 302, 387
Islamic society 67, 71, 105, 106, 112, 114, 186, 220, 239, 354
  guilds 112, 113
Islamic studies 3, 19, 20, 24, 25, 26, 27, 35, 45, 52, 57, 58, 62, 63, 76, 105, 132, 166, 217, 220, 233, 237, 241, 253, 266, 278, 279, 301, 303, 305,
Islamization of Knowledge 22, 23, 24, 37, 296, 297, 303, 305, 307
Islamophobia 181, 183, 184, 187, 188, 363
Isma‘ili 111, 117

K

knowledge production 4, 8, 336
Korean society 177, 179, 180, 182, 183, 184, 186, 187
  Korean Muslims 179, 180, 181, 182, 183, 185, 187
Korean War 175, 179

L

Lings, Martin 27, 147, 208, 310, 314, 323
Logic 59

M

Mamluk dynasty 77
marriage 132, 187, 227, 251, 252, 254, 256, 257, 258, 259, 378
Marx, Karl 106 369
materialism 6
Mawdudi, Abul A'la 41, 42, 226
metaphysics 47, 58, 59, 60, 64, 148, 150, 204, 212, 288, 295, 310, 311, 320, 322, 329, 331, 346, 348, 350, 353, 354
Ming dynasty 189, 190, 193, 195, 196, 197, 199,
modernity 2, 53, 67, 69, 70, 127, 128, 145, 146, 147, 148, 152, 153, 218, 220, 222, 226, 229, 230, 231, 232, 280, 335, 346, 353, 362, 369, 370,
Mongol 177, 189
Mughal Empire 111
multiculturalism 164, 168, 185
Muslim identity 29, 167
Muslim philosophers 19, 21, 30, 58, 105, 107, 164, 294, 299, 300
Muslim reformist movements 26, 74, 78
Muslim scholarship 32
Mutazilite 60

N

Nasr, Seyyed Hossein 1, 2, 3, 4, 7, 9, 12, 14, 15, 27, 30, 32, 46, 57, 108, 109, 111, 113, 121, 122, 163, 164, 166, 224, 281, 286, 296, 297, 298, 299, 304, 310 335, 345, 346, 349, 350, 352, 353,
nationalism 71, 76, 79, 81, 165, 226
natural philosophy 11, 336, 337, 338, 339, 340, 341, 342, 344, 345, 347, 348, 349, 350, 351, 352, 353, 354
Newton, Isaac 150, 151, 341, 352
Nietzsche, Friedrich 148

O

Oil Crisis 180, 183
orientalism 4, 62, 63, 88, 95, 101
Ottoman Empire 84, 88, 89, 103, 105, 111, 113, 123, 124, 178, 230, 326

P

pamphlet journalism 74
Plato 108, 159, 204, 214, 271, 313, 315, 331, 340, 343, 345

postcolonialism 12, 225, 226, 230, 232, 372, 400
postmodernism 147, 148, 152, 279
poverty 92, 109, 229, 233, 267, 275, 276
Prophet Muhammad 129, 130,, 223, 257, 293, 326,, 348
psychology 62, 64, 150, 293, 303

Q

quantum mechanics 151
quantum physics 22, 151
Qur'an 6, 10, 11, 14, 105, 106, 107, 113, 130, 133, 141, 168, 178, 179, 186, 218, 222, 223, 224, 226, 227, 233, 254, 255, 256, 257, 258, 280, 281, 282, 283, 284, 285, 286, 288, 289, 290, 293, 294, 295, 296, 297, 299, 300, 302, 315, 317, 318, 321, 348, 364, 375, 376, 377, 379, 383,

R

Raffles, Stamford 88, 89, 90, 91, 92, 93, 94, 95, 96, 97, 99, 100, 101, 102,
refugees 183, 184
religious studies 10, 19, 23, 24, 26, 62, 264, 275, 278, 279, 280, 281, 283, 290, 362, 394
Renaissance 11, 15, 128, 345, 351,
Rūmī 148, 149, 154

S

Safavid Empire 105, 111, 123
Salafism 229, 230, 241, 243
Sassanid Empire 105, 111, 176
Schuon, Frithjof 5, 209, 210, 211, 213, 300, 309, 310, 317, 320, 322, 324,
science
  Islamic science 2, 11, 12, 30, 31, 44, 48, 178, 296, 300, 301, 302, 304, 335, 349, 350, 351, 352, 353, 375, 376, 381,
  modern science 4, 28, 30, 31, 41, 43, 48, 145, 232, 296, 298, 336, 337, 339, 341, 345, 347, 348, 349, 350, 351, 352, 353, 354
  natural sciences 10, 11, 58, 64, 147, 293, 300, 301, 306, 335, 345, 351
  philosophy of science 43, 45, 50, 62, 164, 279, 284, 290, 298, 302, 304, 305, 335, 336, 348, 352
  Western science 7, 41, 45, 164, 298, 350
scientific racism 99, 100
scientific realism 335, 336, 337, 339, 343, 345, 348, 349, 351, 352, 353, 354
Scientific Revolution 7, 40, 337, 340, 349, 351, 354, 356, 357,
Second World War 225
secularism 6
Shia 107, 111, 122, 170, 224 233
Silk Road 176, 199
slavery 101

social class 5, 96, 105, 106, 108, 109, 110, 111, 114 116, 117, 119, 122, 123
social mobility 115
social media 184
social sciences 10, 11, 22, 28, 35, 63, 263, 268, 269, 284, 304
sociology 62, 293, 336
Soeharto, President 238, 243, 245
Sufism 9, 15, 112, 119, 123, 157, 158, 159, 160, 165, 206, 207, 208, 212, 221 237, 238, 239, 240, 241, 242, 243, 244, 245, 246,, 286, 312, 314, 318, 323, 328, 330, 382,
Sunni 110, 131, 133, 134, 135, 138, 170, 224
sustainable development 10, 252, 275, 277, 278, 281, 282, 284, 285, 286, 287, 288, 289, 290
syncretism 224, 232, 237

T

T'ang Dynasty 176
Tawhid 8, 23, 27, 30, 31, 42, 46, 48, 56, 58, 60, 186, 263, 269, 296, 297, 299, 300, 301, 307, 335,
teleology 149
terrorism 184, 185, 232, 361, 363
theology 5, 29, 59, 60, 62, 64, 67, 108, 123, 134, 137, 139, 140, 156, 157, 172, 203, 226, 238, 243, 284, 285, 286, 294, 348, 370, 371,
theory of evolution 29, 30, 47

U

universalism 6
utilitarianism 11, 73, 295, 351

V

Vietnam War 41

W

women's rights 185, 186, 225, 232, 277

X

xenophobia 184

www.ingramcontent.com/pod-product-compliance
Lightning Source LLC
Chambersburg PA
CBHW030238170426
43202CB00007B/41
9781915025418